MW01617884

PICASSO
PORTRAITS

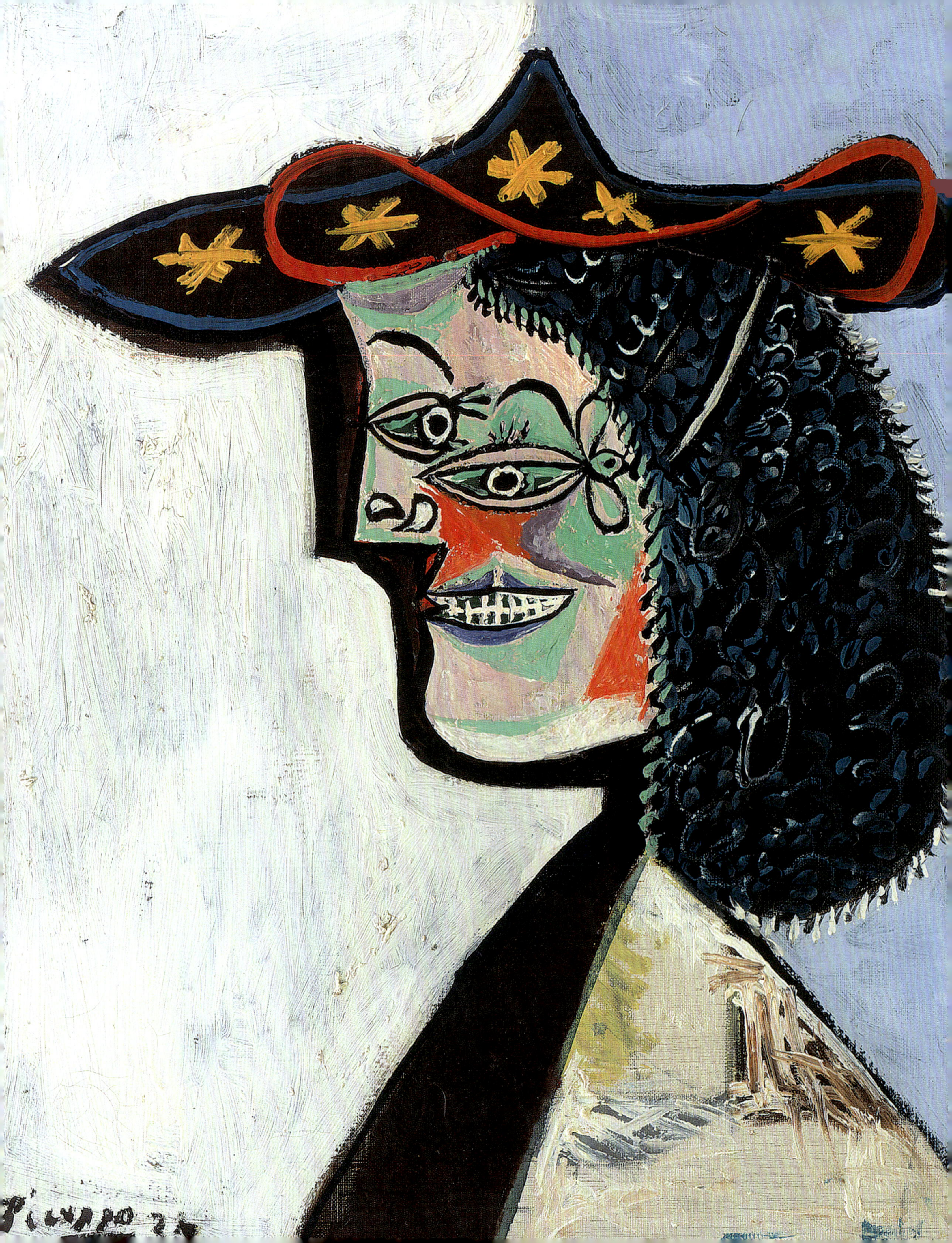

PICASSO PORTRAITS

Elizabeth Cowling

NATIONAL PORTRAIT GALLERY, LONDON
MUSEU PICASSO, BARCELONA

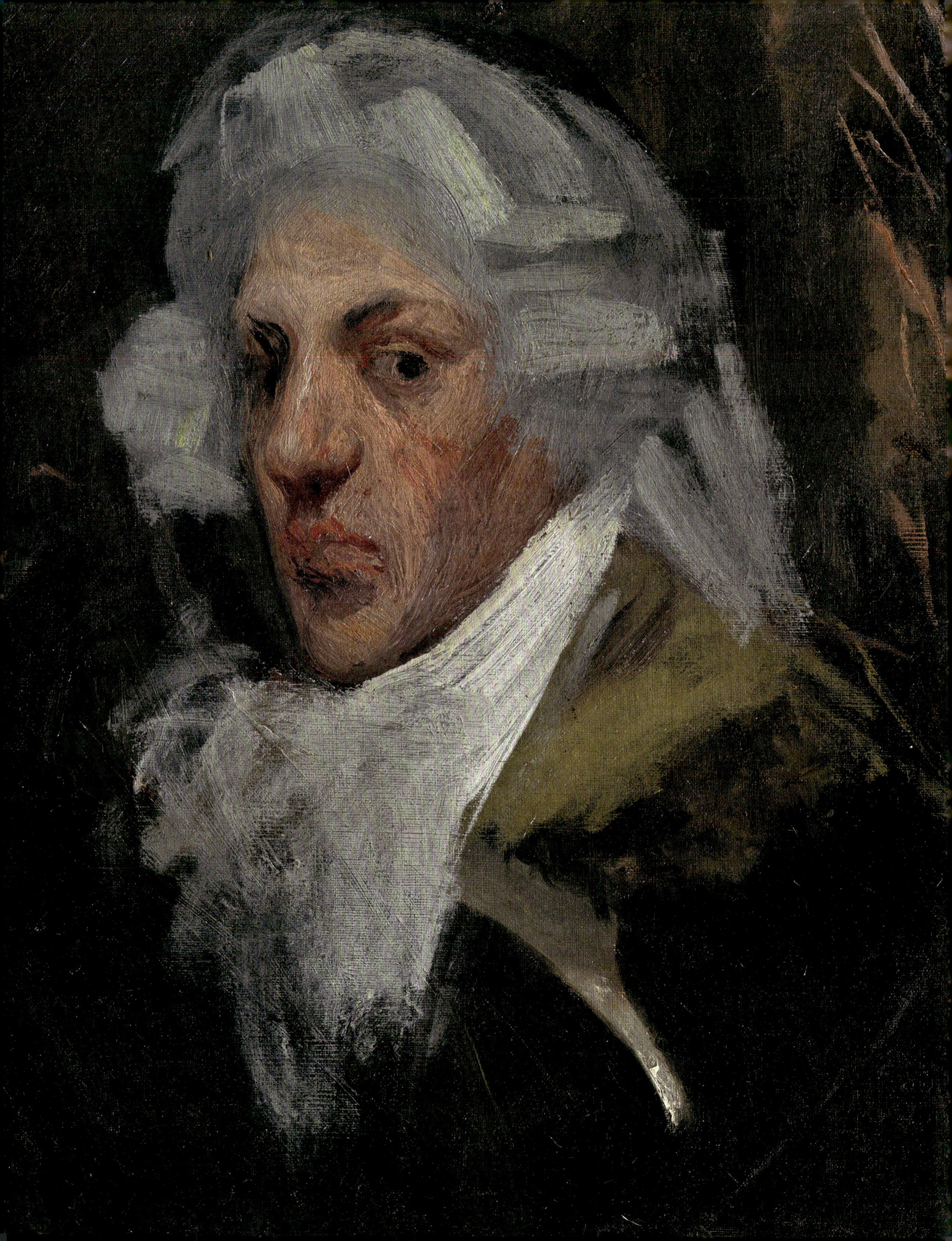

Contents

Directors' foreword

Pablo Picasso's achievement during a long, protean and highly prolific career is undisputed, but the need to understand the precise nature of that achievement is ongoing. The last major exhibition to examine Picasso's engagement with portraiture was William Rubin's magisterial *Picasso and Portraiture* at the Museum of Modern Art, New York in 1996, which then travelled to the Grand Palais in Paris, and remains a landmark in our understanding of Picasso as a portraitist. Twenty years on, it seems timely to revisit this topic with a particular focus on Picasso's manipulation of time-honoured conventions of portraiture, and his genius for caricature.

Our exhibition gathers together major loans from public and private collections that demonstrate the breadth of Picasso's oeuvre and the extraordinary range of styles he employed across all media and from all periods of his career. As well as acknowledged masterpieces, the exhibition also includes lesser-known paintings, drawings, sculpture and prints. It sets Picasso's portraiture in the context of his dialogue with the 'old masters' with whom he identified. As virtually none of these works were commissioned, he was freer to experiment than might otherwise have been the case, and made portraits of the same sitters in many different modes and styles over time.

Like much of Picasso's work, this exhibition is the result of a series of productive collaborations, first and foremost that between the National Portrait Gallery, London, and the Museu Picasso, Barcelona. Sandy Nairne, former director of the National Portrait Gallery, proposed the partnership in 2012, having previously approached the exhibition curator Elizabeth Cowling in 2009. We are immensely grateful to Sandy, and also to Elizabeth, who has worked tirelessly to bring this project to fruition. We are indebted to Elizabeth for her intelligence, scholarship, imagination and commitment.

At the National Portrait Gallery, we would like to thank a number of colleagues including those who have worked most closely with Elizabeth Cowling on shaping and delivering the exhibition: Sarah Tinsley, Rosie Wilson and Michelle Greaves. Our sincere thanks also to Pim Baxter, Nick Budden, Robert Carr-Archer, Jane Chambers, Naomi Conway, Andrea Easey, Neil Evans, Justine McLisky, Paul Moorhouse, Nicola Saunders, Jude Simmons, Fiona Smith, Liz Smith, Christopher Tinker, Denise Vogelsang, Ulrike Wachsmann and Helen Whiteoak.

At the Museu Picasso, Barcelona, we would like to thank particularly the Exhibition Coordinator Mariona Tió. However practically every member of staff has worked on the exhibition. Our gratitude to Palmira Balagué, Lluís Bagunyà, Reyes Jiménez, Anna Vélez, Yolanda Granel, Anna Fàbregas, Anna Rodríguez, Anna Guarro, Mercè Garcia, Mireia Llorella, Anna Bru de Sala, Esther Calvo and Malén Gual. Special mention is due to Guri-Casajuana, Dos de Nou and La Invisible for the installation and lighting design.

Our thanks also go to our colleagues from both the National Portrait Gallery and the Museu Picasso for their work on the catalogue: Sarah Ruddick, Senior Editor; Andrew Roff, Editor; Marta Jové, Coordinator; Ruth Müller-Wirth, Production Manager; Raquel Revuelta, Digital Image Control; and Jason Ellams for the catalogue design.

We would very much like to express our gratitude to the Picasso family for all their support, in particular to Catherine Hutin, Almine and Bernard Ruiz-Picasso, Claude Ruiz-Picasso, Diana Widmaier Picasso and Maya Widmaier-Picasso. Our profound thanks are due to a number of institutions and private collectors, in particular to the Musée national Picasso-Paris and its director Laurence Le Bon. Without their generous loans *Picasso Portraits* would only be an idea.

In London, the exhibition has been made possible by the gracious support of Goldman Sachs, and their commitment to the exhibition and the Gallery is much appreciated.

Nicholas Cullinan
Director, National Portrait Gallery, London

Bernardo Laniado-Romero
Director, Museu Picasso, Barcelona

Sponsor's foreword

Goldman Sachs is proud to partner with the National Portrait Gallery to bring the *Picasso Portraits* exhibition to London. Our two institutions share the fundamental belief that art and culture have the power to bring people together, inspire the exchange of ideas and foster creativity and innovation.

Pablo Picasso is known as a great artistic innovator and one of the most influential artists of the twentieth century. We are delighted that visitors to the exhibition will have the opportunity to explore Picasso's portraits, and see at first hand the wide range of styles and techniques with which the artist experimented over the course of his extraordinary and prolific career.

Goldman Sachs is immensely grateful for the effort and dedication of the staff at the National Portrait Gallery and the generosity of their colleagues at the Museu Picasso in Barcelona, without whose support this project would not have been possible.

We hope you enjoy this landmark exhibition.

Michael S. Sherwood
Richard J. Gnodde
Co-Chief Executive Officers
Goldman Sachs International

Goldman
Sachs

List of lenders

Picasso Portraits would not be possible without the generosity and support of the many lenders. The National Portrait Gallery, London, and the Museu Picasso, Barcelona, are very grateful to all of them. We would also like to thank the many private collectors who have preferred to remain anonymous. Numbers in brackets refer to illustrations.

The Art Institute of Chicago (83)

The British Museum, London (184, 185, 189)

Centre Pompidou, Paris. Musée national d'art moderne/Centre de création industrielle (42, 111, 145)

Colección 'El Conventet', Barcelona (17)

Colección Telefónica, Madrid (190)

Collection of Mr and Mrs J. Tomilson Hill (123)

Fundación Almine y Bernard Ruiz-Picasso para el Arte (65, 72, 79, 97, 98, 107, 108, 112)

Fundación Francisco Godia, Barcelona (32)

Fondation Hubert Looser, Zürich (159)

Horst und Gabriele Siedle-Kunststiftung (167)

Leonard A. Lauder Cubist Collection (77)

Los Angeles County Museum of Art (47)

Maison Jean Cocteau, Milly-la-Forêt (90)

Metropolitan Museum of Art (25, 30, 87)

Musée d'art moderne de la Ville de Paris (67)

Musée national Picasso-Paris (58, 84, 89, 96, 101, 143, 151, 156, 196)

Museu Picasso, Barcelona (2, 3, 7, 8, 9, 10, 11, 13, 15, 18, 19, 20, 21, 22, 29, 31, 33, 34, 45, 48, 49, 50, 56, 61, 140, 141, 152, 155, 172, 173, 174, 175, 176, 177, 181, 182, 184, 186, 188, 189)

The Museum of Modern Art, New York (110, 133, 164)

National Gallery of Iceland (166)

The Penrose Collection (126, 132)

Philadelphia Museum of Art (71)

Prins Eugens Waldemarsudde (68)

Solomon R. Guggenheim Museum, New York (66)

Staatliche Museen zu Berlin, Nationalgalerie, Museum Berggruen (55, 60, 129)

The Syndics of the Fitzwilliam Museum, Cambridge (78)

Tate, London (139)

Note
Unless otherwise stated in captions, all works are by Pablo Picasso.

Works shown at the National Portrait Gallery, London, are marked (L); those shown at the Museu Picasso, Barcelona, are marked (B); those shown at both venues are marked (B, L).

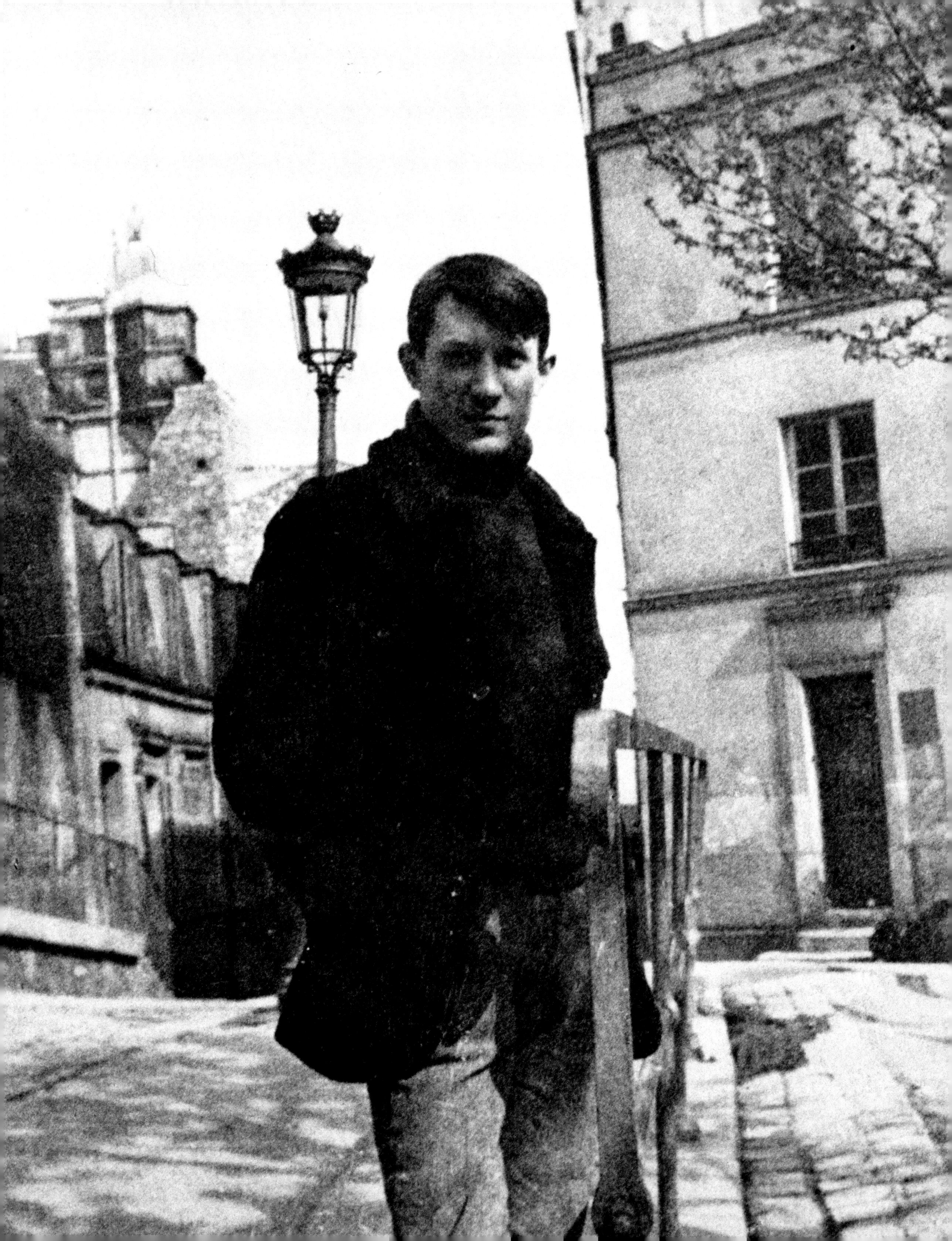

Introduction

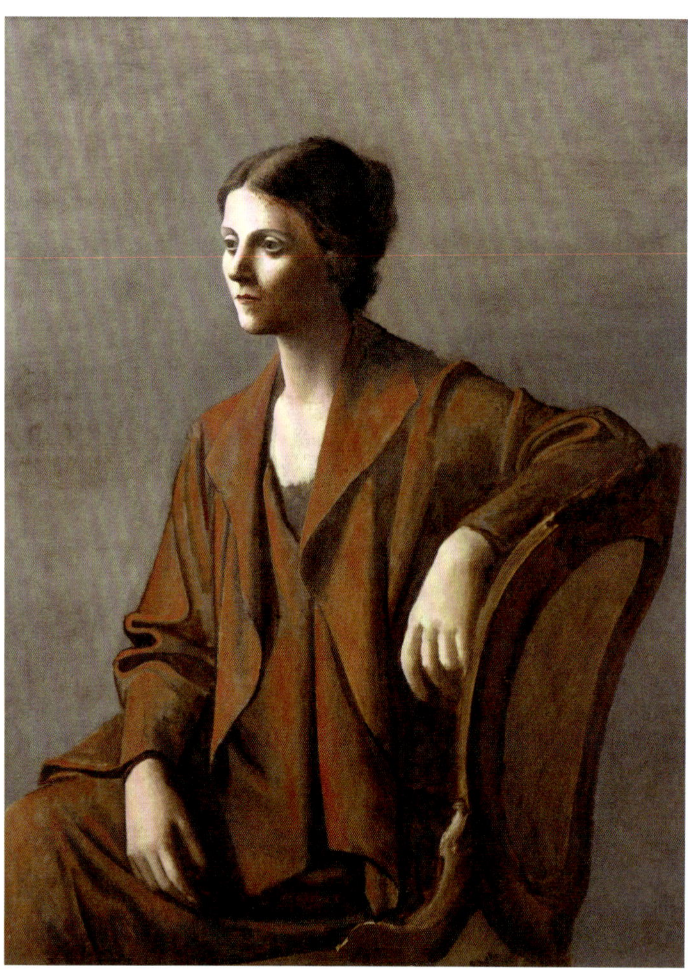

1 *Portrait of Olga Picasso*, 1923 (B, L)

The human figure was always Pablo Picasso's prime subject, and portraiture always had an important place in his art. He made portraits in every medium and in the full range of styles he practised. Beside the solemn, nobly beautiful painting of his first wife that won him the Carnegie Prize in 1930 (1), the torn scrap of paper with his self-caricature as a grinning, scratching monkey (2) comes as a shock. But startling shifts in tone and method of this kind are among the constants of his portraiture.

For art students of Picasso's generation, drawing from reproductions of canonical antique sculpture was the foundation of their training. Drawing and painting from the nude model were the next skills to be mastered, and Picasso followed that orthodox route. But his father, the painter and art-school teacher José Ruiz Blasco, saw to it that the boy also acquired the basic skills of portraiture from life when he was still only in his early teens. The academic emphasis on the classical ideal was thereby leavened with a healthy dose of the Spanish realist aesthetic, to which Don José himself subscribed.[1] Instead of reacting against parental pressure to paint convincing likenesses, Picasso was enthralled, and when completing his academic training in Madrid, he chose to copy the Prado's bust portrait of Philip IV by Velázquez (3 and 4). Lacking all the paraphernalia of kingship, and exceptional for its timeless candour and intimacy, this portrait was an ideal model for an aspiring portraitist concerned with the inner as well as the outer person. For the rest of his life, Picasso remained keenly interested in other artists' portraits, taking inspiration from them and forming a small but choice collection by Corot, Rousseau, Matisse, Modigliani and Miró, among others (5).[2] An occasional photographer himself, he also amassed a huge collection of nineteenth-century photographic portraits that left their mark upon his own work.[3]

Picasso's sharp eye for personal idiosyncrasies – and his precocious ability to describe facial expressions, poses and gestures vividly and accurately – was rooted in the caricatures he drew in childhood. The earliest to survive are crammed in the margins of school textbooks. He was then between ten and twelve years old, and taught himself by imitating caricatures and cartoons published in magazines and newspapers.[4] *Azul y Blanco* and *La Coruña*, the handmade spoof-newspapers he created from time to time between 1893 and 1895 for the amusement of his family (6), are filled with drawings of this kind.[5] In the words of art historian Adam Gopnik, 'Caricature was Picasso's mother tongue.'[6] He learned early that he could make people laugh with his drawings, and he continued to do so for the rest of his life, never regarding comedy as a lower form of expression. Caricature was not a marginal activity for Picasso in the way it has been for most 'fine' artists, ever since the genre was recognised at the end of the sixteenth century.[7] Indeed, some of the most striking portraits of his maturity have an undeniably caricatural quality.[8] As Picasso himself remarked when discussing the impossibility of definitively imitating 'reality': 'There are so many realities that in trying to encompass them all one ends in darkness. That is why, when one paints a portrait, one must stop somewhere, in a sort of caricature.'[9]

Unlike the professional caricaturist, whose usual targets are public figures, Picasso's subjects were almost always his friends. The same is true of his portraits, for he hardly ever worked to commission. Returning repeatedly to the same select band of family members, friends, acquaintances and especially lovers, he used portraiture to develop relationships and strengthen bonds. Certain self-portraits stood in for the manifestos that he never wrote. Sometimes he worked from life and the term 'sitter' is literally apt; sometimes he depended on photographs; sometimes he relied on his formidable memory; sometimes all three processes were involved. The great majority of Picasso's portraits

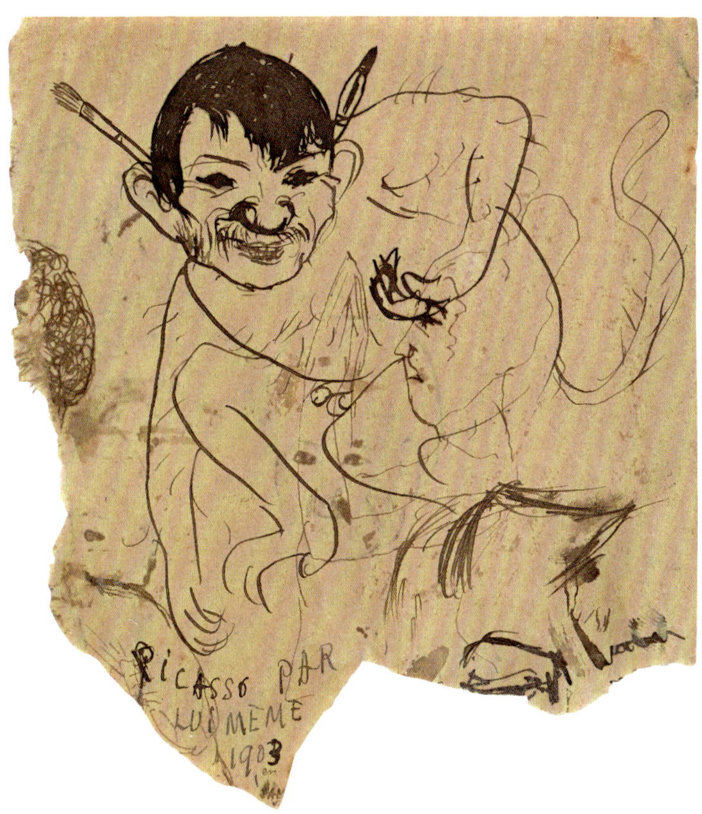

2 *Picasso par lui mème (Picasso by Himself)*, 1 January 1903 (L)

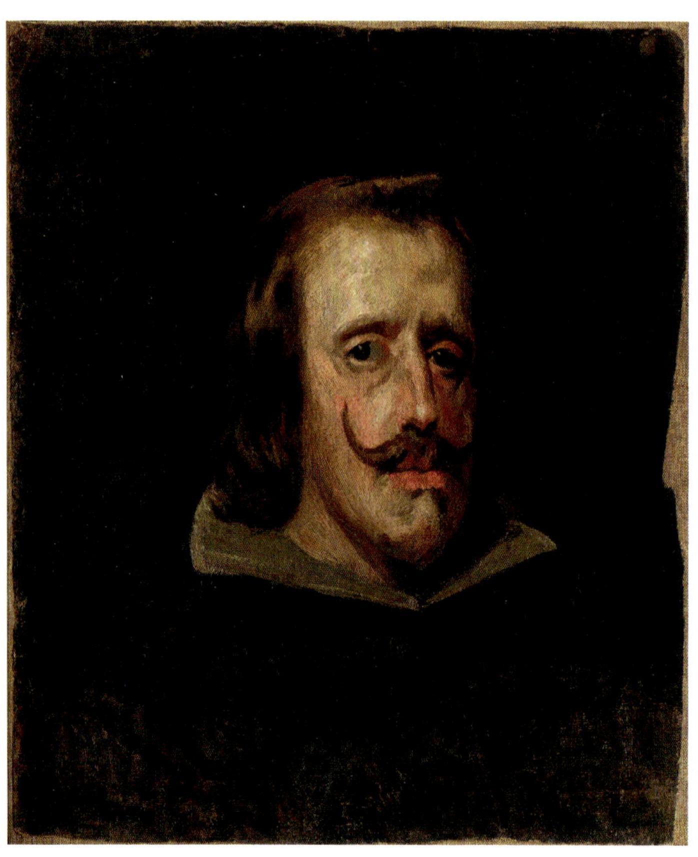

3 *Copy of* Philip IV *by Velázquez,* Madrid, October–November 1897

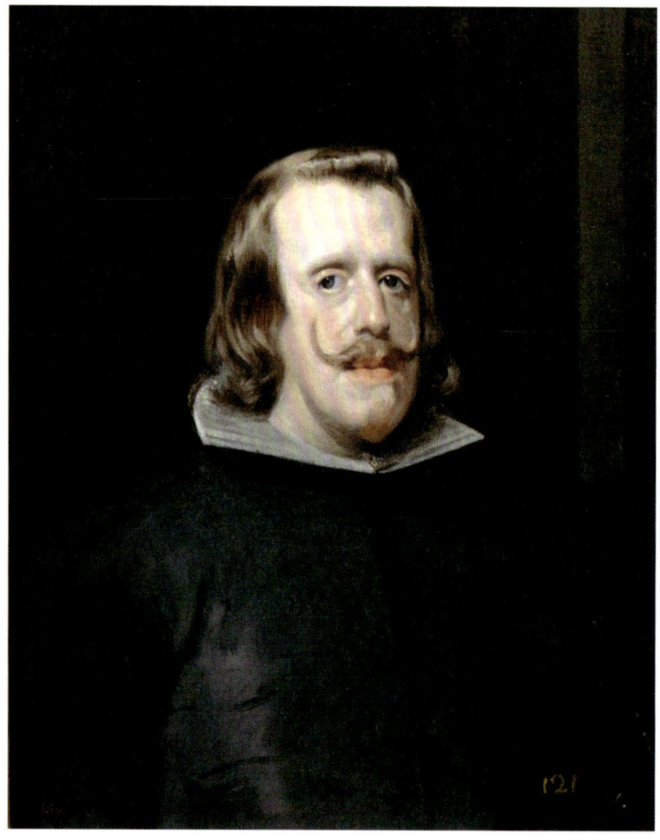

4 *Philip IV* by Diego Velázquez, c.1653

depicted a single figure, and he used again and again the same limited repertoire of time-honoured poses and formats. The chair was a constant – usually the only – prop; most backgrounds were neutral and, because the people were his intimates, he hardly ever felt the need to allude to their occupation or social status. Exceptions to these general rules are mainly to be found in his caricatures, which occasionally have a narrative structure. Without the pressure of demand or expectation that came with a commission, Picasso felt free to depict and interpret his subjects as he wished. His approach to portraiture involved engaging with its ancient traditions whilst simultaneously subverting them.[10]

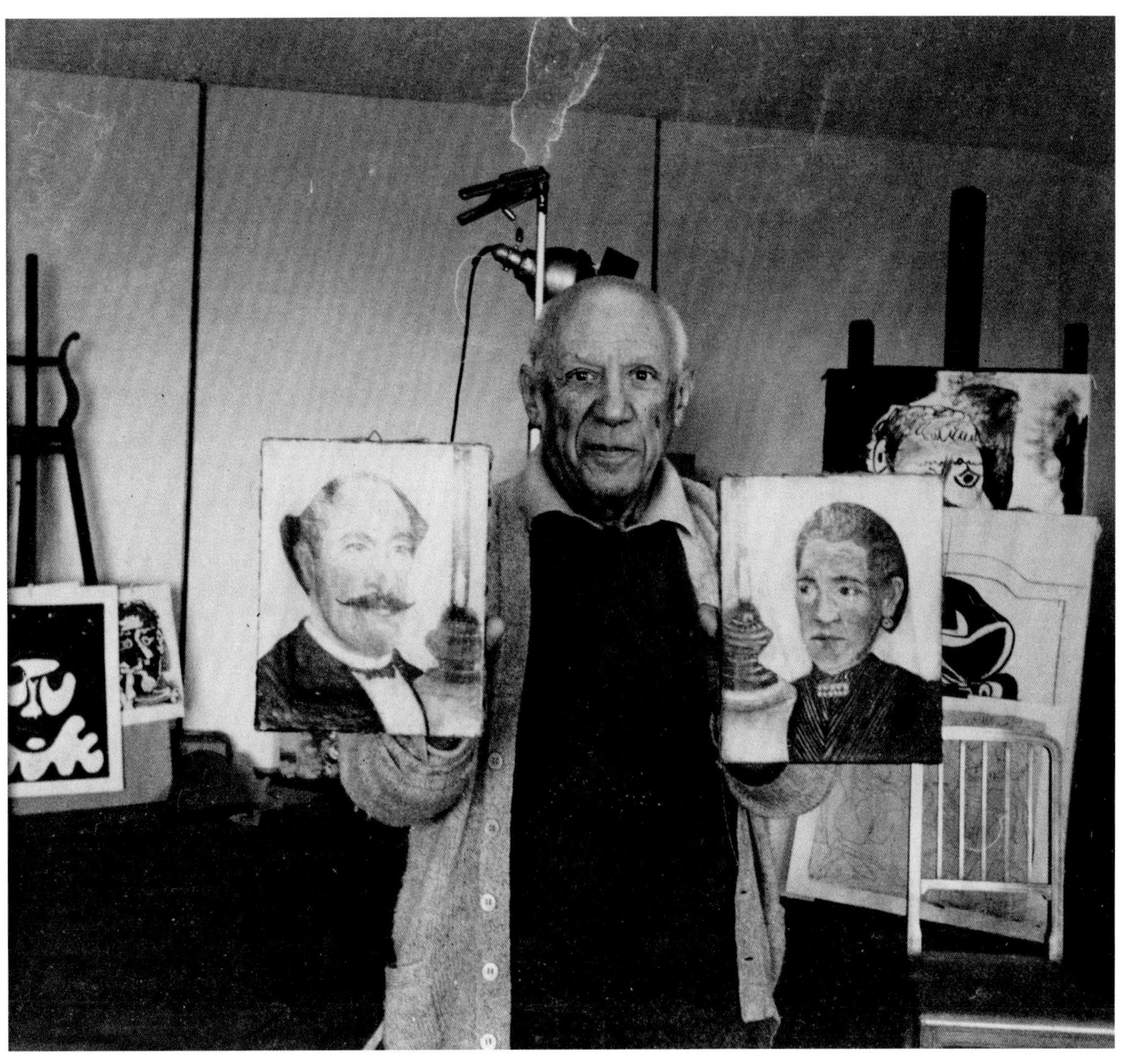

5 Picasso with Henri Rousseau's *Self-portrait* and *Portrait of the Artist's Second Wife (both 1900–3)*. Photograph by André Gomès, Notre-Dame-de-Vie, Mougins, April 1965

Given the freedom Picasso so often took with 'natural appearances', were his 'sitters' merely a convenient pretext for another work of art, merely grist to his mill? Was the style foisted on the person, regardless of his or her looks, personality or life-story? Dora Maar, one of Picasso's long-term companions, took a bitter view of the matter after their relationship had ended: 'All his portraits of me are lies. They're all Picassos, not one is Dora Maar.'[11] Portraiture – especially the portraiture of women – is traditionally associated with a degree

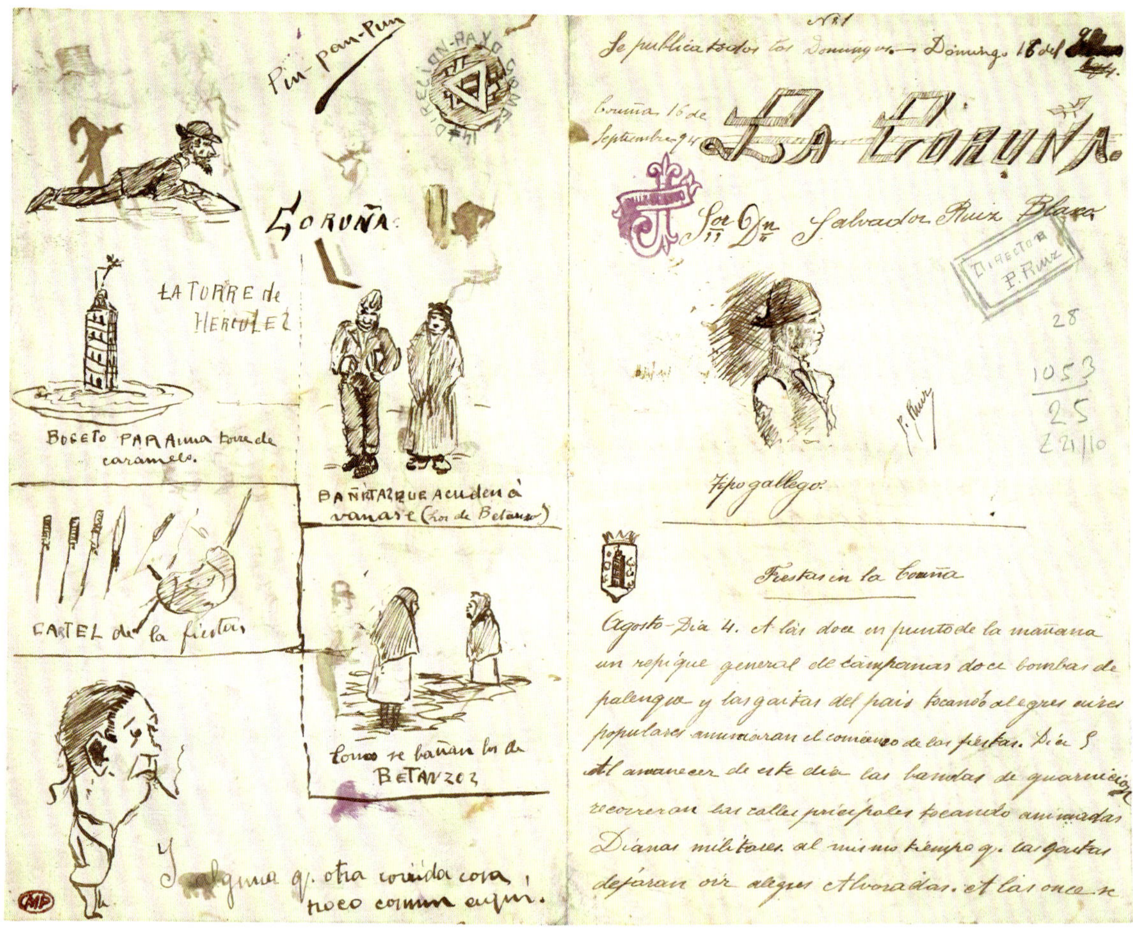

6 *La Coruña*, 16 September 1894

of idealisation and flattery; Picasso's refusal to subscribe to that convention, and his readiness to distort, sometimes grotesquely, his sitter's features, has led to regular accusations of misanthropy or misogyny.[12] Yet an examination of his portraits suggests that Picasso was in fact interested in the individual and chose or adapted his style to express his understanding of that person, using allusions to external sources (and sometimes symbols) to express his idea more completely. Thus the abnormal distortions had a dramatic rather than malevolent purpose. It was *his* vision of that person, certainly, and he was clear on that score: 'Doesn't everyone look at himself in his own particular way? Deformations simply do not exist. Daumier and Lautrec saw a face differently from Ingres or Renoir, that's all. As for me, I see it this way.'[13] Moreover, in order to safeguard that vision, Picasso developed controlling strategies, such as working in the absence of his subject. But the humanity of the individual mattered to him: the monster of egotism of popular legend is a far cry from the subtle, suggestive artist of the portraits.

Defining the limits of Picasso's portraiture is not a simple matter. In the vast and revelatory exhibition curated by William Rubin and mounted in New York and Paris in 1996, the definition was purposefully stretched to include figure paintings that might otherwise have been categorised as purely generic images, or nudes, or narrative scenes, and so on.[14] In *Picasso Portraits*, the focus is confined to works in which the subjects are identified individuals and in which the artist engaged directly – albeit transgressively – with the established compositional norms of European portraiture. On the other hand, an issue Rubin chose to leave aside has been broached: Picasso's portraits and caricatures of the old masters and his free 'variations' after old-master portraits. These great ancestors not only profoundly influenced Picasso's depiction of his intimates, but in his mind also became his intimates themselves.

1 See Marilyn McCully, 'Retratos', in *Primer Picasso* 2015, pp.327–45.

2 See Seckel-Klein 1998.

3 Archives Picasso. Musée national Picasso-Paris. See pp.102–7.

4 See Rubén Ventureira, 'Periódicos y caricaturas', in *Primer Picasso* 2015, pp.164–205.

5 Picasso's models were *Blanco y Negro*, Spain's most popular weekly magazine, and *Teatro Crítico*, to which his parents subscribed (Richardson 1991, p.46).

6 Adam Gopnik, 'Caricature', in Varnedoe and Gopnik 1990, p.123.

7 It is generally agreed that the history of the mock-portrait begins with Annibale and Agostino Carracci c.1590. See, for instance, Gombrich and Kris 1940, p.10; McPhee and Orenstein 2011, p.4.

8 See Michel Melot, 'Stylistic distortion', in *Picasso Caricature* 2003, pp.39–47. Citing Picasso as a prime example, C.R. Ashbee noted how difficult it was to draw a clear-cut distinction between the modernist 'portrait' and 'caricature' (Ashbee 1928, pp.137–8).

9 Picasso in conversation with Daniel-Henry Kahnweiler on 9 November 1959. Cited in Ashton 1972, p.82.

10 For the modernists' subversion of the conventions of portraiture, see Malcolm Warner, 'Portraits about portraiture', in Alarcó and Warner 2007, pp.11–22.

11 Lord 1993, p.123.

12 For contextualised discussion of these physical distortions, see *inter al.* Rudolf Arnheim, 'The rationale of deformation', in *Art Journal*, vol. 43, no.4, Winter 1983, pp.319–24, and Neil Cox, 'Picasso (in)human face', *Angelaki*, vol.16, no.1 March 2011, pp.199–222.

13 Picasso reported by Anatole Jakovsky in 'Midis avec Picasso', *Arts de France*, no.6, 1946. Cited in Ashton 1972, p.110.

14 See Rubin, 'Reflections on Picasso and Portraiture' in Rubin 1996, pp.13–109.

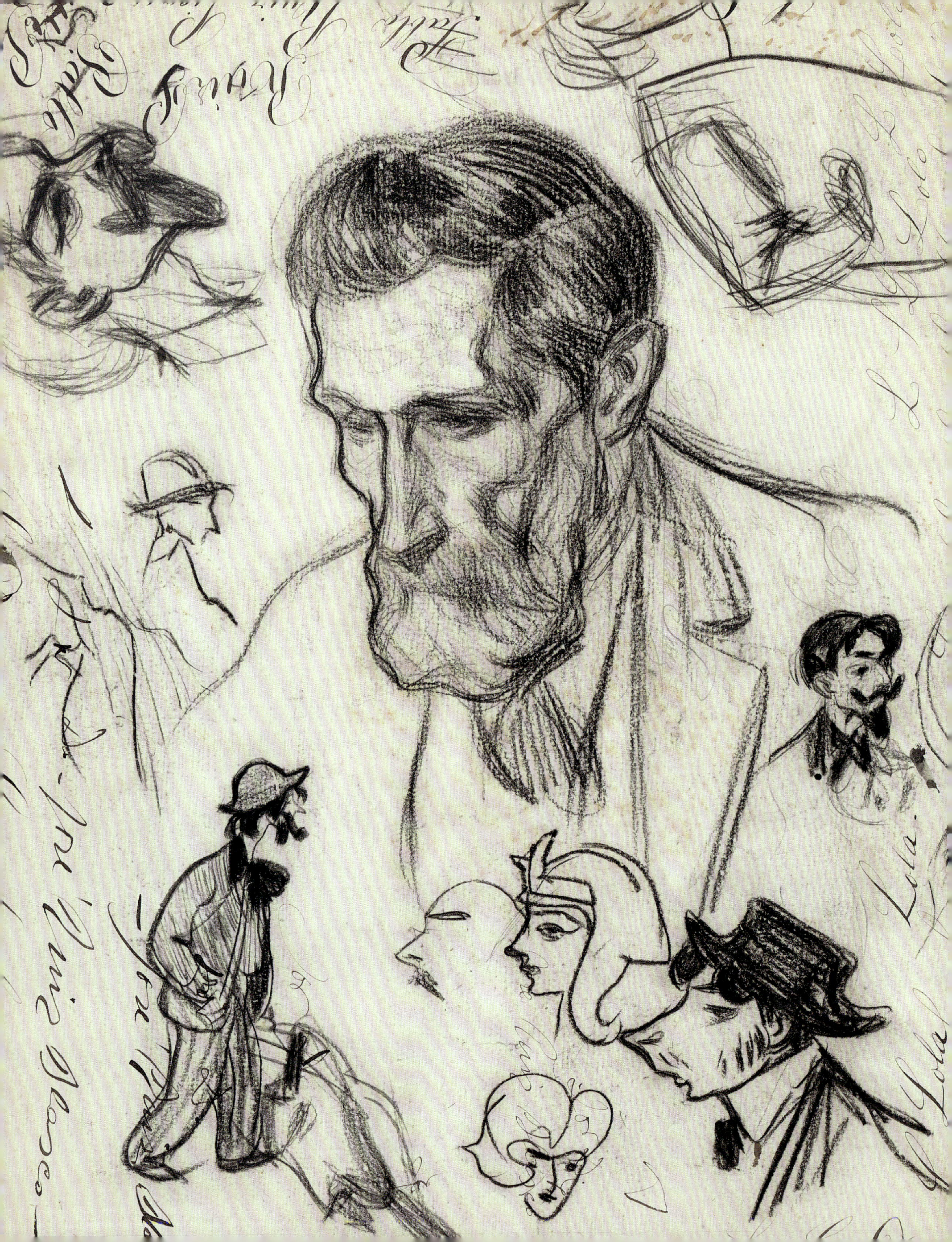

1. Launching a career, 1895–1900

THE ART STUDENT

Picasso's father Don José not only supervised the young artist's first steps as a portraitist, he also masterminded the boy's early attempts to paint Salon-scale genre scenes with a moral or sentimental message.[1] The beneficial effect on Picasso's portraiture was that he grasped early on the importance of evoking a state of mind as well as describing physical appearance. Nowhere is this clearer than in the portraits of his father that he executed after the family moved to Barcelona in 1895. In the masterly watercolour painted entirely in deep pink (7), Picasso described Don José's gaunt but handsome features meticulously: the set of his eyes and mouth, the shape of his cheeks, nose and ear, the growth and lie of his thick hair and wispy beard – all are precisely defined. But it is the suggestion of personality and mood that especially holds the viewer's attention. Don José's erect stance implies pride, but his deeply lined brow and unfocused gaze hint at the depression and anxiety that afflicted him in middle age.[2] Physically, he is diminished by the large expanse of empty paper above and to the sides of his head. It was surely by design that Picasso left so much vacant space and he reinforced the poignant sense of his father's vulnerability by surrounding his head with encroaching shadows.

No less penetrating was the portrait of Josefa Ruiz Blasco, painted in 1896 on a return visit to Málaga, Picasso's birthplace (8). Don José had urged his son to study the great Spanish masters of realism and, although convention normally demanded that women's portraits err on the side of charm and flattery, Picasso felt no compunction about truthfully recording, Ribera-style, the old woman's sagging flesh and thinning hair. Known as Aunt Pepa, she was Don José's reclusive, excessively pious elder sister and had the reputation of being bad-tempered and 'a little crazy'. But she agreed to pose, and according to family legend the portrait was finished in an hour.[3] This claim cannot be taken seriously for the surface betrays the fact that Picasso adjusted the position of the old lady's head and the line of her shoulders, built the face methodically, touch by touch, in a quasi-sculptural manner, and struggled bravely to give a sense of three-dimensionality to the funereal black of Aunt Pepa's utterly plain, all-concealing dress. Evidently, he wanted to catch something of her state of mind, and Velázquez's searching portraits of marginal types proved inspirational. We know those paintings marked him because on his first ever visit to the Prado Museum in the spring of 1895, he had time to make only two quick sketches, choosing to copy the portraits of the jester Calabacillas (9) and the dwarf Francisco Lezcano. In both cases, he concentrated on the pale, looming heads, surrounding them with an aureole of deep shadow, in a manner that anticipates the dramatic lighting of the portrait of his freakish aunt who, mouth firmly closed, avoids her nephew's eye and looks furtively out to her right. Velázquez showed Picasso that no props at all were needed in a portrait that conveyed the always mysterious, endlessly intriguing inner world of someone else, and for the rest of his life, Picasso tended to use suggestive allusion to other works of art, rather than props and accessories, when developing an expressive portrait.

Like many young artists, Picasso was fascinated by his own appearance and, aged fourteen or fifteen, painted a searching self-portrait during his first year at La Llotja, Barcelona's School of Fine Arts (10). His fellow students were all several years older and so he styled himself as a fashionable young man, not a boy, with the darker shade of his chin and upper lip signalling his maturity. Yet the outward evidence of manliness is counteracted by the air of anxious self-interrogation typical of adolescence. The slight downward inclination of the head, the set of the full lips, and above all the deep shadow cast over the right side of the face,[4] combine to suggest

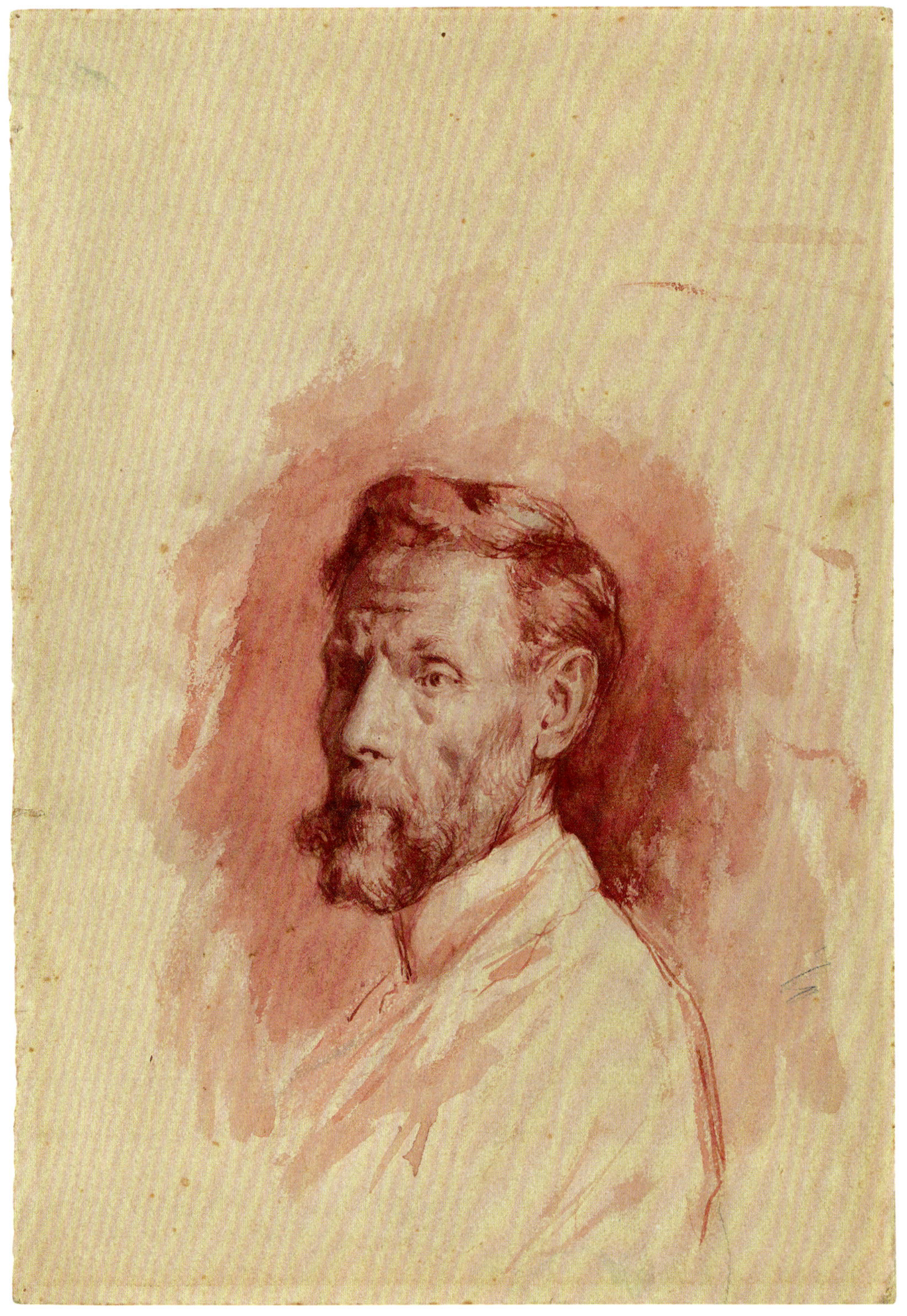

7 *The Artist's Father*, 1896 (B)

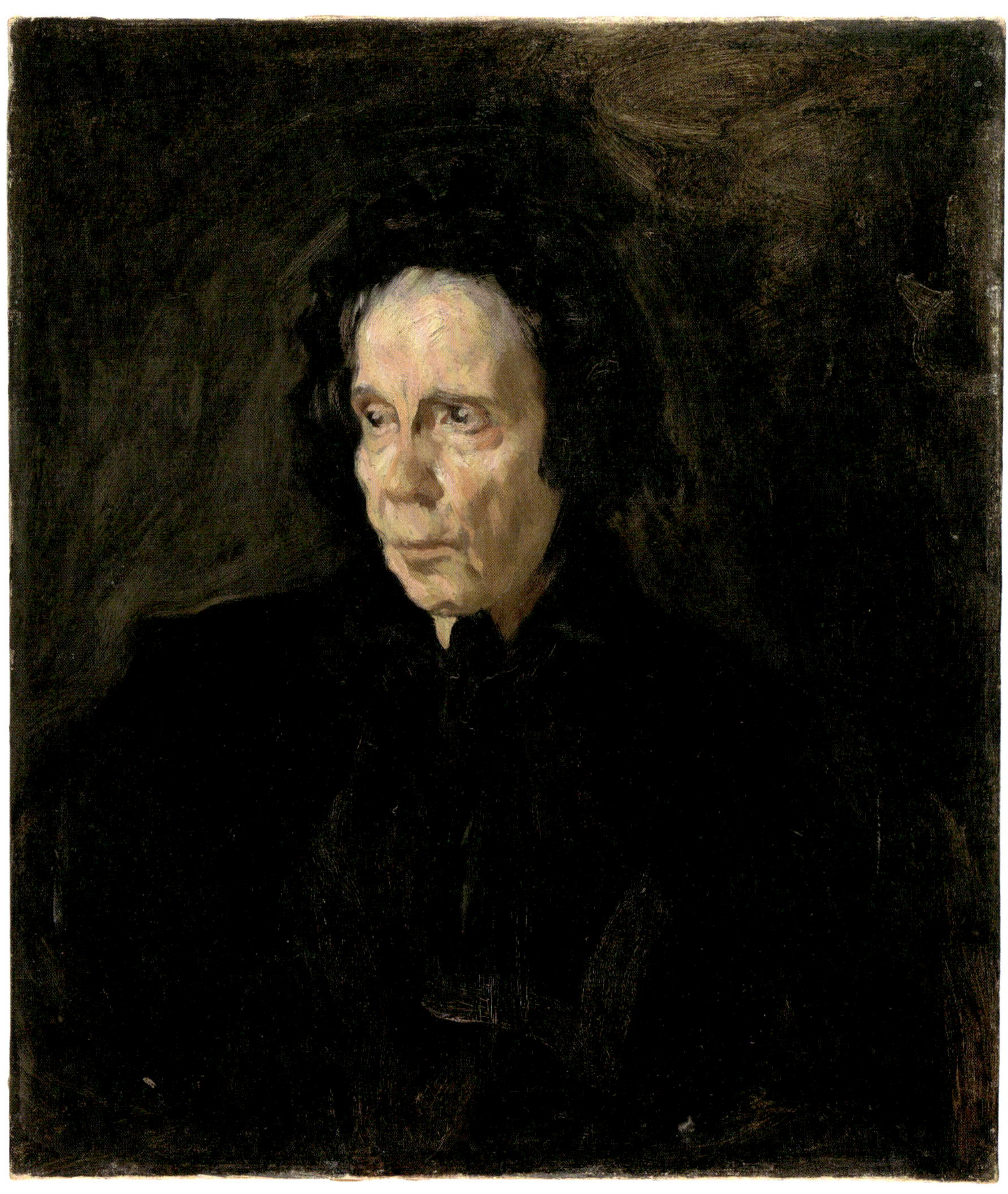

8 *Aunt Pepa*, June–July 1896 (B)

sullenness, if not introspective gloom, the murky dark grey-brown background serving as a metaphor for his inner world. Yet the unruly clumps of hair falling over the brow and the striking inconsistency of the painting's technique – sketchy in some areas, meticulously descriptive in others – point to energy and spontaneity. The account of Picasso's volatile personality provided by Manuel Pallarès, who befriended him when he enrolled in La Llotja in autumn 1895, might almost have been written with this painting in mind:

> Sometimes he got very excited; sometimes he would go for hours without a word. He was quick to anger, just as quick to calm down ... He often seemed melancholy, as if he had just thought of something sad. His face would cloud over, eyes become dark. At fifteen he neither looked nor acted like a boy his age. He was very mature.[5]

In later self-portraits, Picasso made more of the penetrating gaze that mastered, transfixed and seduced so many people he encountered. Here, the white of his downcast left eye is grey and no match in brightness for his wing collar, while the contours of the right eye, occluded by a palisade of dark brown strokes, are barely visible at all. This conception of the face as split into two contrasting zones, one illuminated, sharp-sighted and outward-looking, the other shaded, unseeing and introverted, presages what would become a leitmotif of Picasso's portraiture, and even at this very early stage, the division probably had symbolic meaning.

In *Self-portrait with Wig*, 1900 (11), it is the artist's left eye that is deliberately occluded by a slashing stroke of black paint. But even before Picasso performed that brutal act of cancellation, the place where the eye should have been was no more than a vague blur of greyish paint, as if he had been born without a second socket or

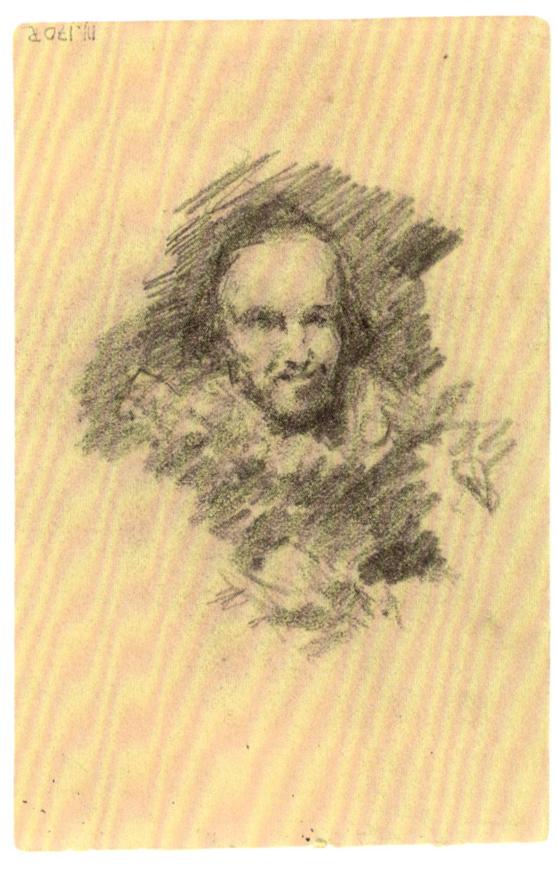

9 *Copy of* The Buffoon Calabacillas *by Velázquez*, 1895

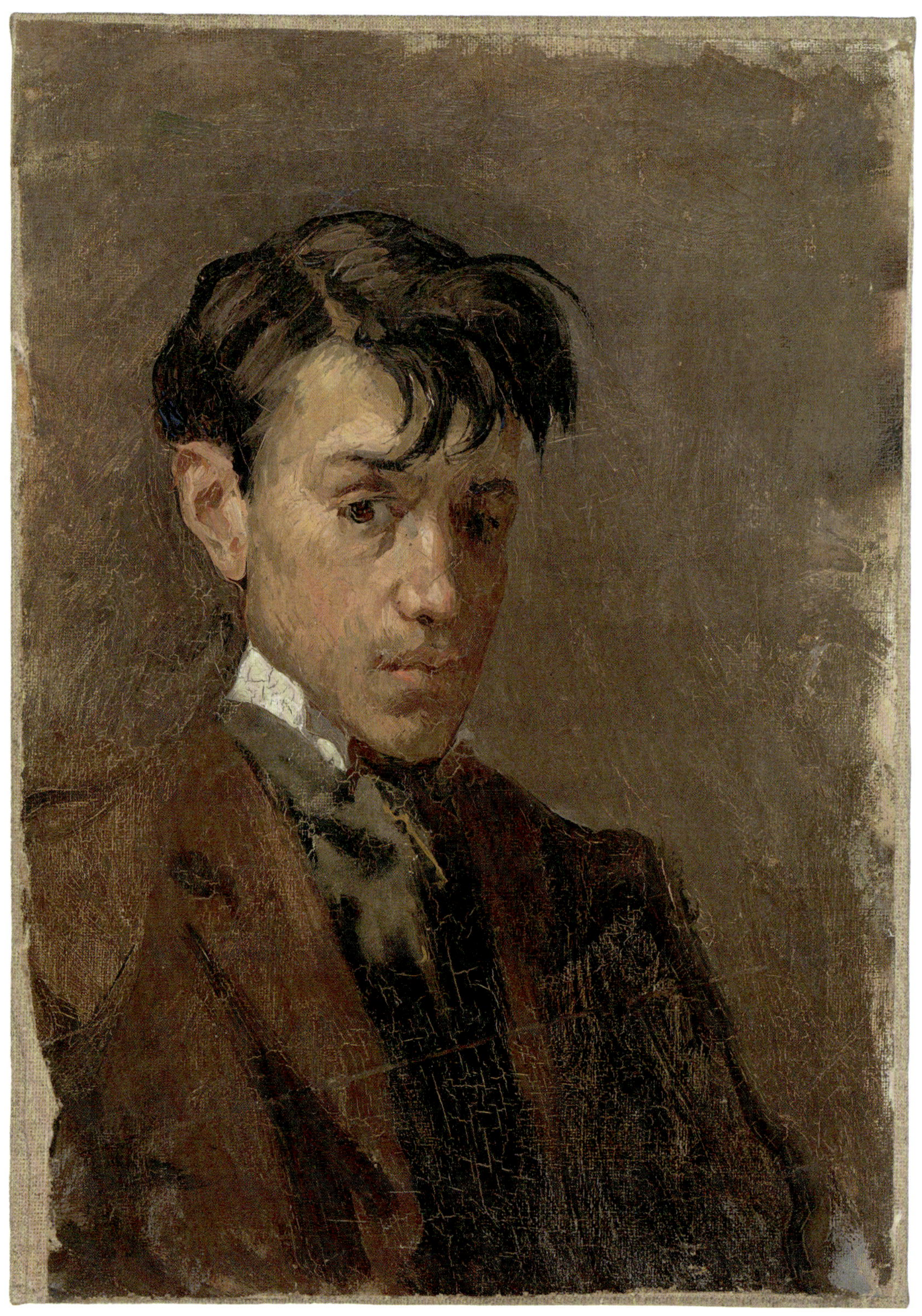

10 *Self-portrait*, 1896 (L)

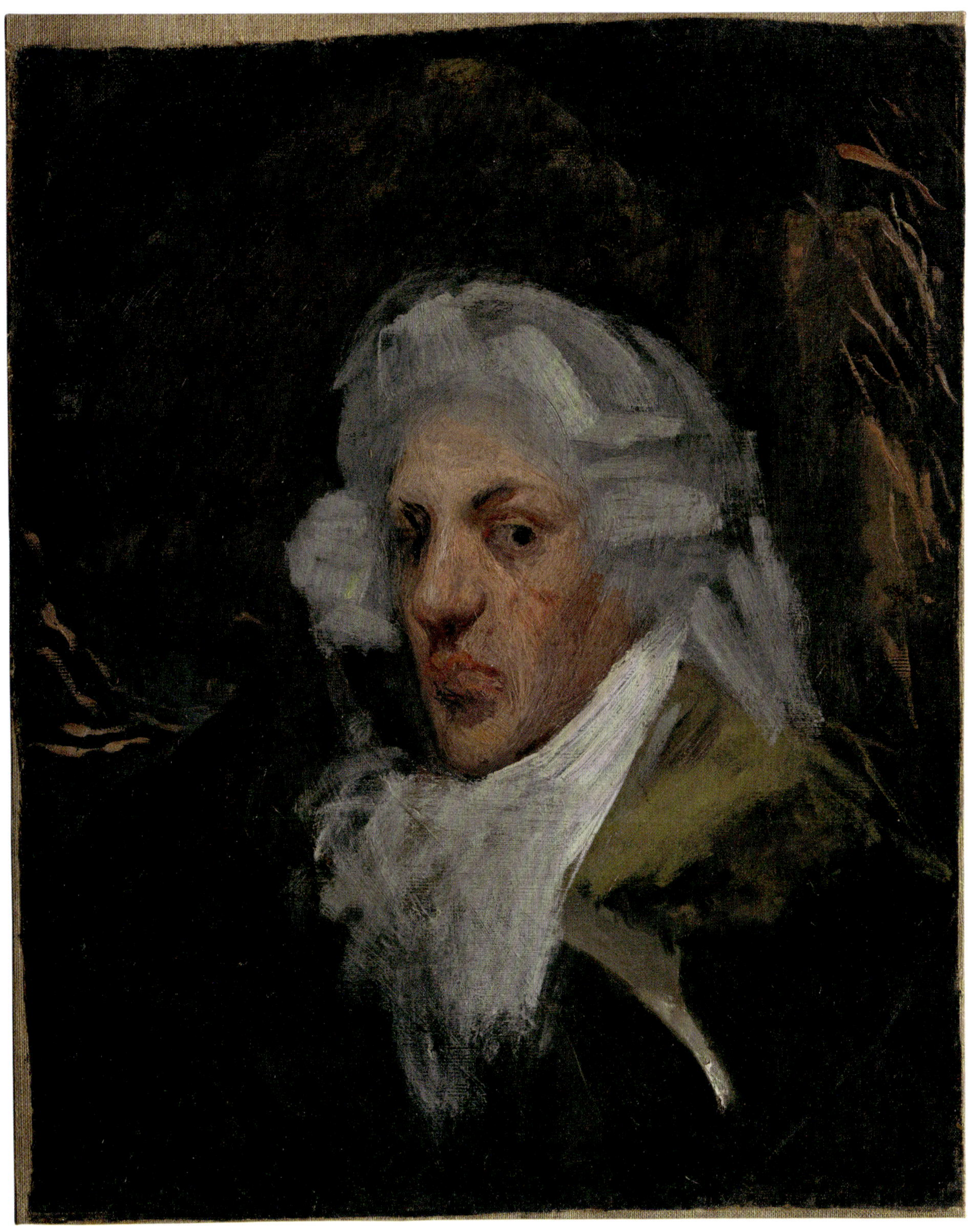

11 *Self-portrait with Wig*, 1900 (B, L)

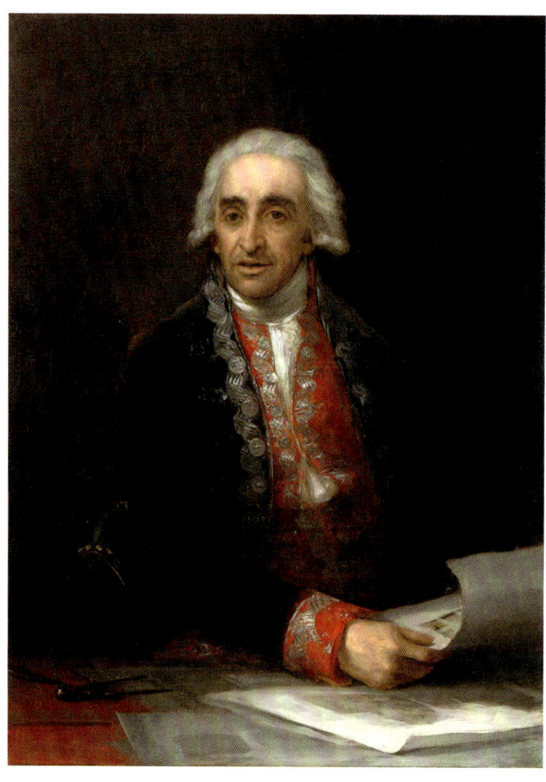

12 *Juan de Villanueva* by Francisco de Goya, 1800–5

had suffered some ghastly accident. The most striking aspect of the picture is, however, the late eighteenth-century costume – a tribute to those portraits by Goya that Picasso had seen in Madrid during his brief attendance at the Academia Real de San Fernando in 1897–8 (12). Contemporary photographs reveal that Picasso depicted his own features naturalistically but, with a mixture of bravado and self-mockery, he presented himself as a confirmed rake in the mould of Laclos's Vicomte de Valmont in *Les Liaisons dangereuses* (1782). Given the uninhibited bravura with which the powdered wig, jabot and olive-green jacket are rendered, perhaps he intended to draw a parallel between the urgency of desire and the urgency of the act of painting, for this parallel was certainly explicit in many of his much later representations of painters with their models. At all events, the masquerade was enacted literally on the canvas, for the wig was swiftly painted over – fitted over – the original crown of his head, and the jabot swept across his neck. Like many of Picasso's early oil paintings, this self-portrait was painted over another composition.[6] He did not bother to efface all traces of this former composition, which depicts a man in a wide-brimmed hat worn at a jaunty angle. Nor did he attempt to conceal his revisions to the new self-portrait. Indeed, he revelled in the discrepancy between the slapdash technique of the wig and costume, and the relative finesse of his painting of the face. This was not a picture intended for public consumption; Picasso could afford to be facetious and experimental.

ELS QUATRE GATS

Picasso's studies in Madrid came to an abrupt end in the spring of 1898 when he contracted scarlet fever and had to go home to recuperate. After his recovery, he refused to resume his formal art training and – despite his father's grave misgivings – gravitated instead towards the bohemian milieu of Els Quatre Gats. Founded in 1897 by Miguel Utrillo, Pere Romeu, Santiago Rusiñol and Ramon Casas – the Four Cats of its name – Els Quatre Gats was the undisputed centre of Barcelona's artistic and intellectual avant-garde at this time, and operated as a bar, restaurant and venue for cultural activities. All four founders had spent long periods of time in Paris, and were also familiar with progressive movements elsewhere in Europe and Scandinavia. Their impact on Picasso was electrifying: having sacrificed the realism inculcated by his father and the classicism inculcated in the art schools he attended, he set about absorbing the painterly and graphic styles of Catalan Modernisme. The prevailing influences on the Modernistes were French Impressionism, Post-Impressionism and Art Nouveau, multinational Symbolism and native Catalan traditions. Picasso was now part of an exclusively masculine set: virtually the only portraits of women he made during this period were of his teenage sister Lola, who, poised between childhood and womanhood, was a stimulating model.[7] Although he did not give up painting on canvas, he concentrated on drawing, partly because the proliferation of little magazines and the fashion for posters provided graphic artists with opportunities for making a modest living.

It was crucial that Picasso establish himself as a force to be reckoned with in the fraternal but competitive atmosphere of Els Quatre Gats, and in a riveting charcoal drawing (13) he cast aside the fantasy of partial blindness he had toyed with in the self-portraits described above and, choosing a strictly frontal pose, unleashed the full hypnotic power of his gaze. On a first, life-changing visit to Picasso's tiny top-floor studio in Carrer d'Escudillers Blancs, his new friend (and future secretary and biographer) Jaume Sabartés was utterly vanquished:

> My eyes were still dazzled by what they had seen among his papers and sketchbooks. Picasso ... intensified my confusion with his fixed stare. On passing before him to go, I sketched a kind of obeisance, stunned as I was by his magical power, the power of a Magi, possessing gifts so astonishingly full of hope and promise.[8]

The torn edges of the drawing and the fact that strokes of charcoal pass beneath the rough borders marked out at the top and bottom of the paper reveal a change of mind: Picasso had originally sketched a bust-length self-portrait, leaving breathing space above the head and to left and right of the shoulders. In that form the drawing would have looked even more like the famous lithograph by Edvard Munch published in 1895, in which the artist's disembodied but wide-eyed head floats in a black void above the skeleton of an arm (14). Munch enjoyed huge prestige in the circle of Els Quatre Gats and contemporary drawings reveal just how enthralled Picasso was by the hagridden melodrama of the Norwegian artist's work.[9] But in the self-portrait, Munch did not get the upper hand: Picasso realised that his head would make a far stronger impact and appear more monumental if he closed in tightly on it. Having quickly mapped out a frame, he tore off the surplus paper: now the eyes, ringed by dark lids and accentuated by black, sloping eyebrows, fell a fraction above the centre of the composition and dominated it completely. As he worked up the thatch of black hair and reinforced the contours of the chin, he made sure to keep the broad nose and full lips soft and vague for, drawn forcefully, they would have struck too crassly earthy a note. Touches of white chalk added

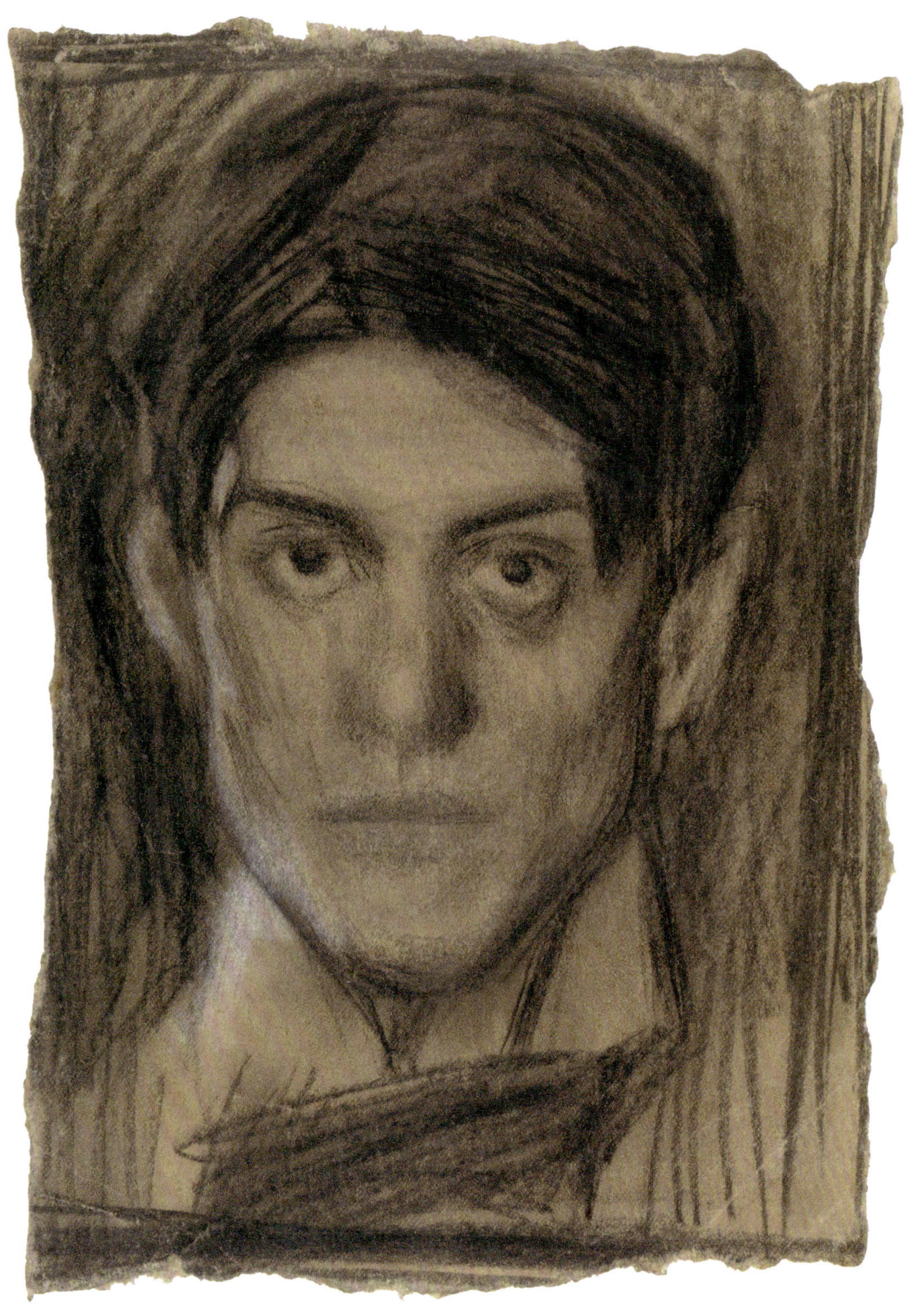

13 *Self-portrait*, 1899–1900 (L)

to the left of the head enhanced its spectral quality. Sabartés's talk of 'the power of a Magi' seems less hysterical when one is face to face with this charismatic image.

Picasso's public career as a portraitist was launched in February 1900 when he held an exhibition of his drawings in the hall adjoining the bar of Els Quatre Gats. According to Sabartés, the impetus for the exhibition was rivalry with Casas, who had held a triumphant exhibition of his portraits, most of them in charcoal and pastel on paper, the previous October at the Sala Parés, Barcelona's leading commercial gallery.[10] Although Picasso 'had already drawn many portraits ... since from morning till night he drew everything that fell before his eyes', he rushed to produce others to cover the walls.[11] The point was to produce distinctive, recognisable likenesses of the tavern's habitués and, unframed, the drawings were simply tacked up with pins. This deliberately amateurish, last-minute approach ruled out the production of a catalogue, and there is no agreement about the number of drawings on show.[12] Sold for next to nothing, a good many were lost or destroyed, and several that survive are torn.

One of the two published reviews was patronising but not unfriendly. Having described Picasso as 'almost a child' and warned him against over-dependence on outside influences, the author conceded that 'many of these portraits have character' and that 'some of them have been executed with conviction and economy'.[13] The other reviewer was less impressed, deploring the 'unsympathetic' impression produced of 'a gallery of melancholy, taciturn and bored characters'.[14] No doubt he would have condemned the portrait of Sabartés on precisely those grounds (15). The latter remembered that it was drawn in the tiny studio in Riera Sant Joan that Picasso began renting in January 1900, and that it was the first portrait Picasso made of him.[15] It bears all the signs of haste

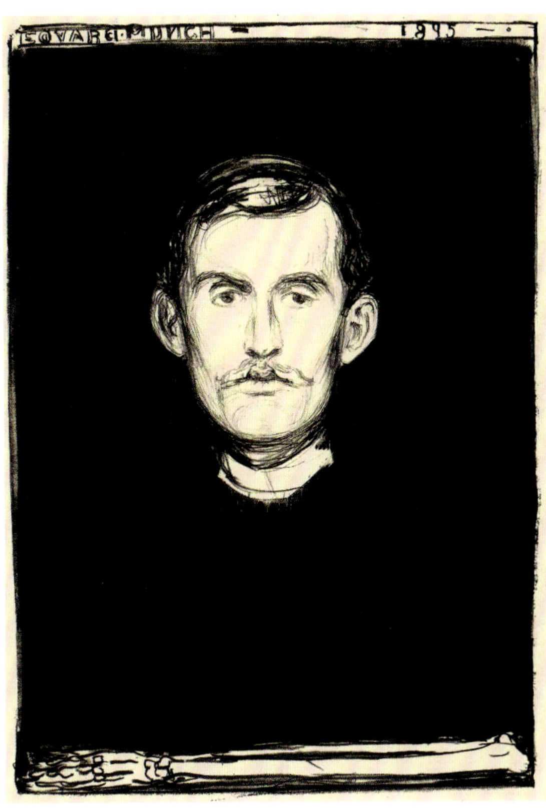

14 *Self-portrait with Skeleton Arm* by Edvard Munch, 1895

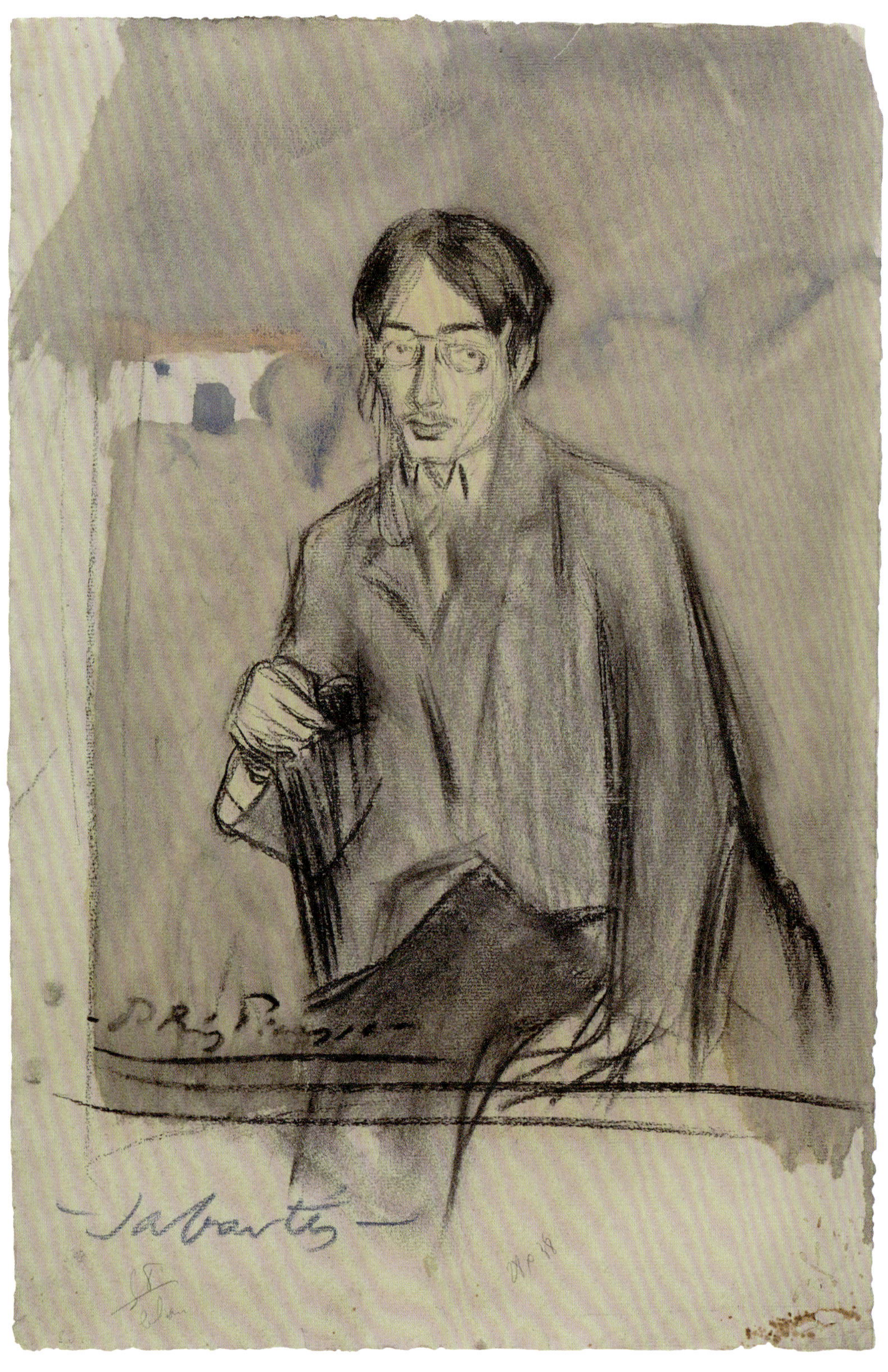

15 *Jaume Sabartés, Seated*, 1900 (B)

that attended the build-up to the exhibition, and the blank left edge of the sheet and impatiently drawn lines beneath the boldly inscribed signature suggest that Picasso planned to cut it down.[16] Even had he done so, the dark grey patch representing Sabartés's crossed leg would still have read oddly. This parade of insouciance and the perfunctory treatment of the torso were in marked contrast to the ingratiating suavity of a typical portrait by Casas, such as his *Pere Romeu* (16). Yet Picasso's characterisation of Sabartés is acute. He hinted at his gauche friend's overawed diffidence using subtle touches to the pose and facial expression: Sabartés shrinks back slightly, hardly daring to maintain the frontal pose, but is unable to resist darting a shy look at his hero though his pince-nez. His habitual gloom is represented symbolically in the rather dismal landscape of the backdrop, while the pooling of the dilute watercolour captures perfectly the effect of a cool, rain-washed afternoon.

The portrait of Sabartés was almost certainly included in the exhibition at Els Quatre Gats. So was the portrait of Santiago Rusiñol (17). Of the four original founders of Els Quatre Gats, Picasso was most attached and indebted to Rusiñol and chose a pure profile view to show off his hooked nose, long ragged beard and slightly stooping gait. Sucking on his pipe, hands behind his back, pacing forwards but so absorbed by his meditations that he is oblivious to his surroundings, Rusiñol is the very picture of the turn-of-the-century, bohemian painter/poet/thinker. The viewer may be reminded – Picasso likely was reminded – of Don José because of certain shared physical traits, but there is no sign of the settled pessimism that makes Picasso's portraits of his father so moving. The background is a vague evocation of the gardens of the Generalife at the Alhambra, the subject of a recent series of paintings by Rusiñol, and a relatively rare instance of Picasso supplying information relevant to the sitter of a portrait.[17]

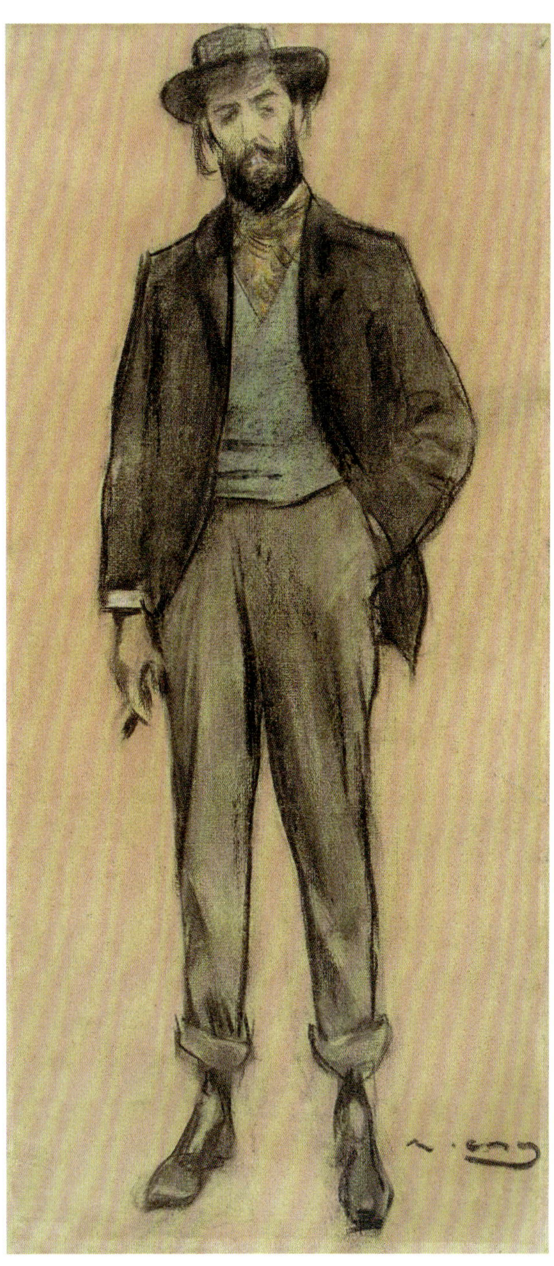

16 *Portrait of Pere Romeu* by Ramon Casas i Carbó, 1897–9

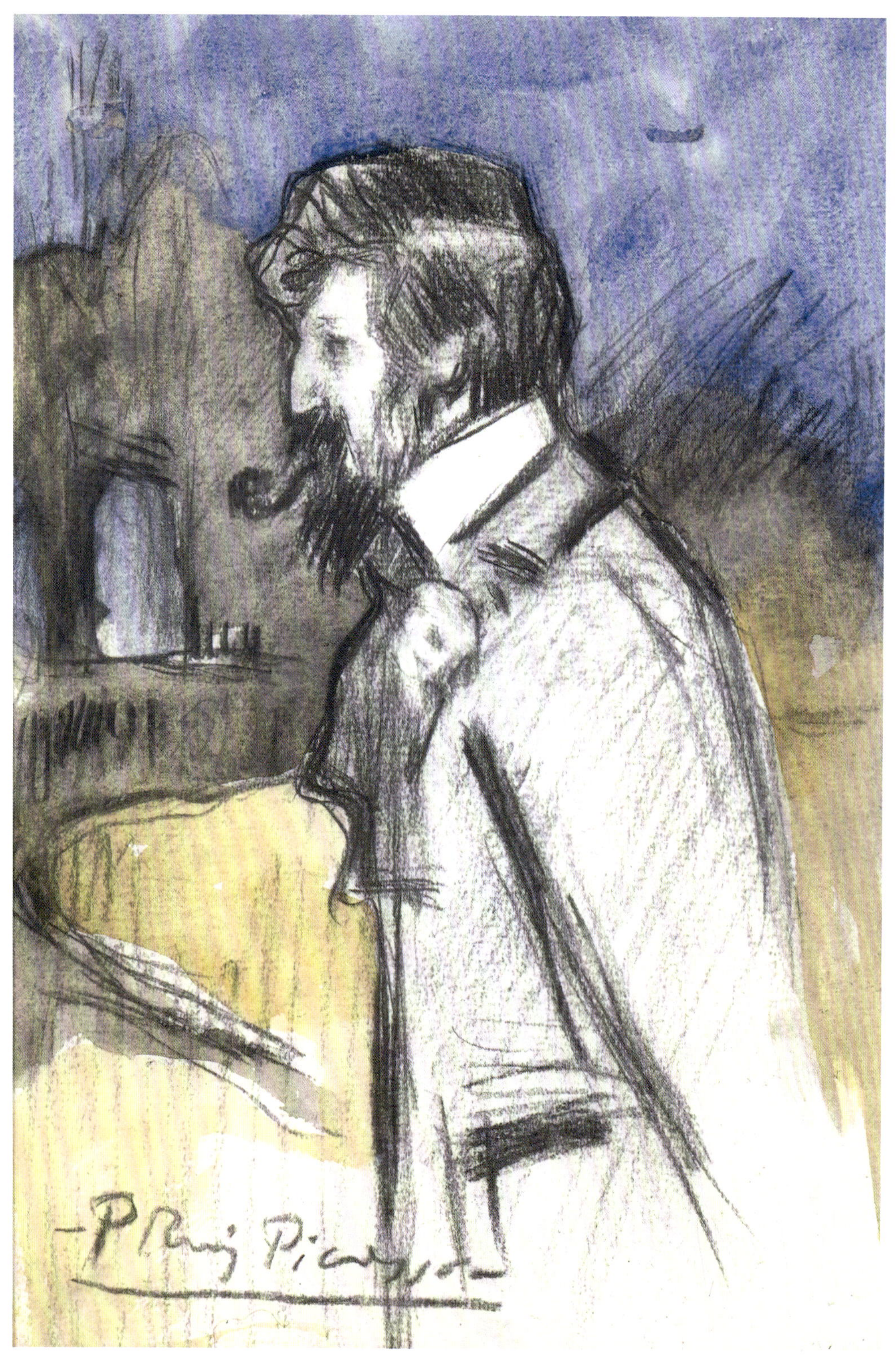

17 *Portrait of Santiago Rusiñol*, c.1900 (B, L)

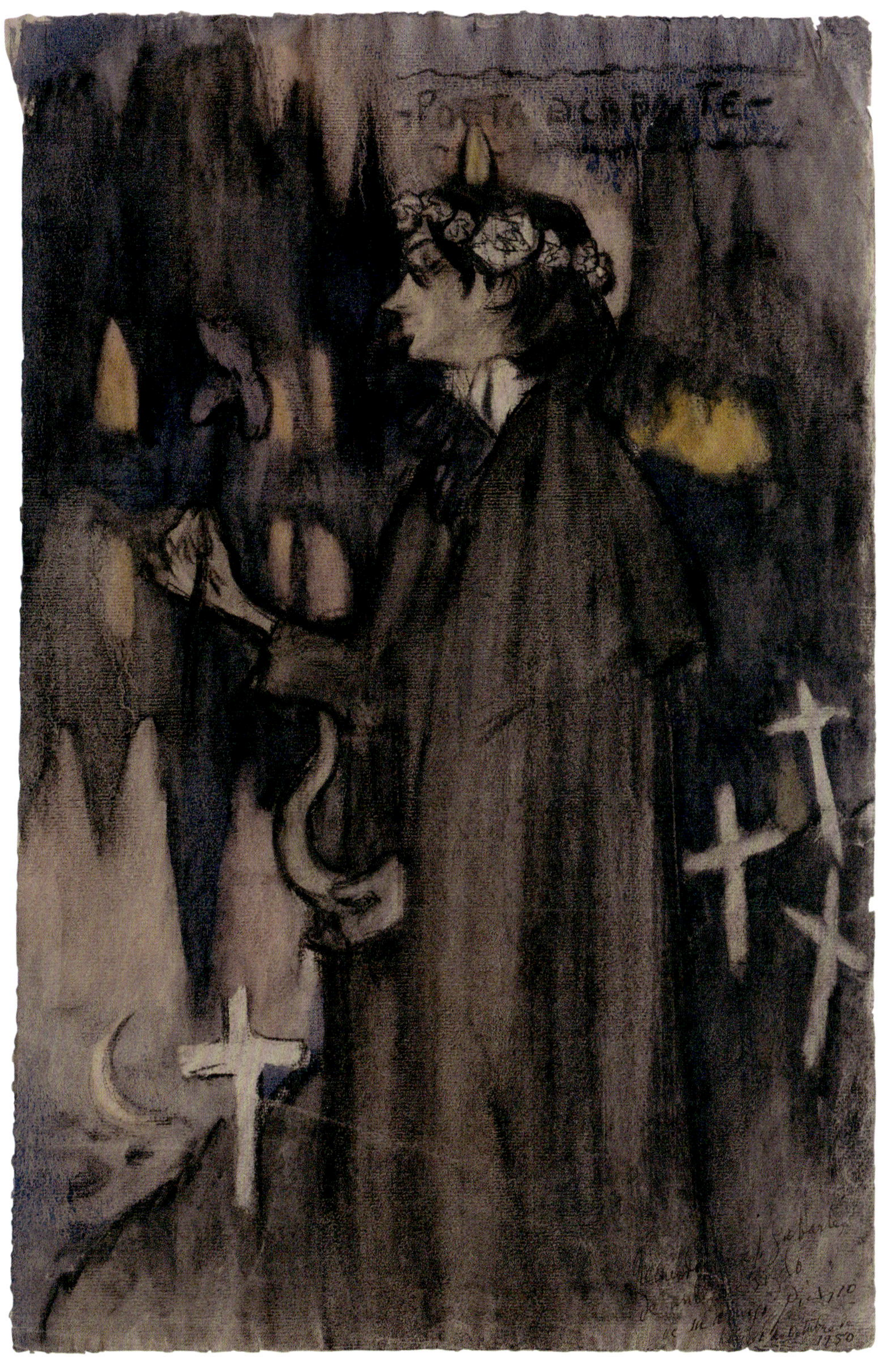

18 *Decadent Poet (Jaume Sabartés)*, 1900 (L)

In the liberal atmosphere of Els Quatre Gats, Picasso's bent for caricature came into its own, and his second portrait of Sabartés (18) is of a different type from the last three drawings. Sabartés was hanging about Picasso's studio one day when he was suddenly handed a paintbrush and told to hold it up before him. The impromptu modelling session was soon over and when he saw what Picasso had done, Sabartés grasped the point at once: 'It was his commentary on the mania for effeteness which pervaded the atmosphere.'[18] The target of Picasso's satire was the Symbolist movement, which was at its height throughout the 1890s. Symbolist clichés for mysticism and the occult abound in this portrait, including the lakeside graveyard, crescent moon, quasi-religious ritual and purple, gold and black colour scheme. Garbed in the voluminous cloak and floppy bow-tie affected by bohemian aesthetes, Sabartés is garlanded like a bridesmaid with the flame of enlightenment bursting through his skull: the result is a grotesque parody of the 'Decadent poet' type. But Picasso simultaneously mocked his friend's odd looks: the myopia that defined him, his mop of lank black hair, long, pointed nose, prominent, rather feminine lips, narrow, jutting chin and delicate frame. The drawing may primarily be the caricature of a type, but it is also the caricature of an individual, and in the years to come the devoted Sabartés would often be the butt of Picasso's caustic humour (see 172–7). He put up with the mockery because being caricatured was a recognised mark of distinction and a backhanded expression of comradeship.[19]

SKETCHES: PLANNING, REHEARSING, PLAYING

The drawings with washes of colour destined for the exhibition in Els Quatre Gats show all the flair, speed and confidence that astonished people who saw Picasso at work. A different Picasso emerges from his contemporary sheets, crammed with private sketches and jottings, where the barriers collapse between portraiture proper, comical caricature and barely conscious doodling. One sheet, executed in pen and ink, is dominated by a self-portrait resembling the charcoal drawing described earlier (see 13), except that the face is split into two halves, with the left side shaded, the right brightly lit (19). The portrait lacks the former's visionary quality and was surely drawn from memory rather than with the aid of a mirror. Having completed it, Picasso proceeded to fill up the empty space with caricatures and doodles, first turning the sheet upside down, then folding it neatly beneath the bow-tie and packing that strip with numerous little figures when the paper was turned on its side. Drawing spontaneously like this was a welcome diversion from more demanding projects, and an outlet for Picasso's irreverent humour, but it was also indispensable as a tool for thinking and planning caricatures that delivered a punch. With the paper upside-down, to the left of his own head, Picasso drew a quick sketch of a raffish, grinning Pompeu Gener sporting his signature wide-brimmed hat – a try-out for the unfinished vignette-portrait in the Museu Picasso de Barcelona.[20] The sketch of the author Oriol Martí to the right of the self-portrait is of a different type: it is a grotesque caricature of the man Picasso portrayed naturalistically in a contemporary head-and-shoulders study.[21] Martí's ludicrously bulging cheeks and popping eyes spawned the obscene buttock-heads with beady eyes that jostle with other doodles on the lower strip of this sheet of drawings (including one of a naked prostitute passing wind).

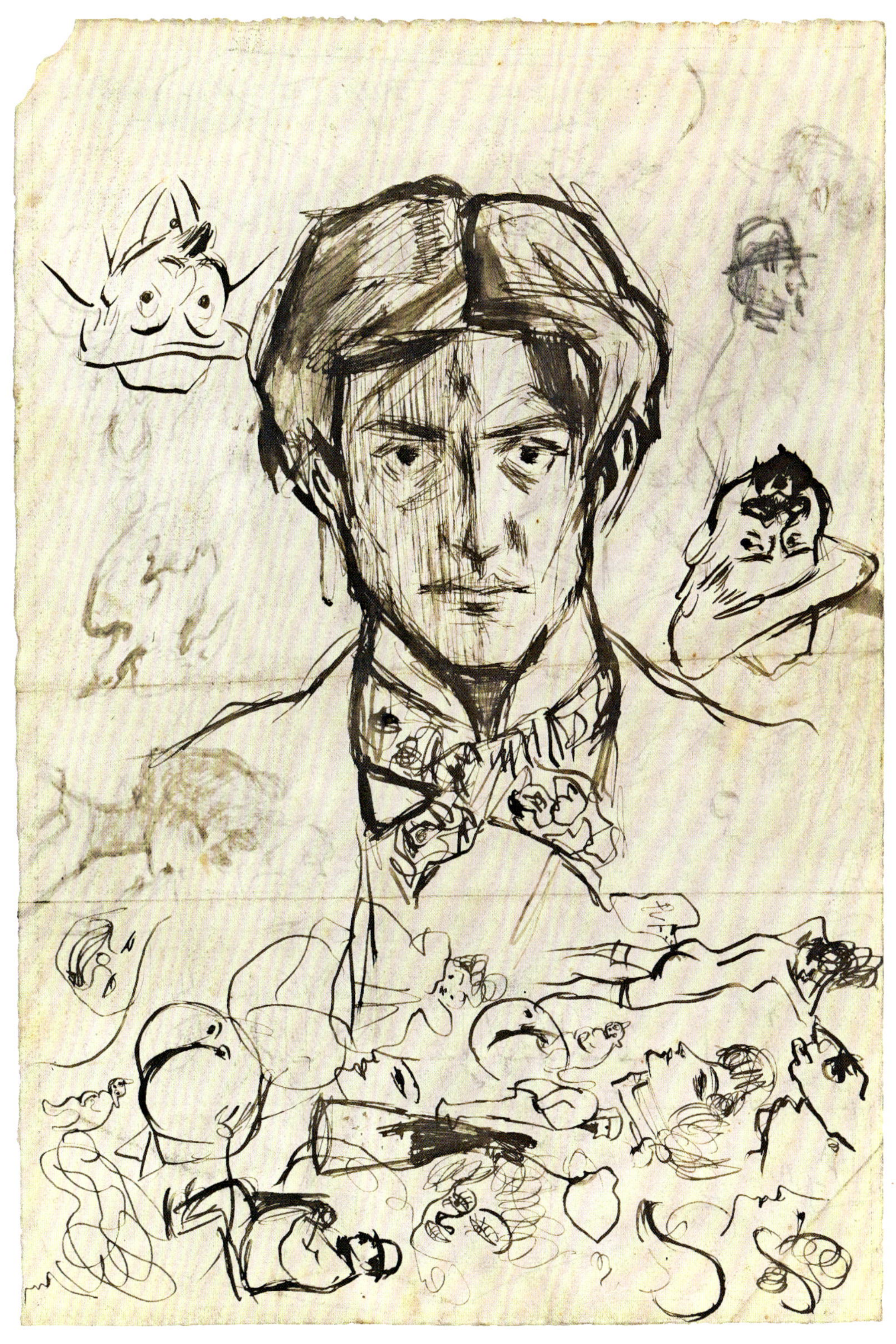

19 *Self-portrait, Pompeu Gener, Oriol Martí and Other Sketches*, 1899–1900 (B)

Rife with coarse schoolboy humour and erotic fantasy, repeats and variations of these little figures are strewn across dozens of contemporary sheets, for drawing was always Picasso's primary medium for thinking, planning, imagining, playing.

In another large sheet of drawings, those disparate modes of representation were complemented by a new element: script (20). Instead of taking an unused sheet of paper, Picasso recycled the cover of a collection of another artist's drawings, inscribed faintly in graphite with a title and name in a fastidious, copperplate hand.[22] The ornamental script, utterly different from Picasso's normal handwriting, evidently caught his attention and stimulated a bout of imitation in pen and ink.[23] Mainly confined to the four edges of the paper so that they function like a picture frame, these calligraphic exercises became increasingly confident as Picasso absorbed and mastered the alien style of the model. The inscriptions are variations of his own name, his father's name and the name of his sister Lola, the latter complemented by a string of Ls. (On the back of the paper, he tried out the first five letters of the alphabet in uppercase and wrote the name of his mother, María, to complete the quasi-ritualistic naming of his closest family members.) Turned vertically, the paper then served for figure drawings executed in Conté crayon.

A portrait of a morose Don José dominates the sheet. It may have been drawn from life, but it also involved wilful Modernista stylisation, for the contours were reinforced to bring out the symmetry of his gaunt and craggy features. If – to use semiotic terminology – these features are Don José's 'iconic sign', the inscriptions of his name, and the names of Lola and Picasso, are 'arbitrary signs', and are an alternative form of representation of three of Picasso's regular subjects at this time – his father, his sister, himself. At top right of the sheet, a male figure ingeniously amalgamates word and image, for his profile is formed from the letters of Don José's name. Circulating round Don José's head are thumbnails of a woman in an Egyptian headdress and a moustachioed dandy – types not individuals – and caricatures of, at the bottom left, the hirsute landscape painter Joaquim Mir and, at the bottom right, Picasso's close friend, the poet and painter Carles Casagemas, with his jutting nose and receding chin grotesquely exaggerated. Like the thumbnails of Gener and Martí mentioned above, these were trials for independent caricatures.[24]

A third sheet of sketches was used in one direction only (21). Picasso's initial idea may have been for some sort of narrative scene centred on himself, for he is seen in profile, wearing a wide-brimmed hat, hand stuffed in pocket, walking forwards. In the event, he filled the space to the left and right of his profile with various disembodied heads and three very rough compositional sketches for a poster advertising the savings bank Caja de Previsión y Socorro.[25] Picasso settled on an Art Nouveau idiom for the symbolic figure group of the poster. The wilful abstraction, distortion and exaggeration of the style made it a natural ally of caricature, and in this sheet it mediated the transition from the naturalistic style of the self-portrait to the grotesquerie of the most reductive of the heads.

One of the most fascinating sheets introduces another weapon in Picasso's graphic armoury: parody (22). *Horror vacui* is the reigning principle but certain figures do stand out from the mêlée. The painter Josep Rocarol i Faura appears in profile three times, helpfully identified by name. All three little drawings are very similar and were done one after the other to sharpen Picasso's caricatural image of his friend. (A finished caricature is discussed below, see 31.) The ludicrous personage in the bottom right corner wearing a large hat, an excessively high collar and a flower in his button-hole is an imaginative invention, albeit a spin-off

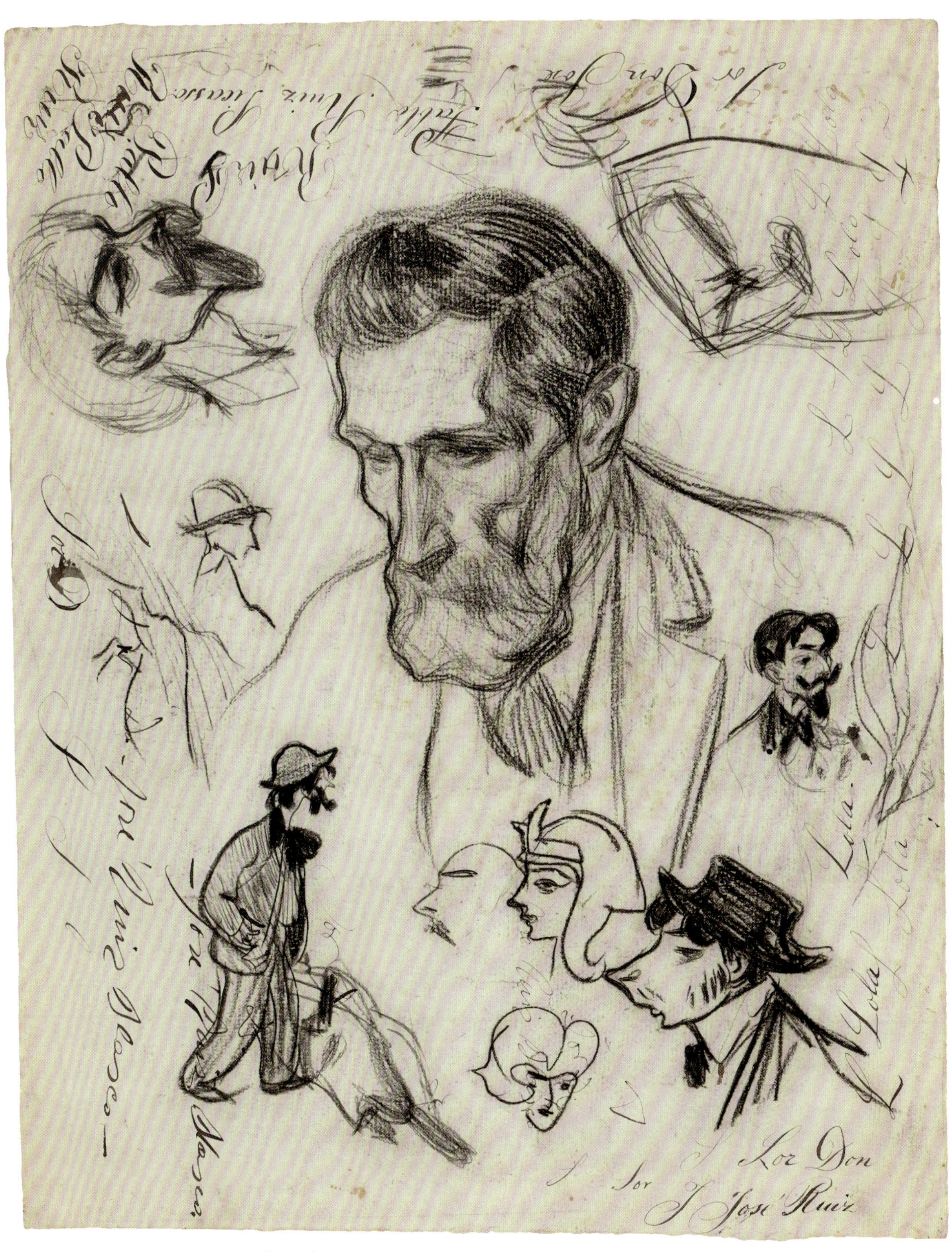

20 *The Artist's Father, Joaquim Mir, Carles Casagemas and Various Caricatures*, 1899–1900 (B)

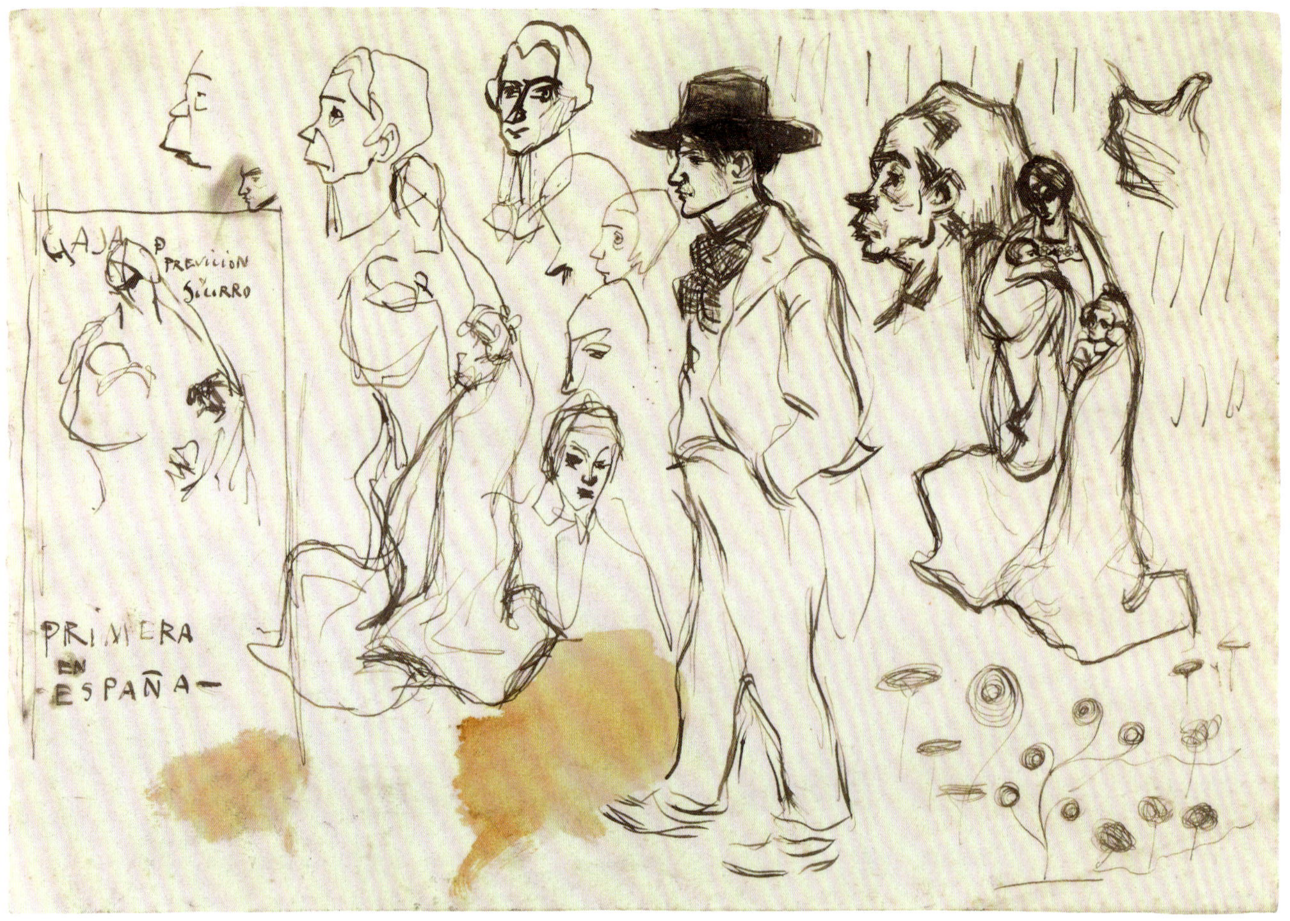

21 *Self-portrait and Studies for a Poster for the Caja de Previsión y Socorro,* May 1900 (L)

22 *Santiago Rusiñol Caricatured as* The Nobleman with His Hand on His Chest *by El Greco, Josep Rocarol i Faura and Other Sketches,* 1899–1900 (B)

from the Rocarol caricatures. Quite different in its miniaturist detail from the other sketches on the sheet, it is a pastiche of illustrations in children's books by the likes of Walter Crane. The other real-life target of Picasso's teasing humour was Rusiñol.[26] Wearing his favourite broad-brimmed hat and smoking a cigar stuffed in his pipe, he is depicted in a vignette at the foot of the sheet in the pose of El Greco's *Nobleman with His Hand on His Chest* (*c.*1580). Picasso knew that Rusiñol identified with this masterpiece in the Prado – that he had painted a life-size copy (in 1897) and that fellow Moderniste Ramon Pichot had depicted him in the same rhetorical pose.[27] To complete his tiny spoof, Picasso gave it an old-master frame.

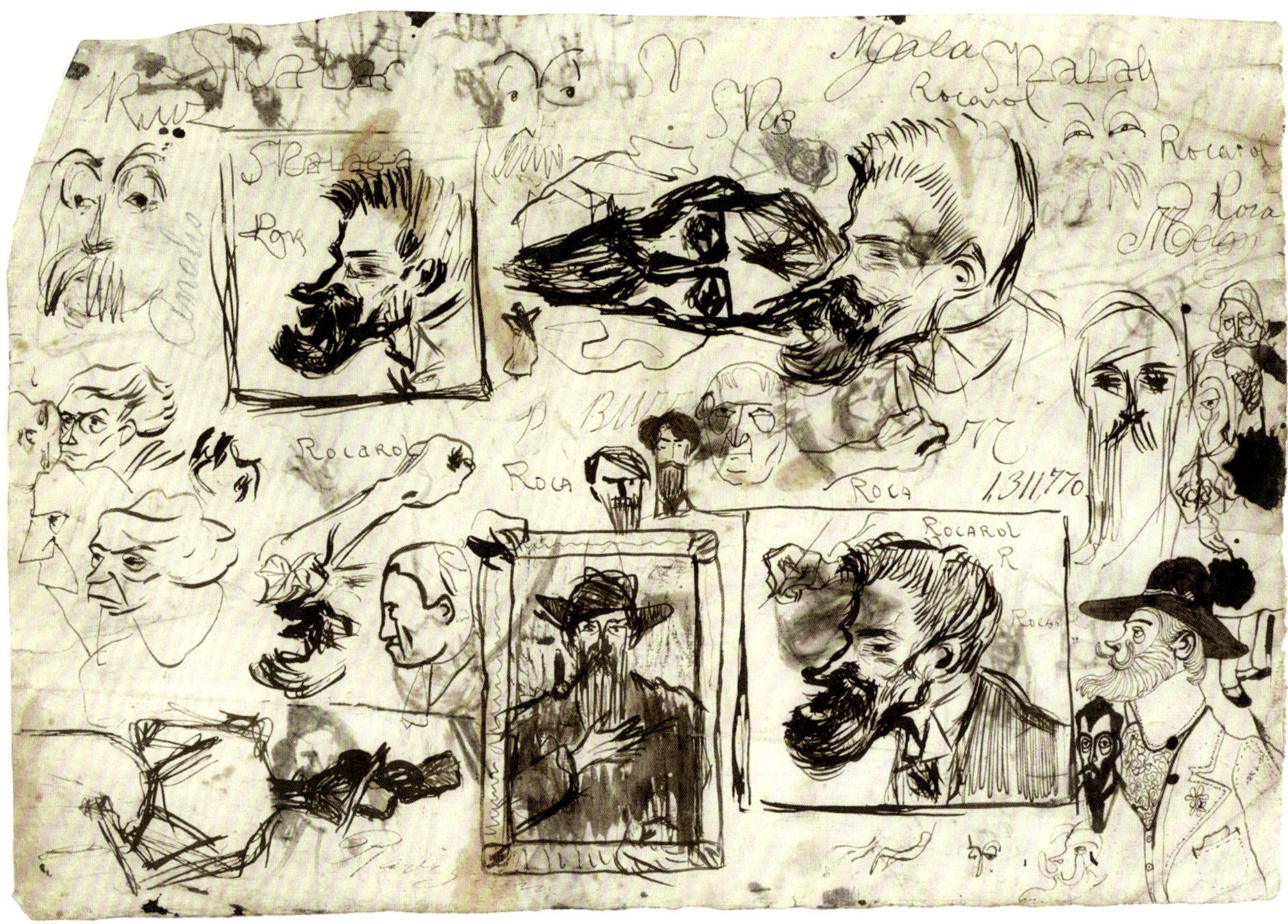

During this period, El Greco meant almost as much to Picasso as to Rusiñol, and a parody of his portraits of bearded, beruffed gentlemen in black floats on its side between two of the sketches of Rocarol. Picasso had made his first pilgrimage to Toledo to see El Greco's *The Burial of the Count of Orgaz* (1586–8) in the autumn of 1897 and, infected by the cult of the maverick artist at Els Quatre Gats, he produced scores of these parodies or pastiches. Indeed, close examination reveals that the pseudo-El Greco head was the very first figure Picasso drew on the present sheet, which at that stage was oriented vertically. One of the Rocarol heads shares certain of its contours, and although the resulting image of symbiotic attachment may have arisen accidentally, it perfectly encapsulates the intimate connection between Picasso's caricatural portraits of his Modernista friends and his absorption of El Greco's unique stylistic mannerisms. Caricature and parody or pastiche are closely related: all three modes claim intimate knowledge of the subject; all three involve schematic condensation and a disconcerting blend (in subtly different measures) of lionising and lampooning.

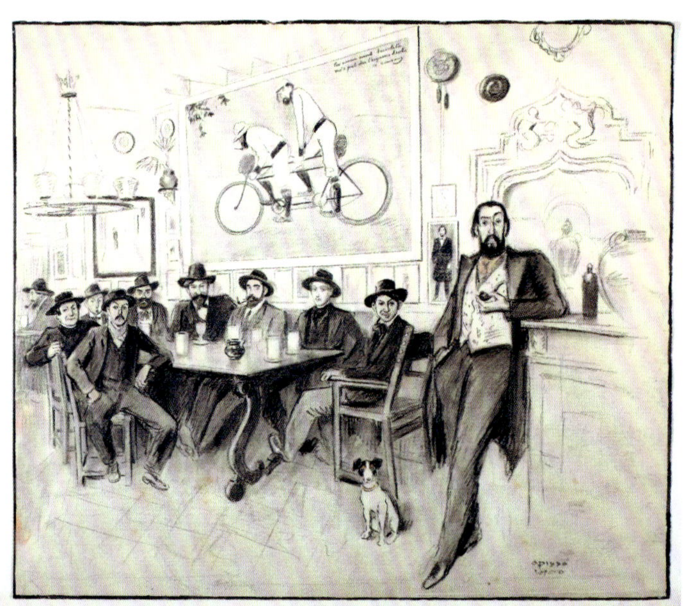

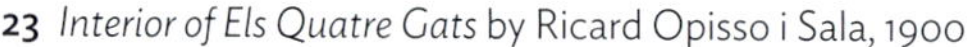

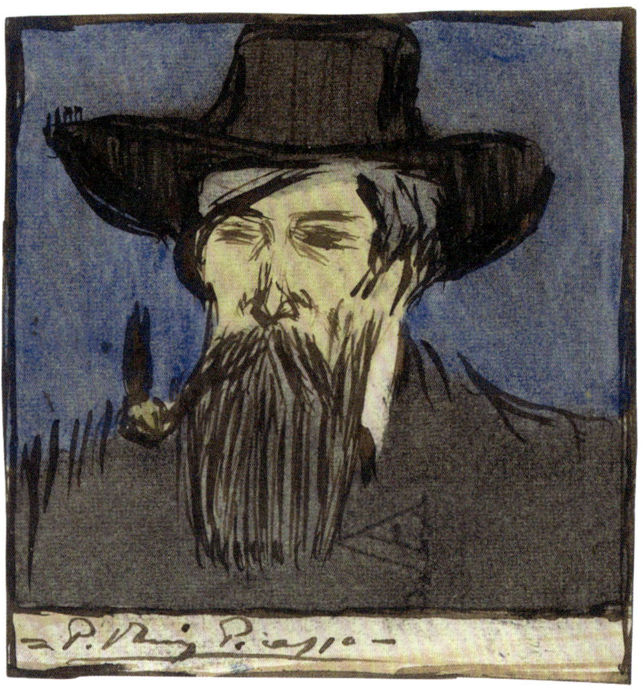

23 *Interior of Els Quatre Gats* by Ricard Opisso i Sala, 1900

24 *Santiago Rusiñol*, 1900

25 *Joaquim Mir*, 1900 (B)

26 *Portrait of Mir* by Ramon Casas i Carbó, reproduced *Pèl & Ploma*, no.81, 1 October 1901

CARICATURES IN MINIATURE

The energy Picasso expended on caricature at this critical moment in his career may strike us now as curious, but as an art form steeped in traditions of protest against the status quo it was held in high esteem in Els Quatre Gats. Casas's enormous, poster-like painting of himself and Pere Romeu speeding on a tandem bicycle was on permanent display in the bar (23), a reminder that mockery was also an instrument for consolidating conspiratorial group-identity. Indeed, caricature functions best when practised within a clique: its effectiveness depends on recognition of the target and also on the viewer's ability to evaluate the balance between truth and falsity in the characterisation.[28] The larger context was the Catalan Modernistes' addiction to all things Parisian – in the words of Sabartés: 'Nothing counted except the fashion from Paris'[29] – for caricature had grown steadily in mass popularity ever since Charles Philipon founded *La Caricature* in 1830 and, importantly, had received ringing

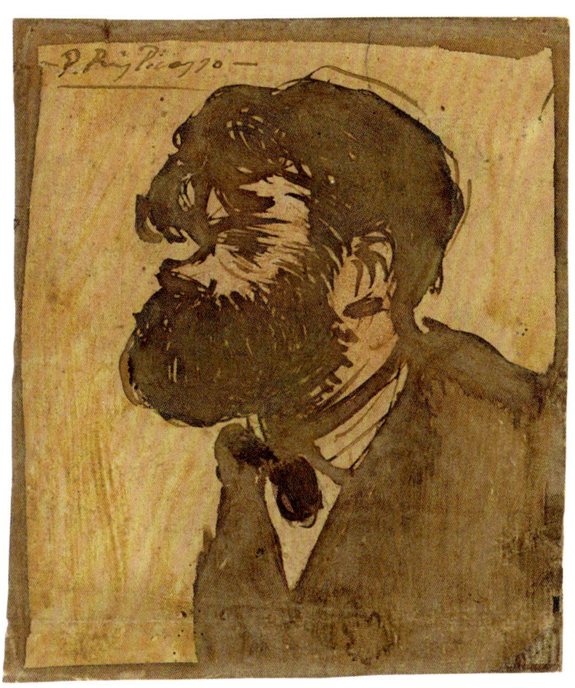

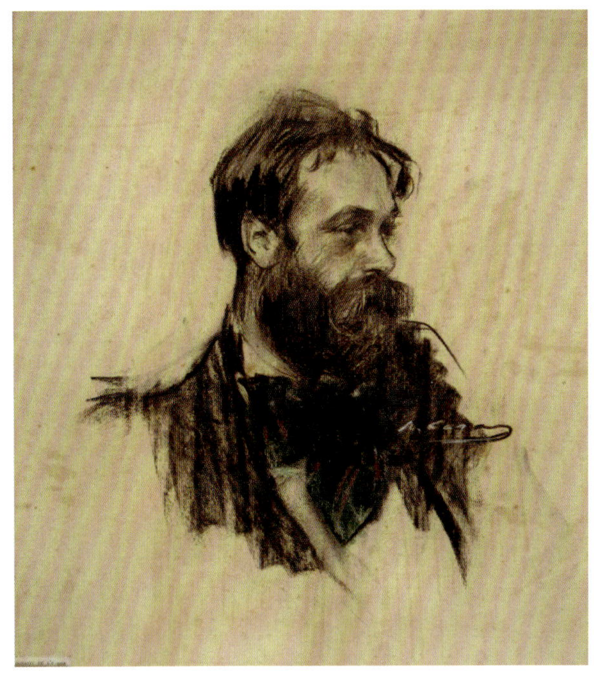

endorsement from Baudelaire.[30] The number of French magazines specialising in caricatures and cartoons is staggering: 139 were published between 1870 and 1900 in Paris alone.[31] By the turn of the century a substantial, well-illustrated literature on the nature, motivation and history of caricature had been published.[32]

Dating Picasso's drawings precisely is impossible, but he does seem to have concentrated on this special field of portraiture after his exhibition at Els Quatre Gats closed. *Pèl & Ploma*, the tavern's in-house magazine published caricatures of Rusiñol (24) and Mir (25) that are now in the collection of the Metropolitan Museum of Art, New York.[33] Lest there be any doubt about their nature, in *Pèl & Ploma* they were labelled 'Caricature of Rusiñol' and 'Caricature of Mir' and implicitly contrasted with full-page reproductions of the flattering, head-and-shoulders likenesses by Casas (26) published in the same issues of the magazine.[34] Caricature was a potential source of income; no doubt Picasso tried to place at least some of the others he prepared so carefully, but without success.

In the words of an English authority on caricature, it was vital to 'get at the soul or pith of the subject' with no sign whatever of hesitation – 'the line must be quick and firm' – and with sufficient wit to pique and amuse the most casual beholder.[35] Picasso's trials scattered across sheets of sketches show how much effort he put into the process of analysis and distillation, alimented by a controlling idea, to achieve this pithiness. His larger, more naturalistic portraits were an altogether easier proposition and he had no need to make preparatory studies. The unsigned portrait of the writer and Esperanto-enthusiast Frederic Pujulà i Vallès is a case in point (27). It preceded the signed version now in the Metropolitan Museum of Art (28), and the differences between the two show Picasso's caricatural guile in action. Colour added to the decorative appeal of the finished portrait but the most significant changes affected the *mise-en-page*

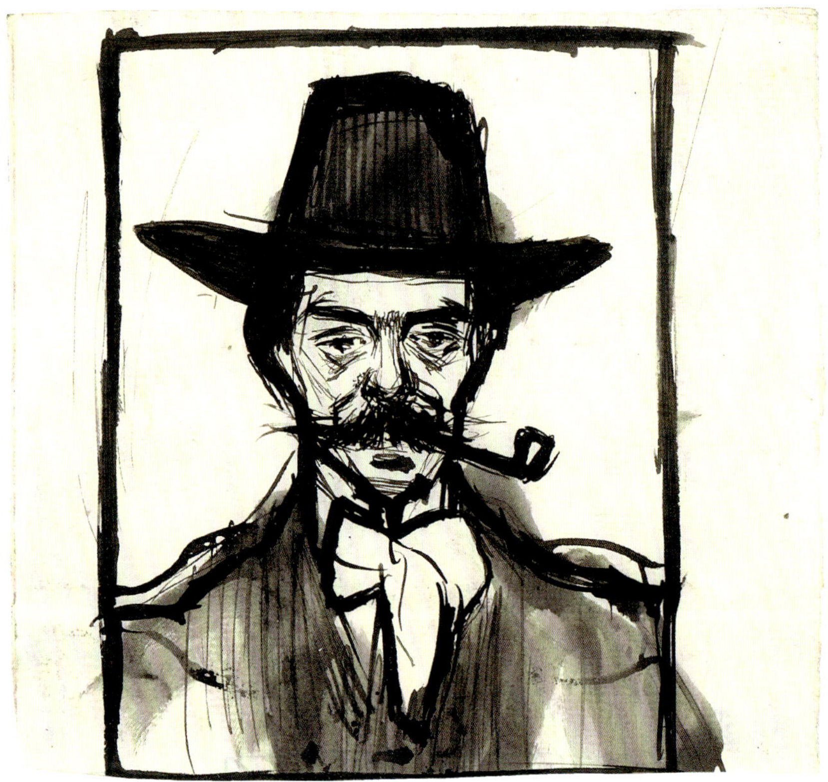

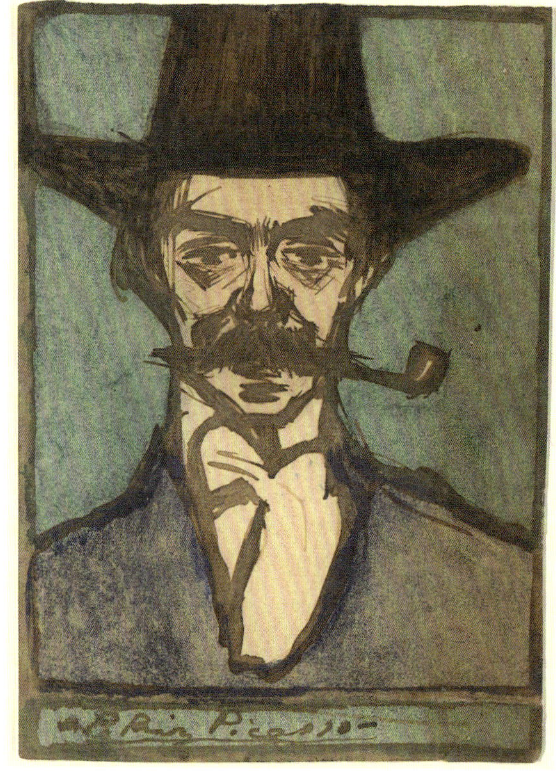

and graphic style. By closing in more tightly on Pujulà's head so that the top and one side of his hat are cropped by the hand-painted frame, by lengthening and simplifying his collar and floppy tie and narrowing the area devoted to the shoulders, Picasso made him appear taller, thinner and gaunter. By placing him slightly off-centre, looking out directly at the spectator, Picasso enhanced the impression of a prim, owlish pedagogue. By abstracting the jacket – sensuously handled in the preliminary version – he ensured that nothing detract from the alert, unsmiling face. Pujulà was only twenty-two or twenty-three at the time, but the caricature predicts how he would look in middle age, and offers a wry assessment of his incipient fanaticism.

The narrow format and strict frontality of the definitive version of the portrait of Pujulà was also deployed in Picasso's portrait of Miguel Utrillo (29), although here the shift away from the centre was to the right, not to the left. One of the more extreme characterisations of the entire set, it was neither washed with colour, nor signed, and may have been the final trial for a caricature that was never executed. Picasso worked over the image, simplifying and reinforcing the principal contours to produce the bold *cloisonné* effect cultivated by Gauguin and Van Gogh and imitated by the Modernistes. Rapid thumbnail sketches that preceded it reveal that Picasso was strongly tempted to present Utrillo in pure profile to show up the extraordinary shape of his long, down-turned nose and the forward thrust of his chin.[36] But determined to vary the viewpoints within the series as a whole, he plumped eventually for a full-face view, focusing on Utrillo's hooded, bloodhound's

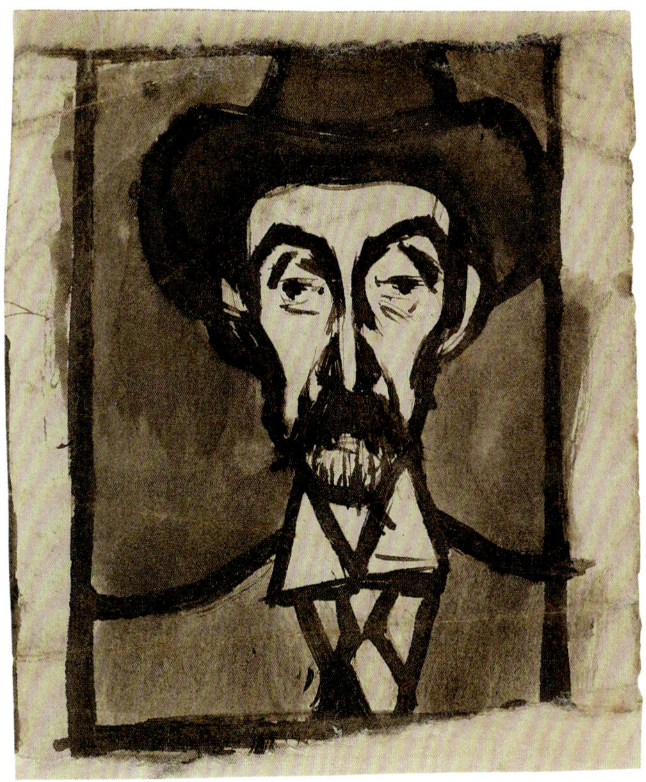

27 *Portrait of the Writer Frederic Pujulà i Vallès*, 1900 (B)
28 *Frederic Pujulà i Vallès*, 1900
29 *Miguel Utrillo*, 1900 (L)

eyes, overhanging brow and the narrow, bony shape of his head. The wilful exaggeration of his idiosyncratic traits is comical, but the suggestion of the dry skull beneath the skin gives the image a chilling edge. No such intimations of mortality attended Casas's contemporary portraits of Utrillo, who was only thirty-eight years old when a sardonic Picasso foresaw his physical decline.[37]

Given Picasso's decision to use a virtually standard format and scale for his gallery of Modernistes, establishing distinctions was all-important to successful characterisation. For the finished, signed and cut-out miniatures of Pichot (30) and Mir (25) Picasso chose the pure profile view preferred for ruler portraits on coins and stamps – an ironic comparison between his resolutely anti-establishment painter-friends and history's Great Men. Pichot's distinctive height and lankiness are wittily suggested by his stooping posture, scrawny neck, baggy clothing and the relatively large area given to the unpainted background; Mir's short, bullish stature is implied by the way in which he fills the composition. These differences are reinforced by the contrast between Mir's snout and Pichot's fine aquiline nose, and between the dense thicket of Mir's hair and beard and the delicate, curling lines of Pichot's soft, wispy beard.

The three vignettes of Rocarol crammed in the sheet of sketches discussed above (see 22) reveal that Picasso originally planned a caricature with exactly the same structure as his profile portrait of Mir. But he realised that distinguishing between these two gruff bohemians would require more than a differentiation of their haircuts. The completed, signed miniature of Rocarol (31) represents him in

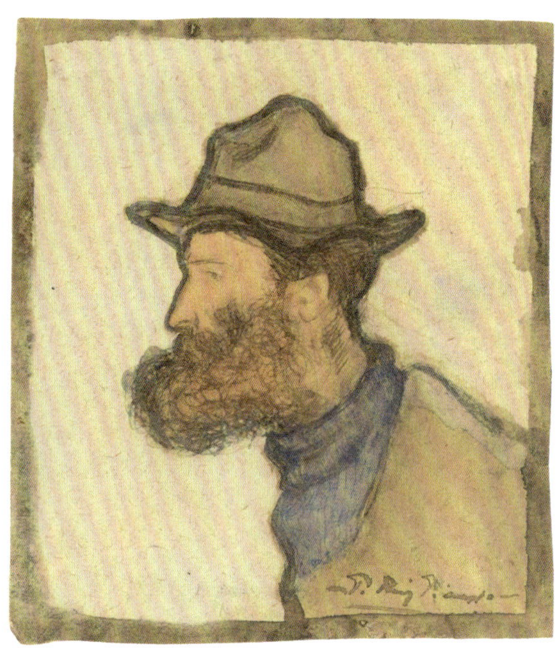

30 *Ramon Pichot*, 1900 (B)

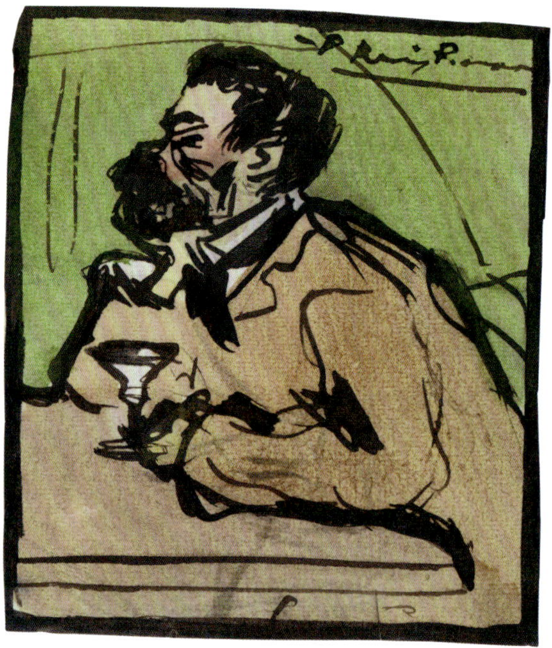

31 *Josep Rocarol i Faura*, 1900 (L)

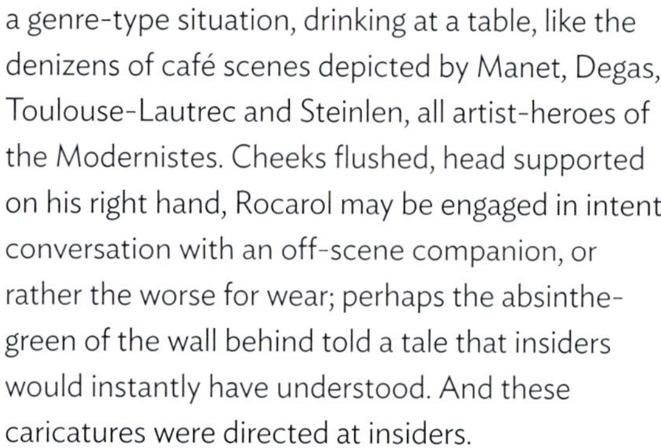

a genre-type situation, drinking at a table, like the denizens of café scenes depicted by Manet, Degas, Toulouse-Lautrec and Steinlen, all artist-heroes of the Modernistes. Cheeks flushed, head supported on his right hand, Rocarol may be engaged in intent conversation with an off-scene companion, or rather the worse for wear; perhaps the absinthe-green of the wall behind told a tale that insiders would instantly have understood. And these caricatures were directed at insiders.

Pere Romeu in a Field of Irises (32) is twice the size of these miniature caricatures and belongs to a different category.[38] With his priestly looks – long, lank hair, full beard, doleful expression, gangling physique, long black coat – Romeu was a favourite target of caricaturists and Picasso did not miss his chance. Kindly, well-intentioned, with a tendency to melancholy and a reputation for utter incompetence in the financial management of Els Quatre Gats, Romeu's personality was equally inviting. In this amusing gouache, Picasso poked fun at his enthusiastic, unworldly temperament, imagining him buried waist-deep in a field of purple irises with eyes raised to heaven in soulful communion with nature. Sabartés gazed raptly at a purple iris in Picasso's elaborate caricature of him as a Decadent poet (see 18); *Pere Romeu in a Field of Irises* should probably be understood as an experiment in bridging the gap between the latter, relatively large drawing and the miniatures.

Santiago Rusiñol (33) has the same format but a rather different tone from these caricatures. A signed-off work of art, it is cut out up to the edges of the hand-painted frame ready for reproduction in a magazine. Rusiñol's thick hair, unkempt moustache and long beard apart, his distinguishing feature for Picasso seems to have been his inwardness, for in this work, and in the caricature chosen for reproduction in *Pèl & Ploma* (24), Rusiñol has the closed, sunken eyes of someone blind since birth. This 'blinding' was no slip of Picasso's draftsmanship but a sign of

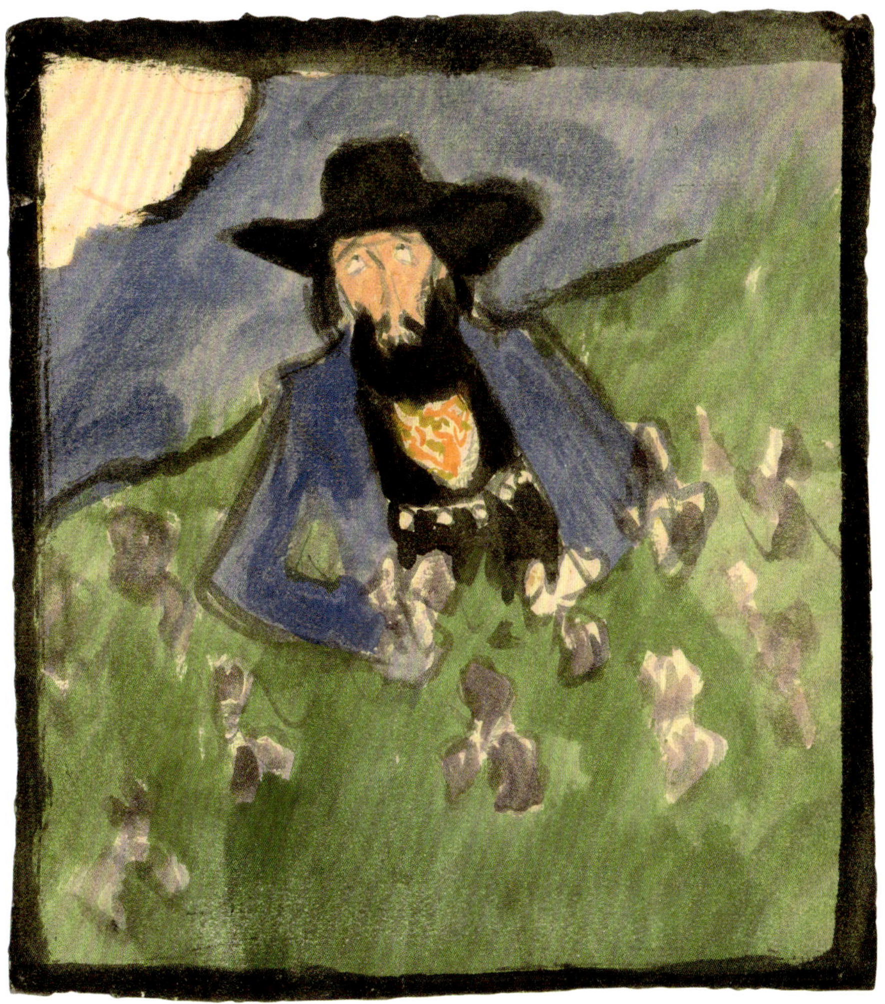

32 *Pere Romeu in a Field of Irises*, c.1900 (B, L)

Rusiñol's dreamy, romantic nature and immersion in the past: his passion for the arts and crafts of medieval Catalonia, his identification with El Greco and his withdrawal into Cau Ferrat – his private museum-cum-studio in the seaside village of Sitges. With its warm brown palette and dark tonality, this diminutive portrait speaks of Rembrandt rather than El Greco, however. A patriarchal figure, the Rusiñol seen here resembles Rembrandt's sympathetic representations of ageing men, traditionally identified as scholars, philosophers or Jews. Picasso's tiny masterpiece is executed with craftsmanly finesse: thread-like vertical lines in sepia cover almost the entire surface, weaving figure and ground together; touches of water were used to blot areas of the beard to create the impression of soft, matted hair. The time and care expended on this exquisite gem reveal a different artist from the one who let his pen run at the speed of thought.

Picasso had developed rapidly in the five years since the family's move to Barcelona in 1895. He had slipped the yoke of his cautious and conservative father and been accepted into the most advanced set of artists in Spain. But like all the Modernistes,

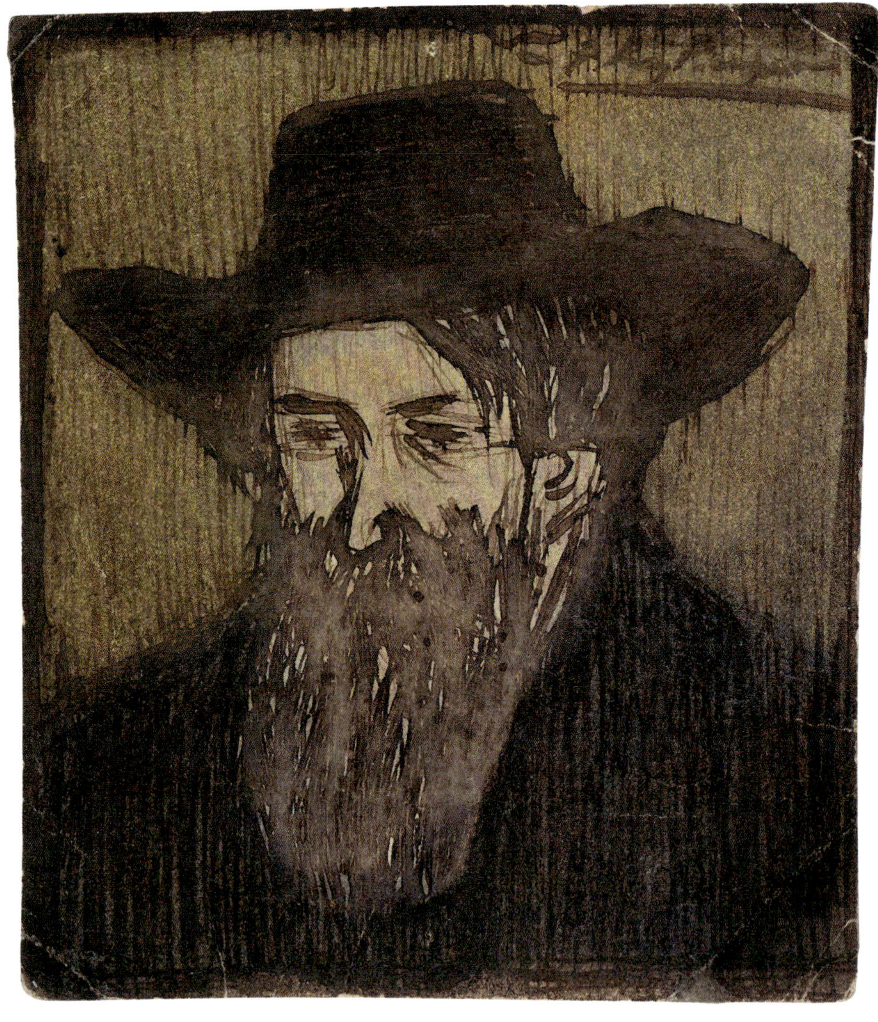

33 *Santiago Rusiñol*, 1900 (L)

he regarded his education as incomplete without time spent in Paris. The perfect opportunity arose when *Last Moments*, the 2-metre-wide deathbed scene he had shown in Málaga the previous summer, was accepted for the Spanish section of the Exposition Universelle, which opened in April 1900.[39] Full of foreboding about the dangerous impact of Paris, Don José financed the trip nevertheless: like Picasso's ever-indulgent mother, he still believed a brilliant career lay ahead for his rebellious son.

1 For instance, *First Communion*, 1895–6 (MPB 110.001). See Maria Teresa Ocaña, 'José Ruiz Blasco versus Pablo Ruiz Picasso', in *Picasso jeunesse* 1991, pp.32–49.

2 For an account of Don José's character, see Sabartés 1954, pp.23–5.

3 See McCully 1997, p.25.

4 Picasso was, presumably, using a mirror.

5 Cited in Richardson 1991, p.67.

6 My thanks to Reyes Jiménez Garnica for information about the underlying composition.

7 Compare, for instance, Lola's childish appearance in a conté crayon sketch (MPB 110.597) with her sultry image in *Lola, the Artist's Sister*, 1899–1900 (MPB 4.265).

8 Sabartés 1949, p.18.

9 E.g. *Allegory: Young Man, Woman and Grotesques*, 1899 (MP 419).

10 Sabartés 1949, p.54.

11 Ibid., p.53.

12 See Richardson 1991, pp.143–9. The number of portraits is sometimes put as high as 150. Picasso also showed three paintings, including *Last Moments* (see below). For illustrations, see also Palau 1981, pp.183–9.

13 Review attributed to Manuel Rodríguez Codolà, *La Vanguardia* (Barcelona), 3 February 1900. Cited in McCully 1981, pp.21–2.

14 Review attributed to Sebastià Trullul i Plana, *Diario de Barcelona*, 7 February 1900. Cited in McCully 1981, p.23.

15 Sabartés 1949, pp.52, 57.

16 The faintly inscribed numbers at centre bottom of the sheet, '28 x 38', are the dimensions the portrait would have had if Picasso had cut it down.

17 In the version of the portrait published in *Arte Joven* (no.1, 31 March 1901), Picasso depicted the garden in greater detail so that it is instantly recognisable. See Vallès 2010, pp.222–39.

18 Sabartés 1949, pp.56–7.

19 See Melot 1975, p.28.

20 *Pompeu Gener in a Wide-brimmed Hat*, 1899–1900 (MPB 110.240). Gener was a playwright, journalist, Catalan nationalist and devoted Nietzschean. For his influence on Picasso, see Gavin Parkinson, 'Incipit Picasso: From *The Birth of Tragedy* to *The Burial of Casagemas*', in Wright 2013, pp.69–80.

21 *Portrait of Oriol Martí*, 1899–1900 (MPB 110.271).

22 The inscription is only partially legible, but one can read '6 Dibujos' and 'Perez'.

23 Picasso's current sketchbook was a recycled ledger with numerous entries in a neat copperplate script – another likely source of inspiration for his inscriptions on the present sheet of drawings. See Léal 1996, cat.1.

24 Notably for *Caricature of Joaquim Mir*, 1899–1900 (MPB 110.365) and *Carles Casagemas*, 1900 (The Metropolitan Museum of Art, New York; Z.XXI.116; see 35).

25 For a more complete compositional design, see MPB 110.825. The closing date of the competition for the poster was 31 May 1900. Picasso did not win.

26 The verso of this sheet is covered with drawings, including caricatures of Casas.

27 Rusiñol's copy of El Greco's painting and Pichot's portrait of Rusiñol are in Museu del Cau Ferrat, Sitges, and reproduced in Vallès 2010, p.200.

28 See David Perkins, 'A definition of caricature and caricature and recognition', *Studies in the Anthropology of Visual Communication*, September 1975, pp.1–24.

29 Sabartés 1949, p.52.

30 The key texts are 'On the Essence of Laughter', first published in 1855, 'Some French Caricaturists' and 'Some Foreign Caricaturists', both first published in 1857. See Baudelaire 1964, pp.147–96.

31 Shikes and Heller 1984, p.11. Between 1900 and 1914 another 94 specialist French journals were published (Judith Wechsler, 'Caricature' in *Grove Art Online*: http://www.oxfordartonline.com/). Catalan art journals regularly juxtaposed caricatures with reproductions of avant-garde French painting.

32 For instance, Champfleury 1865, Alexandre 1893 and Veyrat 1895.

33 For the Metropolitan's entire collection of these caricatures, see Tinterow and Stein 2010, cats 1–11.

34 For Rusiñol, see *Pèl & Ploma*, no.65, 1 December 1900: Casas's portrait of Rusiñol is on the cover, Picasso's 'caricature' on p.4.

35 Ashbee 1928, p.24.

36 The alternative views are juxtaposed in a sheet of ink drawings (MPB 110.303).

37 For instance, Casas's full-length charcoal portrait of Utrillo published in *Pèl & Ploma*, nos 50–2, 26 May 1900, p.3. The caption pointedly states that it was 'drawn from life'.

38 For the Metropolitan Museum's superbly pithy caricature of Romeu seen from the back, see Tinterow and Stein 2010, cat. 11.

39 *Last Moments* was also shown in Picasso's exhibition at Els Quatre Gats in February 1900. *La Vie*, 1903 (The Cleveland Museum of Art; Z.I.179) was subsequently painted over it.

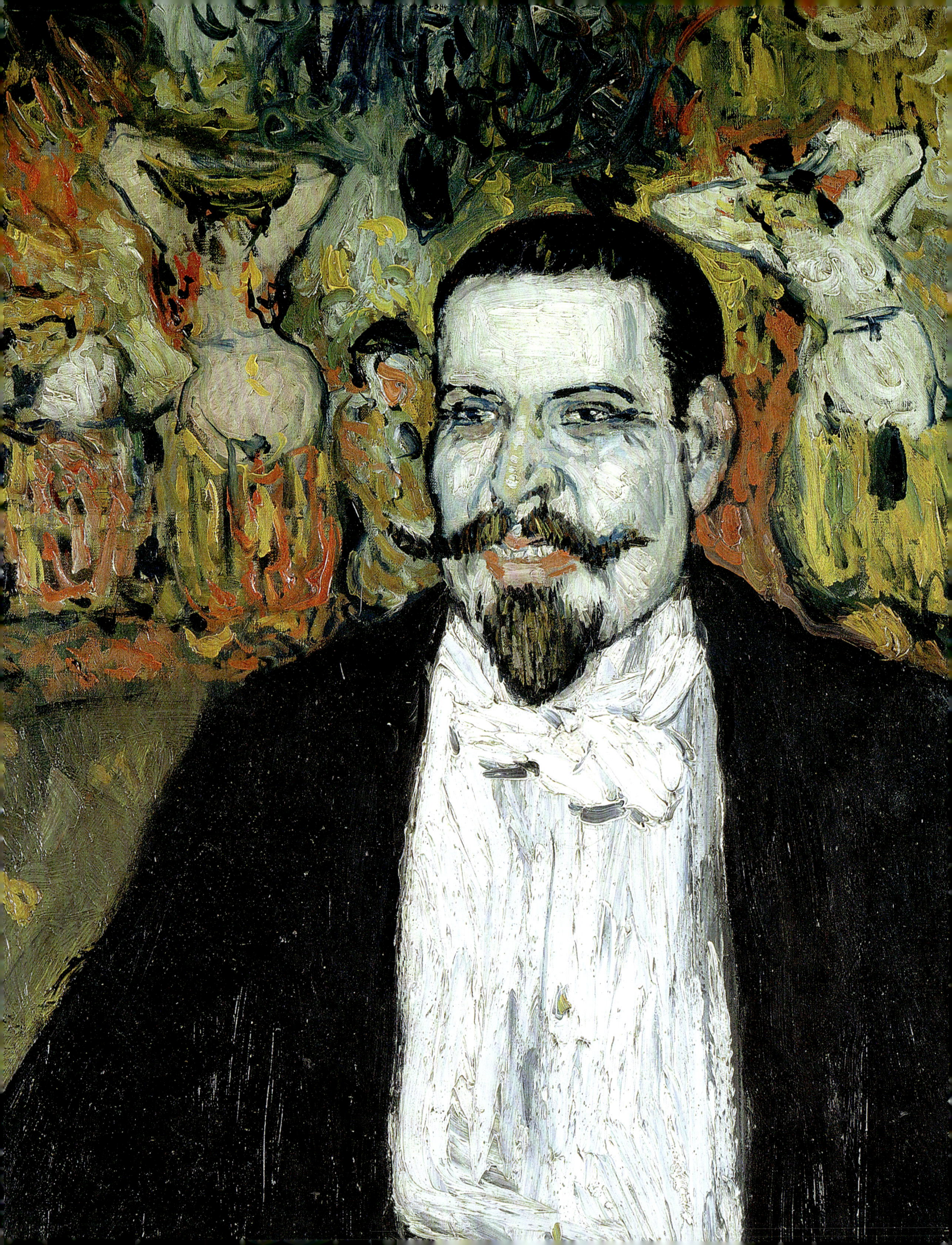

2. Experiments with form: Paris and Barcelona 1900–1904

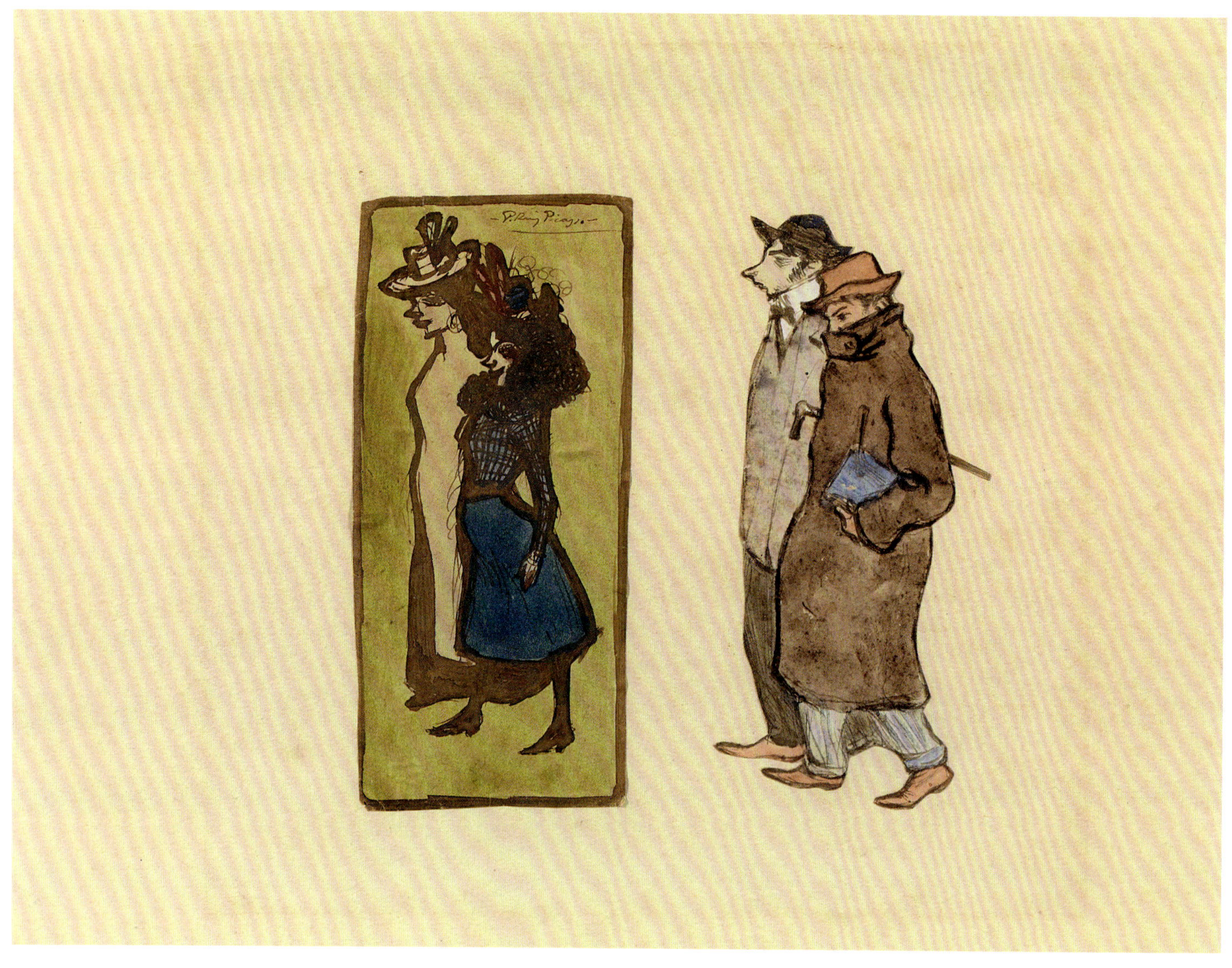

34.i *Two Girls*, 1900 (B)

34.ii *Carles Casagemas and Picasso*, 1900 (B)

PICASSO IN PARIS, 1900 AND 1901

For this first, keenly anticipated trip to Paris, Picasso's travelling companion was Casagemas. They arrived in late October 1900 and settled in a studio in Montmartre, then a cheap, rough, marginal district much favoured by the fluctuating Catalan community. An amusing ink and watercolour drawing of two young women, one dressed like an adolescent but strutting and ogling provocatively, encapsulates the louche allure of the street life of Paris (34.i). Prominently signed and with a hand-painted frame, it was probably destined for one of the scores of Parisian satirical magazines where sexual innuendo was the stock-in-trade. At some point, the vignette of the girls was united with a cut-out watercolour (now rather faded) of Picasso, bundled into a coat against the winter cold, clutching a sketchbook and trudging beside Casagemas (34.ii). The latter's weasel-features, hat and clothing are a virtual repeat of the caricature from the gallery of miniatures Picasso had produced in Barcelona at the beginning of the year (35). Whether he was responsible for cutting out the double portrait and teaming it with the watercolour of the girls to concoct a narrative of pursuit is an unanswered question.[1]

In career terms, the most significant event of Picasso's first trip to Paris was his meeting with Pere Mañach, an astute Catalan runner who made his living by brokering deals with gallerists and collectors. It was Mañach who organised Picasso's breakthrough exhibition at Ambroise Vollard's gallery the following June. Wary of giving the entire gallery over to an unknown nineteen-year-old, Vollard teamed Picasso with the older Basque painter Francisco Iturrino, whose brightly coloured genre scenes had a steady market. Much hung on the success of this exhibition and Picasso put together an extremely varied group of paintings in the hope of appealing to as wide a field of collectors as possible. Typically Spanish scenes transported

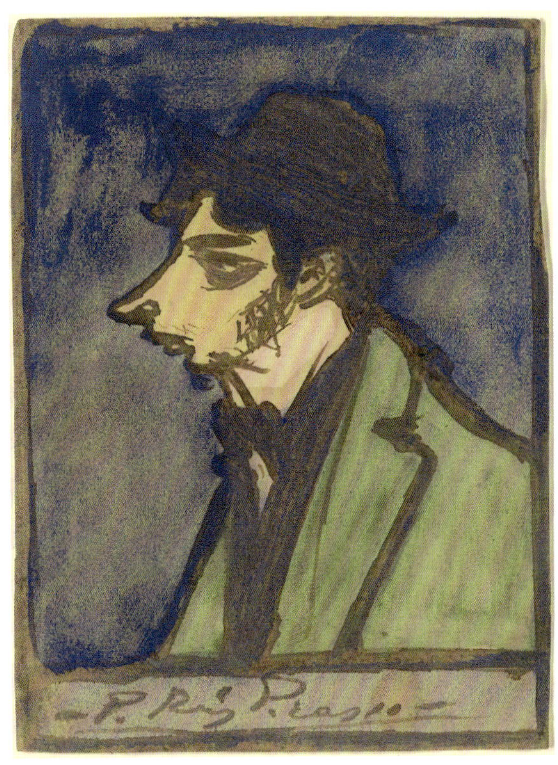

35 *Carles Casagemas*, 1900

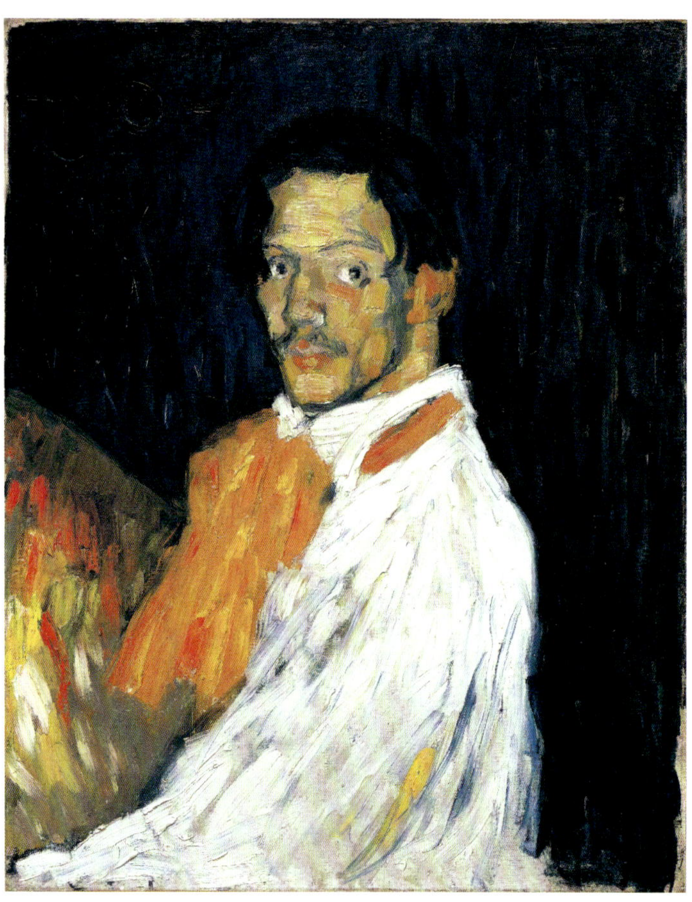

36 *Self-portrait (Yo Picasso)*, 1901

from Barcelona were mixed with newly minted, archetypal French scenes that revealed his recent, first-hand encounter with Impressionist and Post-Impressionist painting. A clutch of six portraits showed what he could do in that line.[2] One of them was *Self-portrait (Yo Picasso)* (36). It appeared in pole position in the catalogue list and could hardly have issued a more brazen demand for attention: the huge letters of the declamatory '– Yo –' (Spanish for 'I') were gouged into the wet paint of the blue–black background like a brand burnt into an animal's hide. *Espagnolisme* had proven appeal in Paris, and Picasso accentuated his blue–black hair, black eyes and sallow complexion, giving himself the swagger of a bullfighter or flamenco dancer.

Self-portrait with Wig (see 11) had demonstrated Picasso's taste for self-dramatisation and his technical daring, but in this new self-portrait he went further, and did so on a public stage. In proto-expressionist manner, he identified himself with paint and its brutally physical application. The combination of pitch-dark background and glaring white smock speaks of burning the midnight oil, and Picasso was in fact working at a frantic pace in the weeks before the show opened on 24 June 1901. He had arrived in Paris too late to see the Van Gogh retrospective mounted at Galerie Bernheim-Jeune in March 1901, but he would have heard talk of the stir it caused among the younger generation of painters. Picasso would also have seen the paintings stocked by Vollard, who had started buying and showing the Dutchman's work in 1895:[3] among those Vollard had at the time was *Portrait of Dr Félix Rey* (37).[4] Although Van Gogh's handling is more systematic and controlled than Picasso's, the emphasis on paint and mark-making may well have emboldened him. Van Gogh's glaring scarlet signature, which followed and reinforced the diagonal thrust of his brushwork at that point, may even have inspired Picasso's vaunting 'Yo'.

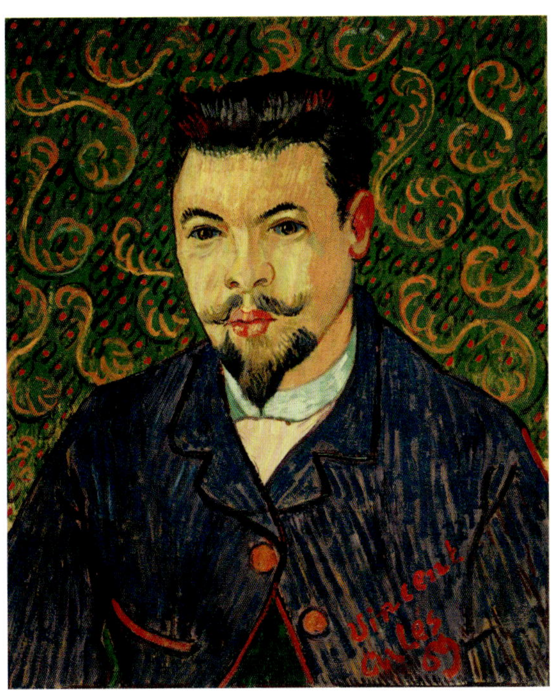

37 *Portrait of Dr Félix Rey* by Vincent Van Gogh, 1889

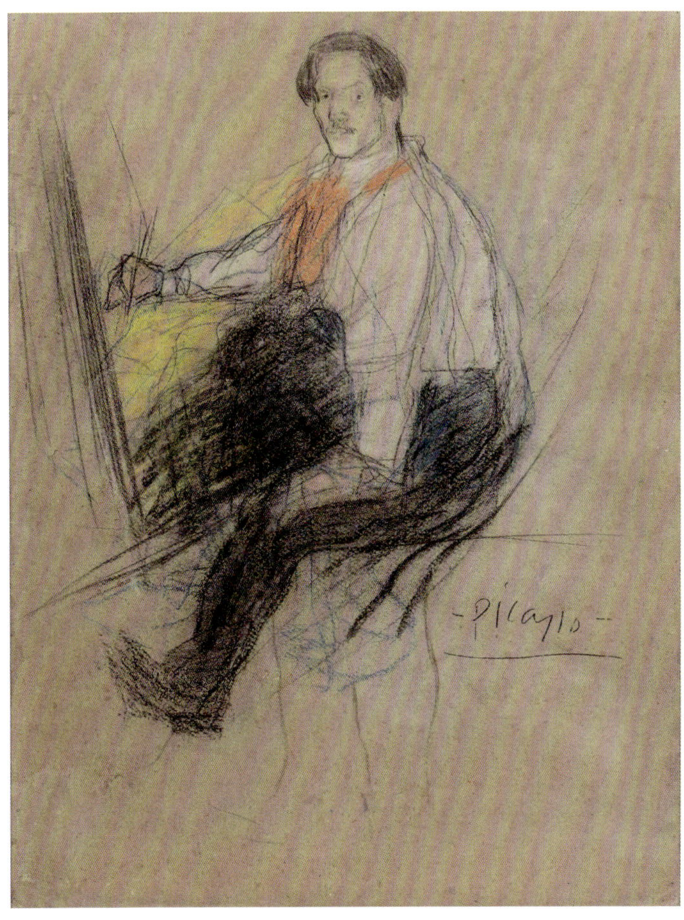

38 *Self-portrait*, 1901

A preparatory pastel and charcoal sketch (38) reveals that Picasso had initially planned to depict himself full-length, seated before his easel, brush in hand. He quickly realised, however, that those accessories were superfluous if paint and brushwork were allowed to speak for themselves. Abandoning the clichéd image of the artist at work in favour of the intimate half-length format, he drew the spectator irresistibly into his orbit. To enhance the dramatic effect of the sharp turn to confront the spectator, Picasso exaggerated the difference in the direction of each eye's dilated and mesmerising gaze. Taken to an extreme, this device for suggesting physical movement resulted in some of the most challenging facial distortions of his much later portraiture.

Picasso in a Top Hat (39) complements *Self-portrait (Yo Picasso)* by again depicting the artist at night. In this guise as a top-hatted Baudelairean *flâneur* – the detached yet constantly alert observer of modern life – it is Picasso himself whom the spectator imagines roaming the city streets, soaking up their sights and sounds and indulging in their dissolute pleasures. Picasso's principal model was evidently Toulouse-Lautrec, whose most original portraits were set up as genre scenes, with the sitter participating in a characteristic activity. Thus Maxime Dethomas, renowned for his theatre decorations, is shown watching the parade of masked dancers at the Bal de l'Opéra (40). Picasso's portrait is more conventional than Toulouse-Lautrec's in that he turns to face the spectator, rather than the bevy of half-naked prostitutes soliciting him. But in choosing dilute

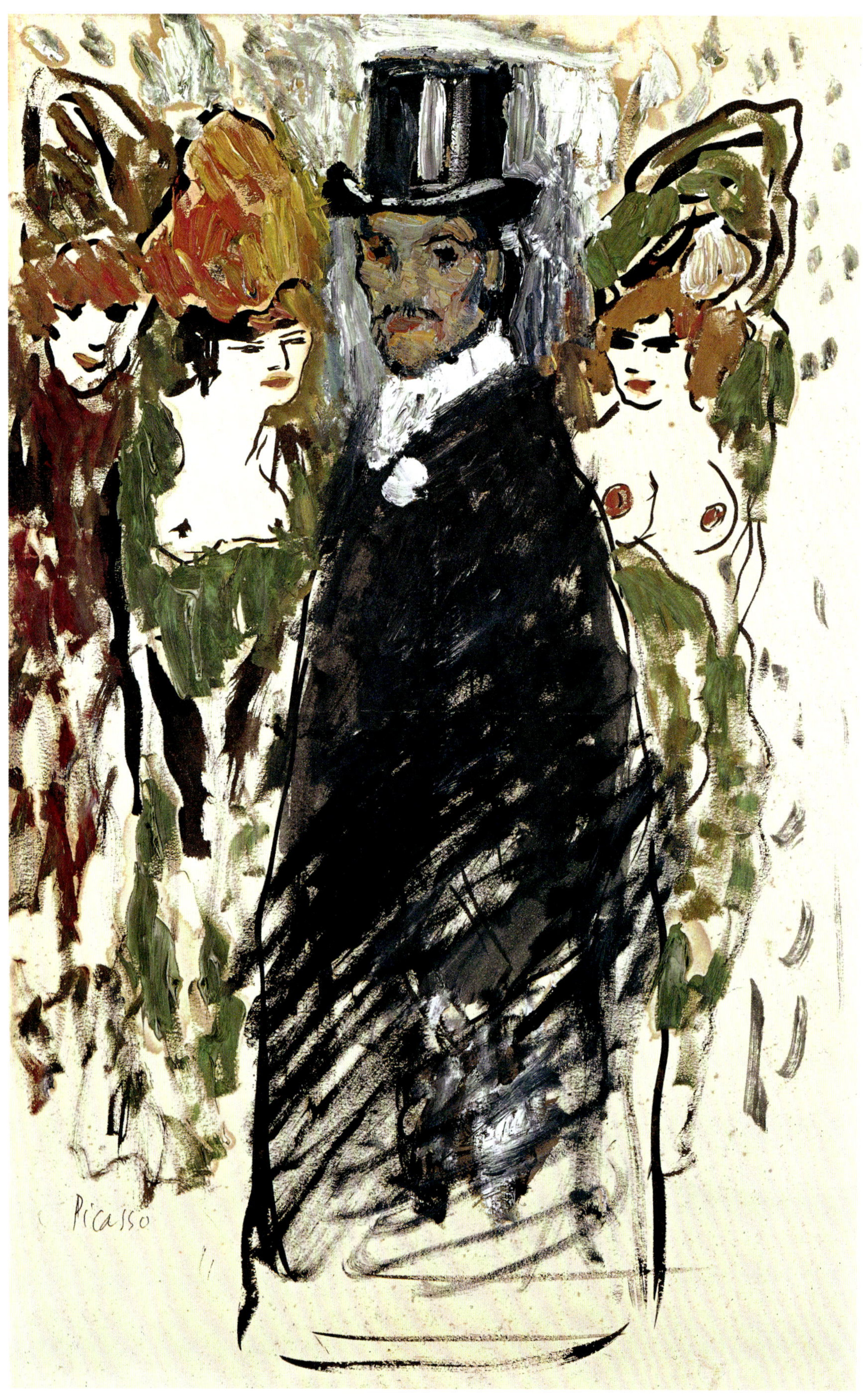

39 *Picasso in a Top Hat*, 1901 (L)

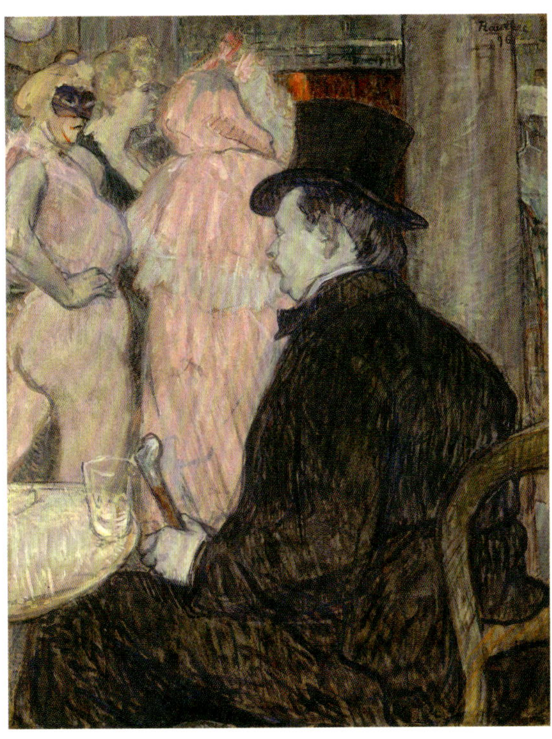

40 *Maxime Dethomas* by Henri de Toulouse-Lautrec, 1896

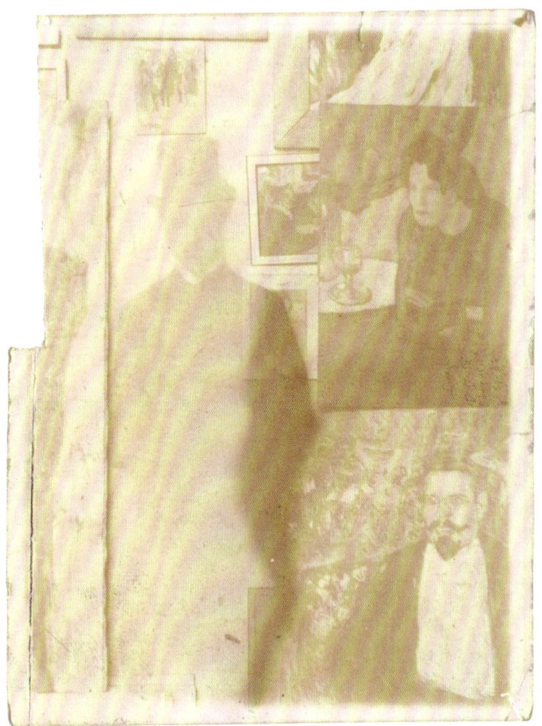

41 *Self-portrait in His Studio*, Paris, 1901

oil paint and paper for his wristy sketch, he approximated the effect of *peinture à l'essence* on cardboard, Toulouse-Lautrec's preferred medium for his most spontaneous paintings of modern life.

Picasso's earliest known photographs were taken with a borrowed camera in his rented studio on Boulevard de Clichy during his second trip to Paris. One of them, postdating his exhibition at Vollard's gallery (41), shows a section of the studio wall thickly hung with paintings, including *Yo Picasso*, and, in a double exposure, his ghost with the gaunt features and evening attire of *Picasso in a Top Hat*. On the back, in Spanish, Picasso scrawled a grandiloquent note: 'This photograph could be titled, "The strongest walls open as I pass. Behold!"'. Anne Baldassari, the authority on Picasso's photographs, is surely right to contend that the superimposition was intentional, and not a darkroom accident.[5] One of Picasso's latest genre scenes depicting a grim-faced absinthe drinker slumped beside a café table is clearly visible.[6] Propped on the studio floor below it is his portrait of Gustave Coquiot in its unrevised state (42). (The principal change affected the treatment of the sofa on which Coquiot is seated: Picasso simplified the pattern of the cover.)

Related in iconography to the dashing self-portrait sketch, this portrait was painted to thank Coquiot for his support, for he had not only written a flattering preface to the Vollard exhibition catalogue but had also contrived to publish it in the wide-circulation newspaper *Le Journal* shortly before the show opened.[7] A prolific and popular writer, Coquiot was famed for his risqué stories as much as for his reporting on the arts and the social scene, and Picasso dared to characterise him as a grinning lecher with a frieze of women in oriental costume performing an arousing dance behind his head, the suggestive position of his hand on his lap leaving little doubt about what was on his mind. (Since Coquiot was evidently responding to some activity beyond the frame, the most likely explanation for this frieze is a stage performance reflected in a mirror above the sofa.) Toulouse-Lautrec was one of Coquiot's favourite artists, and he would have relished and felt flattered by the allusion to the genre-style portraits of fellow *flâneurs*.[8] But unlike Toulouse-Lautrec's *Maxime Dethomas*, Picasso's *Gustave Coquiot* is strikingly inconsistent in technique. The black suit is handled casually, the paint of his white shirt-front trowelled on roughly and his hand a mere beginning. Only the face, painted carefully and in detail, is truly in focus; everything in the periphery is more or less blurred. This device ensured that Coquiot's grimace and the source of his emotion were the central issue for the viewer.

Dubbed 'the king of Bohemia', Bibi-la-Purée (Bibi-the-Down-and-Out) (43) was an actor-turned-vagabond and petty thief. A familiar sight on the streets of Montmartre and the Latin Quarter, he was an excellent subject for a young artist eager to make his mark in Paris.[9] Such was Bibi's local fame that Picasso could have been introduced to him by any number of his new contacts, and his two known drawings of the tramp may have been made with an eye to publication in a magazine.[10] One, a Casas-like charcoal drawing of Bibi in a classic full-length pose, was probably the starting point for the present painting, which is thought to have been one of the nameless *Portraits* shown in the Vollard exhibition.[11] In choosing a bust-length format, Picasso acted as he had when recomposing *Yo Picasso*, and *Bibi-la-Purée* is executed with similar vigour, not to say violence. Although the background is featureless, the painting has a narrative dimension in its strong suggestion that Bibi, costumed like a circus clown and with a lewd grin spreading over his features, is accosting the viewer, just as he did in reality when begging on the streets. Bibi's moist crimson lips, flushed cheeks and the rose in his buttonhole all imply lust and the effect is disturbingly invasive as well as comedic, breaching the normal rules of decorum in portraiture. Like the portrait of Coquiot, the painting verges on caricature.

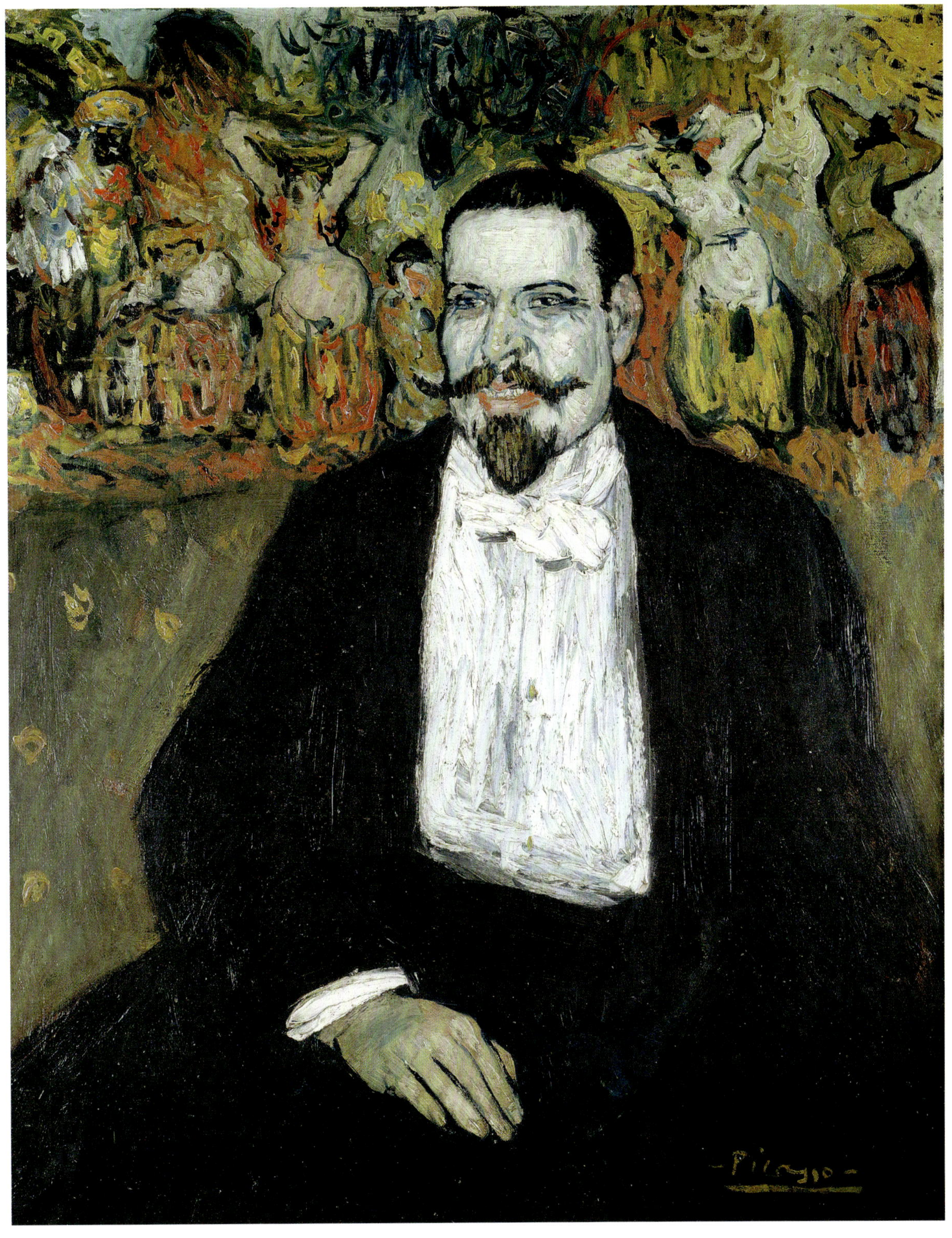

42 *Gustave Coquiot*, 1901 (B, L)

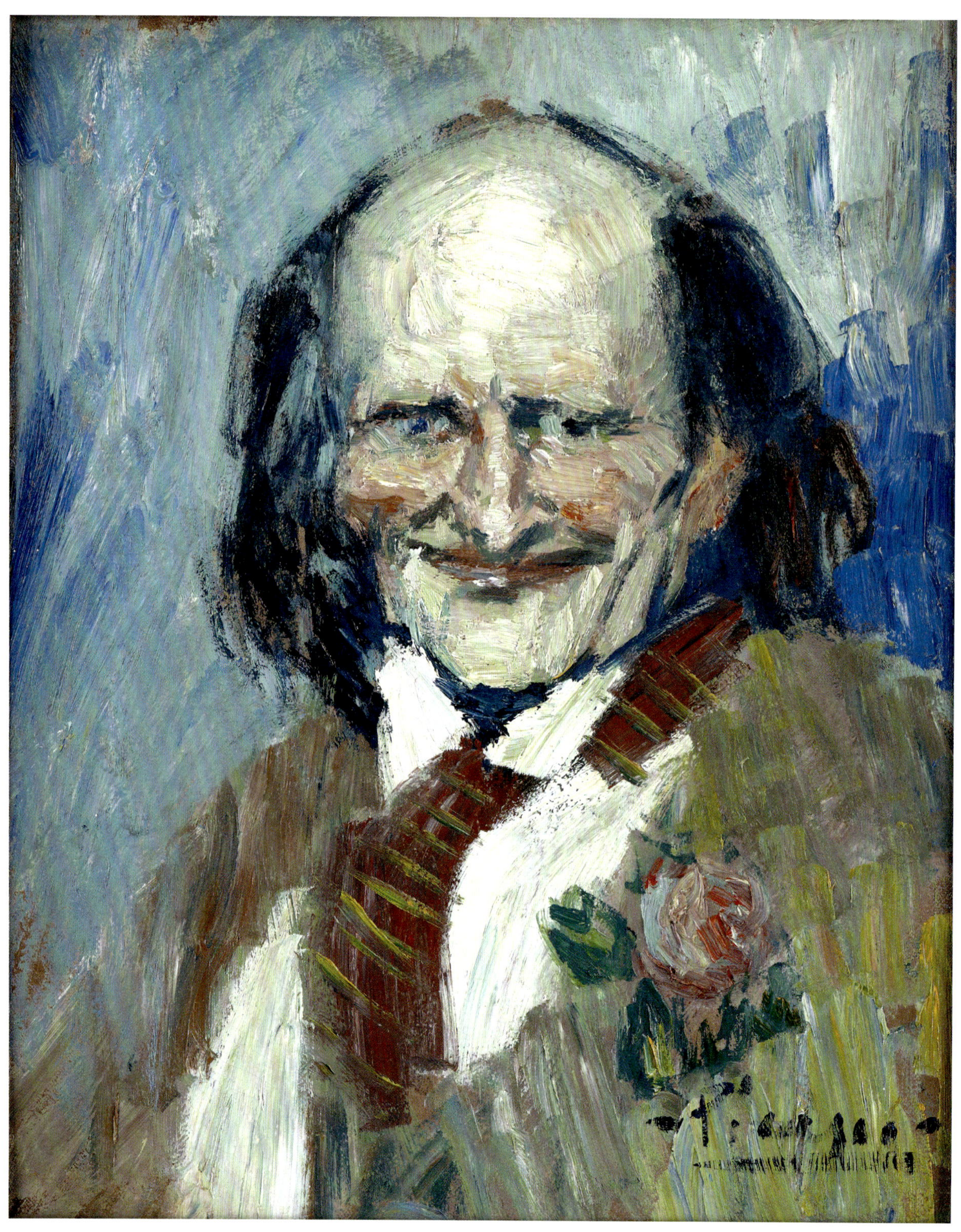

43 *Bibi-la-Purée*, 1901 (B, L)

PORTRAITURE AND CARICATURE IN PICASSO'S 'BLUE PERIOD'

Félicien Fagus, who reviewed Picasso's exhibition at Vollard's gallery for the prestigious *La Revue Blanche*, was stunned by the young artist's 'brilliant' painterly gifts. But he was troubled by the rampant eclecticism, reeling off the names of Delacroix, Manet, Monet, Van Gogh, Pissarro, Toulouse-Lautrec, Degas, Forain and 'perhaps' Rops as 'momentary' influences, not to mention 'the great [Spanish] precursors'. '[Picasso] is clearly in such a feverish hurry that he has not yet had time to forge his own personal style,' Fagus concluded, and he warned that this 'impetuosity' could all too easily lead to 'facile virtuosity', for 'It is one thing to produce and quite another to produce something worthwhile.'[12] Whether or not Picasso was affected by Fagus's criticism, in the months between the closure of the exhibition and his return to Barcelona in January 1902, he noticeably slowed down his rate of production. He also set about absorbing more fully the work of the vanguard artists who had most to say to him (Van Gogh, Gauguin, Degas and Toulouse-Lautrec, especially), while leaving aside those who did not (Monet and Pissarro, for instance).[13] Towards the end of his stay in Paris, the love of brilliant colour for its own sake, noted by Fagus in his review, had been supplanted by a palette dominated by shades of blue, and introspection, inertia and pathos had replaced the febrile gaiety of paintings like *Bibi-la-Purée.* This, Picasso's 'Blue period' manner, was in effect the missing 'personal style'.

Picasso's new portrait of Sabartés, who joined him in Paris in October 1901, registered the shift in palette, mood and technique (44). According to Sabartés, it recorded a particular episode, when he was 'alone, and dreadfully bored', waiting for Picasso at their favourite café: 'Just as my desolation was keenest, Picasso appeared.' On entering the artist's studio a few days later he was surprised to

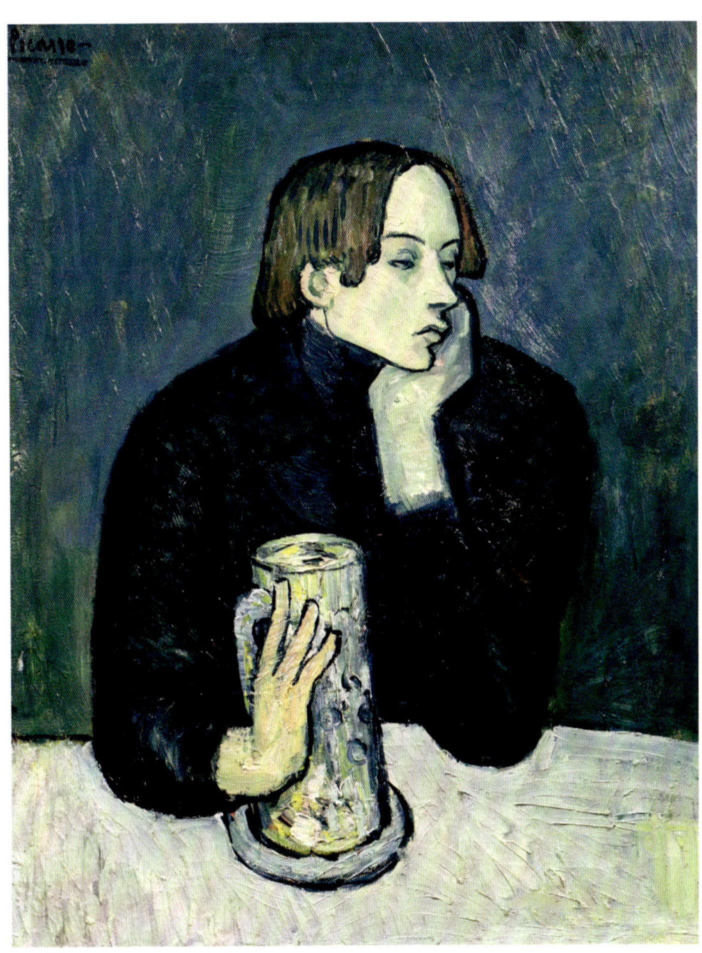

44 *Portrait of the Poet Sabartés*, 1901

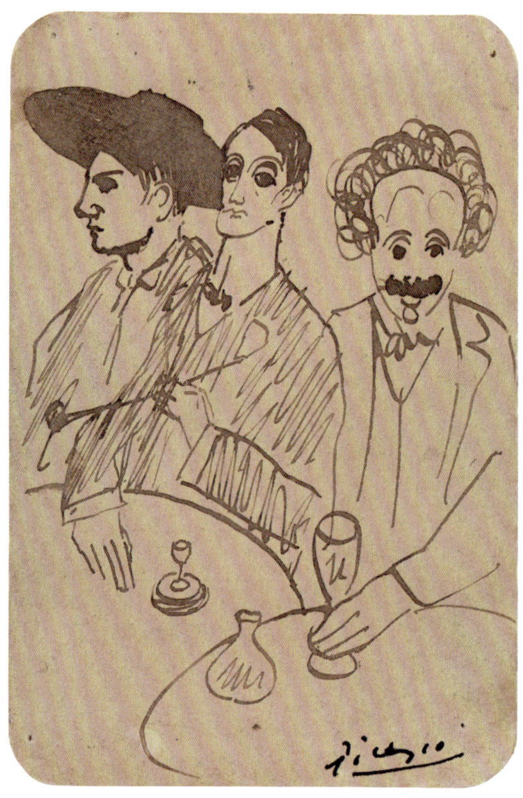

45 *Picasso, Àngel Fernández de Soto and Sebastià Junyer i Vidal in a Café*, c.1903 (L)

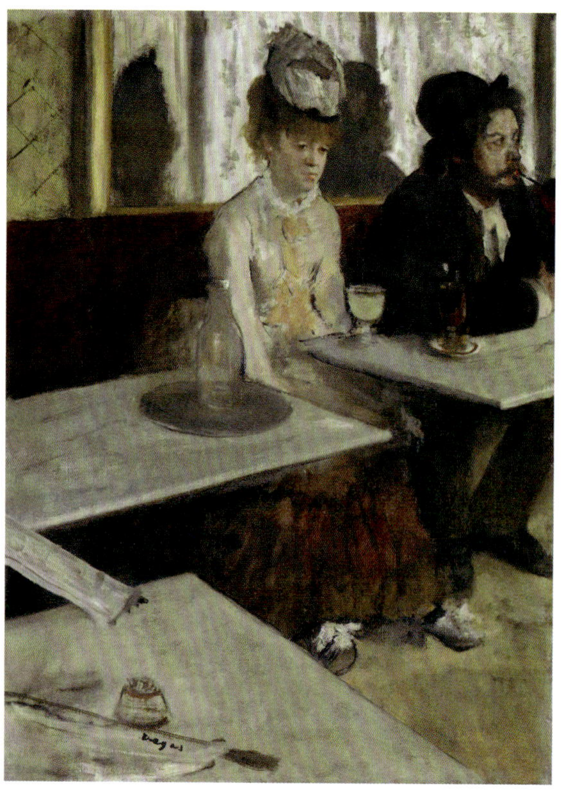

46 *In a Café (L'Absinthe)* by Edgar Degas, 1875–6

discover that he had unwittingly fallen 'like a fly into the trap of Picasso's stare'.[14] Although the setting is generalised, the painting was another essay in the mode of the genre-portrait, which at that time seemed so full of potential to Picasso. Perhaps it was in order to strengthen the connection with scenes of modern urban life that he omitted the spectacles that were Sabartés's normal emblem, thus transforming him into a virtual type, brother to the depressed absinthe drinker in the painting recorded in the studio photograph (41). The Gauguinesque simplification of form and firmly drawn *cloisonné*-style contours, together with the dense handling of the medium, lent the portrait the solemnity of an allegory of melancholy.

On his return to Barcelona, Picasso pursued this path in portraits of other constant companions – men who, unlike Sabartés, were not inveterate pessimists and therefore invited a sardonically humorous approach. Sebastià Junyer i Vidal had the physiognomy to delight the caricaturist in Picasso: a broad bulbous forehead framed by a thick bush of curly hair, eyes with a permanently surprised expression and a handlebar moustache that might have come from a joke shop (see 75). In a quick sketch (45), drawn on the back of a trade card from the yarn and stocking shop that he and his brother had inherited from an uncle,[15] Junyer i Vidal forms an unholy trinity with a supercilious Àngel Fernández de Soto (whom we shall shortly meet again) and a rather severe-looking Pablo wearing a Cordoban riding hat. Done in a flash though it was, the little drawing may have been the starting-point for the heavily worked Blue-period painting

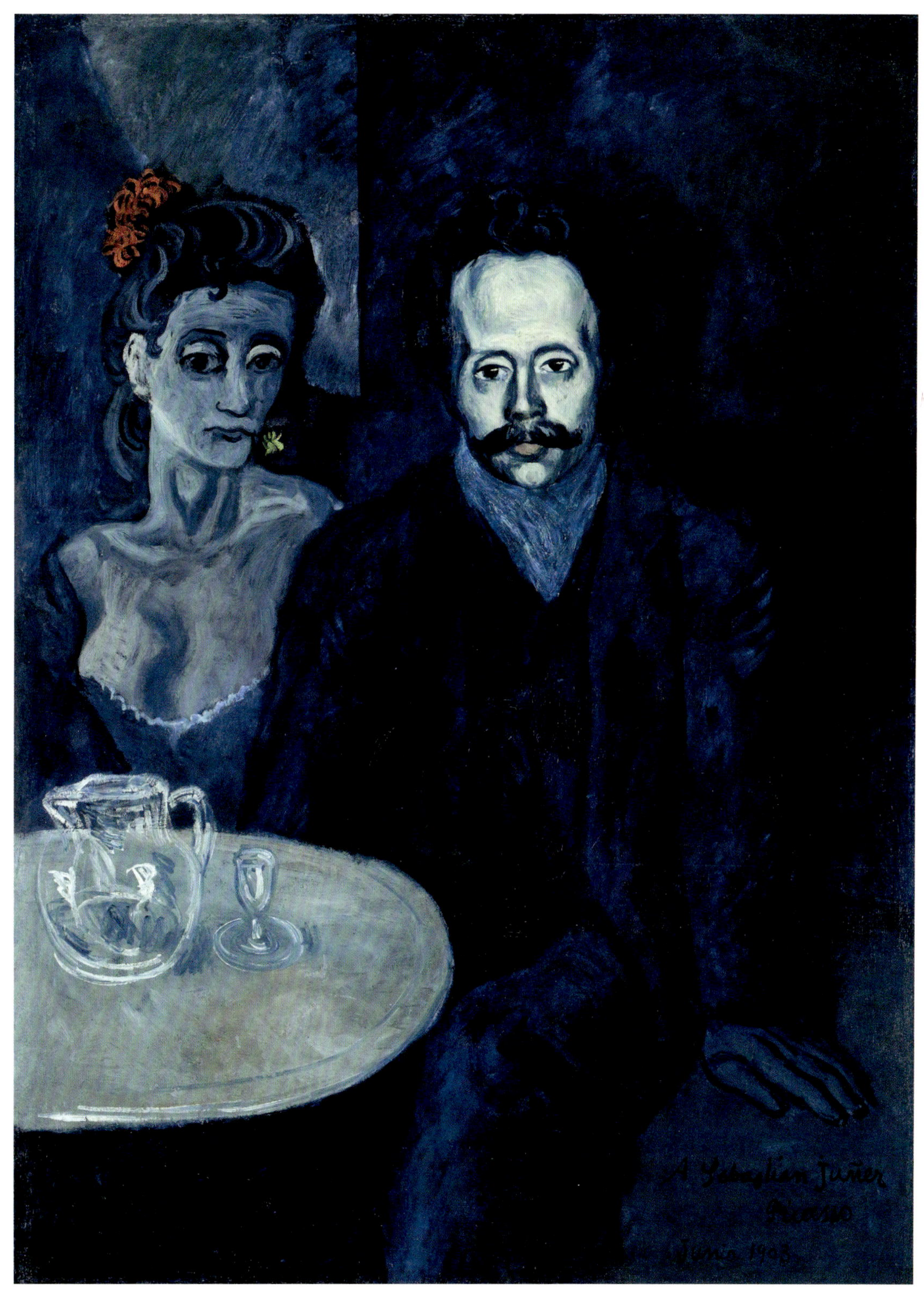

47 *Portrait of Sebastià Junyer i Vidal*, 1903 (L)

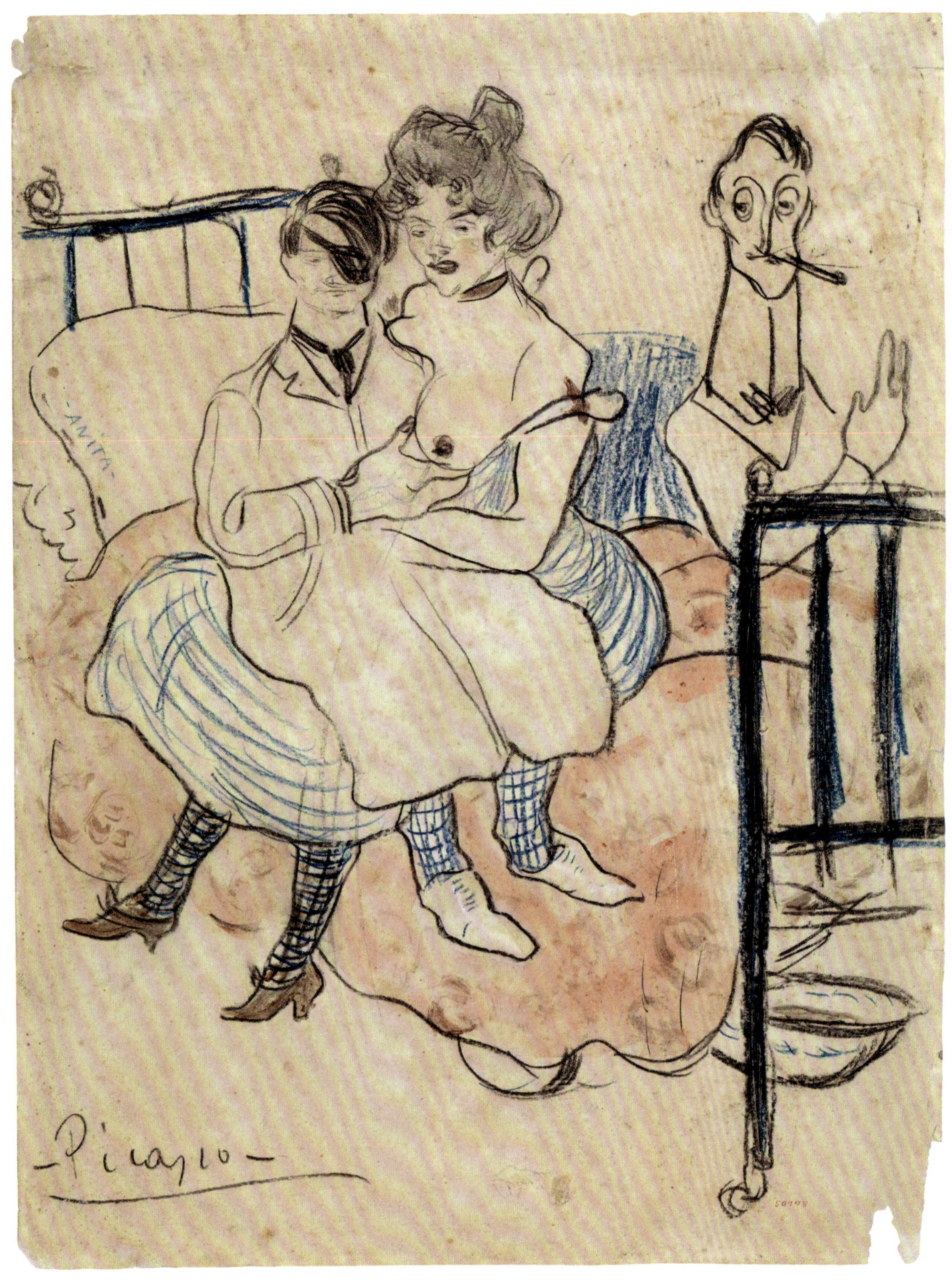

48 *The Brothers Mateu and Àngel Fernández de Soto with Anita*, 1902–3 (B)

of Junyer i Vidal, seated in a bar beside a scrawny prostitute (47). Picasso's main reference-point for this portrait was Degas's *In a Café (L'Absinthe)* (46), which had aroused consternation when first exhibited because of its painfully realistic image of urban alienation and addiction.[16] But whereas Degas's painting is set up as a genre scene, with the oblivious protagonists glimpsed out of the corner of the passing observer's eye, Picasso's painting is set up as a double-portrait, with the two disenchanted protagonists staring back at the spectator. X-rays have revealed that Sebastià's original companion was not a woman but a faithful dog (or two),[17] and therefore that Picasso conceived the painting initially – and ironically – in terms of 'ruler portraits', in which the aristocratic sitter is attended by a devoted hound.[18]

Meanwhile, Picasso produced a steady stream of outright caricatures of his cronies. Their sexual escapades, real or fantasised, formed one strain and when there was no question of publication he could be as raunchy as he liked. The de Soto brothers were fair game and in one scene he imagined them consorting with a prostitute called Anita: in a charming touch, her name is embroidered on the pillow-slip (48). An aficionado of Barcelona's brothels, phallic-necked Àngel, pipe clamped between his lips, presides over Mateu's inexpert fumblings while gesturing lewdly. (The ghost of an erased speech-bubble can just be glimpsed to the right of his head.) Mateu was reputedly the antithesis of his brother in looks and character – small, frail and shabby, diligent, reserved and prone to melancholy[19] – and his canoodling with Anita takes the form of a blasphemous parody of the Virgin nursing the Christ Child. Àngel's debauches inspired another deft caricature, which makes up in obscenity for what it lacks in sacrilege (49). A crease across the centre of the sheet of paper suggests that it was kept concealed in an envelope and, unlike the other drawing, it was not signed.

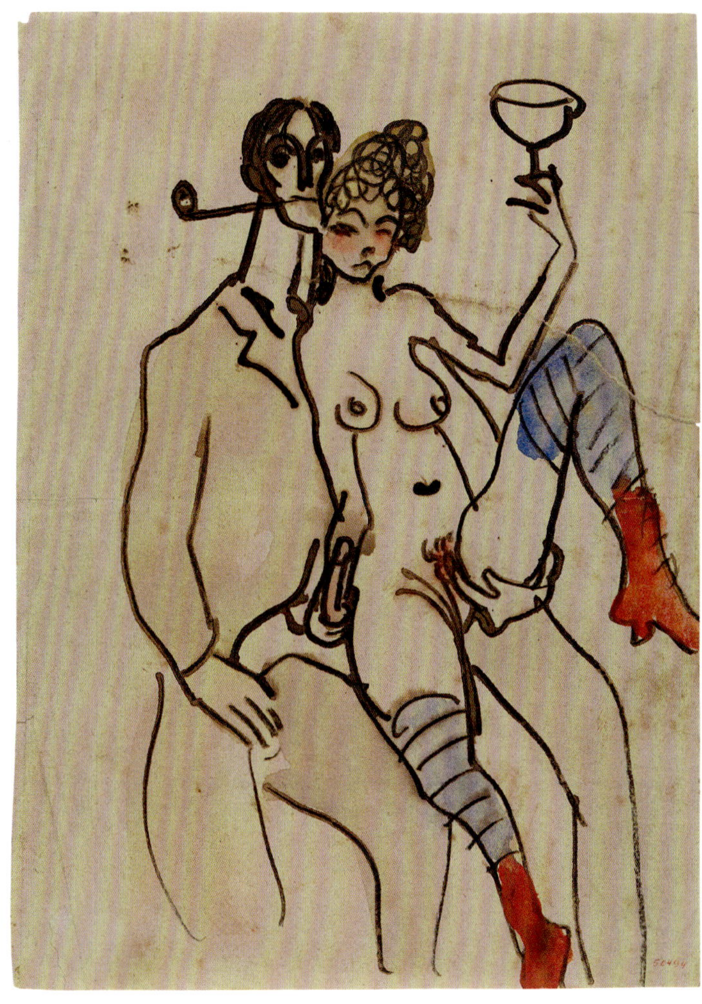

49 *Àngel Fernández de Soto with a Woman*, 1902–3 (L)

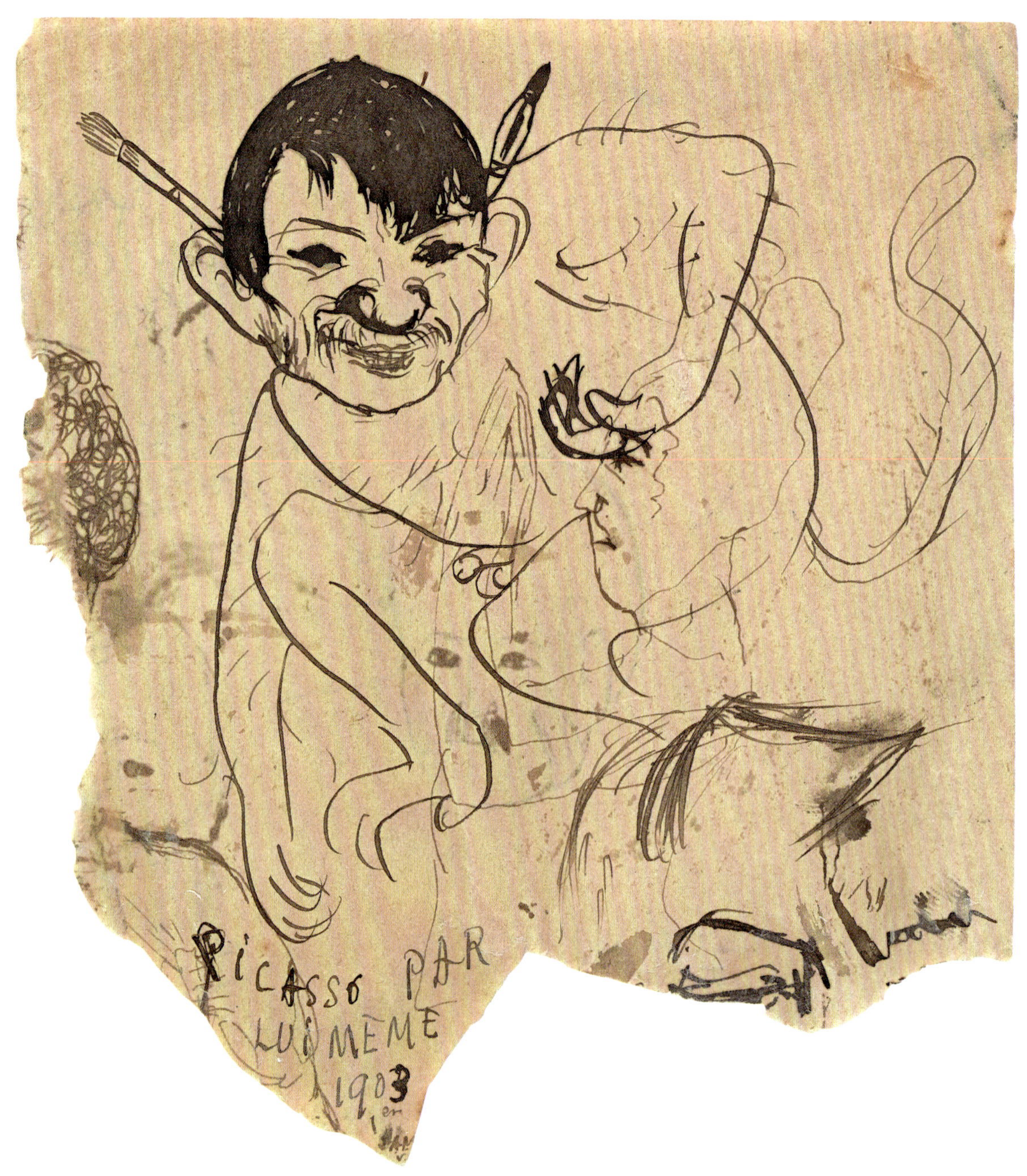

50 *Picasso par lui mème (Picasso by Himself)*, 1 January 1903 (L)

Picasso did not exempt himself from satire, and near the end of his third trip to Paris drew his self-portrait as a hairy, grinning monkey – the evil genius behind the scurrilous caricatures (50). In *Picasso in a Top Hat* (see 39) he had posed as a dashing, sophisticated man about town, potentially a painter of high society in the John Singer Sargent mould. Here he reflected on his base animal nature and its role in his creativity. Although executed at great speed and crammed into the top-right corner of a sheet of paper already covered with doodled heads, the drawing's cultural references are precise. Behind one ear is a paint brush, behind the other a *porte-crayon*: the allusion is to the long tradition of satirical images – by Goya, for one – (51) of the mindlessly imitative 'monkey-painter' or 'ape of nature'. Pleased with his caustic self-assessment, Picasso tore off the corner of the sheet and labelled it with mock-pedantry 'PICASSO PAR/LUI MÈME/1903/1er/JAN' (Picasso by Himself, 1903, 1 January). He was twenty-one years old at the time.

The portrait-as-genre-scene was not the only new form of portraiture Picasso essayed at this period of ambitious experimentation. In the aftermath of the Vollard gallery exhibition he also used portraiture to come to terms with Casagemas's suicide. The tragedy had occurred in Paris in February 1901 while Picasso was in Madrid preparing the first issue of *Arte Joven*, the short-lived periodical he co-edited with their mutual friend Francisco Soler. His immediate response to the news was a profile portrait to accompany the brief obituary published in *Catalunya artística* (52). Drawn from memory after Casagemas's death, as befitted the occasion it was a relatively flattering likeness. The three portraits of the dead Casagemas produced in Paris more than six months later had a private purpose and only came to light during the 1960s when Pierre Daix was preparing his catalogue raisonné of Picasso's early work.

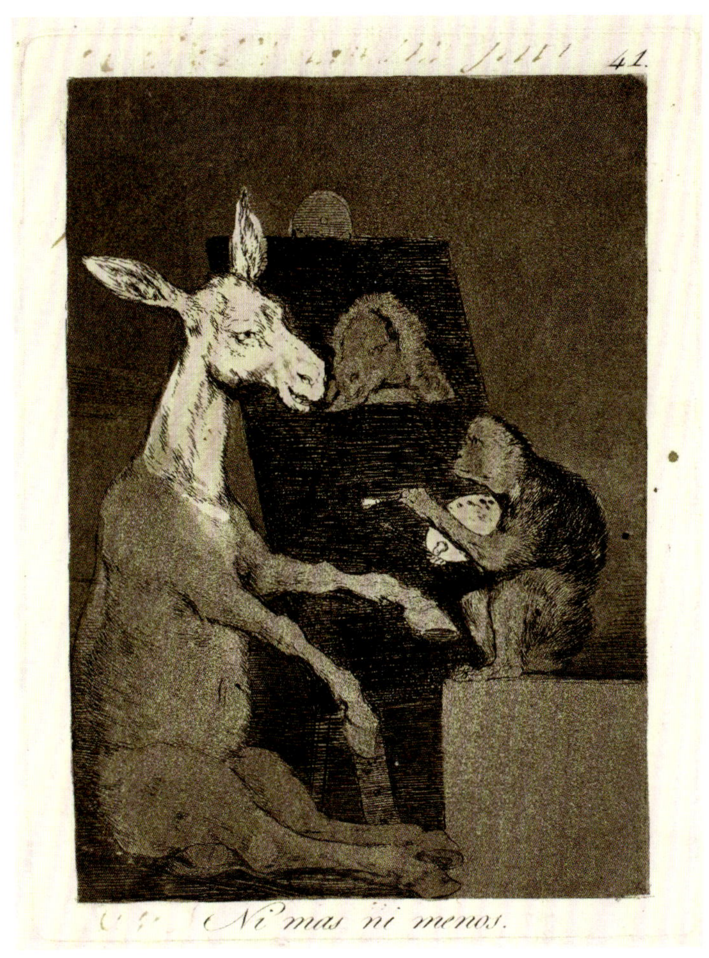

51 *Neither More Nor Less* by Francisco de Goya, 1799

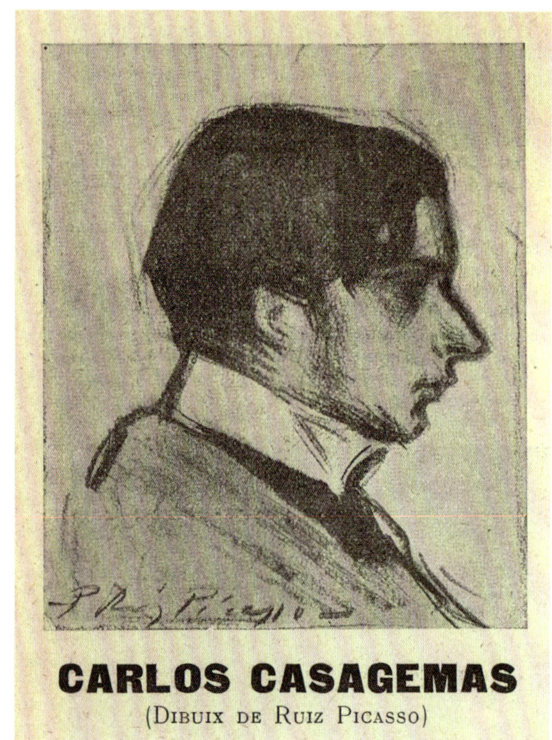

52 *Portrait of Carles Casagemas*, reproduced in *Catalunya artística*, no.38, 28 February 1901

Plausibly interpreted as acts of exorcism for the guilt he felt for abandoning his seriously disturbed friend and heading for Madrid without him,[20] two of the three paintings employed the melancholy blue palette which, years later, he specifically connected with 'thinking about Casagemas'.[21] The relationship of portraiture with commemoration and rituals of death and burial is an ancient one: in painting *Casagemas in His Coffin* (53), Picasso had innumerable precedents to draw upon, from tomb effigies of the deceased to the post-mortem photographs that were commonplace in the second half of the nineteenth century (54).[22] Because it was a private act of mourning, physical resemblance hardly mattered; in death, Casagemas lost his individuality and took on the pathetic anonymity and atavism of the skeleton.

With the bust portrait of Sabartés painted in Barcelona in the spring of 1904 (55), Picasso returned to a format with which he felt entirely comfortable. As usual, Sabartés provided invaluable information about its circumstances. The two friends saw each other almost every day and it often fell to him to assuage Picasso's passing moods of boredom, frustration and bad temper by keeping him company. On one such occasion Picasso invited him back to his studio, 'and suddenly, as if it were fated that only his ill humour or mine would stimulate him to do my portrait, he began to observe me from different angles. He took a piece of canvas, put it on the easel and got ready to paint.' Sabartés stood 'at a certain distance from his easel' and posed patiently until Picasso had 'covered' the canvas. He resumed the pose the following day and the portrait was completed 'in a very brief session': Picasso merely touched up the background, firmed up the line of Sabartés's hair and coloured the lips. He then stopped work because 'his present vision differed from his first,' and if he had carried on he would have had to 'produce something entirely different': his state of mind and Sabartés's mood

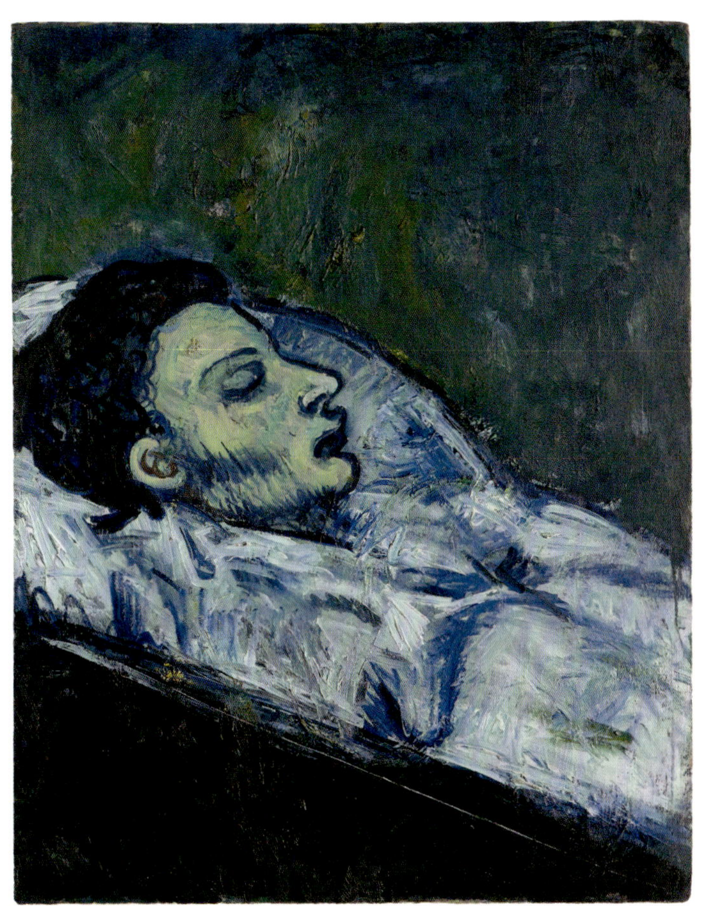

53 *Casagemas in His Coffin*, 1901

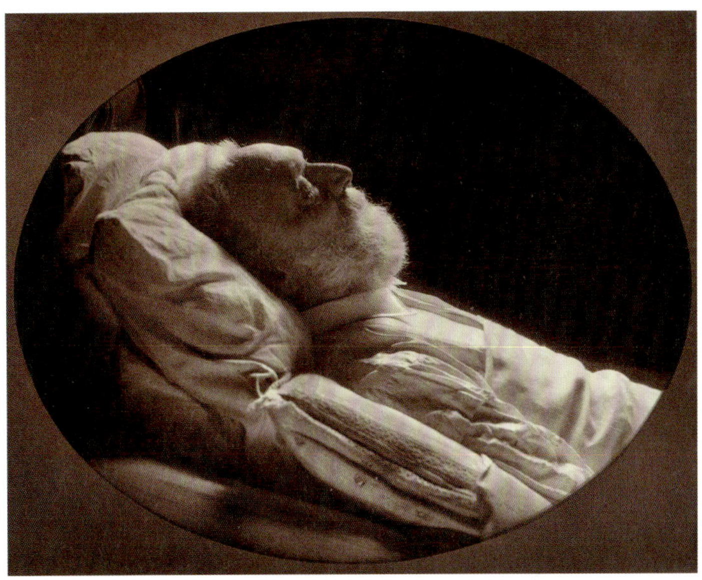

54 *Victor Hugo on His Death Bed*. Photograph by Félix Nadar, 1885

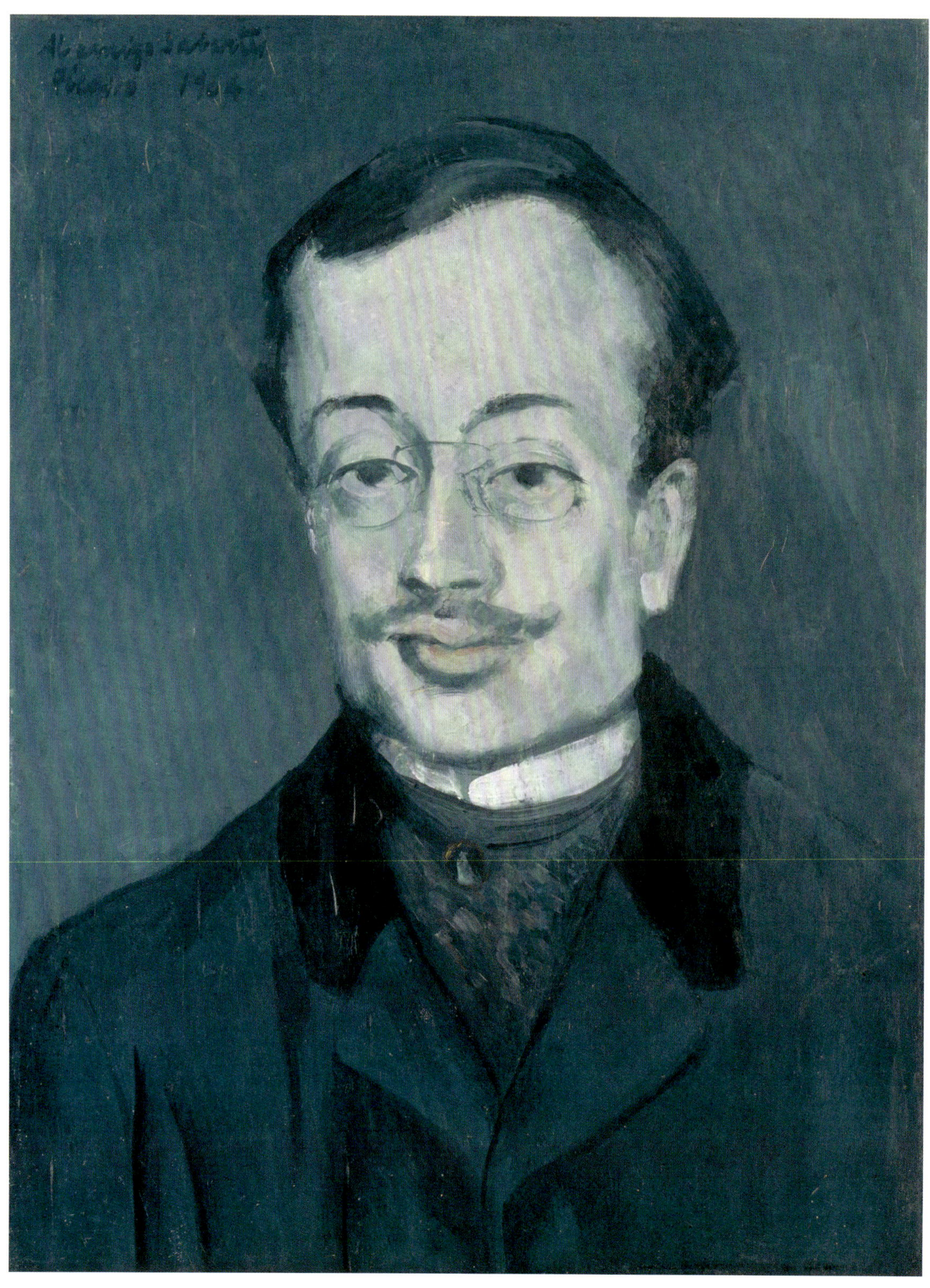

55 *Portrait of Jaume Sabartés*, 1904 (B)

were not what they had been the previous day and he risked destroying what he had achieved.[23]

This was, then, a different type of portrait from any of those described in this chapter and, the monochrome blue of its palette aside, it is a persuasively objective likeness. The expressionless face gazing back through pince-nez provides no clue as to Sabartés's tastes, talents or inner being; the portrait is no more revealing psychologically than a photograph on an official document and no emotional reaction is solicited from the spectator. When Picasso painted the picture he was planning to move to Paris and make his career there and it is possible that he wanted to test out his competence in lifelike portraiture, since although working to commission went against the grain, he might be obliged to paint portraits of strangers to make ends meet. Sabartés was in a somewhat similar situation: he was about to make a decisive move to Guatemala, where through family contacts he had the promise of a secure job; hence his well-groomed, sober, bourgeois appearance. The portrait marked a critical moment in his life as well as a turning-point in his friendship with Picasso, and they had no idea when they would meet again. Under such circumstances, a documentary approach may have seemed right and proper. Dedicating it on the front to his 'amigo', Picasso gave the picture to Sabartés and it travelled with him to Guatemala. It was one of the last portraits Picasso painted before he packed his bags.

1 In its present form, the work was illustrated in Cirici-Pellicer 1946, no.10. However, in 1954 Zervos catalogued the two parts separately: Z.VI.105, Z.VI.219.

2 For a new attempt to identify the paintings exhibited, see Marilyn McCully and Michael Raeburn, 'Appendix: Works in the 1901 Vollard Show', in Wright 2013, pp.176–81.

3 In 1901, Vollard had twenty or so works by Van Gogh in stock, most of them portraits (Nienke Bakker, 'The reputation of Vincent Van Gogh in Paris around 1900', in McCully 2011, p.85).

4 See Rabinow 2006, cat.125, p.380. Entry by Ann Dumas and Jonathan Pascoe Pratt.

5 See Baldassari 1997, pp.19–21.

6 *Woman with Crossed Arms*, 1901. Kunstmuseum Basel (Z.I.100). It was not included in the Vollard exhibition, but other paintings on the theme of the alcoholic prostitute were.

7 'Pablo Ruiz Picasso', *Le Journal*, 17 June 1901. Cited in Palau 1981, p.514.

8 Coquiot illustrated the portrait of Maxime Dethomas in his pioneering monograph on Lautrec, *H. de Toulouse-Lautrec* (A. Blaizot, Paris, 1913).

9 Bibi's real name was André-Joseph Salis. For a recent biography, see Gury 2004.

10 The drawings are Z.VI.355 and Z.VI.1460.

11 See Palau 1981, p.248, and Marilyn McCully and Michael Raeburn, 'Appendix: Works in the 1901 Vollard Show', in Wright 2013, p.179.

12 Félicien Fagus, 'L'invasion espagnole', *La Revue Blanche*, 15 July 1901. Cited in Palau 1981, pp.514–15.

13 For the evolution of Picasso's work during the course of 1901, see Wright 2013.

14 Sabartés 1949, pp.62–4.

15 See Richardson 1991, pp.280–1, for the explicit erotic drawings Picasso made on the back of the shop's trade cards.

16 For detailed discussion of Picasso's preoccupation with Degas's *L'Absinthe*, see Richard Kendall, 'Neighbors in Montmartre', in Cowling and Kendall 2010, pp.88–92.

17 The X-ray is accessible via The Cleveland Museum of Art website: http://www.clevelandart.org/exhibcef/PicassoAS/html/7475296.html

18 Picasso's model at that point may possibly have been Titian's (strikingly blue) *Federico de Gonzaga, Duke of Mantua* in the Prado. For his later promise to paint Sabartés dressed as a sixteenth-century Spanish gentleman with a naked woman and a dog at his side, see p.158.

19 Richardson 1991, p.116.

20 Ibid., pp.173–5, 180–1.

21 Daix 1994, p.27. The third mourning portrait is the brightly coloured panel in the Musée national Picasso-Paris (Z.XXI.178), thought to be the earliest of the three.

22 On the portrait as commemoration and memorial, see for instance West 2004, pp.62–5.

23 Sabartés 1949, pp.97–8.

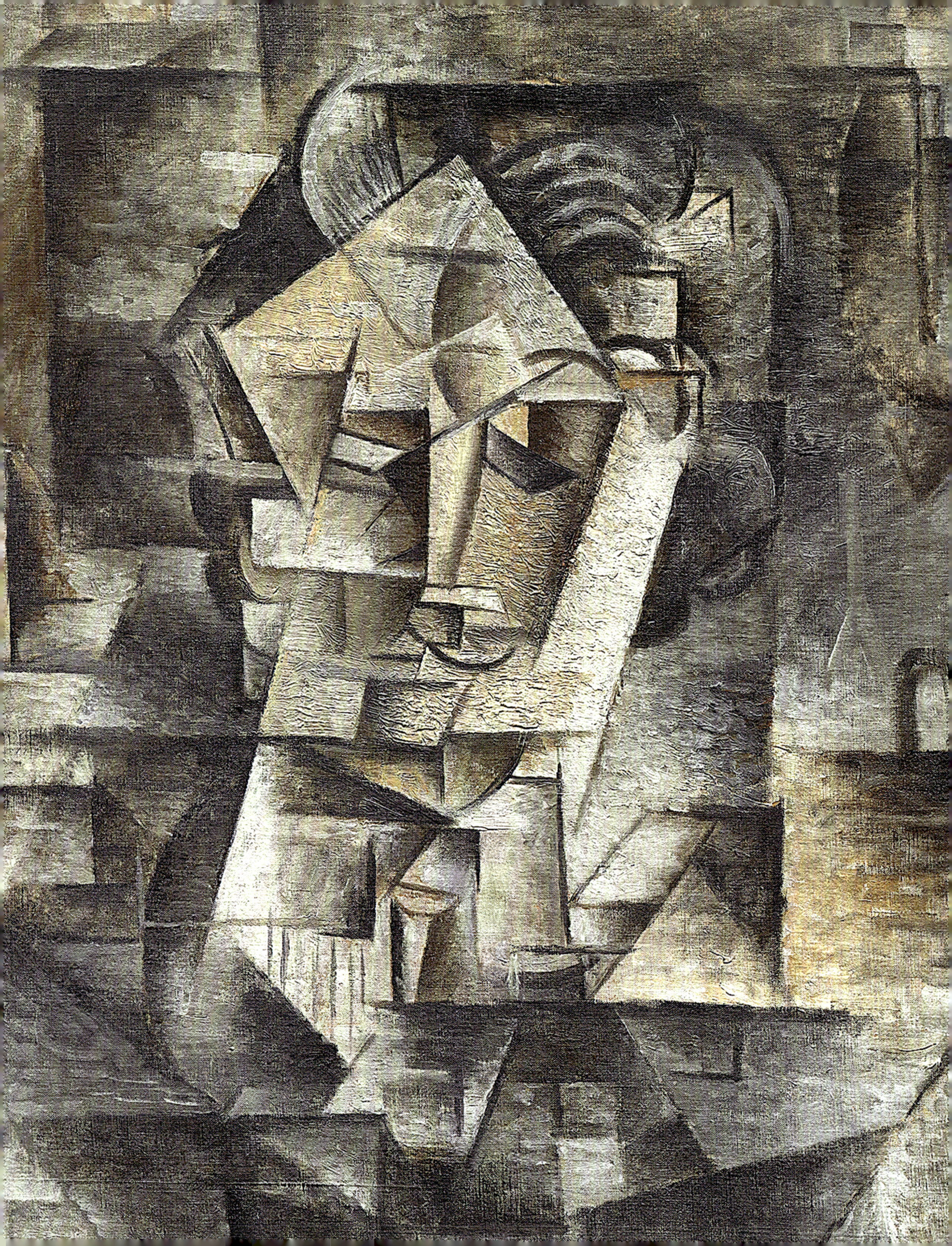

3. Paris: new circles, shifting styles 1904–1910

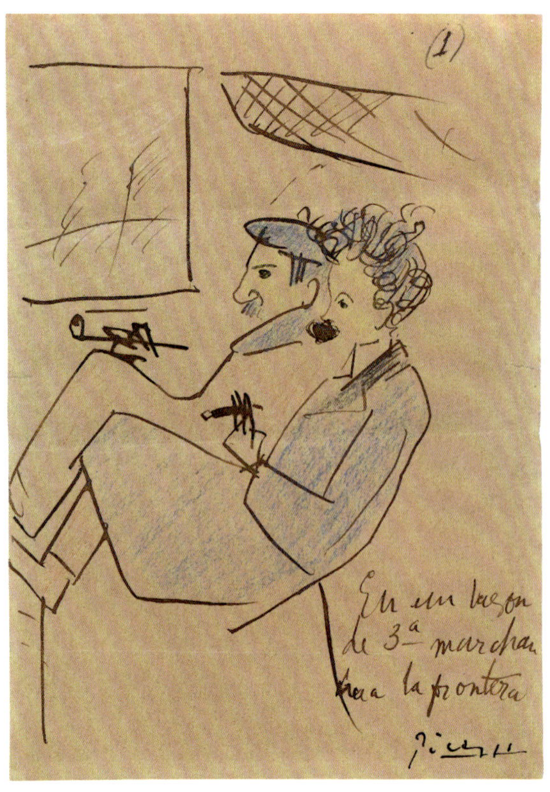

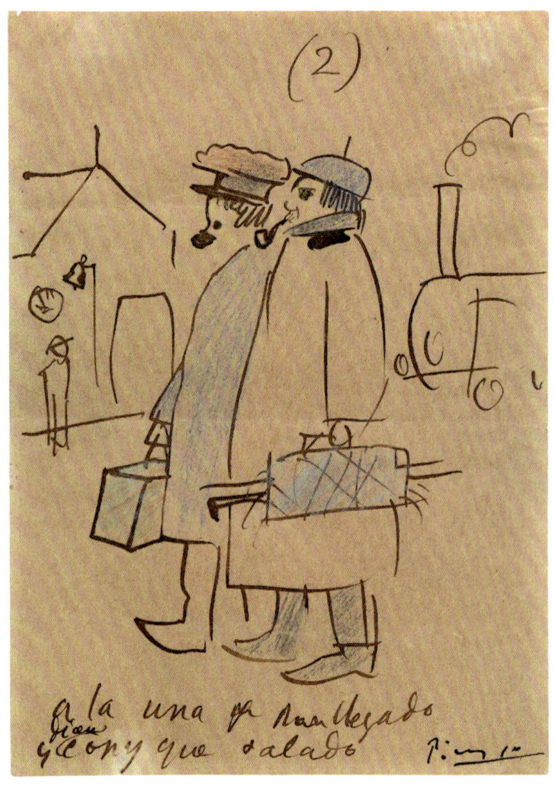

THE *BANDE À PICASSO*

In April 1904, Picasso set off for Paris, accompanied by Sebastià Junyer i Vidal. Within a few days of arriving they had settled into a top-floor studio in the ramshackle artists' colony in Montmartre, nicknamed the Bateau-Lavoir (laundry boat) on account of its shape and creaky wooden construction. In a humorous parody of the traditional Catalan *auca* (strip-cartoon), replete with authentic details of clothing, baggage and location, Picasso summed up their long train journey, arrival in Paris and dreams of worldly success (56). Each of the six numbered vignettes – sadly, the fifth is lost – is captioned with a rhyming text in a mixture of colloquial Spanish and Catalan: (i) 'In a third-class carriage they reach the frontier'; (ii) 'They arrive at one o'clock and exclaim, "Fuck, what a laugh!"' (iii) 'And they arrive at Montauban [misspelt Montaulvant] wrapped in their overcoats'; (iv) 'At nine in the morning they finally arrive in Paris'; (vi) 'He [Junyer i Vidal] got a call from Durand-Ruel [misspelt Duran-Rouel] and collected the dough'. This last was pure wish-fulfilment, for they had no realistic hope of selling to the famous Impressionist dealer, and before long, Junyer i Vidal had taken the train back to Barcelona. For Picasso, the move to Paris proved permanent, but he could hardly have been sure of that at the time since he had no exhibition in view and no dealer or patron to provide support.

The Bateau-Lavoir was home to artists and writers of many different nationalities and Picasso's circle expanded greatly over the next few years. The poet Max Jacob had been a friend since the time of his Vollard gallery exhibition in 1901, and lived next door at 7 Rue Ravignan.[1] Now Picasso met

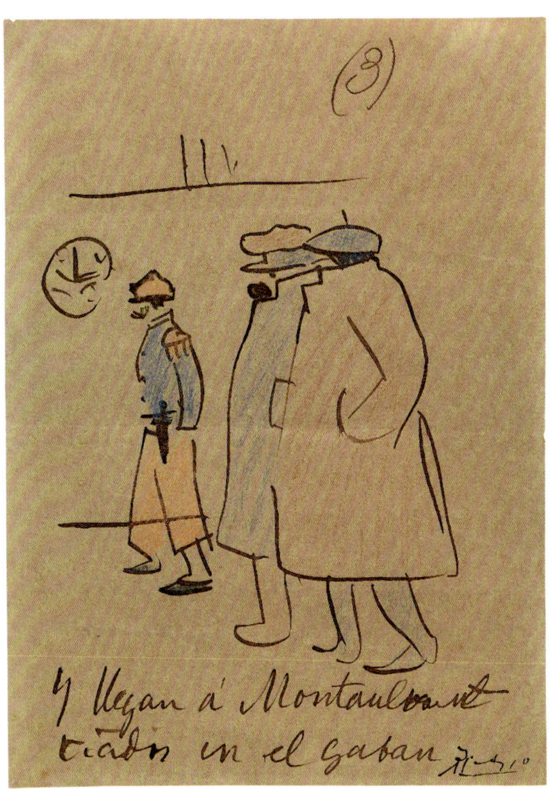

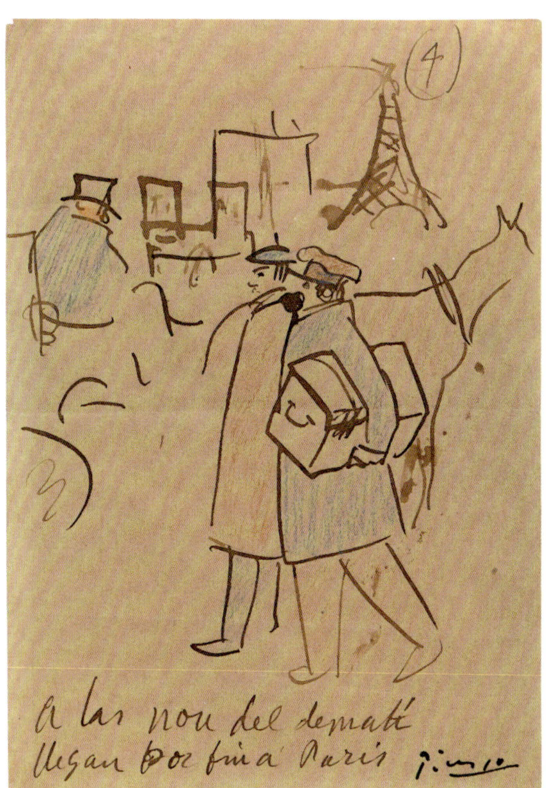

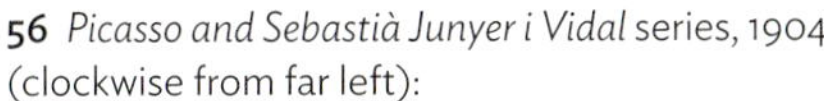

56 *Picasso and Sebastià Junyer i Vidal* series, 1904 (clockwise from far left):

i *Picasso and Sebastià Junyer i Vidal Set Off on a Journey* (L)

ii *Picasso and Sebastià Junyer i Vidal Arrive at the Border* (L)

iii *Picasso and Sebastià Junyer i Vidal Reach Montauban* (L)

iv *Picasso and Sebastià Junyer i Vidal Arrive in Paris* (L)

v [this vignette is lost]

vi *Sebastià Junyer i Vidal Calls on Durand-Ruel* (L)

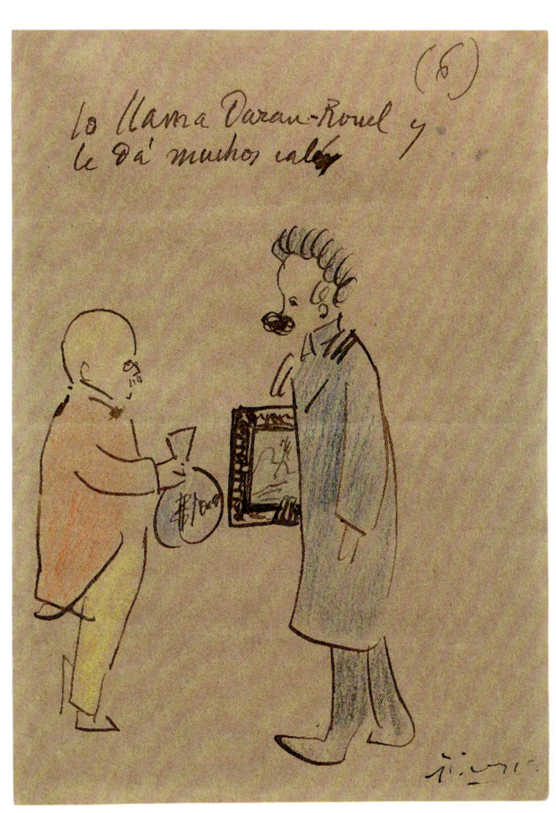

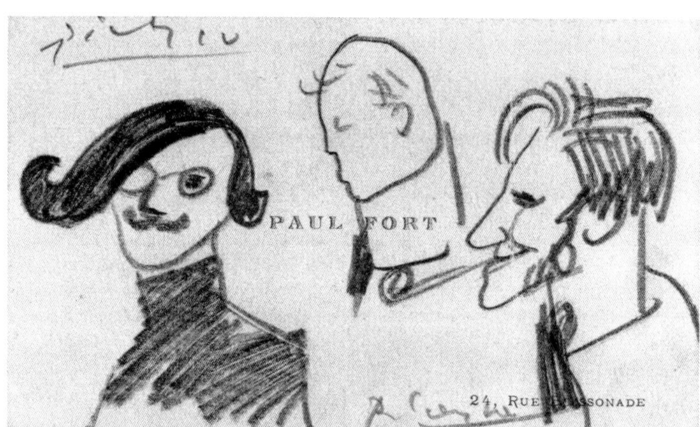

57 *Caricatures of Paul Fort, Henri Delormel and André Salmon*, 1905

other up-and-coming French writers, in particular Guillaume Apollinaire and André Salmon, who, with Jacob, formed the nucleus of the *bande à Picasso*. They introduced him to the *Vers et Prose* coterie headed by Paul Fort, the founder and editor of the journal, which promoted Symbolism and for which Salmon acted as editorial secretary. These new friends and acquaintances challenged, stimulated and sustained Picasso in much the same way as the Els Quatre Gats clan had done; he caricatured them as freely as he had the Modernistes.[2] In the tiny drawings on Fort's calling card (57), Fort is on the left, the author and dealer Louis Libaude (aka Henri Delormel) – always depicted by Picasso with a phallic head poking up from a starched collar – in the centre, and Salmon on the right. The card went into Apollinaire's choice collection of Picasso's humorous drawings.

Thin, gangling, pallid, lantern-jawed, the poet and literary journalist André Salmon was physically not unlike Àngel Fernández de Soto. He too inspired numerous caricatures that drew attention to his memorable jutting profile, hunched posture and the 'long fine hands' remembered by Picasso's lover, Fernande Olivier, who summed him up as '[a] dreamer with an alert sensibility'.[3] Picasso's large charcoal drawing (58) fixed on those defining traits and on the 'gauche and clumsy gestures' that were, Olivier added, 'a mark of his shyness'. Salmon's body looks boneless and rubbery and his arms like tentacles, but his head is configured in terms of the African and Oceanic tribal carvings for which he and Picasso competed in their trawls through Parisian junk shops (in 1907, the collectors' market in tribal art barely existed). Seeing Salmon as like a 'fetish' was equivalent to seeing his Modernista cronies in the light of El Greco.[4]

Picasso and Apollinaire became inseparable and the stream of witty, inventive, occasionally scatological caricatures Picasso made of him helped to consolidate their intimacy and mutual

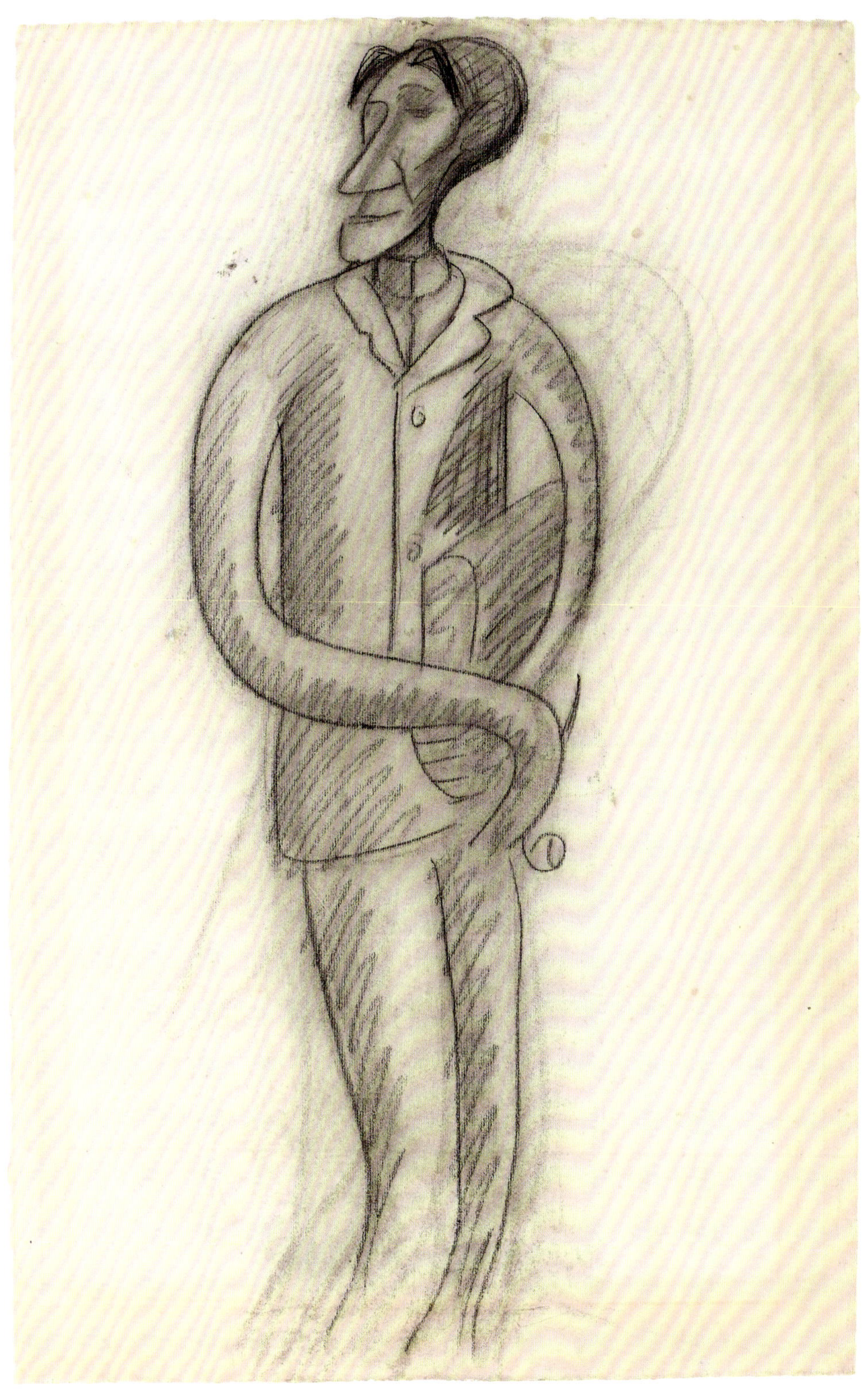

58 *Portrait of André Salmon*, 1907 (B)

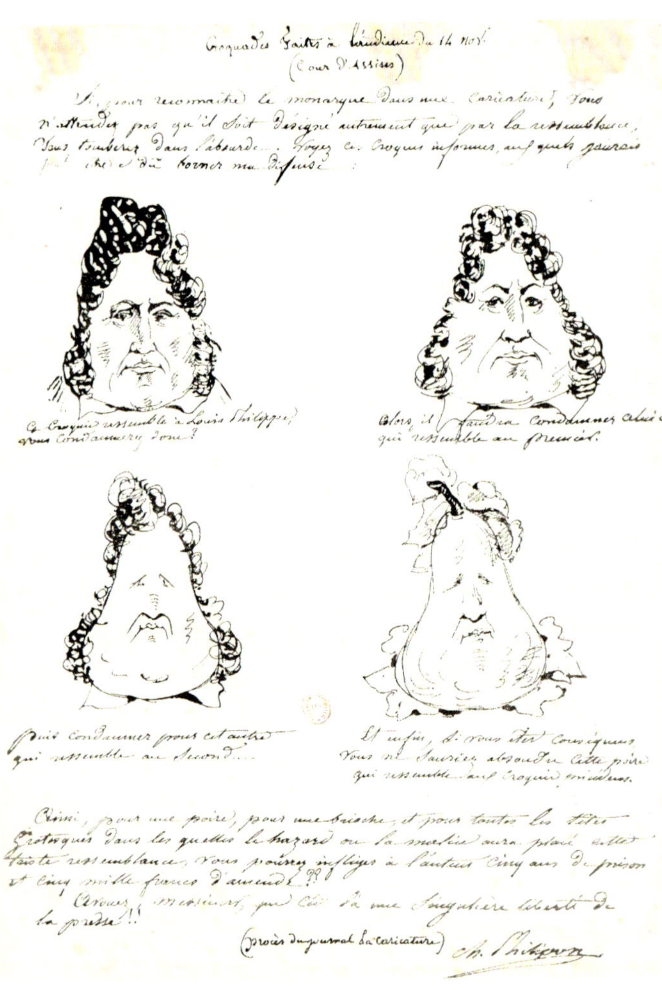

59 *Sketches Made During the Audience of 14 November (Court of Assizes)* by Charles Philipon, 1831

understanding. Many went straight into the poet's collection. The natural shape of Apollinaire's head, narrower at the crown than at the heavy chin, was pear-like and Picasso seized on the chance to echo Charles Philipon's and Honoré Daumier's famous caricatures of Louis-Philippe as a *poire* (59).[5] Picasso's caricatures of Apollinaire are much less insulting but invariably his head is pear-like, his hair a row of bristles, his eyebrows and eyes slanting downwards, his mouth small and his figure portly. There the similarity ends and Apollinaire's principal attribute is his pipe.

A typical example is the rapid ink drawing on a letter-card that Picasso sent Apollinaire on 6 December 1905 (60). The abrupt, scrawled message reads: 'I haven't seen you for ages. Are you dead? Picasso.' Alluding ironically to his day-job as a bank clerk, Picasso depicted the poet garbed and accoutred like a standard-issue businessman, strolling past the colonnaded Stock Exchange just before 1pm. The dog at his heels belonged to his mother, the half-Polish adventuress Olga de Kostrowitzky – a wry comment, as Peter Read has remarked, 'on the fraught but dependent relationship between domineering mother and adult son'.[6] During the summer of 1906 when Picasso was painting in the remote Pyrenean village of Gósol and doubtless missing Apollinaire's stimulating company, it tickled him to imagine his friend as a Spanish gentleman – 'Don Guillermo Apolliner' (61). This was more than a passing fancy, for so picaresque was the poet's early life that he had gone by various names before he chose to be known as Guillaume Apollinaire. His identity was so flexible, his talents so various and his character so complex that in Picasso's caricatures he appeared simultaneously in numerous guises: as Pope, French Academician, swaggering boxer, and so on.

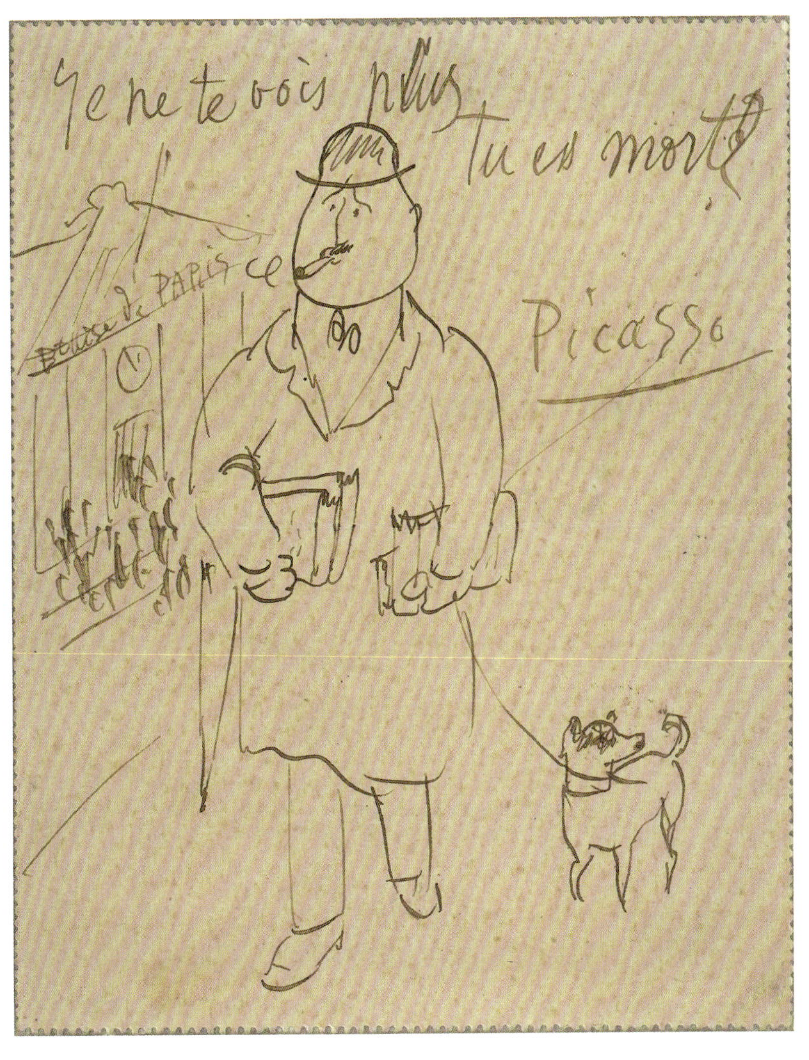

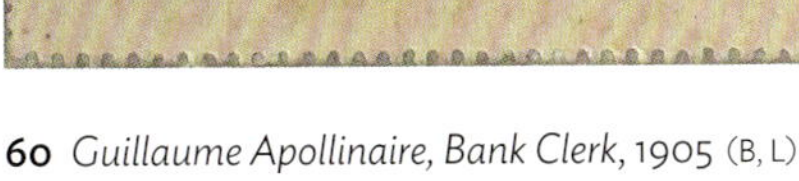

60 *Guillaume Apollinaire, Bank Clerk*, 1905 (B, L)

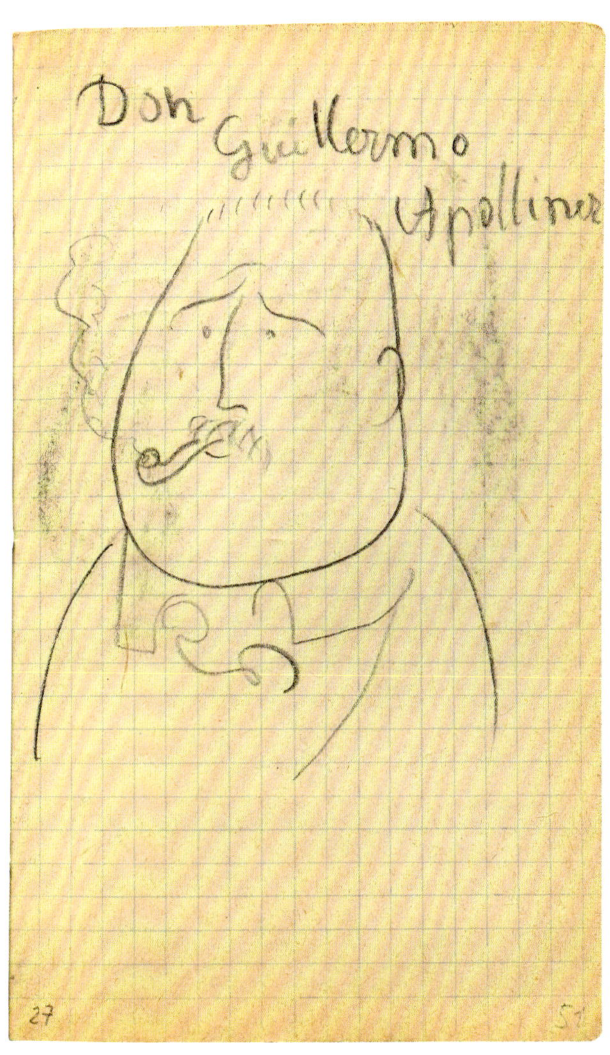

61 *Caricature of Guillaume Apollinaire*, 1906 (B)

PORTRAYING WOMEN: FERNANDE OLIVIER AND GERTRUDE STEIN

The new male friends Picasso made after settling in the Bateau-Lavoir inspired caricatures, not portrait paintings. With women the situation was different: there are very few caricatures of women – a hangover perhaps of the old chivalrous code governing female portraiture[7] – but an increasing number of paintings. The artist's model Fernande Olivier was Picasso's first long-term, live-in lover, and it was during her reign that women began to replace men as his primary subject. But before we consider the portraits of Olivier herself, a telling instance of this sea-change deserves mention. The fact that the Guggenheim Museum's silvery masterpiece *Woman Ironing* (62) was painted over the portrait of a man has been known for years, but thanks to new advances in infrared spectral imaging techniques, the man can now be confidently identified as Ricard Canals, a Catalan painter whom Picasso had met in Barcelona but saw much more of when they became neighbours in the Bateau-Lavoir (63).[8] As far as one can tell, the portrait of Canals standing at his easel was unfinished when Picasso turned the canvas upside down and painted *Woman Ironing* over it. It is symptomatic of the 'feminisation' of his work after he settled in Paris that the portrait of Canals could be sacrificed, but not the slightly later portrait of Canals's partner, the ravishing artist's model Benedetta Bianco (64).

Olivier was a good friend of Benedetta and Canals, and when her affair with Picasso started (casually and intermittently at first) in the summer of 1904, she was staying with them in the Bateau-Lavoir.[9] Exactly when Picasso painted his moody half-length portrait (66) is a matter of conjecture – perhaps at about the same time as his portrait of Benedetta, who may be wearing the very same mantilla.[10] Of the two, the portrait of Olivier is the quicker and sketchier, the face rendered impressionistically instead of with the fine detail devoted to Benedetta's. And whereas Benedetta's coolly appraising expression, her right eyebrow arched quizzically, strongly suggests interaction between artist and posing sitter, Olivier emerges from the vaporous background like a transient vision. Photographs confirm that the pale face framed by the soft, dark folds of fabric resembles Olivier's, but truth to appearances was not Picasso's priority and her role borders on the symbolic. The move to Paris had not severed Picasso's links with *fin-de-siècle* Symbolism, and Olivier may incarnate feminine mystery, or melancholy, or pensiveness: the lack of any tell-tale emblems or accessories leaves one free to speculate. The excessive fluidity of the paint – drips stream down over her shoulders from the top of the canvas like rain down a pane of glass – and the looping and scumbling motion of Picasso's brush foreground his artistic process, his sole agency in the transfer to canvas of this projection of Olivier's wistful image.

The portrait of Olivier was most likely painted in her absence. The sensitive graphite drawing may have served as a study, for the similarities suggest a direct connection (65).[11] In this study, Olivier faces the artist and looks him in the eye. To represent her unique features more precisely – the arch of her brows, the almond shape of her eyes, the straight line of her nose – Picasso went over his initial tentative contours with a finer, sharper pencil. In her presence, he strove to be exact. In the painting, her head is averted and her gaze clouded, and instead of pressing forward assertively she retreats into the cavern formed by the mantilla. All these modifications contribute to the visionary quality of the painting, and in distancing himself from the experience of looking intently at the real woman when he was drawing her, Picasso switched the direction of the lighting. In her absence he could exert greater control over her image and be more suggestive in his

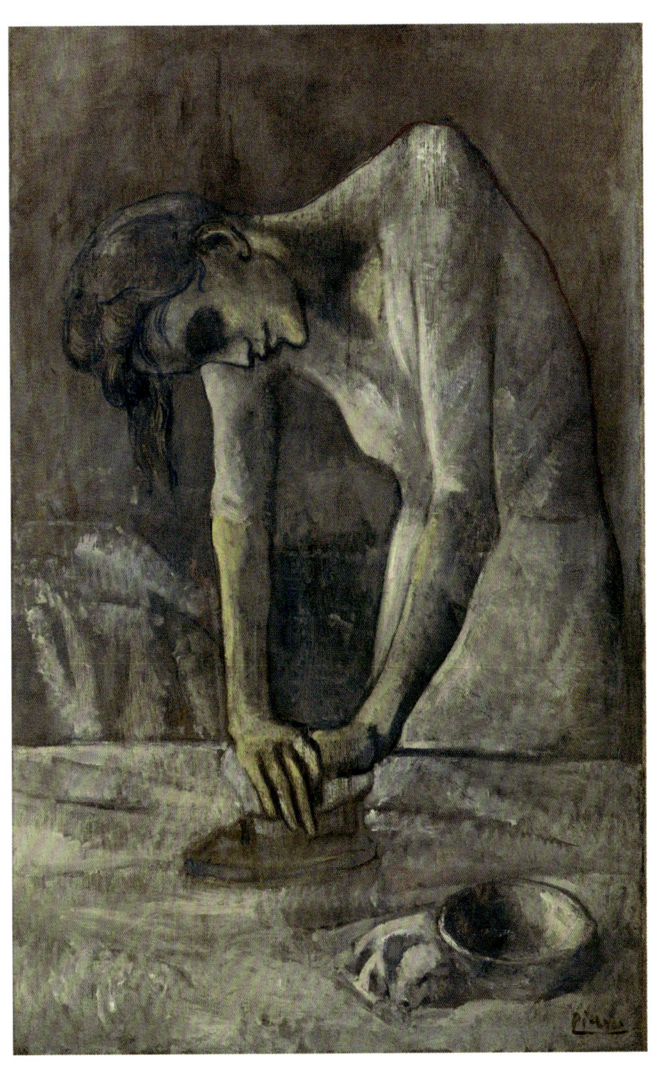

62 *Woman Ironing*, 1904

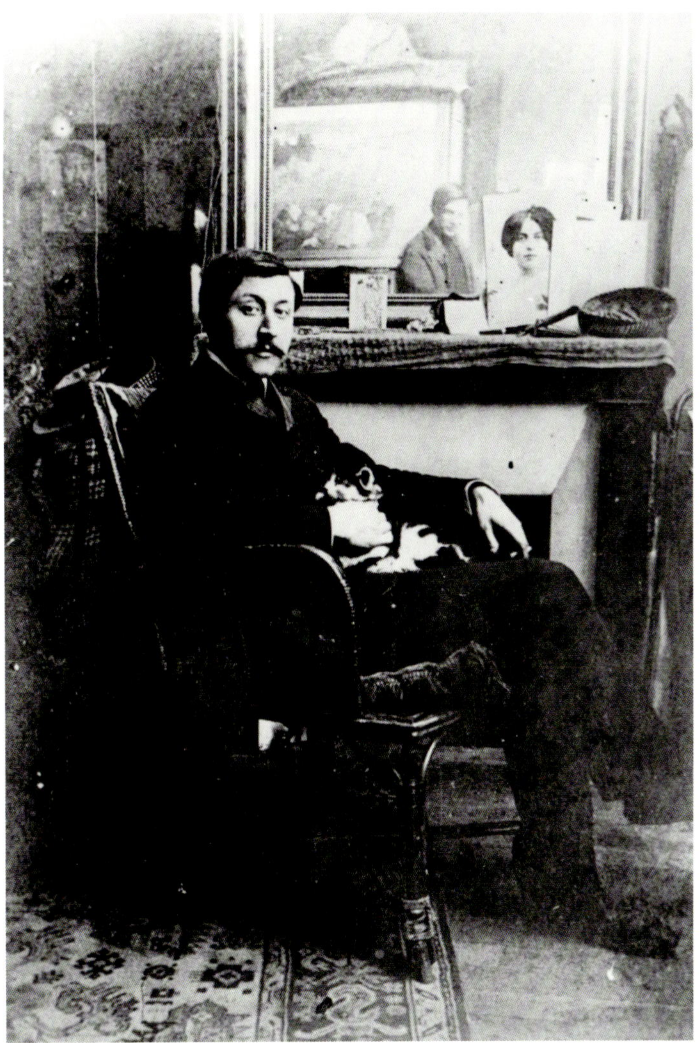

63 *Portrait of Ricard Canals*, Paris, 1904

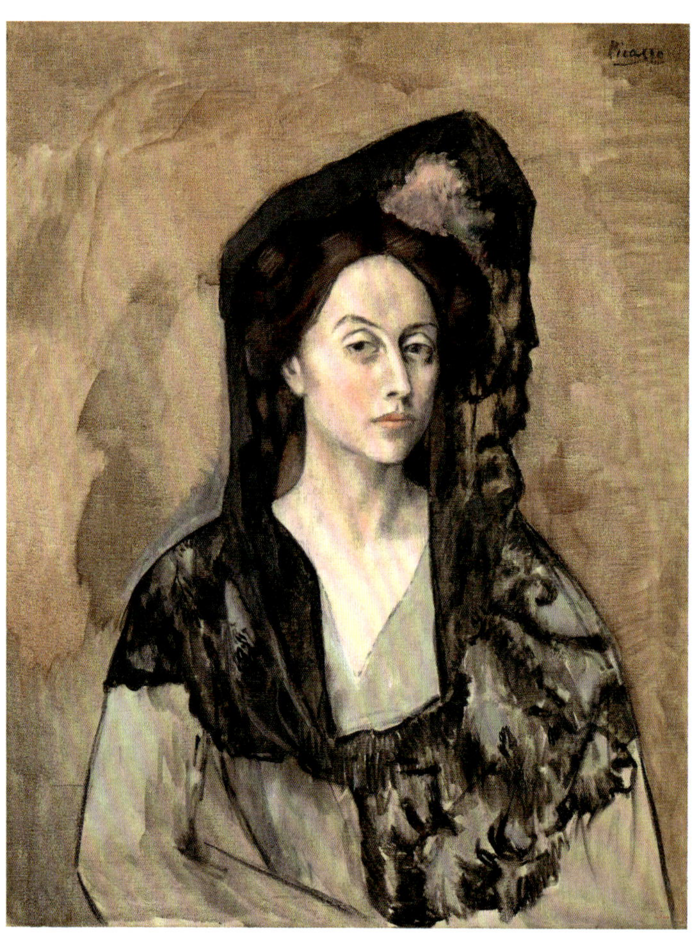

64 *Madame Canals (Benedetta Bianco)*, [autumn] 1905

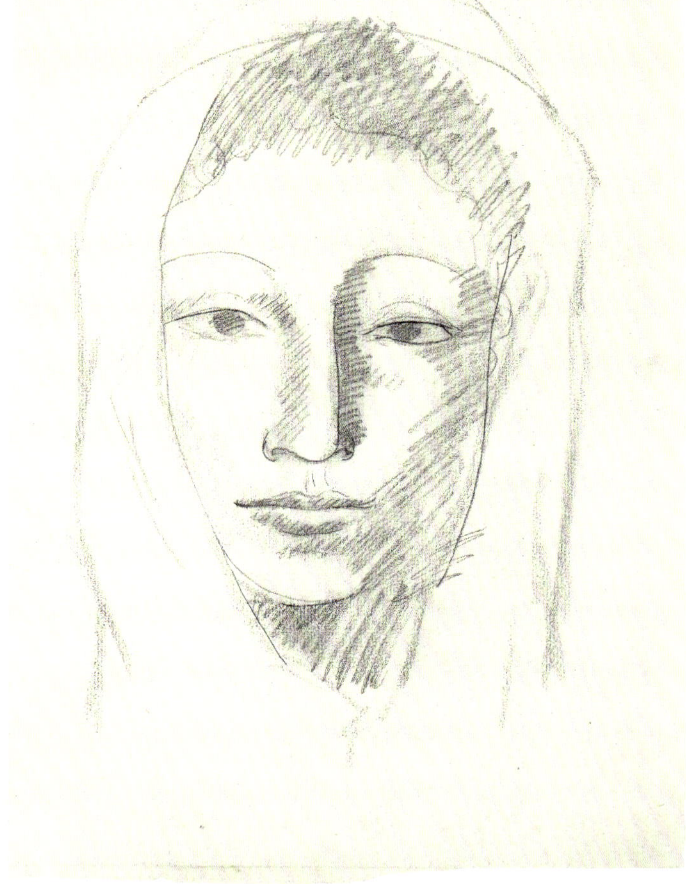

65 *Fernande Olivier*, 1905–6 (B)

interpretation. This would be a recurrent pattern in his portraiture of women.

By his own account, Picasso had modelled 'thousands of crèche figures' as a child.[12] However, his entire training, both at the hands of his father and in the Spanish art schools he attended, was geared to a career as a painter and it was not until 1902 that he took up modelling again. Four years later he began sculpting in a more sustained fashion, trying out different materials and techniques and turning to sculptor-friends for instruction and advice. *Head of a Woman (Fernande)* (67) was modelled in clay in the spring of 1906 in the studio of Paco Durrio – the Basque sculptor, ceramist and disciple of Gauguin – and it was doubtless he who taught Picasso the trick of pressing fine tulle into the surface of the moist clay to evoke the porous texture of skin.[13] In her diary, Olivier refers to the convivial evenings they spent with Durrio, and to his kiln, used for firing his ceramics in his studio near the Bateau-Lavoir.[14] But she does not mention posing for the sculpture, and Picasso very likely worked from memory with the aid of drawings from life. In her portrait, Olivier has the aloof serenity of a classical goddess but Picasso struck a balance between idealisation and reality, for her distinctive

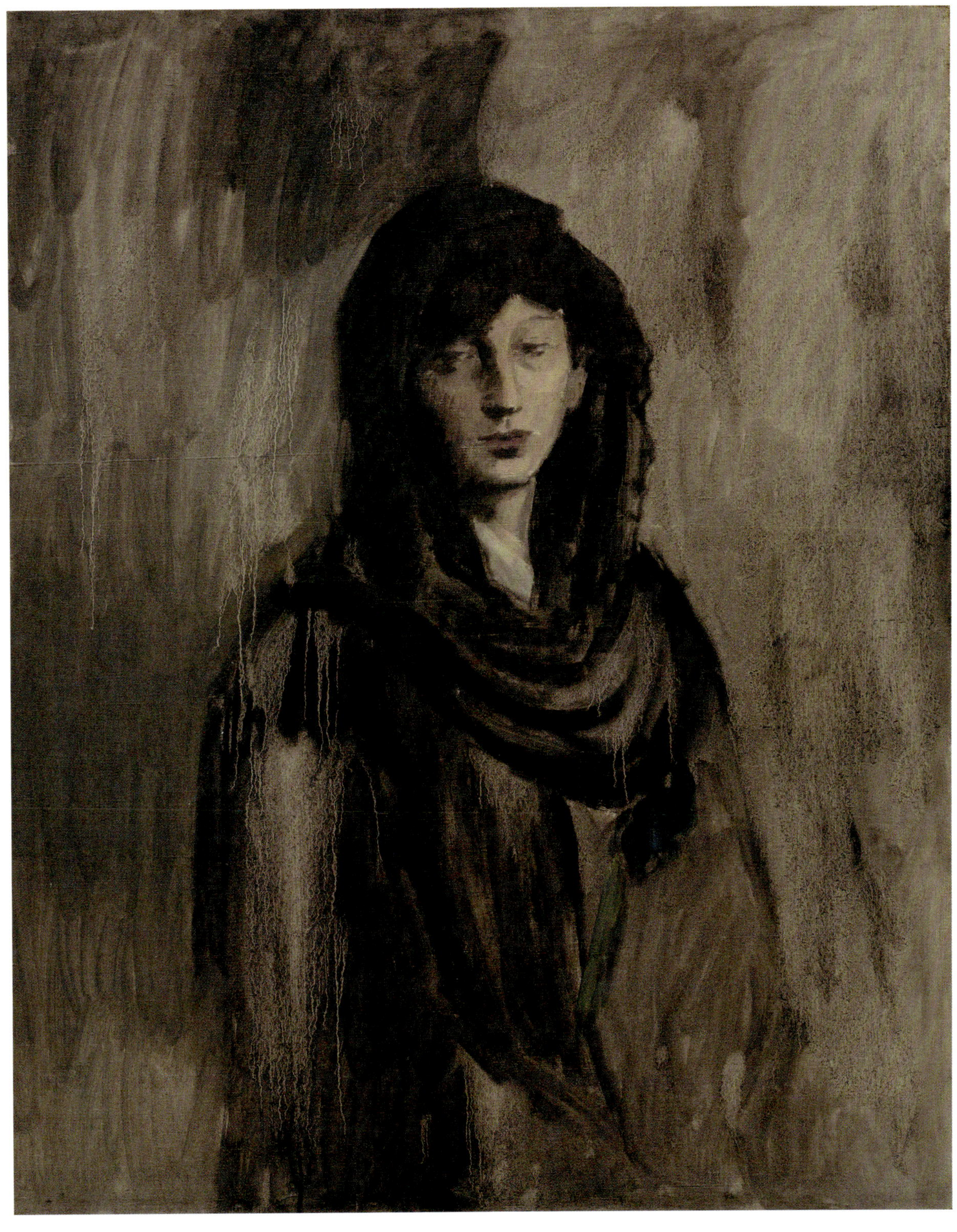

66 *Fernande Olivier with a Black Mantilla*, 1905–6 (B, L)

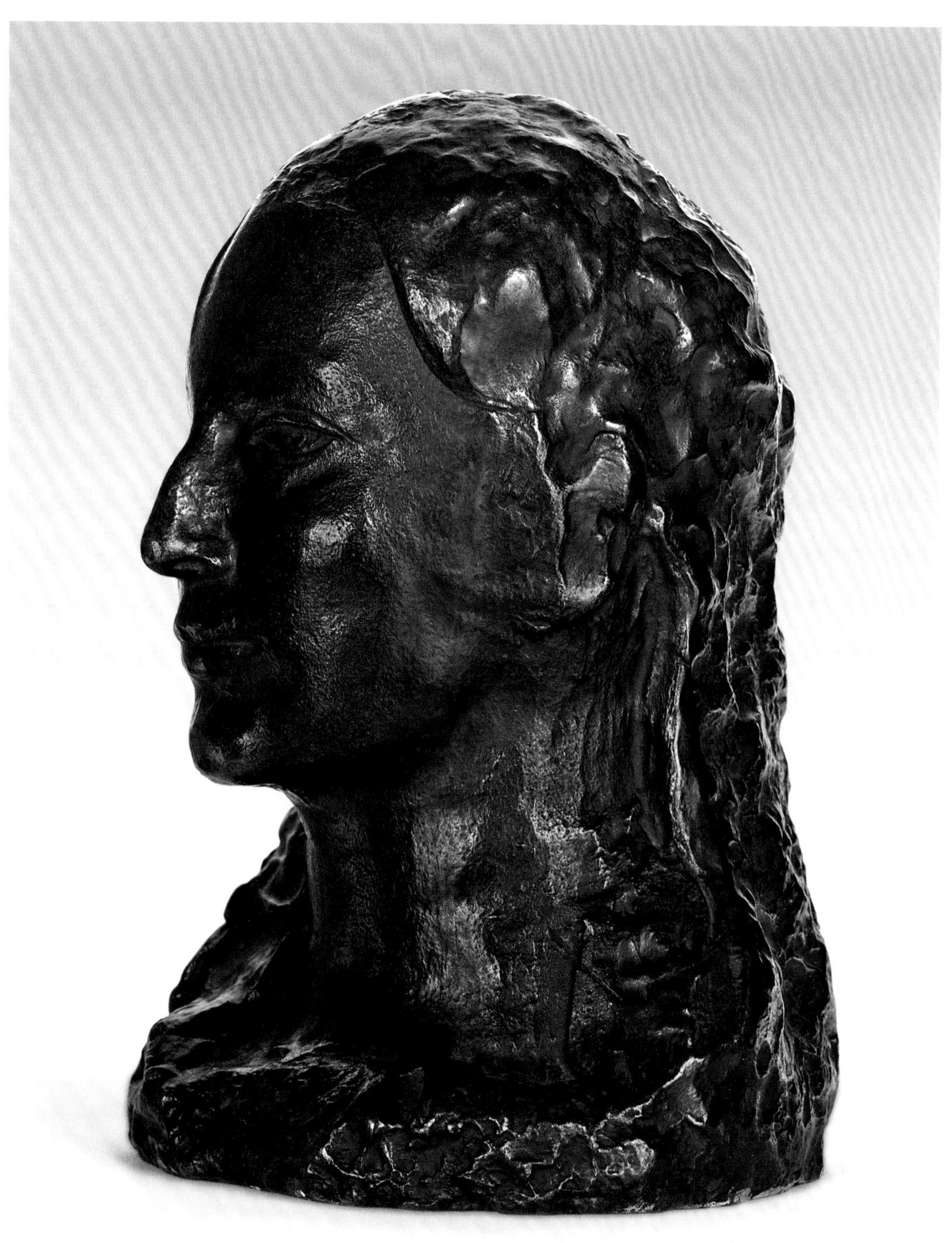

67 *Head of a Woman (Fernande Olivier)*, 1906 (B, L)

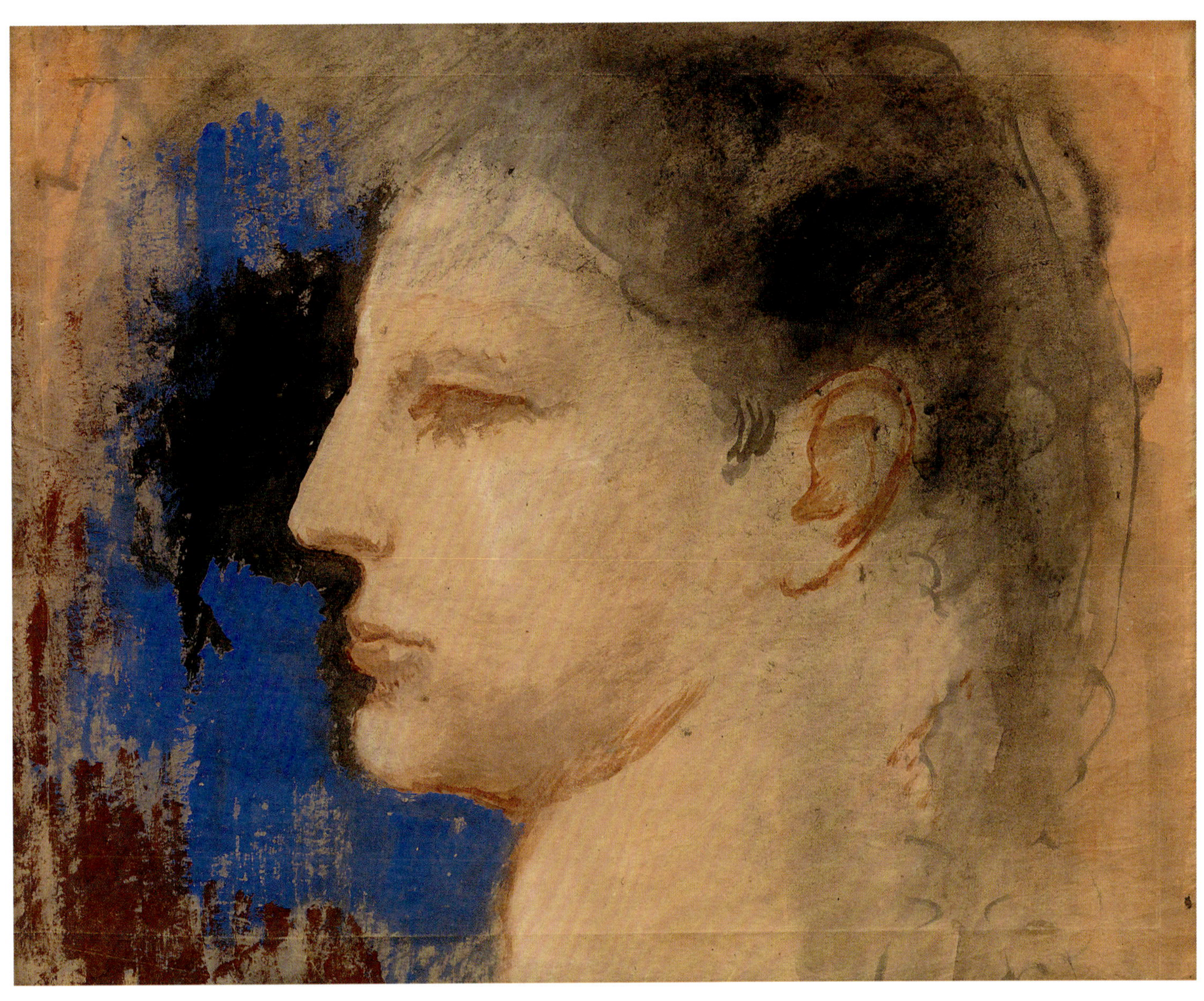

68 *Woman's Head. Portrait of Fernande Olivier*, 1906 (L)

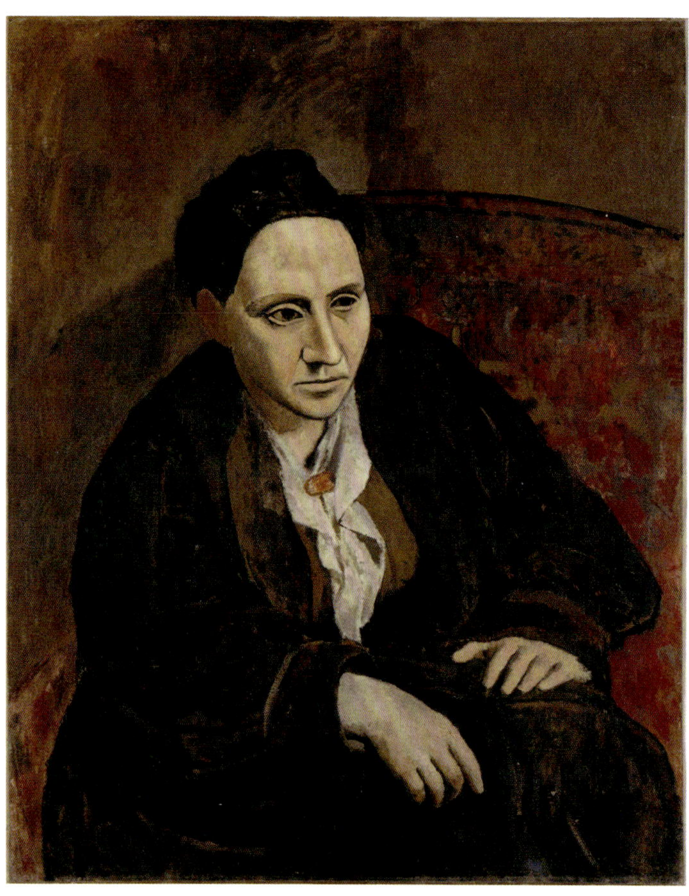

69 *Portrait of Gertrude Stein*, 1906

features are immediately recognizable: the almond eyes, Roman nose, high cheekbones, strong neck and copious, softly waving hair. The right side of the head looks less finished than the left and registers the marks of the sculptor's knife and fingers; her right eye is indicated with the lightest of scratched incisions – a mere beginning. The back of the head, an amorphous accumulation of hundreds of tiny patches of clay, is exploratory in a painterly fashion. By contrast, Olivier's left eye, eyebrow and hairline are finely modelled and incised. This inconsistency was surely intentional, recalling the 'blinded' eyes of self-portraits painted before Picasso's first trip to Paris (see 10 and 11). Here the disparity probably signified Olivier's contrasting public and private faces, the knowable and unknowable aspects of her personality and the shifting moods to which she was prone. But it also arose from Picasso's commitment to the dynamism of the 'provisional' and aversion to the inertia of the 'finished'. Both *Fernande Olivier with a Black Mantilla* and the portrait of Benedetta were left in a seemingly incomplete state for the same compelling motive – to keep them provocatively alive.

Picasso's activity as a sculptor gathered momentum during the course of 1906 and his painting became increasingly sculptural in appearance.[15] Olivier was statuesque and slow-moving, not a slender waif like some of his former Parisian girlfriends; this contributed to Picasso's evolution in style and *Woman's Head. Portrait of Fernande Olivier* exemplifies the tendency (68). Postdating the sculpted head, it was painted either in Gósol, the remote Catalan village in the Pyrenees where the couple stayed from the beginning of June to the middle of August 1906, or in Paris shortly after their return. Although the handling of the gouache is sketchy and the description of the crown and back of Olivier's head provisional, Picasso conferred on his lover the impersonal dignity of a priestess or matron in a Roman relief.

We know from the memoirs of the Italian painter Ardengo Soffici that he was often to be seen pacing about in the Louvre's galleries of antique sculpture 'like a hound in search of game'.[16] By closing in on her expressionless head and silhouetting her profile against the patches of dense blue and black, Picasso enhanced the impression of timeless monumentality. Far from bringing out her unique qualities through the caricatural exaggerations used for his male friends, he made her conform to a certain type and take on the values associated with that type – nobility, solemnity, rectitude. There is no hint here of the indolent, capricious, pleasure-loving woman revealed in Olivier's private diary.

Picasso first met the American writer Gertrude Stein and her brother Leo in the autumn of 1905 and began attending their open-house soirées with his band of friends. He was so taken by this exceptional woman, who claimed equality with men of 'genius' and in no way fitted the normal pattern of the decorative female 'muse', that he immediately proposed painting her portrait (69). Since the Steins had already started buying his work this was also a way to consolidate a promising relationship. Gertrude's vivid description of the first session in the Bateau-Lavoir has the ring of truth: she posed on 'a large broken armchair' and Picasso sat 'very tight' on 'a little kitchen chair' and 'very close to his canvas'. By the end of the afternoon he had completed a sketch, which the members of her family thought so beautiful that they 'begged that it should be left as it was. But Picasso shook his head and said, non.'[17] She claims that 'some eighty or ninety' sittings followed – a gross exaggeration, although X-rays and autoradiographs have revealed successive revisions to the angle of her head that probably were undertaken in her presence.[18] In any case, in the spring of 1906, 'all of a sudden one day Picasso painted out the whole head. I can't see you any more when I look, he said irritably. And so the picture was left like that.'[19] Picasso did not touch it again until he returned to Paris from Gósol in mid-August. Then, while Gertrude was still on vacation in Fiesole, he repainted the head.

Picasso had reached an impasse: he could no longer 'see' Gertrude Stein because he had set himself far more to do than simply communicate a vivid first impression of her unconventional appearance.[20] He was determined to rival acknowledged masterpieces of portraiture by producing a definitive image that would somehow convey profound truths about her through his representation of her head and body alone. Typically, when formulating an interpretation of his subject, Picasso would draw upon works of art and styles of art that seemed to him peculiarly appropriate and revealing. His vision of Stein was mediated through a combination of sources, including Ingres's celebrated portrait of the physically similar newspaper magnate Louis-François Bertin (1832; Musée du Louvre), and the portrait of his wife by Cézanne that Gertrude and Leo prized above all else in their collection.[21] But when Gertrude posed in his studio it proved difficult to preserve that vision intact: strong-willed, intrusive and egotistical, she unsettled Picasso with her passing moods; mercurial by nature, his own frame of mind was equally liable to change. As discussed above, the farewell portrait of Sabartés painted in 1904 (see 55) had to be finished very quickly on the second day because otherwise Picasso would have had to start it all over again. But Gertrude was no awestruck Sabartés and dismissing this formidable woman from his studio was no easy matter. She relished the intense, tussling interaction that posing for him involved; no wonder he lost his way and his patience. New sculptural sources of inspiration – archaic Iberian and Catalan Romanesque sculpture – discovered while the portrait was in process clinched his characterisation, but it was only when she was safely out of the way that Picasso was able to

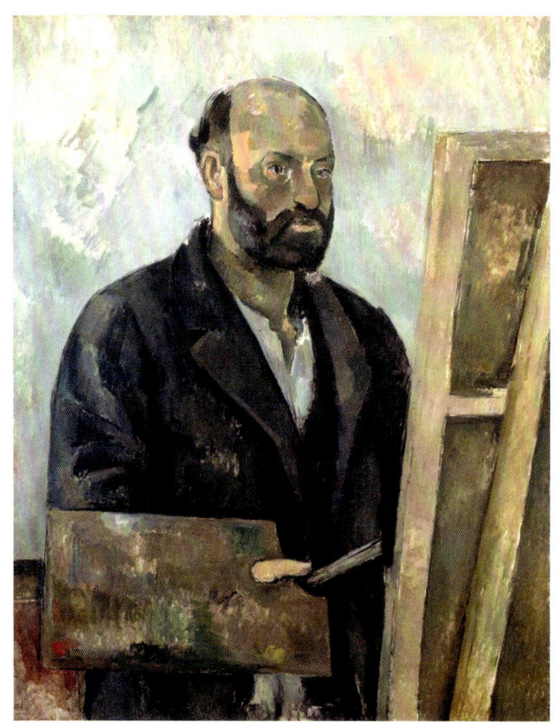

70 *Self-portrait with Palette* by Paul Cézanne, *c.*1890

repaint her head as the adamantine mask that we now know. That mask stood for atavism, profundity, permanence and essence. Picasso made a few minor adjustments to other areas of the composition but left the painting otherwise unchanged: tidying it up by making it consistent stylistically and technically would have deadened its impact disastrously. Stein's proud verdict on the result was categorical: 'For me, it is I, and it is the only reproduction of me which is always I, for me.'[22]

It is sometimes said that Picasso never painted from a posing sitter again. In fact he did, but it is true that – in contrast to, say, Alberto Giacometti – he generally preferred not to. Nevertheless, he continued to make portrait drawings from life. The problematic balance of power between artist and sitter hardly arose when he used the quicker medium. In his next self-portrait (71), projecting a meaningful image mattered to him above all and nothing suggests that he stood before a mirror when painting it. Preparatory sketches recorded different possibilities for the angle of his head and the direction of his gaze.[23] As if to underline his sense of brotherhood with Gertrude Stein, Picasso gave himself the same fixed stare and mask-like, Iberian-style features.[24] Cézanne had played a part in the conception of her portrait and this self-portrait is also an act of homage to Cézanne. The parallels with the latter's *Self-portrait with Palette* are so striking that at the very least, Picasso must have seen a photo of this austere and commanding painting (70).[25] We don't know the exact date of Picasso's self-portrait but it was certainly produced near the time of Cézanne's death on 23 October 1906. If it was painted in the aftermath of that shock, Picasso's spellbound gravity and the bleak grey background may be explained by his wish to express reverence for the artist. 'Cézanne!' he later said. 'He was my one and only master! [...] It was the same with all of us – he was like our father. It was he who protected us.'[26] Picasso's twenty-fifth birthday fell on 25 October, but rather than depict himself brush in hand ready to start work (as he had in the preparatory drawings), he depicted himself standing stock-still as if observing the ritual of a minute's silence.

In the schematic manner typical of caricature, but without humorous flourishes and comic details, Picasso summed up his tough-guy physical appearance by eliminating all nuance and stressing his identifying features: short black hair, large eyes with black dilated pupils, broad, fleshy nose, full lips, bullish neck, four-square torso, muscular arms, workman's collarless shirt and baggy trousers. These traits served as code for Picasso the driven worker-artist, and having hit upon this potent self-image in the autumn of 1906 he played up to it for the next ten years or so in self-portraits, which for the most part took the form of photographs (72–4).

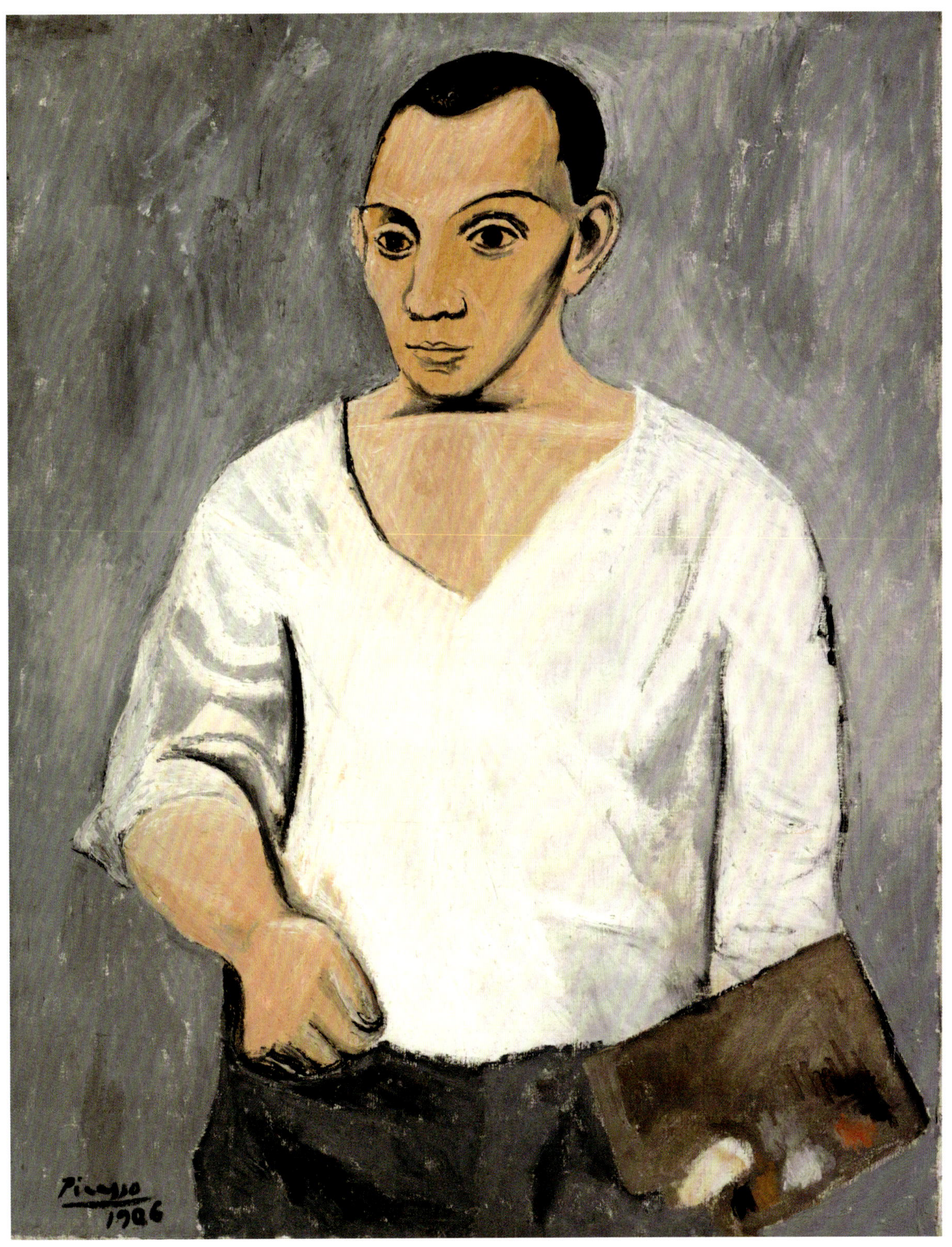

71 *Self-portrait with Palette*, 1906 (L)

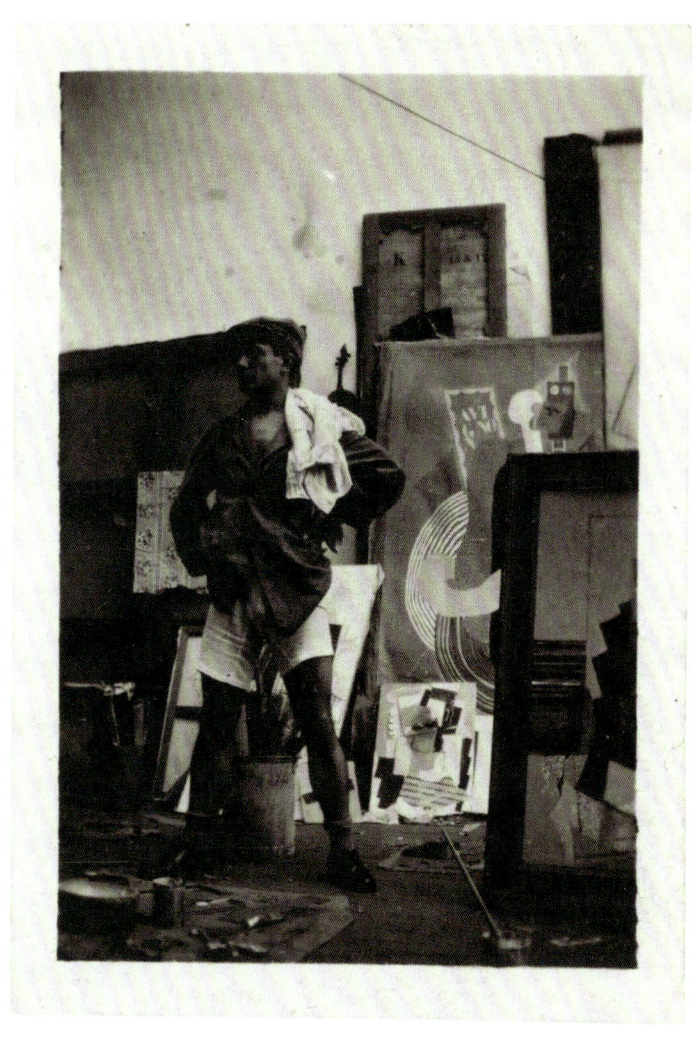

72 *Self-portrait with* Seated Man with Glass, 5 bis Rue Schoelcher, Paris, 1915–16 (B, L)

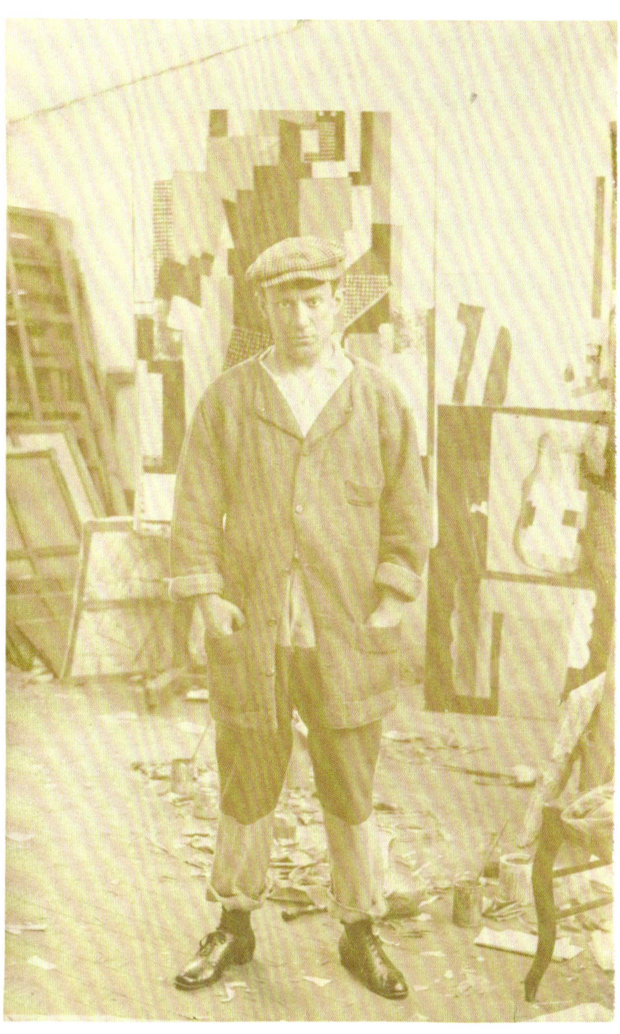

73 *Self-portrait with* Man Leaning on a Table, 5 bis Rue Schoelcher, Paris, 1915–16 (B, L)

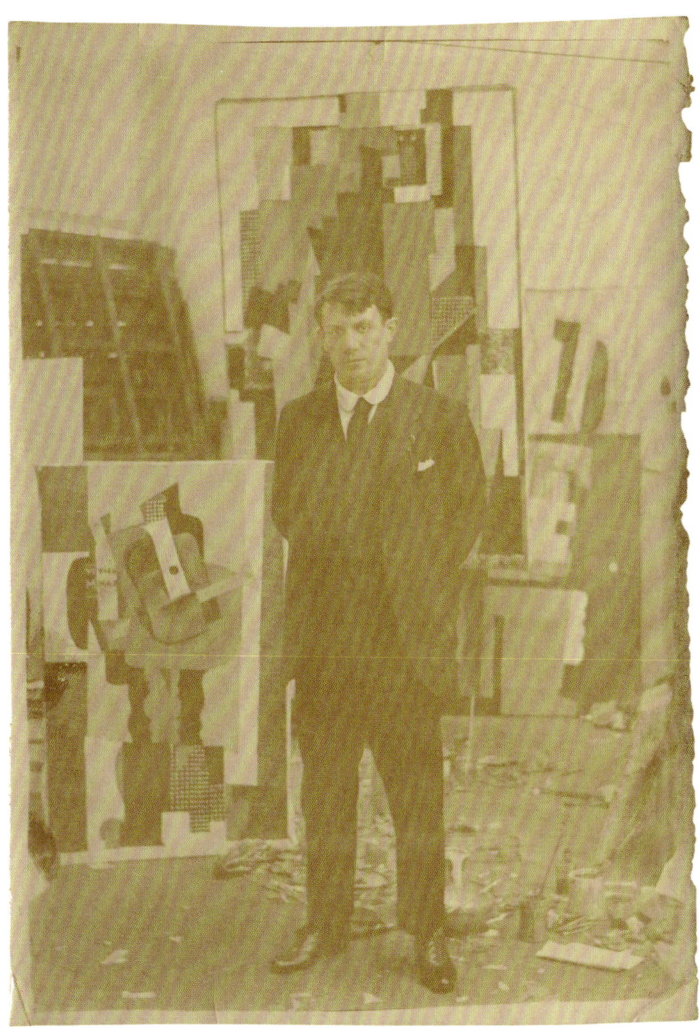

74 *Self-portrait with* Man Leaning on a Table, 5 bis Rue Schoelcher, Paris, 1915–16 (B, L)

PORTRAITURE, PHOTOGRAPHY AND CUBISM

In 1906 Picasso's work manifested clear signs of his response to ancient traditions of sculpture, especially traditions that lay outside the academic canon: Egyptian, Archaic Greek, Archaic Iberian, Etruscan and Romanesque. These so-called 'primitive' sources were then joined by *art nègre* (African and Oceanic art): contemporary with *Les Demoiselles d'Avignon*, his charcoal drawing of Salmon (see 58) was an early case. For artists of Picasso's generation, primitivism necessarily involved rejecting Western traditions of naturalism and illusionism. The sophisticated representational skills taught in art schools were cast aside; portraiture, like scenes of contemporary urban life, suffered an eclipse. Photography, it was said, could perform the task of recording appearances and particularities: art had the nobler purpose of addressing elemental, timeless themes, with the nude as the best universalising vehicle of expression. During the period between Picasso's departure for the ideally backward, peasant environment of Gósol and the beginning of his collaboration with Georges Braque on the creative adventure of Cubism during the winter of 1908–9, the number of his painted portraits decreased and the nude dominated his figure painting. To compensate, he began photographing Olivier and their friends posing in the Bateau-Lavoir in front of uncompromisingly primitivist paintings like the State Hermitage Museum's *Three Women* (75).[27]

The experiment with photography satisfied Picasso only up to a point, however, and in 1909–10 he began to explore how Cubism might be used to reinvent the portrait. Since Braque had no interest in portraiture, Picasso was on his own in this venture. Fernande Olivier was the obvious ready-made subject for this purpose, and after three years of cohabitation he had no qualms about laying aside the traditional obligations of

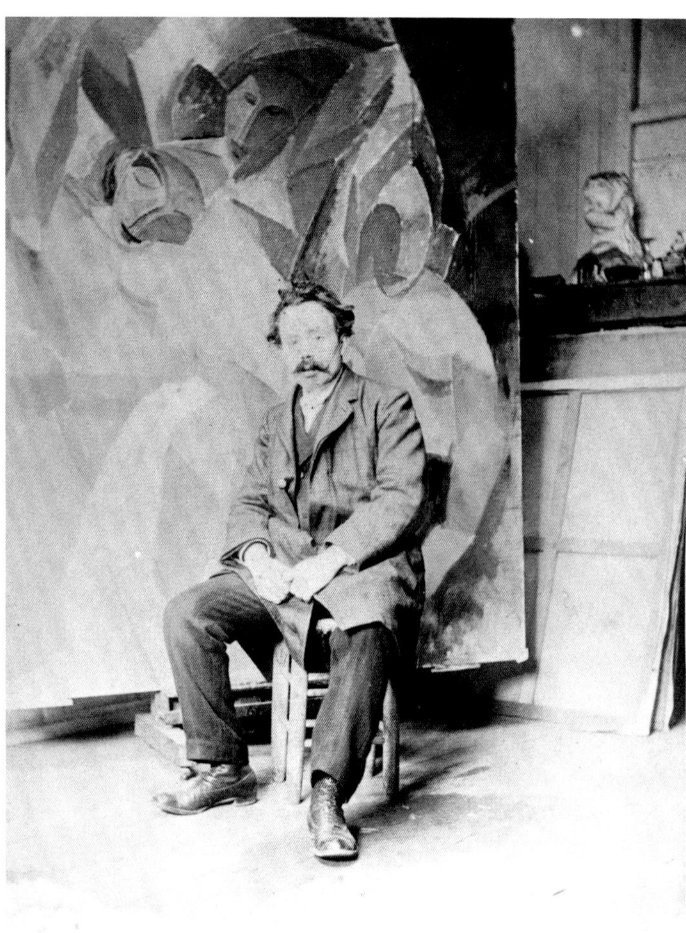

75 *Sebastià Junyer i Vidal in front of* Three Women, Bateau-Lavoir, Paris, 1908

the portraitist. For only the second time since settling in Montmartre, he decided to spend the summer of 1909 in Spain. After a few weeks in Barcelona the couple arrived in Horta de Sant Joan in early June and for the next ten weeks or so he worked with great intensity in rented rooms in the historic hilltop village. Apart from views of Horta itself, Olivier was his main subject, with the head and bust his most frequent formats.[28]

The Städel Museum's powerful study is typical of the series (76). Massively enlarged, Olivier's head is set against the backdrop of the harsh, rocky landscape of the region – a landscape that influenced the painting's earthy palette and Picasso's conception of her head as a terrain of peaks and ravines. In spite of the subtlety of his handling and the airy, uneven coverage of the canvas, the sensation of sculptural relief is almost oppressive. Defining characteristics from earlier portraits of Olivier – her piled-up hair, broad brow, Roman nose and strong neck – recur in a more abstracted form, but here her gaze and the set of her lips are sullen and reproachful. From letters she sent to Gertrude Stein and Stein's partner Alice Toklas, we learn that Olivier was unwell, depressed and disgruntled for much of the trip.[29] Adept since childhood at representing transient facial expressions, Picasso caught her resentful look with merciless accuracy.

He returned to Paris in September, resolved on taking to their logical conclusion the sculptural implications of the paintings and drawings executed in Horta. Modelling a lifesize Cubist head of Olivier also offered a perfect opportunity to gauge the distance he had travelled since sculpting his first portrait of her in 1906 (see 67). This time he used the studio of his sculptor-friend Manolo (Manuel Hugué), whom he had known since before the turn of the century when both belonged to the Els Quatre Gats set. Judging by the two surviving plaster casts, Picasso worked the clay vigorously and fast.[30] Although the Cubist sculpture (77) is more impersonal than most of the Horta paintings, the slight downward inclination of Olivier's head is a time-honoured indication of melancholy reflection, and is in marked contrast to the sublime serenity of the earlier, forward-facing sculpture. The strongly marked torsion of the neck and unpredictable twists and turns of the multiple jutting forms that make up the head imbue the sculpture with dynamism and drama that, one senses, have a psychological origin. The play of light and shadow over its rugged surface, which has reminded more than one writer of an anatomical écorché, increases that feeling of straining tension. Like the Horta paintings, this sculpture confirmed that the abstracted formal language of analytical Cubism was compatible with evoking personality and emotion.

On their return to Paris in September 1909, Picasso and Olivier moved out of the squalid Bateau-Lavoir and into a comfortable, well-appointed apartment with a large studio on the top floor of 11 Boulevard de Clichy. It was in this more bourgeois environment that Picasso painted *Cubist Head (Portrait of Fernande)* during the winter of 1909–10 (78). It derives from the recently completed sculpture, but its tone is quieter, gentler and more contemplative. The head is like a sculpted bust, with the rectangular shoulders (near the bottom edge of the canvas) serving as a plinth. The pale tones of brown, yellow and bluish-grey suggest plaster, rather than flesh – the plaster of the casts taken from Picasso's original clay model. Compared to the Cubist sculpture, the head in the painting is more geometric: the planes are fewer in number, flatter, sharper edged and more regular in shape. Moreover, the brow is treated like ascending steps and the neck like flaps of folded paper, while diagrammatic V-shapes replace the sculpture's relatively naturalistic eyes, nose and mouth. But Picasso humanised the overall effect by representing the soft waves of Fernande's hair

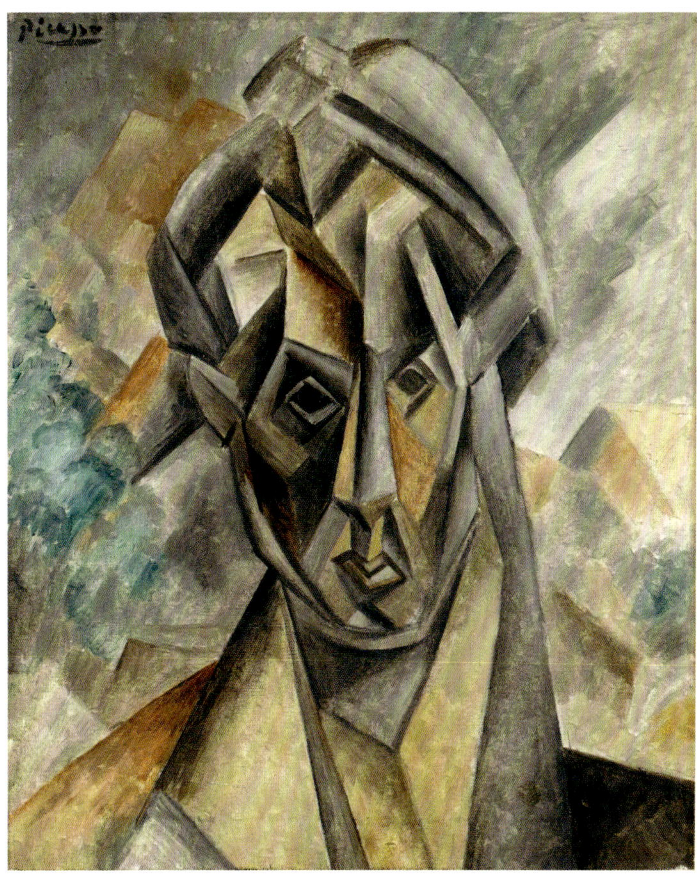

76 *Head of a Woman (Fernande Olivier)*, 1909

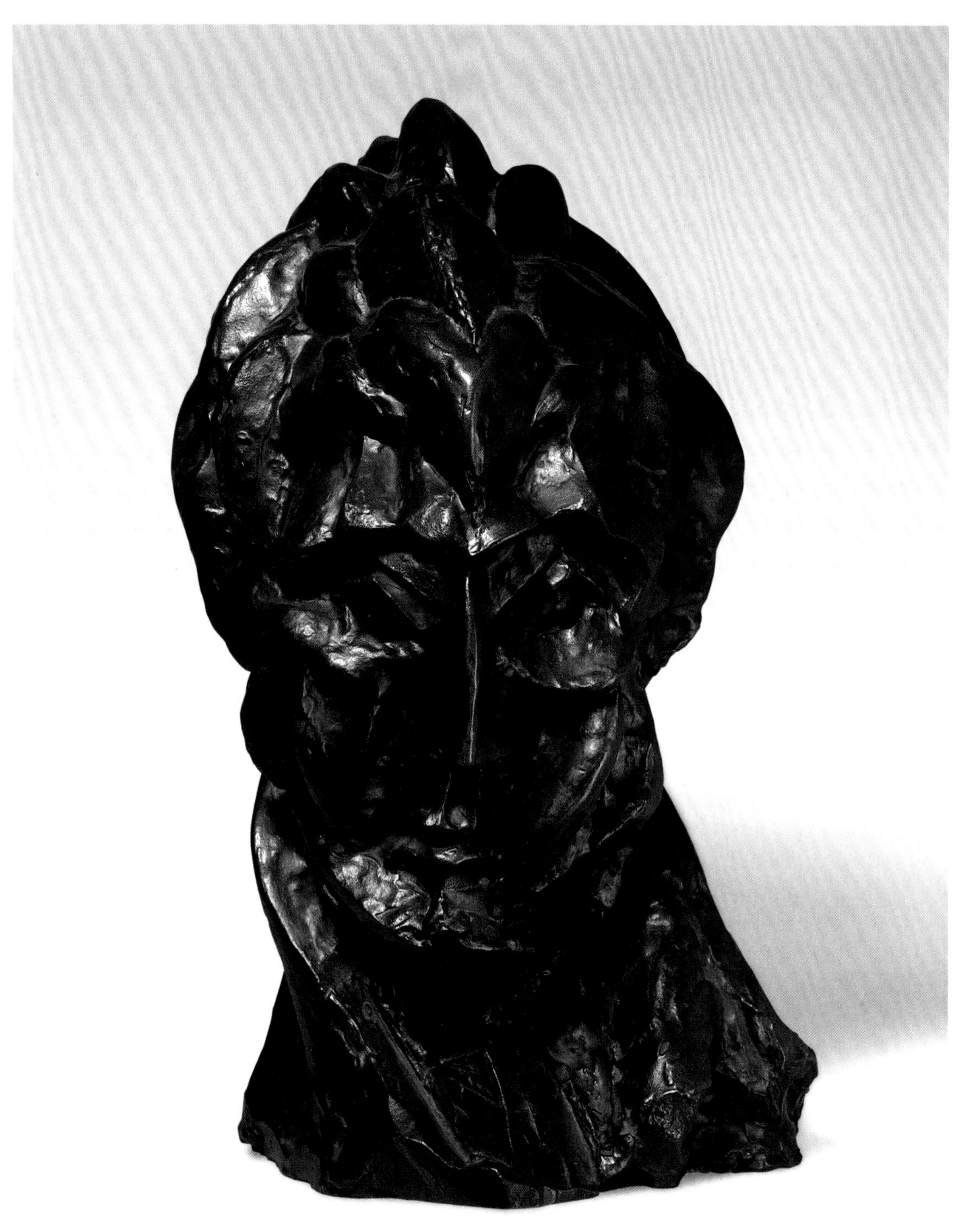

77 *Head of a Woman (Fernande)*, 1909 (B, L)

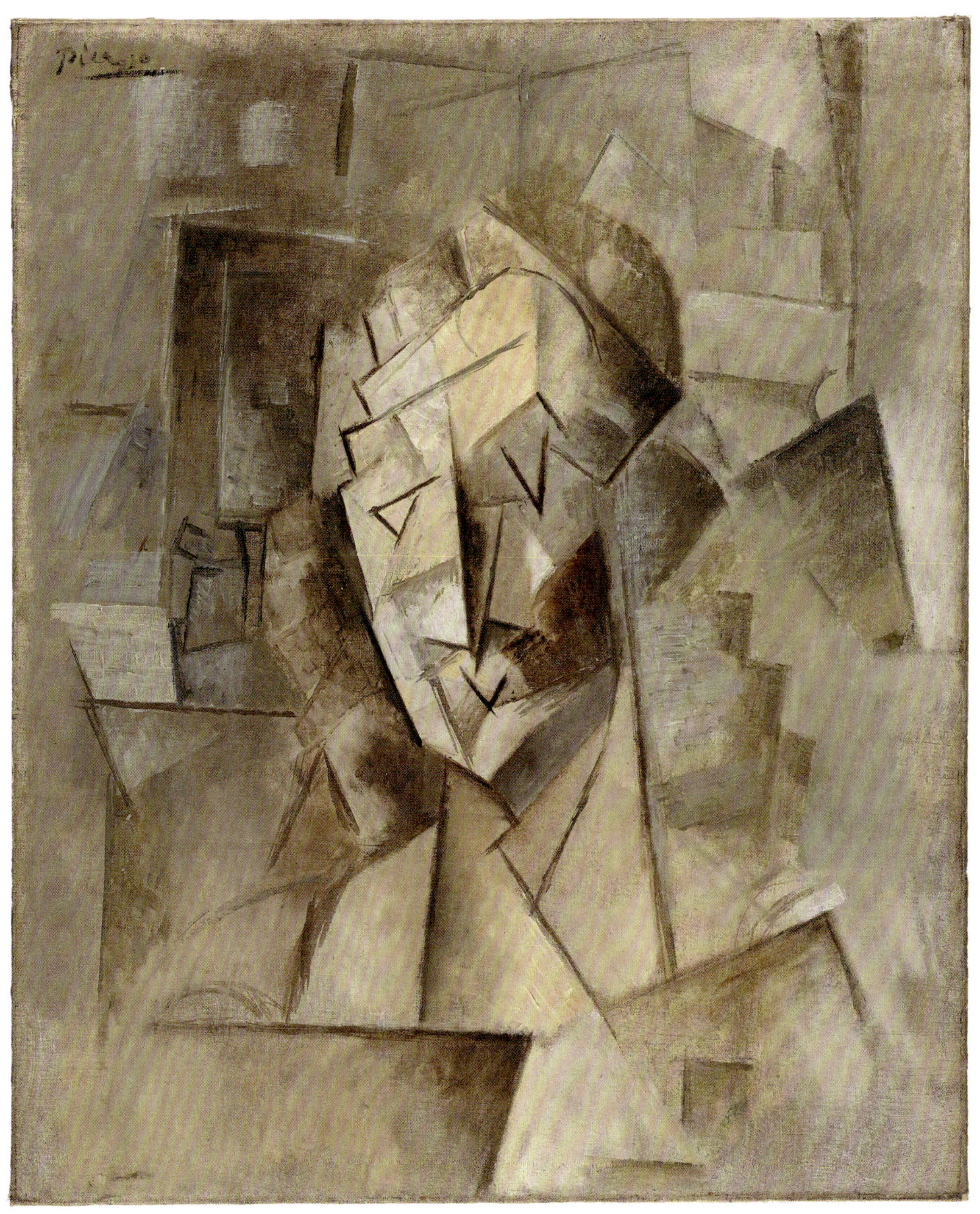

78 *Cubist Head (Portrait of Fernande)*, 1909–10 (B, L)

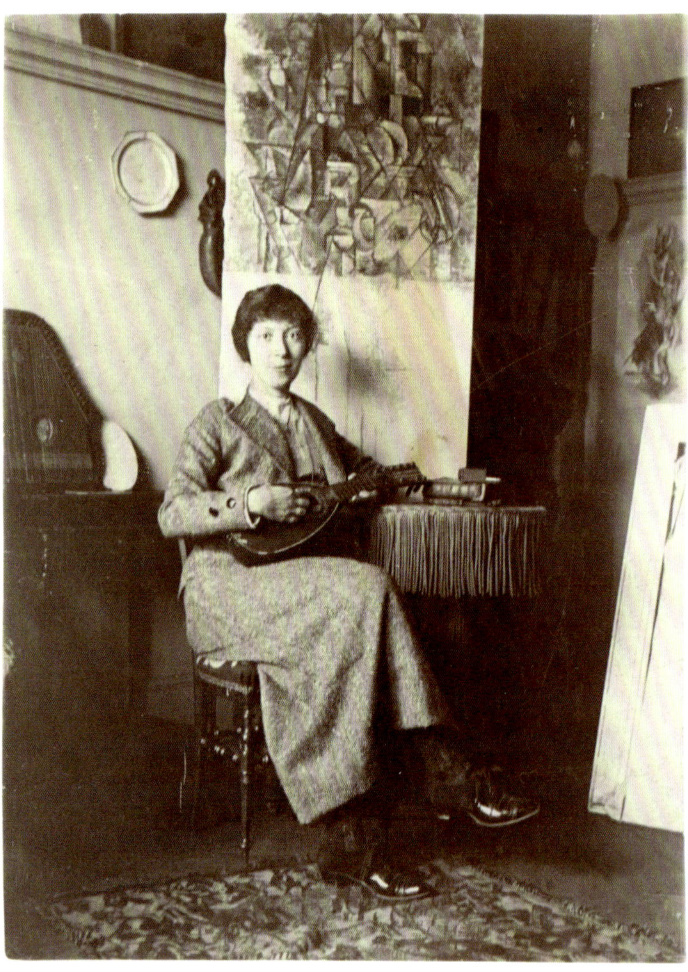

79 *Marie Laurencin with* Man with Mandolin, 11 Boulevard de Clichy, Paris, 1911 (B, L)

flowing down her back as rounded, puffy forms and faintly delineated zig-zags. Behind her head, a shadowy, framed, rectangular object probably represents a mirror and the small cubic object in front of it a box standing on a ledge – perhaps the very dressing-table to which he devoted a fine Cubist painting some months later.[31] The delicate, impressionistic handling and pearly lighting affirm the femininity of the subject matter of this lyrical canvas.

In the Boulevard de Clichy apartment Picasso resumed his habit of photographing friends. Apollinaire (80), Jacob, Salmon, Braque and Marie Laurencin (79) all posed beside recent paintings or were seated in the salon surrounded by the textiles, tribal carvings and bric-à-brac that Picasso had picked up from junk shops and flea markets.[32] Like those taken in the Bateau Lavoir, these photos stood in for the portraits that Picasso was *not* painting of his friends. They also had an autobiographical function: all these people were photographed in his constantly evolving environment, not theirs. Meanwhile, Picasso pursued his ambition to revolutionise portraiture by painting the three dealers on whom he relied at the period: Ambroise Vollard, Daniel-Henry Kahnweiler and Wilhelm Uhde.[33]

Vollard's support had been crucial in 1901 and from time to time he made substantial purchases after Picasso settled in the Bateau-Lavoir.[34] The dealer made several interventions in 1910: he purchased Cubist paintings executed during Picasso's trip to Cadaqués that summer; he also purchased five of Picasso's original sculptures, including both portraits of Olivier, with the right to issue bronze casts on demand; and in December he opened a mixed exhibition of Picasso's work that included Cubist paintings and probably the first bronze cast of the Cubist head. (We cannot be sure because there was no catalogue.) These events coincided with the painting of the lifesize,

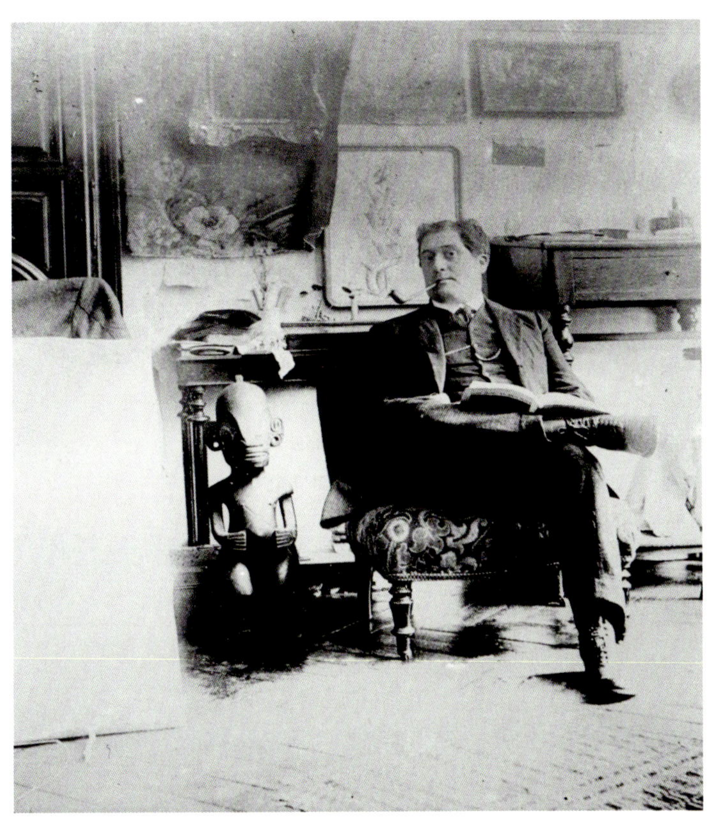

80 *Guillaume Apollinaire*, 11 Boulevard de Clichy, Paris, 1910

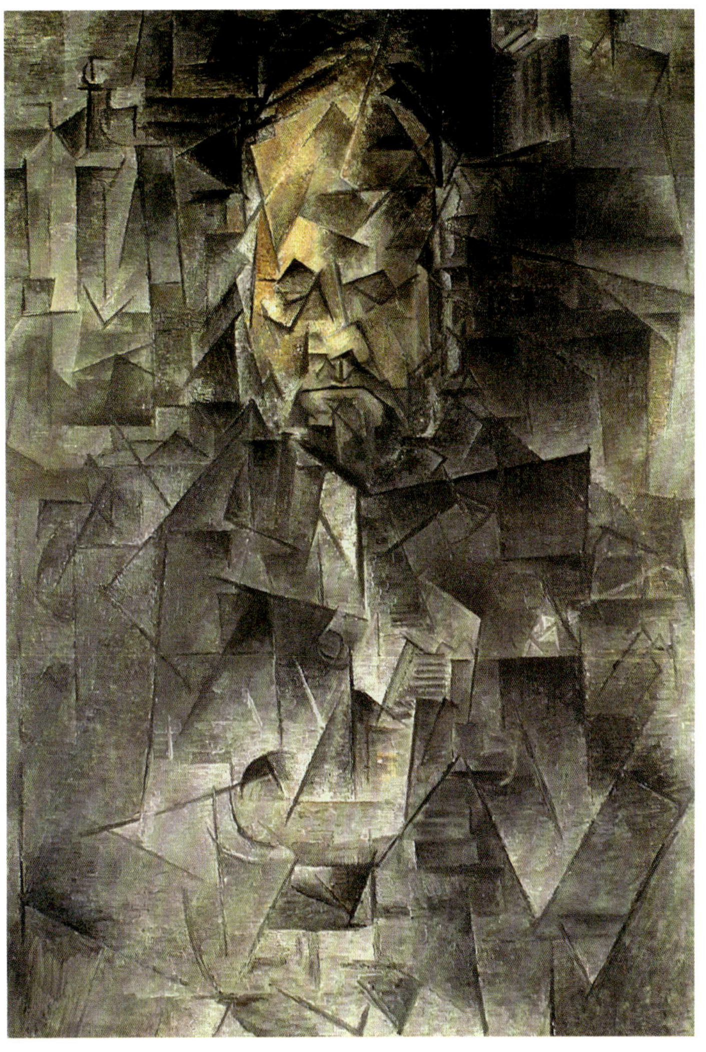

81 *Portrait of Ambroise Vollard*, 1910

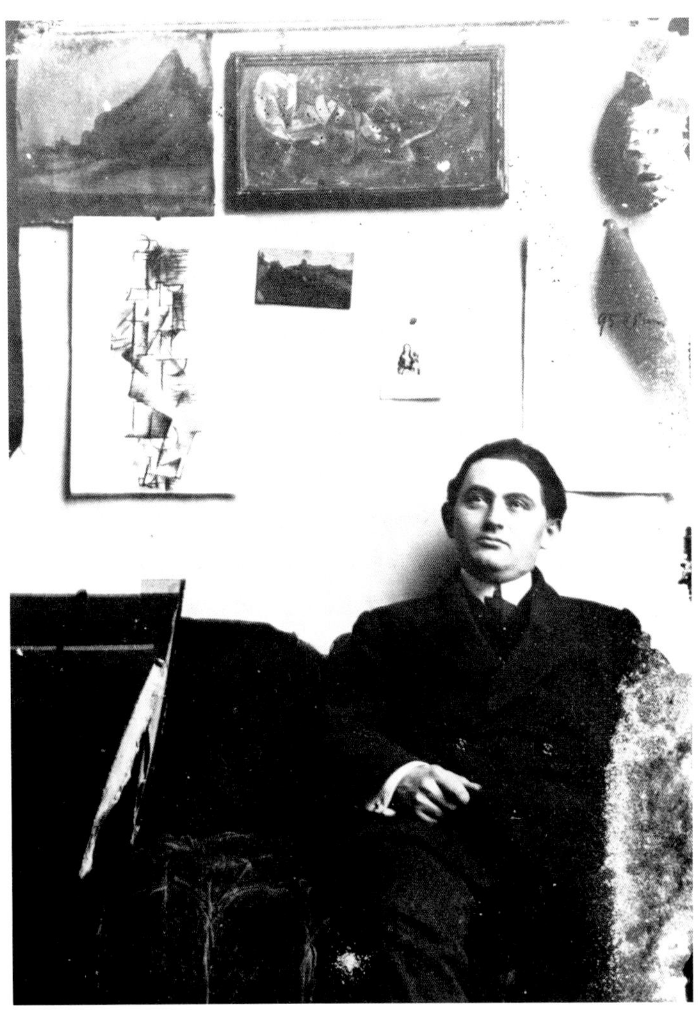

82 *Daniel-Henry Kahnweiler*, 11 Boulevard de Clichy, Paris, 1910

half-length *Portrait of Ambroise Vollard* (81). A letter Picasso sent to Gertrude Stein on 16 June 1910 confirms that the picture was then underway but not finished,[35] and Olivier remembered that it 'dragged over several months', costing Picasso more effort than the portraits of Kahnweiler and Uhde.[36] Much of the work was probably done in Vollard's absence and Picasso probably made use of photographs as an *aide-mémoire*. The dealer's domed, balding head, bulbous nose, thin lips, neatly trimmed beard and the set of his features are admirably characterised and easily deciphered. Vollard was notorious for his tendency to drop off to sleep in company and Picasso showed him behaving true to form: his eyes are closed, his head droops, his body has settled and slumped a little, the bulge of his stomach catching the light.

It is often assumed that the photograph of Kahnweiler lounging on Picasso's massive Louis-Philippe divan (82) was a source for the famous portrait painted during the autumn of 1910 (83). But since Kahnweiler actually posed for the painting on numerous occasions,[37] the photo may have had an independent existence. The setting of the portraits is certainly different. The New Caledonian ridgepole figure owned by Picasso, and beneath it the medicine bottles which, Kahnweiler said, were always present during his sittings, can be deciphered in the painting, to the left of the dealer.[38] But these objects do not appear in the photo, and for Kahnweiler to maintain his stiff, upright stance he must have posed on a straight-backed chair rather than rested against the divan's soft cushions. Like Picasso, Kahnweiler collected *art nègre* and displayed it in his home alongside contemporary art, so the New Caledonian figure was a fitting bystander. As for the medicine bottles that supplant the wine bottle and glass featured in so many Cubist still-lifes, they may have been Picasso's sly joke: Kahnweiler was famously abstemious and painfully out of his element in the smoky cafés and

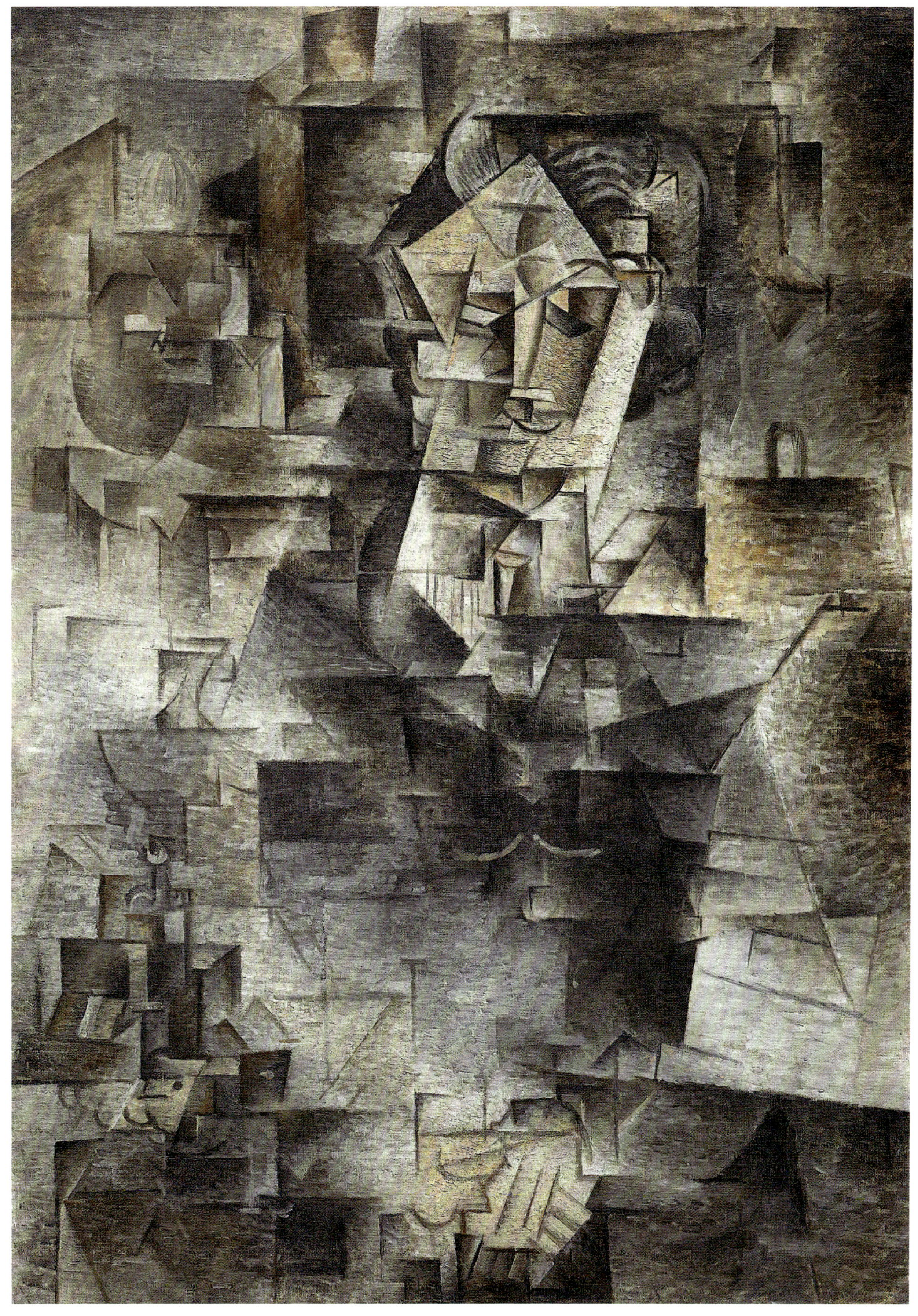

83 *Daniel-Henry Kahnweiler*, 1910 (B, L)

cabarets frequented by his stable of bohemian artists.[39] Probably the photograph was conceived as an alternative to the painting – a means to test the cheap, speedy, popular, mechanical medium against the labour-intensive, high-art medium it threatened to kill off.

To match the conventional medium of oil on canvas, Picasso chose the time-honoured frontal pose and half-length format for the painting, which at one metre high is approximately life-size. Its revolutionary aspects lie in its style, which Picasso felt no pressure to attenuate since Kahnweiler was wholeheartedly committed to promoting Cubism and enjoyed 'explaining' it to potential clients.[40] This subtle and complex picture depends upon the 'sign language' that replaced descriptive naturalism in the analytical Cubism of Picasso and Braque for its evocation of Kahnweiler's appearance and personality. Together, the signs for Kahnweiler's oiled, wavy hair, broad brow, hooded eyes, beaky nose, thin lips and strong chin build a lifelike impression of his head – as Picasso's portrait photograph confirms – but an impression that drifts into and out of focus with the elusiveness of the memory image. (Vollard's head is notably more volumetric and less evanescent.) Meanwhile, Kahnweiler's punctilious time-keeping and legendary patience are epitomised by the eye-catching sign for the watch-chain straddling the waistcoat of his immaculate dark suit and the prominence given to his neatly clasped hands resting in his lap. This sign language depends upon a graphic shorthand that has common ground with the abbreviations and exaggerations of classic caricature. The touch of mockery in this evocation of Kahnweiler's fastidious demeanour and the contrast between his alert expression and Vollard's somnolence remind us of Picasso's maxim: 'All good portraits are in some degree caricatures.'[41] The portraits proved that photography could not match the suggestiveness and wit of analytical Cubism, which demanded an actively enquiring and imaginative response from the spectator. Many years later, Picasso summed up the value of photography in rather negative terms, as 'capable of liberating painting from all literature, from the anecdote, and even from the subject,' and it shocked him that Brassaï had chosen photography when he was a 'born draftsman'. He ought to go back to drawing, Picasso said, because, 'You own a gold mine, and you're exploiting a salt mine.'[42]

1 Picasso painted over a portrait of Jacob soon after completing it. It lies beneath *Mother and Child*, 1901 (Fogg Museum, Harvard Art Museums; Z.I.115). See Seckel 1994, pp.3–4.

2 See Peter Read, '"Au Rendez-vous des poètes": Picasso, French Poetry, and Theatre, 1900–1906', in McCully 1997, pp.211–23.

3 Olivier 1964, p.75.

4 Subsequent drawings of Salmon push the identification with tribal 'fetishes' further. See Adam Gopnik, 'High and Low: Caricature, Primitivism, and the Cubist Portrait', *Art Journal*, vol.43, no.4, pp.374–5.

5 Jacob recalled giving Picasso his collection of Daumier lithographs soon after they first met (Seckel 1994, p.208).

6 Read 2008, p.30.

7 See Alexandre 1893, p.37, for condemnation of the practice of caricaturing women.

8 Convincing arguments for the identification of the subject as Ricard Canals were provided in Julie Barten's lecture 'Woman Ironing Unveiled: Research and Treatment', co-authored by John Delaney and delivered at the Museu Picasso de Barcelona on 30 January 2015. Marilyn McCully was the first to suggest that the man might be Ricard Canals.

9 For Olivier's indiscreet private diary, see Olivier 2001. For her published account of life with Picasso, see Olivier 1964.

10 Pierre Daix attributed it to Gósol and summer 1906 (Daix 1995, p.368). The first half of 1905 is, in my view, more likely.

11 I am grateful to Julie Barten for her insights on the relationship between these two works.

12 Reported in Spies 2000, p.17.

13 Spies 2000, p.28.

14 Olivier 2001, esp. p.163. Durrio was the previous tenant of Picasso's studio in the Bateau-Lavoir.

15 For this evolution, see Cowling 2002, pp.131–57.

16 Ardengo Soffici, *Ricordi di vita artistica e letteraria* (A. Vallecchi, Florence, 1942). Cited in McCully 1997, p.49.

17 Stein 1966, pp.52–3.

18 See Lucy Belloli, 'The evolution of Picasso's portrait of Gertrude Stein', *The Burlington Magazine*, Vol.141, No.1150, January 1999, pp.12–18); also Giroud 2007.

19 Stein 1966, p.60.

20 In contrast, Picasso's contemporary *Portrait of Leo Stein*, painted in gouache on cardboard (Baltimore Museum of Art; Z.I.250), has the immediacy of a one-session sketch.

21 Paul Cézanne, *Portrait of the Artist's Wife*, *c.*1879–82. Foundation E.G. Bührle, Zurich.

22 Quoted in Tinterow and Stein 2010, p.108.

23 See MP 524R, 524V, 526R, 526V.

24 For compelling evidence of Picasso's identification with Gertrude Stein provided by an X-ray of *Three Nudes* (summer 1906; The Leonard A. Lauder Collection; Z.I.340), see Christine Poggi, 'Double Exposures: Picasso, Drawing, and the Masking of Gender, 1906–1908' in Braun and Rabinow 2014, pp.28–30.

25 See Rewald 1996, no.670. Vollard had an archive of photos of Cézanne's work.

26 Overheard by Brassaï on 12 November 1943. Brassaï 1967, p.79.

27 For a selection, see Baldassari 1997, pp.62 ff.

28 See Weiss 2003.

29 See Richardson 1991, pp.123–37.

30 See Valerie J. Fletcher, 'Process and Technique in Picasso's Head of a Woman (Fernande)', in Weiss 2003, pp.165–91.

31 *The Dressing-Table*, 1910. Private collection (Z.II.220).

32 For a selection of these photographs, see Baldassari 1997, pp.89 ff.

33 For *Portrait of Wilhelm Uhde*, 1910 (Private collection; Z.II.217), see Pierre Daix, 'Portraiture in Picasso's Primitivism and Cubism', in Rubin 1996, pp.278–81.

34 See Gary Tinterow, 'Vollard and Picasso', in Rabinow 2006, pp.100–17, 388–93; also Diana Widmaier Picasso, 'Vollard and the Sculptures of Picasso', in ibid., pp.182–8.

35 Excerpt quoted in Judith Cousins, 'Documentary Chronology', in Rubin 1989, p.365.

36 Olivier 1964, p.144.

37 Kahnweiler told Roland Penrose that it required 'some thirty sittings' ('Picasso's Portrait of Kahnweiler', *The Burlington Magazine*, Vol.116, No.852, March 1974, p.129); Isabelle Monod-Fontaine believes 'about twenty' sittings more likely ('Chronologie et documents', *Kahnweiler* 1984, p.103).

38 For the medicine bottles, see Roland Penrose, 'Picasso's Portrait of Kahnweiler', *The Burlington Magazine*, Vol.116, No.852, March 1974, p.129. Failing to see its long body, some writers (e.g. Richardson 1996, p.176) have mistakenly identified the ridgepole figure as Picasso's Mukuyi mask (Punu, Gabon).

39 Assouline 1991, pp.63–6.

40 Composed in 1915, Kahnweiler's pioneering study of Cubism was published in 1920 as *Der Weg zum Kubismus* (Delphin-Verlag, Munich).

41 Picasso reported in Penrose 1958, p.126.

42 Brassaï 1967, pp.46–7. The conversation took place in September 1939.

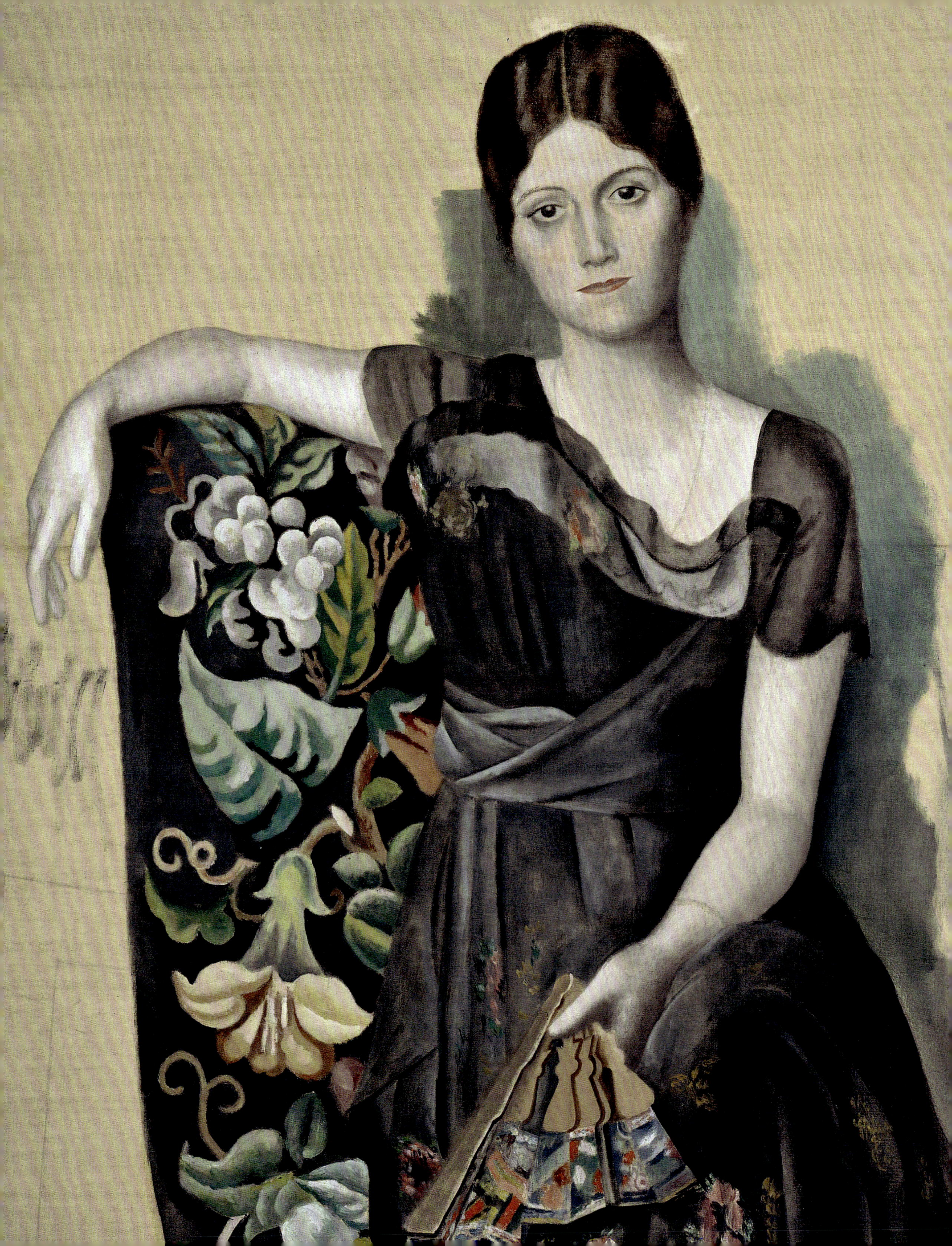

4. Photography and the return to classic styles 1915–1927

PORTRAITS OF MEN

After 1910, portraiture proper virtually disappeared from Picasso's repertoire for several years. Very occasionally he depicted celebrities who caught his fancy – Buffalo Bill, for example.[1] Apollinaire was the subject of a masterly analytical Cubist drawing that bewildered critics when it was published in April 1913 as the frontispiece to *Alcools*, Apollinaire's new collection of poems (Mercure de France, Paris).[2] But for the most part generic figures occupied Picasso: *The Aficionado*, *The Poet*, *The Girl from Arles*, *The Student*, numerous musicians, and so on. His temporary abandonment of portraiture is highlighted by the case of Eva Gouel, whose love affair with him began in the winter of 1911–12. There were none of the tender naturalistic drawings he usually made at the beginning of a lasting liaison. Initially this renunciation may have been motivated by the need for secrecy, but by the late spring of 1912 it had hardened into an aesthetic decision to use language – 'I love her very much and I shall write this in my painting,' he told Kahnweiler – and metaphor (typically, a guitar stands in for her body).[3] Only later did her image surface in his work.[4]

Portraiture proper made a sudden and controversial return in January 1915 with the naturalistic drawing of Max Jacob (84), then about to be received into the Catholic Church with – strange as it may seem – Picasso as his godfather. On display were all the skills in classical draftsmanship Picasso had acquired in boyhood and consciously laid aside when joining the circle of Els Quatre Gats. From Jacob's letter to Apollinaire, we know that he sat for the portrait in Picasso's studio in Montparnasse and, like the portrait of Kahnweiler, the drawing includes faint but precise details of the actual setting, including the kitschy iron pedestal table with its integral beaded and fringed cloth familiar from many of Picasso's photos (including 79).[5] Though 'very beautiful', Jacob wryly observed that the drawing made him look 'simultaneously like my grandfather, an old Catalan peasant and my mother'.[6] He did not mention Ingres, but did so later that year when telling a sceptical Francis Picabia about the even more refined and polished *Portrait of Ambroise Vollard* (87).[7] Picasso's Ingrism extended to materials, for he used the very type of paper and hard graphite pencil favoured by the master himself. Journalists and critics, who assumed that Picasso was wedded exclusively and forever to Cubism, were stunned by these exquisite drawings and references to Ingres were *de rigueur* in their commentaries.[8]

Vollard had sold his Cubist portrait (see 81) to the Moscow collector Ivan Morosov in 1913 and commissioned the drawing to replace it. He may not have posed at all, for in most respects it closely follows a photograph by Thérèse Bonney, even reproducing its exaggerated foreshortening.[9] Since Ingres had made use of photographs in the latter part of his career, the wilful fusion of Ingresque classicism with photography had perfect legitimacy, and in mapping out a schematic setting for Vollard, Picasso imitated the artificial domestic settings typical of the *cartes de visite* of Ingres's day. He was entirely conversant with the conventions of these calling-card photographs for he owned hundreds of them, including some by André-Adolphe-Eugène Disdéri, who patented the standard format in 1854 (86). *Portrait of Max Jacob* was also composed with them in mind: a *carte de visite* by Charles-François Jalabert in Picasso's collection is strikingly similar in pose and set-up and in the rough appearance of its (unnamed) subject (85).

During the First World War, Picasso occasionally photographed himself with his personal art collection (88) and in his studio surrounded by recent paintings (see 72–4).[10] Otherwise, he was interested exclusively in other photographers' portraits, using them as a catalyst or reference-point. Instead of reproducing their essential qualities, he often worked against the photographs,

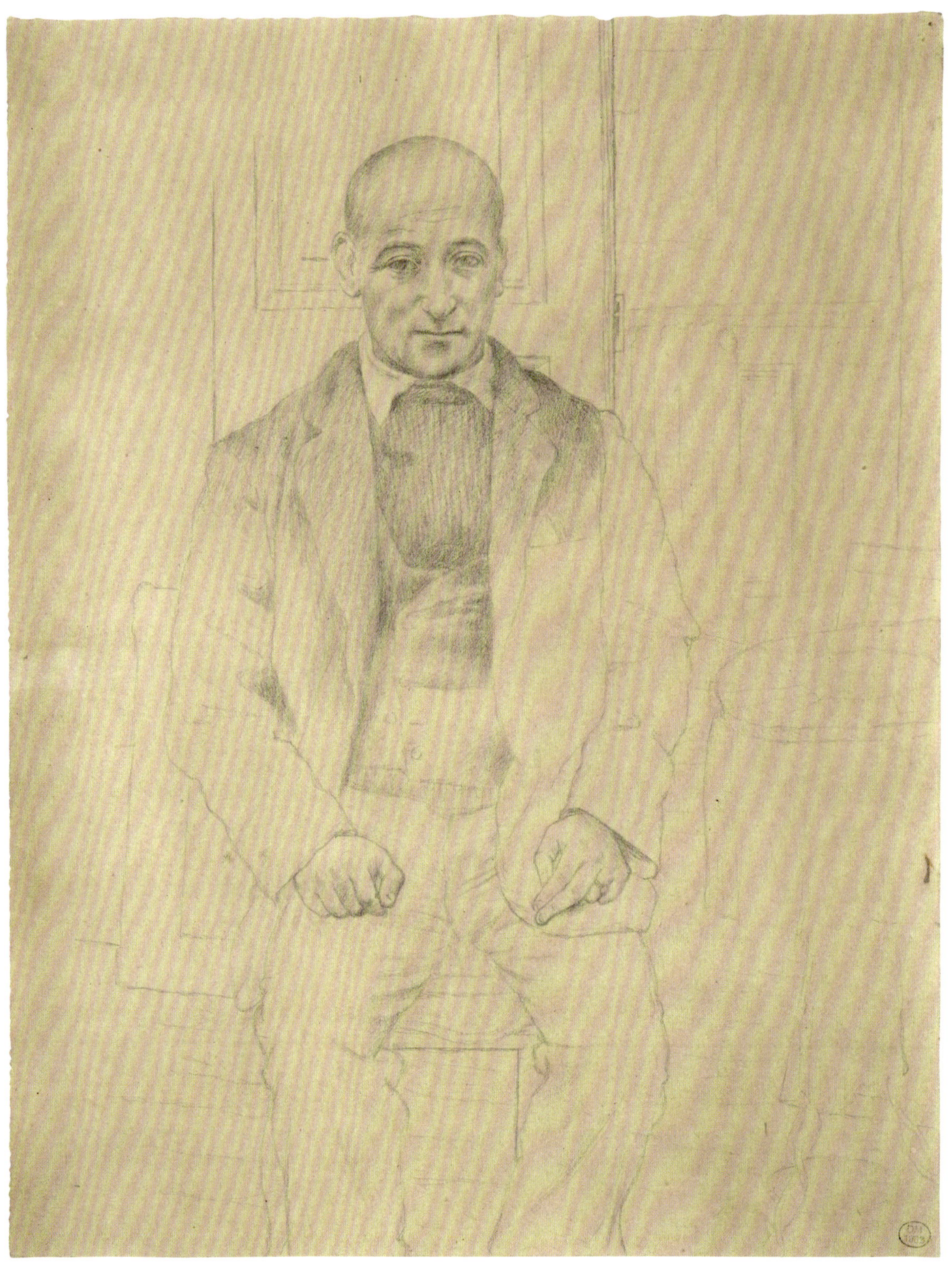

84 *Portrait of Max Jacob*, 1915 (B)

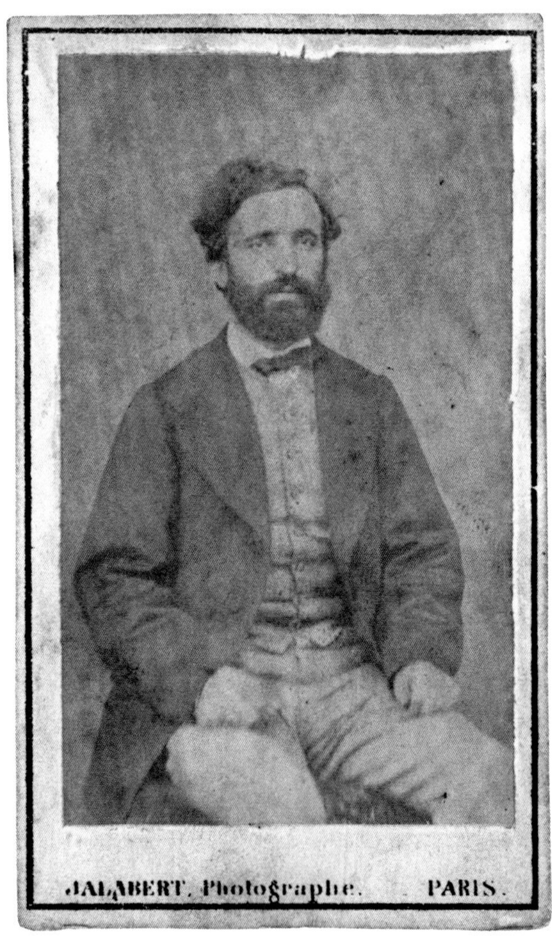

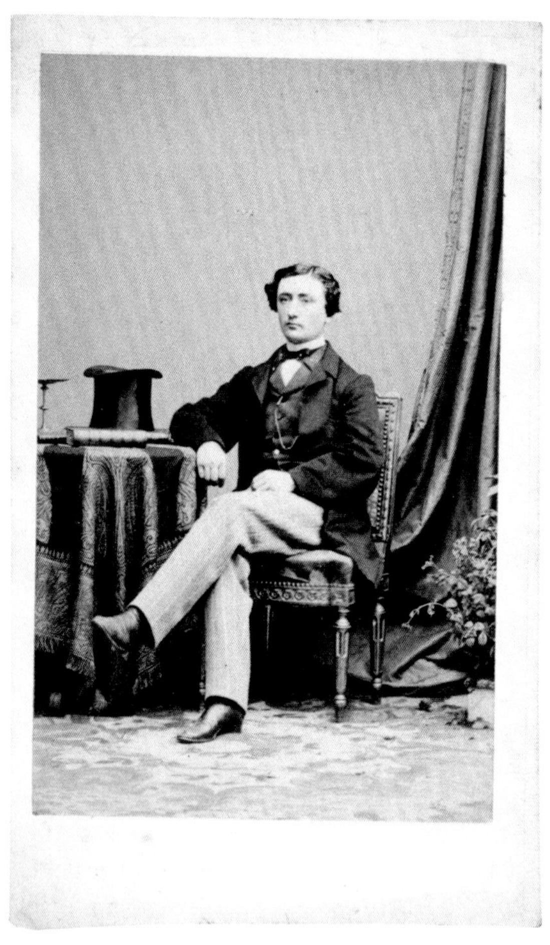

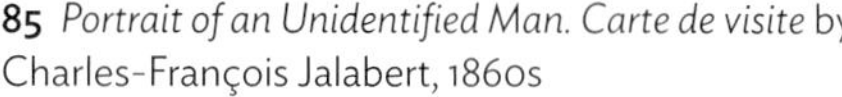

85 *Portrait of an Unidentified Man. Carte de visite* by Charles-François Jalabert, 1860s

86 *Portrait of an Unidentified Man. Carte de visite* by André-Adolphe-Eugène Disdéri, c.1860

distorting anatomy, reducing detail drastically, and generally stamping the image with the unique personality of the handmade. How he acquired his vast collection of late nineteenth-century photos remains a mystery: did he buy entire albums during the excursions to junk shops and flea markets described by Fernande Olivier;[11] did he collect rather than amass; was the hoard acquired in a concentrated phase, or slowly and fitfully; when he based a drawing closely on a particular photo, had he just got it, or owned it for several years; was there any pattern to the lag between acquiring and responding? Although we don't yet have answers to these questions, we do know that the period of Picasso's most intense involvement with Sergei

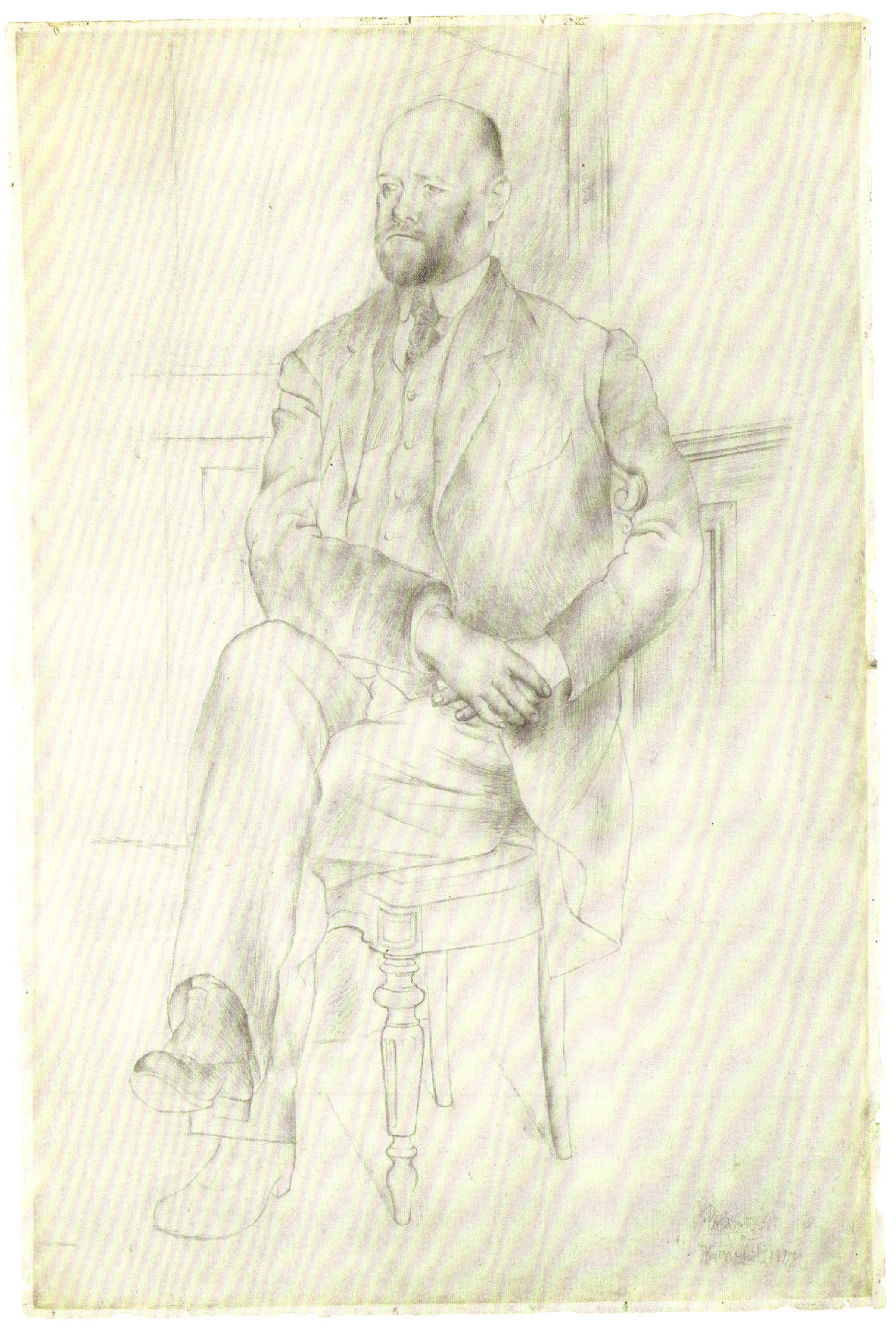

87 *Portrait of Ambroise Vollard*, 1915 (B)

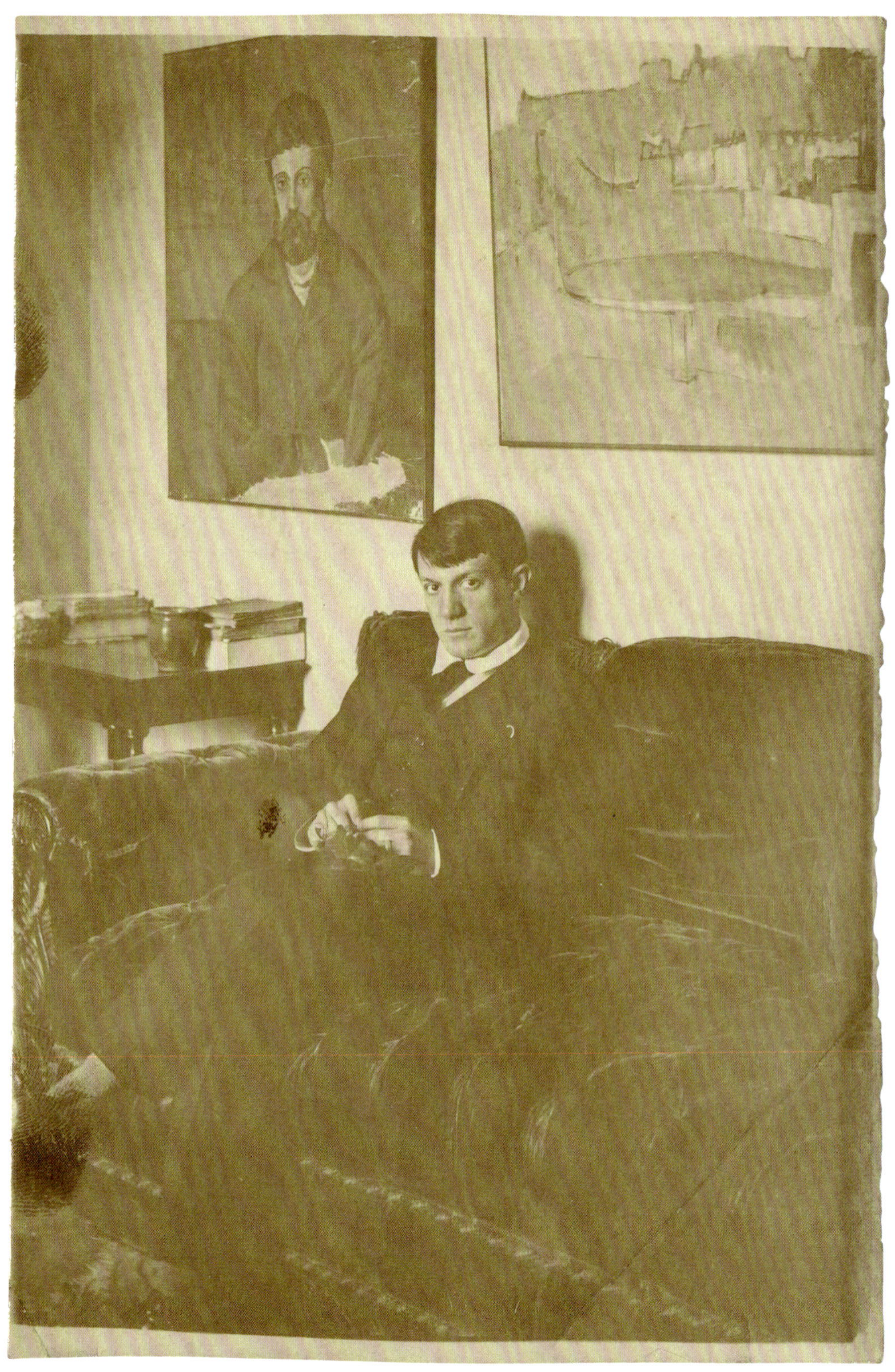

88 *Self-portrait with* Portrait of a Man,
5 bis Rue Schoelcher, Paris, 1915–16 (B, L)

Diaghilev's Ballets Russes, 1917–21, coincided with the creation of numerous variations on photographs he owned, some of them portraits, others images of types.[12] Still photography played a vital promotional role in the world of the Ballets Russes and this can only have fortified Picasso's fascination with the medium.

Some of Picasso's drawings of members of the ballet company were derived from publicity photographs, but the new friendships he formed also led to a spate of more intimate portraits. His introduction to Diaghilev came through the multi-talented Jean Cocteau, who proposed him as the designer for *Parade* – a short, wilfully avant-garde ballet with a scenario by Cocteau himself, music by Erik Satie and choreography by Léonide Massine. In February 1917, Cocteau and Picasso left for Rome together to join the company. It was Picasso's first visit to Italy and in April he wrote cheerfully to Gertrude Stein summarising his adventures and the tally of his work, including 'caricatures of Diaghilev, the dancer Massine and the ballerinas'.[13] A gifted caricaturist himself, Cocteau was the subject of an amusing gouache (89) mocking the angular profile and graceful figure he was so proud of, as well as his fastidious attention to matters of dress. On Easter Day, Picasso dedicated a more flattering drawing to him (90). Its reductive style was adapted from the abstract planes of synthetic Cubism and faint *pentimenti* allow one to witness the process of refining and strengthening its principal contours. *Cartes de visite* played their part, for the set-up with Cocteau, notebook in hand and resting his elbow on the nearby table, reproduces their awkward imitation of 'real-life' situations. But that mundane source is crossed with another of nobler lineage, for Cocteau's hieratic bearing and the seamless marriage of profile, frontal and three-quarter views amount to code for Ancient Egyptian art. Even the poet's dressing-gown and slippers supported the gratifying comparison with an Old Kingdom dignitary. More discreetly than in the caricature, Picasso was gently teasing his narcissistic friend, whose appetite for portraits of himself was insatiable.

Igor Stravinsky was also in Italy working on projects with Diaghilev, and in his memoirs he gave a vivid account of his escapades in Rome and Naples with Picasso. The riveting portrait Picasso dedicated to him was drawn in Rome in the Hôtel de la Russie, where many of the ballet dancers were staying (91).[14] Subsequently, it was the centre of a barely credible drama. Stravinsky was on his way home to Switzerland but the military authorities at the frontier town of Chiasso refused to allow him to take the drawing any further, insisting that it was 'a plan' not a portrait:

> 'Yes, the plan of my face, but of nothing else,' I replied. But all efforts failed to convince them, and I had to send the portrait [...] to the British Ambassador in Rome, who later forwarded it to Paris in the diplomatic bag.[15]

Laughably obtuse though they were, the frontier guards did at least recognise that Picasso had used a form of code in summarising Stravinsky's features. Renouncing the exquisite, quasi-photographic detail of the portraits of Jacob and Vollard, Picasso stripped back ruthlessly, erasing inessential information (certain lines on Stravinsky's face and the lapels of his jacket, for instance), clarifying the main contours and paying special attention to the form of his left ear, the musician's all-important organ. This reductive process, also applied to the presentation-portrait of Cocteau, is reminiscent of his approach to caricature in Barcelona at the turn of the century; the difference is that then, instead of reworking the master drawing, he refined and codified his characterisation through drawing the same head repeatedly.

Portrait of Igor Stravinsky in Profile (92), drawn on New Year's Eve 1920 in Paris was, Stravinsky recalled, 'conceived as a mutual gift from Picasso and myself to our friend Eugenia Errázuriz'[16] – the Chilean collector and balletomane who had done so much to promote Picasso's association with Diaghilev. More informal and less severe than the full-face portrait, it depicts Stravinsky in his shirt-sleeves, apparently deep in thought. Since the chair faces forward he must have swivelled round to present the peculiar geometry of his features in profile – almost diamond-shaped thanks to the ascending and descending diagonal thrusts of ear and jaw, hairline, forehead and nose, mouth and chin. Having drawn him full-face, Picasso was keen to capture his profile. The composer's huge hands grasping his forearms may seem grotesquely enlarged, but serve to hint at his narrow chest and short stature, while simultaneously enhancing the impression of energy and power. Like the first portrait, it is a compelling characterisation: not in the least flattering, but testament to the precision of Picasso's eagle eye, to Stravinsky's lack of vanity and to their mutual understanding.

The portrait of Russian scene-painter Vladimir Polunin (93) was made in London in 1919 in gratitude for his expert repairs to the damaged set of *Parade*, and also for his work on the curtain and sets designed by Picasso for the Spanish-themed ballet *Le Tricorne* (*The Three-Cornered Hat*).[17] Posed during a break from the work, the drawing captures Polunin's long, handsome head, the rather mournful set of his features and his tall, supple figure. According to Polunin, Picasso possessed an instinctive and infallible understanding of theatre design.[18] For his part, Picasso was delighted to work alongside a specialist in an unfamiliar method of painting that had its own aesthetic and *savoir-faire*. Their instant rapport resulted in a particularly sympathetic portrait, lacking the teasing wit present in many of Picasso's drawings of more intimate male friends.

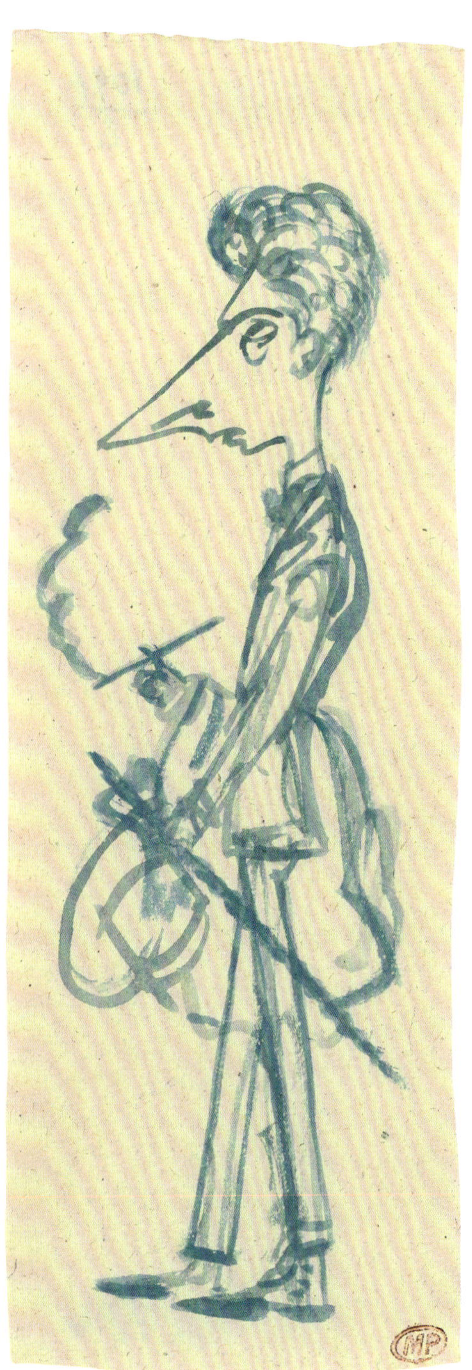

89 *Caricature of Jean Cocteau*, 1917 (B)

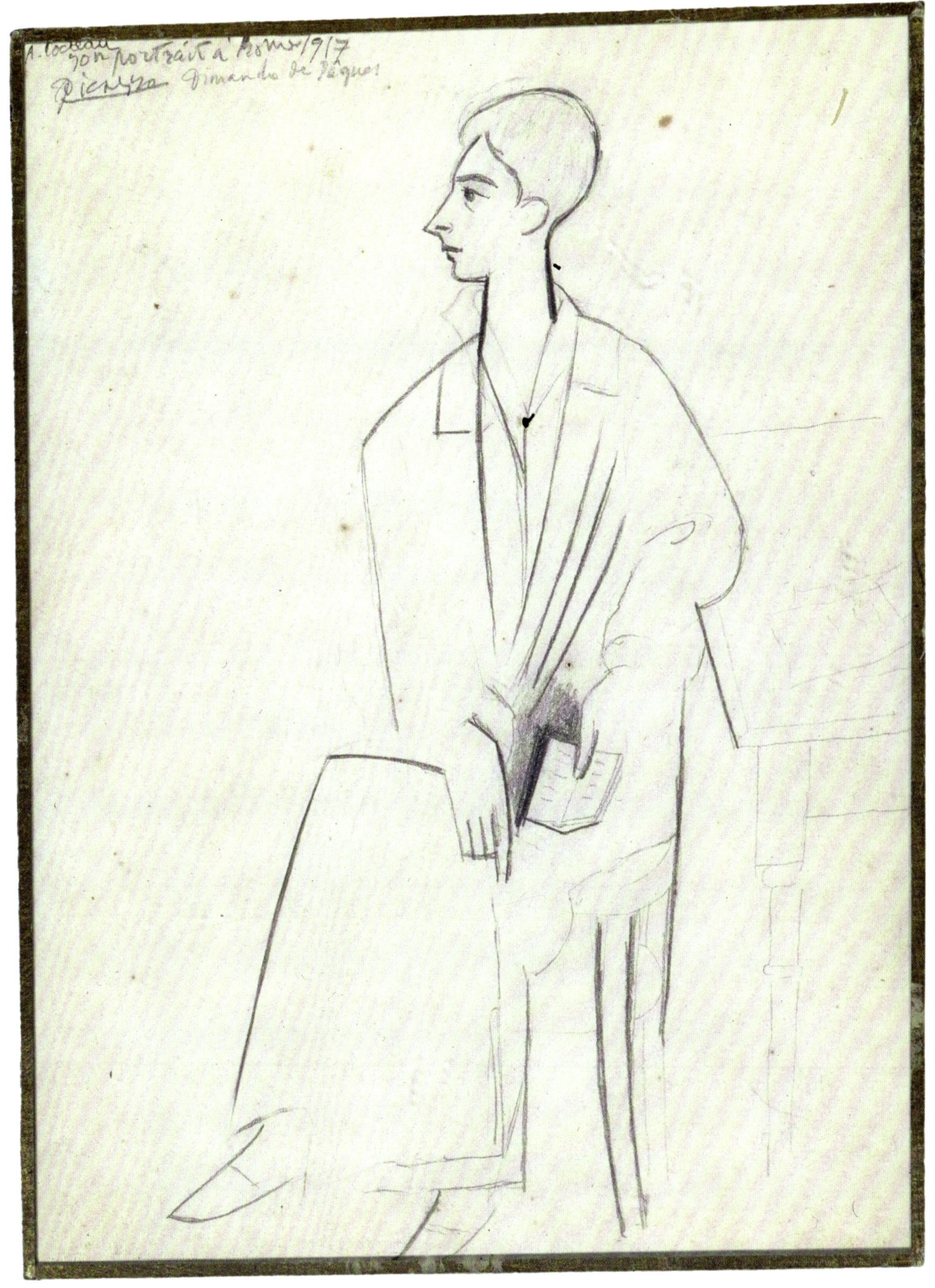

90 *Jean Cocteau*, 1917 (B, L)

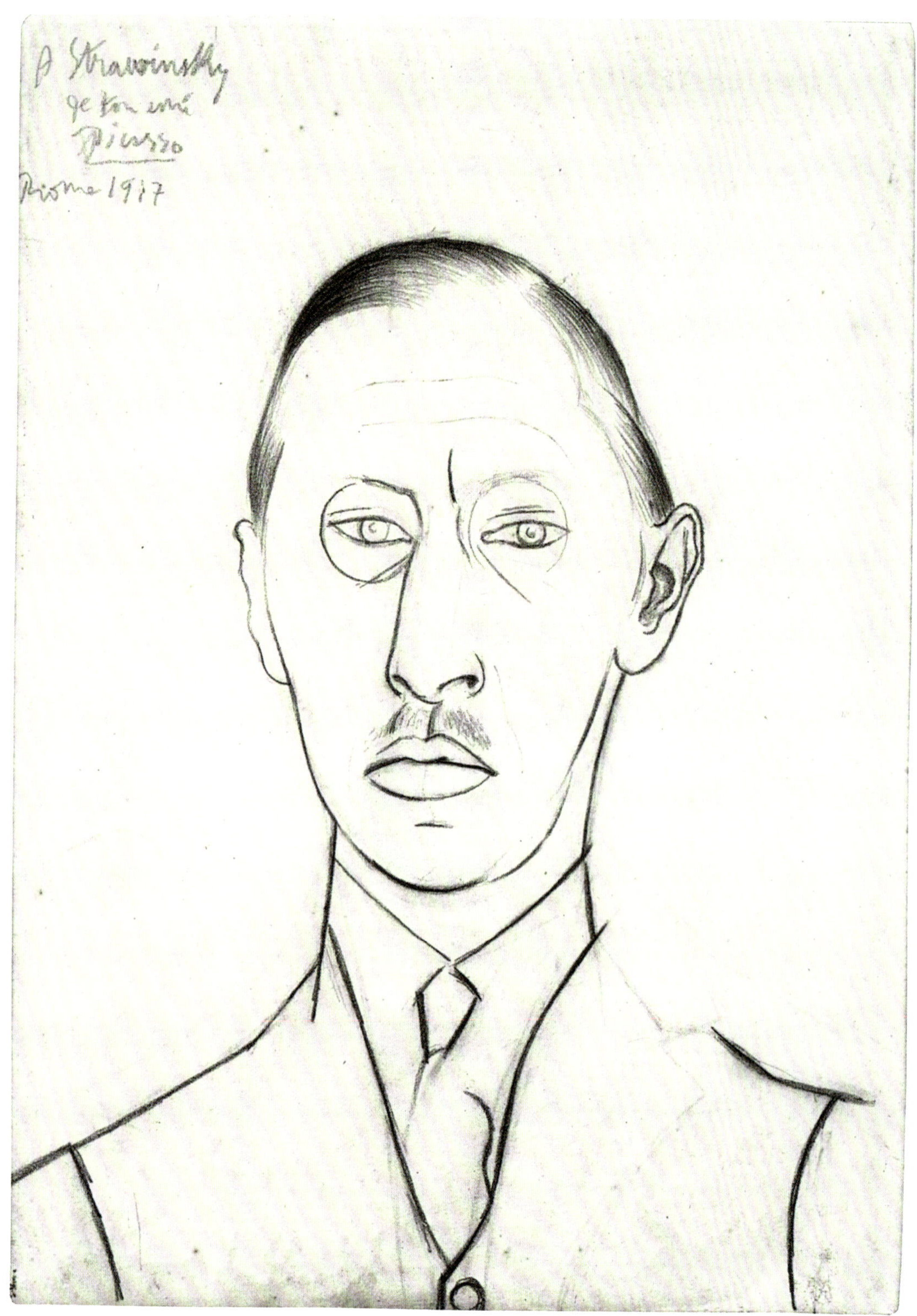

91 *Portrait of Igor Stravinsky*, 1917 (L)

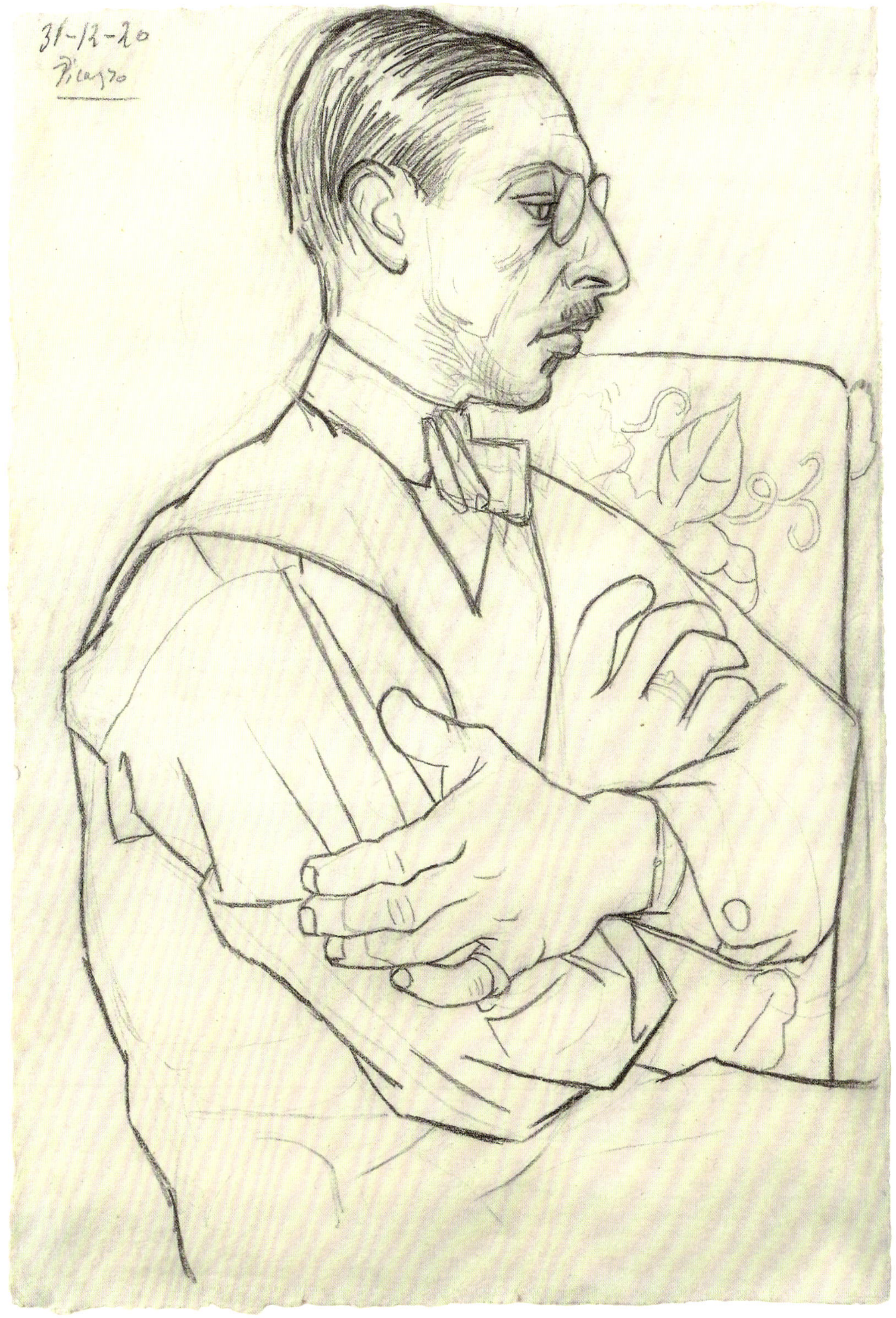

92 *Portrait of Igor Stravinsky in Profile*, 31 December 1920 (B)

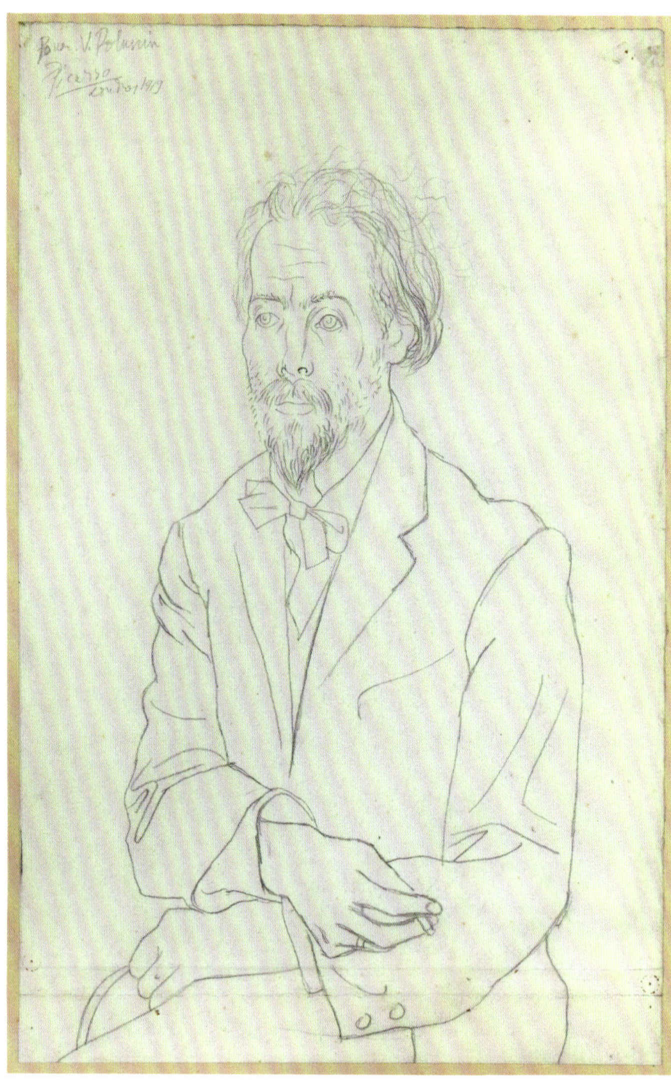

93 *Portrait of Vladimir Polunin*, 1919 (L)

By 1920, having one's portrait drawn by Picasso had become a badge of honour in the art world. Writers solicited him for portraits as frontispieces for their forthcoming books, and some were lucky.[19] The doctor, art lover and prolific author Élie Faure had met Picasso before the outbreak of the First World War, but only began to see him with any regularity in 1921, when he wrote an article about Picasso's drawings and started (protracted) negotiations to purchase a pastel. He also appealed to Picasso for his help in raising money for the Basque painter Francisco Iturrino, who had exhibited alongside Picasso in Vollard's gallery in 1901 but had fallen on very hard times.[20] That mission of mercy accomplished, the indefatigable Faure wrote again to Picasso on 7 June 1922 – '*J'ai quelque chose à vous demander*' (I have something to ask you) – proposing to visit exactly one week later. The favour this time was his portrait, and Picasso graciously obliged (94). Just enough of the chair is visible to confirm that Faure posed in the studio at 23 Rue La Boétie on the simple, rush-bottomed armchair that Picasso habitually used for distinguished sitters. Relying on minimalist but firm contours to conjure up Faure's stocky torso, Picasso allowed himself the luxury of precise detail only when depicting Faure's head, although even there he depended solely on small, individual strokes. Portrayed in a rare moment of inactivity, Faure's alert intelligence is suggested by the watchfulness of his eyes and the tortoise-like turn of his head. If Picasso's approach seems a trifle detached – the rendering of the hands is, for instance, inexpressive and generalised – he had good reason to be on his guard: in the recently published *L'Art moderne* volume of his multi-volume *Histoire de l'art*, Faure had voiced the very dim view he took of Cubism. He went on to describe Picasso as 'dangerous' and 'disconcerting', his work 'brilliant one minute, adroit the next'.[21] But he also expressed warm approval of Picasso's post-war return to classic styles of

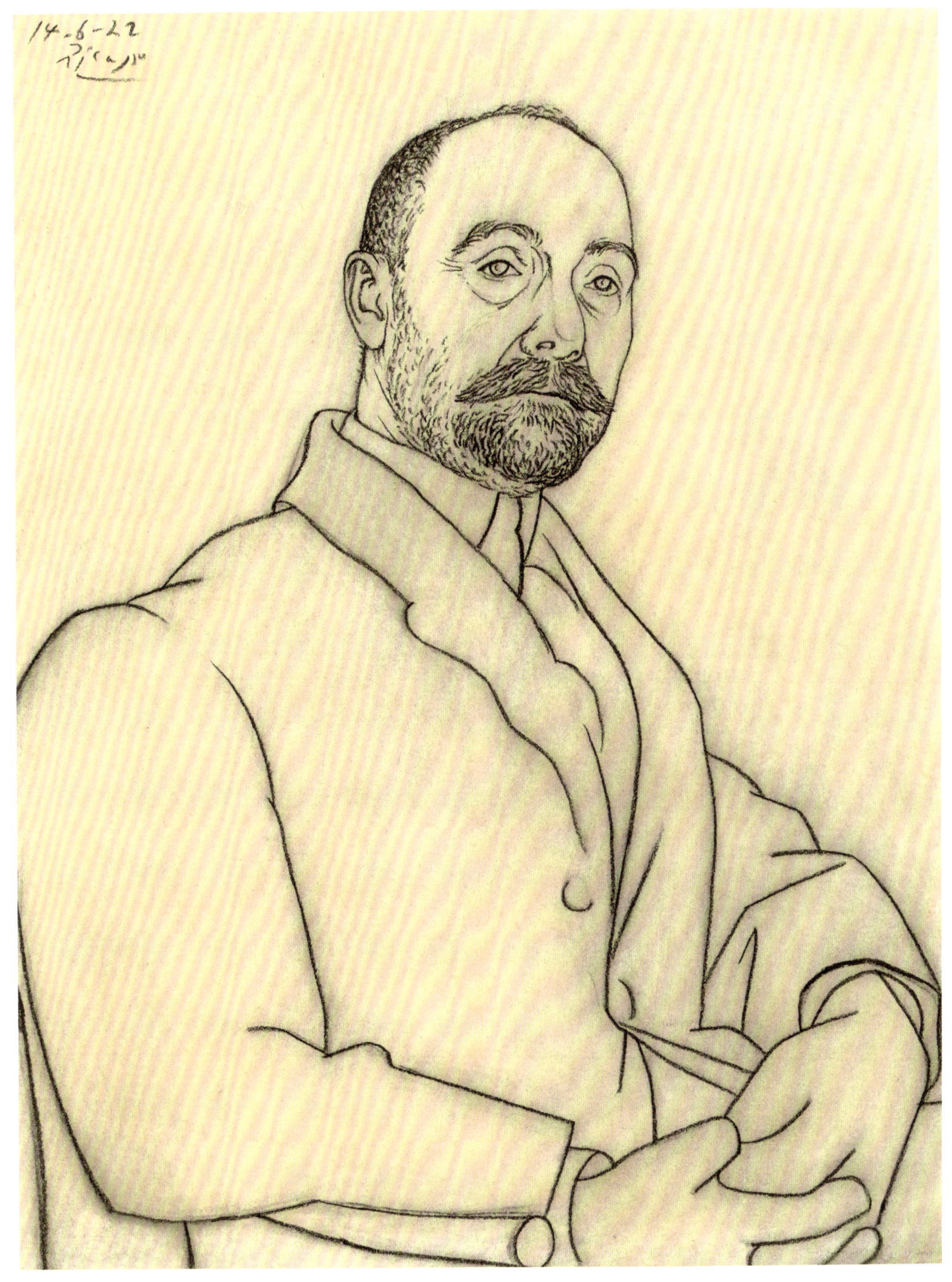

94 *Portrait of Élie Faure*, 14 June 1922 (B, L)

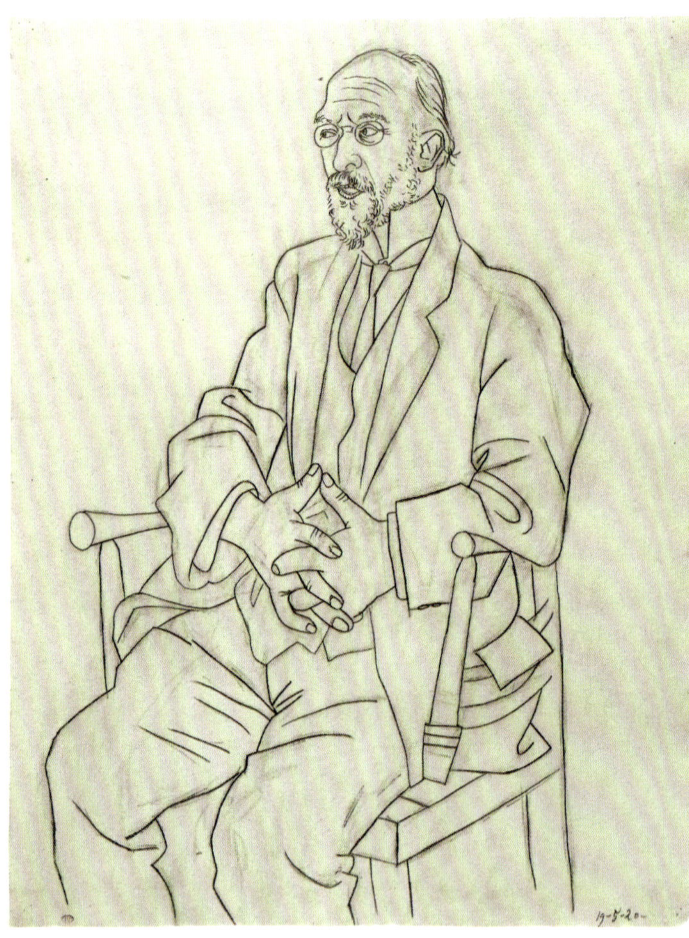

95 *Portrait of Erik Satie*, 19 May 1920

representation, and the portrait pleased him greatly. He thanked Picasso with a case of fine red wine.[22]

The portrait of the composer Francis Poulenc (96), drawn in Cannes on 13 March 1957, is introduced here since it was through their mutual friends Satie and Cocteau that Poulenc and Picasso first met in 1918 or 1919. They saw much of each other during the 1920s when both were involved on and off with Diaghilev's Ballets Russes. The portrait was connected with another mutual friend: Poulenc had set to music seven poems from Paul Éluard's anthology *Voir: poèmes, peintures, dessins* (1948), each one dedicated to a different painter. The first poem, '*Entoure ce citron de blanc d'œuf informe*' (Encircle this lemon with shapeless white of egg), was dedicated to Picasso. The cycle was about to be performed for the first time in Paris, and Poulenc had come to Cannes to collect Picasso's design for the cover of the sheet music.[23]

Nostalgia informed the composition of the portrait, for Picasso posed Poulenc at the identical angle and in the same armchair used for the trio of portraits he drew in May–June 1920 of Satie (95), Stravinsky and Manuel de Falla.[24] He had never parted with those drawings and the reprise was intended as a high compliment to the younger composer. The chief difference lies in Picasso's exploitation of familiar caricatural conventions for Poulenc's portrait: his head is disproportionately large, his defining features exaggerated for comic effect, and his waistcoat and tweed jacket treated playfully. Mouth open, hooded eyes roving, he appears to be gossiping – reminiscing amusingly perhaps, for he was a witty raconteur – while his raised, active hands play an invisible piano. The complicity between the two old friends sanctioned the caricatural approach – it would have been inappropriate for the portrait of Faure, a mere acquaintance – and the drawing of Poulenc joined those of the three older composers in Picasso's private, commemorative collection.

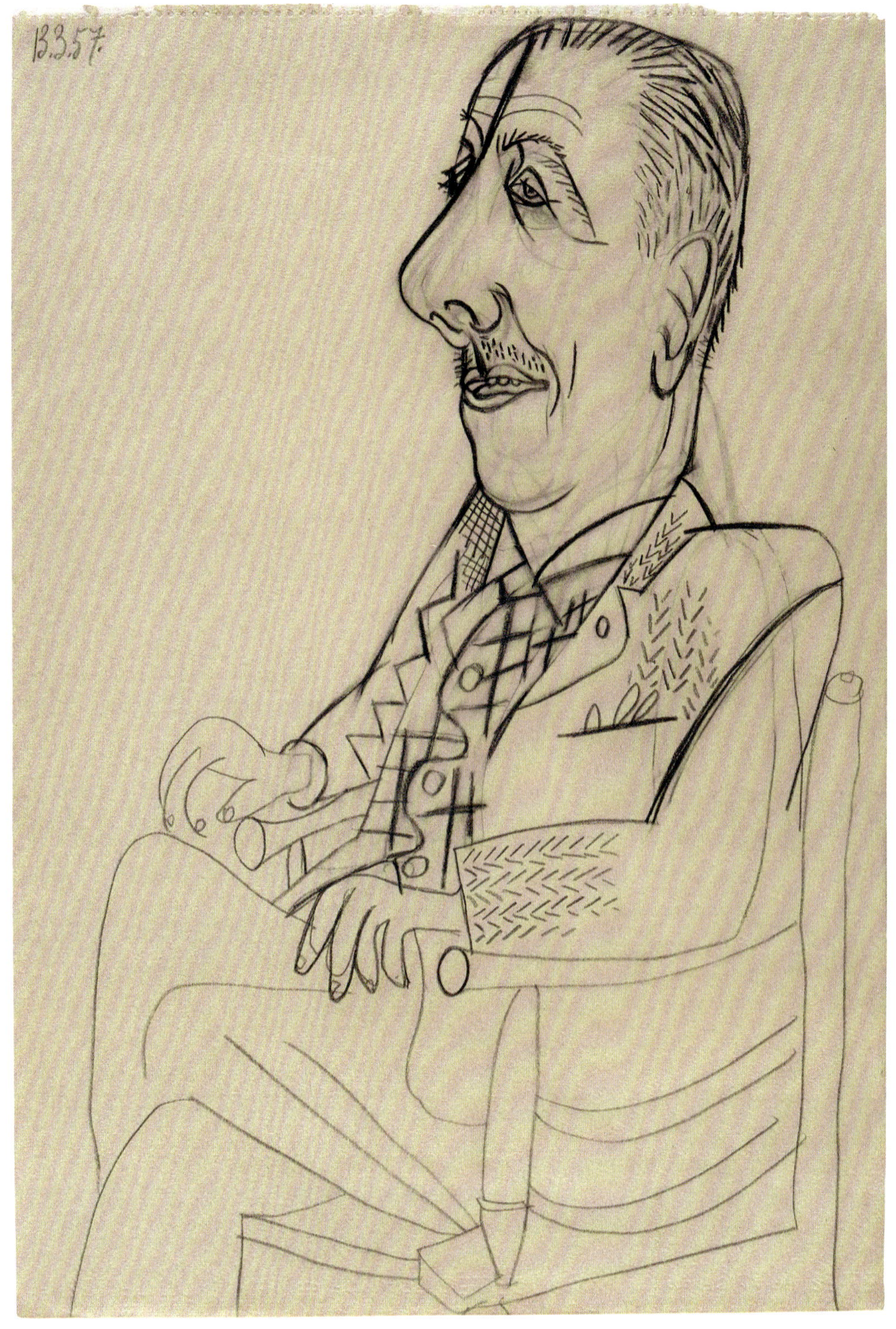

96 *Portrait of Francis Poulenc*, 13 March 1957 (L)

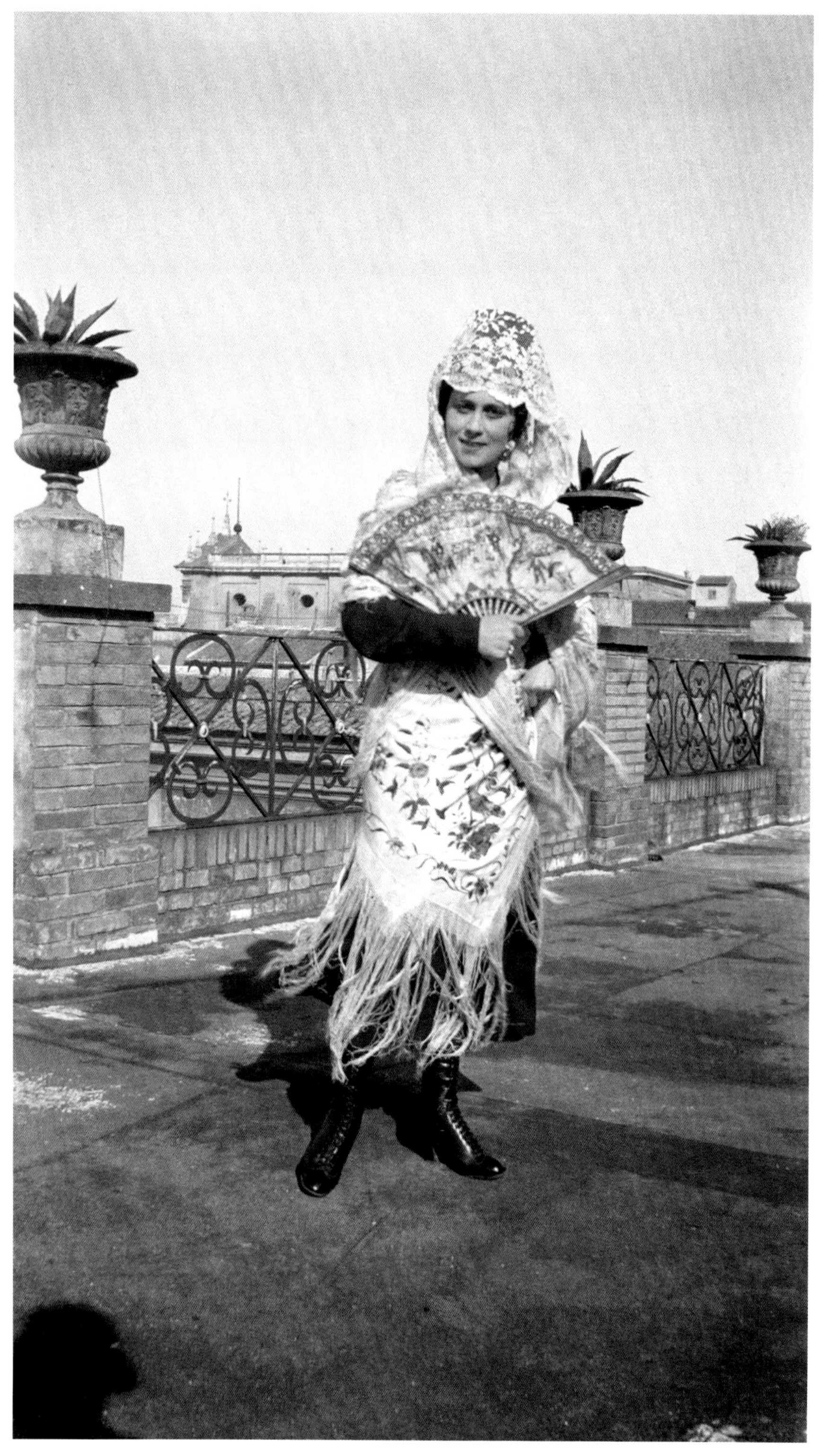

97 *Olga Khokhlova on the Roof of the Minerva Hotel*, Rome, 1917 (B, L)

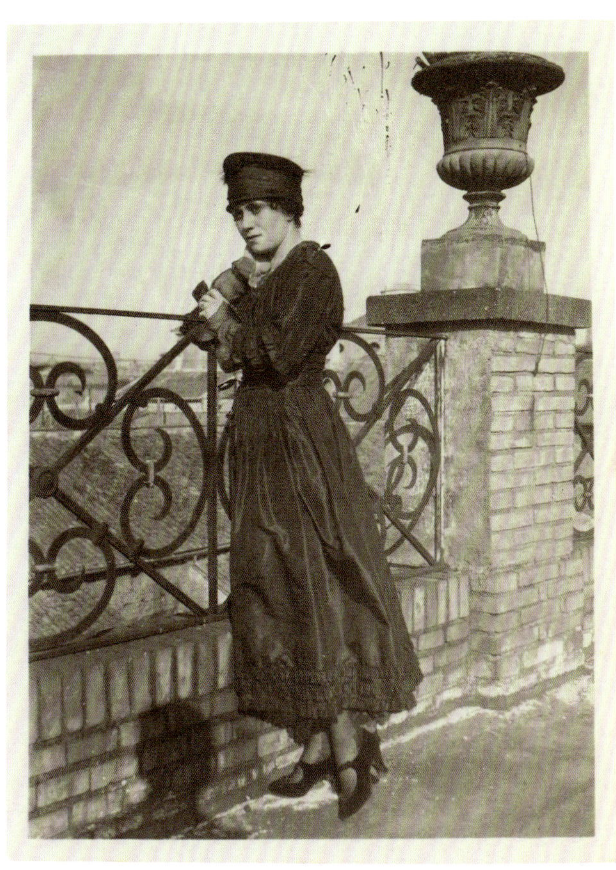

98 *Olga Khokhlova on the Roof of the Minerva Hotel*, Rome, 1917 (B, L)

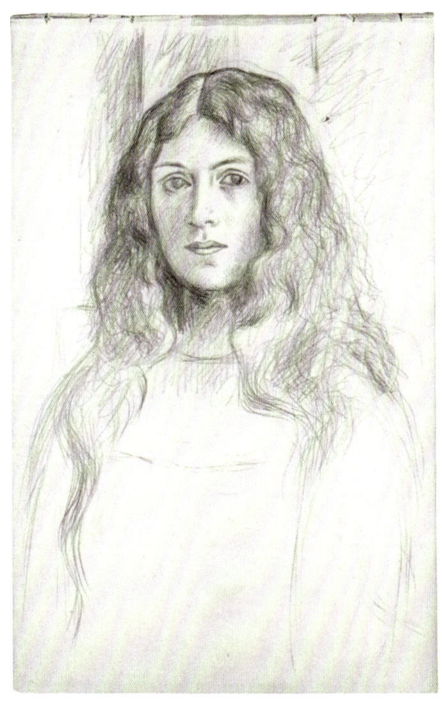

99 *Olga with Her Hair Down*, 1917

100 *Olga on a Balcony Overlooking the Ramblas*, 1917

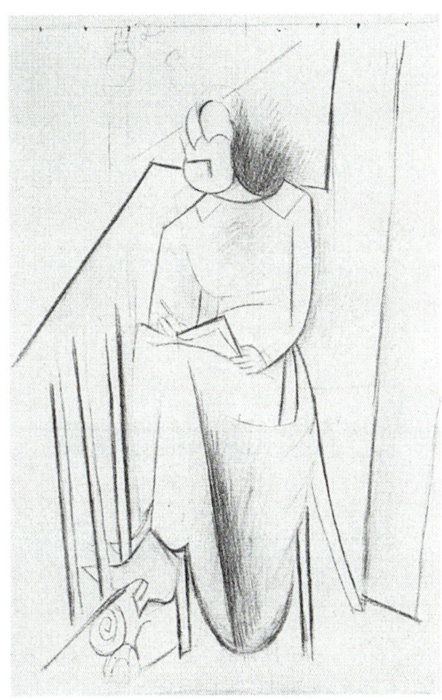

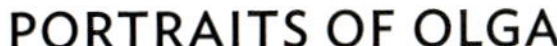

PORTRAITS OF OLGA

It was through Diaghilev that Picasso met his first wife, the Ukrainian ballerina Olga Khokhlova, when he was working on the designs for *Parade* in Rome in the spring of 1917. Like all the dancers, she was used to posing before a camera and a smitten Picasso photographed her repeatedly in Rome (97–8), in Paris where *Parade* was premièred in May, and in Madrid and Barcelona where the Ballets Russes had engagements that summer.[25] He also drew her repeatedly, sometimes naturalistically (99), sometimes in an abstracted style derived from synthetic Cubism (100). Drawing her was a way of getting to know her and, by experimenting with different approaches, discovering the right image

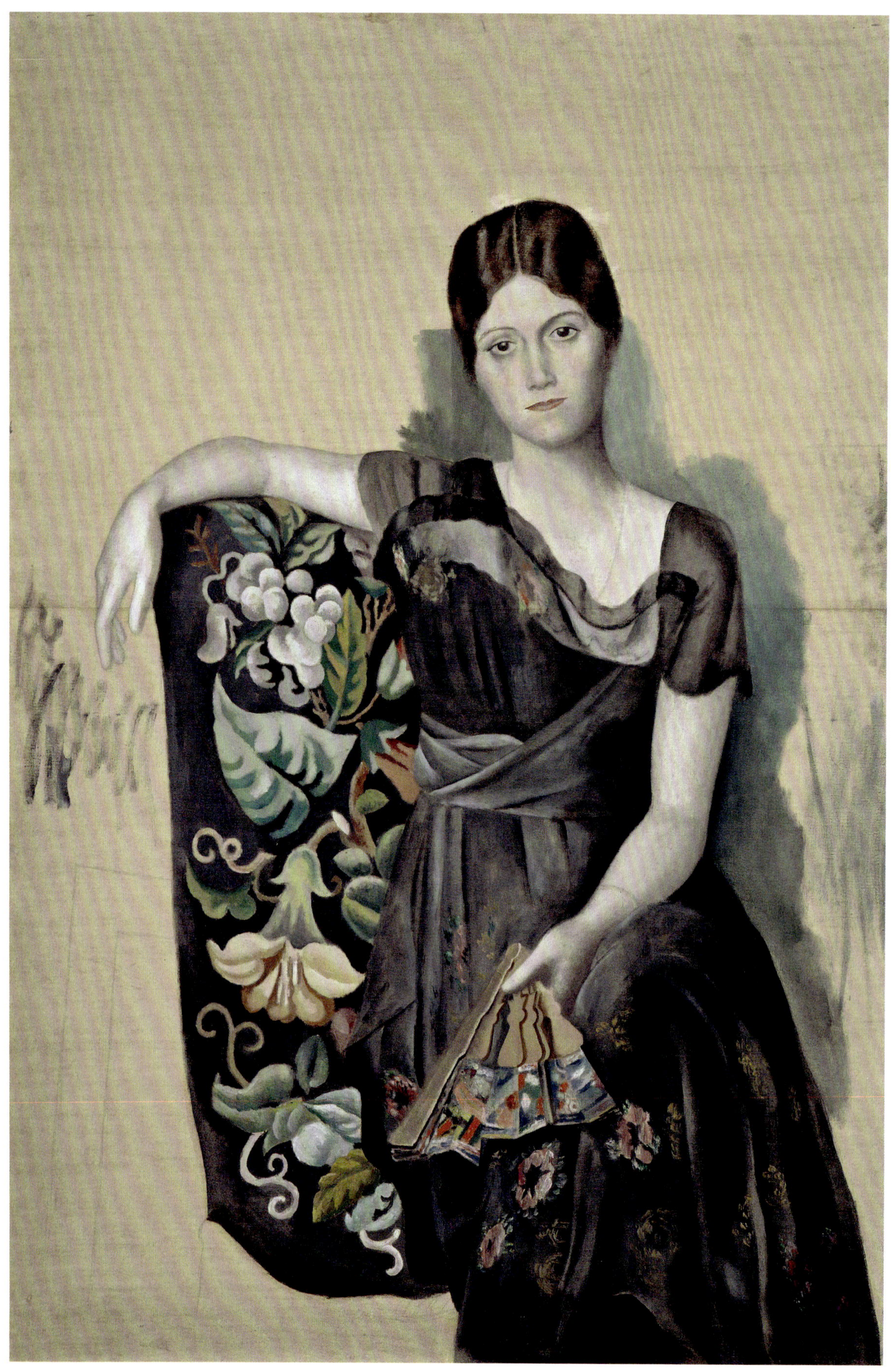

101 *Portrait of Olga in an Armchair*, 1918 (L)

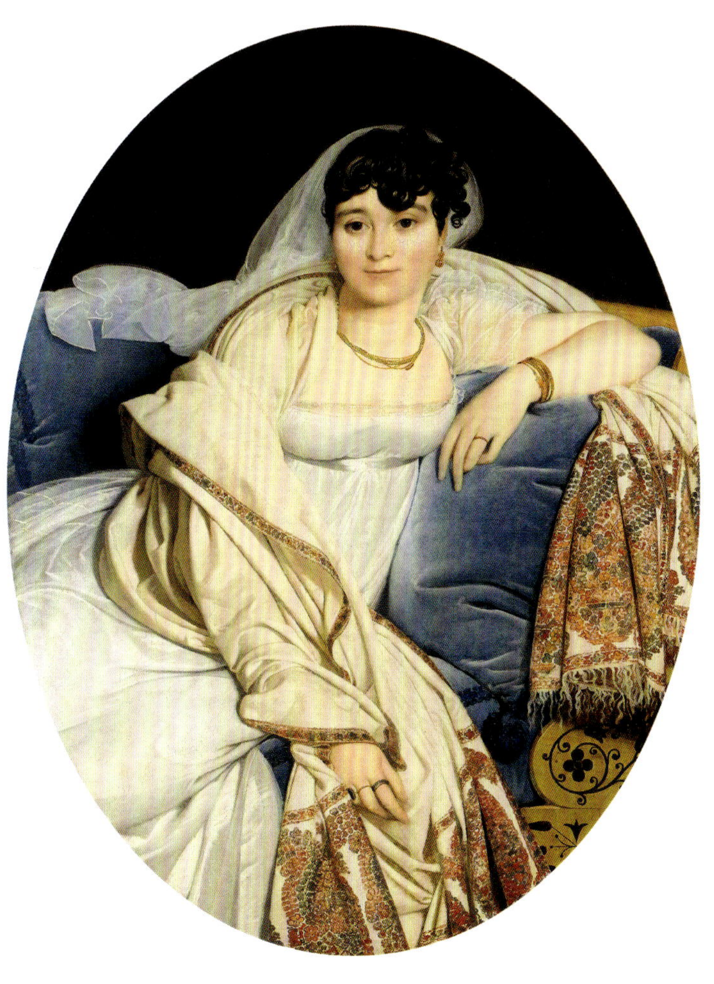

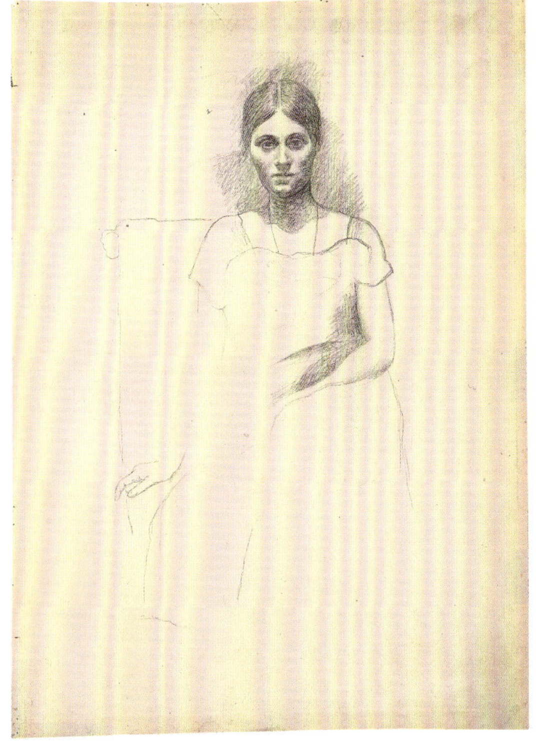

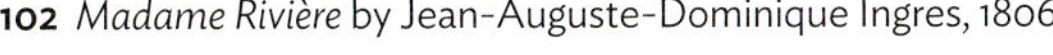

102 *Madame Rivière* by Jean-Auguste-Dominique Ingres, 1806

103 *Portrait of Olga, Seated*, 1918

104 *Olga Khokhlova in Picasso's studio in Montrouge.* Photographer unknown, 1918

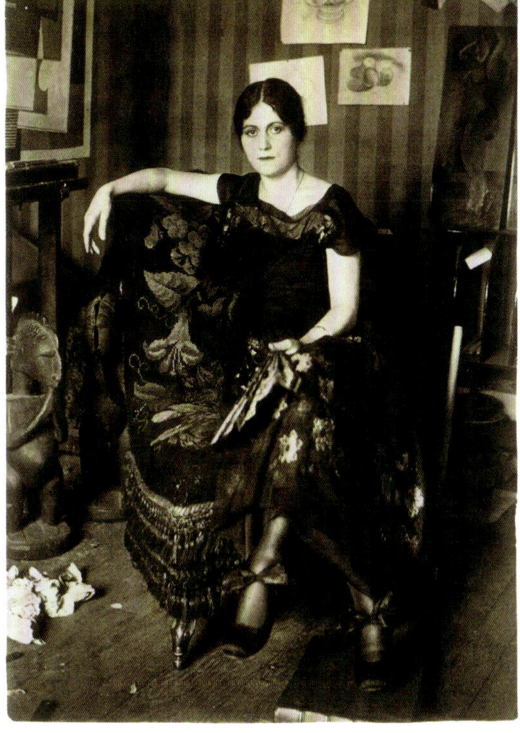

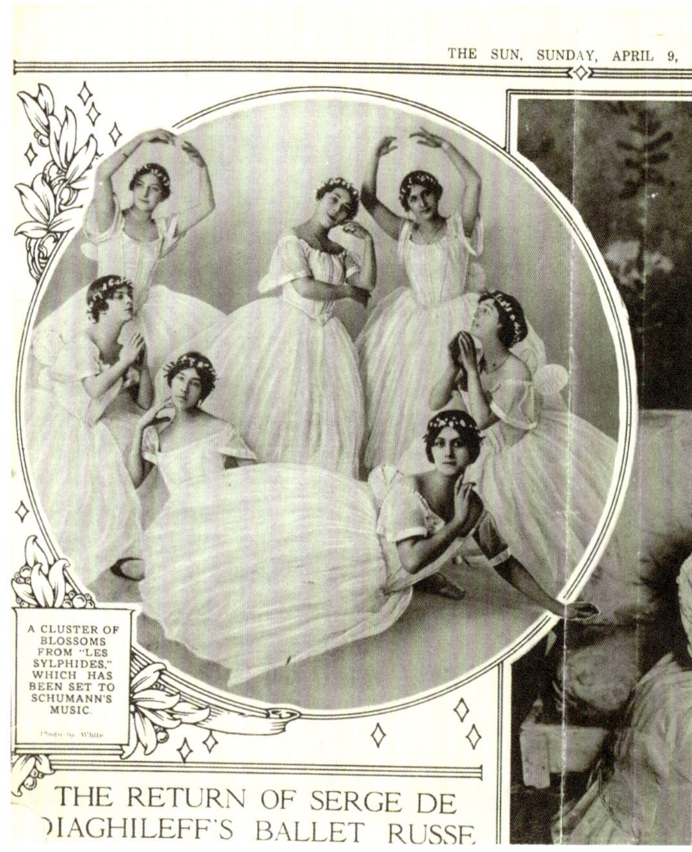

105 Olga Khokhlova (reclining in the foreground) with Members of the Ballets Russes Corps de Ballet in *Les Sylphides*, New York, 1916

for her in his painting. By the time he embarked on the famous engagement portrait (101) he had decided that an Ingresque style suited Olga best of all, and the painting has always reminded art historians of Ingres's portraits of Madame Rivière (102) and Madame Duvaucey (1807; Musée Condé, Chantilly). A delicate drawing made from life of Olga wearing the same dress (which they had chosen together on a shopping spree in Barcelona),[26] but in a slightly different pose and without the fan (103), was probably the starting-point for the painting. In the end, however, Picasso relied on a photograph (104) taken in his studio in Montrouge soon after the couple returned to Paris from Spain at the end of November 1917. In the painting Picasso omitted all the studio paraphernalia recorded in the photo, as having no relevance to Olga herself and being at odds with her elegant appearance. Yet far from concealing its actual photographic source, when Picasso sent a photo of the painting to Gertrude Stein he described it as 'in the manner of a photographic enlargement'.[27]

Portrait of Olga in an Armchair was always destined for display in the couple's home (see 112) and Picasso could please himself when it came to 'finish'. It was by definition an artificial construct and, transcending its purpose as a representation of his fiancée, the portrait became his manifesto-cum-demonstration of the painterly process. Large areas of bare canvas announce how it began life; faint charcoal lines show the first steps Picasso took to map out the composition; seemingly casual brush-wipings at the left and right edges signal the activity of mixing and laying on the paint; the finished areas testify to what can be accomplished, after sufficiently dedicated labour, in the way of conjuring up an illusion. The areas of bare canvas and the careless brush-wipings intentionally injected a salutary dose of rebarbative 'ugliness' into a picture that risked being too soothingly 'beautiful'. That too was part of his credo: 'Academic training in beauty is a sham,' he told Christian Zervos, the editor of *Cahiers d'Art* and compiler of the complete catalogue of his work. 'Art is not the application of a canon of beauty, but what the instinct and the brain can conceive beyond any canon.'[28]

Perhaps because of the crisis Picasso experienced when painting Stein's portrait in 1906 (see 69), he was content to work from a photograph rather than Olga herself. In the pose and many of its incidental details, such as the pattern of the chair-cover and the embroidery and cut of her dress, the painting sticks closely to the reality it recorded, but her characterisation is strikingly different. In the photo she appears alert and confident, and the pliancy and strength of her well-trained dancer's body is evident to the viewer. In the portrait, by contrast, her body is flattened and the anatomy fudged, making her seem frail and insubstantial – an effect heightened by leaving a hollow void where her left ankle should be and reducing the chair to its cover, which seems to float like a magic carpet in mid-air. Rather than looking back directly at the spectator/artist, she languishes, drooping like the folds of her dress, in danger of letting the fan fall from her hand. This was Picasso's poeticised vision of Olga as delicate and melancholic, whereas in the snapshots he took of her (see 97–8) – and indeed in certain drawings made from life (see 99) – she appears animated, cheerful and flirtatious. Had she been face to face with him, staring beadily back, he might no longer have been able to 'see' her. With only the photo to hand, he remained in full control of Olga's image.

Olga suffered a serious injury to her right foot in April 1918. It took months to heal and put a brutal end to her career as a dancer.[29] Picasso compensated by making drawings, based on Ballets Russes publicity photographs, of her in costume mimicking a performance on stage. His response to the artificiality of the photos (105) was to poke fun at the mannered poses and stereotyped gestures,

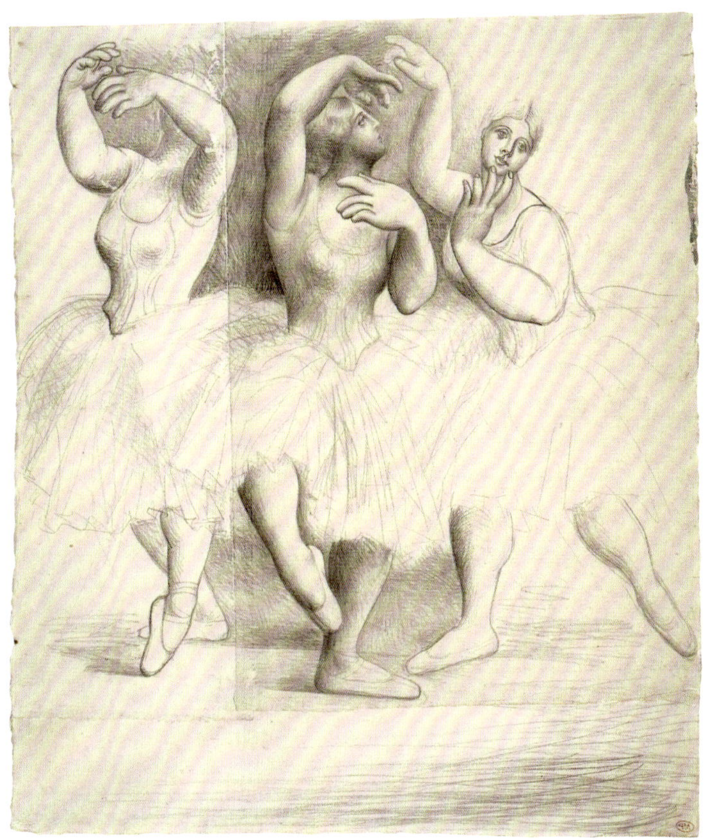

106 *Three Dancers*, 1919–20

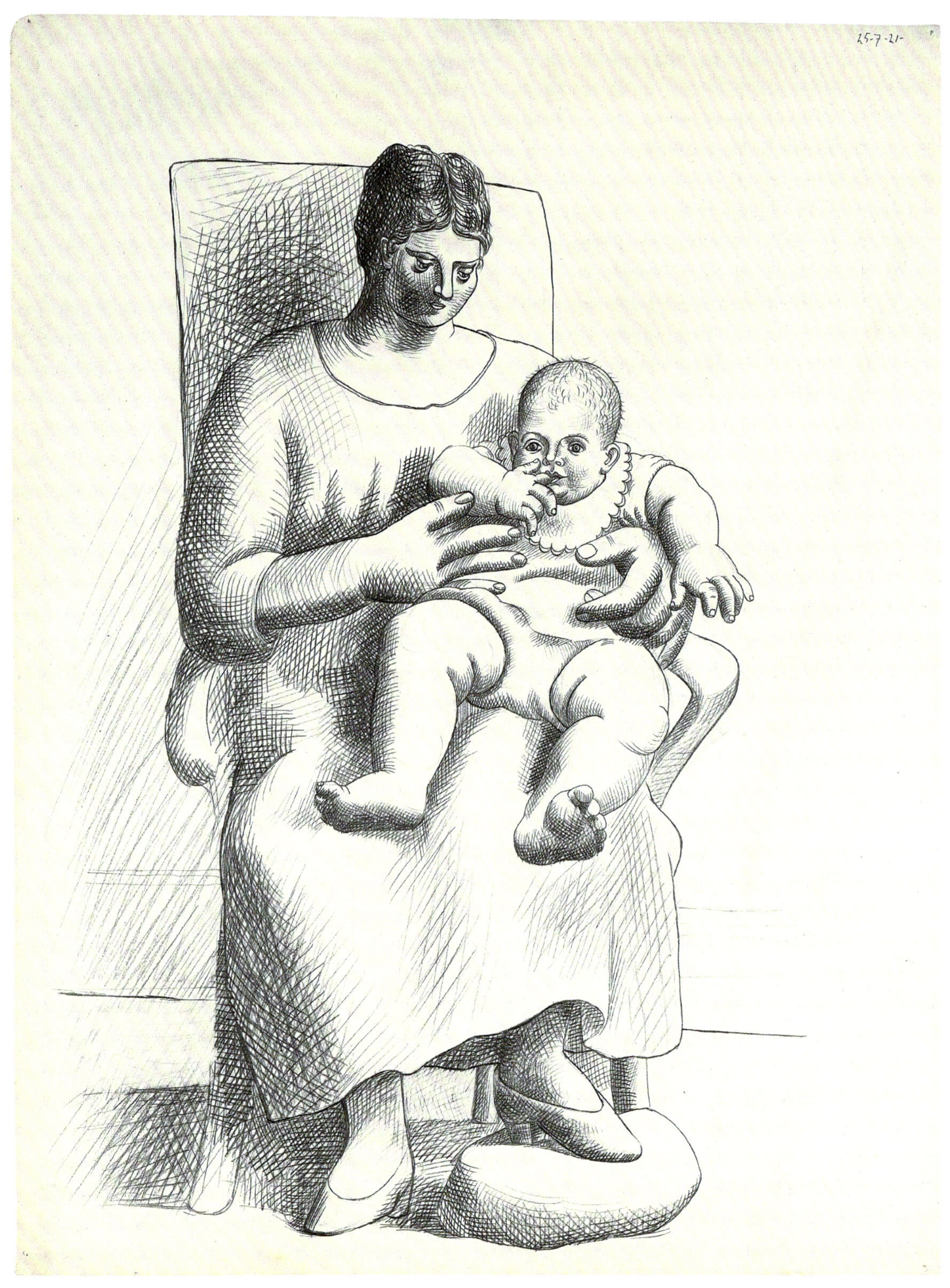

107 *Mother and Child (Olga and Paulo)*, 25 July 1921 (L)

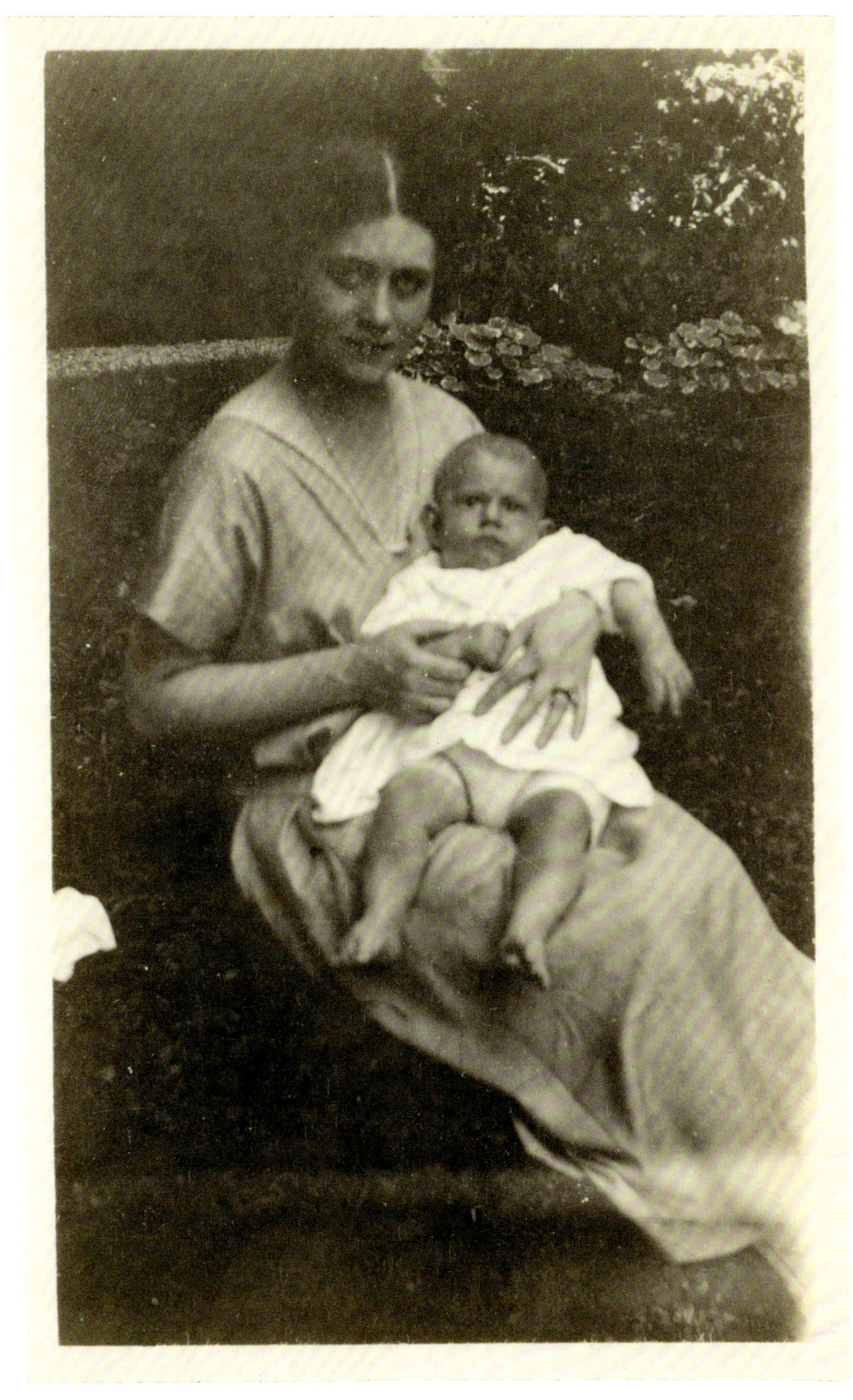

108 *Olga and Paulo, Fontainebleau*, 10 August 1921 (B, L)

grossly inflating the dancers' limbs and comically exaggerating their simpering expressions (106). (Olga is the dancer on the right in this drawing.) In *Mother and Child (Olga and Paulo)*, he took that caricatural approach again (107). The drawing was made in Fontainebleau when the couple's son Paulo, born in February 1921, was almost four months old. Its source was very likely a photo, similar to the one illustrated here (108), taken in the villa they had rented for the summer.[30] Presenting his elegant, figure-conscious wife and the infant son of whom they were both so proud in this unsentimental, unflattering manner may astonish, even shock, until we remember that Picasso reserved his caricatural humour for those who were closest to him. In Fontainebleau, his paintings alternated between a highly decorative form of synthetic Cubism and a monumental, neoclassical style strongly influenced by Graeco-Roman sculpture and the paintings of Poussin.[31] *Mother and Child* was an ironic exercise in the latter style – the 'grand manner' applied incongruously to the banal domestic subject of a baby in bib and nappy sucking his thumb, watched over by his solicitous mother.

Portrait of Olga Picasso has, by contrast, a good claim to be considered Picasso's most formal statement as a portrait painter (109). Small tonal studies of Olga's head seen at the same angle were painted in preparation for the portrait and, leaving nothing to chance, Picasso also made a charcoal sketch of the full composition.[32] Shown for the first time in Paris in 1928 in a vast survey resonantly entitled *Portraits et figures de femmes: Ingres à Picasso*,[33] it was subsequently shipped to the United States to represent him at the prestigious Carnegie International Exhibition in 1930.[34] Picasso duly won first prize, supported by Matisse, who was on the jury and had won the prize himself in 1927. These public accolades come as no surprise, for the painting is the masterpiece of Picasso's classicising images of his wife during the first six years of their marriage, when he underlined her conformity to the aesthetic ideals of the Great Tradition. He had used pastel for some of the most perfect of these images, and here he handled the oil paint as gently as if it were pastel, covering the canvas lightly and with a restrained touch to create a surface of admirable delicacy and economy.[35] The subtle colouristic harmony and perfect balance of the composition must have astonished visitors to the exhibitions in Paris and Pittsburgh, many of whom were used to thinking of Picasso as the *enfant terrible* of contemporary art. A supremely dignified representation of Olga, the portrait expresses Picasso's appreciation of her poise, grace and refinement. The marriage, however, was doomed, and Olga's statuesque immobility and the absence of the least sign of interaction between sitter and painter hint at the couple's growing estrangement. The women in Ingres's portraits may be unreal in their immaculate perfection of body and dress but they are never as remote and untouchable as Olga in this painting.

Executed in the same year as the prize-winning portrait, Picasso's sensitive drypoint (110) caught Olga in a moment of reverie, dressed in the silk coat with a fur collar seen in some of his photographs of her in their living-room in Rue La Boétie (112).[36] There too her expression is grave and tinged with sadness, in keeping with the image he had formed for her in his earliest portraits. Her melancholy was no doubt real enough, for quite apart from the strains within their relationship, Olga endured constant anxiety on behalf of her family, who were on the losing side in the Russian Revolution and in real danger as well as serious financial difficulties. Although the overall effect of the drypoint is evanescent, and the mark-making, even in the shady areas with dense cross-hatching, extremely delicate, the portrait possesses a paradoxical grandeur thanks to its over-lifesize scale – a grandeur that serves to heighten rather than diminish its poignancy.

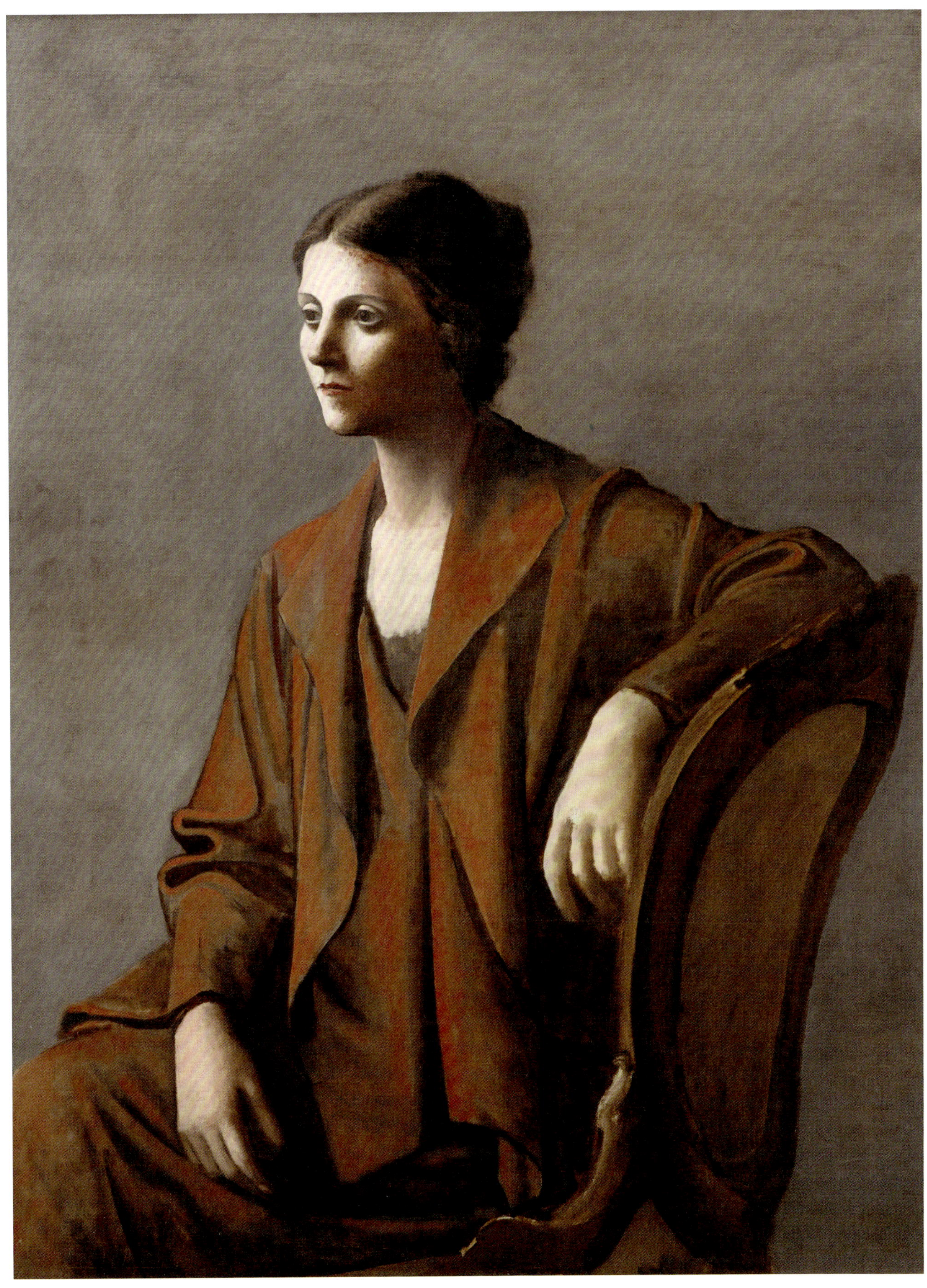

109 *Portrait of Olga Picasso*, 1923 (B, L)

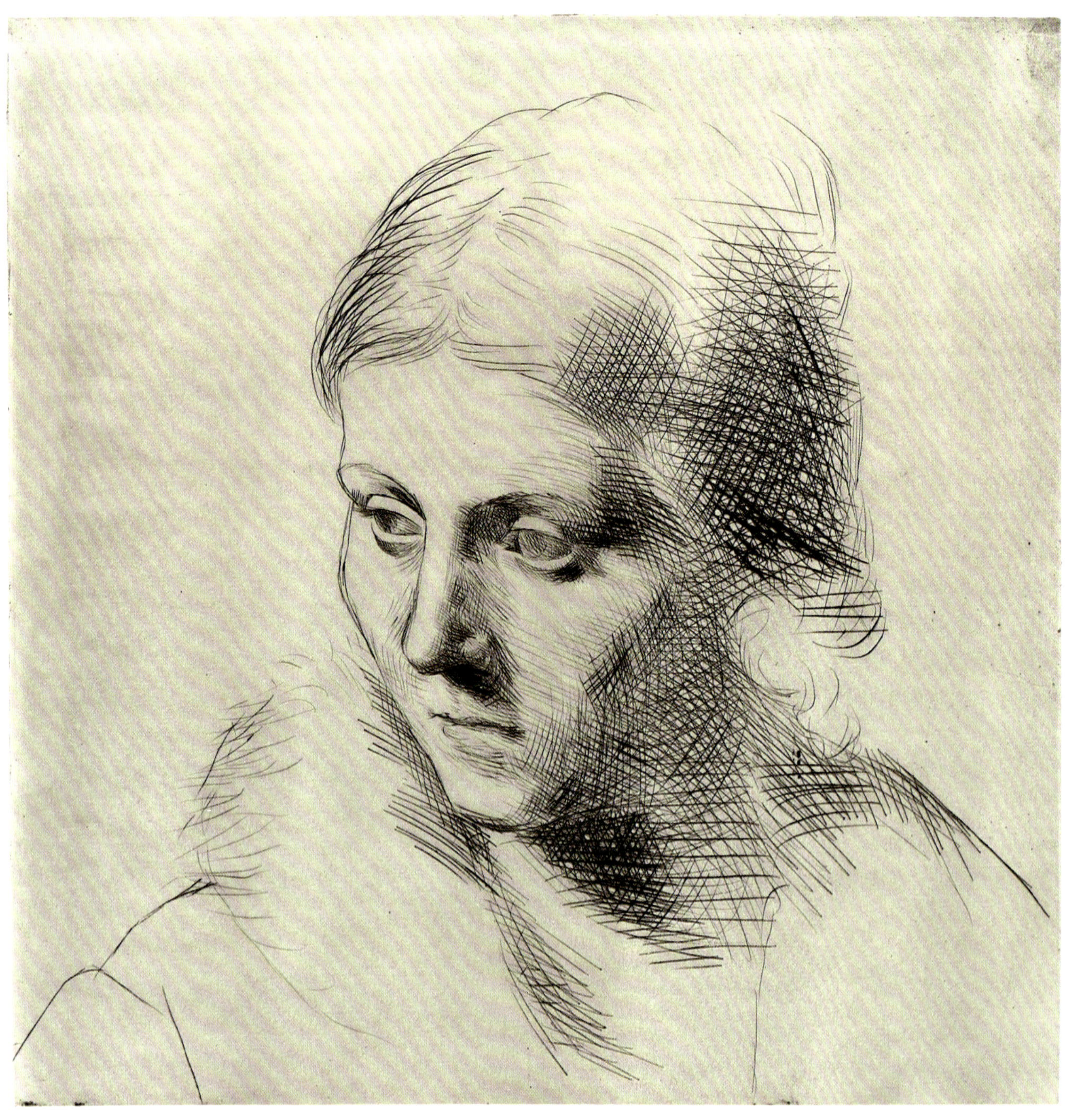

110 *Olga with a Fur Collar*, 1923 (B, L)

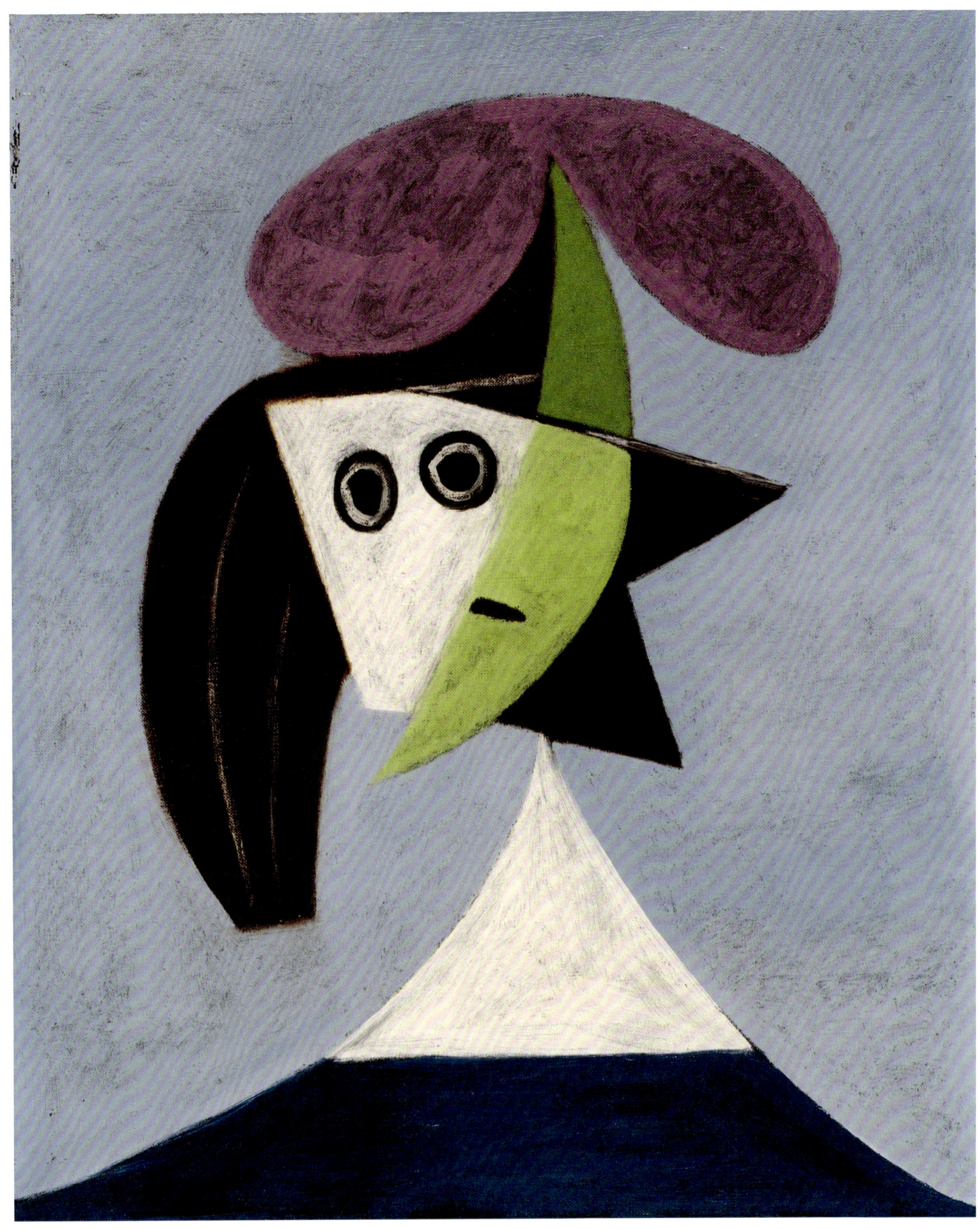

111 *Woman in a Hat (Olga)*, 1935 (B, L)

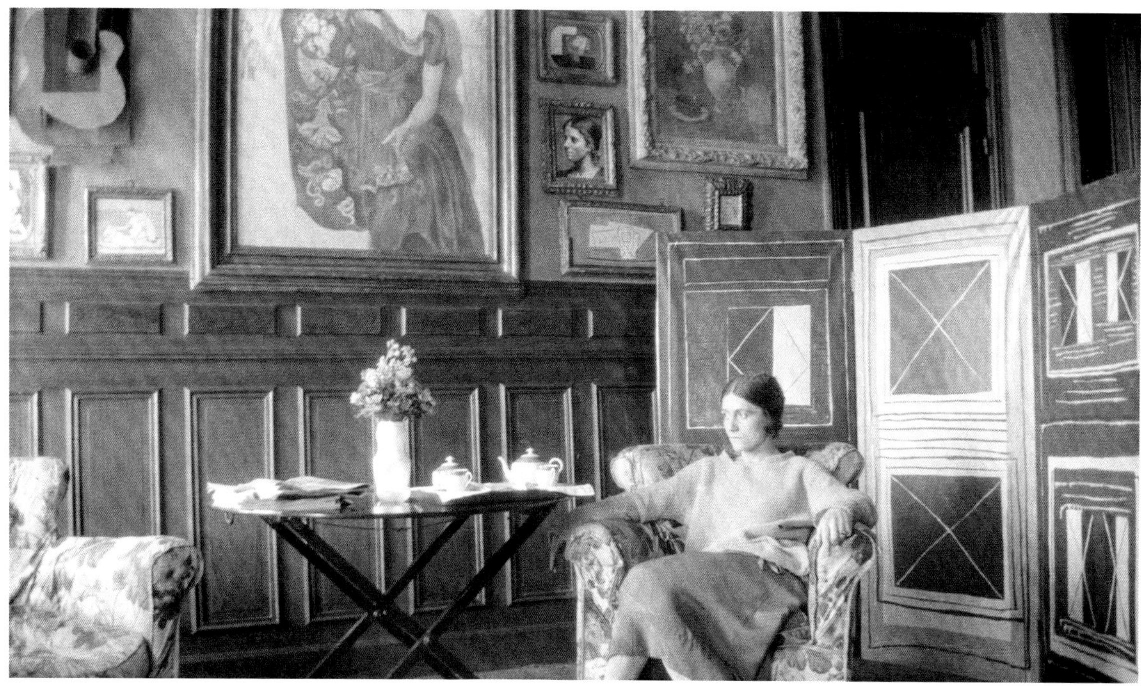

112 *Olga Picasso in the Living Room at 23 Rue La Boétie, Paris, c.1923* (B, L)

Knowledge of Olga's family circumstances and a better understanding of Olga herself, her relationship with Picasso and her influence on his art will be possible only when the extensive correspondence and other documents preserved in her archive become available and are studied with an open mind. However, it does seem that, with the exception of his photographs and home movies, Olga largely disappeared from Picasso's portraiture in the mid-1920s, supplanted by Marie-Thérèse Walter, with whom he began a passionate affair in 1927. One of Olga's final appearances was in *Woman in a Hat* (111), painted in the crisis year of 1935, when his daughter by Walter was born and the couple's marriage came to an acrimonious end.[37] In reductive, caricatural fashion, the picture itemises the large dark eyes, small pursed mouth, broad pale features and *soignée* appearance that Picasso recorded in his earlier 'straight' portraits, while mocking the chic hats seen in innumerable photographs. Placed alongside the drypoint of 1923, its essential similarity to the 'real' Olga is painfully apparent: even the blue strip of her dress refers to a favourite blue dress depicted in paintings and pastels. Grotesque, certainly, but *Woman in a Hat* is also tragic in the sadness and bewilderment written on Olga's ashen, mask-like face. Picasso's pictorial farewell is barbed, but also imbued with pity and sorrow.

1 Picasso, *Buffalo Bill*, 1911. Private collection (Z.II.255).

2 See Read 2008, pp.106–9.

3 For Picasso's letter to Kahnweiler, dated 12 June 1912, see Judith Cousins, 'Documentary Chronology', in Rubin 1989, p.395. Relevant paintings include: *Female Nude: 'J'aime Eva'*, 1912 (Columbus Museum of Art, Columbus, Ohio; Z.II.364); *Violin: 'Jolie Eva'*, 1912 (Staatsgalerie Stuttgart; Z.II.342).

4 To judge by surviving photographs, the nude in *The Painter and His Model*, summer 1914 (MP 53), is a likeness of Eva Gouel. But paintings of women in fashions of the 1890s that are often said to portray her (for instance, *Portrait of a Girl*, 1914; Centre Pompidou, Paris. Musée national d'art moderne/Centre de création industrielle. Z.II.528), were almost certainly based on old postcards or photos in outdated women's magazines.

5 This curious table survives. See *Picasso Camera* 2014, p.50.

6 Letter from Max Jacob to Guillaume Apollinaire, 7 January 1915. Quoted in Seckel 1994, p.116.

7 Undated letter from Max Jacob to Francis Picabia, autumn 1915. Quoted in Seckel 1994, p.120.

8 See Michael FitzGerald, 'The Modernists' Dilemma: Neoclassicism and the Portrayal of Olga Khokhlova', in Rubin 1996, pp.299–301.

9 For Vollard's letter to Picasso enclosing the agreed sum of 500 francs and a surviving print of the Bonney photograph (printed in reverse), see Tinterow and Stein 2010, cat.61, pp.172–5.

10 See Baldassari 1997, pp.134–7, 139–41.

11 Olivier 2001, pp.178–82.

12 See Baldassari 1997, pp.146 ff. The classic study of Picasso's ballet designs is Cooper 1968.

13 Madeline 2005, no.137, p.204.

14 Stravinsky and Craft 1959, p.104.

15 Stravinsky 1936, pp.114–15.

16 Stravinsky and Craft 1959, p.104.

17 This ballet premiered at London's Alhambra Theatre on 22 July 1919. For photographs of Picasso and Polunin painting the curtain, see *Picasso Tricorne* 1992, pp.79–89.

18 Polunin 1927, pp.53–5, 79–80.

19 For instance, Picasso provided portrait frontispieces for: Paul Valéry, *La Jeune parque*. NRF, Paris, 1921 (lithograph); Pierre Reverdy, *Les Cravates de chanvre*. Éditions Nord-Sud, Paris 1922 (etching); André Breton, *Clair de terre*. Presses du Montparnasse, Paris, 1923 (drypoint).

20 Fifteen letters from Faure to Picasso documenting their contacts are preserved in the Archives nationales Picasso (Série B 12). Faure's essay, 'Les dessins de Picasso', was eventually published in *Les Feuillets d'Art*, vol.6, September 1922, pp.267–70.

21 Faure 1921, pp.444, 446, 457–9.

22 Courtois and Morel 1989, p.20.

23 Francis Poulenc, *Le travail du peintre. Sept mélodies sur des poèmes de Paul Éluard pour chant et piano* (Éditions Max Eschig, Paris, 1957).

24 *Portrait of Igor Stravinsky*, 24 May 1920 (MP 911); *Portrait of Manuel de Falla*, 9 June 1920 (MP 915). Faure also posed in this chair.

25 For a selection of Picasso's snapshots and publicity photographs of Olga in costume for her dancing roles, see *Picasso Camera* 2014, pp.83–95.

26 Richardson 2007, p.59.

27 Letter dated 26 April 1918. Madeline 2005, no.152. Picasso noted that the photograph of the painting was taken by Émile Delétang, who may also have been responsible for the studio photo of Olga (Baldassari 1997, p.253, note 441).

28 Christian Zervos, 'Conversation with Picasso', 1935; Cited in Ashton 1972, p.11.

29 Richardson 2007, pp.79–81.

30 The photograph (108) is dated 10 August 1921, whereas Picasso's drawing is dated 25 July 1921.

31 The classic contrast is between *Three Musicians*, 1921 (The Museum of Modern Art, New York; Z.IV.331) and *Three Women at the Spring*, 1921 (The Museum of Modern Art, New York; Z.IV.322).

32 See Palau 1999, nos 1426, 1427, 1429. Like the painting, these studies are not dated. Palau i Fabre attributes all of them to autumn 1923.

33 Galerie de La Renaissance, Paris, June 1928, no.142. In his conclusion to his flowery dual-language catalogue text, Arsène Alexandre wrote: 'The final chord is struck by Picasso, a classic Picasso, Ingresque in his way, which permits us to remark that Ingres was a Picasso in his' (*La Renaissance*, vol.11, no.7, July 1928, p.308).

34 *Twenty-ninth International Exhibition of Paintings*, Carnegie Institute, Pittsburgh, October–December 1930, no.247.

35 Compare, for instance, the exquisite pastel and black crayon *Olga in Pensive Mood*, 1923 (MP993).

36 See *Picasso Camera* 2014, pp.120–2.

37 Picasso told Georges Salles, who owned the painting, that it was a portrait of Olga (Michael FitzGerald, 'The Modernists' Dilemma: Neoclassicism and the Portrayal of Olga Khokhlova', in Rubin 1996, p.334, note 80).

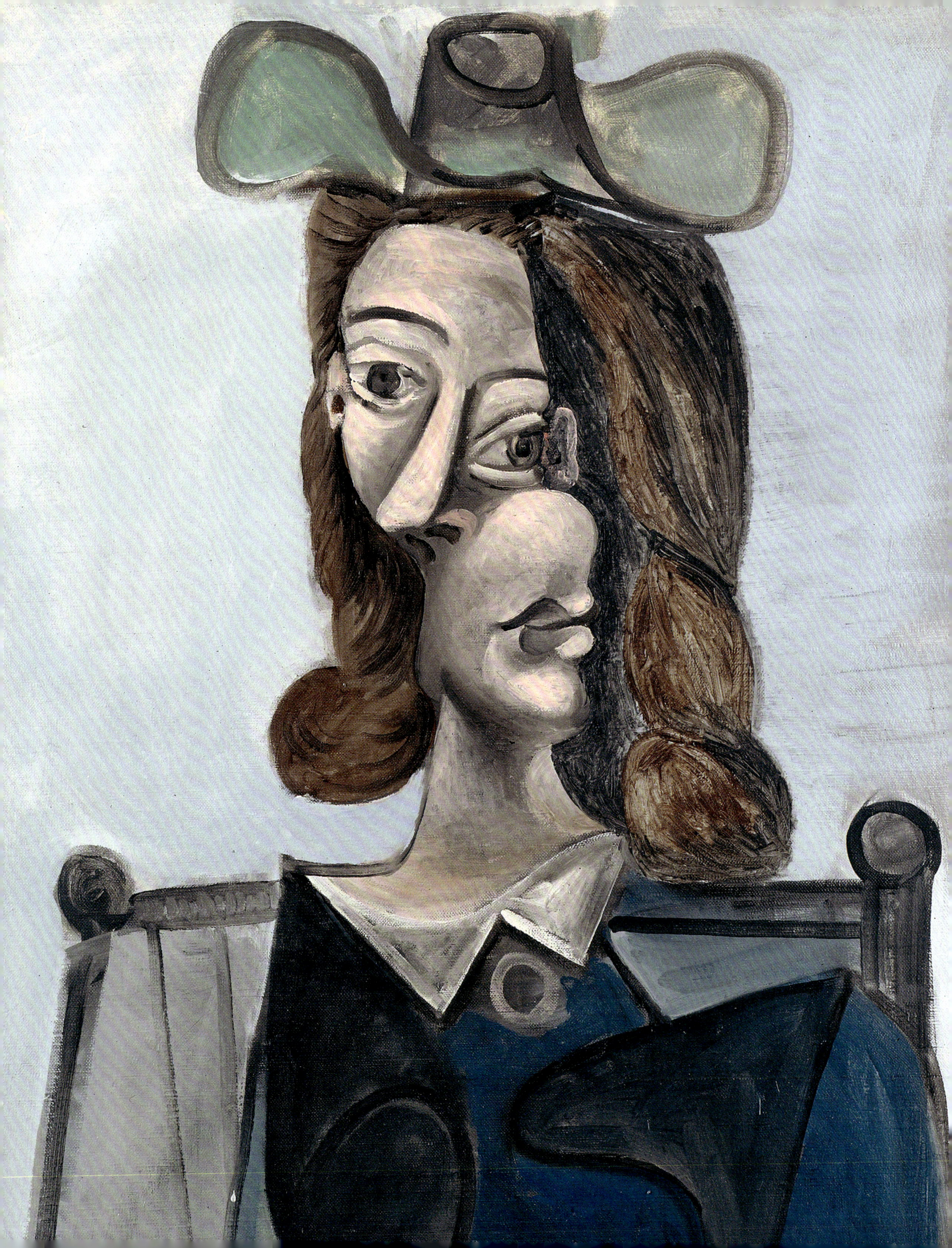

5. The many faces of Picasso's portraiture 1927–1944

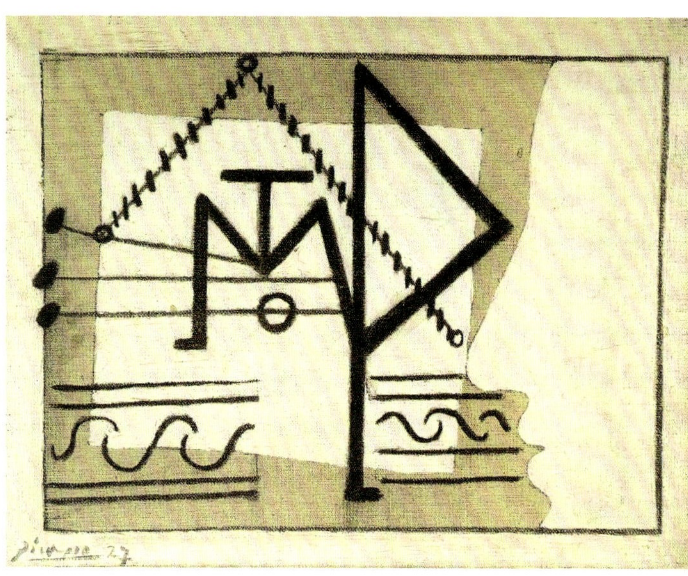

113 *Guitar Hanging on a Wall with Profile*, 1927

Women dominated Picasso's imagery from the mid-1920s until the Liberation of France in 1944. Yet Picasso did not cease to enjoy the friendship of men or to form new friendships with men: at the very moment, 1925, when he pulled back from his association with the world of the ballet, he drew close to the poets and painters in the Surrealist movement – a society in which all the key figures at that time were men. The powerful influence of the women with whom he was involved provides the obvious explanation for this striking bias in his imagery. But his interest in representing the many facets of their differing personalities was accompanied by the desire to marshall their potential as vehicles for the expression of emotion and drama that transcended the strictly personal or individual. For Picasso, women possessed the capacity to represent the human condition in a way that men did not. It was also women who embodied the tragedy of the Spanish Civil War and the Second World War in his art.

MARIE-THÉRÈSE WALTER

Picasso's chance meeting with Marie-Thérèse Walter outside the Galeries Lafayette in Paris on 8 January 1927 had major consequences for his art as well as his life. His opening gambit – 'You have an interesting face. I would like to do a portrait of you. I feel we are going to do great things together. I am Picasso' – had the desired effect even though the magic name meant nothing to her.[1] But painting portraits of Walter was hardly a realistic option since secrecy was vital if the affair were to be more than a passing fling, and he resorted to symbolism and code (typically the letters M, T and P) in the earliest paintings dedicated to her (113).[2] There are, however, some private drawings. On one sheet, possibly the earliest of all, he acquainted himself with the classic form of Marie-Thérèse's head by drawing it from four different angles (114). The limpid full-face view, and especially the softly modelled three-quarter view, reveal that he instinctively saw her as the incarnation of a Raphael Madonna – serene, innocent, gentle, candid – and in later drawings that analogy still holds true. In the rapt head and shoulders drawing of her from *c.*1930, she gazes back steadily through pale, almond-shaped eyes (115); transcending the banal reality of beret, sweater and thick jacket, she transmits radiance like the blonde Virgin of Raphael's *La belle jardinière* in the Louvre (116). The melancholy air Picasso had associated with Olga is absent, and even though he refined Walter's features he did not conceal her strong, broad shoulders – signs of the keen sportswoman that she was.

The close-up drawing of Marie-Thérèse's profile, dated 27 December 1935 on the reverse, was made at a watershed in their relationship (117). Their daughter Maya was almost four months old and mother and baby were established in an apartment at 45 Rue La Boétie, a stone's throw from Picasso's studio and apartment at No. 23. Distracted and traumatised by the wrangling that preceded his legal separation from Olga, Picasso had stopped painting and plunged into writing surrealist poetry instead. Now and then, however, he broke off from writing to make drawings of Marie-Thérèse with the baby.[3] For this drawing, he used a soft pencil and exploited the slight texture of the paper to give the portrait the velvety sensuousness that he felt suited her best of all. Its intimacy is remarkable: intently and tenderly, Picasso recorded the set of her eyes and mouth, the 'Roman' nose that lent her face nobility, the intricate form of her ear, the growth and fall of her baby-fine hair, the smoothness of her skin, the shaft of her neck. He also recorded her faraway glance. One senses a desire to penetrate her thoughts at that moment, but his recognition of the inaccessibility of her inner world.

The loving tenderness of these private drawings was not replicated in work of a more public character. Picasso had a sentimental, gracious tendency but usually kept it under very strict control, just as he guarded against the allure of conventional beauty and introduced discordant notes to energise an image that risked becoming too sweet-toned. Cocteau was fascinated by this aspect of Picasso's character and reflected acutely on it in the diary he kept during the 1950s. In the entry for 28 May 1955, he noted: 'a true feminine beauty threatens to make him fall into the aestheticism against which he struggles *out of weakness*, from fear of losing his hardness, his intensity. From fear of charm.'[4]

Picasso purchased the Château de Boisgeloup, a secluded country house with a large walled garden near Gisors in Normandy, in the summer of 1930, and immediately set about converting the stables into a sculpture studio. He had undertaken to design a monument for the grave of Apollinaire in Père Lachaise cemetery, but none of his proposals to date had been accepted.[5] This unfulfilled commission was a major incentive to make sculpture, but it was not the only one for, like

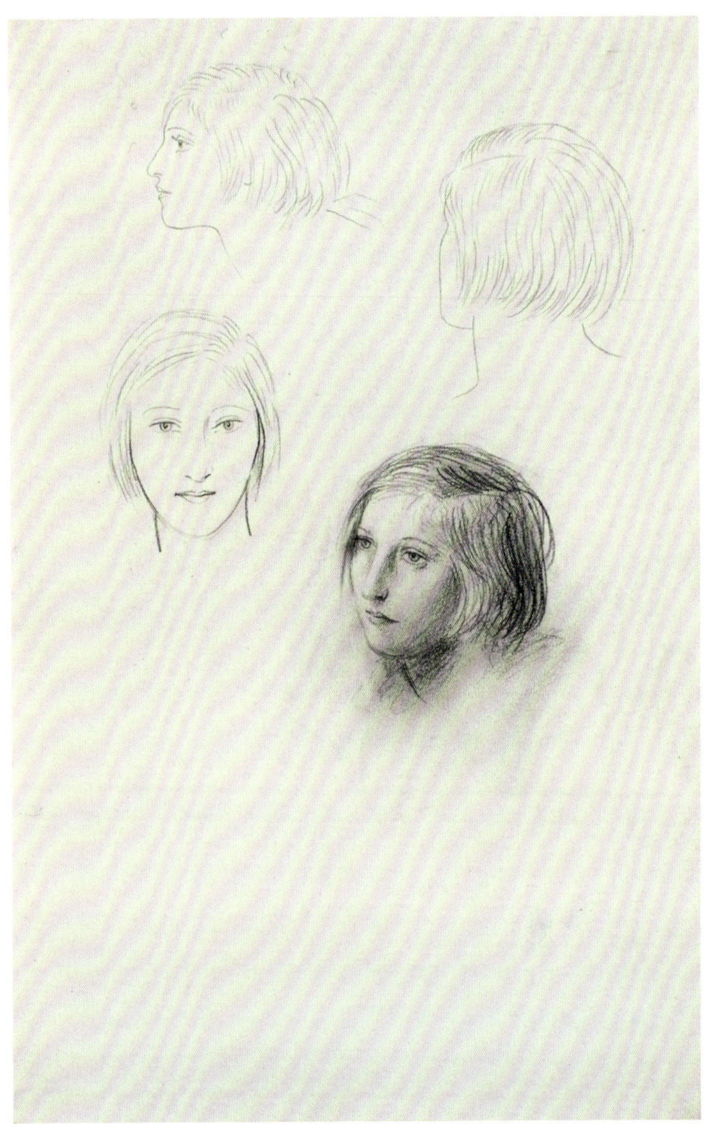

114 *Marie-Thérèse Walter*, 1927

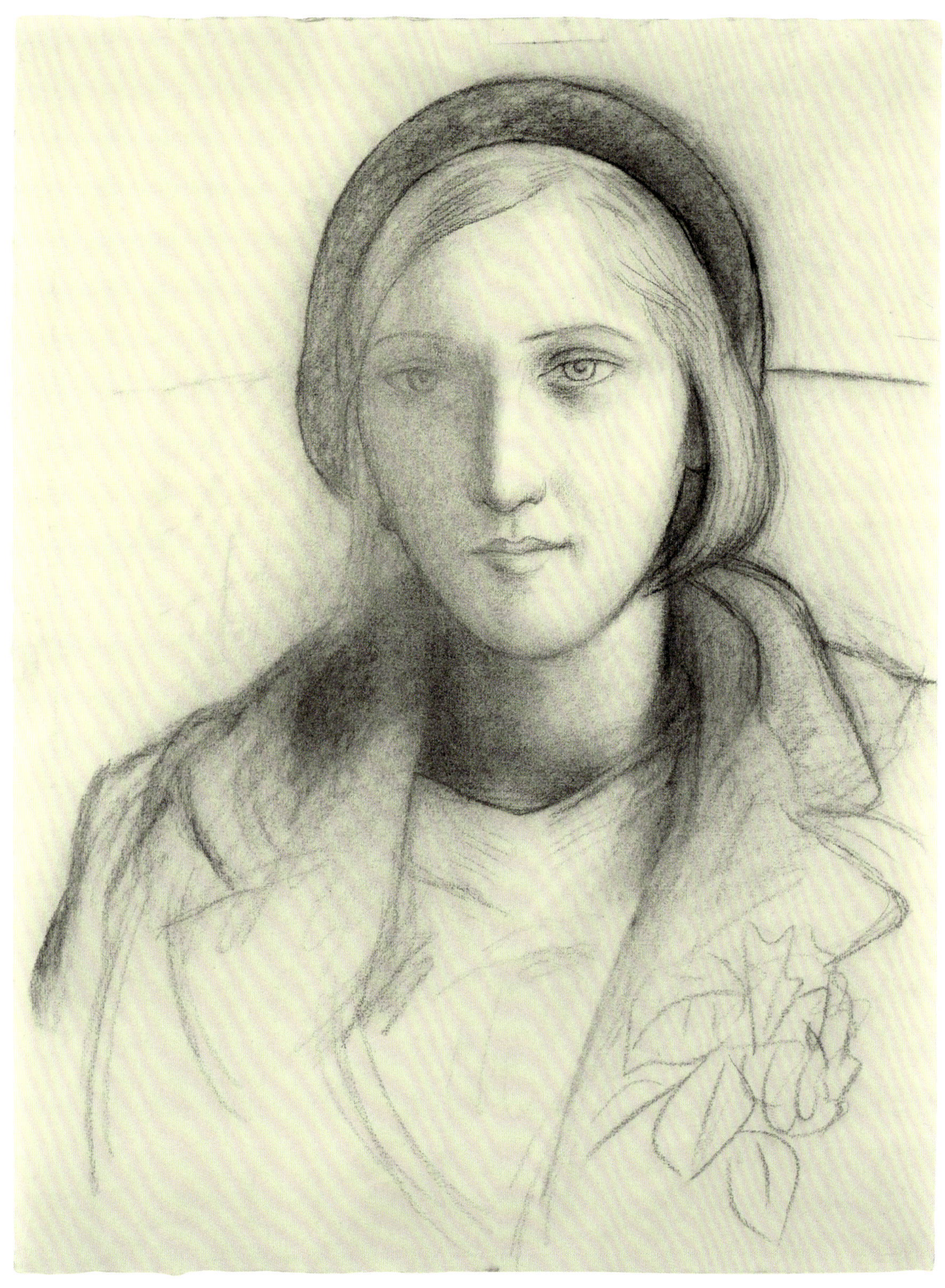

115 *Marie-Thérèse in a Beret*, c.1930 (B)

Fernande Olivier, Marie-Thérèse Walter appealed strongly to his sculptural imagination. The drawing in which he surveyed her head from all sides shows that he saw her in three-dimensional terms from the start. *Head of a Woman* (118) was created in Boisgeloup, probably in the spring of 1931.[6] The most classical in style and finish of all the sculptures Walter inspired, it is reminiscent of the smooth neoclassical sculpture of Aristide Maillol, then at the height of his fame. The pensive angle of the head recalls that of the Cubist head of Fernande Olivier (see 77) but in every other respect the sculpture is entirely different: the dramatic tension of the earlier work has been replaced by contemplative serenity. Although *Head of a Woman* exhibits Marie-Thérèse's distinctive traits – her broad, regular features with unusually smooth transitions between brow, nose and cheek, her prominent 'Roman' nose, her bobbed hair clinging to her spherical skull – it is more generalised and impersonal than the drawings made from life. Like the other heads and busts she inspired, it was modelled in plaster. The flexibility of plaster – which can be modelled like clay when damp, but chiselled and filed like stone when dry – suited Picasso's driven, quick-fire, venturesome temperament perfectly. Its whiteness gave it the look of unpolished marble, reinforcing the purposeful allusion to classical sculpture.

On 16 June 1932, Picasso's first thoroughgoing retrospective exhibition opened at the Galeries Georges Petit in Paris – an enormous affair with 236 catalogued items and a substantial, illustrated catalogue.[7] It was organised by a consortium of dealers but Picasso took a leading role in the selection, lent many works from his own collection and was responsible for the startling, non-chronological hang. The new Boisgeloup sculptures were not included, but were unveiled publicly a year later in Brassaï's atmospheric photographs published in *Minotaure* in June 1933.[8] Instead, Picasso showed twenty-seven large new paintings,

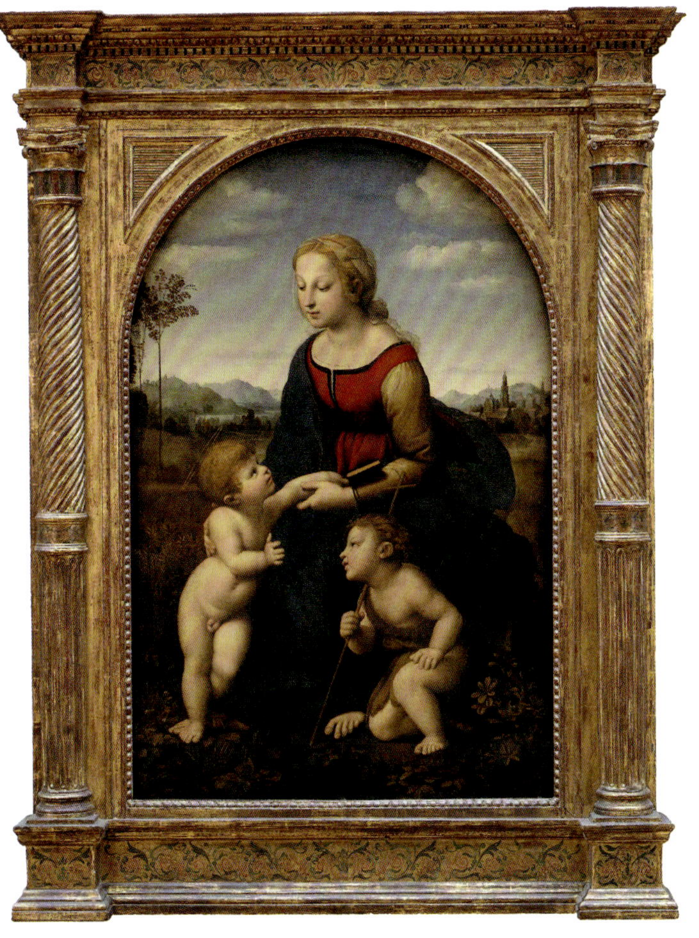

116 *La belle jardinière* by Raphael, 1507

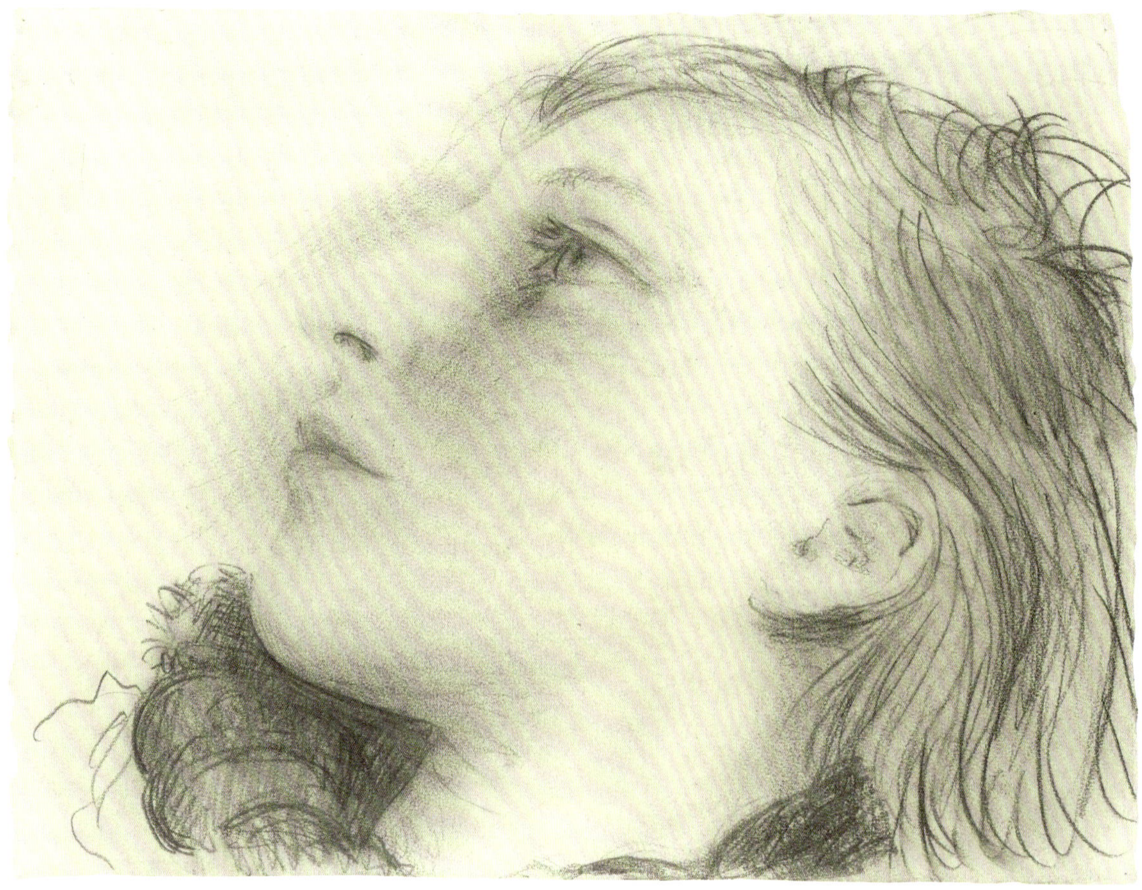

117 *Portrait of Marie-Thérèse*, 1935 (L)

the majority executed between December 1931 and April 1932. It is certain that *Marie-Thérèse, Full-face and Profile* (119) was painted at the beginning of that intensely productive period because a study for it appears in a sketchbook he used in Boisgeloup in the autumn of 1931.[9] It was not, however, included in the exhibition, probably because its austere grisaille palette was at odds with the brilliant prismatic colours of the pictures he chose from the mass of new work.

Picasso's fascination with the motif of a head seen simultaneously from different angles, as if it were turning or the viewer were circling around it, can be traced back to the Cubist period. It became obsessive during the mid-1920s when he was on close terms with the Surrealists and, responding

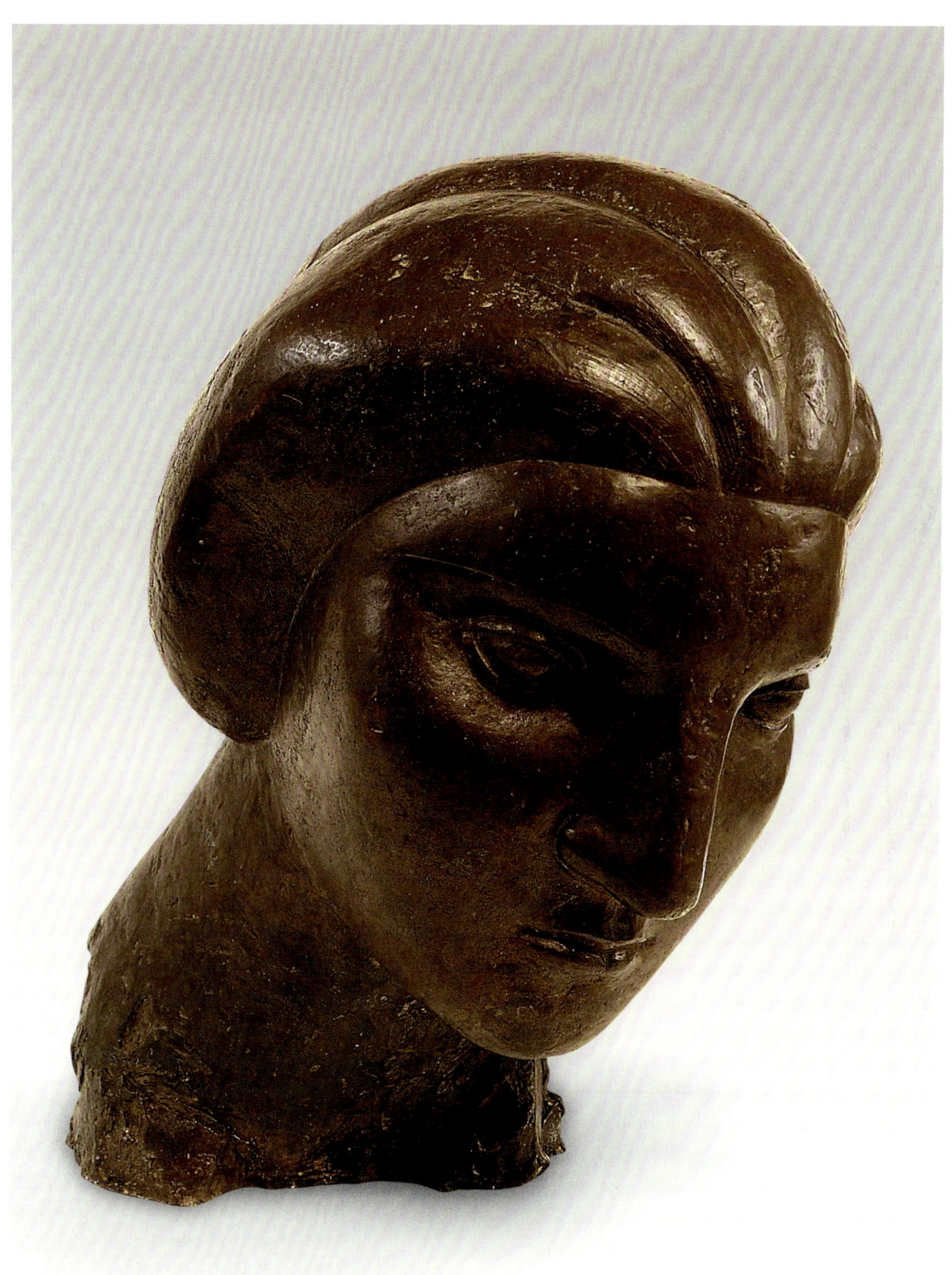

118 *Head of a Woman (Marie-Thérèse)*, 1931 (B, L)

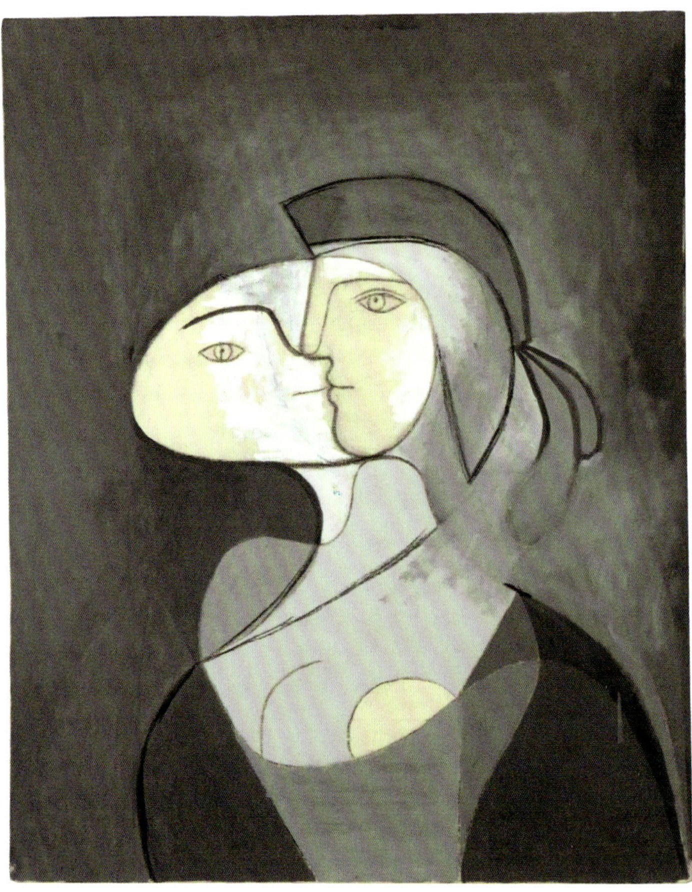

119 *Marie-Thérèse, Full-face and Profile*, 1931

to their experiments with 'psychic automatism' and identification with the phenomenon of metamorphosis, used the motif to suggest the interplay between the conscious and subconscious mind. In sketchbooks used between the summer of 1925 and the early autumn of 1926 he made numerous drawings in pen and ink of these split, multi-view heads, exploiting the natural fluidity of ink to enhance the impression of boundless transformation.[10] The experience of making sculpture in the round encouraged him to push forward with this imagery in his paintings of Walter. In highly simplified form, the characteristic physical traits recorded in the full-face portrait drawn *c.*1930 (see 115) reappear in *Marie-Thérèse, Full-face and Profile*, but in this mysterious canvas her image has an otherworldly, mythological dimension. With its gleaming silvery centre and foggy, near-black periphery, the painting evokes a moonlit night, the gradual turn of Walter's head from pure profile to full-face suggesting the phases of the moon or the passage of the moon across the night sky, now and then obscured by dark clouds. Her pale breast, shaped like a half-moon, amplifies the lunar metaphor, and the sweeping contours traversing her body strengthen the theme of planetary revolution in space.

Woman in a Yellow Armchair (121) was included in the Galeries Georges Petit exhibition.[11] The show opened exactly one year after the retrospective celebrating Matisse held in the same venue.[12] Matisse was on Picasso's mind as he painted the picture, which takes to an almost caricatural extreme the painterly characteristics particularly associated with his name: brilliant colour, flatness and decorative organisation of the surface (120). At this time, Matisse was wholly absorbed by the commission to paint murals for Dr Albert Barnes's Foundation on the outskirts of Philadelphia and was, in Isabelle Monod-Fontaine's words, 'absent from the arena of painting'. Picasso, she argues, 'then took it upon himself to paint for two, for himself and his main rival.'[13] The flagrantly Matissean paintings Picasso exhibited in June 1932 constituted a challenge to his old friend and competitor, but also expressed homage and brotherhood.

Walter was the reigning muse of this resplendent series of sensual, Matisse-like paintings. In some she was transformed into a voluptuous, sleeping odalisque, but *Woman in a Yellow Armchair* is composed as a portrait and summarised the traits of body as well as face that Picasso identified as specific to her. At a superficial level, the image is down-to-earth: a comely woman wearing a wristwatch is seated in an armchair with her arms crossed over her stomach. But the 'Egyptian' combination of face in profile with frontal eye is unnerving, as are the subhuman, paw-like hands and the mysterious mirror – or is it a picture? – at the top-left corner, which calls across to the equally mysterious black shadow at the bottom-right edge of the composition. Sandwiched between these sinister elements, Walter could be seen as a victim or prisoner were it not for the fact that she is sphinx-like and dauntless – less benign than the moon-goddess of *Marie-Thérèse, Full-face and Profile*. The painting's dazzling patchwork of coloured shapes has instant decorative appeal but these ambiguities at its core constitute its lasting power to challenge and intrigue.

Raphael Madonna, idealised classical type, moon-goddess, sphinx: these were only some of Picasso's imaginative transformations of Walter's image. In *Woman in a Beret and Fur Coat* (122), he retained certain aspects of her moon-goddess persona but combined them with incongruous, earthbound details of clothing – beret, blouse with lace-trimmed collar, bulky winter coat – and domestic setting – chair, table, vase. Walter's staring eyes, with their flap-like, colourless irises, have a haunted, baleful expression, and the bands of

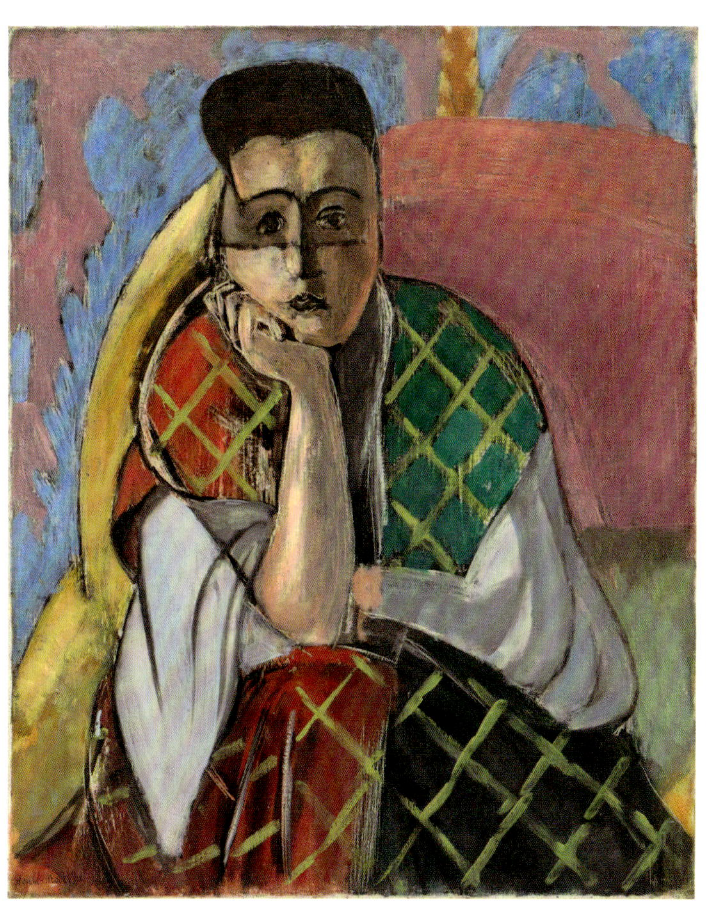

120 *Woman with a Veil* by Henri Matisse, 1927

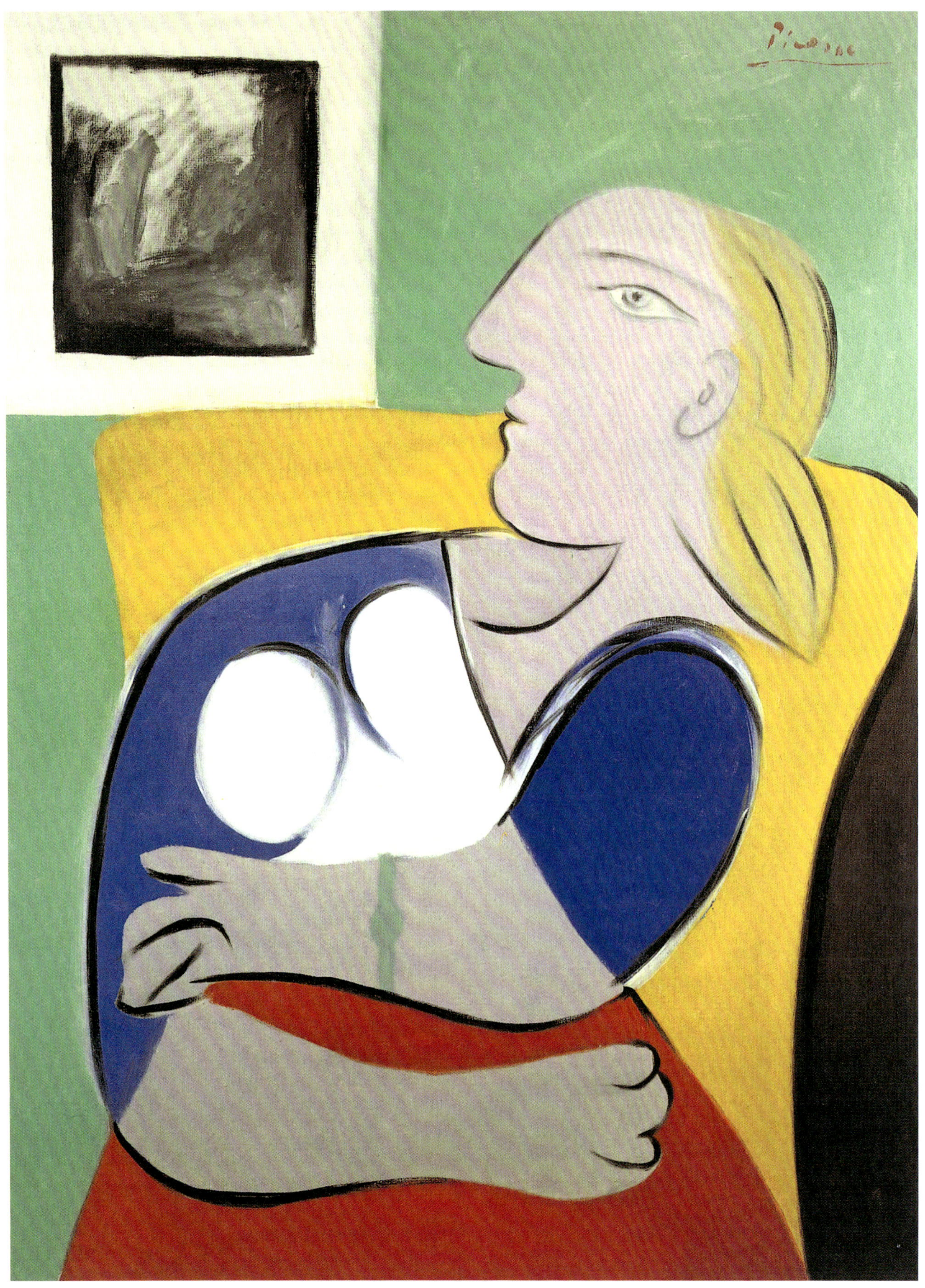

121 *Woman in a Yellow Armchair*, 1932 (L)

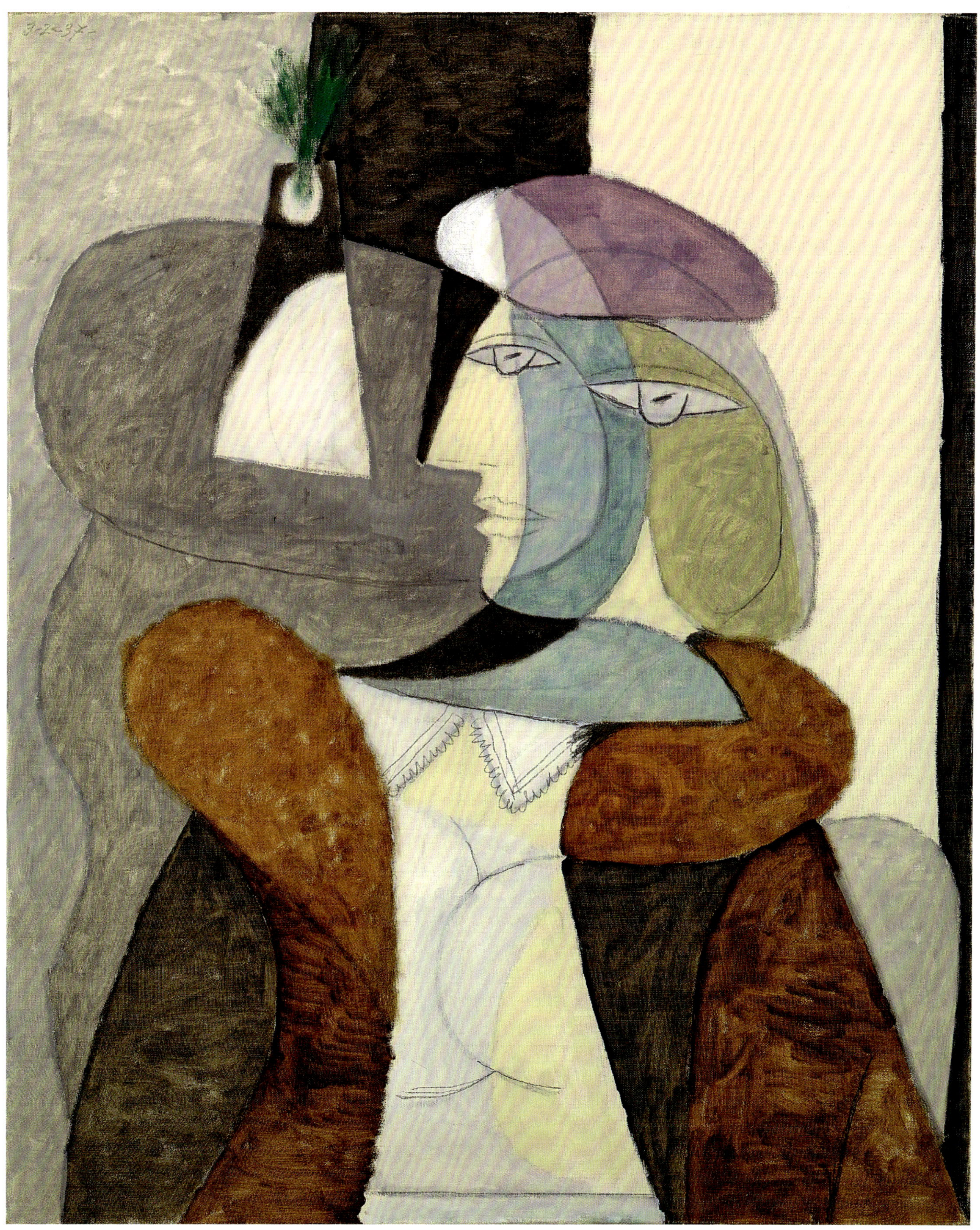

122 *Woman in a Beret and Fur Coat*, 3 February 1937 (B)

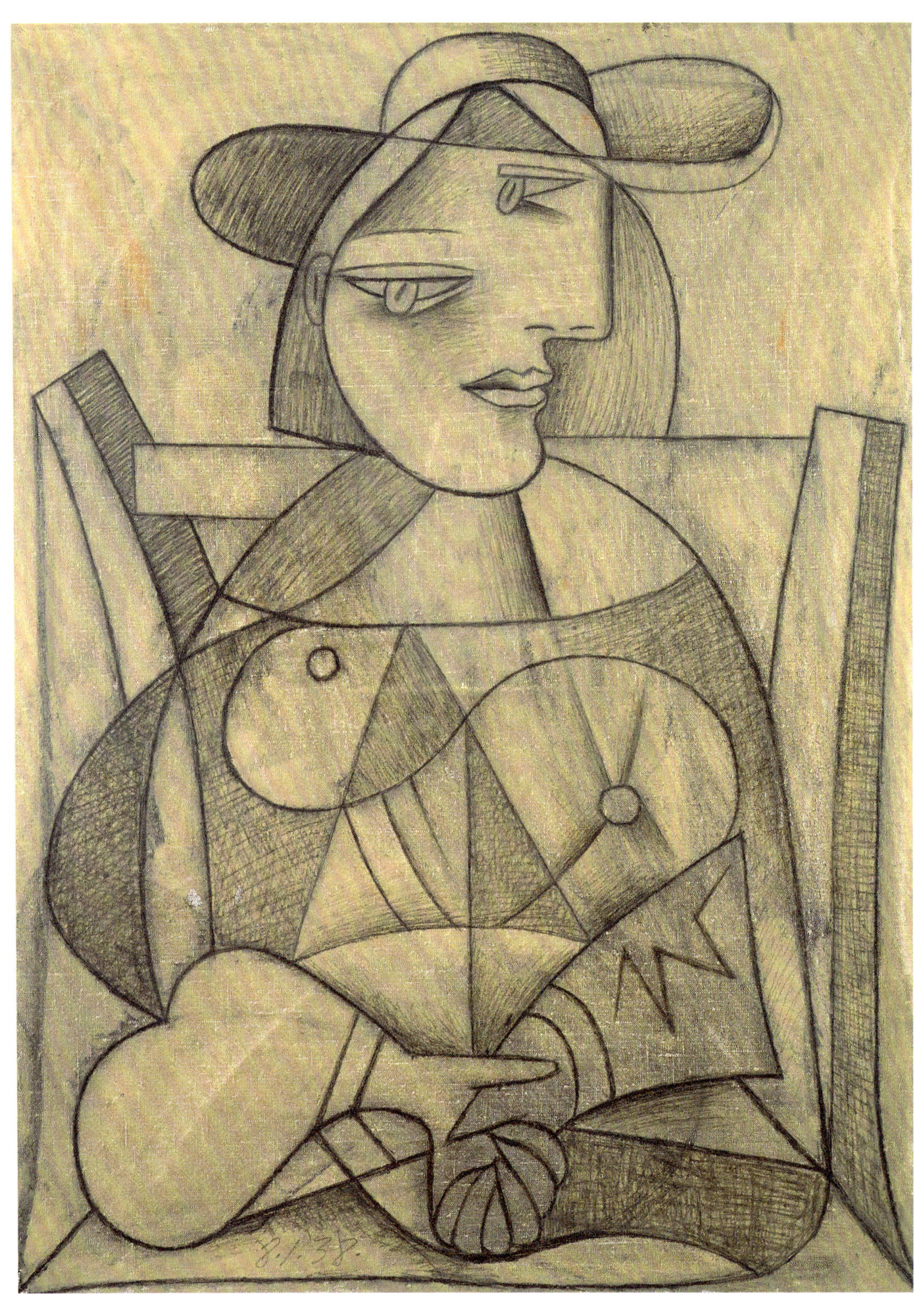

123 *Woman with Joined Hands (Marie-Thérèse Walter)*, 8 January 1938 (B, L)

coloured shadows traversing her face contribute to the sinister effect created by the funereal blacks and greys of the background. The date inscribed on the canvas – 3 February 1937 – provides a clue to the painting's ominous mood. The Nationalists had been advancing rapidly towards Málaga since the middle of January, but it was on that day that their assault on the city began. Ill-prepared to defend Málaga, where their navy was based, the Republicans were utterly defeated by Franco's troops a few days later. Wearing a coat and hat indoors implies readiness to leave home; in this portrait, Walter may have stood for all those citizens who were anxiously preparing their escape.

Woman with Joined Hands (123) is a far more sanguine representation of Marie-Thérèse Walter. Seated squarely on a hard kitchen chair, she looks placid and matronly. Her whole torso, with its separate zones, folds and creases and its passages of tightly woven hatching, resembles a comfortably padded sofa. That cushiony quality is partly the result of the over-painting of the surface and the layering and smudging of the charcoal: the medium has literal density and depth, and the residual streaks of red and orange lend a warm glow to the blacks and greys, mitigating the austerity of pure draftsmanship. Yet there is an erotic charge to the painting: the direction and position of Walter's eyes, and the sweep of the brim of her hat, suggest the seductive lowering, raising and turning of her head. The serpentine contours that map out the curvaceous forms of her body suggest surging movements akin to the twists and turns of the supine dreaming nudes who haunted Picasso's imagination in 1932 (124) and were his embodiment of the Surrealists' ideal of *amour fou*. The shaded wedge above the tightly clasped hands reads as her naked pubes and her humped right sleeve as buttocks: the spectator is invited to play the Freudian dream-analyst and interpret the hidden erotic content of the composition. Taken together,

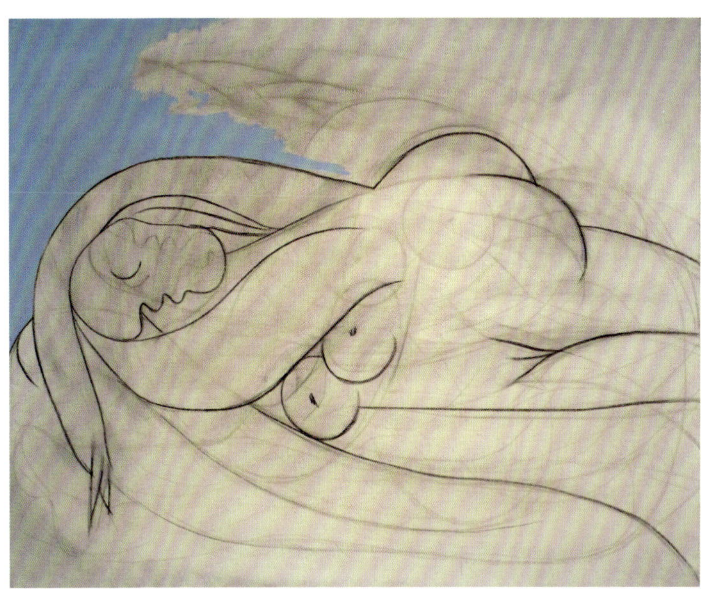

124 *Sleeping Nude*, 13 March 1932

these strikingly different portraits of Marie-Thérèse amount to an evocation of a complex, mutable personality: the longer and better Picasso knew her, the older and more experienced she grew, the more she eluded a consistent representational formula.

The flat, cubistic geometry of Picasso's contemporary portrait of an elegantly languid Nusch Éluard (125) is strikingly different from the sensual organic style of *Woman with Joined Hands*. Only a month separated the two pictures, and the differences between them reveal how important it was to Picasso to find a style that matched the individual portrayed. Nusch had been a travelling acrobat and captivated her future husband, the Surrealist poet Paul Éluard, when he saw her performing a circus routine on the street. Slender and delicate, unlike the broad-shouldered, sporty Marie-Thérèse, she also captivated Picasso, whose friendship with Éluard deepened after his split from Olga in 1935. She was the subject of many portraits that vary markedly in style and tone, but in all of them her defining attribute was her mass of dark, tightly curled hair, usually kept back from her brow by a ribbon. In this ultra-refined drawing on canvas, Nusch's hair is wittily represented by means of innumerable little squiggles – a form of graphic mark used nowhere else in the composition. To evoke the lightness of her body, Picasso represented it in terms of flat, wafer-thin planes with sharply drawn contours and pointed extremities, reminiscent of cut and folded paper. The rectilinear forms of the hard wooden chair, nearby table and window behind her head reinforce the impression of boniness, and the airily delicate application of the charcoal – no sign here of the dense layering of Walter's portrait – reiterates the ethereal theme: Nusch seems brittle and translucent. Yet she also possesses feline litheness with a touch of feline ferocity: her paw-like left hand spreads out its claws and the viewer is reminded that cats – nature's acrobats – have nine lives.

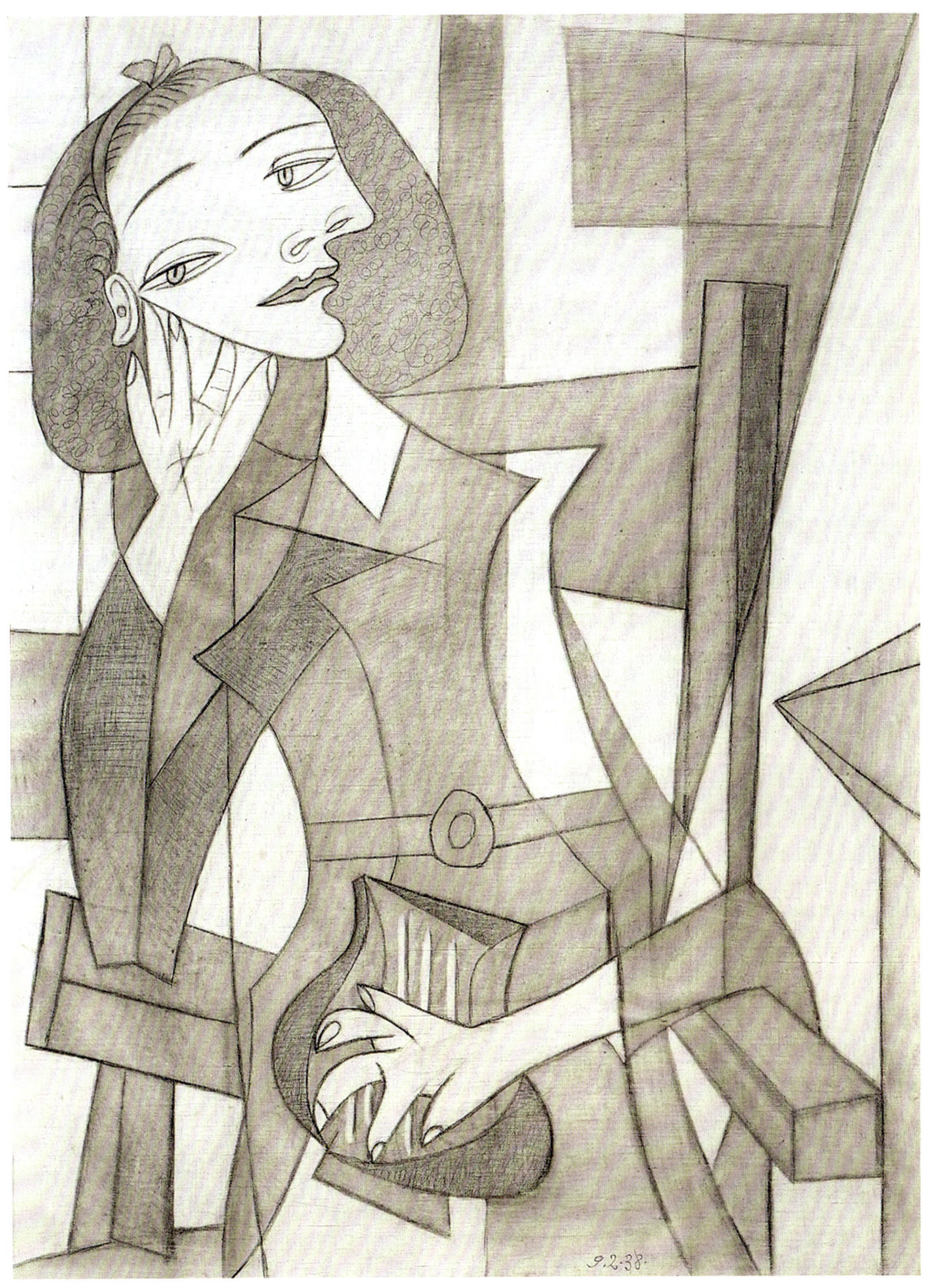

125 *Portrait of Nusch Éluard*, 9 February 1938 (B, L)

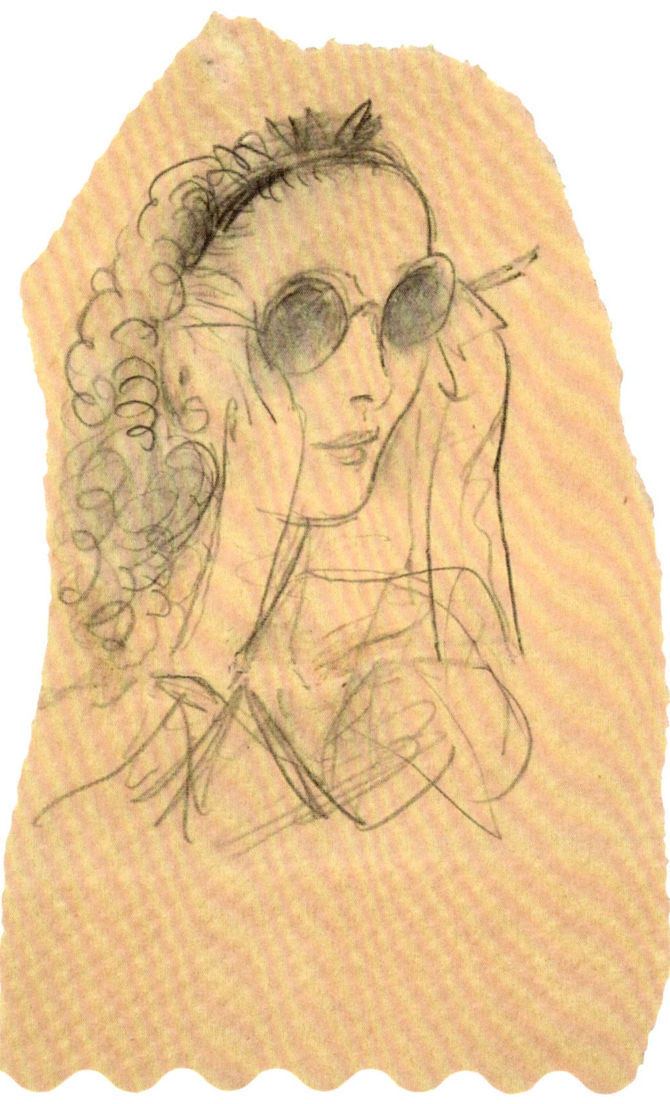

126 *Portrait of Nusch Éluard*, 1937 (L)

THE COMIC MUSE

Paul and Nusch Éluard had discovered the (then unspoiled) village of Mougins in the hills above Cannes. In 1937 Picasso spent his summer vacation there with them, as well as his new companion Dora Maar and a changing cast of mutual friends, including Roland Penrose, the leader of the Surrealist group in England and Penrose's lover, the American photographer and former fashion model Lee Miller. Their *bonheur de vivre* as they idled on the beach or lunched in the shade of vines was captured in scores of photographs, but as usual Picasso insisted on making time to work. He produced some instantaneous sketches, like the charming vignette on a scrap torn from a paper serviette of a chic Nusch Éluard – identified by her crinkly hair – adjusting her sunglasses (126). No doubt it was sketched during an outdoor meal.

Penrose recalled that Picasso was 'seized with a diabolical playfulness' during this holiday. He described the 'ludicrously recognisable' portraits that Picasso painted to entertain the assembled company as a reaction against the strain of completing the enormous *Guernica* mural for the Spanish pavilion at the Exposition Internationale in Paris.[14] As the situation in Spain became ever more critical, the friends' pursuit of pleasure was punctuated by agonised discussions about the likely outcome. Little wonder that the comedy of Picasso's paintings has a hysterical edge, and his technique a violent urgency: catharsis as much as relaxation was involved. In the most outrageous of these brazen caricatures (127), Paul Éluard, dressed in the traditional cap and costume of an Arlésienne and with the bright green skin of a lizard, suckles a tabby kitten. In her portrait (129), Nusch Éluard wears the hat of the women of Nice and, like her husband, grins wickedly, her eyes transformed into 'bright-coloured Mediterranean fish'.[15] Choosing to ignore her ethereal beauty, this time Picasso focused on Nusch's vivacity and ringing laughter, captured so memorably in the photograph Lee Miller took during the same holiday (128). *Nusch Éluard* may look as if it was dashed off, and passages like her blue curls and the yellow stars decorating her hat were obviously brushed with the uninhibited energy of a child scribbling, but in fact it involved substantial revision. The background was originally dark brown,[16] and by painting it over in white and pale blue, Picasso lightened the overall mood. He took care to frame Nusch's profile with a black shadow so that the pastel pinks, blues and greens composing her face commanded attention. The result is like a playing-card with Nusch as Queen of Misrule.

Lee Miller was the subject of several of these high-voltage pictures. Penrose bought the best of them as a gift for her to commemorate the auspicious beginning of their romance (132). It was painted very spontaneously: there are drips, lots of hairs from Picasso's brush caught in the paint, and details like her green lips and dangling earring were done in a moment. In his memoirs Penrose called it 'an astonishing likeness ... put together in such a way that it was undoubtedly her but with none of the conventional attributes of a portrait.' And when he showed it to their two-year-old son for the first time, 'His instant cry of delight was "Mummy, Mummy".'[17] Whether or not Picasso had met Miller when she was living with Man Ray (and sometimes acting as his assistant) in 1929–32, he would have seen some of the latter's hundreds of photographs of her, both nude and clothed, and possibly also some of the many fashion photographs published in *Vogue*. In the great majority of these images Miller was idealised as the incarnation of perfect beauty, grace and serenity, and nobody – Man Ray included – could resist introducing allusions to classical sculpture and Renaissance painting, or lighting her in such a way that she appears almost divine. Picasso was having none of this. He knew that the real woman was more than a beautiful

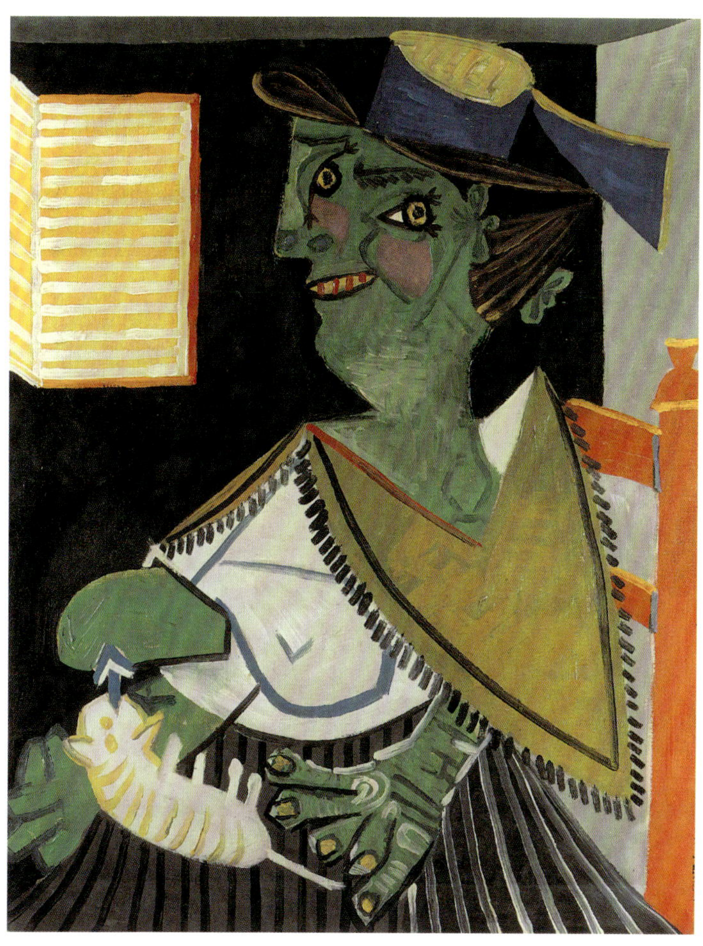

127 *Woman with a Cat (Portrait of Paul Éluard)*, 30 August 1937

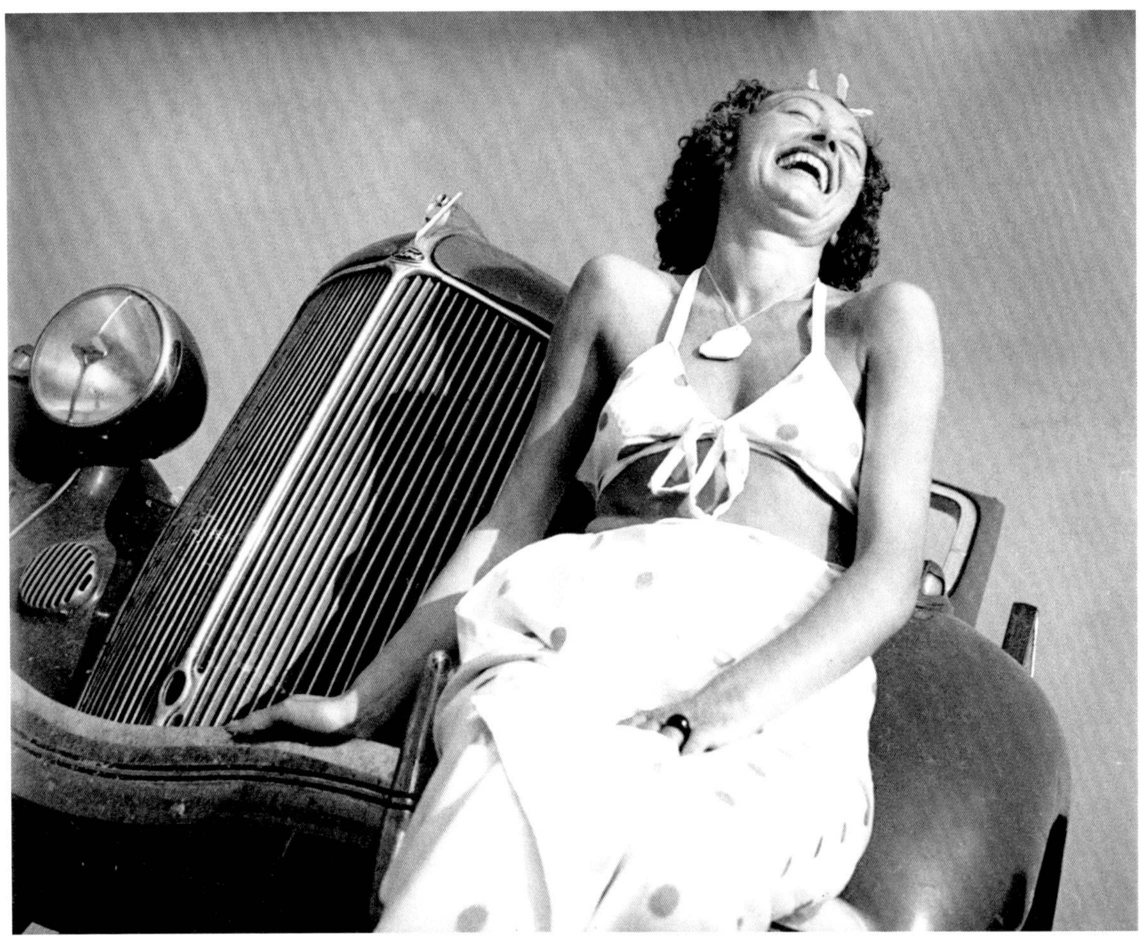

128 *Nusch Éluard*. Photograph by Lee Miller, 1937

face and body, more than a graceful clothes-horse, and he apparently felt that, with her racy wit and libertine sexuality, Miller deserved to be treated with friendly banter rather than awestruck homage. So, although he exactly reproduced the undulation of her profile – as can be seen if his painting is compared with Man Ray's famous, solarised profile portrait (130)[18] – he showed her grinning broadly. The idealising photographs never did this, partly because goddesses do not grin, partly because her teeth had gaps. Picasso also endowed her with spiky, club-like hands that look nothing like her own, but give a sense of the ruthless courage with which she pursued her desires. Perhaps, moreover, he was struck by Miller's ability to put on a performance

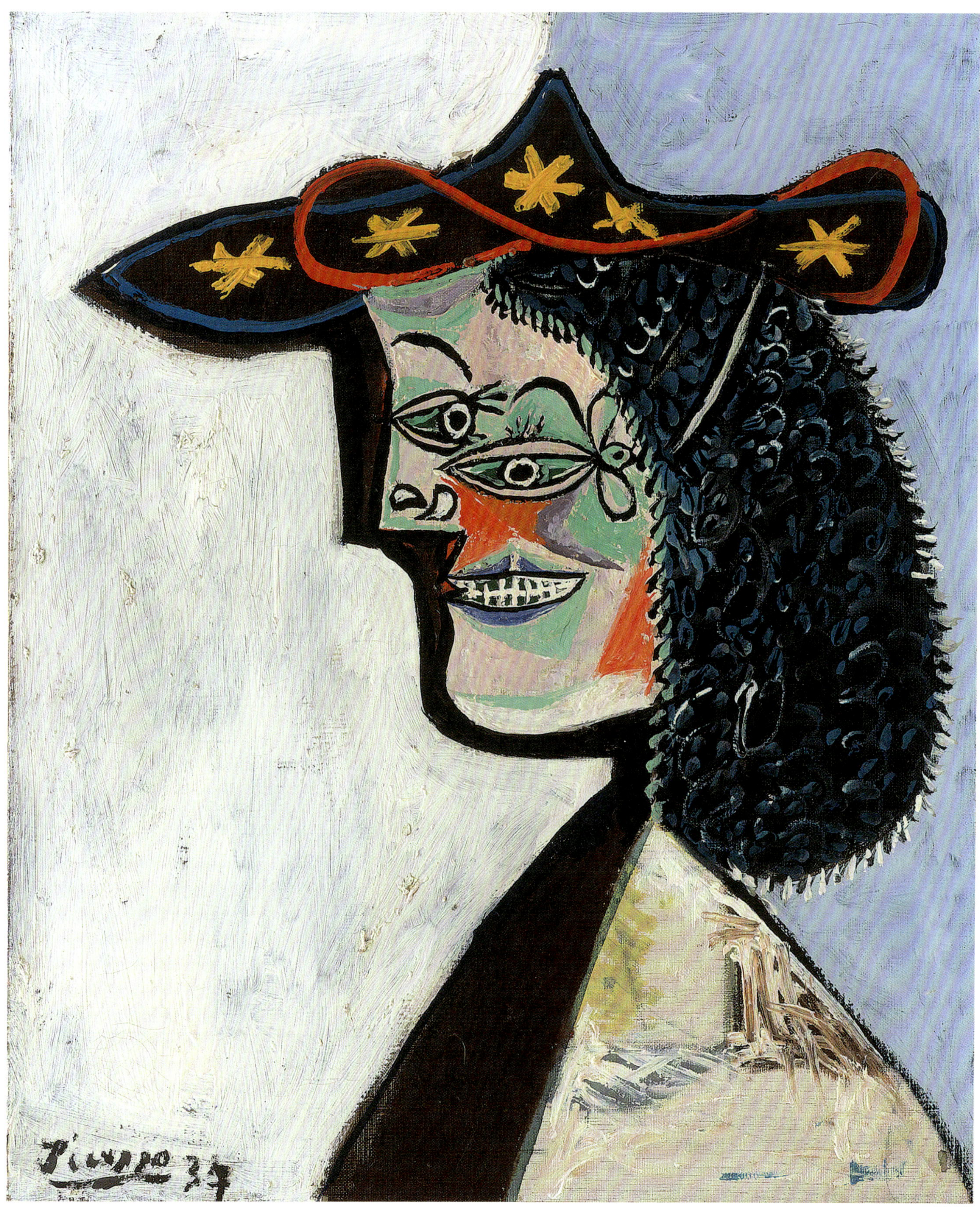

129 *Nusch Éluard*, 1937 (B, L)

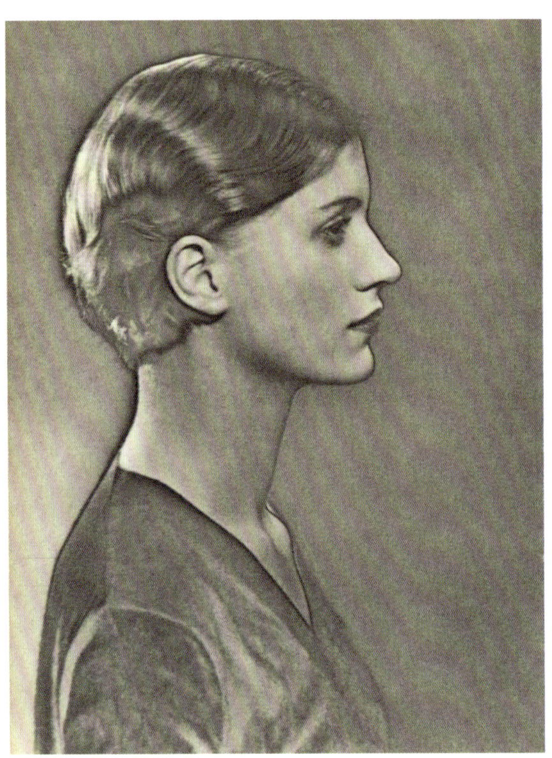

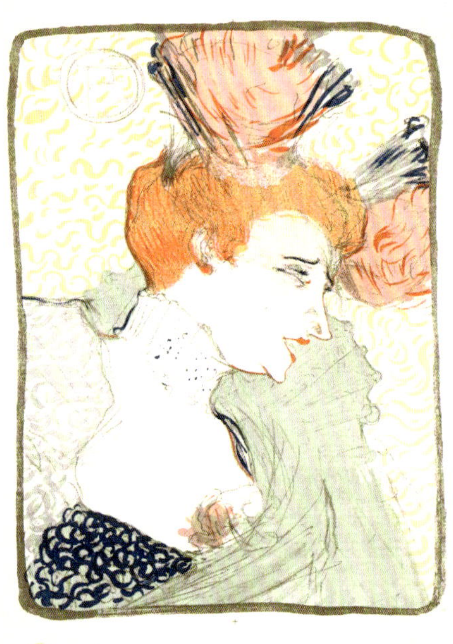

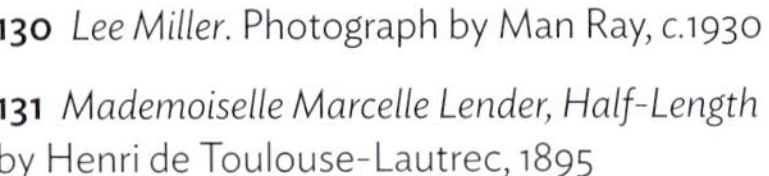

130 *Lee Miller*. Photograph by Man Ray, *c.*1930

131 *Mademoiselle Marcelle Lender, Half-Length* by Henri de Toulouse-Lautrec, 1895

– to look like an angel while remaining a devil inside (to paraphrase her own account of herself in her heyday).[19] If so, this would account for the similarities to Toulouse-Lautrec's lithographs of famous cabaret *artistes* like Yvette Gilbert, Jane Avril and Marcelle Lender (131). Like Toulouse-Lautrec, Picasso united caricatural exaggeration of his vivacious subject with eye-catching decorative design to produce an irresistibly animated image.

The comic mode of the Mougins series was carried over into the painting of Maya in a sailor suit, when the child was nearly two and a half years old (133). She bears the imprint of both parents: her father's name emblazoned on her sailor's cap, her mother's fair skin and hair. To please her, Picasso dressed her like her favourite doll – she did not have a sailor suit herself.[20] And lest anyone mistake the boisterous child for a boy, Picasso stamped the log seen between her open legs with

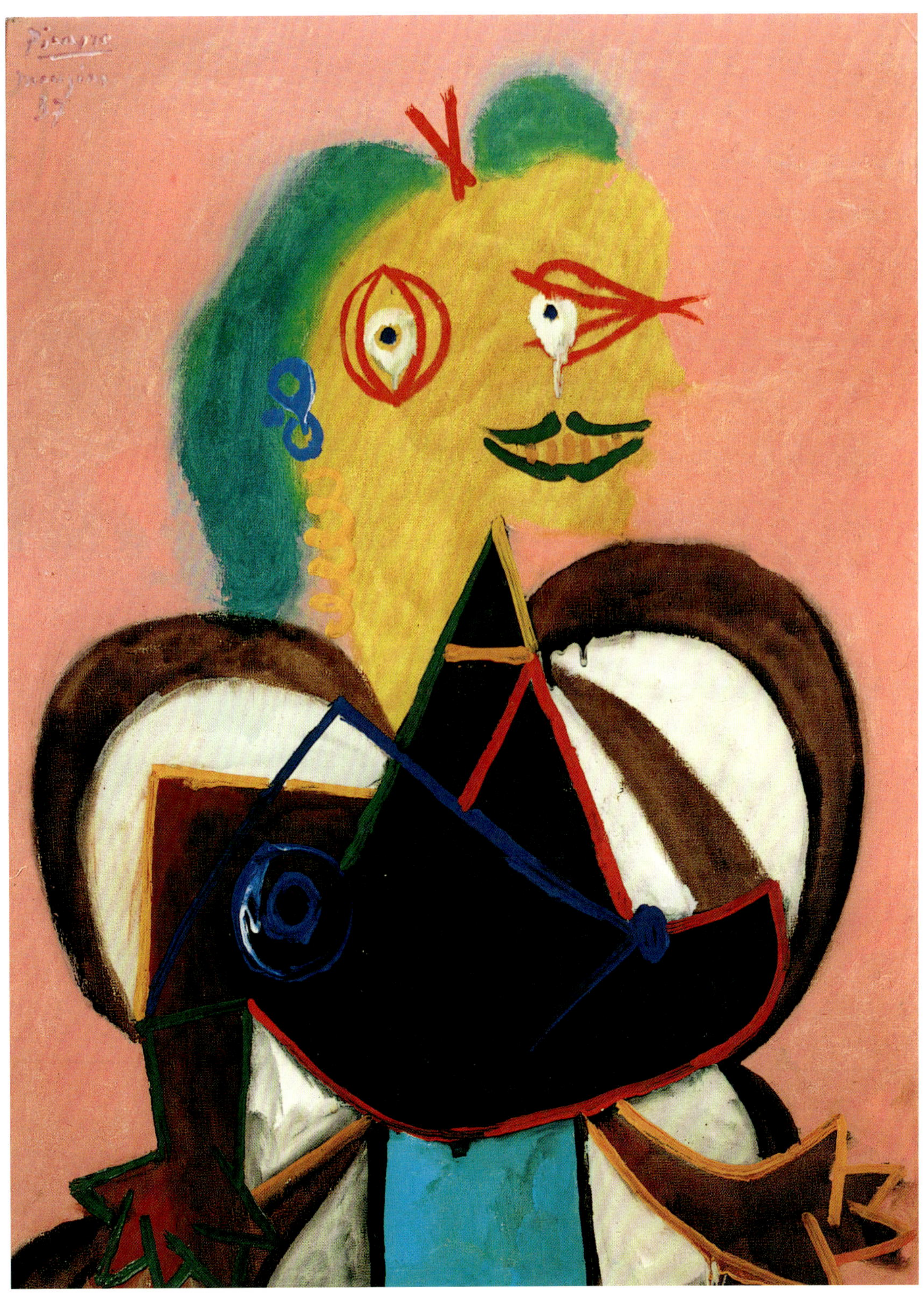

132 *Portrait of Lee Miller à l'Arlésienne*, 1937 (B, L)

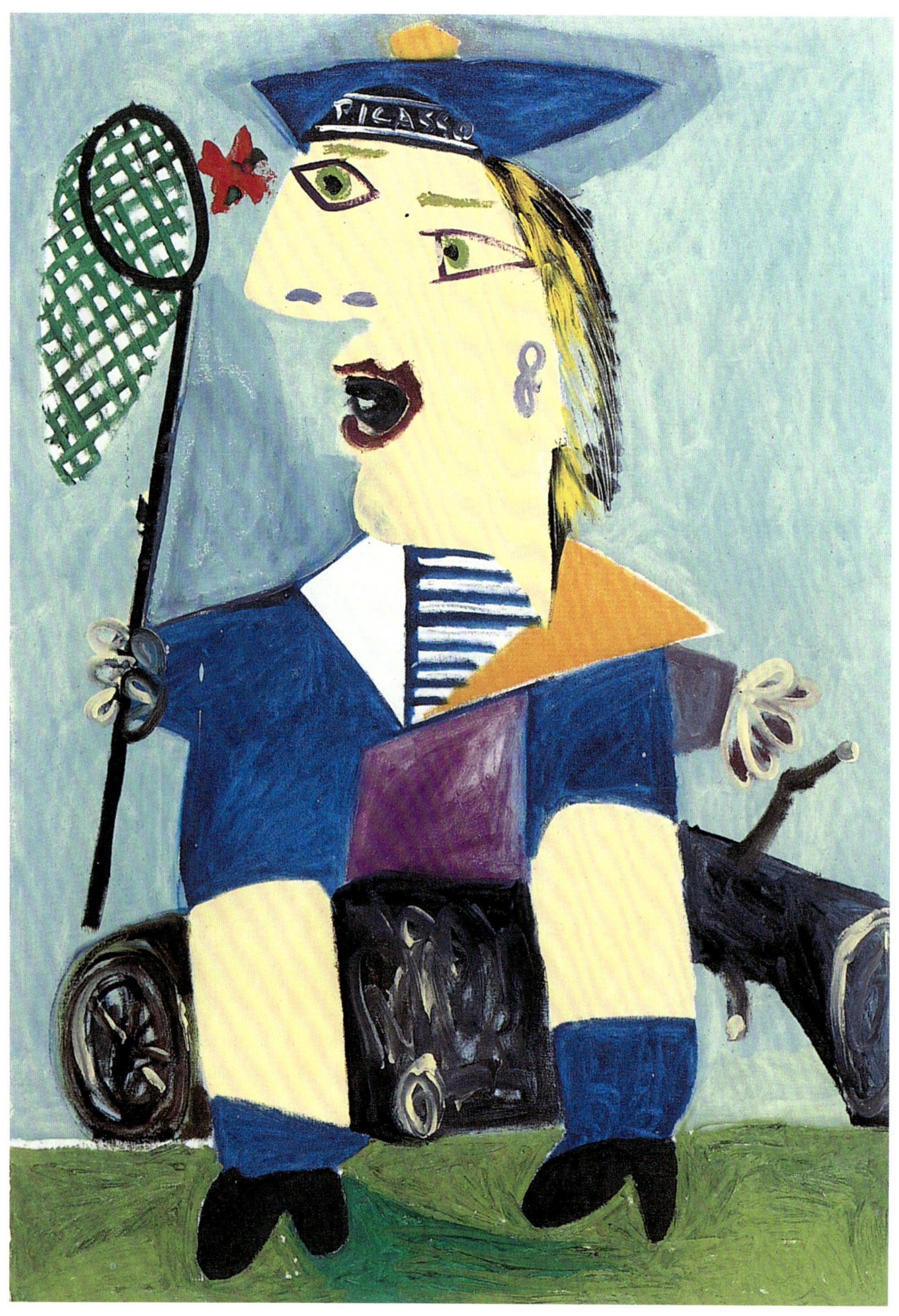

133 *Maya in a Sailor Suit*, 23 January 1938 (B, L)

a vagina-shaped knot. The simplified rendering of her head, body and costume, and the crude technique of the painting constitute a virtual pastiche of child art. This was yet another case of Picasso purposefully matching style to subject, and there are clear echoes of Matisse's portrait of his daughter Marguerite (1906; Musée national Picasso-Paris). Greatly admiring its radical simplifications, Picasso had obtained this painting by exchange with the artist in 1907. Like Matisse and like his Surrealist friends, Picasso considered the art of children of kindergarten age a prime model of pure, liberated creativity. But for him it had special meaning beyond this, for when still a child, he had been taught to 'draw like Raphael', and 'It took me many years to learn how to draw like ... children.'[21]

A very different Maya is portrayed in the drawing executed at the end of August 1943 in the ominous third year of the Nazi Occupation of France (134). She was then nearing her eighth birthday and living with her mother in an apartment near the Bastille, a short walk from Picasso's rambling two-floor domain at 7 Rue des Grands-Augustins. Father and daughter saw each other regularly and he liked to record the changes in her appearance as she grew older. On this occasion, he scrutinised her profile intently, interested to gauge which traits she had inherited from him, which from her mother, and where a seamless blending took place. After all, Picasso had often portrayed himself and Marie-Thérèse in profile and knew the peculiar ripple of each of those contours by heart. Maya behaves impeccably: no sign here of the shrieks of pleasure or rage evoked in the painting of her in a sailor suit. Nor is there any pretence of naïvety on Picasso's part. On the contrary, the precision of the contour of her profile – as sharp as a silhouette cut out with a pair of scissors – the refined description of eye, nostril and mouth, and the delicate handling of the pastel suggest that exquisite Renaissance portraits by François Clouet (135) and Hans Holbein were his

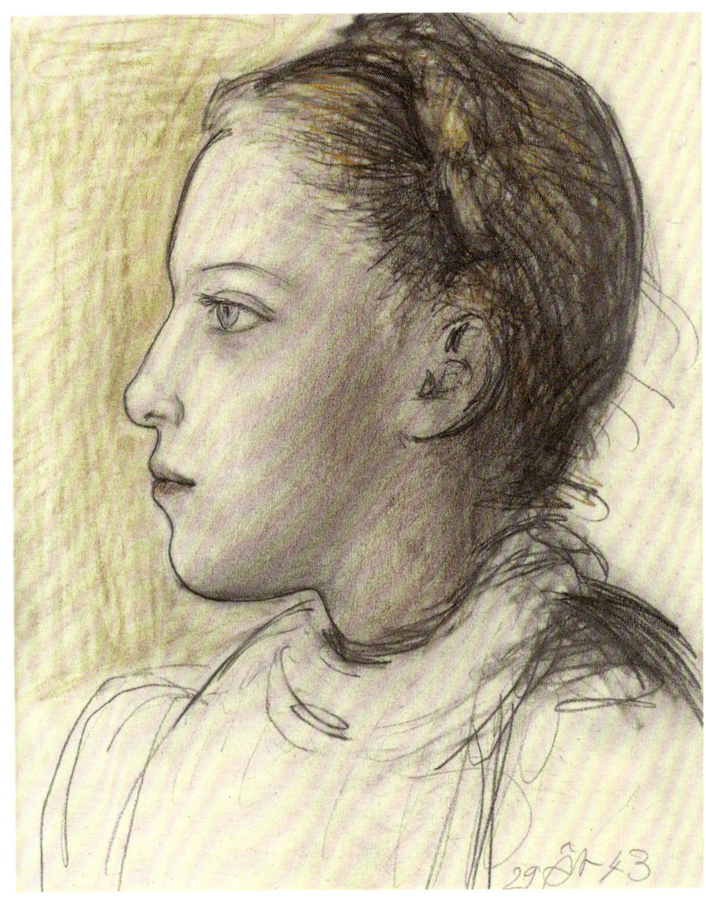

134 *The Artist's Daughter, Maya*, 29 August 1943

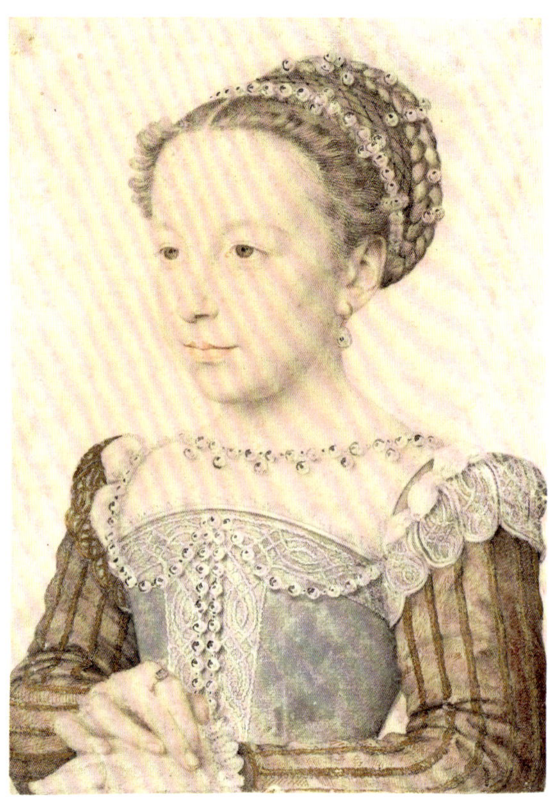

135 *Marguerite de France, Reine de Navarre* by François Clouet, *c.*1559

models. Maya's personality was not the issue in this drawing, whereas it had been in the caricatural painting. For once, Picasso behaved like a professional portraitist, documenting her appearance without cloying sentimentality, but with the degree of tactful idealisation normally required from a commissioned portrait.

DORA MAAR AND THE FACE OF WAR

Marie-Thérèse Walter never became Picasso's publicly acknowledged partner after his separation from Olga in 1935. She had no part in his professional or intellectual life in Paris and never accompanied him to meetings with the Surrealists, whom he saw much of before the outbreak of the war. The position of recognised *maîtresse* was occupied instead by the painter and photographer Dora Maar, who participated actively in this avant-garde milieu and already knew many of his friends. They were introduced by Paul Éluard in the autumn of 1935. That winter Maar photographed Picasso in her studio and he photographed her in Boisgeloup the following March.[22] Portraits and symbolic images celebrating her entry into his life proliferated from August 1936 onwards. Some, in Picasso's charming phrase, were *'fait par coeur'* (made by heart),[23] but others were done from life.

His profile portrait of Dora Maar (136) is not dated – the dedication in red ink (dated '22.11.50') was added later – but it is similar to one of the photos Picasso took of Maar in Boisgeloup in March 1936.[24] Both express his appreciation of the classic nobility of her profile, her brow lining up perfectly with her chin. She was a highly intelligent, cultivated woman, whose former lovers included the 'dissident' Surrealist Georges Bataille, and in this drawing he gave her an attentive, farsighted gaze, the slight lift of the head suggesting her independence of mind. Its essential truthfulness is confirmed by Lee Miller's photograph of Maar alone in her apartment displaying that strong, brave, reserved profile some twenty years later, with the drawing hanging on the wall behind as a poignant reminder of the passage of time (137). Above the fireplace is the expressively distorted portrait now in the Berggruen Museum that hints at the emotional instability Picasso found equally stimulating.

Like the contemporary drawings on canvas of Marie-Thérèse Walter (see 123) and Nusch Éluard

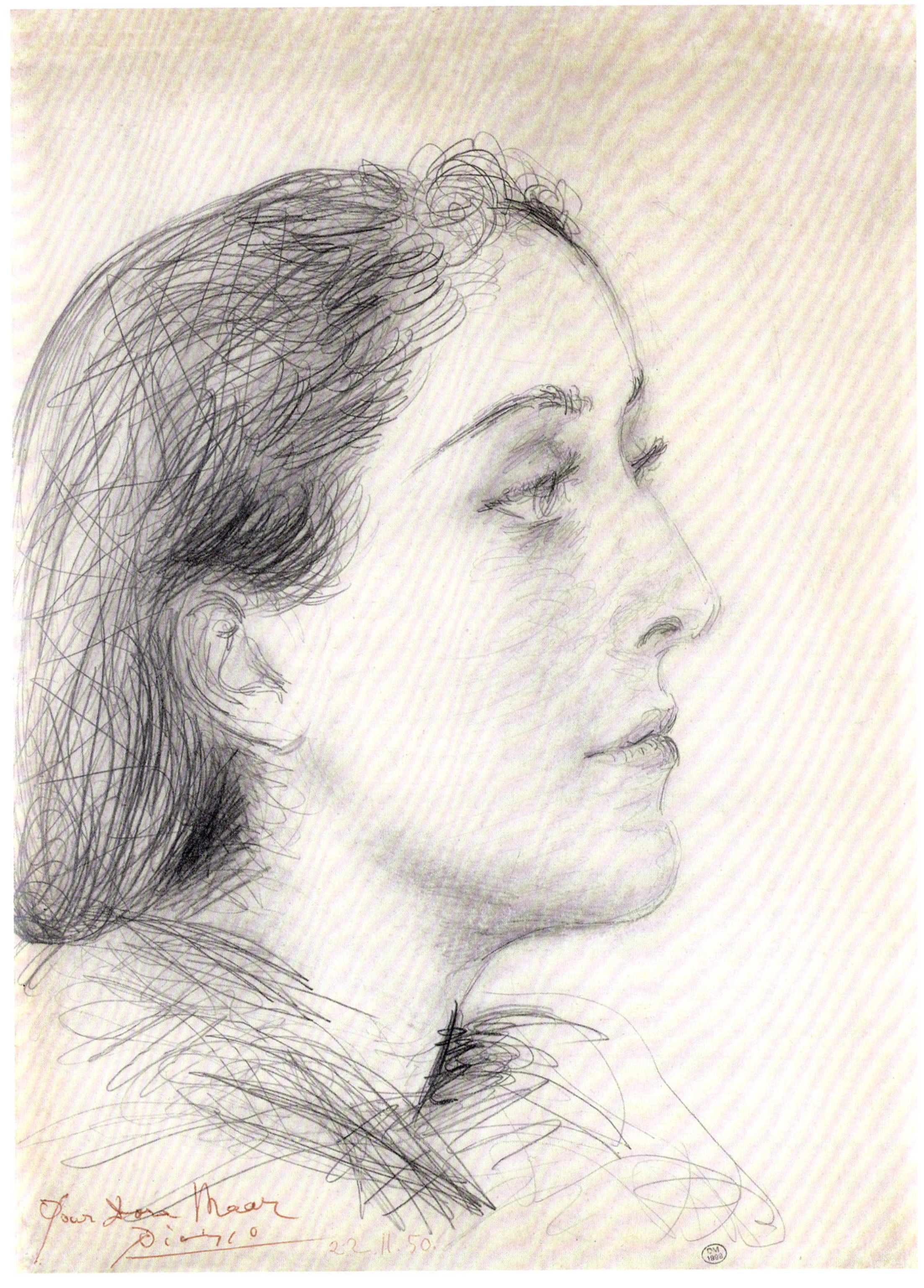

136 *Dora Maar*, c.1937 (B, L)

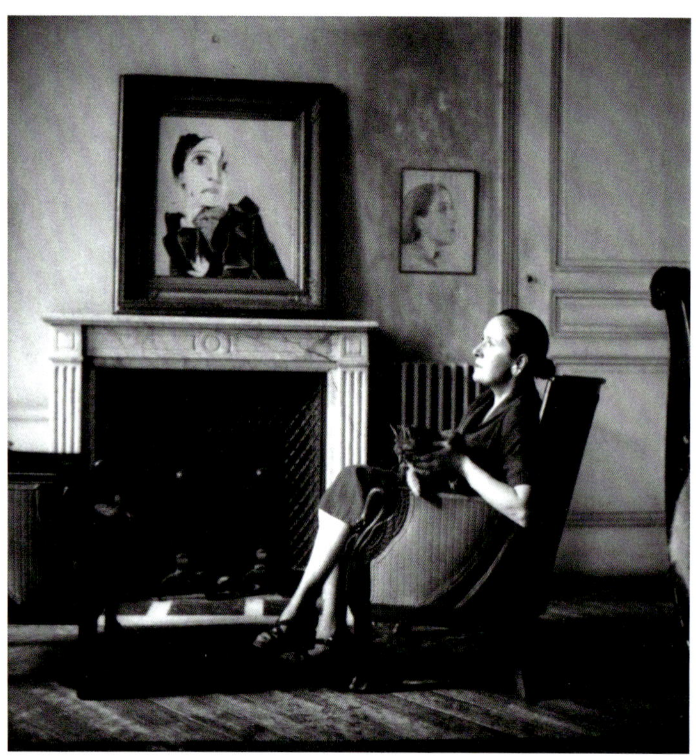

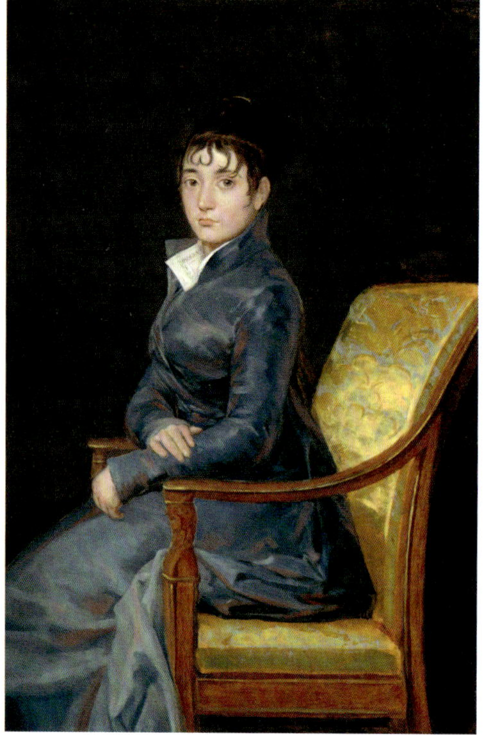

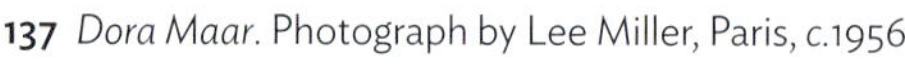

137 *Dora Maar*. Photograph by Lee Miller, Paris, *c.*1956

138 *Thérèse Louise de Sureda* by Francisco de Goya, *c.*1803–4

(see 125), *Dora Maar Seated* (139) is set up as a formal, posed portrait. Picasso chose paper, not canvas, as his support, and began by drawing freely in pen and ink with a spidery line. Afterwards, he covered over much of the pen-work of her head and torso with gouache and very dilute oil paint, but the calligraphic swirls and flourishes beneath the thin washes of colour can still be glimpsed. In 1938 this ornamental and at times excessively intricate graphic style was developed specifically to express what he judged to be Maar's neurotic, 'Kafkaesque' personality: he told Françoise Gilot that, with Kafka in mind, he would use his fountain pen to transform little spots and stains on the walls of her apartment into minutely detailed insects.[25] Gilot's own slightly tart description of the woman she supplanted fits Maar's image in this portrait rather well:

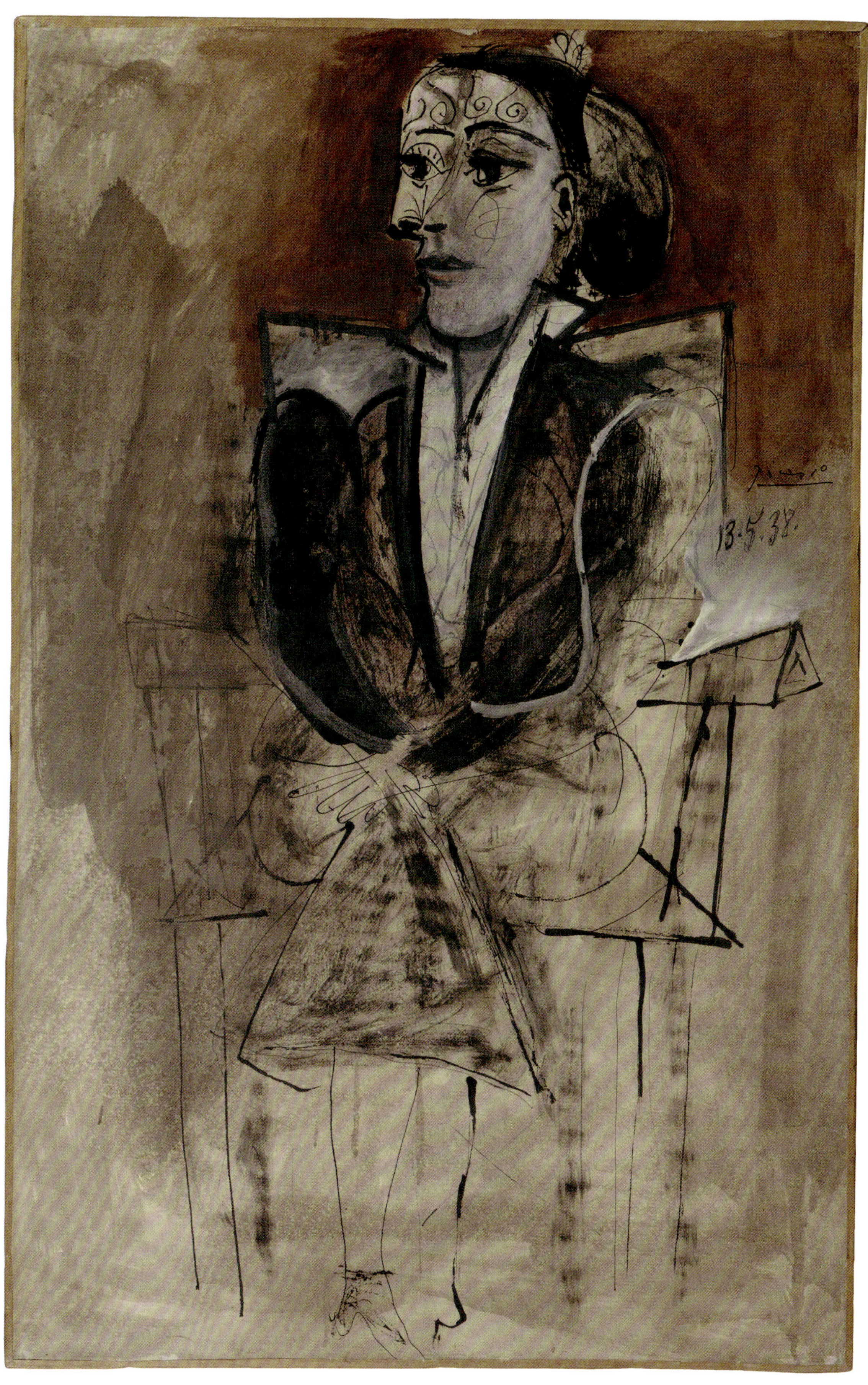

139 *Dora Maar Seated*, 13 May 1938 (B, L)

> She had a beautiful oval face but a heavy jaw .... The most remarkable thing about her was her extraordinary immobility. She talked little, made no gestures at all, and there was something in her bearing that was more than dignity – a certain rigidity. There is a French expression that is very apt: she carried herself like the holy sacrament.[26]

In *Dora Maar Seated* Dora's distinctive features – large eyes, broad brow, straight nose, full mouth, heavy chin, dark hair – are treated in a formulaic manner and, as in a traditional *portrait-charge*, her head is disproportionately large and the lower half of her body represented in a cursory fashion.[27] Her rigid carriage, neatly crossed hands and especially her tightly clamped legs betray the nervousness normally concealed by her 'holy sacrament' aloofness. Equally telling in Picasso's characterisation is the Spanish quality of the portrait. Maar had lived in Argentina in her youth and spoke Spanish fluently, and when they first met he encouraged her to grow her hair so that she could dress it in the Spanish style he loved. To see her in terms of Spanish painting came naturally to him, and on this occasion Picasso's probable point of reference was Goya's portrait of the ramrod-stiff Thérèse Louise de Sureda (138).[28] Picasso began by giving Maar the black kiss-curls of Señora de Sureda, and all the modifications he made to the initial ink drawing brought the portrait ever closer to Goya's: the washes of colour applied to Dora's head to make it more fleshy and painterly; the V-shape of the starched white blouse under the tight-fitting black jacket; and the contrasting, coloured background to offset the figure. Neither Walter nor Nusch Éluard was treated in this manner: each woman was accorded the graphic style that suited Picasso's vision of her.

Picasso and Dora Maar never cohabited. When their affair began, his live-in companion was Jaume Sabartés. They had seen hardly anything of each other after Sabartés left Barcelona for Guatemala, but had remained in touch by letter and when Picasso begged him to come to Rue La Boétie to be his confidant, assistant and secretary, Sabartés readily agreed. He and his wife arrived in Paris in November 1935 in the midst of the crisis that followed the birth of Maya, when writing had replaced painting as Picasso's principal form of creative expression. One of Sabartés's main duties was to decipher and type up the chaotic manuscripts of the surrealistic prose-poetry that poured from Picasso's pen – texts hailed by the Surrealists as equal in importance to his paintings.[29] Another was to keep him company and Picasso's first portrait of him since 1904 derived from one such occasion (140). On Christmas Eve 1938, Picasso was in bed suffering from a severe attack of sciatica and to pass the time they discussed portraiture. Frustratingly, Sabartés offers no summary of what was said beyond remarking that 'as usual' Picasso took the lead, but he implies that Spanish painting was a topic because at one point he confessed that he had always wanted to be portrayed 'with ruffs, like those gentlemen of the sixteenth century, and with a plumed hat to cover up my bald head.'[30] Picasso knew that Sabartés had immersed himself, to the point of total identification, in the visual arts and literature of Spain in the Golden Age and immediately promised to paint 'a full-size portrait, with a nude woman, and a very lean dog by your side ... a dog like Kazbek' (Picasso's Afghan hound). Fully expecting that nothing would come of this flight of fancy, Sabartés was gratified to discover the next day that, in his absence, Picasso had made a drawing corresponding to his whim, pressing so hard with his pencil that he almost tore the cheap paper. Because his friend's features were indelibly etched on his memory, the drawing, though flippant, is an excellent likeness as well as a clever pastiche

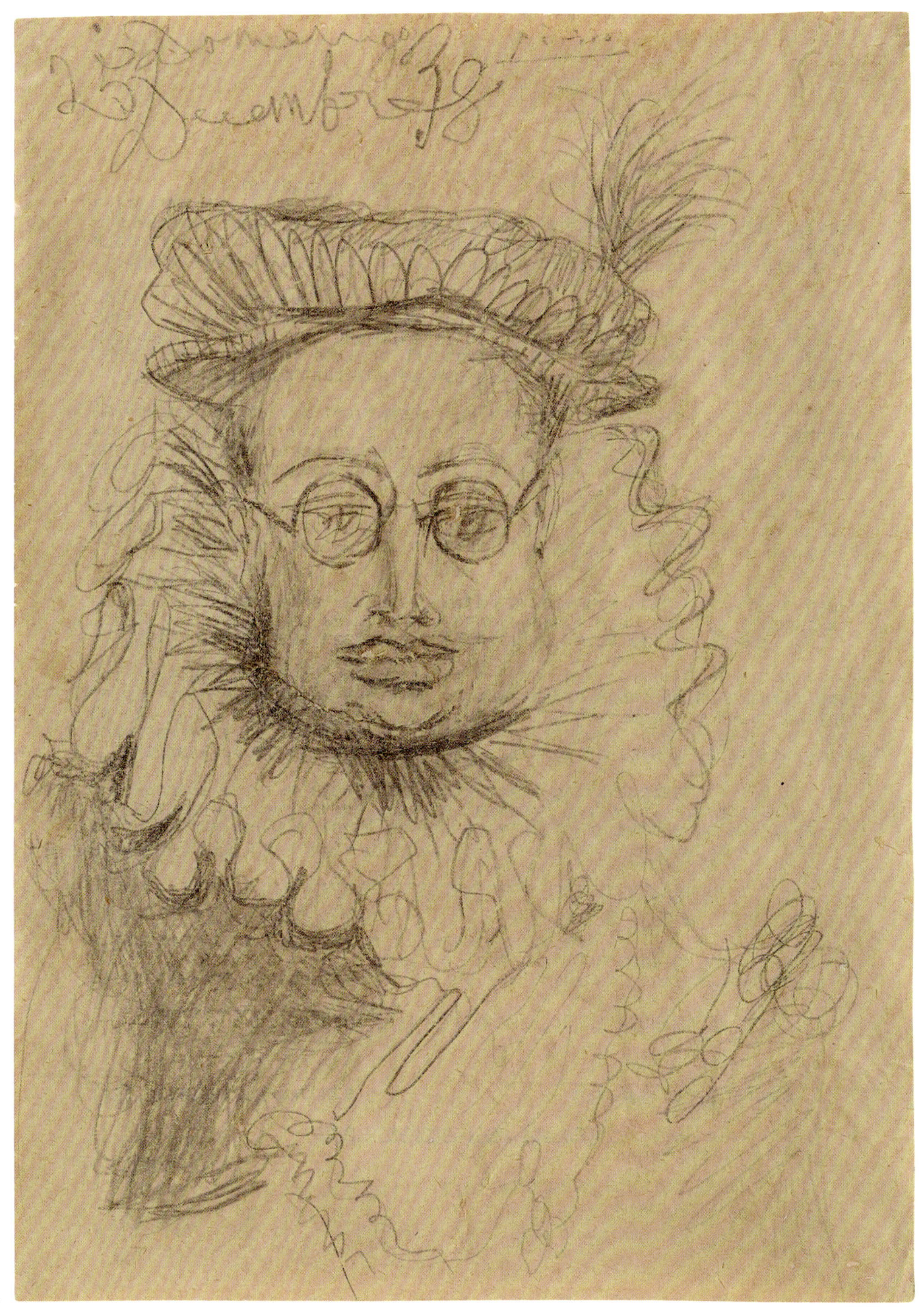

140 *Jaume Sabartés as a Gentleman of the Age of Philip II,*
25 December 1938 (B)

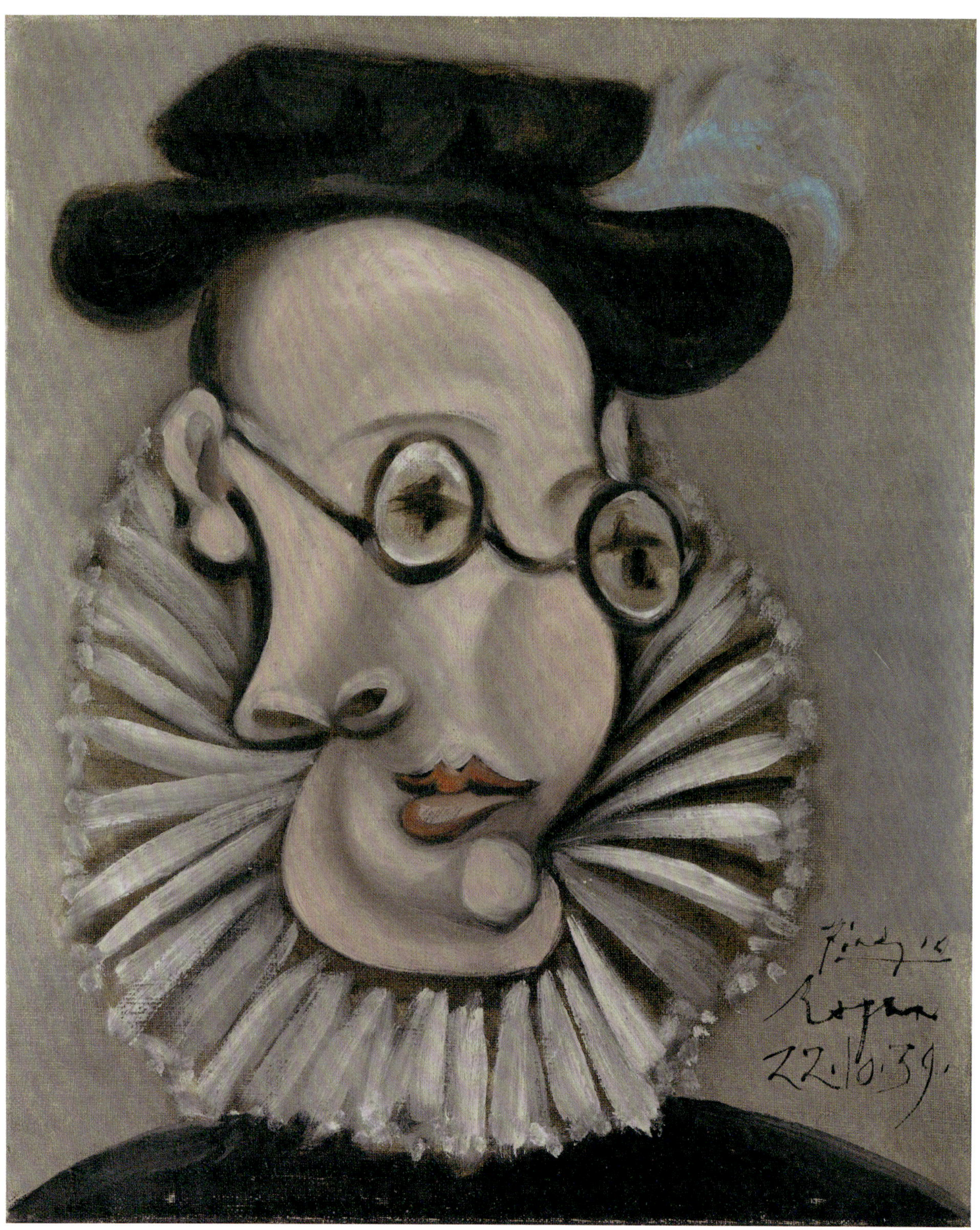

141 *Jaume Sabartés with Ruff and Cap*, 22 October 1939 (B, L)

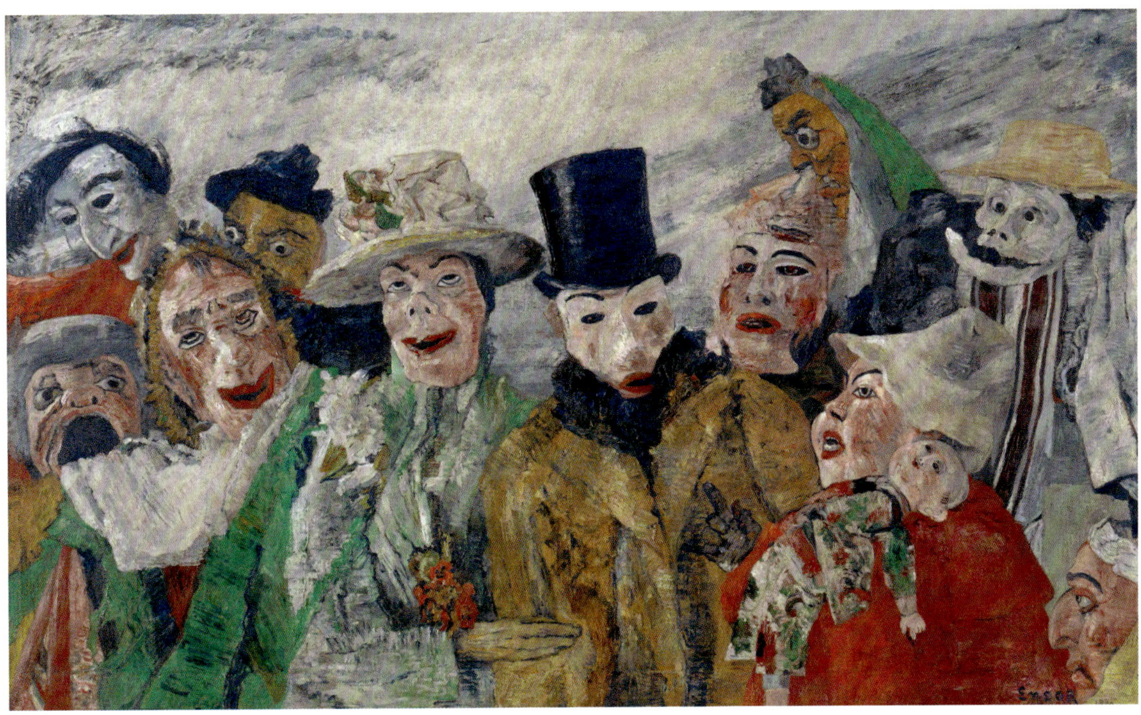

142 *The Intrigue* by James Ensor, 1890

of court portraits by Golden-Age artists such as Sanchez Coello.

The follow-up to this episode took place in October 1939 when Picasso, Maar, Sabartés and his wife – and in separate lodgings, Walter, her mother and Maya – were all staying in Royan on France's Atlantic coast, waiting nervously to see how the war between France and Germany would develop. It took the form of a painting (141) with exactly the same format and almost the same dimensions as the naturalistic portrait of Sabartés Picasso had painted in 1904 (see 55). Like many of the contemporary paintings of Walter and Maar, the head is a synthesis of a range of viewpoints, as if Sabartés were turning this way and that, and in consequence is disturbingly monstrous. Other aspects of the painting that are unique to it toy with Sabartés's desire for a portrait in period costume, and its tone is provokingly hard to gauge. How should one interpret the fact that his head is not attached to his shoulders but, like a moulded and painted carnival mask, seems to hang in front of the ruff, with his spectacles placed upside down and the plumed hat balanced precariously on top? (These absurdities were absent from the drawing made on Christmas Day 1938.) By treating his head as a hollow mask, was Picasso simply flagging up the fact of masquerade? Or was he suggesting something disquieting about Sabartés's personality – or about human nature in general? Was this portrait effectively a Symbolist painting in the tradition of James Ensor's terrifying paintings with carnival masks (142)?

Sabartés admitted that he was initially nonplussed. Previous portraits had not been flattering but none had exhibited such outlandish deformations. However, he soon realised that 'My portrait has truly all the characteristics of my physiognomy, and only the most essential ones' – namely, his severe myopia, the curious form of his lips that had always fascinated Picasso, his pointed nose and jutting chin, and his smooth, bald, domed head. He also recognised that it possessed a formal and colouristic harmony of 'great lyricism' inspired, appropriately, by Spanish painting.[31] So, when some weeks later an acquaintance described the painting as a 'caricature', Sabartés objected:

> A caricature is a kind of 'minimum' portrait, done with the avowed purpose of ridiculing a person, whereas a portrait is the 'maximum' expression of a personality, the qualities of which the painter emphasizes by means of lines, colours or both, as in this case, without, however, overlooking certain features which might seem ridiculous to anyone else; for no one is perfect .... But when we are caught upon the canvas by a real artist we are surprised to find what he discovers, and prefer to consider it a caricature.[32]

Here, Sabartés drew a crucial distinction between the caricaturist's intention to 'ridicule' and the artist's intention to achieve a psychologically deeper, non-photographic kind of likeness; but he also suggested that catching the likeness of someone in a 'maximum' portrait necessarily involves identifying the very traits of physiognomy, physique, gesture and dress that the caricaturist exaggerates for humorous or satirical purposes. This shrewd assessment of the fundamentals of portraiture is in line with Picasso's remark that 'all good portraits are in some degree caricatures.'[33] Neverthess, it is fair to say that Picasso eroded the boundary of decorum between the two genres to a degree that few other artists have dared.

Picasso's outrages against 'nature' and pictorial decorum climaxed in paintings made of Maar during the Occupation in which the classic beauty of her features – honoured in his drawings from life (see 136) – was violently travestied. The context was all-important for, as Picasso explained to an American war correspondent who interviewed him shortly after the Liberation of Paris, although he had not documented the events of the war like a photographer, 'I have no doubt that the war is in these paintings I have done.'[34] Because Maar was highly strung, sensitive and often wracked by anxiety, she perfectly exemplified the prevailing atmosphere of dread. Inscribed 9 June 1941, *Woman in a Hat* (143) was executed almost exactly a year after Nazi troops marched into Paris (14 June 1940). Picasso and Maar had returned to Paris towards the end of August 1940 and they experienced the effects of the Occupation at first hand, including the mounting persecution of the Jews. In the painting, Maar embodies psychic tension, her head and body registering the corkscrew twisting of someone in the grip of acute distress. In a nightmarish metamorphosis, the wooden chair has fused with her torso, acting simultaneously as a necessary support and a rack-like instrument of

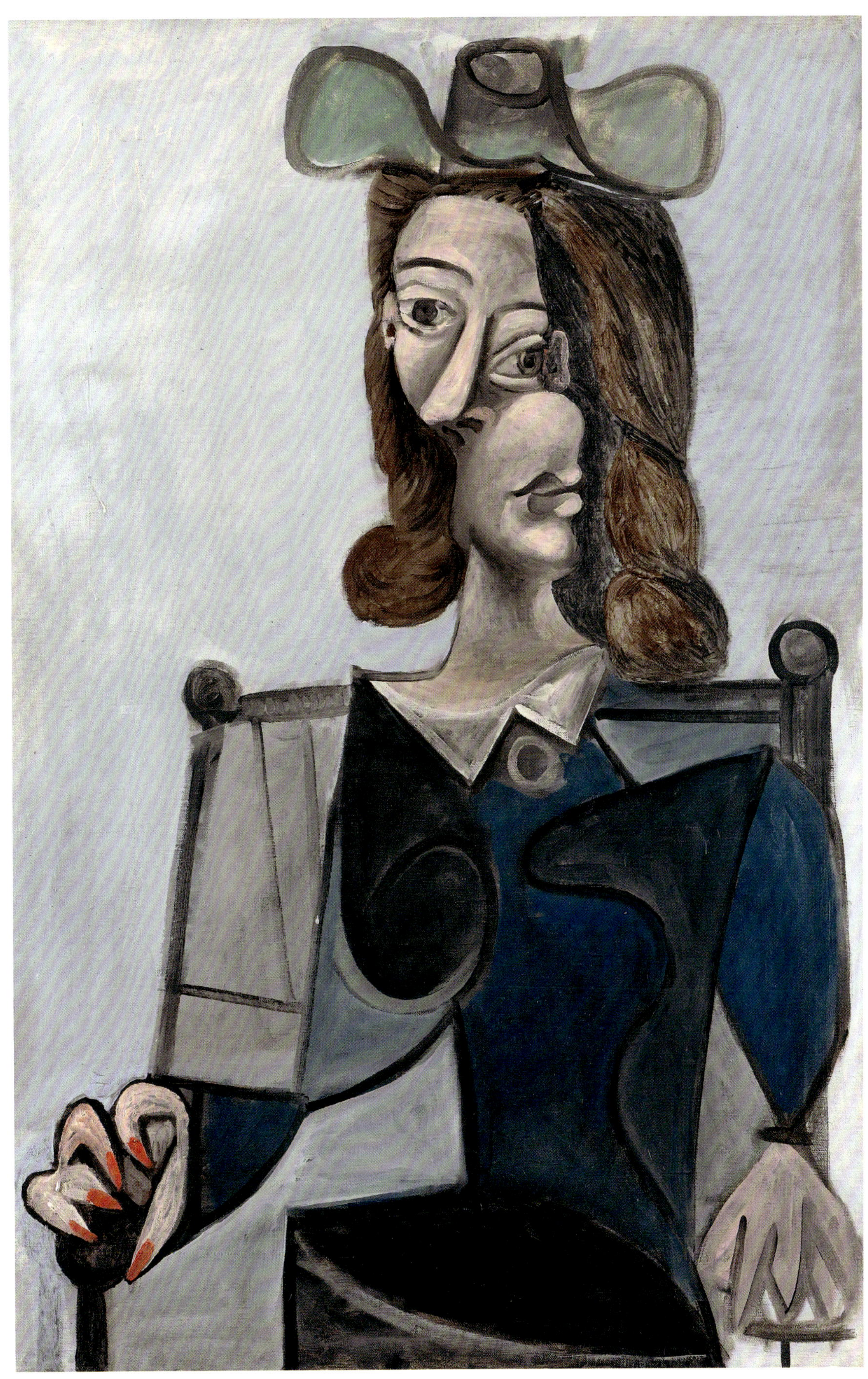

143 *Woman in a Hat*, 9 June 1941 (B, L)

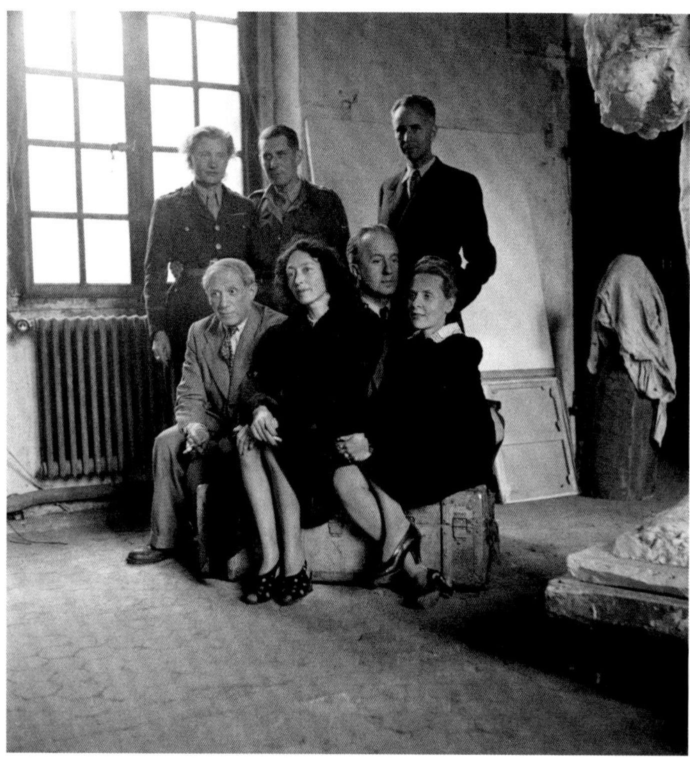

144 Left to right (back row): Lee Miller, Roland Penrose, Louis Aragon; (front row): Pablo Picasso, Nusch Éluard, Paul Éluard and Elsa Triolet. Photograph by Lee Miller, September 1944

torture. The predominately blue-grey palette of the painting harks back to Picasso's Blue period, where it symbolised misery, deprivation and the imminence of death. The skeletal structure of the chair and grey cast of her flesh suggest a body in the process of decomposition. Yet the Dora of this painting strives to keep up appearances, for her hairstyle, hat, fitted blue dress and painted, claw-like finger-nails are Picasso's knowing caricature of the fashions of the moment, and her stiffly formal frontal pose is that of an enthroned Spanish Infanta. The pitiful comedy of these worldly pretensions heightens the sense of existential conflict. When Picasso showed Françoise Gilot this and other 'very tortured' paintings of Maar in 1943, she realised instantly that the deformations were 'symbolic of human tragedy'.[35]

Not all of Picasso's Occupation-period portraits were of this overtly expressionist type. In the nude portrait of Nusch Éluard (145) dated 19 August 1941, he reverted to the romantic style of his Saltimbanque series of 1905. This was appropriate, given her past as an acrobat, but Picasso chose a deathly blue-grey monochrome in preference to the warm palette of the Saltimbanque pictures. Nusch was thirty-four years old when Picasso painted this picture, but no longer the laughing Niçoise of her Mougins portrait (see 129) or the elegant sophisticate of the drawing on canvas (see 125). Here she is the *femme-enfant* idolised by the Surrealists. This vision of adolescent frailty and vulnerability, communicated as much through the extreme delicacy of the handling as through the image itself, was not pure fantasy: the Éluards led an extremely precarious existence throughout the Occupation owing to their active engagement in the Resistance. Thinner than ever, Nusch visibly suffered from the deprivations they endured (144) and her premature death aged thirty-nine in November 1946 was attributed by her friends to the drastic effect of her wartime experiences.[36]

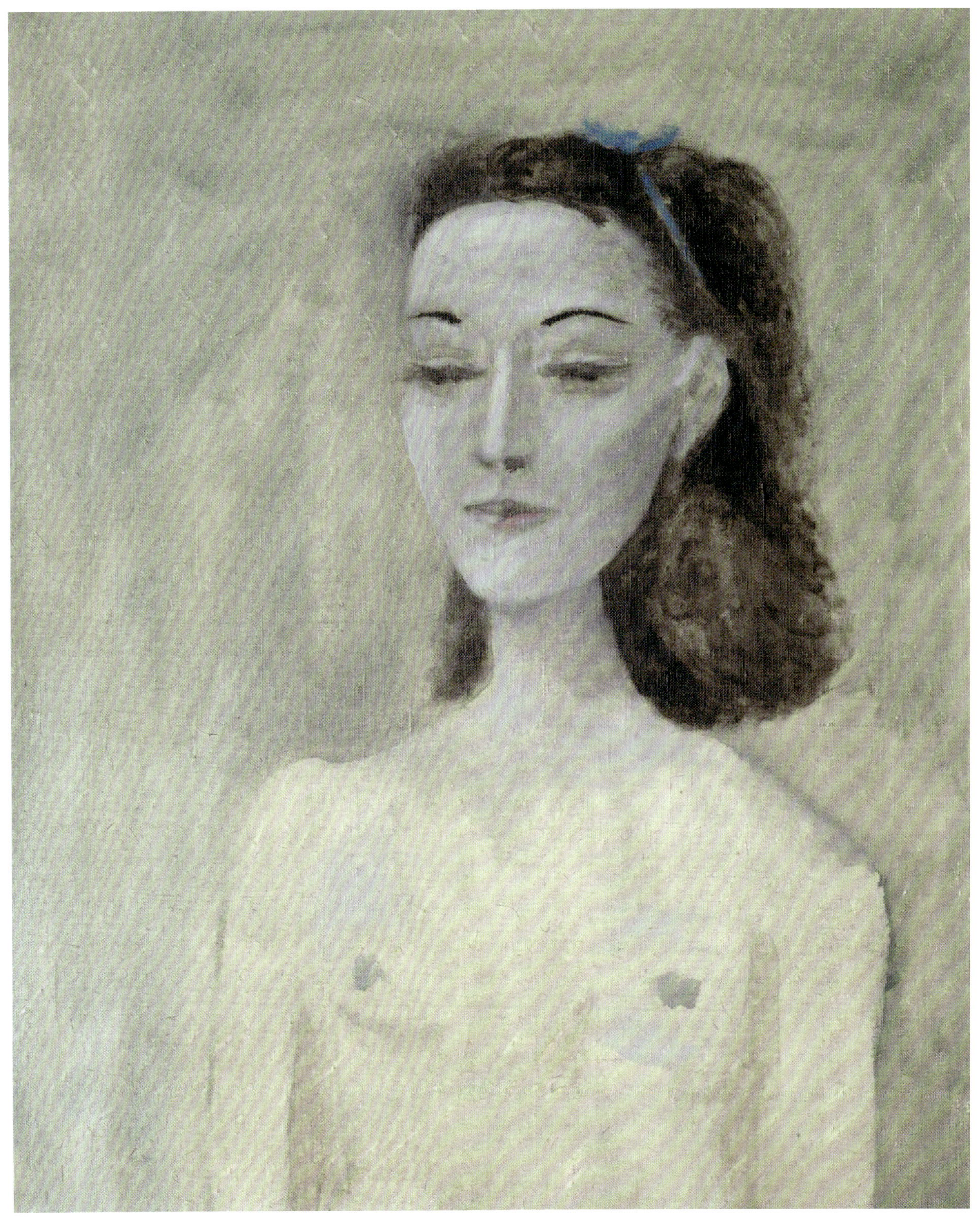

145 *Madame Paul Éluard*, 19 August 1941 (B, L)

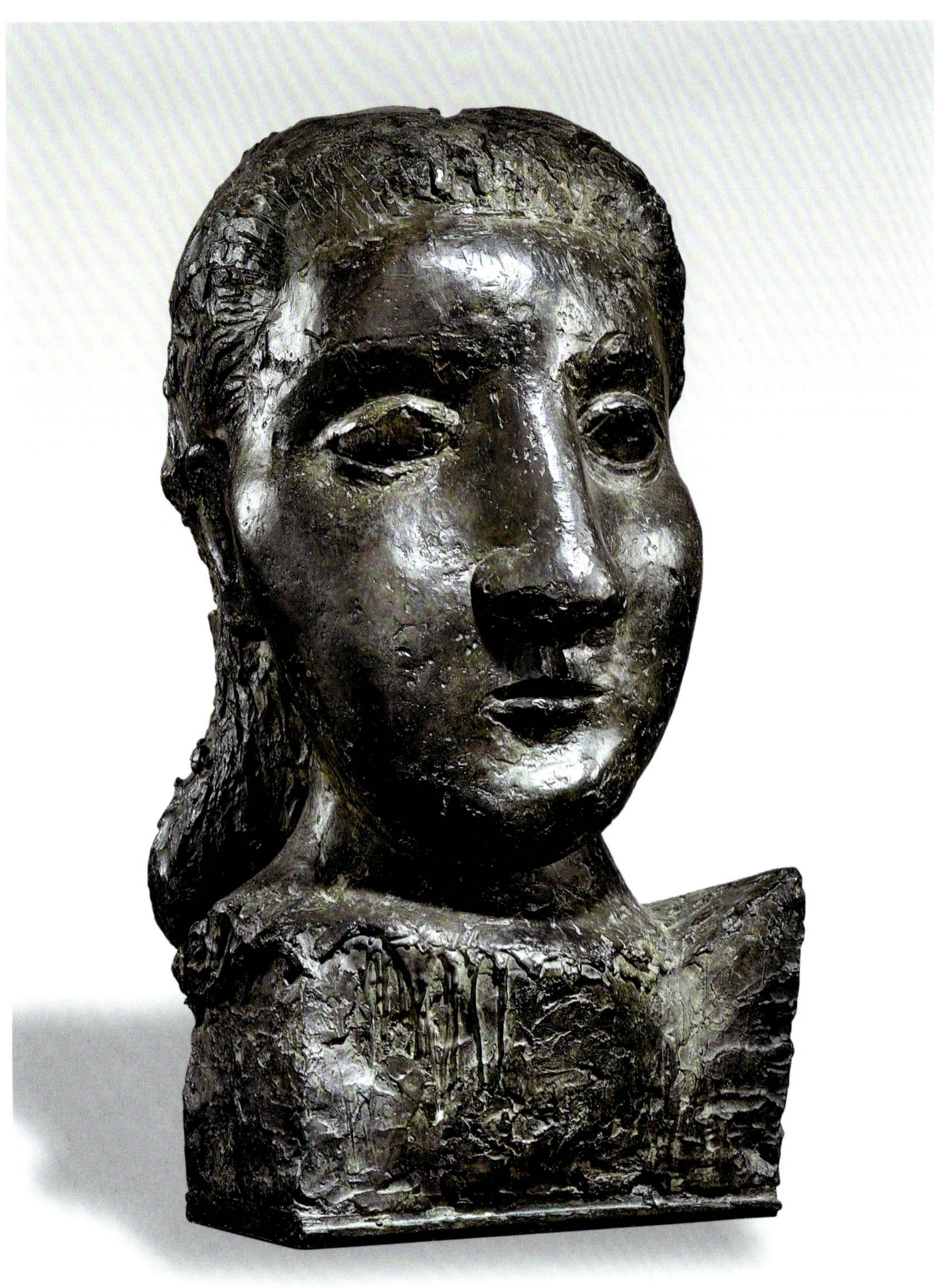

146 *Head of a Woman (Dora Maar)*, 1941 (B, L)

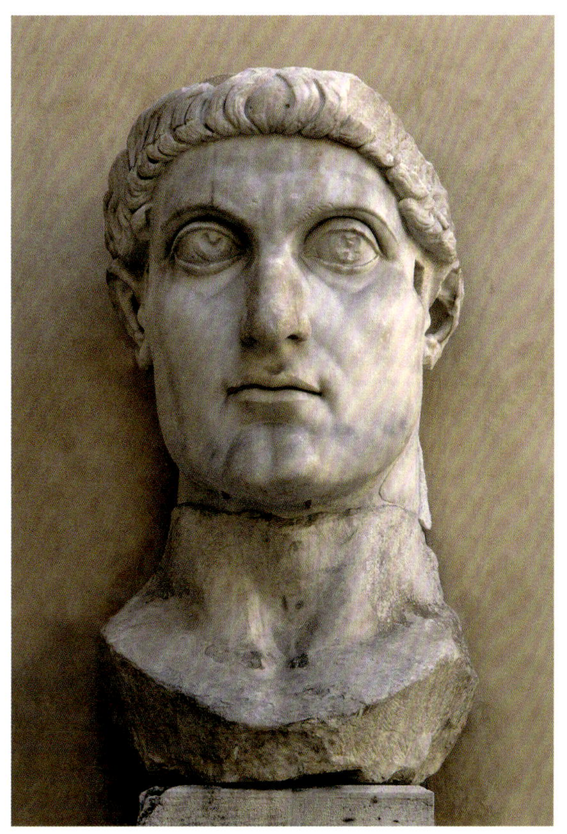

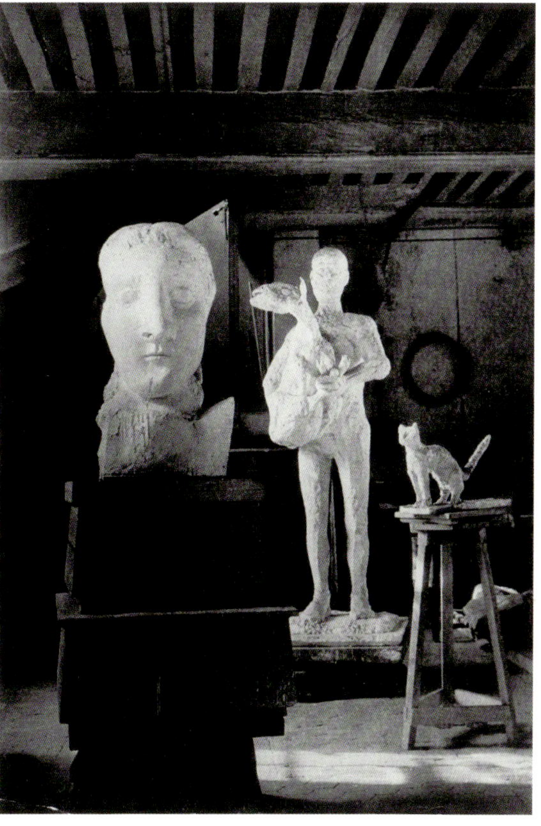

147 *Colossal Statue of Constantine: Head*, AD 313–24

148 *Picasso's Studio, 7 Rue des Grands-Augustins, Paris, with* Head of a Woman (Dora Maar) *and* Man with a Sheep. Photograph by Brassaï, 1943

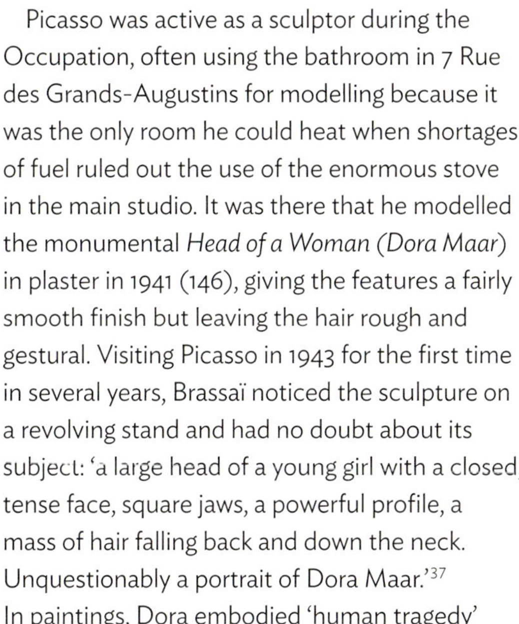

Picasso was active as a sculptor during the Occupation, often using the bathroom in 7 Rue des Grands-Augustins for modelling because it was the only room he could heat when shortages of fuel ruled out the use of the enormous stove in the main studio. It was there that he modelled the monumental *Head of a Woman (Dora Maar)* in plaster in 1941 (146), giving the features a fairly smooth finish but leaving the hair rough and gestural. Visiting Picasso in 1943 for the first time in several years, Brassaï noticed the sculpture on a revolving stand and had no doubt about its subject: 'a large head of a young girl with a closed, tense face, square jaws, a powerful profile, a mass of hair falling back and down the neck. Unquestionably a portrait of Dora Maar.'[37]
In paintings, Dora embodied 'human tragedy'

but her dignified bearing also cut her out to be the model for a freestanding, classicising sculpture. Picasso emphasised the symmetry and volume of her head to bring it closer to imperial Roman prototypes, enhancing its monumental impact by means of the cubic plinth from which it rises up vertically. Formal similarities to the colossal head of Constantine in the Capitoline Museum in Rome are surely not fortuitous (147). With lips closed and eyes open but unfocused, facing forward in hieratic fashion, the Dora Maar of this portrait expresses no transient emotion and, in the context of the Occupation, can be read as incarnating the spirit of stoical resistance and fortitude. The sculpture has an heroic presence in the photographs Brassaï took in Rue des Grands-Augustins (148), where it partners *Man with a Sheep*, the great full-length statue which Picasso modelled early in 1943 as a humane riposte to the gigantic, grossly muscular male nudes of Arno Breker, Hitler's favourite sculptor.

In 1959 the head took on a different symbolic meaning: a bronze cast was set up in a square beside the church of St-Germain-des-Prés as a memorial to Guillaume Apollinaire, thus bringing to an honourable conclusion the tragi-comic saga of Picasso's efforts to fulfil the commission for a monument for the poet's tomb. The choice of this particular sculpture for the memorial was a compromise, for it bore no relation to any of Picasso's original designs. In the documents relating to its selection and inauguration, Maar's name was never mentioned, and in its new situation the sculpture was no longer the portrait of an individual woman, or a symbol of Resistance, but in some vague sense an allegory of Poetry.[38]

1 Richardson 2007, pp.323–4.

2 Ibid., pp.330–3. See also Robert Rosenblum, 'Picasso's Blond Muse: The Reign of Marie-Thérèse Walter', in Rubin 1996, pp.336–83.

3 According to Diana Widmaier Picasso, some of these drawings were based on photographs ('The Marie-Thérèse Years: a Frenzied Dialogue for the Sleeping Muse, or the Rebirth of Picasso's Plastic Laboratory', in *Amour fou* 2011, pp.71–9).

4 Jean Cocteau, *Le passé défini. Journal*. Cited in *Picasso Mediterranean* 2010, p.331.

5 See Read 2008, Part II, for the full story of the commission for the Apollinaire monument.

6 The sculpture was certainly completed by 6 September 1931, when Picasso made a dated sketch of it propped up on wooden blocks near the studio wall. See Glimcher 1986, cat.101.

7 *Exposition Picasso* (Galeries Georges Petit, Paris, 16 June–30 July 1932). See FitzGerald 1995, pp.190–204.

8 Brassaï's photographs accompanied André Breton's seminal essay on Picasso's sculpture, 'Picasso dans son élément', *Minotaure*, no.1, 1 June 1933, pp.8–29.

9 The sketchbook (Glimcher 1986, cat.103) is dated 8 October–12 December 1931. The study for *Marie-Thérèse, Full-face and Profile* is reproduced in *Picasso intime* 1981, cat.14 (n.p).

10 See Léal 1996, vol.2, cats 31–3.

11 *Exposition Picasso* (Galeries Georges Petit, Paris, 16 June–30 July 1932), cat.218.

12 *Henri Matisse* (Galeries Georges Petit, Paris, 16 June–25 July 1931).

13 Isabelle Monod-Fontaine, in *Matisse Picasso* 2002, pp.248–9. For the artistic exchanges between Matisse and Picasso in the early 1930s, see also Bois 1998, chapter III.

14 Penrose 1958, p.279.

15 Ibid.

16 Kendall 1991, cat.59, p.160.

17 Penrose 1981, pp.108–9.

18 I owe this observation to Antony Penrose.

19 She made this remark to the author in the early 1970s.

20 My thanks to Maya Widmaier-Picasso for this information. A portrait painted on 16 January 1938 shows the little girl cradling this very doll (*Maya with a Doll*; MP 170).

21 Picasso quoted by Herbert Read in a letter to *The Times*, 27 October 1956, p.27. Picasso made the remark when viewing an exhibition of children's drawings with Read in Paris in April 1945.

22 For their convergence and the early photographs they took of each other, see Baldassari 2006, pp.25–53.

23 *Dora Maar with Windswept Hair* (Private collection; Z.VIII.289) is inscribed 'Mougins 11 septembre/XXXVI/fait par coeur'.

24 Baldassari 2006, fig.20, p.48.

25 Gilot and Lake 1965, pp.81–2, 85. Examples of Picasso's excessively ornamental portraits of Dora Maar include *Dora Maar Seated*, 2 February 1938 (MP 1201) and *Seated Woman*, 14 June 1938 (MP 1204).

26 Gilot and Lake 1965, p.14.

27 Picasso's later *portrait-charge* of Poulenc (see 96) followed the same conventions.

28 The portrait of Thérèse Louise de Sureda had been acquired for the Havemeyer collection, New York, in 1897, but was illustrated in the standard literature on Goya. It is now in the National Gallery of Art, Washington.

29 See André Breton, 'Picasso poète', and Jaume Sabartés 'La literatura de Picasso', in *Picasso 1930–1935*, pp.49–55, pp.89–102 respectively.

30 Sabartés 1949, p.143.

31 Ibid., pp.201–2.

32 Ibid., p.217.

33 Penrose 1958, p.126.

34 Peter D. Whitney, 'Picasso is Safe', *San Francisco Chronicle*, 3 September 1944. Quoted in Nash 1998, p.13.

35 Gilot and Lake 1965, p.20.

36 Penrose 1958, p.319.

37 Brassaï 1967, p.52. Initially Picasso modelled a hat similar to the one seen in contemporary paintings, but wisely decided to remove it. For a photograph of the sculpture in that state, see Spies 2000, p.232.

38 See Read 2008, pp.226–43. The inauguration ceremony on 5 June 1959 was attended by many of Picasso's old friends but not by the artist himself.

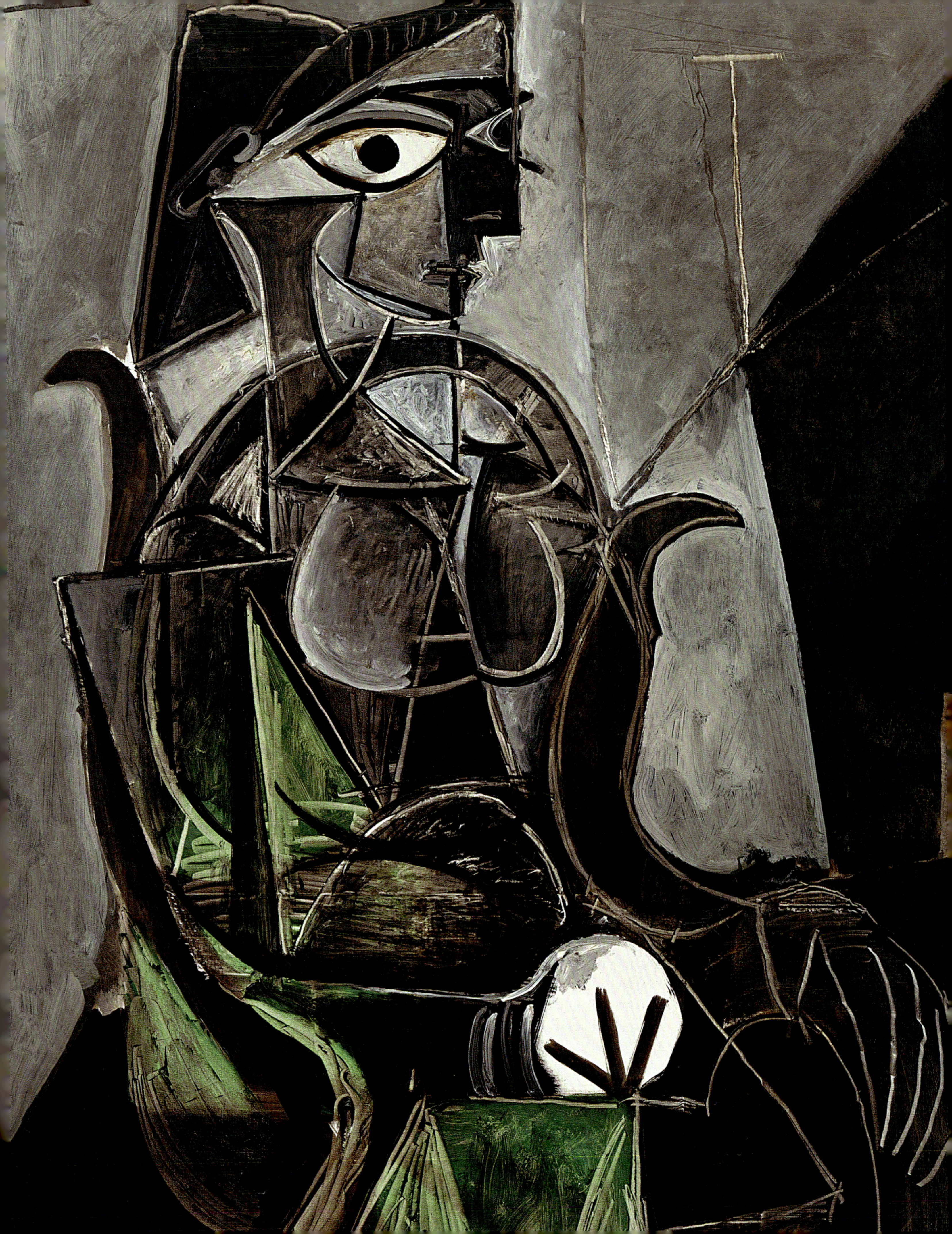

6. Picasso's post-war portraiture

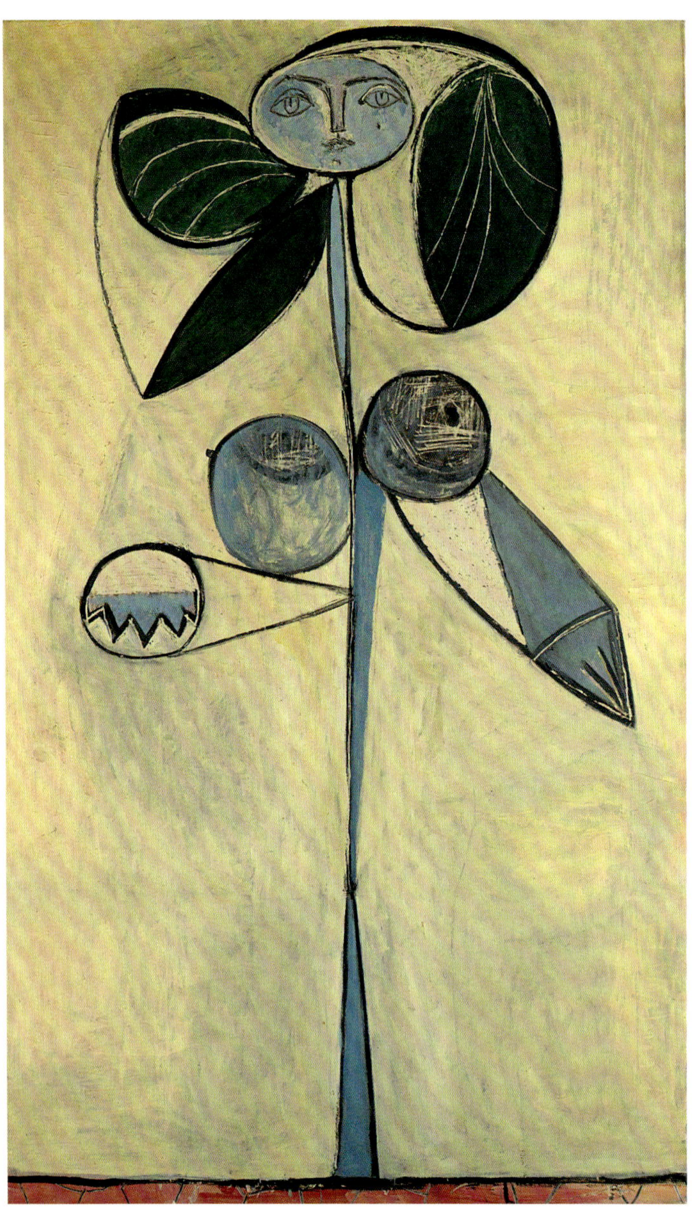

149 *La femme-fleur (Françoise Gilot)*, 5 May 1946

During the last decades of Picasso's life his approach to portraiture remained largely unchanged. Most portraits depicted his lovers and his children, but his high profile in the French Communist Party, which he joined in October 1944, meant that he was occasionally called upon to contribute portraits of political figures to Communist publications. This obligation did not bring out the best in him. Picasso was far more at home in the field of caricature, where his comic verve never deserted him and, as usual, male friends were his target.

PORTRAYING FRANÇOISE GILOT AND THEIR CHILDREN

Françoise Gilot's witness-account of the execution of *La femme-fleur* is the most detailed for any of Picasso's portraits (149). Although the painting is atypical in the degree to which symbolism governed its imagery, her description of his exploratory methods and openness to outside influence applies to his portraiture more generally.[1] Begun soon after she started living with him, *La femme-fleur* is dated 5 May 1946 but was worked on over a period of several weeks and underwent substantial revision. Picasso prepared by making drawings from life of Gilot seated on a low stool, but these displeased him and he destroyed them. The following day he asked her to pose in the nude, standing upright with her arms at her sides. Without making any drawings, he looked intently at her for over an hour and then told her to get dressed, remarking, 'You won't have to pose again.' The next day he began work on the canvas: it was not the only painting he had on the go and he switched between it and several still-lifes – his usual procedure at this period, she noted.

In its first state, *La femme-fleur* was 'fairly realistic', with Gilot seated on the stool. But Picasso decided that realism did not suit her personality; nor did a 'passive' seated pose: 'I only see you standing,' he said. The crucial transformation of young nude woman into 'woman-flower' was sparked by an outside source: the couple had paid a visit to Matisse during which the latter had announced that if he were to paint Gilot's portrait he would paint her hair green. Not to be outdone – 'Matisse isn't the only one who can paint you with green hair' – Picasso transformed Gilot's luxuriant chestnut hair into large green leaves and from then on, 'the portrait resolved itself in a symbolic floral pattern.' The wide blue oval shape of her face – contradicting the long oval of her actual face – was reached by experimenting with paper cut-outs and Picasso described it as 'like a little blue moon'. Matisse was cutting out shapes in coloured paper when they visited him and, clearly, that fascinating spectacle left its mark. In a later account of the same visit Gilot implies that Matisse was also the source of the choice of light blue for her flesh.[2] Thus the visit and her unconcealed enthusiasm for Matisse's painting – 'Matisse was indeed my favorite among the moderns'[3] – conditioned Picasso's evolving poetic vision. But an evolution of this kind was not unusual for him: we have seen already how a portrait by Goya changed the course of a portrait of Dora Maar (see 138–9).

When at last Picasso felt satisfied with the painting, he remarked:

> We're all animals, more or less, and about three-quarters of the human race look like animals. But you don't. You're like a growing plant and I've been wondering how I could get across the idea that you belong to the vegetable kingdom rather than the animal. I've never felt impelled to portray anyone else in this way.[4]

Representing people as animals, giving animals human faces, drawing analogies between people and animals: these are among the commonest devices of caricature and Picasso's self-portrait as a monkey (see 50) was an exercise in that long

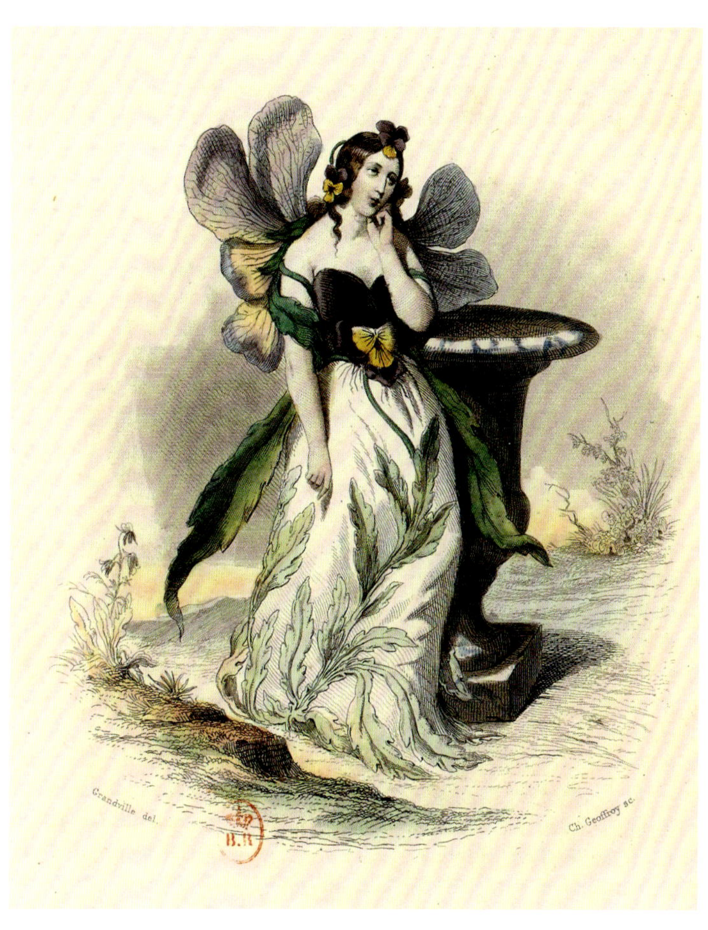

150 *'Pansy', Les fleurs animées* by J.J. Grandville, 1847

tradition. But he rarely spelled out the animal analogy so clearly, normally leaving it to the spectator to notice that, for instance, Cocteau's nose was like a bird's beak (see 89) or Nusch Éluard's hand like a cat's paw (see 125). The explicit equation of Gilot with a flowering plant suggests that Picasso had in mind the witty *femmes-fleurs* of J.J. Grandville's celebrated caricatural illustrations for *Les fleurs animées* (150), or similar composite images turning on the woman/flower analogy.[5]

According to Gilot, Picasso had great difficulty in seeing her in any other way after this: 'he kept coming back to the oval moon-shape and the plant forms. It exasperated him.'[6] *Woman in an Armchair* (151) underwent extensive revision as Picasso strove to rid himself of the moon/plant imagery. In the process, it became daringly diagrammatic, with Gilot's face rendered in the most elementary and generalised way, and her body as quasi-geometric shapes linked by sweeping lines. The painting is dated 2 April 1947, a matter of weeks before the birth of Claude on 15 May, and Gilot's pregnant belly is given due emphasis as a deep red triangular shape on which her left hand rests protectively. Her forearm is a continuation of the vertical back of the green chair, but here the fusion of body and chair lacks the sinister implications it had had in the wartime portrait of Maar (see 143): her face expresses perfect serenity, her hieratic stance perfect command. Picasso had transcended the botanical metaphor of *La femme-fleur* and created what is in effect a hieroglyph for Françoise.

Picasso's lithographic portraits of Gilot were never as radically abstracted.[7] In October 1945 the master-printer Fernard Mourlot, who specialised in lithography, invited him to make prints in his workshop on the Rue de Chabrol. Always delighted to collaborate with artisans who could help him extend his technical range, Picasso made his first lithographic portraits of Gilot in early November 1945. The most important sequence came later, during the winter of 1948–9 when she was pregnant with Paloma. In November 1948 he produced a five-colour lithograph of her wearing the embroidered sheepskin jacket he had bought for her when he attended the Peace Conference held in Wrocław, Poland. He did not authorise an edition of the image but instead reworked each of the separate zinc plates used for the five colours. In all, some thirty different variations (all printed in black) resulted from this intense engagement with the printmaking process. Although artist's impressions were pulled from every state, Picasso authorised editions of only two, including the fifth and final state of the zinc plate used for the violet of the original five-colour lithograph (152).

Like so many of Picasso's other portraits of the women in his life, *Woman in an Armchair. No.4 (From the Violet)* involved allusions that worked on both a public and a private level. On the day their affair was consummated, and knowing full well what would happen, Gilot had arrived at 7 Rue des Grands-Augustins 'wearing a black velvet dress with a high white lace collar, my dark-red hair done up in a coiffure I had taken from a painting of the Infanta by Velázquez.'[8] The reference to Velázquez was not lost on Picasso, and in the lithograph Gilot possesses the hauteur of an Infanta, while her hair, curiously decorated with ribbons, resembles the braided and beribboned hair of Mariana of Austria, Philip IV's teenage second wife, in Velázquez's full-length court portrait in the Prado (153).[9] The patterns on Gilot's sleeves and bodice recall the gorgeous silver braid decorating the Queen's black dress quite as much as the peasant embroidery of her Polish jacket.
Her admiration for Matisse was undimmed and she had promoted further meetings, engaged in a correspondence with him and brought Claude to see him.[10] In response, Picasso gave the portrait a Matissean flavour: Gilot's face, body and hands and the contrasting patterns recall decorative paintings of

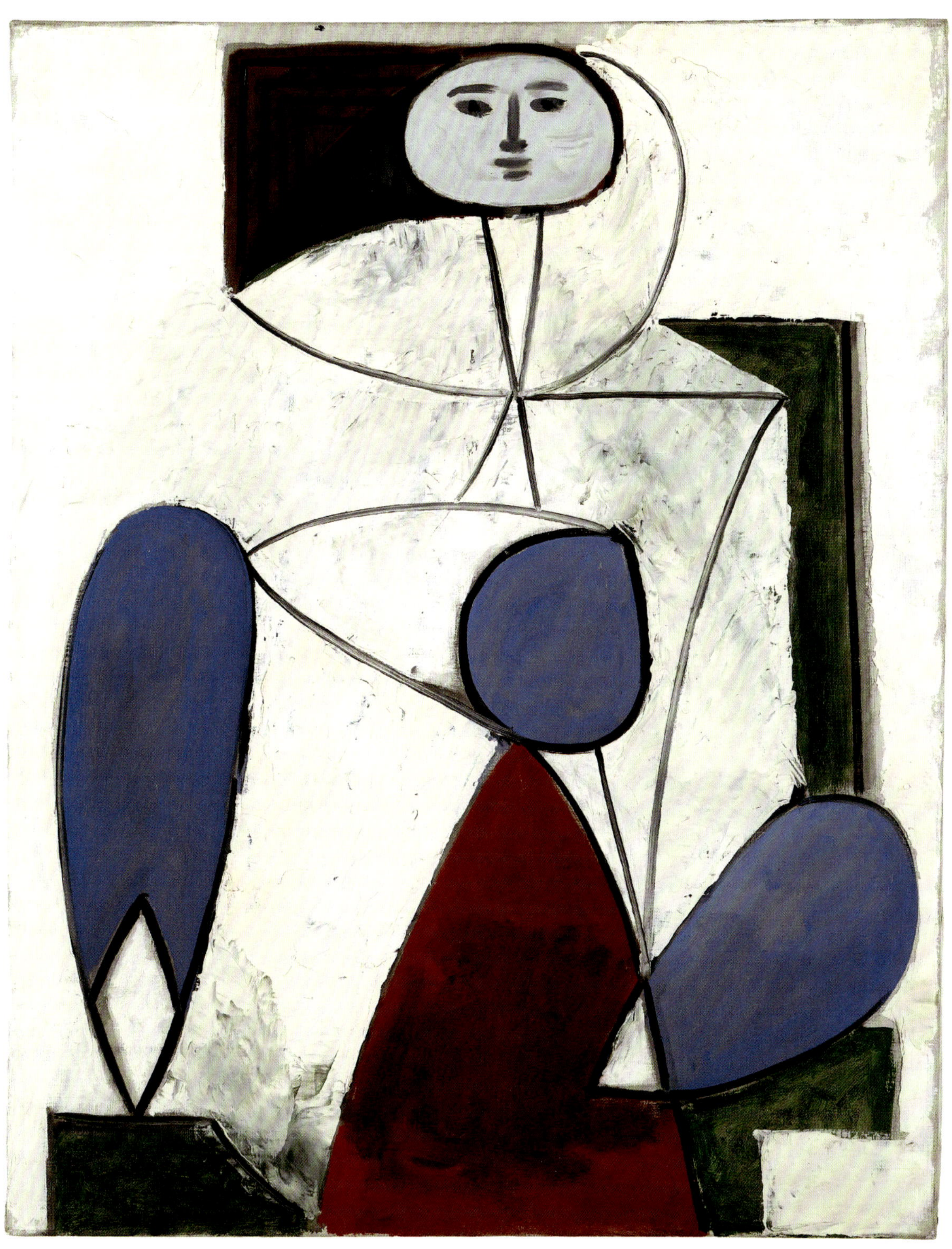

151 *Woman in an Armchair*, 2 April 1947 (B, L)

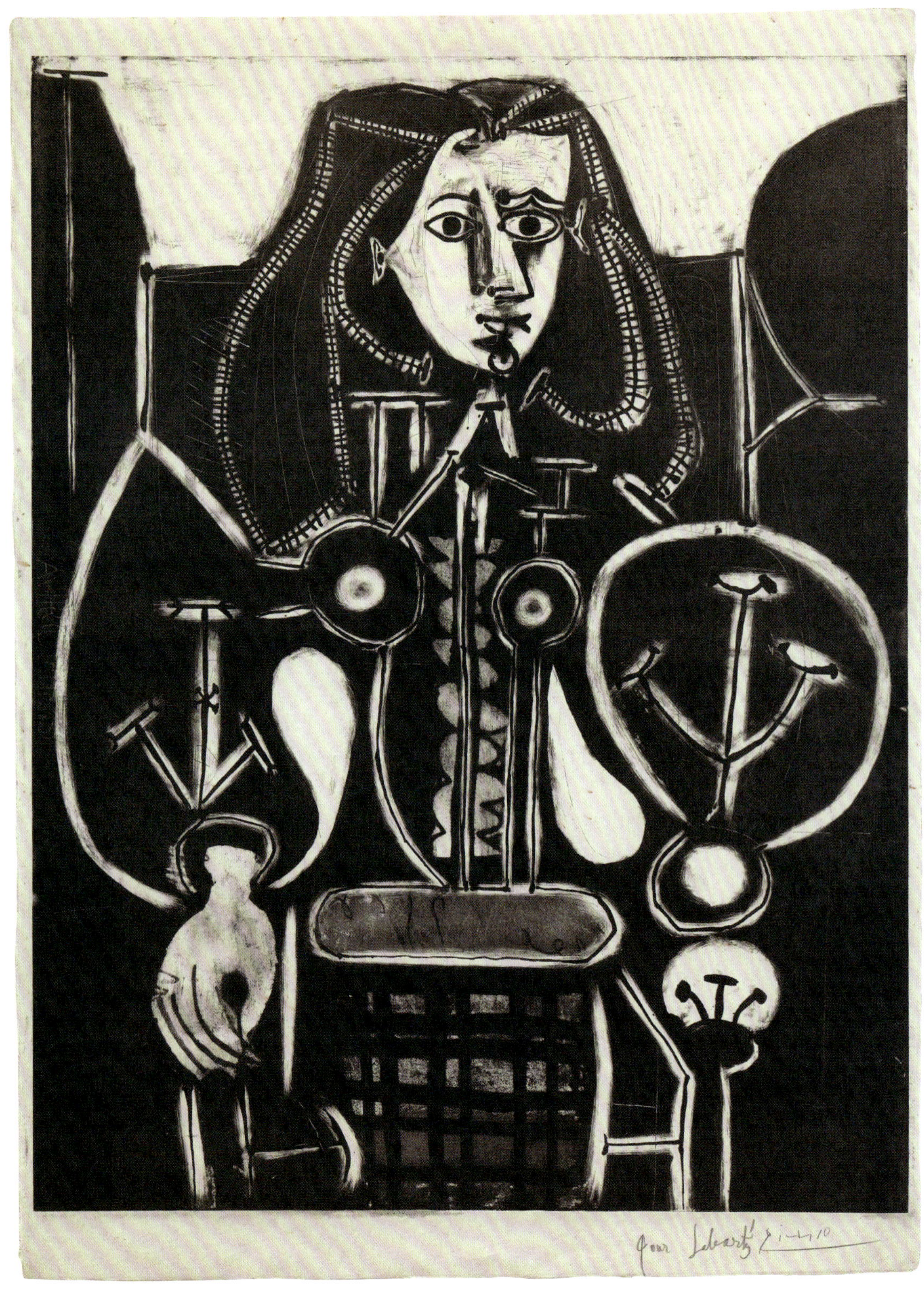

152 *Woman in an Armchair. No. 4 (From the Violet)*, 3 January 1949 (B, L)

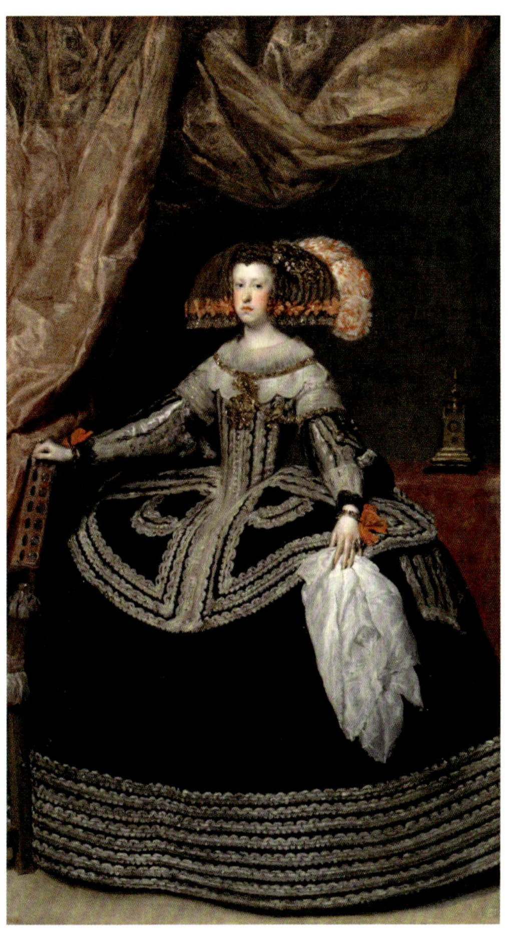

153 *Queen Mariana of Austria* by Diego Velázquez, 1652–3

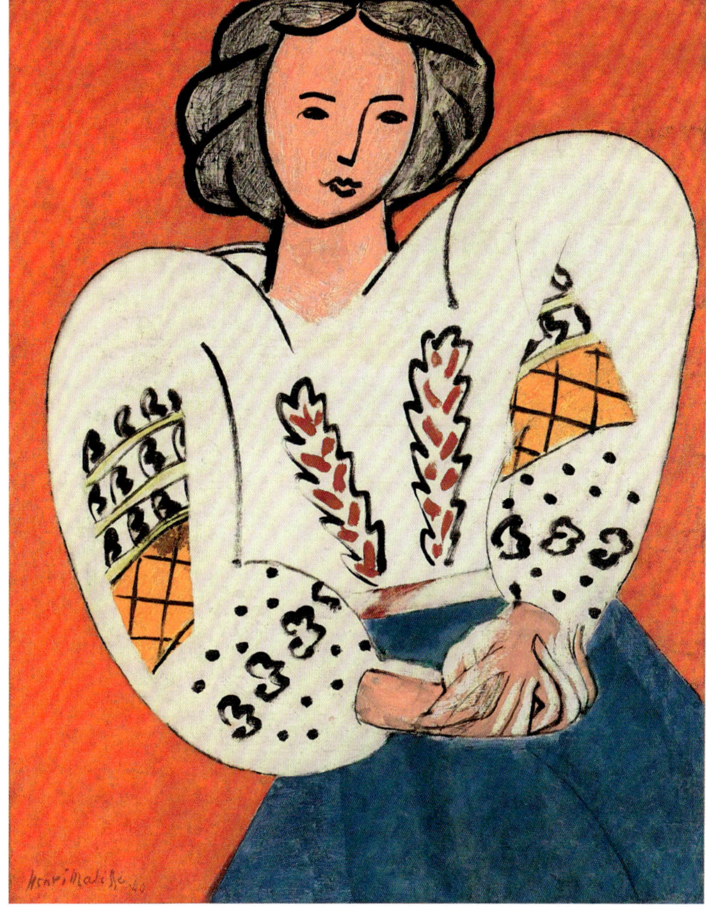

154 *The Romanian Blouse* by Henri Matisse, 1939–40

women, such as *The Romanian Blouse* (154). Not that Picasso was overwhelmed by these external sources: the rectilinear structure of the portrait and the 'sign language' governing its abstraction have their origin in his Cubism. The 'order' of Cubism was a subject he discussed with Gilot, who told him frankly that she thought 'he had done nothing greater than his work of the Cubist period'.[11] These allusions to Velázquez, Matisse and Cubism are accessible to any spectator with a reasonable knowledge of art history, but without Gilot's candid memoirs we would not know why Picasso may have associated her with this unusual trio.

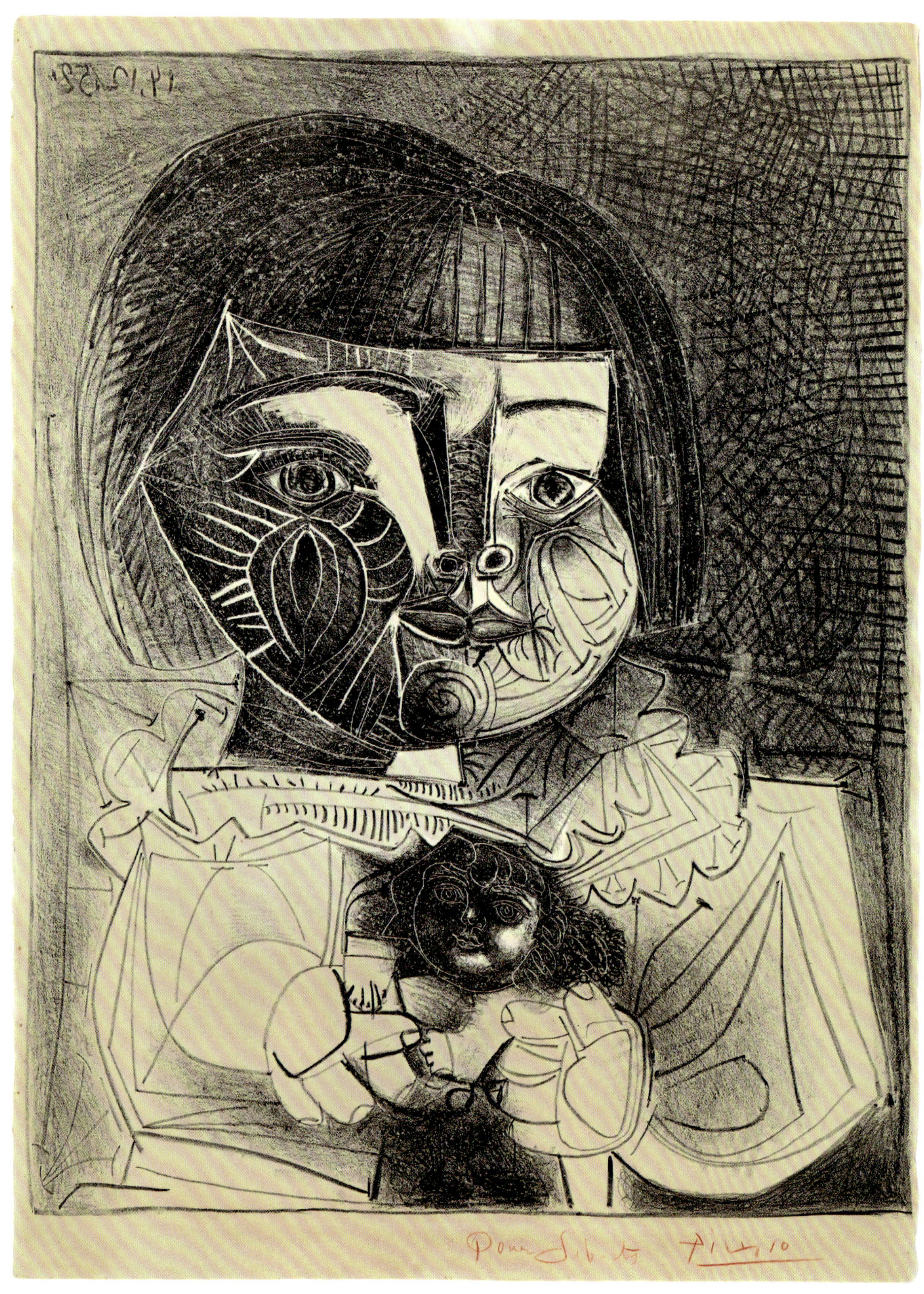

155 *Paloma and Her Doll on a Black Background*,
14 December 1952 (L)

While Picasso and Gilot continued to live together, their children were the subject of numerous portraits. This surprisingly monumental lithograph of Paloma (155) is one of a clutch of portraits executed in various media and styles in mid-December 1952, when she was just over two and a half years old. Calm and self-possessed, Paloma holds her doll towards the spectator in unconscious mimicry of the Virgin with the Christ Child. The patterning of the surface – Paloma's plump cheeks are tattooed like a Maori's, while the dark background is dense with superimposed meshes of lines – exhibits the *horror vacui* that overcame Picasso from time to time, particularly at periods of stress when the cleansing process of simplification was beyond him. Certain ornamental patterns are disturbingly aggressive, notably the sharp nail- or tack-like details of Paloma's lace collar and similar marks wrinkling and scarring her left cheek, as well as the gaping wound-like form (a sign for the vagina) that engulfs her right cheek. Picasso was greatly disturbed by the Korean War and his still-lifes during this period turned obsessively on *memento mori* themes. The disintegration of his relationship with Françoise, however, was probably the main source of the lithograph's baneful undertones.

The couple separated in the autumn of 1953. *Claude Drawing, Françoise and Paloma*, dated 17 May 1954 (156), was painted soon after the Easter holiday, which had temporarily reunited the family in Vallauris, and is one of several pictures on the same theme, mostly done after the children's return to Paris with their mother. Picasso was as fascinated by the spectacle of children painting and drawing as he was by the paintings and drawings they produced. This was due partly to his sense that he had never drawn like a child when he was a child,[12] and partly to his abiding fascination with the mystery of the creative act: watching young, untaught children draw might afford some revelation. Edward Quinn captured one family session with his camera: the two children draw on a large sheet of paper laid on the floor, with Picasso involved at one point (157). The communal effort was signed by all three, and by Gilot, and dated proudly in Picasso's hand '16.4.53.'[13] Four years later, David Douglas Duncan photographed Paloma drawing after a family lunch while Picasso worked on a linocut: 'They treated each other as equals – without questions, advice or criticism,' Duncan noted.[14]

In *Claude Drawing, Françoise and Paloma*, it is Claude, crouched on the floor, who is about to draw. Head bowed, drawing arm outstretched in readiness, he appears to be in a mediumistic trance; the brilliant light striking his back, his eye and the virgin sheet of paper sanctifies both him and the imminent deed. Paloma watches intently, focused on the act of drawing, not her brother. Françoise is equally attentive, leaning over Paloma, determined to miss nothing. On all fours, providing shelter and protection for both children, Françoise is like some large animal with its cubs. Represented in negative – her white outline is not painted over the dark violet background, but is a track left in the bare canvas – she seems more like a ghost than a physical presence, and in some other paintings in this series she is omitted altogether. The children, too, are represented as outlines scratched into or painted in black over the zones of colour – colours that show through them as if they were transparent. Thus the entire image is conjured up through the act of drawing and we are shown that, like Claude's virgin sheet of paper, it began as bare white canvas. Evidently, Claude is a cipher for Picasso himself – the fourth, unseen member of the family.

Knowing the circumstances of the painting, the viewer is bound to connect the insubstantiality of the three figures depicted with their actual absence: they were memories. The fact that in the Catholic Church the colour violet is associated with Lent and with repentance may also be relevant: the parents'

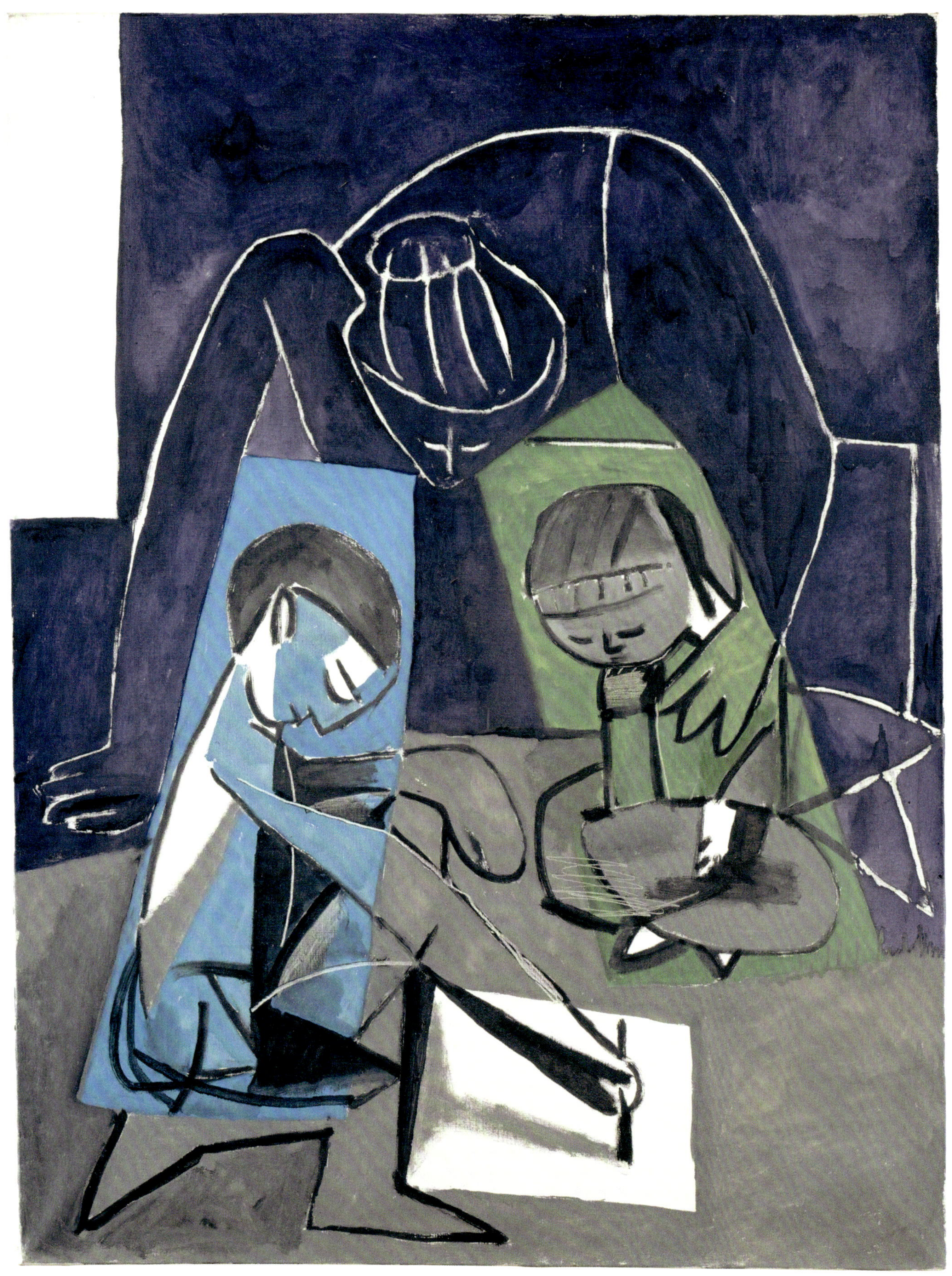

156 *Claude Drawing, Françoise and Paloma*, 17 May 1954 (B, L)

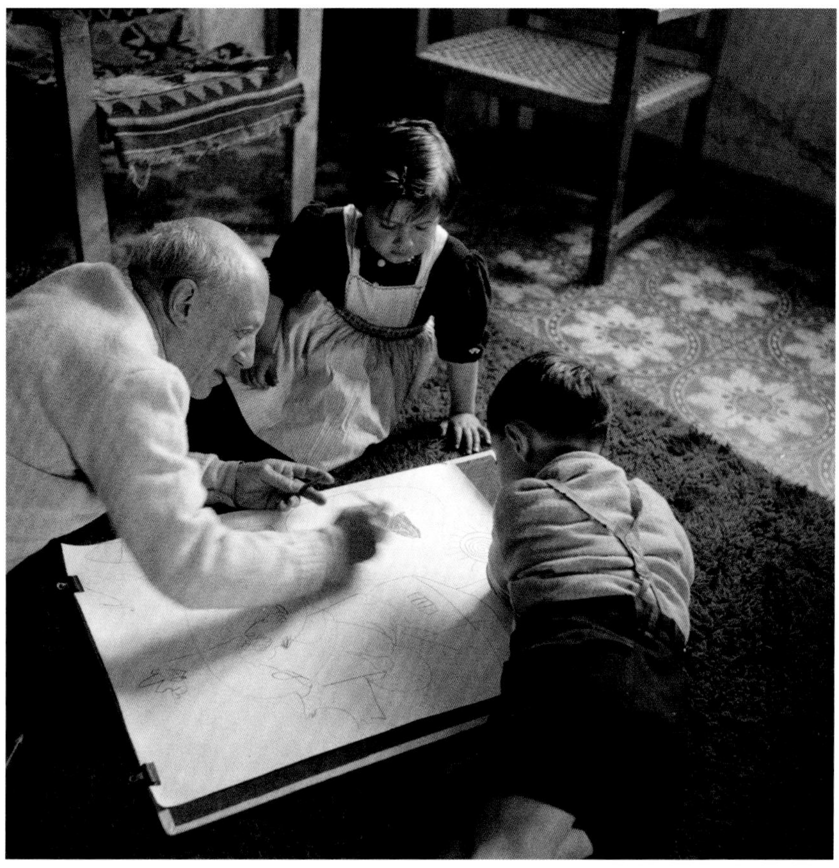

157 *Picasso Drawing with Claude and Paloma*. Photograph by Edward Quinn, La Galloise, Vallauris, 16 April 1953

separation brought sorrow and remorse and the painting is as much about loss as about the creative act. Portraiture has always had a memorial function and this nostalgic painting belongs to that branch of the genre. In that sense it is linked with the portraits of Casagemas on his deathbed painted half a century before (see 53).

Claude Drawing, Françoise and Paloma was contemporary with an unusual episode in Picasso's career: his decision to work with a model. She was a beautiful, 19-year-old blonde called Sylvette David, who was living in Vallauris and who posed occasionally for him between late April (158) and the end of June 1954. The more abstracted portraits were painted in her absence.[15] Picasso had settled in Vallauris in order to have immediate access to the Madoura pottery, where he had worked intensively for the first time in the summer of 1947. This activity led to a resurgence of his passion for sculpting. For the first few years he either modelled small figures in clay or constructed large sculptures (like the famous *Goat*, 1950) with a multitude of found objects. But Sylvette David inspired a new kind of planar sculpture made with cut, bent and painted sheet-iron – sculpture that in conception and technique harked back to Picasso's Cubist paper and metal constructions of 1912–14. The technical breakthrough was facilitated by Sylvette's fiancé, Tobias Jellinek, who used iron in his furniture and sheet-metal in his sculpture and had access to the workshop and machinery of the local metalworker Joseph-Marius Tiola.

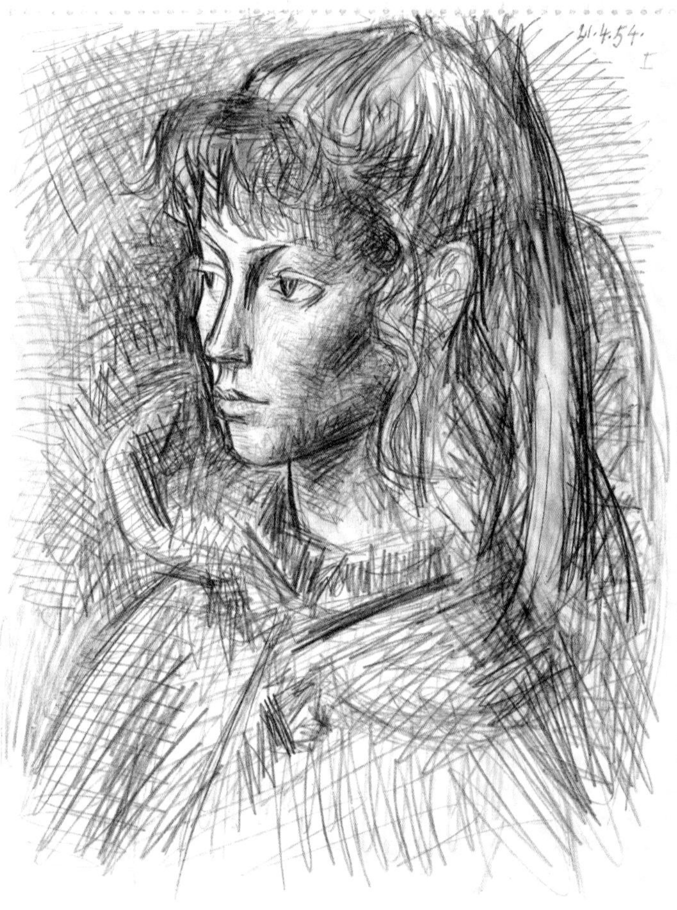

158 *Sylvette David*, 21 April 1954

Jellinek's task was to copy exactly in sheet-iron the cardboard maquettes Picasso gave him, bending the metal where Picasso had folded the cardboard. The flat shape of the original cut-outs did not require intricate cutting, but the folds introduced volume and spatial complexity, and when Picasso painted the metal he worked both with and against the concertina of planes. In the sculpture featured here (159), he painted the two sides in contrasting styles. The style of the more complex 'front' view is close to that of the decorative Cubist paintings he created during the years when he was designing ballets for Diaghilev (1917–21):[16] Sylvette's face is seen simultaneously from different viewpoints and the back of her head and her signature pony-tail are mapped out in an approximation to Cubist faceting. But the graphic style of the 'back' view is wilfully naïve, reminiscent of child art in its use of dots, lines and squiggles. Picasso had good reason to be especially attuned to child art at this moment, but the connection he drew between it and Sylvette was purposeful. In between posing for Picasso, she sometimes played with Claude and Paloma while they were staying in Vallauris.[17] A more significant factor was her immaturity, for she has described herself as very naïve for her age and Picasso as 'like a father'.[18] That little-girl innocence is captured in the back view of the sculpture, whereas she appears more grown-up and self-aware in the Cubist-style front view. As the spectator circulates around the sculpture, her image undergoes transformation and her personality evolves – a reflection of Picasso's sense of the liminal state of David herself.

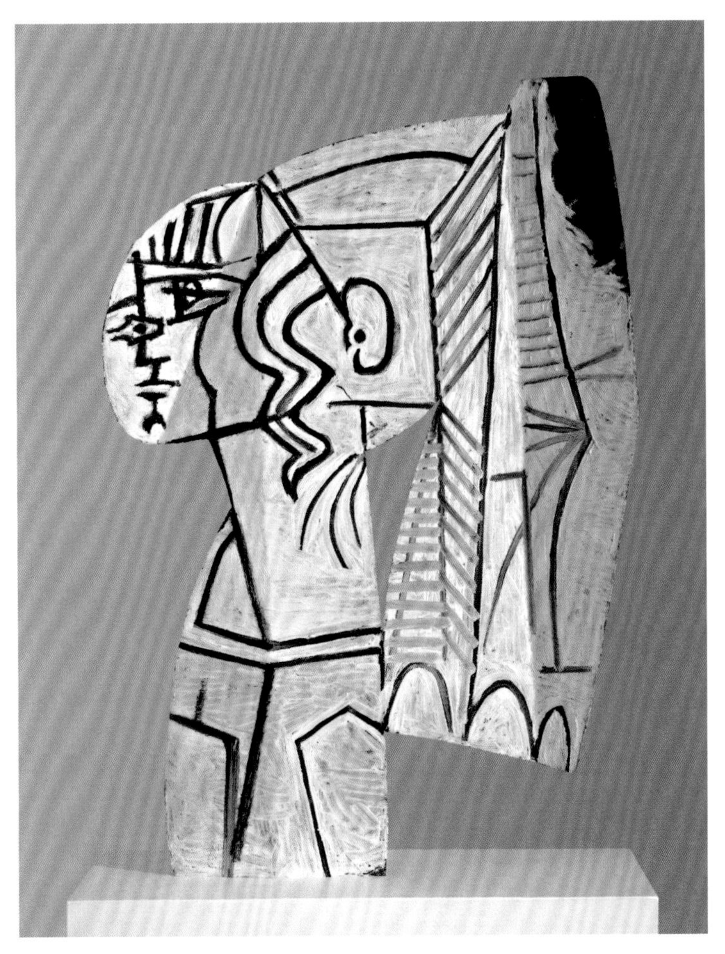

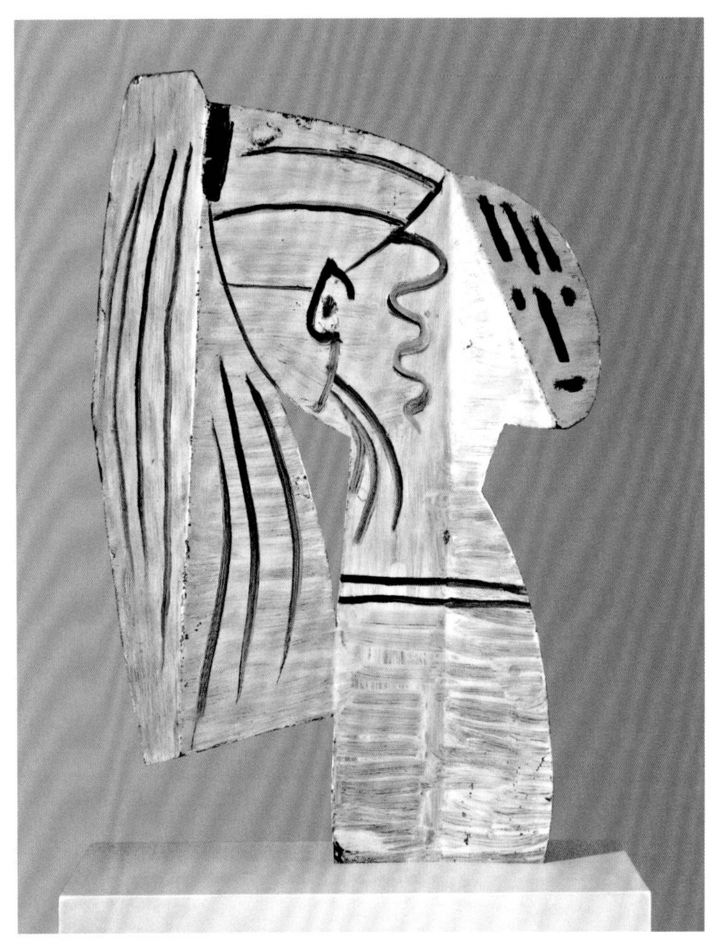

159 *Sylvette*, 1954 (B, L)

PORTRAYING JACQUELINE

Jacqueline Roque worked in the shop of the Madoura pottery and it was there that Picasso got to know her in 1952 or 1953 (accounts differ). By the end of the summer of 1954 she had become a permanent fixture in his life. This meticulous drawing of her profile (160) is one of his earliest portraits and served as the preparatory sketch for the decorative painting known as *Madame Z.* or *Jacqueline with Flowers*.[19] Picasso recorded the large, slanting eyes, arched brows, straight nose and strongly marked bone structure seen in contemporary photographs. He also lent Roque the long neck, slender torso and girlishness of Sylvette David, who was still posing for him at the time. (Jacqueline was of shorter, stockier build than she appears in this drawing – a classic 'Mediterranean' type, strikingly different from the willowy, 'Nordic' Sylvette.) The long neck acts as a graceful pedestal lifting her above crass reality, and it is possible that Picasso already planned to make sculptures in sheet metal along the lines of those he eventually made with Tiola in 1957.[20]

In *Portrait of Jacqueline in a Black Scarf* (161), the gamine of the profile portrait has been transformed into the archetypal Spanish woman in mourning. From contemporary photographs (and Picasso's other portraits), we know that this was not how Jacqueline habitually dressed: in this painting she is 'in costume' – a costume redolent especially of Picasso's boyhood in provincial Spain. The rippling contours of her face and figure and the format and composition of the portrait suggest that Picasso also had in mind El Greco's portraits of men dressed in black, and one can imagine the portrait as the feminine counterpart to El Greco's *Portrait of a Painter*, which Picasso had paraphrased in a free 'copy' in 1950.[21]

Dressed as if for a funeral though she is, Jacqueline does not look melancholy. On the contrary, the hint of a Mona Lisa smile suggests complicity in the charade and the flush suffusing her pale face speaks of sensual pleasure. The portrait's pressing intimacy – the spectator is privy to an intense but mute dialogue between artist and sitter – reflects the fact that it was at this moment, October 1954, that she began living with Picasso. The cane and bentwood rocking-chair – her seat of choice – became her personal emblem and from this time on featured in many other portraits (including 164). The sheer fluency of Picasso's brushwork and the harmony of the painting's restricted but not austere colour scheme speak of a rare (for him) sense of relaxation and concord.

One of Jacqueline's attractions for Picasso was her uncanny ability to inhabit and blend with now one picture in his *musée imaginaire*, now another. She could look like the perfect subject for El Greco yet also remind him of the beautiful squatting woman to the right of Delacroix's voluptuous harem painting, *Women of Algiers*. It was partly because she did so that in the winter of 1954–5 he embarked on an extended series of variations after Delacroix's painting.[22] By the beginning of October 1955, Jacqueline had assumed the identity of Manet's *Lola de Valence* (163) – yet another costume role. Picasso must often have seen Manet's painting of the Spanish dancer in the Louvre, or latterly in its Jeu de Paume outpost,[23] but the immediate prompt was the temporary loan of the picture to the Musée Masséna in Nice.[24] In *Picasso Plain* Hélène Parmelin gives a vivid description of the excitement caused by this event, how Picasso and her husband, the painter Édouard Pignon, could talk of nothing but Manet, and then of their trip to Nice to see 'the beautiful, the incomparable, the unique Lola de Valence'.[25] She also mentions the book of reproductions that Picasso and Pignon pored over before setting off to see the painting. Photographs of people gave Picasso control over their image and the same was true of reproductions of paintings, which left him free to invent and imagine, whereas

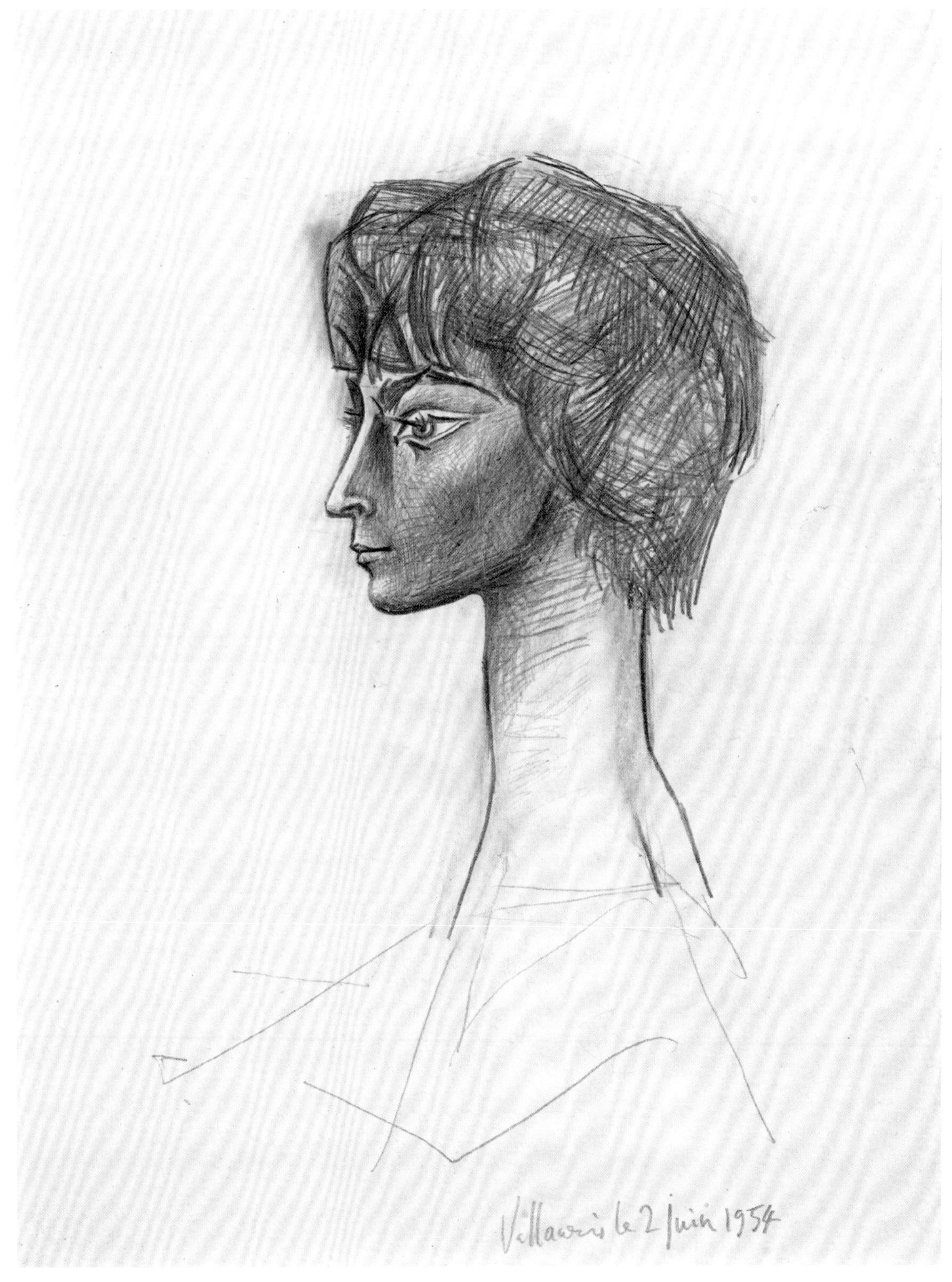

160 *Jacqueline*, 2 June 1954 (B)

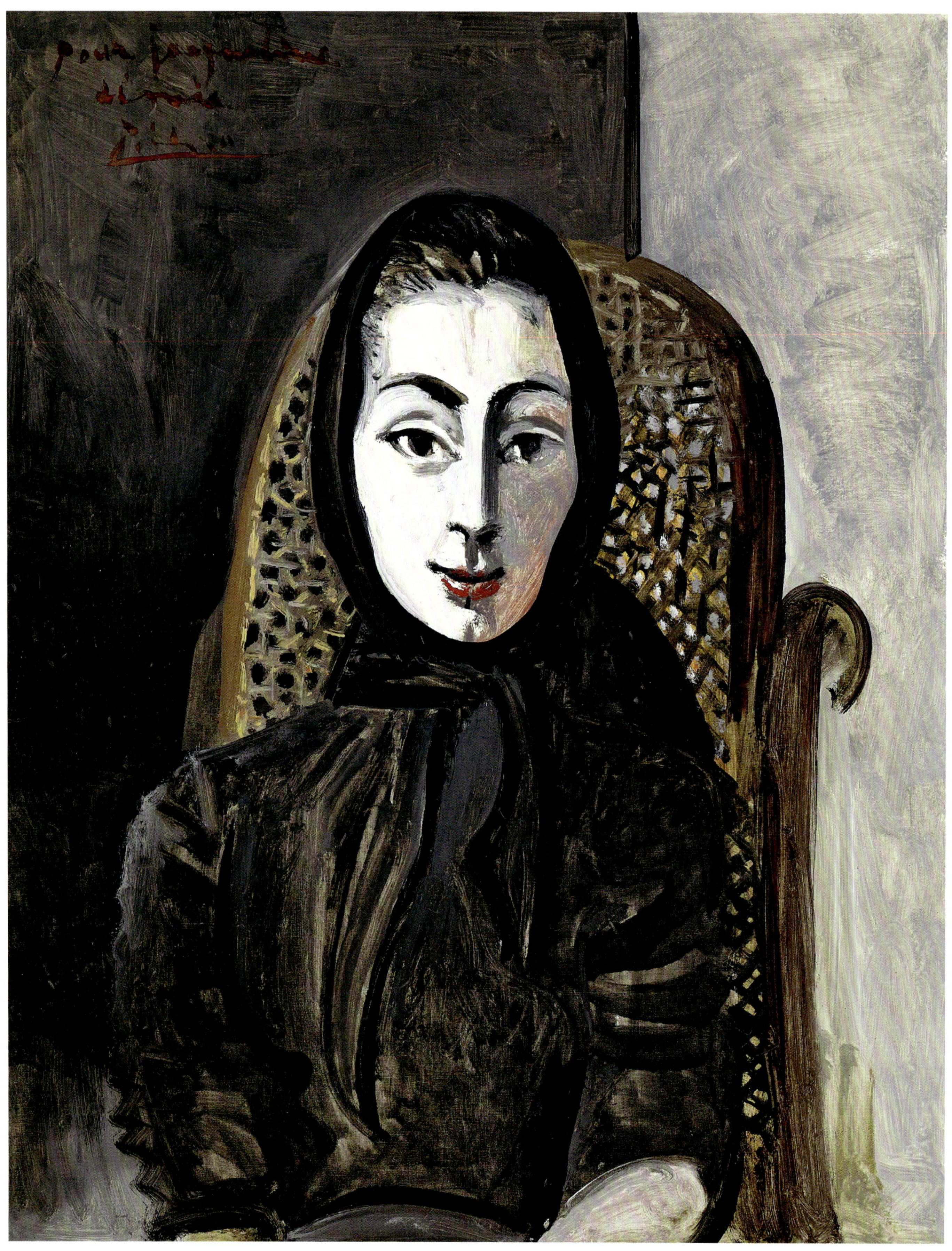

161 *Portrait of Jacqueline in a Black Scarf*, 11 October 1954 (B, L)

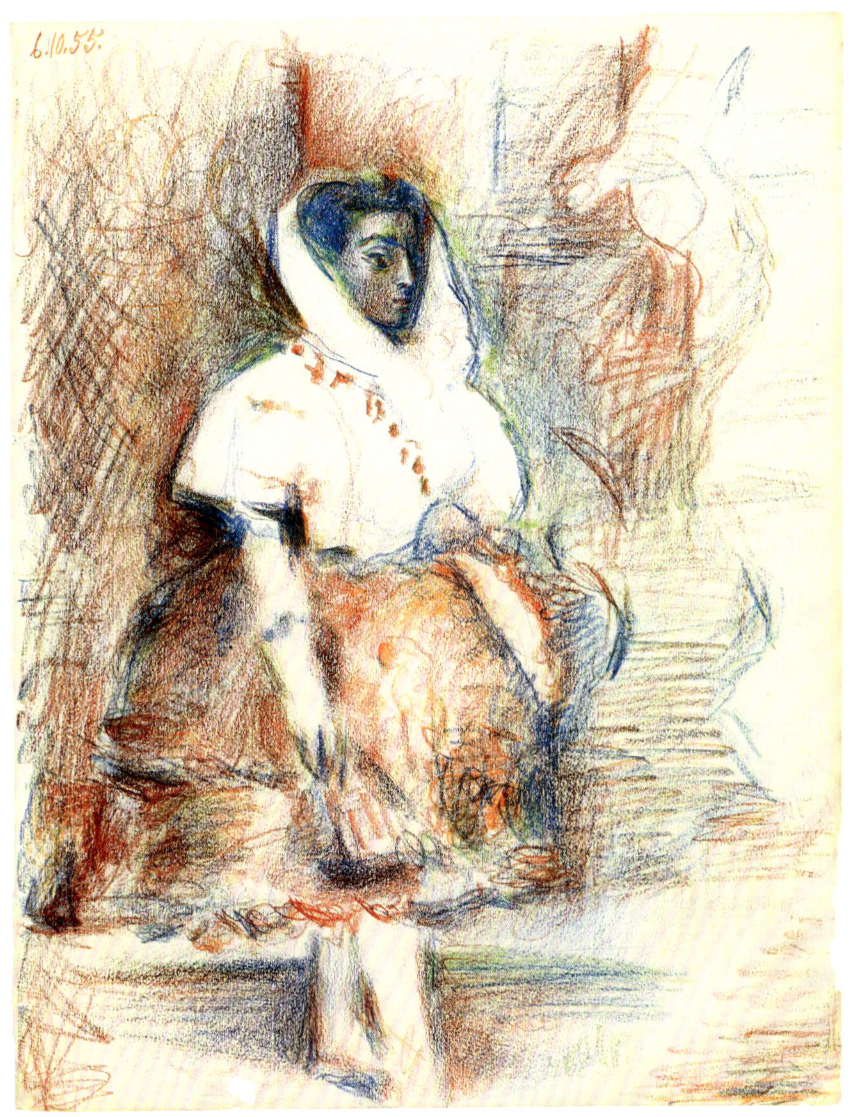

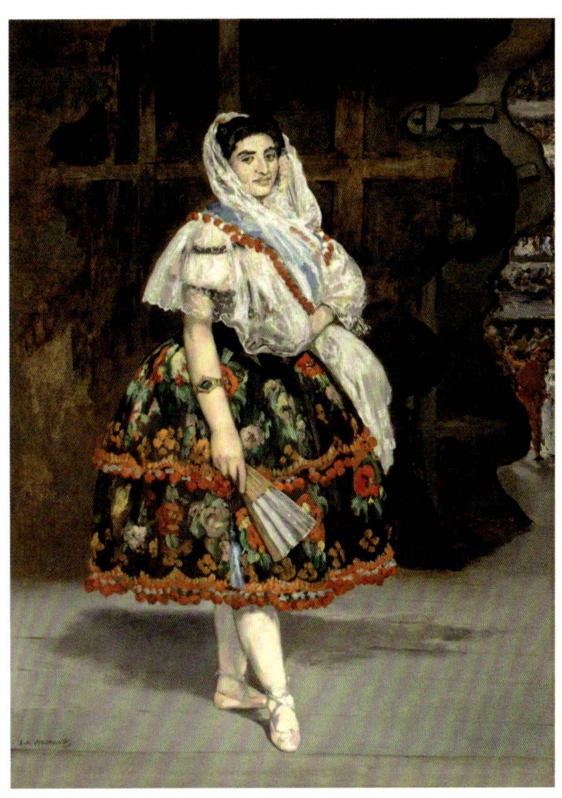

162 *Jacqueline (after* Lola de Valence *by Manet),* 6 October 1955 (L)

163 *Lola de Valence* by Édouard Manet, 1862

the original might overwhelm – or, worse, leave him cold. The drawing in coloured crayons of Jacqueline as Lola de Valence follows the composition of Manet's painting so closely that Picasso must have had a photo to hand, but his interpretation is typically and wittily independent (162). Using a light, feathery stroke and high-key prismatic colour, he gave a Renoiresque look and style to Manet's solidly brushed and relatively dark painting. Thus Jacqueline is at one and the same time Manet's heroine, a Spanish beauty in the tradition of Goya – Manet's source was Goya's portraits of the Duchess of Alba – and a sensual, sun-drenched Renoir type.

The drawing was made shortly after the couple moved into La Californie, a sprawling Art Nouveau villa in Cannes. The house was surrounded by a huge garden with palm trees, where Picasso installed bronze casts of his sculpture. He set up

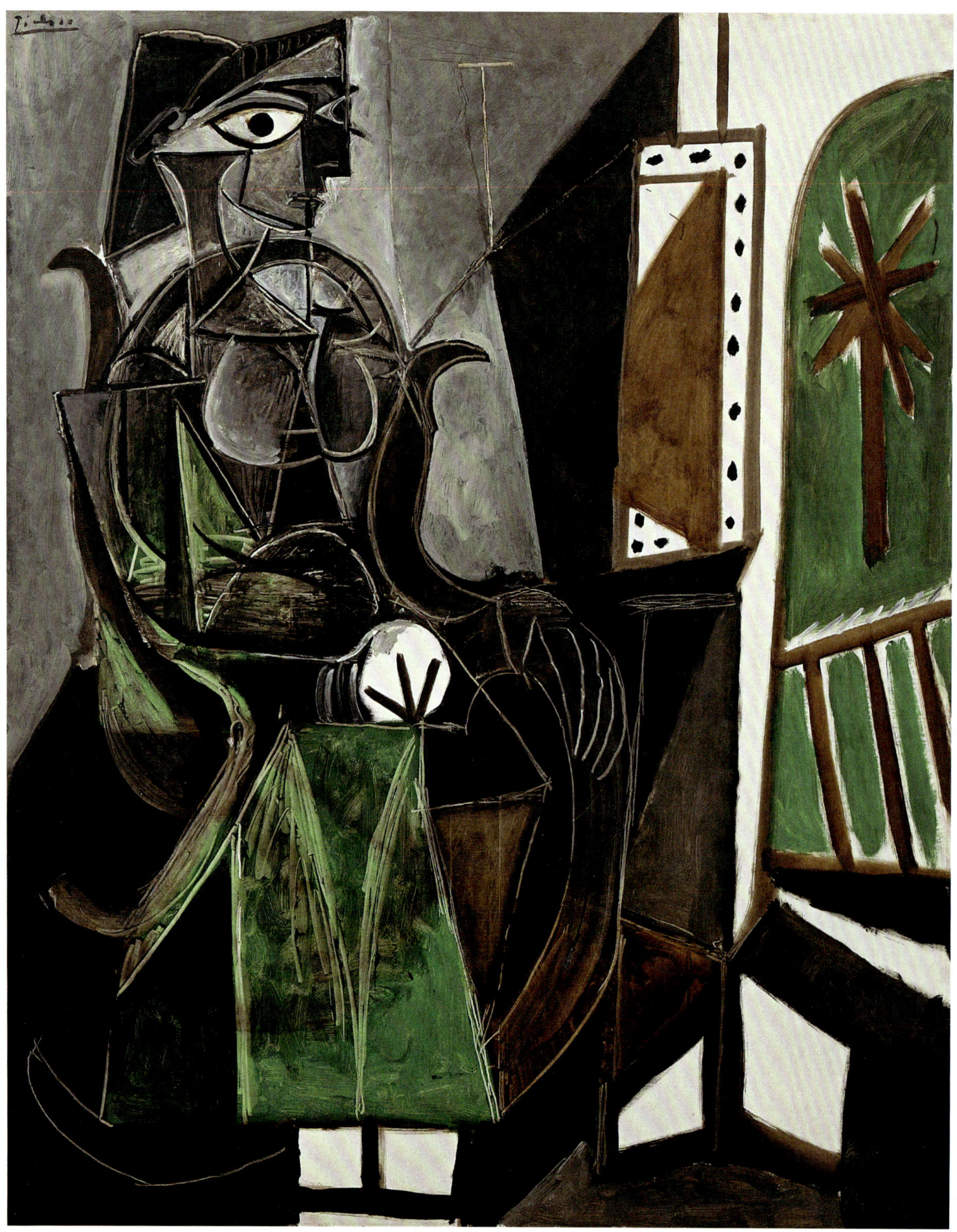

164 *Woman by a Window*, 11 June 1956 (B, L)

his painting studio in one of the large ground-floor rooms. Fascinated by this spacious new environment and the light that poured through the arched French windows, he made his studio the subject of the first major series of paintings executed there in the autumn of 1955.[26] The following spring, the studio theme was modified to include the image of a woman wearing a black headscarf seated in a rocking chair. *Woman by a Window* (164) is the masterpiece of this series. The woman is of course Jacqueline Roque, whose devotion to Picasso was such that, like the archetypal Spanish duenna, she would sit for hours on end in the studio while he worked – so constant a presence, indeed, that in this painting she has completely fused with the rocking-chair in a reprise of the sinister motif of the wartime portrait of Dora Maar (see 143). Unlike the Jacqueline of the earlier, naturalistic portrait of her dressed in black, the Jacqueline of *Woman by a Window* is rigid with the tension of her vigilance, her enormous, dilated right eye fixed on the artist, her left eye, in profile, scanning the studio like a searchlight. This anxious duenna is also the Sphinx and it is debatable whether she is a benign presence or not. But there can be no doubting her regality: the painting has the conventional structure of portraits of rulers and aristocrats enthroned beside a window or doorway that opens out onto their domain.[27]

The left two-thirds of the composition containing Jacqueline are painted in a notably different style from the remainder – a style ultimately derived from Cubism of the 1908–12 period. Picasso built up the surface and then scored the contours into the wet paint with the wooden end of his brush or some other sharp tool; he then adjusted the light and made revisions to the salient forms of her neck, breasts, stomach and skirt in order to enhance the sculptural effect of the figure. The right third of the composition, the sunlit outdoors, contrasts with the Escorial-like gloom of Jacqueline's territory and was painted quickly and thinly in the wilfully naïve style used in some of the earlier studio scenes; some areas of the canvas are left completely bare. Stylistic discrepancy of this kind is common in Picasso's work, serving not only to draw attention to the physical process of painting but also to allude to time in a metaphysical sense. And themes of process and time are crucial to the conception of *Woman by a Window* and to the psychological tension at the core of this grand but ambiguous effigy.

Much more sanguine in mood are the two cut and folded sheet-iron portraits created in 1962, a year after Picasso and Jacqueline were married and moved to Notre-Dame-de-Vie, a secluded farmhouse outside Mougins. The huge frontal eye blazoned on one side of each sculpture seems benign, not baleful like her eyes in *Woman by a Window*, and Lee Miller immortalised their friendly aspect in her photograph of Picasso cheerfully saluting the one Jacqueline later donated to

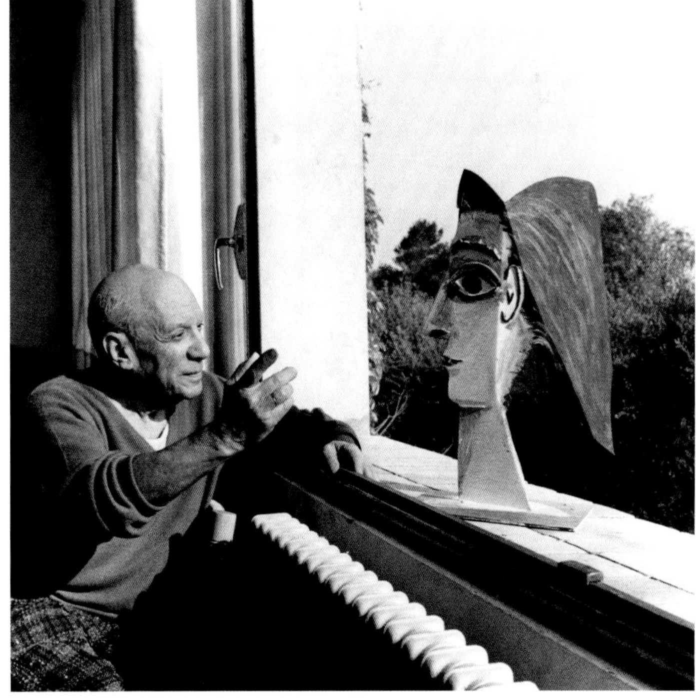

165 *Picasso with* Jacqueline with a Yellow Ribbon *in Notre-Dame-de-Vie, Mougins*. Photograph by Lee Miller, May 1963

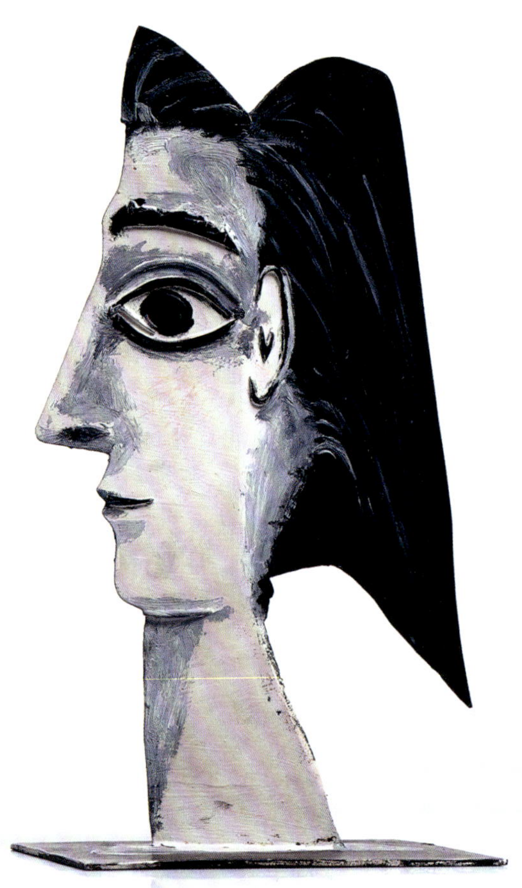

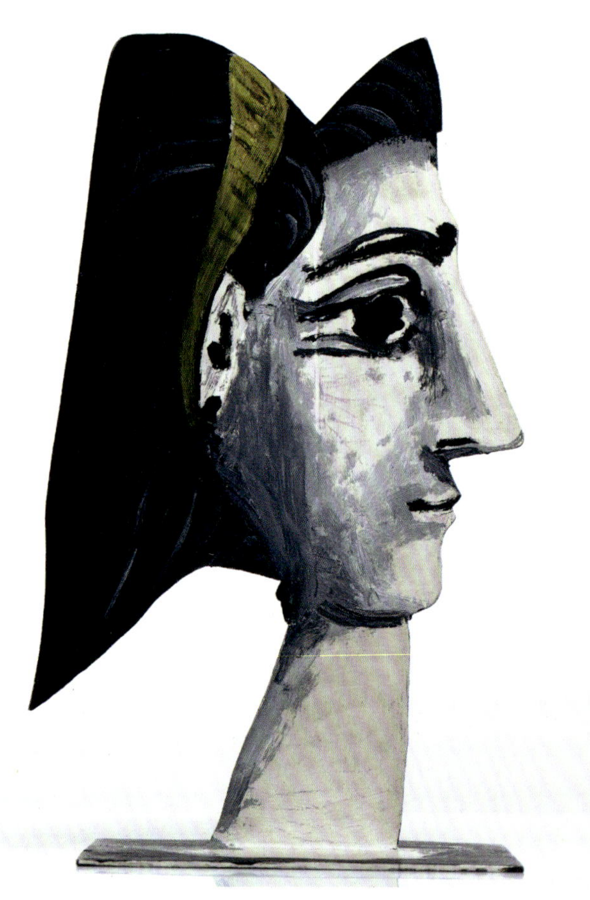

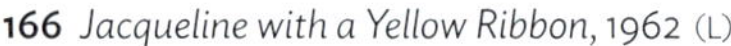

166 *Jacqueline with a Yellow Ribbon*, 1962 (L)

the National Gallery of Iceland (165). The two sculptures are differently decorated versions of the same head. For their realisation, Picasso depended upon the expertise and resources of Tiola, but, exceptionally, instead of providing him with a cut-out maquette in paper or cardboard, Picasso supplied a tracing from a recent, highly simplified painting.[28] Of the two, *Jacqueline with a Yellow Ribbon* (166) is the more naturalistic. On both its sides, Picasso counteracted the flatness of the sheet-iron by using colour and chiaroscuro modelling to give a painterly illusion of volume. The flat rectangular base from which Jacqueline's head rises up is painted with tongue-in-cheek

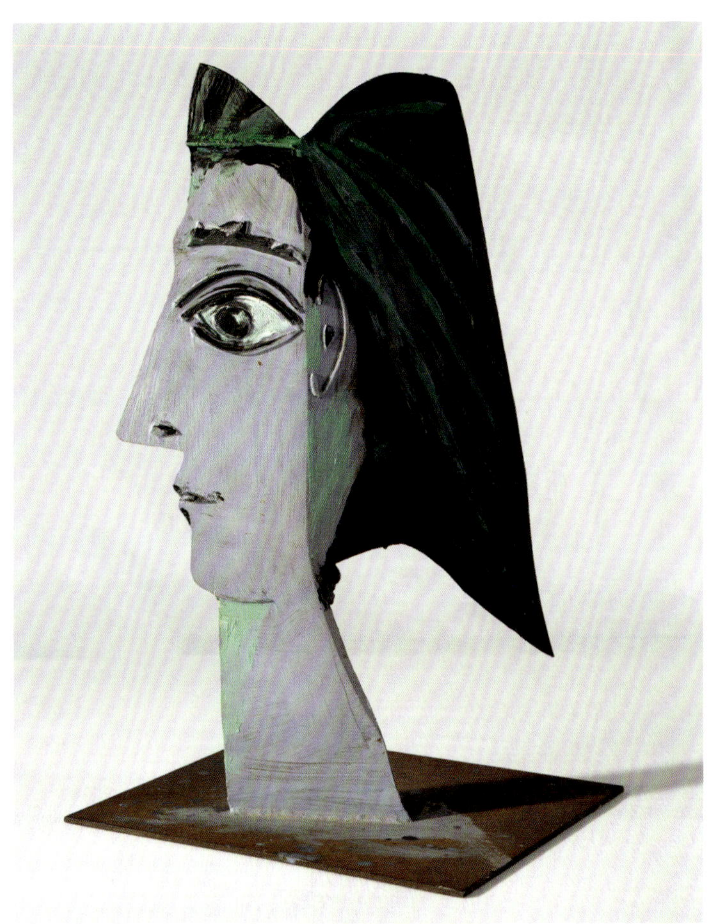

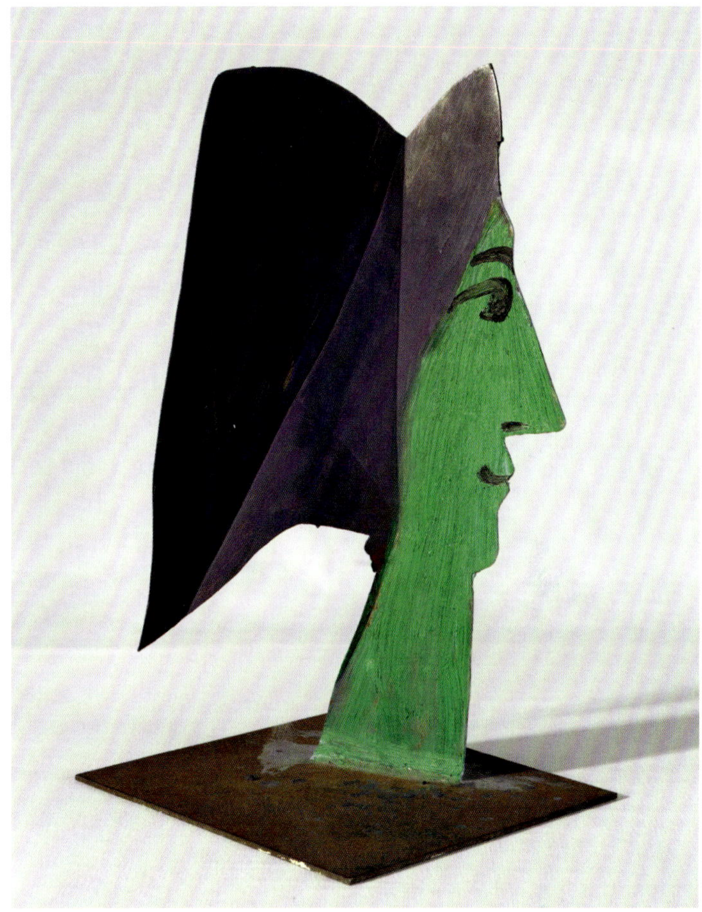

167 *Head of a Woman (Jacqueline)*, 1962 (B)

naturalism to represent her shoulders, the circle delineating the neck of her dark sweater.

Its twin (167) is equally painterly but in a more abstracted vein. The sculpture turns on the relationship between varying tones of emerald green and purple – the colours of the flag of Málaga. The unwitting spectator is surprised and amused by the dramatic contrast between the two sides, but a closer look reveals that exactly the same limited palette was used for both, in greater or lesser saturation. The greys were formed by mixing purple and green, with black and white as the only other pigments used. Rather than make the rectangular base serve as Jacqueline's shoulders, in this sculpture Picasso treated it like a palette and did not bother to wipe off the accidental drips and splashes. The 'front' view – the head stands at the front of the rectangular base and Jacqueline's blade of hair folds away from the viewer – is strongly lit and painted with the speed and spontaneity of Picasso's contemporary canvases. He accentuated the features he had associated with Jacqueline's image from the start – large dark eyes, long straight nose, neatly formed mouth, clearly defined bone structure and thick black hair. The strongly coloured but shaded 'back' view is comically abbreviated, with just a few graphic touches to define eyebrow, eye, nostril and mouth. Two different aspects of Jacqueline are presented: the wide-eyed, protective Muse whose devotion to Picasso and his art was absolute, and the resourceful, witty partner who smiled benevolently on the childish antics with which, in old age, he entertained their visitors.

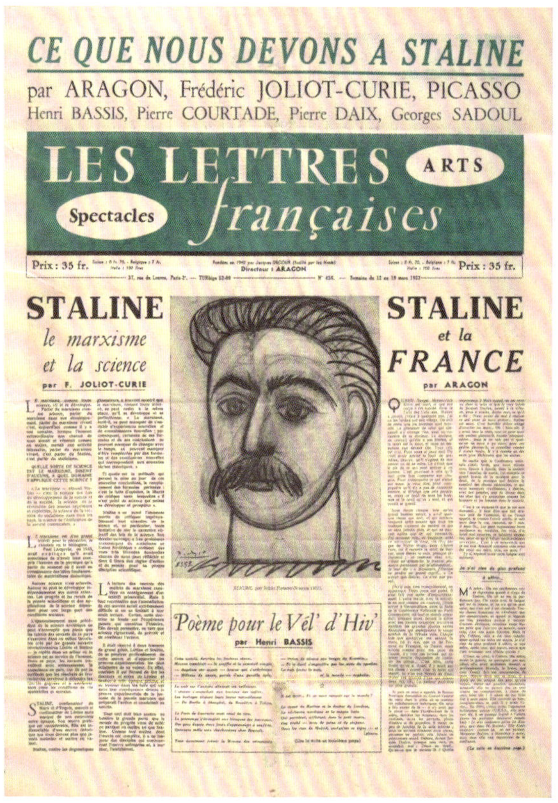

CE QUE NOUS DEVONS A STALINE

par ARAGON, Frédéric JOLIOT-CURIE, PICASSO
Henri BASSIS, Pierre COURTADE, Pierre DAIX, Georges SADOUL

LES LETTRES françaises

ARTS

Spectacles

Prix : 35 fr.

Directeur : ARAGON

Prix : 35 fr.

STALINE
le marxisme et la science
par F. JOLIOT-CURIE

STALINE
et la FRANCE
par ARAGON

'Poème pour le Vél' d'Hiv'
par Henri BASSIS

168 *Portrait of Stalin*, 8 March 1953. Reproduced on the front cover of *Les Lettres françaises*, no.456, 12–19 March 1953

PROPAGANDA VERSUS CARICATURE

Producing a flattering portrait to order was not something that came easily to Picasso and on one of the few occasions when he set out to please he failed to do so. The occasion was the death of Stalin on 5 March 1953. The following day, Picasso's old friend Louis Aragon sent a telegram beseeching him to produce a text or drawing for the commemorative issue of the Communist newspaper *Les Lettres françaises*. The portrait, based on photos Aragon supplied, duly appeared in the centre of the front page (168). Hagiography was the order of the day and it did not occur to Picasso that he would cause offence by portraying Stalin as a handsome young man, rather than as the venerable 'Father of the people', but the bland

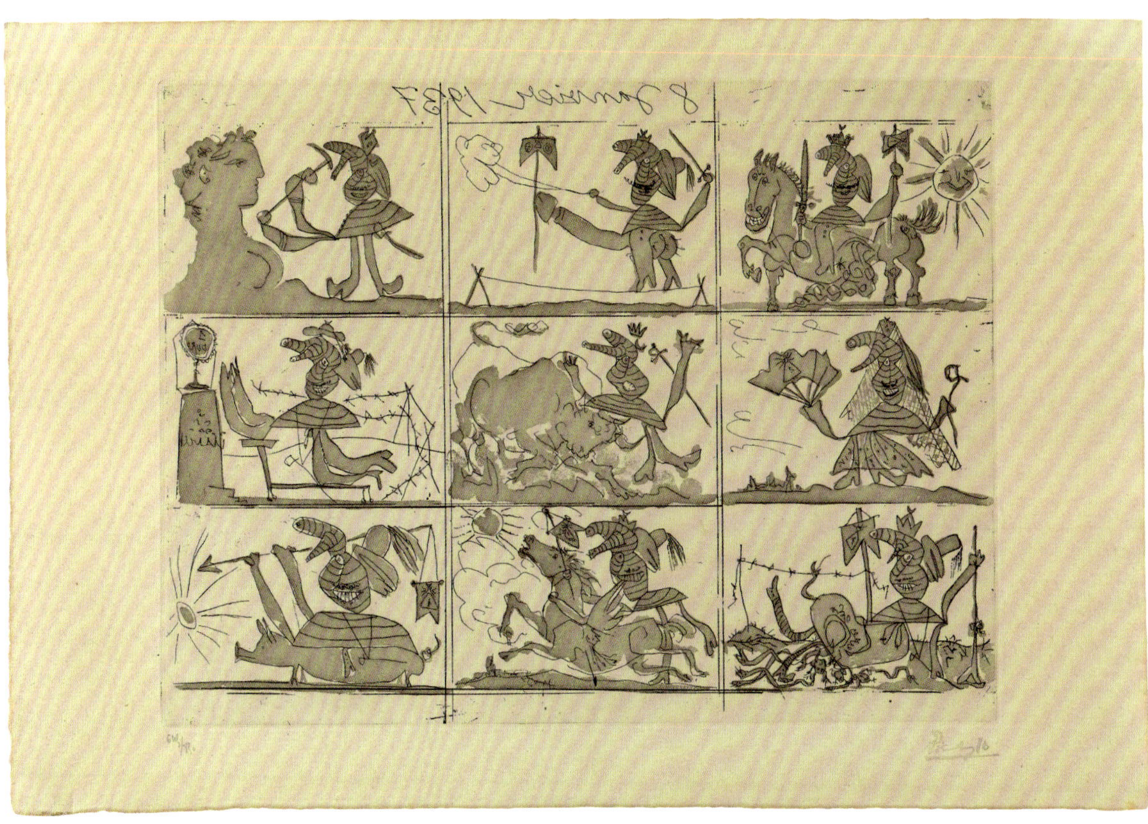

169 *Dream and Lie of Franco I*, 8 January 1937

image provoked disgust and rage and Picasso was accused of mockery and travesty.[29] The intensity of the criticism baffled him – as well it might, given how offensive he could be when he so wished. The obvious parallel is with his other 'portrait' of a political leader – the savage strip-cartoon, produced for sale at the Exposition Internationale in Paris in 1937 to raise money for the Republican cause, in which Franco is satirised as a repulsive and grotesque 'polyp' (Picasso's word) (169).

Fortunately, Sabartés knew better than to expect emollience. After Picasso settled in Cannes and Jacqueline assumed many of the organisational duties he had once performed, Sabartés focused on the creation of a museum dedicated to Picasso's work in Barcelona. (The Museu Picasso was eventually inaugurated in March 1963.) In return for his dedication – the mission was fraught with difficulties, not least those of political origin – Picasso presented Sabartés with dozens of portrait-caricatures. While poking fun at his appearance, they also referred ironically to aspects of his personality and tasks he had performed on Picasso's behalf, and were thus in-jokes that only they or their intimates could fully appreciate.

Picasso took two impressions of one monotype before reusing the zinc plate for one of the satirical aquatints featuring Sabartés produced on the same day, Sunday 5 May 1957 (170).[30] The combination of narrative subject, printmaking process and small scale tells us that he had Degas's brothel monotypes in mind. The prostitute in Picasso's

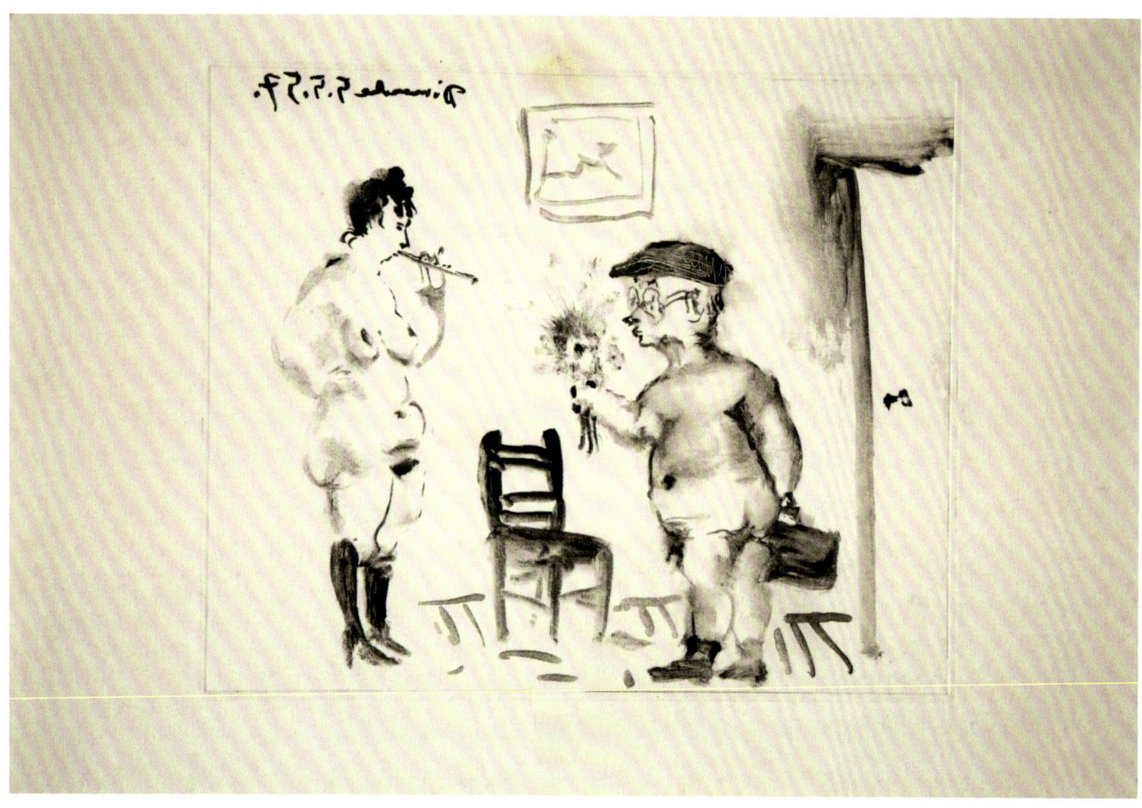

170 *Sabartés and His Neighbour*, 5 May 1957 (B, L)

monotype resembles her counterparts in Degas's prints – naked except for stockings and shoes, coarse-looking, charmless, running to fat (171). Sabartés, on the other hand, looks very different from Degas's fully dressed clients: unlike them he is polite and diffident, naked save for his favourite cloth cap, socks and shoes and the attaché case that accompanied him on all his trips to Cannes and Barcelona to further the cause of the future museum. The setting is also different from Degas's Parisian brothels, with their mirrors, padded sofas, patterned carpets and gas lighting: it is the kind of simple, homely establishment of small-town Spain that Picasso remembered from his youth. In 1971, three years after Sabartés's death, Picasso engaged in a protracted dialogue with Degas's brothel monotypes (see 186–8). This monotype is like a dry-run.

Sabartés was the subject of more caricatures, by a considerable margin, than anyone else in Picasso's entourage. Caricaturing him became something of a party-piece whenever Picasso was asked to sign the title page of one of Sabartés's books about his work, as happened rather often. In this case (172), in Paris on Christmas Day 1958 Sabartés dedicated a copy of his book about Picasso's series of variations after Velázquez's *Las Meninas* (see 179 and 181–2) to Dr Joseph Jaffé, and in Cannes on 3 January 1959, Picasso added a comical drawing of the author in the guise of an elderly Pinocchio – the puppet in Carlo Collodi's children's story whose nose stretches when he is telling lies – a joke, presumably, about the credibility of Sabartés's text.

Some of the funniest caricatures of all were drawn rapidly on pin-ups of movie stars distributed

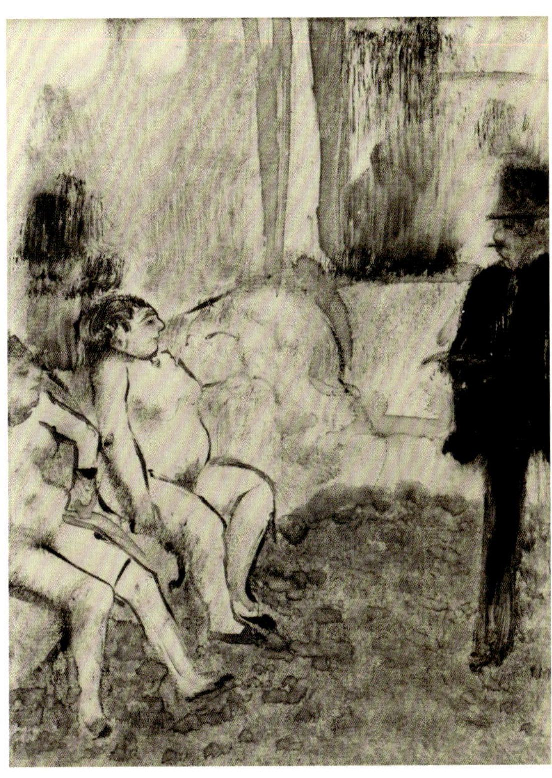

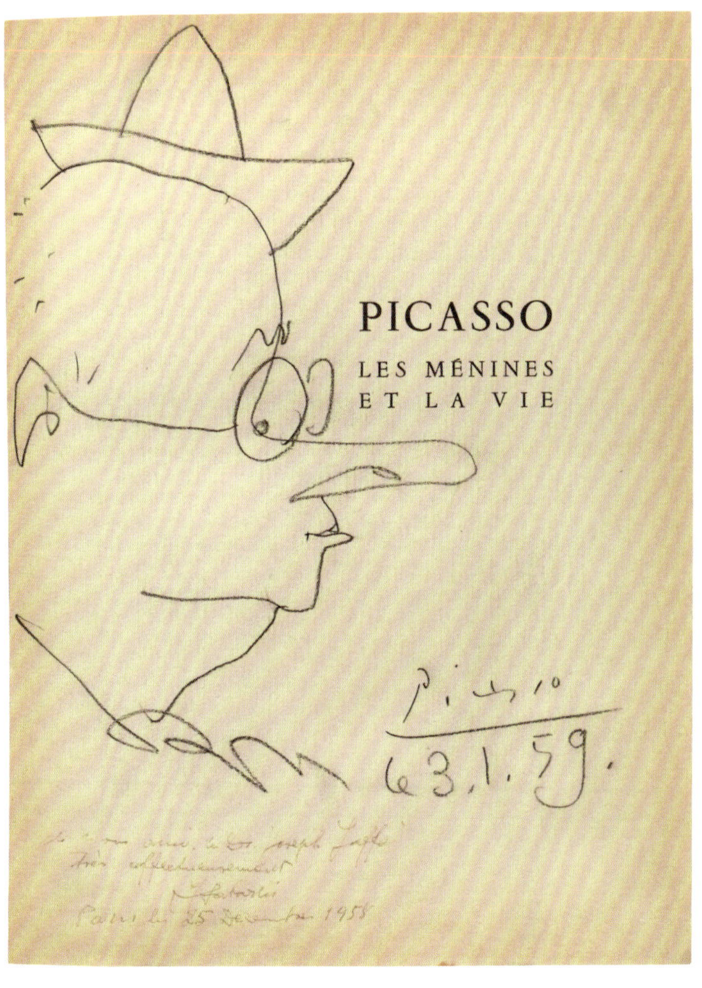

171 *The Client* by Edgar Degas, c.1876–7

172 *Caricature of Jaume Sabartés,* 3 January 1959. Dedication on title-page of Jaime Sabartés, *Picasso. Les Ménines et la vie*, Paris, Éditions Cercle d'Art, 1958 (B)

in issues of *Ciné-Révélation*, which claimed to be 'Le plus grand hébdomadaire du cinéma' (The greatest weekly devoted to the cinema) and was one of dozens of popular magazines founded by the publishing magnate and film producer Cino del Duca. The association of Cannes with the movie industry provides the immediate context for the series: in the 1950s Picasso had superstar status himself and being seen with him was considered excellent publicity by rising stars such as Brigitte Bardot.[31] But hoarding pin-ups from movie magazines of the 1950s was no different from collecting photos and postcards of entertainers and celebrities, as Picasso had begun doing before the First World War.

Esther Williams (173) is in one of her classic swimming roles as the heroine of MGM's *Dangerous When Wet*, directed by Charles Walters (released in 1953). The cut-out of the hugely successful MGM star Lana Turner (174) seems to be one of the many bikini or swimsuit photos for which she was famed, rather than a publicity still from one of her movies, while the cut-out of Neile Adams (175) celebrates her dazzling nightclub routine in MGM's comedy-drama *This Could be the Night*, directed by Robert Wise (released in May 1957). In the only European

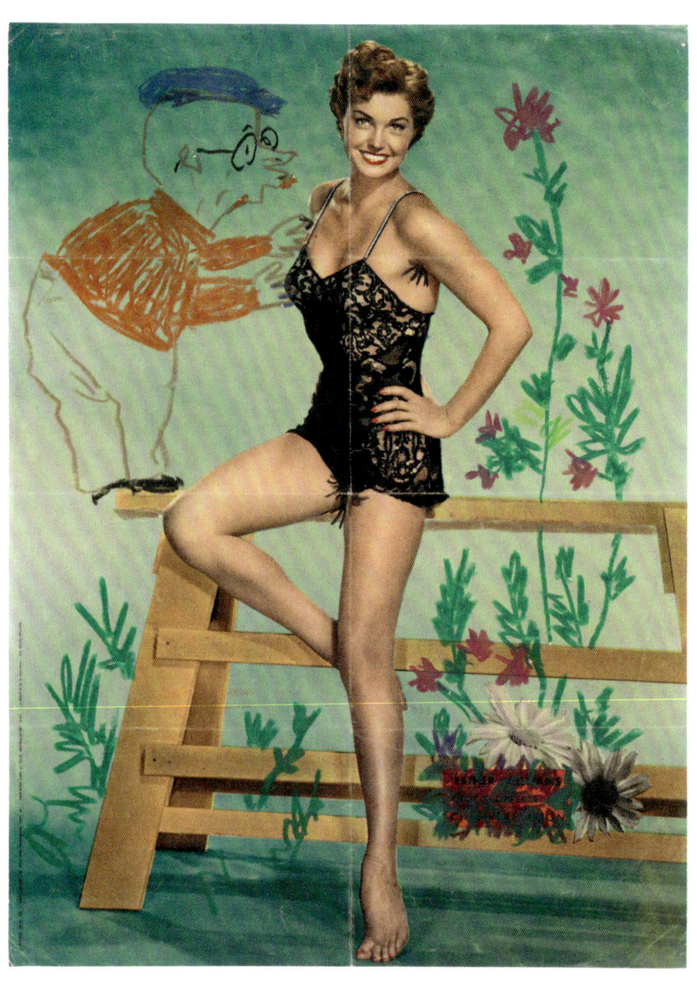

173 *Humorous Composition: Jaume Sabartés and Esther Williams*, 23 May 1957 (L)

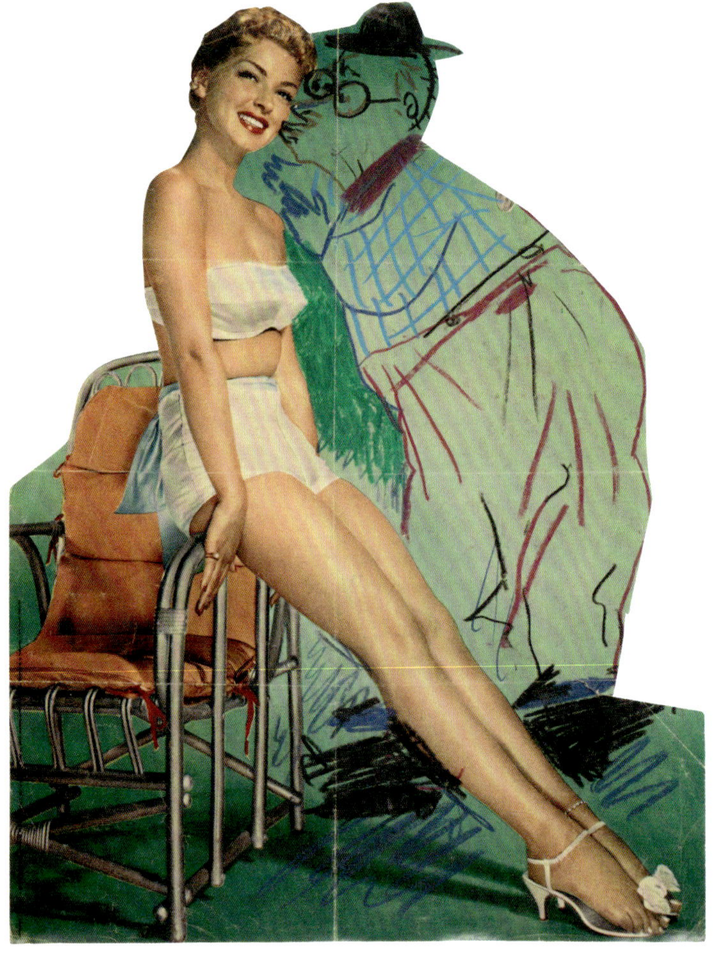

174 *Humorous Composition: Jaume Sabartés and Lana Turner*, 22 May 1957 (B)

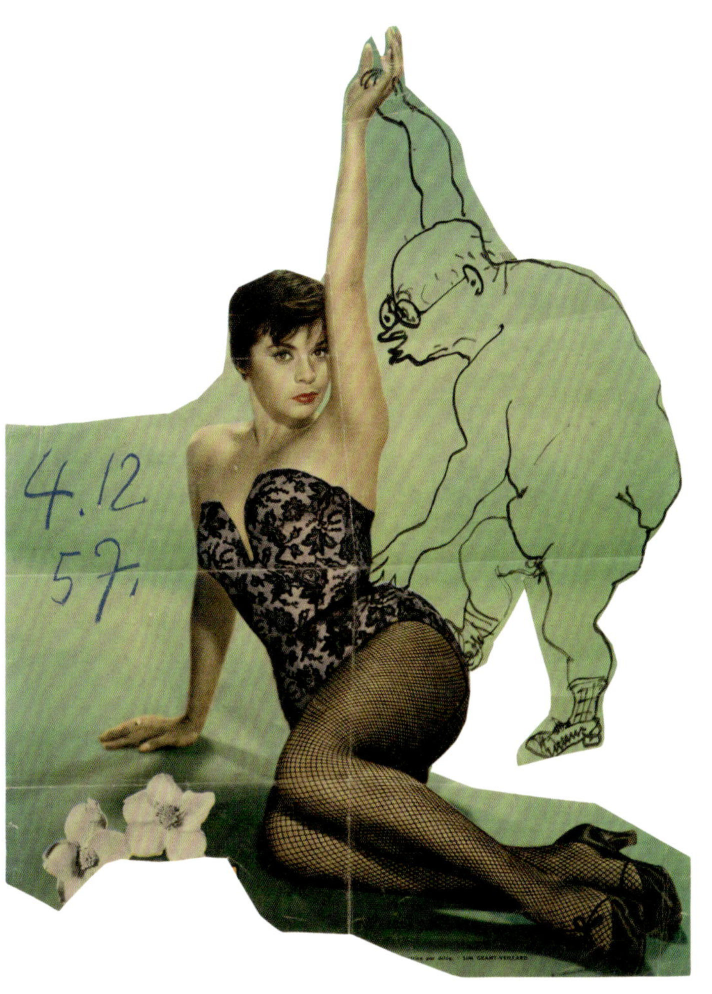

175 *Humorous Composition: Jaume Sabartés and Neile Adams*, 4 December 1957 (B)

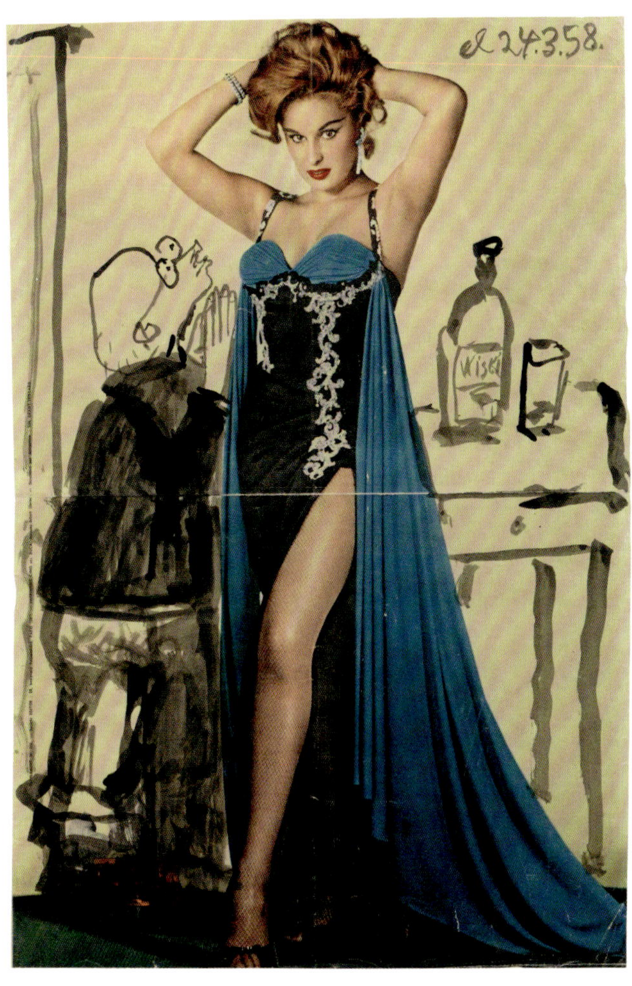

176 *Humorous Composition: Jaume Sabartés and Sylvia Lopez*, 24 March 1958 (L)

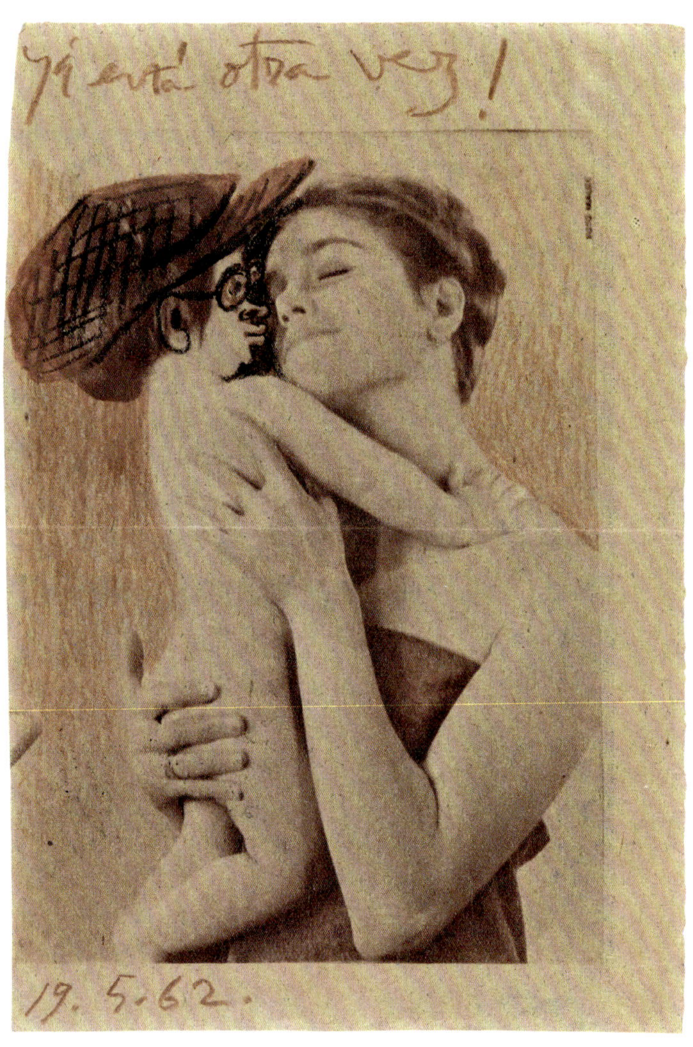

177 *Humorous Composition: Jaume Sabartés as a Baby and a Model*, 19 May 1962 (L)

production featured in this foursome, Sylvia Lopez (176) is in her role as the music-hall dancer Florence Didier, in the about-to-be-released French-Italian movie *Tabarin*, directed by Richard Pottier. Each time, Picasso created a different farcical scenario in which an ardent, gnome-like Sabartés attempts to kiss the sexy actress – or, rather, her effigy. Usually fully clothed, although once memorably naked save for socks and shoes, and never without his spectacles, his position is hopeless: directing all her attention and her charms towards the spectator, the object of his passion is indifferent to the manikin beside her. An uxorious husband while his wife was still alive and never a Don Juan, Sabartés used to grumble and utter dire warnings whenever Picasso became entangled with yet another woman, so the running joke of the pin-up series and the monotype turns on the disparity between his real persona and the persona Picasso foisted on him. The later caricature of Sabartés as a naked, bespectacled, cap-wearing baby in the arms of his adoring mother (177) has a different source – a photo from an unidentified Spanish newspaper.[32] Here for once the roles are reversed and it is Sabartés who is the object of a woman's adoration.

1 See Gilot and Lake 1965, pp.109–13.

2 Gilot 1990, p.23.

3 Ibid., p.21.

4 Gilot and Lake 1965, p.113.

5 The first edition of Grandville's *Les fleurs animées* was published in 1847 (Gabriel de Gonet, Paris). Further editions followed in 1857, 1867 and 1899. Grandville was a favourite of the Surrealists.

6 Gilot and Lake 1965, p.116.

7 See Charles Stuckey, 'The Face of Picasso's Lithography', in *Picasso and Gilot* 2012, pp.164–89.

8 Gilot and Lake 1965, p.40.

9 Stuckey points out that a workshop version of Velázquez's portrait of Queen Mariana was acquired by the Louvre in 1941 ('The Face of Picasso's Lithography', in *Picasso and Gilot* 2012, p.178).

10 See Gilot 1990, pp.100–39.

11 Gilot and Lake 1965, pp.68–70.

12 See p.169, note 21.

13 Quinn 1965, chapter 4, non-paginated.

14 Duncan 1958, pp.159, 164–5. Picasso was by then living in Cannes with Jacqueline Roque.

15 For the full story and a catalogue of all the works depicting her, see *Sylvette* 2014. Sylvette David later changed her name to Lydia Corbett.

16 For instance, *Harlequin with Violin ('Si tu veux')*, 1918 (Cleveland Museum of Art; Z.III.160).

17 For one of the snapshots taken by Tobias Jellinek, see *Sylvette* 2014, p.118.

18 Lydia Corbett/Sylvette David reported by Martin Gayford in 'The Old Man and his Muse', *Sunday Telegraph*, 30 January 1994.

19 *Madame Z. (Jacqueline with Flowers)*, 2 June 1954 (Private collection; Z.XVI.365).

20 For instance, *Head of a Woman*, 1957. Painted sheet-iron (Private collection; S.492).

21 El Greco's *Portrait of a Painter*, c.1603 (Museo de Bellas Artes, Seville) is presumed to represent his son Jorge Manuel Theotocópuli. For the juxtaposition with Picasso's *Portrait of a Painter, after El Greco*, 1950 (Museum Sammlung Rosengart, Lucerne; Z.XV.165), see Galassi 1996, pp.122–3.

22 See Penrose 1958, p.350, for an early reference to her role in the series.

23 The Impressionist collection was removed to the Musée du Jeu de Paume in 1947. It is now in the Musée d'Orsay.

24 *La peinture française dans la seconde moitié du XIXe siècle et au début du XXe siècle*. Musée Masséna, Nice, August–September 1955, no.11. *Lola de Valence* was illustrated (in black and white) on the cover of the catalogue, which bore the title *Chefs-d'oeuvre du Musée du Louvre*.

25 Parmelin 1963, pp.120–1.

26 For instance, *The Studio at La Californie*, 23 October 1955 (Centre Pompidou, Paris. Musée national d'art moderne/Centre de création industrielle; Z.XVI.486).

27 For example, Titian's posthumous portrait of Empress Isabel of Portugal, 1548 (Museo Nacional del Prado, Madrid).

28 *Head of a Woman in Profile*, 19 February 1960 (Private collection; Z.XIX.176). The tracing is S.630.1.

29 For a summary of the scandal, see Utley 2000, pp.181–90.

30 See Baer, vol.IV, cats 965–9.

31 Brigitte Bardot was photographed at La Californie during the Cannes Film Festival in 1956, the year in which Henri Clouzot's film *Le mystère Picasso* was awarded the Prix spécial du Jury.

32 On the reverse is an advertisement for a new production of Alejandro Casona's *La Dama del alba* (1944), directed by José Tamayo Rivas at Madrid's Teatro Bellas Artes.

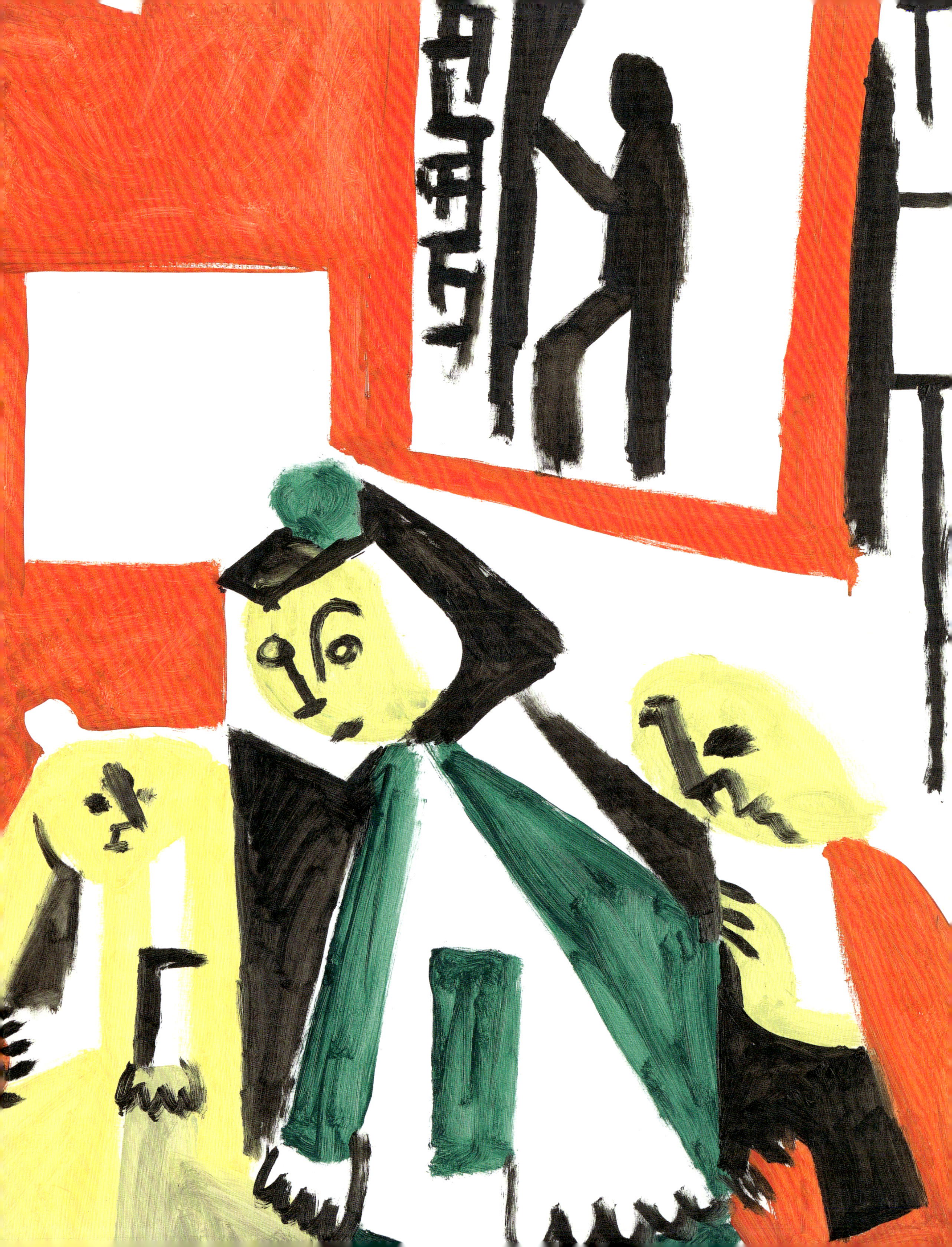

7. Picasso with the old masters

'Straight' copies of old-master paintings are a great rarity in Picasso's work. One of the very few is his student copy of Velázquez's *Portrait of Philip IV* (see 3). But free, personal transcriptions are common and after the Liberation they consumed much of his creative energy.[1] Sometimes Picasso's responses were one-offs, but his longstanding habit of producing multiple variations on the same theme was extended to this special body of work.

WITH VELÁZQUEZ

The paintings Picasso chose were always by artists he particularly admired and on themes that had special meaning for him. Portraits had their fair share. He had executed hardly any group portraits,[2] and it was perhaps partly to make amends that he committed himself to grappling with one of the greatest group portraits of all time, Velázquez's *Las Meninas* (178). Knowing this would test him to the limits, he set up a special studio on the unused top floor of La Californie and initially forbade entry to anyone other than Jacqueline. The dialogue with this notoriously enigmatic painting occupied him for four intense months, August to December 1957, and, feeling exposed and under pressure, his temper was volatile.[3] Picasso's sense of his Spanish identity was profoundly involved and he eventually gave the entire series to the museum dedicated to his work that Sabartés was at that very time striving to set up. It was also Sabartés who undertook to write the first fully illustrated account for immediate publication in 1958.[4]

The dynamics of the dialogue were established in the powerful first variation (179), which is by far the most faithful of the entire set in that it includes all the elements in Velázquez's composition. But so much is wilfully altered – starting with the horizontal instead of vertical orientation of the huge canvas and the decision to paint exclusively in monochrome – that the spectator may initially sense a spirit of irreverent contradiction. In fact, Picasso's approach was exploratory and empathetic, for he was not only intent on remaking the composition according to his own artistic preoccupations but also fusing his identity with that of his great ancestor. He imagined, for instance, what the cavernous room in the Alcázar – the setting for *Las Meninas* – would be like if all the shutters were opened and more light allowed to flood in, as the light flooded into the spacious rooms of La Californie. And, comically, he replaced the somnolent mastiff with his yapping, much-loved dachshund Lump, depicted in a passable imitation of child art.[5] This process of identification is wittily captured in a doctored photo of *Las Meninas*, with Picasso in the place of Velázquez and Sabartés as a marvelling spectator (180). On 1 April 1959 the two friends – together with 'Diego' (Velázquez) – dedicated it to Joan Gaspar, who with his cousin Miguel, ran the Sala Gaspar art gallery in Barcelona.[6]

In interpreting *Las Meninas* Picasso recast it in terms of his own recent work. So, like the portrait of Jacqueline overseeing his studio (see 164), his version shifts in style from the dense, complex and cubistic (on the left) to the rapid, simple and faux-naïf (on the right). This blatant inconsistency of style and finish is at odds with the unity and harmony of *Las Meninas*, but is consistent with Picasso's personal cult of stylistic and technical variety and obsession with the fluidity of the creative process. Nevertheless, he also explored essential aspects of *Las Meninas*. The play of light and shade, on which its mesmerising illusionism largely depends, was one of Picasso's chief concerns in this spacious, perspectival first variant, and his decision to work in grisaille was conditioned at least as much by his engagement with the lighting of *Las Meninas* as by his investment in grisaille as an expressive tool.[7] With his acute sensitivity to personality, expression and gesture, Picasso was also responsive to Velázquez's evocation of the *comédie humaine* of court life, humorously playing up the anxious fussing of the maids of honour. Realising that Velázquez's pride in his privileged status at Philip's court underpinned the unique conception of *Las Meninas*, Picasso enlarged him to the full height of the canvas, so that he towers above the pygmy figures of the Infanta, her attendants and the cartoon-like mirror-reflections of the King and Queen. Beneath the humour of Picasso's version lies a shrewd mixture of updating – how might *Las Meninas* have looked had it been painted in 1957 instead of 1656? – and analysis – what motivated Velázquez when he painted *Las Meninas*? Underlying the dialogue was Picasso's conviction that great art is always of today: 'To me there is no past or future in art. If a work of art cannot live always in the present it must not be considered at all.'[8] The fact that he found the 300-year-old painting so stimulating and provocative was proof of its timelessness.

In the string of variations that followed, Picasso allowed himself equal latitude: dismantling the composition; focusing on parts not the whole; pushing to extremes the Cubist and kindergarten styles he had juxtaposed in this first painting; reimagining the scene in different palettes of colour; and experimenting with different painterly techniques. Only two are discussed here. For his second variation (181), dated 20 August 1957, Picasso retained the grisaille palette of the first and, reverting to his preferred form of portraiture, homed in on Infanta Margarita María. As the pivotal figure of *Las Meninas*, she was an obvious choice, but for Picasso this was also a way of revisiting the portraiture of his children, especially eight-year-old Paloma, who had just spent part of the summer holidays in La Californie. He cut the Infanta's figure off at the edge of the platter-like top of her farthingale skirt to create an intimate half-length image comparable to the lithograph of Paloma with her doll (see 155). But in its ultra-simplified style, the painting is closer to the sheet-metal portraits of Sylvette David (see 159). Indeed, one can imagine Picasso's Infanta cut out in sheet-metal, bent along a couple of the strongly marked contours, with the top of her skirt folded out to form the base. Picasso was excited by the potential of this radically new type of sculpture and shortly before embarking on the *Las Meninas* series had realised in painted sheet-iron several large heads of Jacqueline raised on tall poles and stands.[9] Imagining the Infanta as a sheet-metal sculpture came naturally to him. But it was not a wholly self-centred response, for, lit more brightly than her companions and separable from the darker frieze of supporting characters, Velázquez's Infanta is the one truly statuesque figure in the ensemble. Picasso was probing the sculptural implications of *Las Meninas*.

Dated 15 November 1957, our other painting was the last of the large canvases in the *Las Meninas* series (182). Throughout the autumn, Picasso had grappled with the issue of colour, ringing the changes in the dominant hue of his multi-figure versions: blue-green, blue-violet, black, yellow and in this, one of the freshest and most luminous of all, bright red. As several writers have pointed out, the use of red to flood the background and unify the surface is a clear reference to Matisse, who often occupied Picasso's thoughts and conversation in the years following his death in 1954. *Large Red Interior* of 1948 (Centre Pompidou, Paris. Musée national d'art moderne/Centre de création industrielle) is often cited as Picasso's source, but he would not have forgotten the great *Red Studio* of 1911 (The Museum of Modern Art, New York). By appropriating Matisse's favourite red, Picasso played the game of imagining what Matisse might have done had he chosen to paint a highly personal version of *Las Meninas*.

The painting is equally redolent of Picasso's own recent work, particularly the scenes depicting Françoise, Claude and Paloma painted in 1953–4 when he and Françoise were splitting up (see 156). Velázquez's portrayal of Margarita María, her

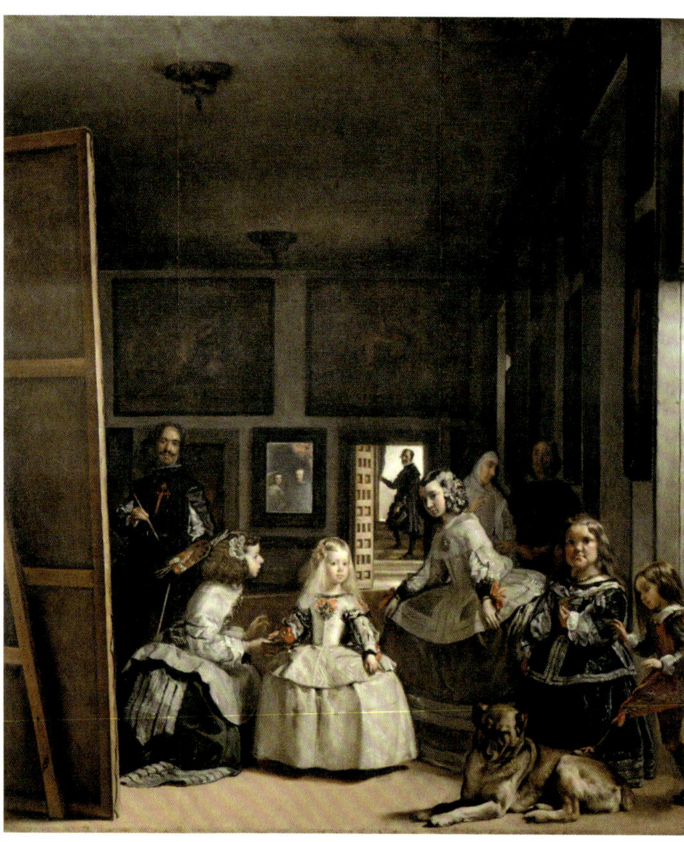

178 *Las Meninas* by Diego Velázquez, 1656

attendants and the dog, with her parents as distant, sidelined figures and himself as observer and recorder, had certain poignant similarities to his own domestic situation. In the present variant, the two maids of honour, Margarita and the dwarf Nicolás Pertusato are all reacting to the barking dachshund, and Lump, pampered and obstreperous, was often the focus of attention in La Californie. Whether or not we are entitled to attribute a fixed identity to each figure – the Infanta as Paloma, the boy-dwarf as Claude, and so on – the Queen's chamberlain, poised in the doorway observing the scene but resembling an artist at his easel, is surely a stand-in for Picasso. With Matisse at his elbow, he had inhabited *Las Meninas* once again.

The Velázquez/Matisse elision is typical of Picasso's variations after old-master paintings, for whenever he 'wrestled' with a particular painter other painters interposed themselves. His *musée imaginaire* had always been of huge proportions, but as he grew older it seemed to him that a host of artists had joined him in his studio: 'I have a feeling that Delacroix, Giotto, Tintoretto, El Greco, and the rest, as well as all the modern painters, the good and the bad, the abstract and the non-abstract, are all standing behind me watching me at work.'[10] The sensation was most acute whenever he was occupied with a suite of variations: the artist in question never left his side and he imagined debates and arguments breaking out with the other painters who dropped by to check out the latest developments.[11] To Roland Penrose he spoke of these multi-voiced dialogues as 'collaborations'[12] – a revealing choice of word because it implies comradeship and equality, transcending time and place. To André Malraux, with whom he discussed the latter's concept of 'a museum without walls', he explained that living 'with' his brother-painters never involved deference or self-effacement because the whole point was to create something new, not to conserve:

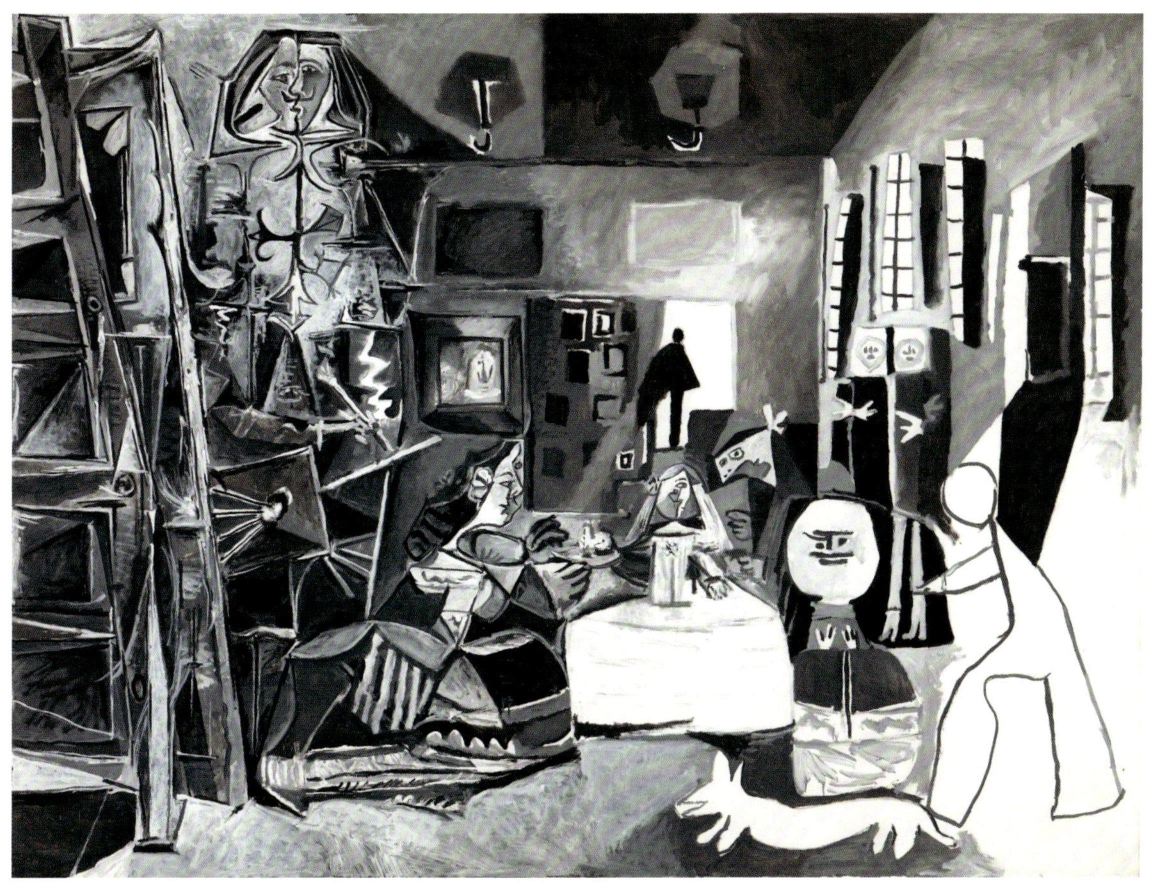

179 *Las Meninas, after Velázquez,* 17 August 1957

180 Photomontage with Velázquez's *Las Meninas,* dedicated to Joan Gaspar by Jaume Sabartés and Picasso, 1 April 1959

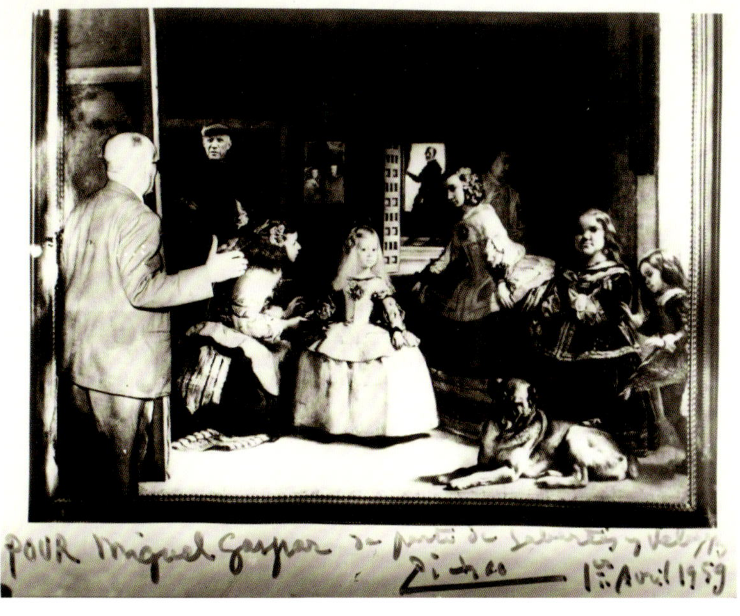

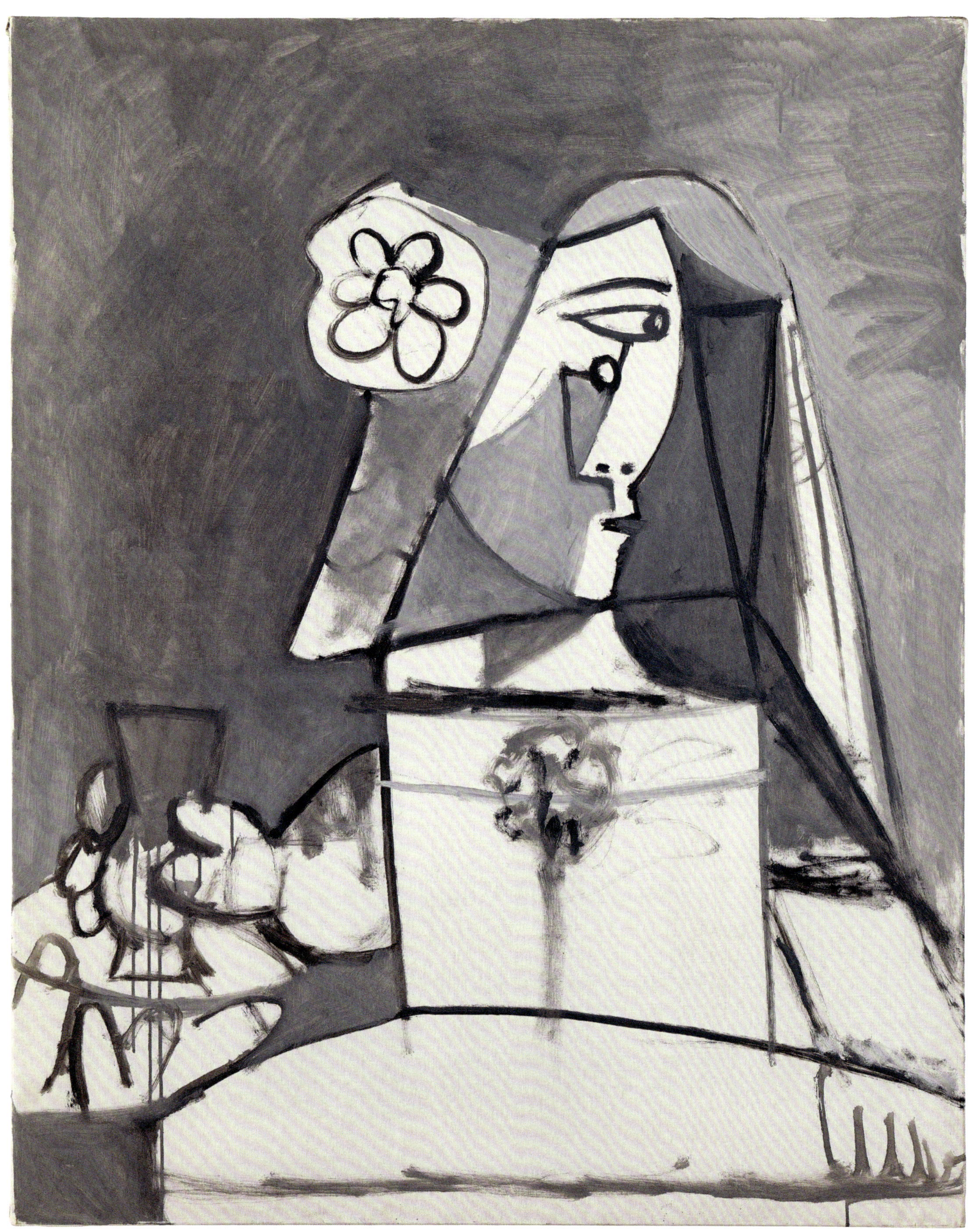

181 *Las Meninas (Infanta Margarita María)*, 20 August 1957 (B, L)

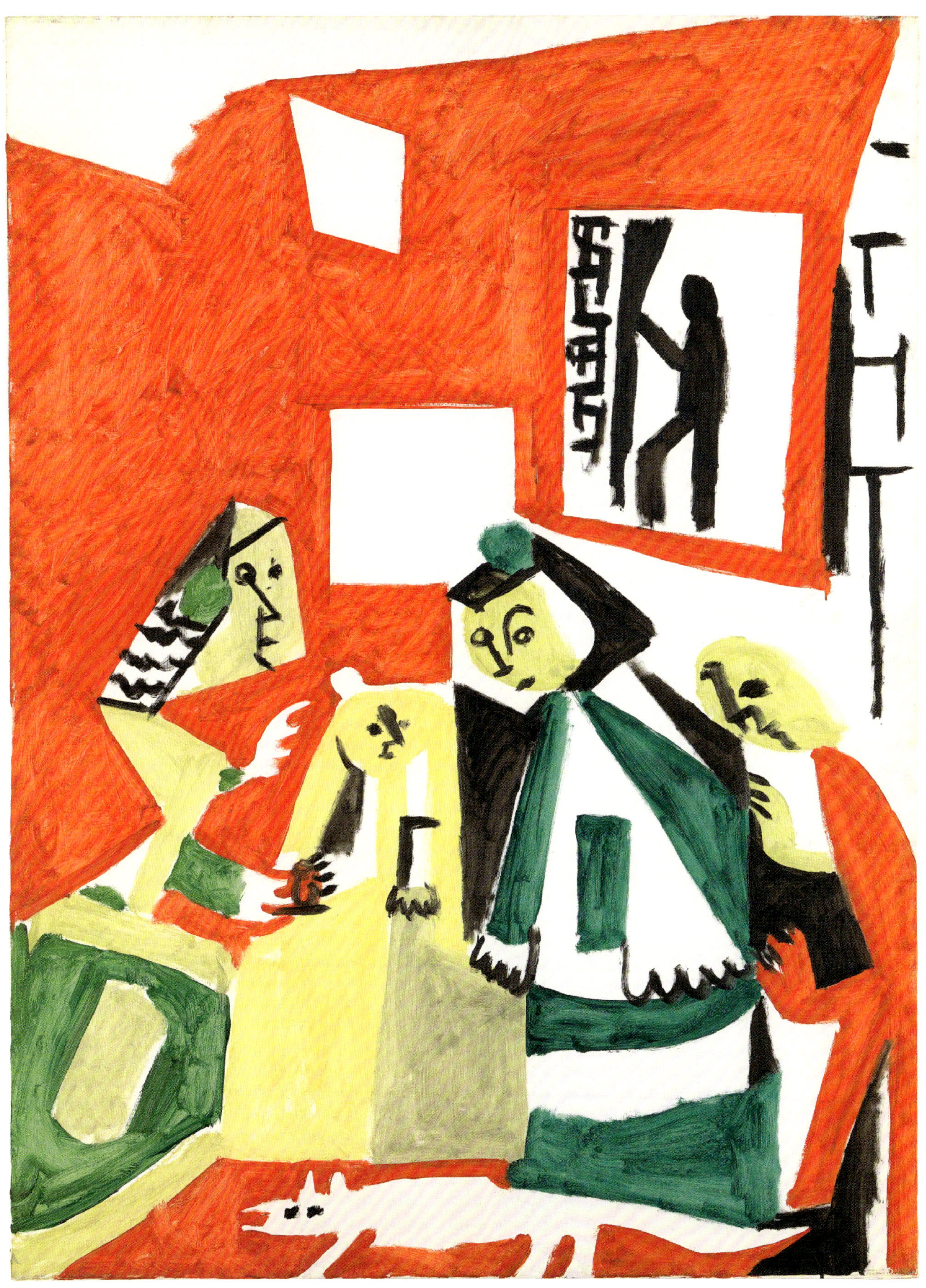

182 *Las Meninas*, 15 November 1957 (B, L)

> I paint against the canvases that are important to me, but I paint in accord with *everything that's still missing* from that Museum of yours. [...] You've got to make what doesn't exist, what has never been made before. That's painting: for a painter it means wrestling with painting.[13]

In essence, Picasso's treatment of old-master paintings, and by extension the old masters themselves, was no different from his treatment of the family members, friends and lovers he portrayed. He described one of his earliest portraits of Jacqueline as *'raté'* (a failure) *'parce qu'elle m'a dominé'* (because she dominated me).[14] He would have regarded a submissive copy as a failure to 'wrestle with painting'.

WITH EL GRECO, RAPHAEL AND DEGAS

At the turn of the century, one of the artists who 'stood behind' Picasso was El Greco and, as we saw, he filled pages of his sketchbooks with pastiches of El Greco-type heads and teased Rusiñol for *his* obsession with the artist (see 22). His one-off variation after El Greco's *Portrait of a Painter*, c.1603, has already been mentioned.[15] In old age, as Picasso was flooded with memories of his childhood and youth in Spain, El Greco came back to haunt him. He told Kahnweiler that he had always preferred El Greco's portraits – 'those men with pointed beards'[16] – and when working on the great suite of 347 prints that absorbed him between March and October 1968, every now and then bearded, beruffed and soulful men in black insisted on appearing in a mixed company of characters, or on having an entire plate to themselves.[17] The etching made on 29 June 1968 (184) is derived from the row of mourners in *The Burial of the Count of Orgaz* (183) and, as with the early pastiches, in converting El Greco's painterly style into a linear language Picasso exaggerated the artist's mannerisms, mimicking his agitated contours and the rhythmic upwards and downwards angling of the heads, and maximising

183 Detail from *The Burial of the Count of Orgaz* by El Greco, 1586–8

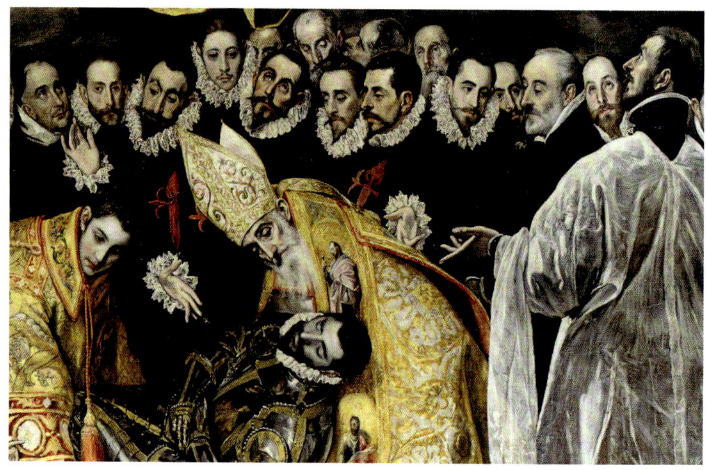

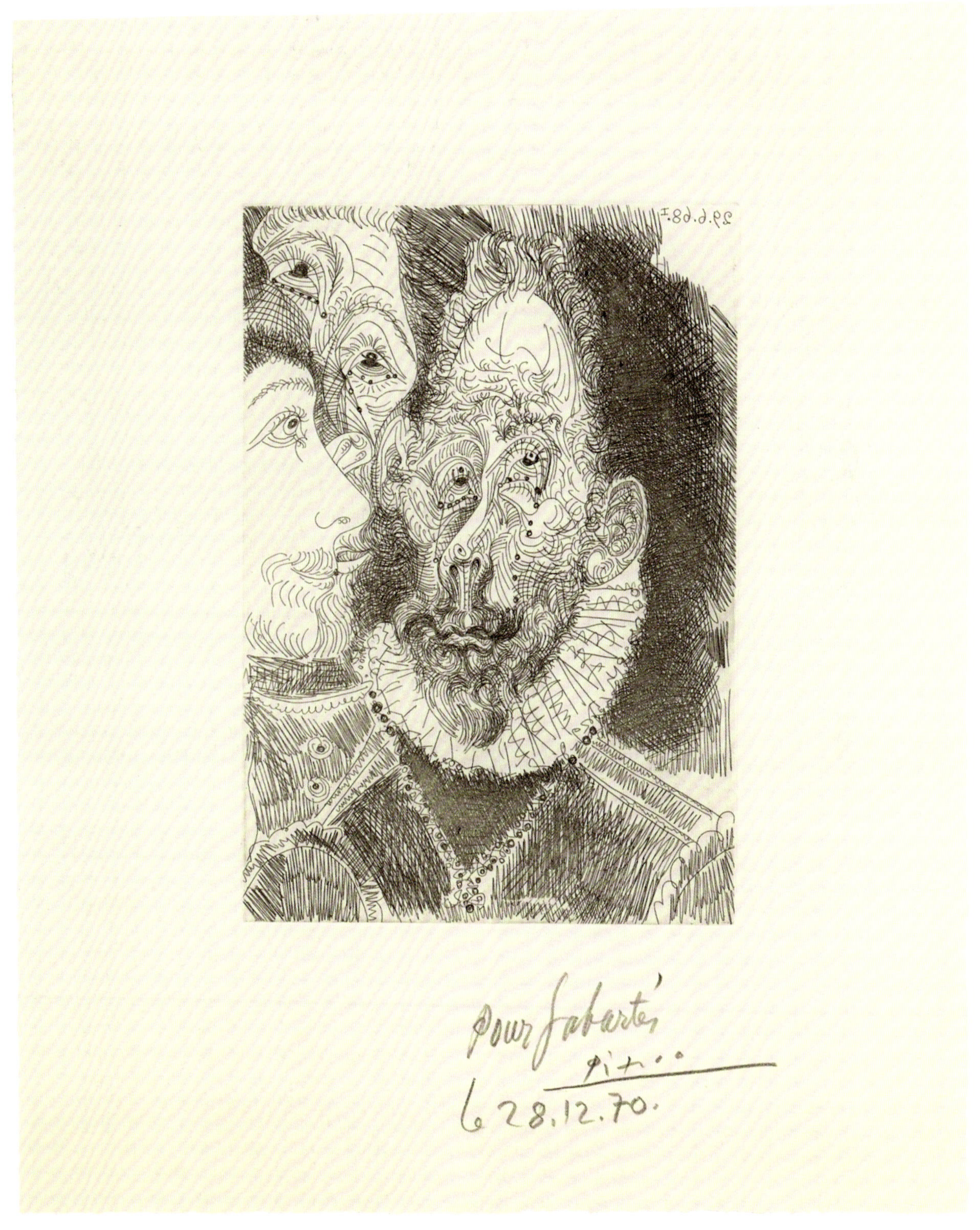

184 *Caricature of One of the Characters in* The Burial of the Count of Orgaz, *Weeping. Suite 347*, plate 194, 29 June 1968 (B, L)

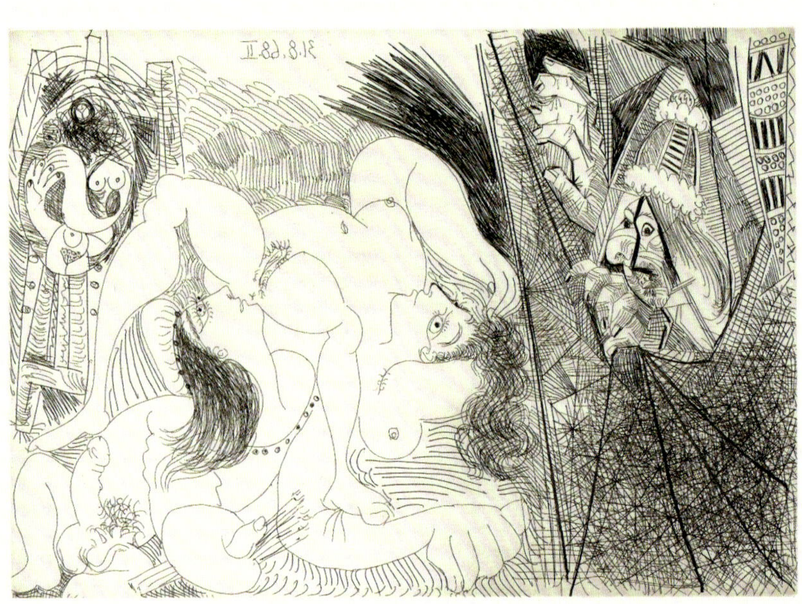

185 *Raphael and the Fornarina IV: with the Pope Pulling Back the Curtain. Suite 347*, plate 299, 31 August 1968 (B, L)

his emotionalism. In playful mood, he exercised all his ingenuity in building up the contour-map of wrinkles on his central mourner's face, curling his lips and beard and turning his tears into tiny pearls indistinguishable from the jewels decorating his chain of office. El Greco was the jumping-off point for a pleasurable, imaginative excursion.

Because he considered them his comrades Picasso did not scruple to caricature the old masters themselves. In a notorious group of etchings in *Suite 347* he fantasised about Raphael's lovemaking with his mistress Margherita Luti, better known as La Fornarina. In the fourth print in the sequence (185), the couple are intently observed through parted curtains by the Pope – the scopophiliac who stands for all of us peeping at the forbidden images. (When *Suite 347* was first exhibited in Paris at Galerie Leiris in the winter of 1968–9, the Raphael prints were deemed too obscene for public display and were shown only to trusted clients in a private office.)[18] Early biographers made much of Raphael's love of women, Giorgio Vasari going so far as to suggest that his premature death was brought about by a surfeit of sex. Picasso took this as licence to treat Raphael as irreverently as he had treated friends like Àngel Fernández de Soto (see 48–9).

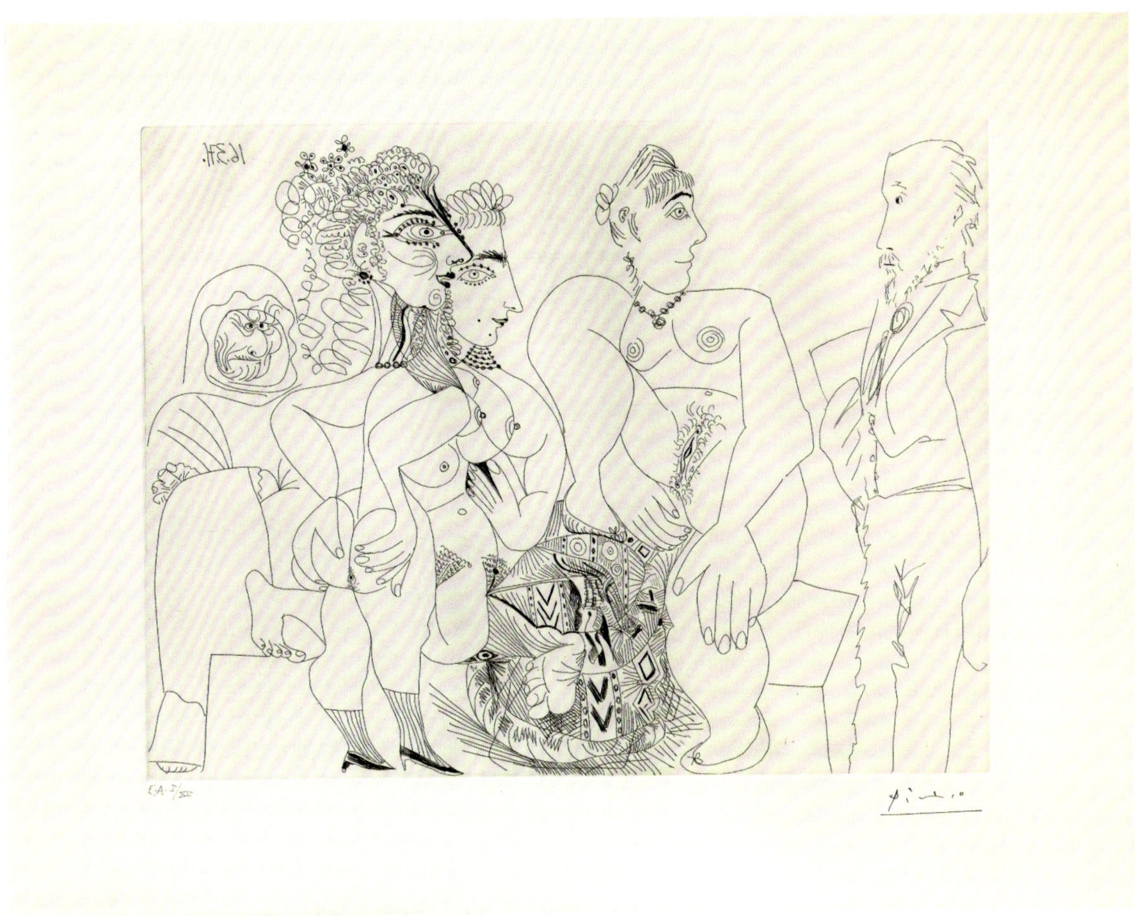

186 *Brothel. Degas with His Sketchbook, Bawd, Three Prostitutes, and a Moroccan Pouffe. Suite 156*, plate 87, 16 March 1971 (B)

His initial source was Ingres's paintings of Raphael with La Fornarina sitting on his lap, gazing raptly not at her but at an unfinished painting. Instead of sticking closely to these decorous compositions, Picasso imagined what would have happened had Raphael given in to his legendary lust and in so doing drew freely on Ingres's voluptuous and voyeuristic odalisque paintings.[19] In a sense, Picasso was liberating Ingres from inhibitions in his thinking about Raphael – the artist he, Ingres, admired above all others – and licensing him to think as he, Picasso, did about the relationship between art and sex. For whereas in Ingres's paintings Raphael seems to be torn between his duty to art and his passion for his mistress, in Picasso's etchings Raphael makes love to La Fornarina in his studio without letting go of his palette and brushes: there is no conflict between desire and creativity, lovemaking and painting; the relationship is blissfully symbiotic.

The priapic Raphael was a natural alter ego for Picasso in his prime. Imagining Raphael with his mistress, he relived his own most ardent love affairs, and by introducing various peeping Toms into the unbridled scenes reflected wryly on the pleasures that remained to him now that he was in his mid-eighties: fantasising, remembering and of course

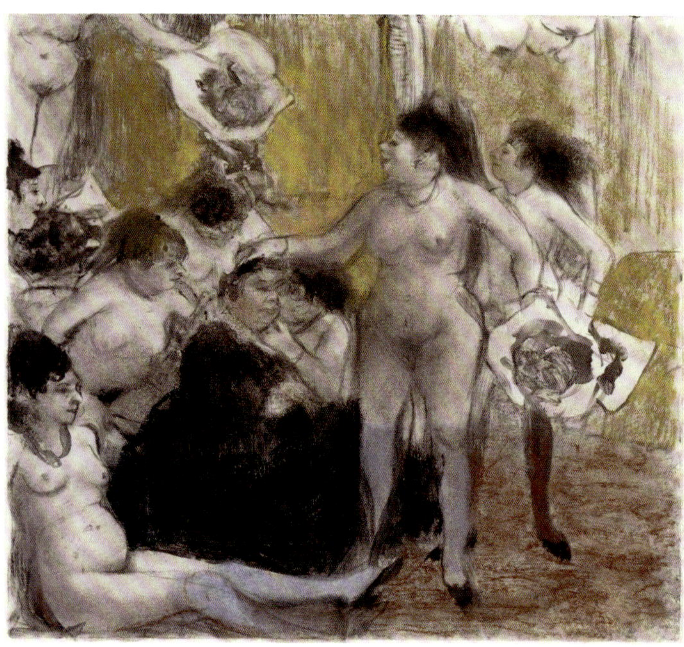

187 *The Madame's Name Day* by Edgar Degas, c.1876–7

looking. In his final collection of prints, known as *Suite 156*, Picasso turned his attention to Degas, who was reputed to have been celibate from an insurmountable fear of sex and therefore the polar opposite of Raphael in his private life. Picasso's immediate source was his own collection of Degas's brothel monotypes and his key intervention was to place Degas himself in the brothel. The monotype that left the deepest imprint on his Degas series was the masterpiece of his collection, *The Madame's Name Day*, in which the *filles* gather around and present bouquets to the motherly madame, with no client in sight (187); but Picasso was never faithful to its composition and elements from other monotypes blended with it in his homage. When he showed them to visitors he enjoyed speculating bawdily about Degas's investment in the brothel scenes: 'What do you think he was doing in those places?' 'Do you think he came just to take notes? No one really knows what he did with women.'[20] In the etchings in which Degas appears in person, Picasso dramatised answers to those questions with subtlety and sympathy, as well as humour. Each scene tells a story and since he never showed Degas so much as touching the prostitutes, but always intently looking at them, we surmise that voyeurism was Degas's motive. As he neared his ninetieth birthday, Picasso felt more affinity with Degas, the man, than ever before.

There are many photographs of Degas – Picasso owned one that is believed to be a self-portrait[21] – and his depictions of Degas are instantly recognisable likenesses – in a caricatural vein. In the etching dated 16 March 1971 (186), a formally dressed Degas, with his famous 'ski-slope' nose silhouetted against the blank background, visits the brothel gripping a sketchbook. At the far left, the toothless, wrinkled Celestina – the traditional Spanish bawd, who had appeared often in *Suite 347* – looks on angrily because she knows no money will be made from this Baudelairean 'painter of

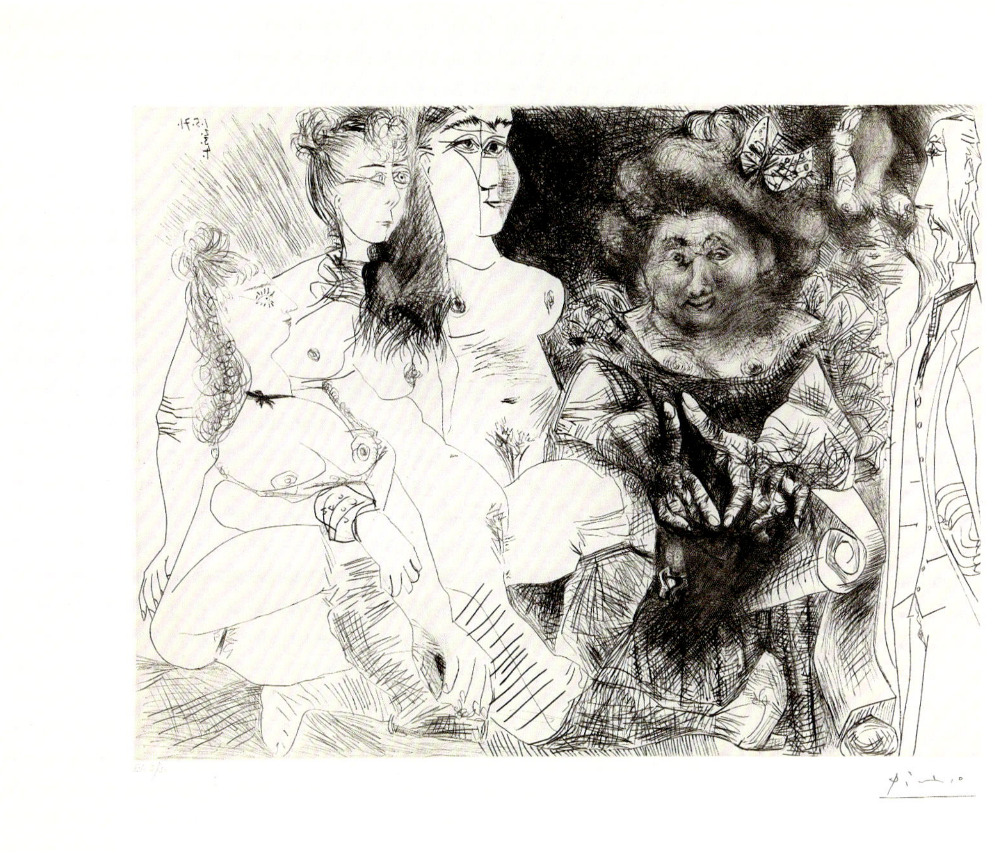

188 *The Madame-Abortionist and Three Prostitutes. Degas with His Hands behind His Back. Suite 156*, plate 117, 1–4 May 1971 (L)

modern life'. The prostitutes display themselves nonchalantly; one of them propositions Degas boldly. The trembling line Picasso used for his trousers tells us he is shaking uncontrollably, but from his rigid stance we know that he will stay put. The drypoint dated 1–4 May 1971 (188) is less fluent, and, like the print from the Raphael series described above, is inconsistent in style. The madame (like the Pope) is more intensely worked than the three scratchily drawn prostitutes/anti-Graces at the left, and in building up her figure with dense chiaroscuro Picasso approximated to the tonal contrasts and sensual smudging of Degas's monotype technique. Enthroned in a massive chair, facing towards the spectator, not Degas, with her grotesquely knarled hands she mimics the shape of a vagina, a complicitous smile crossing her face. Unaware of the lewd joke at his expense, Degas stands rigidly to attention, immaculately dressed as usual, with his hands locked behind his back. Repeated throughout the series, this gesture signifies puritanical self-censorship: if he were to relax he might not be able to resist reaching out. But he cannot tear his eyes away from the girls, and in print after print that is what we are shown: the act of looking that led to the creation of the searingly truthful monotypes, which Picasso considered Degas's greatest achievement as an artist.

WITH REMBRANDT

Rembrandt figured largely as a more or less explicit point of reference in Picasso's paintings, drawings and prints in the last decade of his life, but he had appeared occasionally earlier on, most famously in several prints in *Suite Vollard*.[22] Talking about them to Kahnweiler on 6 February 1934, Picasso explained that the head of Rembrandt had arrived accidentally when the varnish on the plate he was working on cracked. He decided to 'scratch on it' and it 'became Rembrandt' – a natural metamorphosis given Rembrandt's supremacy as a printmaker. He followed it up with a plate in which he set out to portray Rembrandt, 'complete with his turban, his fur coat and his eye, that elephant eye of his'.[23] Speaking of the same prints to Françoise Gilot almost exactly a decade later Picasso talked of Rembrandt as one of the great figures, writers as well as artists, in the 'colony' that formed his being ('Every human being is a whole colony, you know').[24]

The print from *Suite Vollard* dated 31 January 1934 (189) provides insight into the more personal side of Picasso's Rembrandt-cult: he found the Dutchman so sympathetic partly because he too had been enthralled and inspired by his lovers and evoked their desirability and physicality with great frankness. In Picasso's portrait a portly, ageing but splendidly dressed Rembrandt holds the hand of a beautiful young woman, naked save for a long diaphanous veil held in place by a garland of flowers. With his other hand he grips his palette and brushes: love and art belong together. The set-up suggests a wedding ceremony and the sun beaming through the window bodes well. That the bride looks rather like Marie-Thérèse Walter should come as no surprise since, in mythologised form, she haunted the imagery of *Suite Vollard*. The contrast between youth and age, between the artist's lovely muse and his unlovely self, is both poignant and comical, but identifying with an ageing Rembrandt on a sensual level was reassuring.

The early 1960s saw a spate of drawings and paintings inspired by the Louvre's masterpiece, *Bathsheba with King David's Letter*, but Rembrandt became a truly obsessive presence when Picasso slowly resumed work after recovering from a serious ulcer operation in November 1965. During his convalescence, he led a hermitic life in Notre-Dame-de-Vie and, Jacqueline reported, studied albums of reproductions of Rembrandt's work.[25] Occasionally an evening was spent gazing at colour slides blown up to a gigantic scale on the studio wall.[26] Rembrandt's *Night Watch* was one of the paintings in which Picasso immersed himself, and it was a catalyst for the stream of paintings of Musketeers he produced in the late 1960s.

Men resembling Rembrandt proliferated in Picasso's drawings and, in a transparent gesture of identification, he sometimes drew a quick caricature of the artist next to his signature when dedicating a book to friends, such as Angela Rosengart (191). In the moving ink and wash drawing dated 4 July 1967 (190), Rembrandt appears three times sporting his famous floppy beret: on the left, full-length and in profile, smoking a pipe while contemplating his nude model – a vignette that recalls the 'marriage' scene in *Suite Vollard*; in the centre in profile grinning mischievously – an outright caricature; and on the right, in a full-face, close-up, head-and-shoulders sketch reminiscent of Rembrandt's unflattering self-portraits. (Whether the head of the child in the top-right corner has any connection with these images is an unanswered question.) The fact that the female nude is represented in a Picassoesque style wholly at variance with the rest of the drawing is a candid statement of Picasso's claim to parity. Executed with great freedom, the drawing unfolds dynamically as a stream of consciousness and has the irrational quality of an hallucination; the spectator has the thrilling illusion of being privy to Picasso's innermost thoughts.

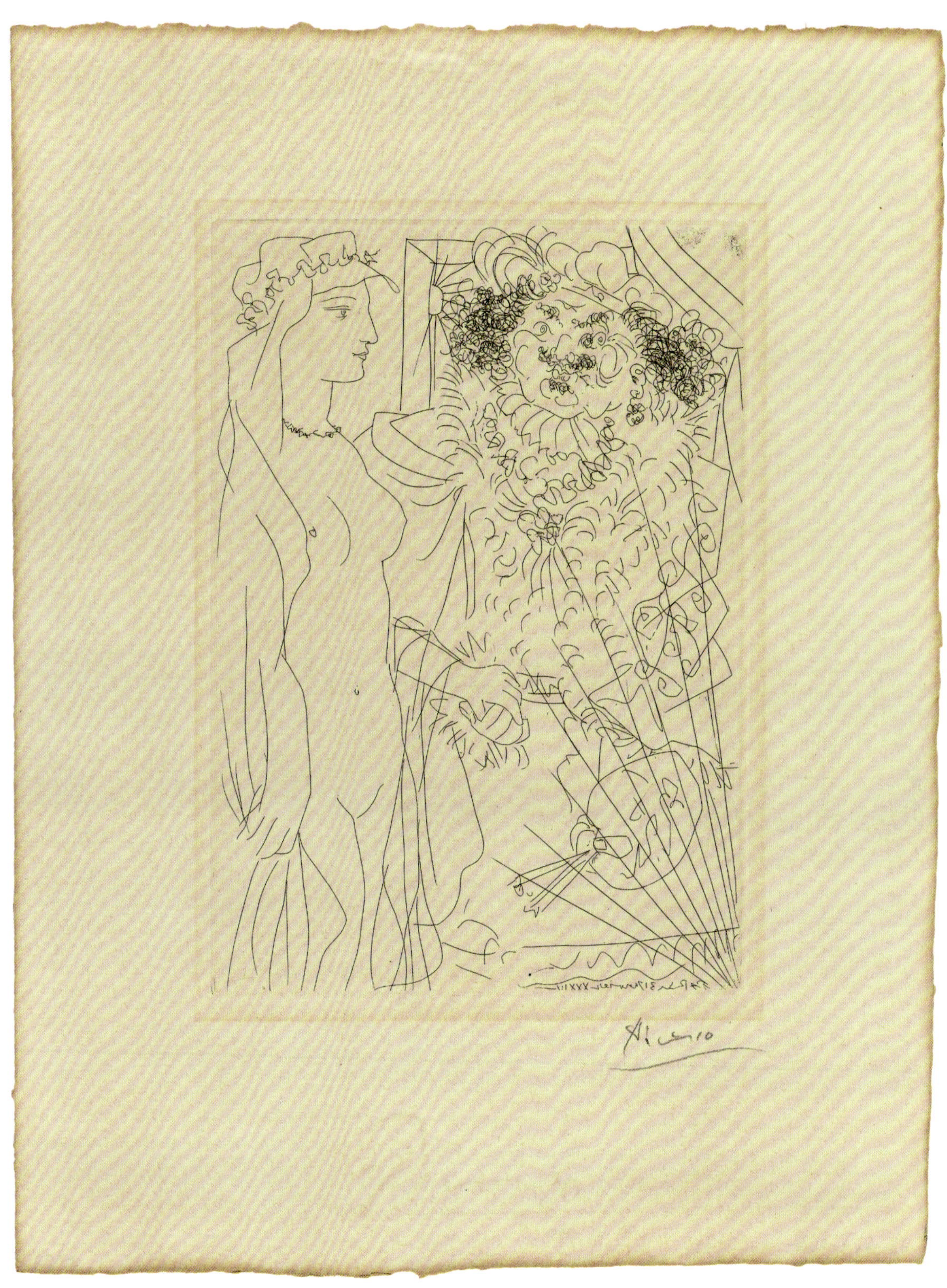

189 *Rembrandt Holding the Hand of a Young Woman with Veil. Suite Vollard*, plate 36, 31 January 1934 (B, L)

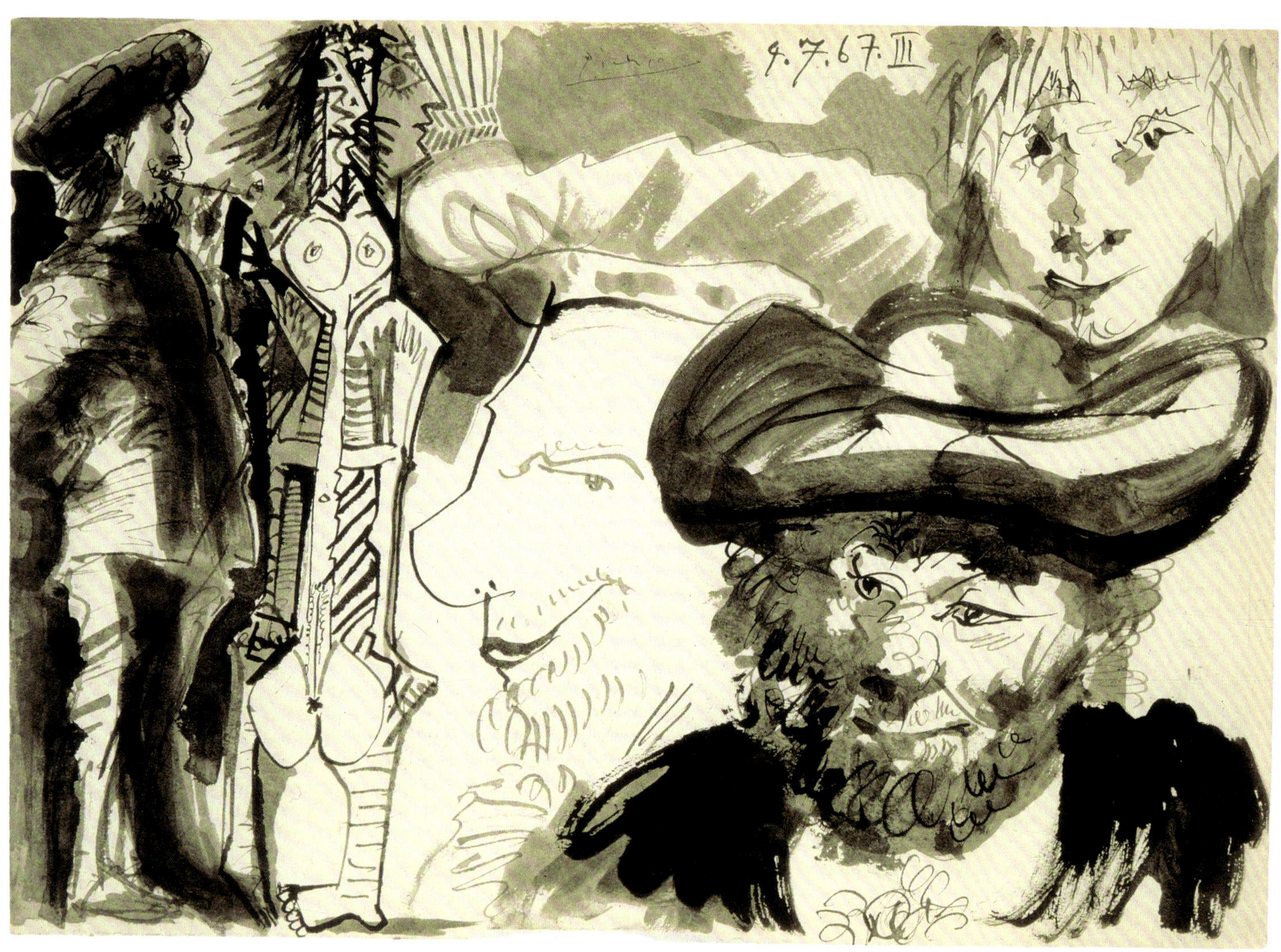

190 *Figure in the Style of Rembrandt*, 4 July 1967 (III) (B, L)

Rembrandt's *The Prodigal Son in a Tavern*, c.1635, fascinated Picasso (192). The amorous subject rendered in so humane and dramatically immediate a manner was irresistibly attractive, but was rendered yet more so by the fact that the models for the Prodigal Son and the prostitute were believed to be Rembrandt and his wife Saskia.[27] Picasso had always used artistic and literary sources to achieve aesthetic distance from private subject matter and appreciated the significance of Rembrandt's masquerade. He engaged directly with the painting in mid-March 1963 when he suddenly interrupted a prolific series on the theme of the artist painting his model to complete a large canvas combining that subject with a free version of Rembrandt's composition.[28] *Rembrandt and Saskia* of 1963 was a one-off, but *The Prodigal Son in a Tavern* was on his mind after his recovery from illness and inspired several major canvases. No doubt its life-affirming exuberance was especially meaningful as Picasso experienced a new lease of energy after his brush with death and the long, frustrating, enforced sabbatical from work.

One of the grandest of these paintings was also one of the last, *Couple*, dated 9 October 1970 (193). Subsidiary details Picasso remembered and retained include the white feathers in the Son's hat, his sword, the swagged curtain behind him to the right, the decorative band holding back the prostitute's hair, and the peacock pie – transformed into a pet bird flapping its wings. He omitted the flute of wine the Son raises in a joyous toast, but by giving his characters huge dilated eyes that instantly attract our attention, Picasso pointed up the crucial role in Rembrandt's narrative played by the gazes of the Son and the prostitute: he looks at an oblique angle in the direction of the unseen new arrival whom he is toasting, and she looks over her shoulder at the spectator. Through the energy generated by the contrast of bright blue and orange, and his ultra-spontaneous painterly technique,

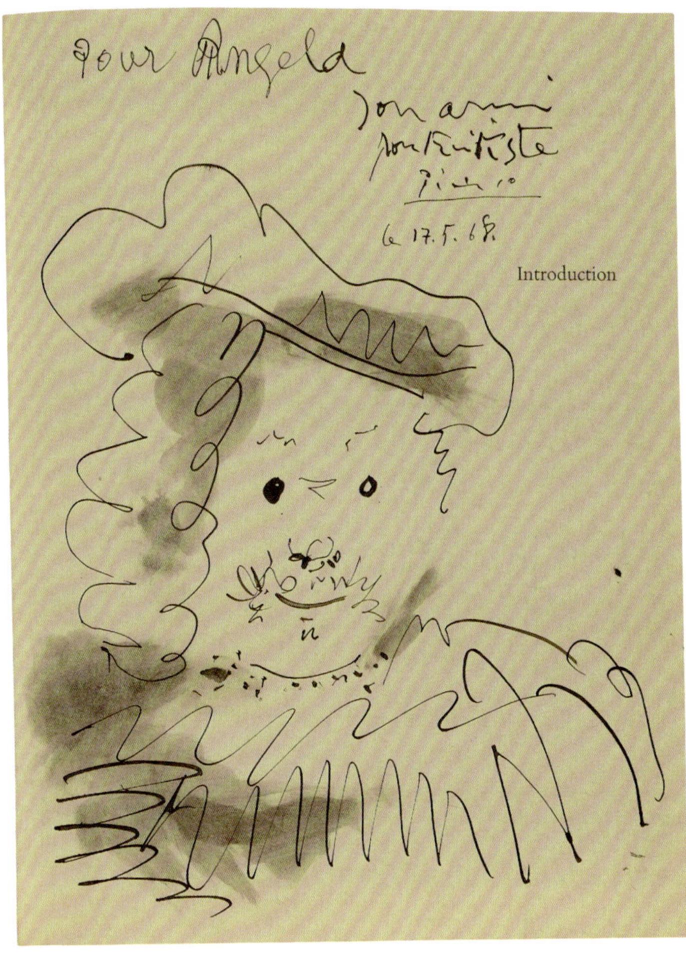

191 *Head of Rembrandt*, 17 May 1968

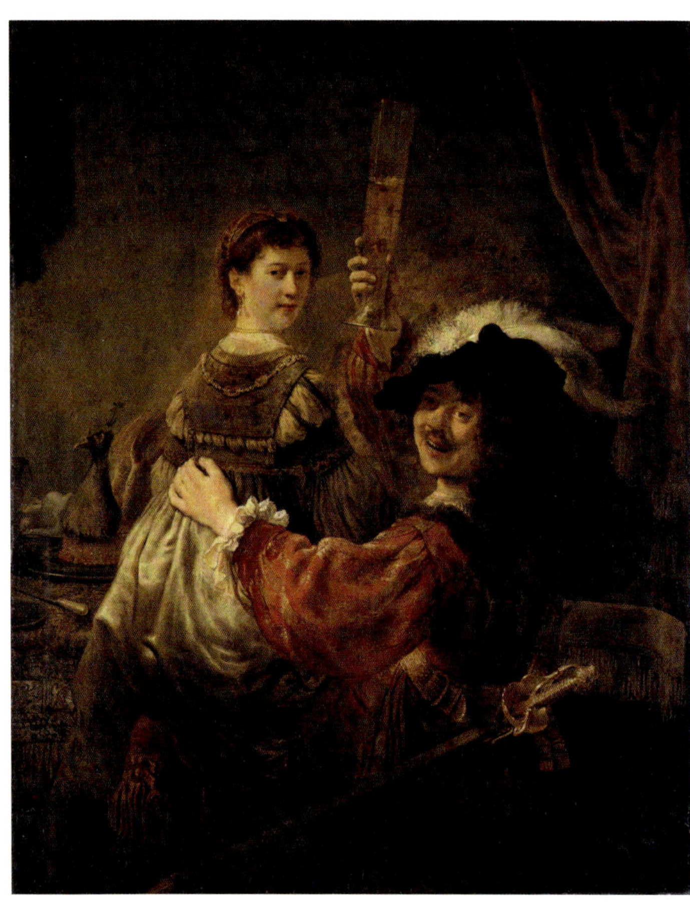

192 *The Prodigal Son in a Tavern* by Rembrandt, c.1635

Picasso approximated the vitality of Rembrandt's tavern scene. For all its assertive independence and grotesquerie, *Couple* is testimony to Picasso's close and affectionate attention to the composition.

Begun a couple of weeks before *Couple* but worked on again a year later, *Old Man Seated* (196) took a very different self-portrait by Rembrandt as its starting point: the majestic painting dated 1658 in the Frick Collection (195). As usual, Picasso's version is independent, but the pose of his old man and crucial details, like the massive right hand resting on the arm of his chair, are surprisingly close to his source. He replaced Rembrandt's large black velvet beret with a straw hat, omitted the sceptre-like maulstick, seated his old man in a rustic wicker chair, and radically altered the overall tonality. The transfer of the gold of the robe to the background of his painting, where it burns as brightly as fire, and the use of green, where Rembrandt had used browns for the cloak, suggest the simultaneous presence of Van Gogh at the forefront of Picasso's mind – especially the self-portraits in which the artist wears a broad-brimmed straw hat (194). And from first-hand reports, we know that in old age Picasso talked constantly about Van Gogh, describing him as 'the one painter whose life was exemplary, up to and including his death'.[29] It was a marriage of two sources characteristic of Picasso in that it rested on the knowledge that Van Gogh was powerfully affected by Rembrandt's work.

Two artist-heroes are, then, fused in *Old Man Seated*. The painting is also a self-portrait by proxy. There is pride in the affirmation of lineage and continuity, but, completed a month after Picasso's ninetieth birthday, it is also unsparing in its evocation of decline. Unlike the commanding figure of Rembrandt in the Frick self-portrait, the old man slumps in his chair and his face expresses something of the desperation, confusion and helplessness of senility. Picasso fought death right to the end with the weapon of work – painting, drawing, printmaking

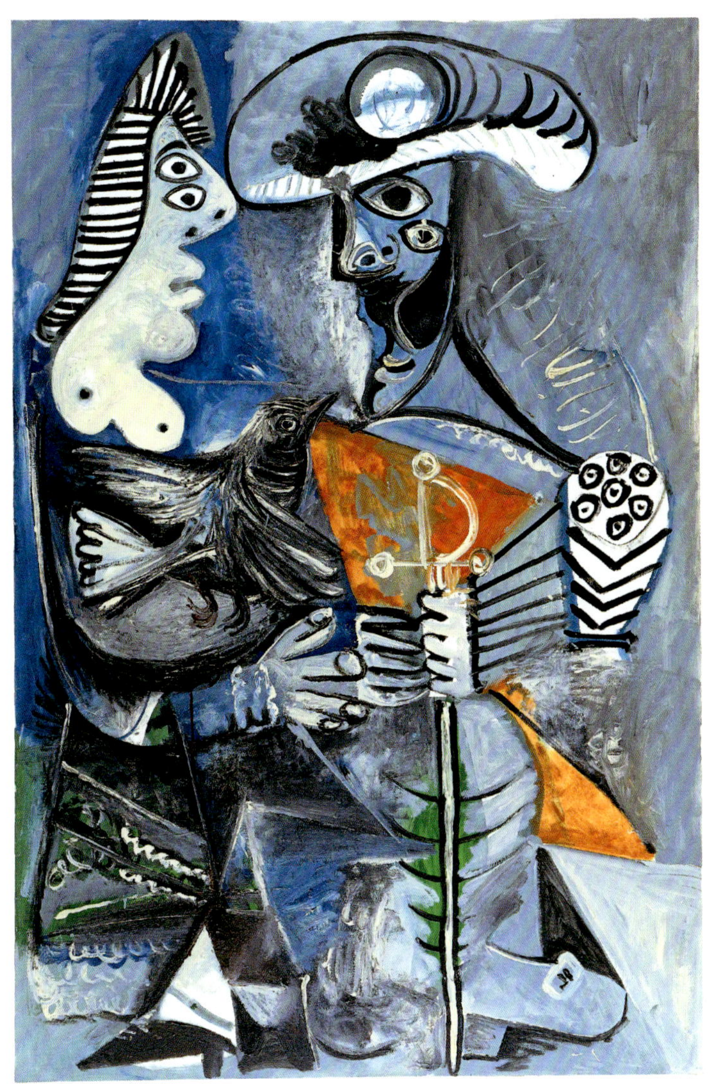

193 *Couple*, 9 October 1970

194 *Self-portrait* by Vincent van Gogh, 1887

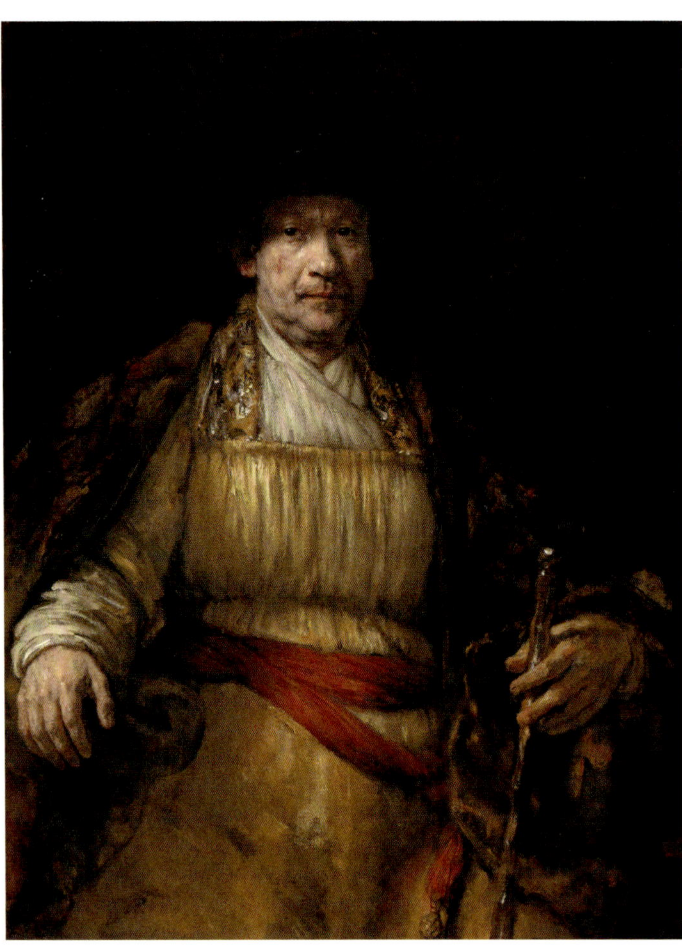

195 *Self-portrait* by Rembrandt, 1658

with a defiant, frenetic energy that astonished everyone around him. But in surrogate self-portraits like this he not only faced the truth about his age but also foresaw, with frightening clarity, what would happen to him if he lived too long.

Facing death is just what Picasso did in the harrowing drawing dated 2 July 1972 – a self-portrait this time, not a self-portrait by proxy (197). Pierre Daix published a moving account of visiting Picasso and being shown the equally monumental, but less skull-like drawing with coloured crayons.[30] Picasso held it up beside his face to show Daix that the fear written in the staring eyes was 'an invention', and remarked: 'I think maybe I touched on something. It's not like anything I've done before.' Three months later Daix saw the drawing again and realised that 'like a good Spaniard, [Picasso] was looking his own death in the face.'[31] Roland Penrose was the first owner of the present, monochrome drawing and likened the monolithic head to 'a great rock set against the sky, the crowning feature of a mountain range'.[32] This captures the indestructible, atavistic aspect of the head, which seems to be losing flesh and returning to bone before our eyes. Yet its fundamental truth to Picasso's appearance in old age is proved by contemporary photographs, such as the unflinching portrait taken by Lee Miller in the late 1960s (198). Symbolism had not taken over completely from reality and one is reminded of the resolute self-examination Picasso undertook when making his intense charcoal self-portrait just before his first trip to Paris in 1900 (see 13). For Picasso, making art was tantamount to being alive and in this self-portrait-as-skull he simultaneously acknowledged the imminence of death and warded it off for just a little longer.

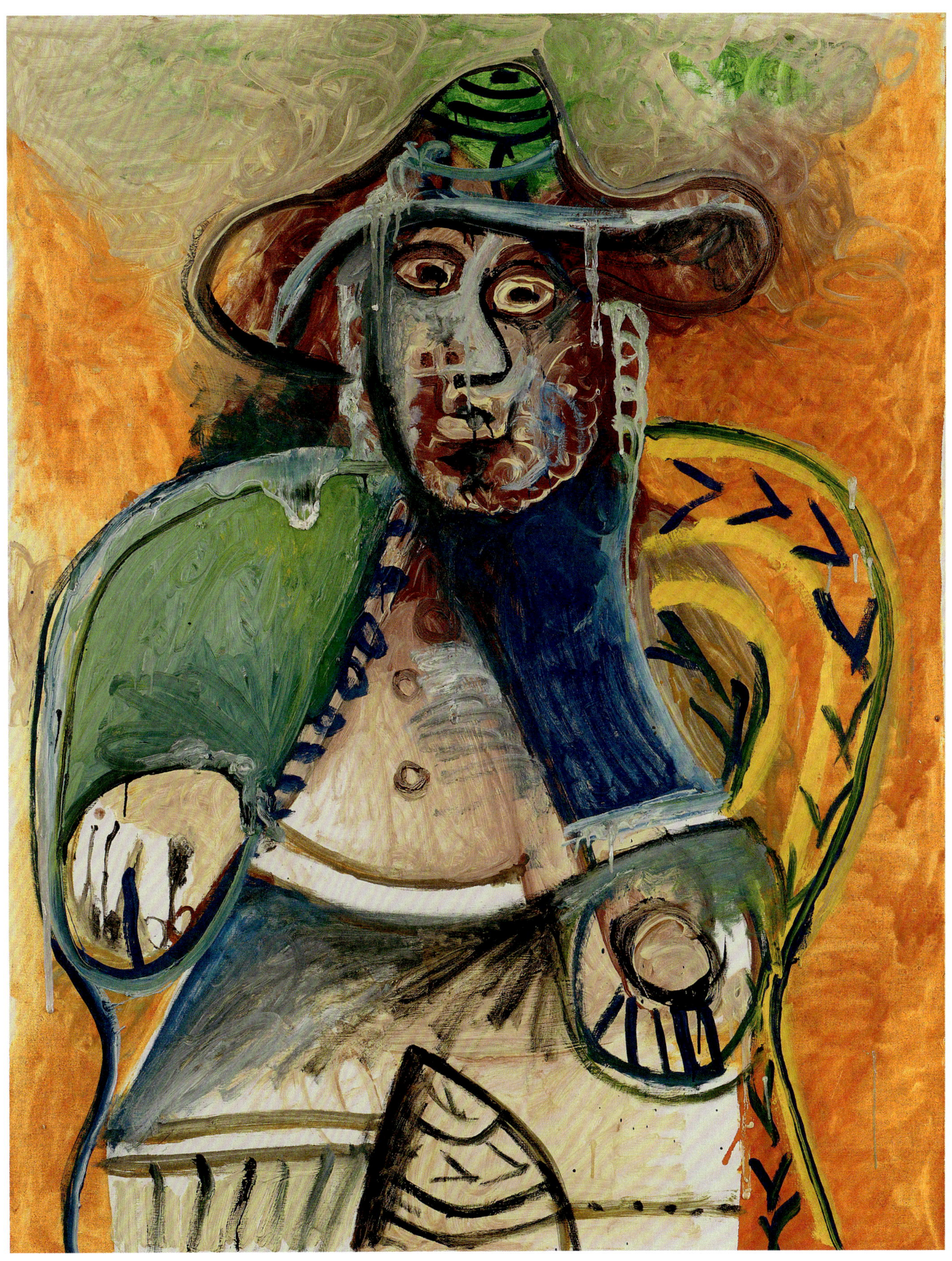

196 *Old Man Seated*, 26 September 1970–14 November 1971 (B, L)

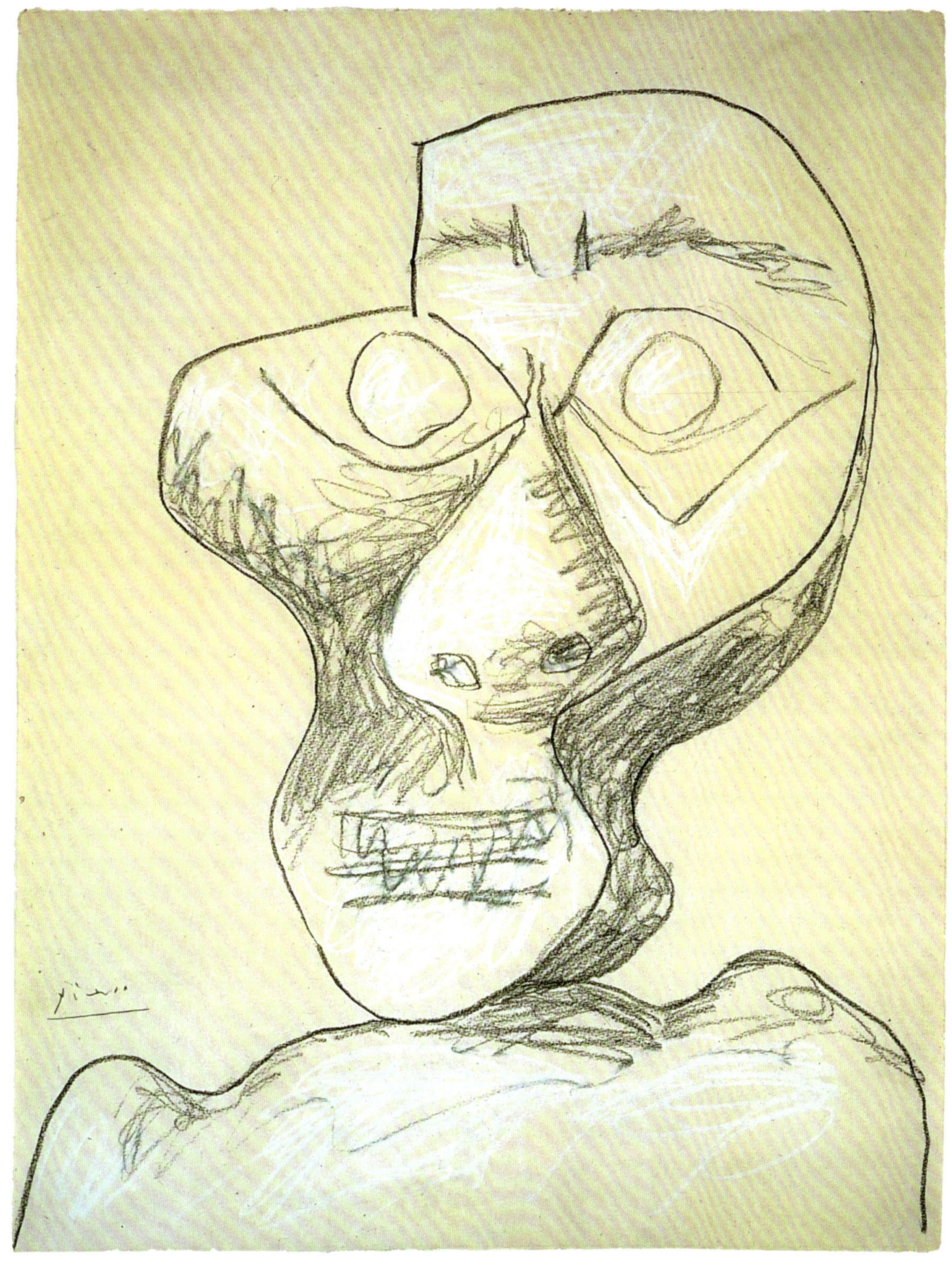

197 *Self-portrait*, 2 July 1972 (L)

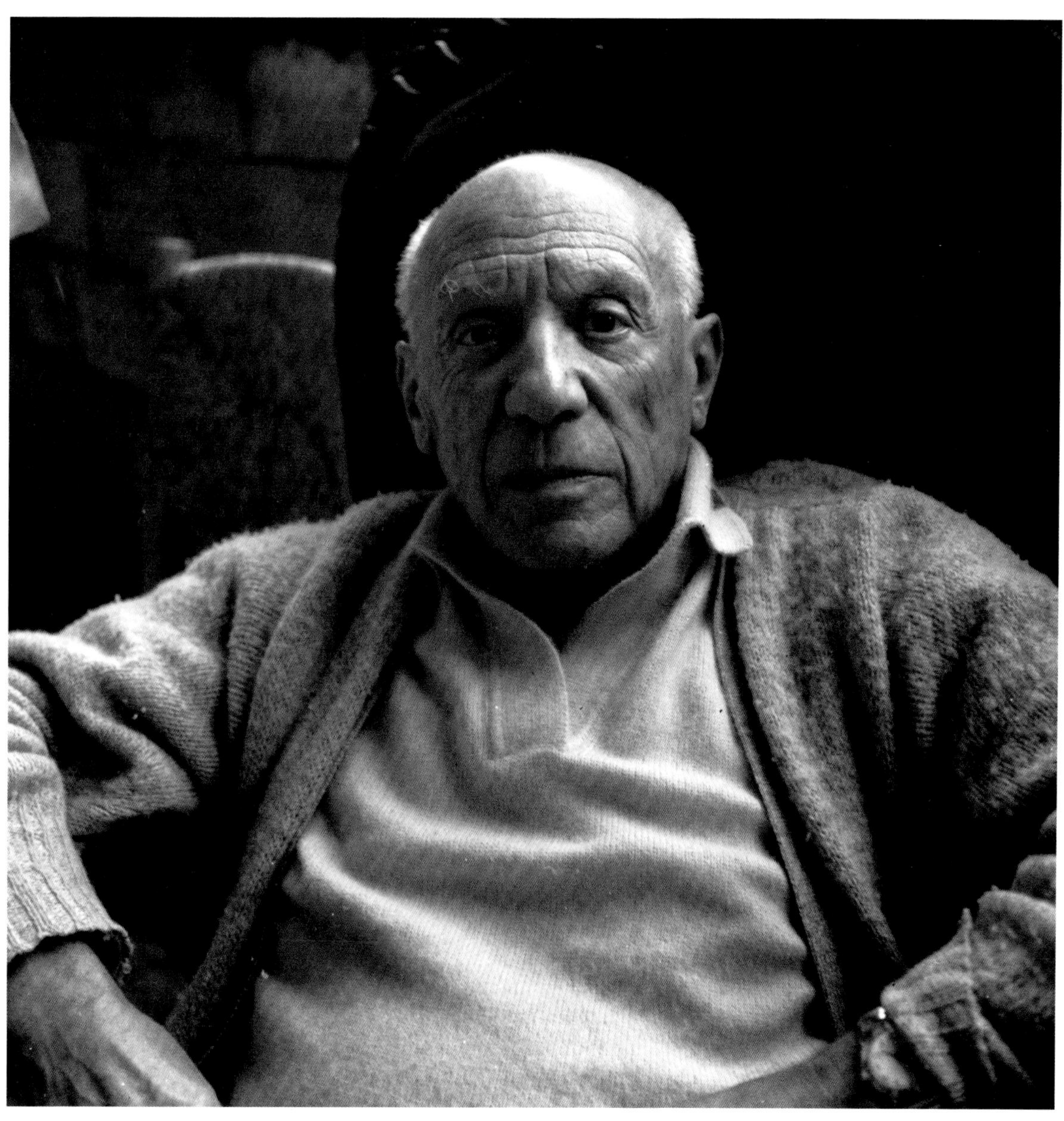

198 *Picasso in Notre-Dame-de-Vie*. Photograph by Lee Miller, late 1960s

1 See Galassi 1996.

2 *The Soler Family*, 1903 (Musée des Beaux-Arts, Liège; Z.I.203) is the major exception to the rule. For its chequered history, see Richardson 1991, p.285.

3 See Parmelin 1963, pp.227–43.

4 Sabartès 1958. See also 172.

5 Lump originally belonged to the photographer David Douglas Duncan. See Duncan 2006.

6 In France, 1 April is the day for pranks and hoaxes but the equivalent day in Spain, *el Día de los Santos Inocente*, is 28 December.

7 On Picasso and grisaille, see Giménez 2012.

8 Marius de Zayas, 'Picasso Speaks', 1923. Cited in Ashton 1972, p.4.

9 For instance, *Head of a Woman* (MP 351). It is seen in a photograph by André Gomes taken in La Californie in July 1957 (MP Ph. 1071).

10 Parmelin 1963, p.77.

11 Parmelin 1969, p.40.

12 Cowling 2006, p.105. The conversation with Penrose took place on 24 February 1955, and turned on the role played by Matisse's odalisque paintings in the recently completed set of variations after Delacroix's *Women of Algiers*.

13 Malraux 1976, p.135. (Malraux's emphasis.)

14 Picasso reported by Roland Penrose in July 1956 (Cowling 2006, p.172).

15 See p.184.

16 Daniel-Henry Kahnweiler, interview with Picasso, Rue des Grands-Augustins, 11 January 1955. Quoted in Bernadac and Michael 1998, p.70.

17 Plates in *Suite 347* with El Greco-type heads include nos 40, 41, 115, 130, 194 and 196.

18 For the Raphael series as a whole, see Holloway 2006, pp.139–53.

19 Picasso's collection of Japanese erotic woodcuts was another source for the Raphael prints. See *Imágenes secretas* 2009.

20 For these quotations and fuller discussion of the Degas series, see Elizabeth Cowling, '"The best things he ever did": Picasso and Degas's *Maisons closes*', in Cowling and Kendall 2010, pp.236–67.

21 Cowling and Kendall 2010, p.224.

22 Although this seems to have escaped notice, the Cubist collage *Man with a Moustache*, spring 1914 (Musée national Picasso-Paris; Z.II.468) is a caricature of Rembrandt.

23 Cited in Ashton 1972, p.165.

24 Gilot and Lake 1965, p.41.

25 Malraux 1976, p.86. Among the books Picasso owned was Otto Benesch's six-volume catalogue raisonné of Rembrandt's drawings (Phaidon, London, 1954–7). See John Richardson, 'L'Époque Jacqueline', in *Late Picasso* 1988, p.34.

26 Parmelin 1969, pp.48–50. The slide shows Parmelin describes took place in the winter of 1963–4.

27 See *Rembrandt Corpus* 1989, pp.142–7.

28 *Rembrandt and Saskia*, 13 March 1963 (Present whereabouts unknown; Z.XXIII.171).

29 Parmelin 1969, p.37.

30 *Self-portrait*, 30 June 1972 (Private collection; Z.XXXIII.435).

31 Daix 1994, p.369.

32 Penrose 1981, p.252.

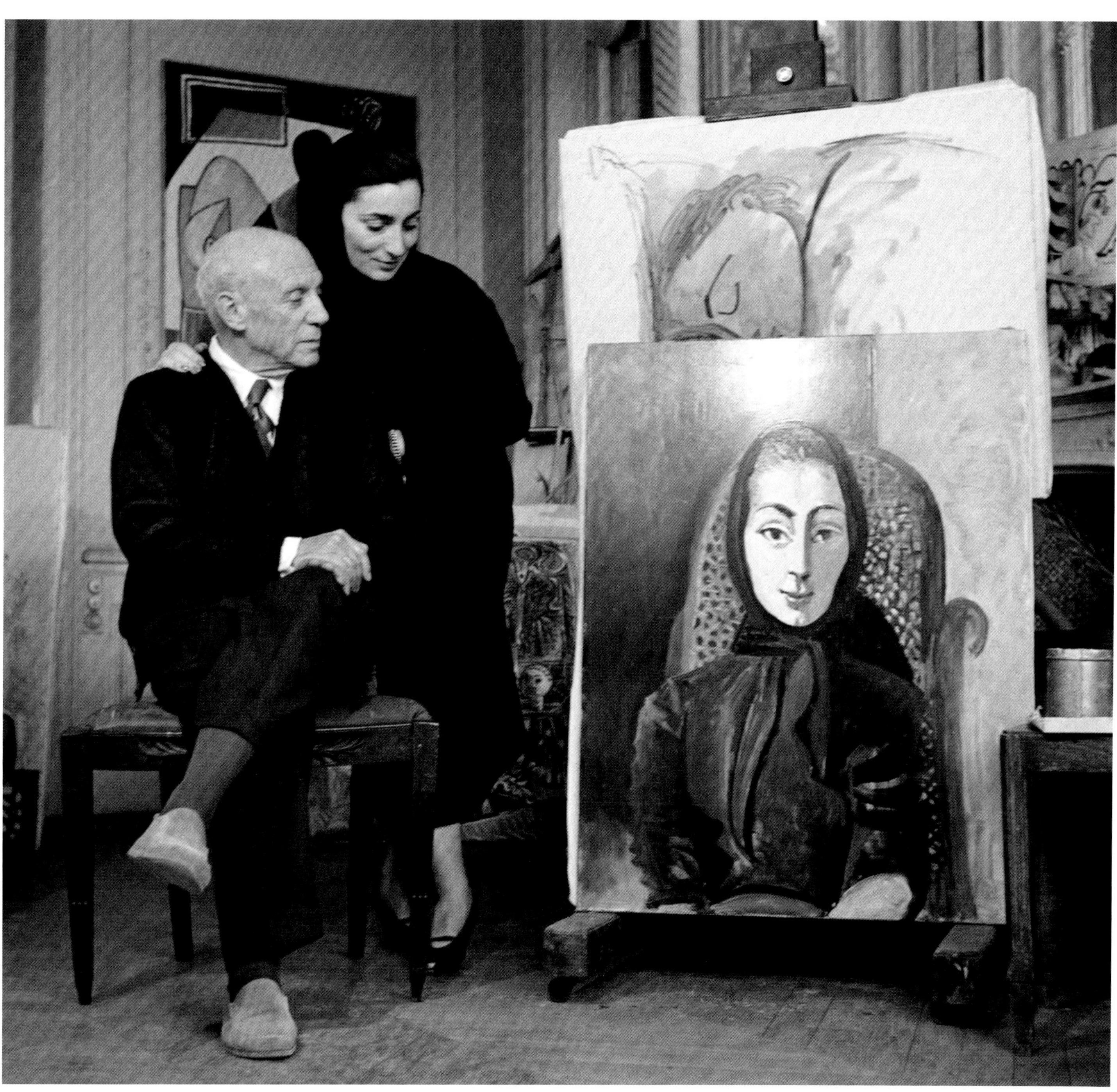

Picasso with Jacqueline and Her Portrait.
Photograph by Edward Quinn, 1955

Bibliography

Abbreviations in bold are used in the notes at the end of each chapter.

Alarcó and Warner 2007 • Paloma Alarcó and Malcolm Warner (eds), *The Mirror & the Mask: Portraiture in the Age of Picasso* (exh. cat., Museo Thyssen-Bornemisza and Fundación Caja, Madrid, and Kimbell Art Museum, Fort Worth; in association with Yale University Press, New Haven and London, 2007)

Alexandre 1893 • Arsène Alexandre, *L'art du rire et de la caricature* (Librairies-Imprimeries réunies, Paris, 1893)

***Amour fou* 2011** • *L'Amour Fou: Picasso and Marie-Thérèse*, curated by John Richardson and Diana Widmaier Picasso (exh. cat., Gagosian Gallery, New York; in association with Rizzoli International Publications, 2011)

Ashbee 1928 • C.R. Ashbee, *Caricature* (Chapman and Hall, London, 1928)

Ashton 1972 • Dore Ashton, *Picasso on Art: A Selection of Views* (Thames & Hudson, London, 1972)

Assouline 1991 • Pierre Assouline (trans. Charles Ruas), *An Artful Life: A Biography of D.H. Kahnweiler, 1884–1979* (Fromm, New York, 1991)

Baer • Brigitte Baer, *Picasso: Peintre-Graveur*, 7 vols (original editions of vols I–II by Bernhard Geiser) (Kornfeld, Bern, 1933–96)

Baldassari 1997 • Anne Baldassari (trans. Deke Dusinberre), *Picasso and Photography: The Dark Mirror* (exh. cat., The Museum of Fine Arts, Houston; in association with Flammarion, Paris, 1997)

Baldassari 2006 • Anne Baldassari, *Picasso/Dora Maar: Il faisait tellement noir...* (exh. cat., Musée Picasso, Paris, and National Gallery of Victoria, Melbourne; Réunion des musées nationaux, Paris, in association with Flammarion, Paris, 2006)

Baudelaire 1964 • Charles Baudelaire (trans. and ed. Jonathan Mayne), *The Painter of Modern Life and Other Essays* (Phaidon, London, 1964)

Bernadac and Michael 1998 • Marie-Laure Bernadac and Androula Michael (eds), *Picasso: Propos sur l'art* (Gallimard, Paris, 1998)

Bois 1998 • Yve-Alain Bois, *Matisse and Picasso* (exh. cat., Kimbell Art Museum, Fort Worth; in association with Flammarion, Paris, 1998)

Brassaï 1967 • Brassaï (trans. Francis Price), *Picasso & Co.* (Thames & Hudson, London, 1967)

Braun and Rabinow 2014 • Emily Braun and Rebecca Rabinow (eds), *Cubism: The Leonard A. Lauder Collection* (exh. cat., The Metropolitan Museum of Art, New York; in association with Yale University Press, New Haven and London, 2014)

Champfleury 1865 • Champfleury, *Histoire de la caricature moderne* (E. Dentu, Paris, 1865)

Cirici-Pellicer 1946 • Alexandre Cirici-Pellicer, *Picasso antes de Picasso* (Iberia - Joaquin Gil, Barcelona, 1946)

Cooper 1968 • Douglas Cooper, *Picasso Theatre* (Weidenfeld and Nicolson, London, 1968)

Courtois and Morel 1989 • Martine Courtois and Jean-Paul Morel, *Élie Faure: Biographie* (Librairie Séguier, Paris, 1989)

Cowling 2002 • Elizabeth Cowling, *Picasso: Style and Meaning* (Phaidon, London, 2002)

Cowling 2006 • Elizabeth Cowling, *Visiting Picasso: The Notebooks and Letters of Roland Penrose* (Thames & Hudson, London, 2006)

Cowling and Kendall 2010 • Elizabeth Cowling and Richard Kendall, *Picasso Looks at Degas* (exh. cat., Sterling and Francine Clark Art Institute, Williamstown, and Museu Picasso, Barcelona; in association with Yale University Press, New Haven and London, 2010)

Daix 1994 • Pierre Daix (trans. Olivia Emmet), *Picasso: Life and Art* (Thames & Hudson, London, 1994)

Daix 1995 • Pierre Daix, *Dictionnaire Picasso* (Robert Laffont, Paris, 1995)

Duncan 1958 • David Douglas Duncan, *The Private World of Pablo Picasso* (The Ridge Press, New York, 1958)

Duncan 2006 • David Douglas Duncan, *Lump: The Dog who Ate a Picasso* (Thames & Hudson, London, 2006)

Faure 1921 • Élie Faure, *Histoire de l'art*, vol. IV, *L'Art moderne* (Crès, Paris, 1921)

FitzGerald 1995 • Michael C. FitzGerald, *Making Modernism: Picasso and the Creation of the Market for Twentieth-Century Art* (Farrar, Straus and Giroux, New York, 1995)

Galassi 1996 • Susan Grace Galassi, *Picasso's Variations on the Masters: Confrontations with the Past* (Abrams, New York, 1996)

Gilot 1990 • Françoise Gilot, *Matisse and Picasso: A Friendship in Art* (Bloomsbury, London, 1990)

Gilot and Lake 1965 • Françoise Gilot and Carlton Lake, *Life with Picasso* (Nelson, London, 1965)

Giménez 2012 • Carmen Giménez (ed.), *Picasso: Black and White* (exh. cat., The Solomon R. Guggenheim Museum, New York, and The Museum of Fine Arts, Houston; in association with Delmonico Books/Prestel, Munich, London, New York, 2012)

Giroud 2007 • Vincent Giroud, *Picasso and Gertrude Stein* (The Metropolitan Museum of Art, New York; in association with Yale University Press, New Haven, 2007)

Glimcher 1986 • Arnold Glimcher and Marc Glimcher (eds), *Je Suis le Cahier: The Sketchbooks of Picasso* (exh. cat., Royal Academy of Arts, London; in association with Pace Gallery, New York, 1986)

Gombrich and Kris 1940 • E.H. Gombrich and E. Kris, *Caricature* (Penguin Books, Harmondsworth, 1940)

Gury 2004 • Christian Gury, *Bibi-la Purée, Compagnon de Verlaine* (Kimé, Paris, 2004)

Holloway 2006 • Memory Holloway, *Making Time: Picasso's* Suite 347 (Peter Lang, New York, 2006)

***Imágenes secretas* 2009** • *Imágenes secretas: Picasso y la estampa erótica japonesa* (exh. cat., Museu Picasso, Barcelona; Ajuntament de Barcelona, 2009)

***Kahnweiler* 1984** • *Daniel-Henry Kahnweiler: marchand, éditeur, écrivain* (exh. cat., Centre Georges Pompidou, Musée national d'art moderne, Paris, 1984)

Karmel 2003 • Pepe Karmel, *Picasso and the Invention of Cubism* (Yale University Press, New Haven and London, 2003)

Kendall 1991 • Richard Kendall, *Van Gogh to Picasso: The Berggruen Collection in the National Gallery* (exh. cat., The National Gallery, London, 1991)

***Late Picasso* 1988** • *Late Picasso: Paintings, Sculpture, Drawings, Prints 1953–1972* (exh. cat., The Tate Gallery, London, 1988)

Léal 1996 • Brigitte Léal, Musée Picasso. *Carnets: Catalogue des dessins*, 2 vols (Réunion des musées nationaux, Paris, 1996)

Lord 1993 • James Lord, *Picasso & Dora: A Memoir* (Weidenfeld and Nicolson, London, 1993)

Madeline 2005 • Laurence Madeline (ed.), *Gertrude Stein, Pablo Picasso: Correspondance* (Gallimard, Paris, 2005)

Malraux 1976 • André Malraux (trans. and ed. June Guicharnaud with Jacques Guicharnaud), *Picasso's Mask* (Macdonald and Jane's, London, 1976)

***Matisse Picasso* 2002** • Anne Baldassari, Elizabeth Cowling, John Elderfield, John Golding, Isabelle Monod-Fontaine, Kirk Varnedoe, *Matisse Picasso* (exh. cat., Tate Publishing, London, 2002)

McCully 1981 • Marilyn McCully (ed.), *A Picasso Anthology: Documents, Criticism, Reminiscences* (Arts Council of Great Britain, London, 1981)

McCully 1997 • Marilyn McCully (ed.), *Picasso: The Early Years, 1892–1906* (exh. cat., National Gallery of Art, Washington, and Museum of Fine Arts, Boston; National Gallery of Art, Washington, 1997)

McCully 2011 • Marilyn McCully, *Picasso in Paris 1900–1907: Eating Fire* (exh. cat., Van Gogh Museum, Amsterdam and Museu Picasso, Barcelona; in association with Mercatorfonds, Brussels, 2011)

McPhee and Orenstein 2011 • Constance C. McPhee and Nadine M. Orenstein, *Infinite Jest: Caricature and Satire from Leonardo to Levine* (exh. cat., The Metropolitan Museum of Art, New York; in association with Yale University Press, New Haven and London, 2011)

Melot 1975 • Michel Melot, *L'oeil qui rit: Le pouvoir comique des images* (Office du Livre, Freiburg, 1975)

MP • *Musée Picasso: Catalogue sommaire des collections*, 2 vols (Réunion des musées nationaux, Paris, 1985, 1987)

MPB • *Museu Picasso: Catàleg de pintura i dibuix* (Ajuntament de Barcelona, 1984)

Nash 1998 • Stephen A. Nash (ed.), *Picasso and the War Years 1937–1945* (exh. cat., Fine Arts Museums of San Francisco and The Solomon R. Guggenheim Museum, New York; in association with Thames & Hudson, London, 1998)

Olivier 1964 • Fernande Olivier (trans. Jane Miller), *Picasso and His Friends* (Heinemann, London, 1964). Originally published as *Picasso et ses amis* (Stock, Paris, 1933)

Olivier 2001 • Marilyn McCully (ed.) (trans. Christine Baker and Michael Raeburn), *Loving Picasso: The Private Journal of Fernande Olivier* (Harry N. Abrams, New York, 2001)

Palau 1981 • Josep Palau i Fabre (trans. Kenneth Lyons), *Picasso: Life and Work of the Early Years, 1881–1907* (Phaidon, London, 1981)

Palau 1999 • Josep Palau i Fabre (trans. Richard-Lewis Rees), *Picasso: From the Ballets to Drama (1917–1926)* (Könemann, Hagen, 1999)

Parmelin 1963 • Hélène Parmelin (trans. Humphrey Hare), *Picasso Plain: An Intimate Portrait* (Secker & Warburg, London, 1963). Originally published as *Picasso sur la place* (R. Julliard, Paris, 1959)

Parmelin 1969 • Hélène Parmelin (trans. Christine Trollope), *Picasso says …* (Allen & Unwin, London, 1969). Originally published as *Picasso dit …* (Éditions Gonthier, Paris, 1966)

Penrose 1958 • Roland Penrose, *Picasso: His Life and Work* (Victor Gollancz, London, 1958)

Penrose 1981 • Roland Penrose, *Scrap Book 1900–1981* (Thames & Hudson, London, 1981)

Picasso 1930–1935 • *Picasso 1930–1935* (Editions 'Cahiers d'Art', Paris, 1936)

***Picasso and Gilot* 2012** • *Picasso and Françoise Gilot: Paris-Vallauris, 1943–1953*, curated by John Richardson in collaboration with Françoise Gilot (exh. cat., Gagosian Gallery, New York; in association with Rizzoli International Publications, 2012)

***Picasso Camera* 2014** • *Picasso and the Camera*, curated by John Richardson (exh. cat., Gagosian Gallery, New York; in association with Rizzoli International Publications, 2014)

***Picasso Caricature* 2003** • *Picasso: from Caricature to Metamorphosis of Style* (exh. cat., Museu Picasso Barcelona; Ajuntament de Barcelona, in association with Lund Humphries, Aldershot, 2003)

***Picasso intime* 1981** • *Picasso intime: Collection Maya Ruiz-Picasso* (exh. cat., Navio Gallery, Tokyo, 1981)

***Picasso jeunesse* 1991** • *Picasso, jeunesse et genèse: Dessins 1893–1905* (exh. cat., Musée Picasso, Paris, and Musée des Beaux-Arts, Nantes; Réunion des Musées Nationaux, Paris, 1991)

***Picasso Mediterranean* 2010** • *Picasso: The Mediterranean Years, 1945–1962*, curated by John Richardson (exh. cat., Gagosian Gallery, London; in association with Rizzoli International Publications, 2010)

***Picasso Tricorne* 1992** • *Picasso: Le Tricorne. Dessins pour le décor et les costumes du ballet de Manuel de Falla* (exh. cat., Musée des Beaux-Arts, Lyon, Museu Picasso, Barcelona, and Fundación Juan March, Madrid; Réunion des musées nationaux, Paris, 1992)

Polunin 1927 • Vladimir Polunin (ed. Cyril W. Beaumont), *The Continental Method of Scene Painting* (C.W. Beaumont, London, 1927)

***Primer Picasso* 2015** • *El primer Picasso: A Coruña 2015* (exh. cat., Museo de Belas Artes da Coruña; Ayuntamiento de A Coruña, 2015)

Quinn 1965 • Edward Quinn, *Picasso at Work* (W.H. Allen, London, 1965)

Rabinow 2006 • Rebecca A. Rabinow (ed.), *Cézanne to Picasso: Ambroise Vollard, Patron of the Avant-Garde* (exh. cat., The Metropolitan Museum of Art, New York; in association with Yale University Press, New Haven and London, 2006)

Read 2008 • Peter Read, *Picasso & Apollinaire: The Persistence of Memory* (University of California Press, Berkeley, Los Angeles, London, 2008)

Rembrandt Corpus 1989 • J. Bruyn et al. (trans. D. Cook-Radmore), *A Corpus of Rembrandt Paintings*, vol.III, *1635–1642* (Rembrandt Research Project, Stichting Foundation; Martinus Nijhoff, Dordrecht, Boston, London, 1989)

Rewald 1996 • John Rewald, with Walter Feilchenfeldt and Jayne Warman, *The Paintings of Paul Cézanne: A Catalogue Raisonné*, 2 vols (Harry Abrams, New York, 1996)

Richardson 1991 • John Richardson, with the collaboration of Marilyn McCully, *A Life of Picasso*, vol.1, *1881–1906* (Random House, New York, 1991)

Richardson 1996 • John Richardson, with the collaboration of Marilyn McCully, *A Life of Picasso*, vol.2, *1907–1917: The Painter of Modern Life* (Jonathan Cape, London, 1996)

Richardson 2007 • John Richardson, with the collaboration of Marilyn McCully, *A Life of Picasso*, vol.3, *The Triumphant Years, 1917–1932* (Jonathan Cape, London, 2007)

Rubin 1989 • William Rubin, *Picasso and Braque: Pioneering Cubism* (exh. cat., The Museum of Modern Art, New York, 1989)

Rubin 1996 • William Rubin (ed.), *Picasso and Portraiture: Representation and Transformation* (exh. cat., The Museum of Modern Art, New York, and Grand Palais, Paris; in association with Thames & Hudson, London, 1996)

Sabartés 1949 • Jaime Sabartés (trans. Angel Flores), *Picasso: An Intimate Portrait* (W.H. Allen, London, 1949)

Sabartés 1954 • Jaime Sabartés (trans. Félia Leal and Alfred Rosset), *Picasso: Documents iconographiques* (Pierre Cailler, Geneva, 1954)

Sabartès 1958 • Jaime Sabartès, *Les Ménines et la vie* (Cercle d'Art, Paris, 1958)

Seckel 1994 • Hélène Seckel, *Max Jacob et Picasso* (exh. cat., Musée des Beaux-Arts, Quimper, and Musée Picasso, Paris; Réunion des Musées Nationaux, Paris, 1994)

Seckel-Klein 1998 • Hélène Seckel-Klein, *Picasso collectionneur* (Réunion des Musées Nationaux, Paris, 1998)

Shikes and Heller 1984 • Ralph E. Shikes and Steven Heller, *The Art of Satire: Painters as Caricaturists and Cartoonists from Delacroix to Picasso* (Pratt Graphics Center and Horizon Press, New York, 1984)

Spies 2000 • Werner Spies (trans. Melissa Thorson House and Margie Mounier), *Picasso: The Sculptures* (exh. cat. Centre Georges Pompidou, Paris; in association with Hatje Canz, Ostfildern/Stuttgart, 2000)

Stein 1966 • Gertrude Stein, *The Autobiography of Alice B. Toklas* (Penguin Books, Harmondsworth, 1966). Originally published by Harcourt, Brace, New York, 1933

Stravinsky 1936 • Igor Stravinsky, *Chronicle of My Life* (Gollancz, London, 1936)

Stravinsky and Craft 1959 • Igor Stravinsky and Robert Craft, *Conversations with Igor Stravinsky* (Faber and Faber, London, 1959)

***Sylvette* 2014** • *Sylvette, Sylvette, Sylvette: Picasso and the Model* (exh. cat., Kunsthalle, Bremen; in association with Prestel, Munich, London, New York, 2014)

Tinterow and Stein 2010 • Gary Tinterow and Susan Alyson Stein (eds), *Picasso in the Metropolitan Museum of Art* (exh. cat., The Metropolitan Museum of Art, New York; in association with Yale University Press, New Haven and London, 2010)

Utley 2000 • Gertje R. Utley, *Picasso: The Communist Years* (Yale University Press, New Haven and London, 2000)

Vallès 2010 • Eduard Vallès (ed.), *Picasso versus Rusiñol* (exh. cat., Museu Picasso, Barcelona; Ajuntament de Barcelona, 2010)

Varnedoe and Gopnik 1990 • Kirk Varnedoe and Adam Gopnik, *High and Low: Modern Art and Popular Culture* (exh. cat., The Museum of Modern Art, New York, The Art Institute of Chicago and Museum of Contemporary Art, Los Angeles; The Museum of Modern Art, New York, 1990)

Veyrat 1895 • Georges Veyrat, *La caricature à travers les siècles* (C. Mendel, Paris, 1895)

Weiss 2003 • Jeffrey Weiss et al., *Picasso: The Cubist Portraits of Fernande Olivier* (exh. cat., National Gallery of Art, Washington, and Nasher Sculpture Center, Dallas; National Gallery of Art, Washington, in association with Princeton University Press, Princeton and Oxford, 2003)

West 2004 • Sheerer West, *Portraiture* (Oxford University Press, 2004)

Wright 2013 • Barnaby Wright (ed.), *Becoming Picasso: Paris 1901* (exh. cat., The Courtauld Gallery, London; in association with Paul Holberton Publishing, London, 2013)

Z. • Christian Zervos, *Pablo Picasso*, 33 vols (Cahiers d'Art, Paris, 1932–78)

Acknowledgements

It has been a great pleasure and privilege to curate *Picasso Portraits* and in the process I have incurred a multitude of debts. The support of the artist's heirs has been invaluable and I thank Catherine Hutin, Almine and Bernard Ruiz-Picasso, Claude Ruiz-Picasso, Diana Widmaier Picasso and Maya Widmaier-Picasso most warmly for their generosity.

The inspired idea of mounting the exhibition within the National Portrait Gallery was that of its former director, Sandy Nairne, and I am extremely grateful both to him and to his successor, Dr Nicholas Cullinan, for their commitment and encouragement. The Museu Picasso has been the ideal partner, lending to London with great liberality, providing indispensable help with research and participating in the burdensome administration with admirable efficiency and good humour. Its director, Bernardo Laniado-Romero, has been the perfect collaborator, helping to shape the selection and sharing his profound knowledge, understanding and love of Picasso's work. The staff of both institutions who have contributed so significantly to the realisation of the project are named in the Directors' Foreword, but I must make special mention of Sarah Tinsley, Michelle Greaves, Mariona Tió and Ulrike Wachsmann: their support over the years has been indispensable and invigorating.

The universal appeal and inexhaustible richness of Picasso's oeuvre generate countless schemes for exhibitions and the demands on museums, galleries and private collectors increase year by year. Without the generosity of lenders these projects remain in the realm of pure fantasy and I am immensely grateful to all the following for their gracious response to our request to borrow the precious works in their care, and for their cooperation in the planning and organisation of the exhibition: Douglas Druick, Stephanie d'Alessandro and Anna Simonovic, Art Institute of Chicago; Natasha Austin; Roly Keating and Lesley Thomas, The British Library; Neil MacGregor, Hugo Chapman, Stephen Coppel and Jordina Diaz Ferrando, The British Museum; Bernard Blistène, Sennen Codio and Brigitte Léal, Centre Pompidou, Paris. Musée national d'art moderne/ Centre de création industrielle; Carmen Godia and Manel Riera, Colección 'El Conventet', Barcelona; César Alierta, Laura Ramón Brogeras and Elena Valderrábano, Colección Telefónica; Hubert Looser, Fondation Hubert Looser, Zürich; Bernard and Almine Ruiz-Picasso, Iro Biehler, Marie Brisson and Claire Guérin, Fundación Almine y Bernard Ruiz-Picasso para el Arte; Liliana Godia, Nadia Hernández and Mercè Obón Mateos, Fundación Francisco Godia, Barcelona; Mr and Mrs J. Tomilson Hill and Julia Lee; Leonard A. Lauder and Emily Braun, Leonard A. Lauder Cubist Collection; Michael Govan, Stephanie Barron and Cynthia Tovar, Los Angeles County Museum of Art; Pierre Bergé, Pascale Léautey and Françoise Leonelli, Maison Jean Cocteau, Milly-la-Fôret; Thomas P. Campbell, Rachel Mustalish, Rebecca Rabinow, Pari Stave and Sheena Wagstaffe, Metropolitan Museum of Art, New York; Fabrice Hergott, Sophie Krebs, Justine Tonelli and Véronique Rustici, Musée d'Art Moderne de la Ville de Paris; Laurent Le Bon, Sarah Lagrevol and Violette Andres, Musée national Picasso-Paris; Jean-Louis Andral and Isabelle Le Druillennec, Musée Picasso, Antibes; Glenn D. Lowry, Eliza Frecon, Ann Temkin and Anne Umland, The Museum of Modern Art, New York; Halldór Björn Runólfsson and Dagný Heiðdal, National Gallery of Iceland; Antony Penrose and Ami Bouhassane, The Penrose Collection; Timothy Rub, Matthew Affron, Nancy Leeman and Joseph Rishel, Philadelphia Museum of Art; Ivan Polunin; Mme Poniatowski and Evelyne Ferlay, Marie-Anne Krugier-Poniatowski Collection; Karin Siden and Catrin Lundeberg, Prins Eugens Waldemarsudde; Horst and Gabriele Siedle and Eva Spitz, Horst und

Gabriele Siedle-Kunststiftung; Richard Armstrong, Julie Barten, Tracey Bashkoff, Susan Davidson and Matt Heffernan, Solomon R. Guggenheim Museum, New York; Udo Kittelmann, Olivier Berggruen, Felicia Rappe and Manuela Bethke, Staatliche Museen zu Berlin, Nationalgalerie, Museum Berggruen; Tim Knox, Jane Munro and David Packer, The Syndics of the Fitzwilliam Museum, Cambridge; Nicholas Serota, Matthew Gale, Christopher Higgins and Helen Little, Tate, London. I am equally indebted to those private collectors who have preferred to remain anonymous.

Numerous individuals have assisted with essential research, information and advice and I sincerely thank them all: William Acquavella, Juan Manuel Albendea, Denise Allen, Doris Ammann, Stephanie Ansari, Yve-Alain Bois, Chris Breward, Rupert Burgess, Philippe Büttner, Roger Cardinal, Michael Cary, Laure Collignon, Laura Couvreur, Emily Crowley, Estrella de Diego, Sofía Diez, Ann Dumas, Dominique Dupuis-Labbé, Isabelle Duvernois, Lucy Economakis, John Elderfield, Patrick Elliott, John Finlay, Clare Finn, Michael FitzGerald, Valerie Fletcher, Peggy Fogelman, Simonetta Fraquelli, Larry Gagosian, Susan Grace Galassi, Scott Gerson, Carmen Giménez, Cécile Godefroy, Brett Gorvy, Christopher Green, William Griswold, Christoph Grunenberg, Tracy Hamilton, Martin Hammer, James Harwood, Diana Howard, Ania Jozefacka, Pepe Karmel, Richard Kendall, Hélène Klein, Felix Krämer, Astrid Le Nay, Stuart Lochhead, Silvia Loreti, Marina Loshak, Nicholas Maclean, Luise Mahler, James Mayor, Marilyn McCully, Ewi Montgomery, Frederick Mulder, Maria Teresa Ocaña, Vlasta Odell, Carina Plath, Sandra Poole, Artur Ramon, Ruth Rattenbury, Peter Read, John Richardson, Christopher Riopelle, James Roundell, Justin T. Russo, Carmen Schjaer, Simon Shaw, Reinhard Spieler, Jeanne-Yvette Sudour, Jane Suitor, Vérane Tasseau, Emmanuelle Terrel, Montse Torras, Giulia Trabaldo Togna, Neisha Tucker, Gertje Utley, Kerry Watson, Deborah Winard, Barnaby Wright, Florence Half-Wrobel, Miki Yoda, Nina Zimmer and Aurora Zubillaga. Christine Pinault of Picasso Administration, Paris, deserves special thanks for her unfailing readiness to answer every question immediately and to offer wise counsel whenever requested. I am also most grateful to Michael Bury, Peter Bury and Gabrielle and Roger Turner for their kindness and constant support.

Elizabeth Cowling

Exhibition works and other illustrations

The National Portrait Gallery, London, and the Museu Picasso, Barcelona, would like to thank the copyright holders for granting permission to reproduce works illustrated in this book. Every effort has been made to contact the holders of copyright material, and any omissions will be corrected in future editions if the publisher is notified in writing. Unless otherwise stated, all works are by Pablo Picasso and © Succession Picasso/DACS, London 2016. Dimensions are given height before width, followed by depth.

Only exhibited works are reproduced below. Those shown at the National Portrait Gallery, London, are marked (L); those shown at the Museu Picasso, Barcelona, are marked (B); those shown at both venues are marked (B, L).
We are most grateful to all the lenders.

Introduction

Picasso in Montmartre, place Ravignan, by an unknown photographer, c.1904
Archives Picasso, Musée national Picasso-Paris

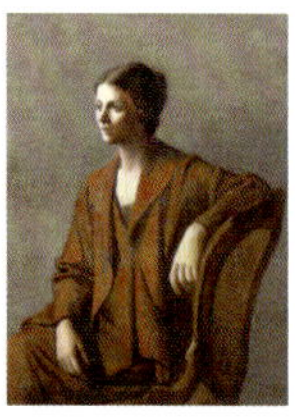

1 *Portrait of Olga Picasso*, 1923
Oil on canvas, 1300 x 970mm
Private Collection
(B, L)

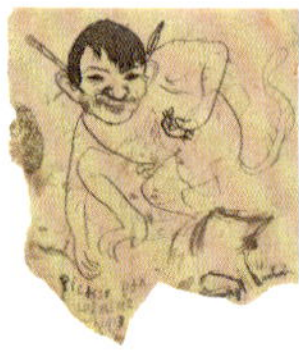

2 *Picasso par lui mème (Picasso by Himself)*, Paris, 1 January 1903
Pen and ink on paper, 118 x 107mm (irregular)
Museu Picasso, Barcelona, Gift of Pablo Picasso, 1970.
MPB 110.440
(L)

3 *Copy of* Philip IV *by Velázquez*, Madrid, October–November, 1897
Oil on canvas, 542 x 467mm
Museu Picasso, Barcelona, Gift of Pablo Picasso, 1970.
MPB 110.017

4 *Philip IV* by Diego Velázquez, c.1653
Oil on canvas, 693 x 565mm
Museo Nacional del Prado, Madrid

5 Picasso with Henri Rousseau's *Self-portrait* and *Portrait of the Artist's Second Wife* (both 1900–3)
Photograph by André Gomès, Notre-Dame-de-Vie, Mougins, April 1965
© André Gomes. Archives Picasso, Musée national Picasso-Paris

6 *La Coruña*, 16 September 1894
Back and front pages of a manuscript newspaper
Pen and brown ink and pencil, 210 x 260mm
Musée national Picasso-Paris
MP 402R

1. Launching a career, 1895–1900

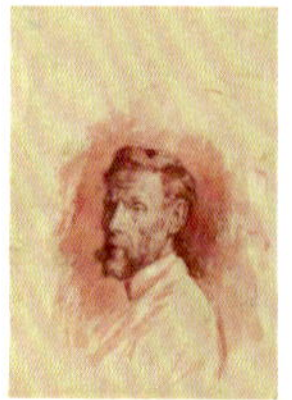

7 *The Artist's Father*, Barcelona, 1896
Watercolour on paper, 255 x 178mm
Museu Picasso, Barcelona, Gift of Pablo Picasso, 1970.
MPB 110.331
(B)

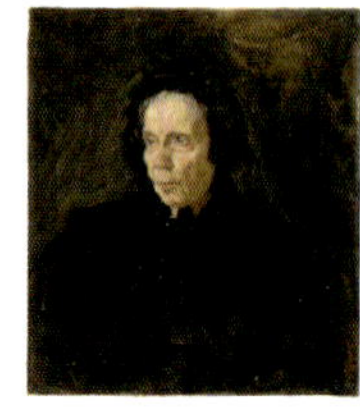

8 *Aunt Pepa*, Málaga, June-July 1896
Oil on canvas, 575 x 505mm
Museu Picasso, Barcelona, Gift of Pablo Picasso, 1970.
MPB 110.010
(B)

9 *Copy of* The Buffoon Calabacillas *by Velázquez*, Madrid, sketchbook, 1895
Graphite pencil on paper, 120 x 80mm
Museu Picasso, Barcelona, Gift of Pablo Picasso, 1970.
MPB 111.170R

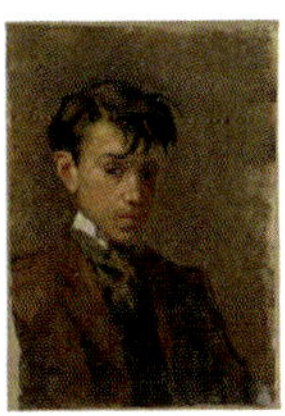

10 ***Self-portrait***, Barcelona, 1896
Oil on canvas,
329 x 235mm (irregular)
Museu Picasso, Barcelona,
Gift of Pablo Picasso, 1970.
MPB 110.076
(L)

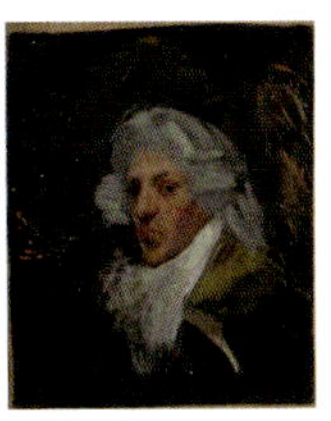

11 ***Self-portrait with Wig***,
Barcelona, 1900
Oil on canvas, 558 x 458mm
Museu Picasso, Barcelona,
Gift of Pablo Picasso, 1970.
MPB 110.053
(B, L)

12 ***Juan de Villanueva***
by Francisco de Goya, 1800–5
Oil on poplar, 900 x 600mm
Museo de la Real Academia de Bellas
Artes de San Fernando, Madrid

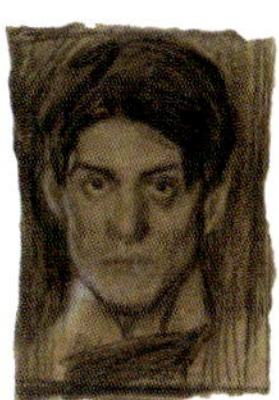

13 ***Self-portrait***, Barcelona, 1899–1900
Charcoal and chalk on paper,
225 x 165mm (irregular)
Museu Picasso, Barcelona,
Gift of Pablo Picasso, 1970.
MPB 110.632
(L)

14 ***Self-portrait with Skeleton Arm***
by Edvard Munch, 1895
Lithograph, 450 x 320mm
The British Museum, London

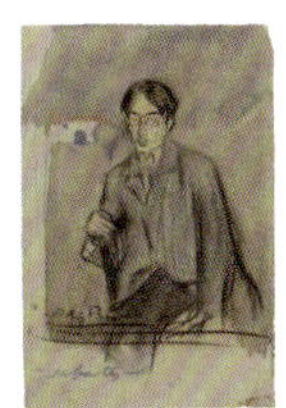

15 ***Jaume Sabartés, Seated***,
Barcelona, 1900
Charcoal and *peinture à l'essence*
on laid paper, 485 x 324mm
(irregular)
Museu Picasso, Barcelona,
Gift of Jaume Sabartés, 1962.
MPB 70.228
(B)

16 ***Portrait of Pere Romeu***
by Ramon Casas i Carbó, 1897–9
Charcoal, pastel and watercolour
on paper, 640 x 300mm
Museu Nacional d'Art de Catalunya,
Barcelona

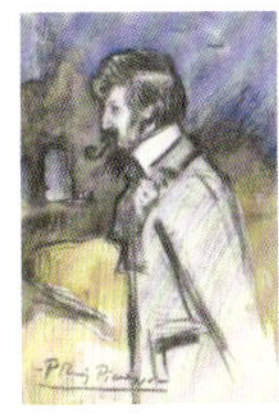

17 ***Portrait of Santiago Rusiñol***, c.1900
Charcoal and watercolour on
paper, 330 x 230mm
Colección 'El Conventet', Barcelona
(B, L)

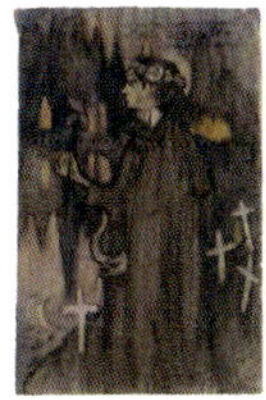

18 ***Decadent Poet (Jaume Sabartés)***,
Barcelona, 1900
Charcoal and *peinture à l'essence*
on laid watermarked paper,
483 x 322mm (irregular)
Museu Picasso, Barcelona,
Gift of Jaume Sabartés, 1962.
MPB 70.232
(L)

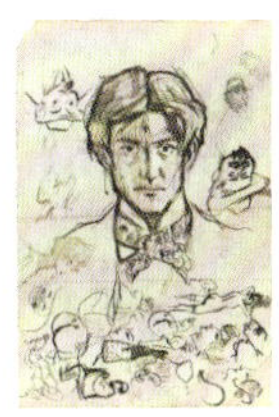

19 ***Self-portrait, Pompeu Gener, Oriol Martí and Other Sketches***,
Barcelona, 1899–1900
Pen and ink and graphite pencil
on watermarked paper,
320 x 220mm (irregular)
Museu Picasso, Barcelona,
Gift of Pablo Picasso, 1970.
MPB 110.676
(B)

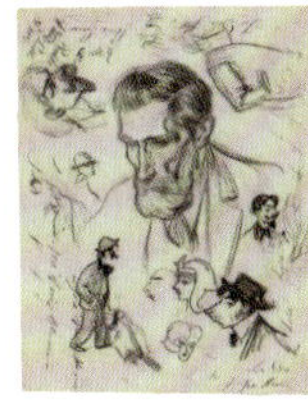

20 ***The Artist's Father, Joaquim Mir, Carles Casagemas and Various Caricatures***, 1899–1900
Conté crayon on watermarked
paper, 409 x 320mm (irregular)
Museu Picasso, Barcelona,
Gift of Pablo Picasso, 1970.
MPB 110.590
(B)

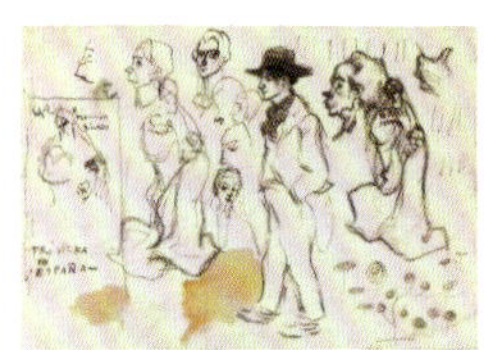

21 *Self-portrait and Studies for a Poster for the Caja de Previsión y Socorro*, Barcelona, May 1900
Pen and sepia ink and touches of watercolour on watermarked paper, 222 x 320mm (irregular)
Museu Picasso, Barcelona, Gift of Pablo Picasso, 1970. MPB 110.814
(L)

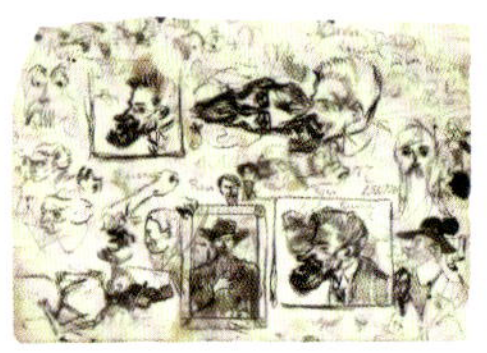

22 *Santiago Rusiñol Caricatured as* The Nobleman with His Hand on His Chest *by El Greco, Josep Rocarol i Faura and Other Sketches*, Barcelona, 1899–1900
Sepia and Indian ink, wash and graphite pencil on watermarked paper, 230 x 334mm (irregular)
Museu Picasso, Barcelona, Gift of Pablo Picasso, 1970. MPB 110.683
(B)

23 *Interior of Els Quatre Gats* by Ricard Opisso i Sala, 1900
Charcoal, ink and coloured crayons on paper, 419 x 491mm
Museu d'Història de la Ciutat de Barcelona

24 *Santiago Rusiñol*, 1900
Ink and essence on wove paper, 108 x 102mm
Metropolitan Museum of Art. Gift of Raymonde Paul, in memory of her brother, C. Michael Paul, 1982 (1982.179.23)

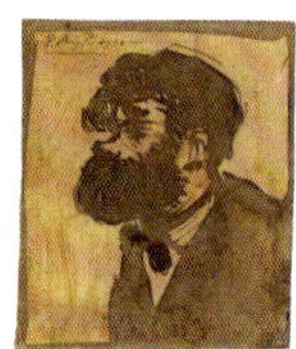

25 *Joaquim Mir*, 1900
Ink and essence on wove paper, 89 x 79mm
Metropolitan Museum of Art. Gift of Raymonde Paul, in memory of her brother, C. Michael Paul, 1982 (1982.179.27)
(B)

26 *Portrait of Mir* by Ramon Casas i Carbó,
Reproduced *Pèl & Ploma,* no.81, 1 October 1901
Museu Nacional d'Art de Catalunya, Barcelona

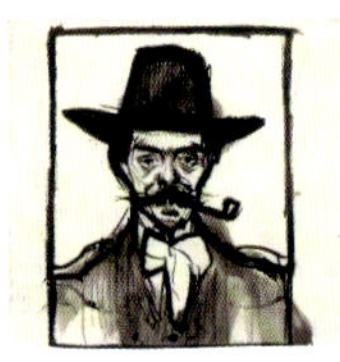

27 *Portrait of the Writer Frederic Pujulà i Vallès*, 1900
Ink and wash on paper, 130 x 140mm
Private Collection
(B)

28 *Frederic Pujulà i Vallès*, 1900
Ink and essence on wove paper, 127 x 92mm
Metropolitan Museum of Art. Gift of Raymonde Paul, in memory of her brother, C. Michael Paul, 1982 (1982.179.20)

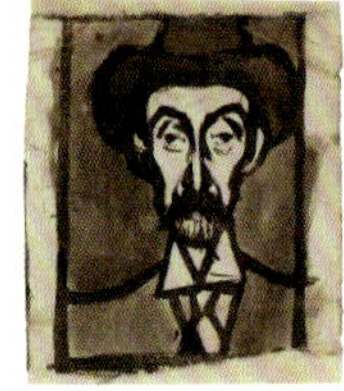

29 *Miguel Utrillo*, Barcelona, 1900
Pen and sepia ink and wash on paper, 92 x 78mm (irregular)
Museu Picasso, Barcelona, Gift of Pablo Picasso, 1970. MPB 110.260
(L)

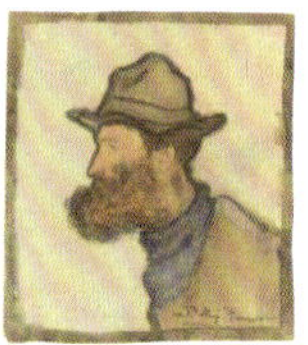

30 *Ramon Pichot*, 1900
Ink and essence on wove paper, 98 x 92mm
Metropolitan Museum of Art. Gift of Raymonde Paul, in memory of her brother, C. Michael Paul, 1982 (1982.179.24)
(B)

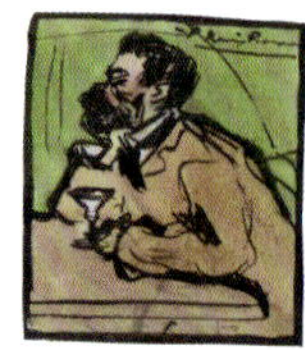

31 *Josep Rocarol i Faura*, Barcelona, 1900
Pen and ink and brush and watercolour on paper, 90 x 79mm (irregular)
Museu Picasso, Barcelona, Gift of Pablo Picasso, 1970. MPB 110.435
(L)

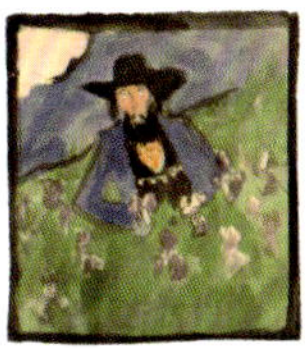

32 *Pere Romeu in a Field of Irises*, Barcelona, c.1900
Gouache and pencil on paper, 190 x 170mm
Fundación Francisco Godia, Barcelona
(B, L)

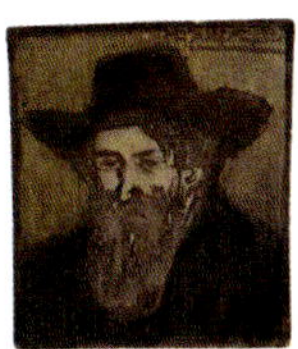

33 *Santiago Rusiñol*, Barcelona, 1900
Pen and ink and watercolour on paper, 103 x 92mm (irregular)
Museu Picasso, Barcelona, Gift of Pablo Picasso, 1970.
MPB 110.433
(L)

2. Experiments with form: Paris and Barcelona 1900–1904

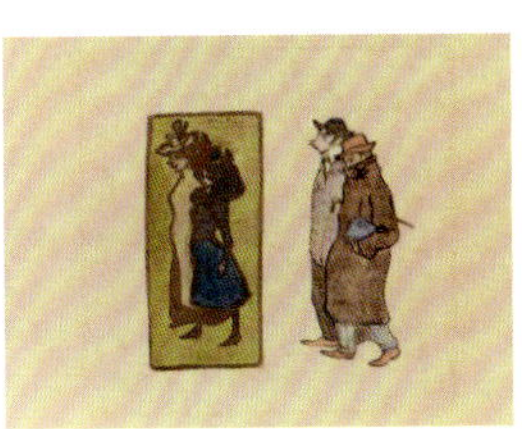

34.i *Two Girls*, Paris, 1900
34.ii *Carles Casagemas and Picasso* Paris, 1900
Pen and sepia ink, watercolour and gouache on paper pasted onto cardboard, 380 x 430mm
Museu Picasso, Barcelona, Acquisition, 1995.
MPB 113.003c
(B)

35 *Carles Casagemas*, 1900
Ink and essence on wove paper, 105 x 79mm
Metropolitan Museum of Art. Gift of Raymonde Paul, in memory of her brother, C. Michael Paul, 1982
(1982.179.19)

36 *Self-portrait (Yo Picasso)*, 1901
Oil on canvas, 735 x 605mm
Private Collection

37 *Portrait of Dr Félix Rey* by Vincent Van Gogh, 1889
Oil on canvas, 640 x 530mm
Pushkin State Museum of Fine Arts, Moscow

38 *Self-portrait*, 1901
Pastel and charcoal on board, 678 x 520mm
Private Collection

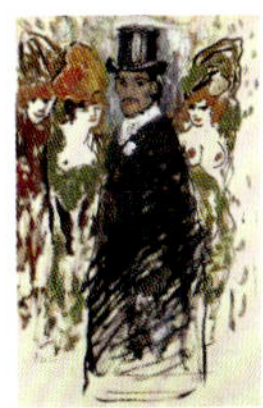

39 *Picasso in a Top Hat*, 1901
Oil on paper, 500 x 330mm
Private Collection
(L)

40 *Maxime Dethomas* by Henri de Toulouse-Lautrec, 1896
Oil on cardboard, 675 x 509mm
National Gallery of Art, Washington. Chester Dale Collection

41 *Self-portrait in His Studio*, Paris, 1901
Gelatin silver print (superimposition), 120 x 90mm
Archives Picasso, Musée national Picasso-Paris

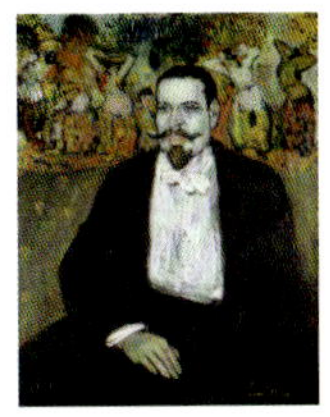

42 *Gustave Coquiot*, 1901
Oil on canvas, 1000 x 810mm
Centre Pompidou, Paris. Musée national d'art moderne/Centre de création industrielle. Achat des Musées nationaux, 1933 (inv. no. JP 652 P)
(B, L)

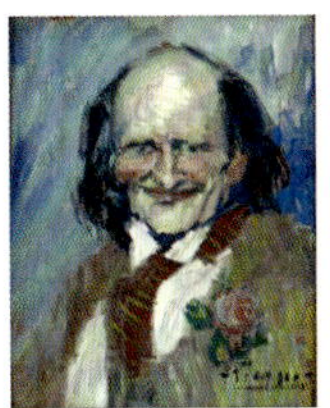

43 *Bibi-la-Purée*, 1901
Oil on cardboard, 490 x 390mm
Private Collection
(B, L)

44 *Portrait of the Poet Sabartés*, 1901
Oil on canvas, 820 x 660
Pushkin State Museum of Fine Arts, Moscow

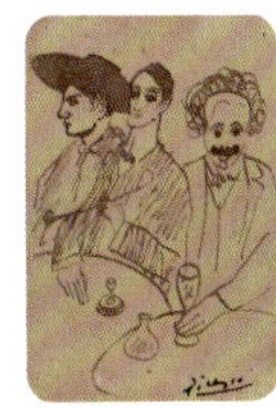

45 *Picasso, Àngel Fernández de Soto and Sebastià Junyer i Vidal in a Café*, Barcelona, c.1903
Pen and sepia ink on paper on cardboard printed card, 132 x 90mm
Museu Picasso, Barcelona, Gift of Sebastià Junyer i Vidal, 1966.
MPB 70.808
(L)

46 *In a Café (L'Absinthe)* by Edgar Degas, 1875–6
Oil on canvas, 920 x 685mm
Musée d'Orsay, Paris. Bequest of Count Isaac de Camondo, 1911

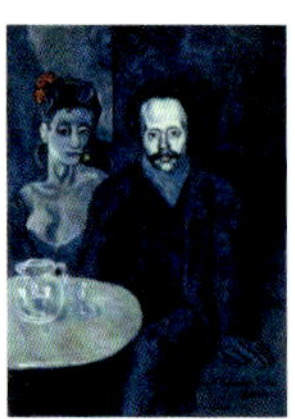

47 *Portrait of Sebastià Junyer i Vidal*, 1903
Oil on canvas, 1264 x 939mm
Los Angeles County Museum of Art. David E. Bright Bequest (M.67.25.18)
(L)

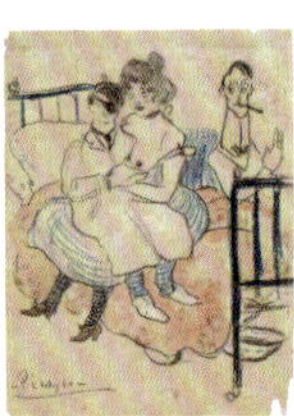

48 *The Brothers Mateu and Àngel Fernández de Soto with Anita*, Barcelona, 1902–3
Conté crayon, blue coloured pencil and watercolour on paper, 310 x 237mm (irregular)
Museu Picasso, Barcelona, Given by the Barcelona City Council, 1963.
MPB 50.498
(B)

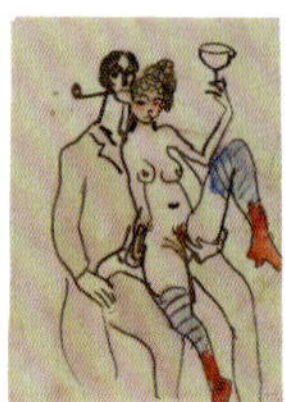

49 *Àngel Fernández de Soto with a Woman*, Barcelona, 1902–3
Pen and sepia ink, wash, watercolour and Conté crayon on paper, 210 x 152mm (irregular)
Museu Picasso, Barcelona, Given by the Barcelona City Council, 1963.
MPB 50.494
(L)

50 [see 2, p.232]

51 *Neither More Nor Less (Ni mas ni menos)* by Francisco de Goya, 1799
Etching, drypoint, polished aquatint on bone-coloured vergé paper, 246 x 212mm
Museo Nacional del Prado, Madrid

52 *Portrait of Carles Casagemas*, reproduced in *Catalunya artística*, no.38, 28 February 1901, p.104
Arxiu Històric de la Ciutat de Barcelona (AHCB)

53 *Casagemas in His Coffin*, 1901
Oil on cardboard, 725 x 578mm
Private Collection

54 *Victor Hugo on His Death Bed*
Photograph by Félix Nadar, 1885
Woodburytype, 165 x 125mm
Musée d'Orsay, Paris
PHO 1985.226

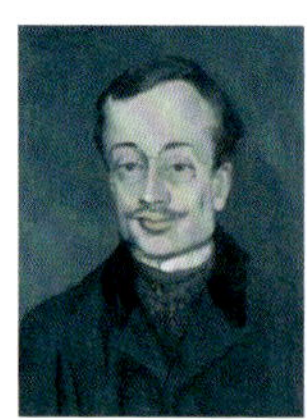

55 *Portrait of Jaume Sabartés*, 1904
Oil on canvas, 495 x 375mm
Staatliche Museen zu Berlin, Nationalgalerie, Museum Berggruen
(B)

3. Paris: new circles, shifting styles, 1904–1910

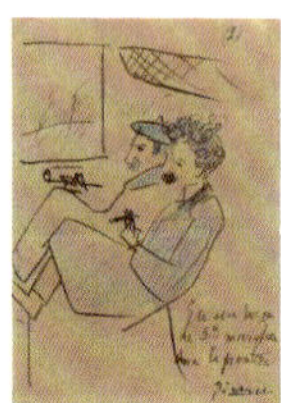

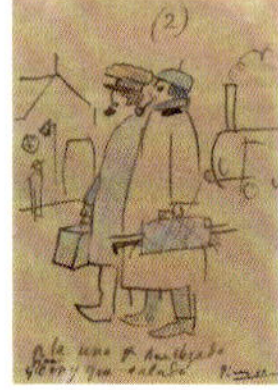

56 *Picasso and Sebastià Junyer i Vidal* **series**, Paris, 1904:

i *Picasso and Sebastià Junyer i Vidal Set Off on a Journey* (L)

ii *Picasso and Sebastià Junyer i Vidal Arrive at the Border* (L)

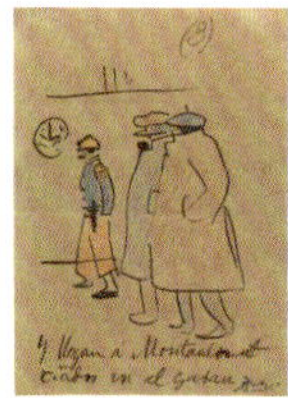

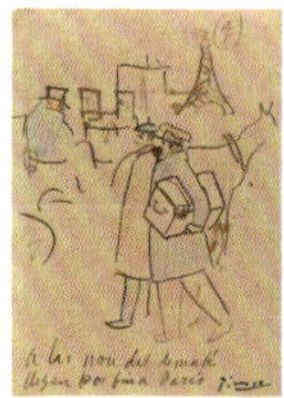

iii *Picasso and Sebastià Junyer i Vidal Reach Montauban* (L)

iv *Picasso and Sebastià Junyer i Vidal Arrive in Paris* (L)

v [this vignette is lost]

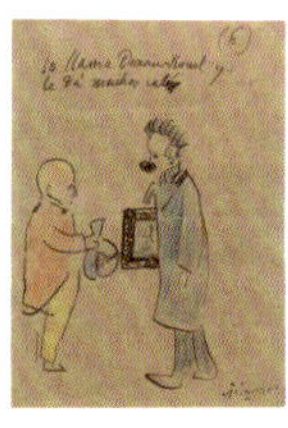

vi *Sebastià Junyer i Vidal calls on Durand-Ruel*
Each drawing: pen and ink and coloured pencils on paper, 220 x 160mm
Museu Picasso, Barcelona, Gift of Sebastià Junyer i Vidal, 1966.
MPB 70.803, 70.804, 70.805, 70.806, 70.807
(L)

57 *Caricatures of Paul Fort, Henri Delormel and André Salmon*, 1905
Pencil on Paul Fort's calling card, 56 x 88mm
Acquisition 1986, formerly collection Apollinaire.
Musée national Picasso-Paris.
MP 1986-44

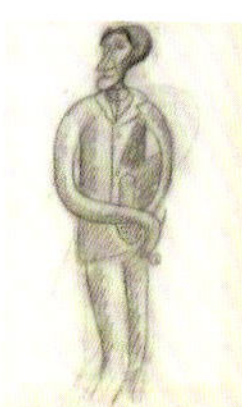

58 *Portrait of André Salmon*, 1907
Charcoal on laid paper, 626 x 405mm
Musée national Picasso-Paris
MP 2000-2R
(B)

59 *Sketches Made During the Audience of 14 November (Court of Assizes)* by Charles Philipon, 1831
Lithograph, 333 x 256mm
Bibliothèque nationale de France, département estampes et photographie

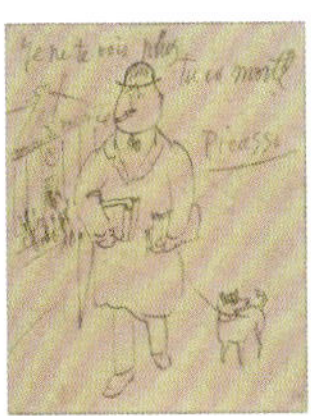

60 *Guillaume Apollinaire, Bank Clerk*, 1905
Pen and ink on postcard, 140 x 110mm
Staatliche Museen zu Berlin, Nationalgalerie, Museum Berggruen
(B, L)

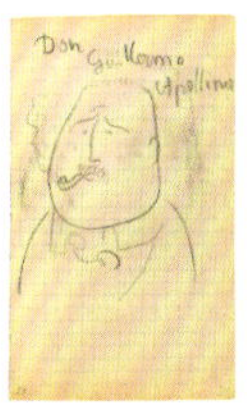

61 *Caricature of Guillaume Apollinaire*
Catalan Sketchbook, Gósol, 1906
Black pencil on graph paper, 120 x 73mm
Museu Picasso, Barcelona, Acquisition, 2000.
MPB 113.039c
(B)

62 *Woman Ironing (La repasseuse)*, Paris, 1904
Oil on canvas, 1162 x 730mm
Solomon R. Guggenheim Museum, New York. Thannhauser Collection, Gift, Justin K. Thannhauser, 1978

63 *Portrait of Ricard Canals*, Paris, 1904
Gelatin silver print, 153 x 107mm
Musée national Picasso-Paris

64 *Madame Canals (Benedetta Bianco)*, Paris, [autumn] 1905
Oil and charcoal on canvas, 900 x 700mm
Museu Picasso, Barcelona, Given by the Barcelona City Council, 1963.
MPB 4.266

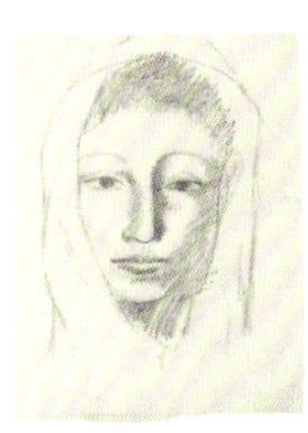

65 *Fernande Olivier*, 1905–6
Charcoal or black chalk on paper, 315 x 245mm
Private Collection. Courtesy Fundación Almine y Bernard Ruiz-Picasso para el Arte
(B)

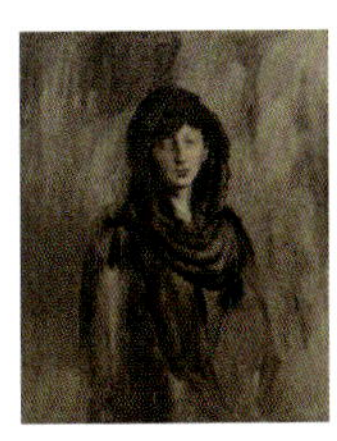

66 *Fernande Olivier with a Black Mantilla*, 1905–6
Oil on canvas, 1000 x 810mm
Solomon R. Guggenheim Museum, New York. Thannhauser Collection, Bequest, Hilde Thannhauser, 1991
(B, L)

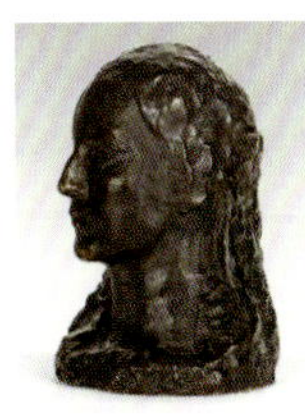

67 *Head of a Woman (Fernande Olivier)*, Paris, 1906
Bronze, 350 x 240 x 230mm
Musée d'Art Moderne de la Ville de Paris
(L)

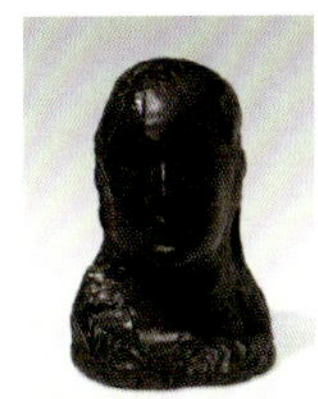

Head of a Woman (Fernande Olivier), Paris, 1906
Bronze, 357 x 248 x 254mm
Museu Picasso, Barcelona, Acquisition, 2000.
MPB 113.035
(B)

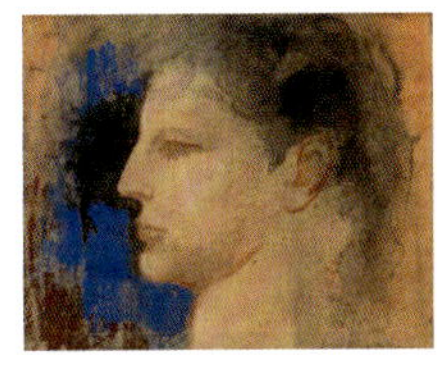

68 *Woman's Head. Portrait of Fernande Olivier*, 1906
Gouache on paper, 320 x 400mm
Prins Eugens Waldemarsudde
(L)

69 *Portrait of Gertrude Stein*, 1906
Oil on canvas, 996 x 813mm
Metropolitan Museum of Art. Bequest of Gertrude Stein, 1946

70 *Self-portrait with Palette* by Paul Cézanne, *c.*1890
Oil on canvas, 920 x 730mm
Foundation E.G. Bührle Collection, Zürich

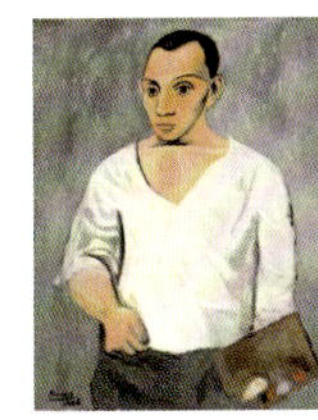

71 *Self-portrait with Palette*, 1906
Oil on canvas, 919 x 733mm
Philadelphia Museum of Art: A.E. Gallatin Collection, 1950
(L)

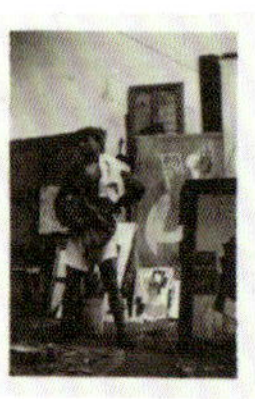

72 *Self-portrait with* **Seated Man with Glass**, 5 bis Rue Schoelcher, Paris, 1915–16
Vintage photograph, 66 x 45mm
Private Collection. Courtesy Fundación Almine y Bernard Ruiz-Picasso para el Arte
(B, L)

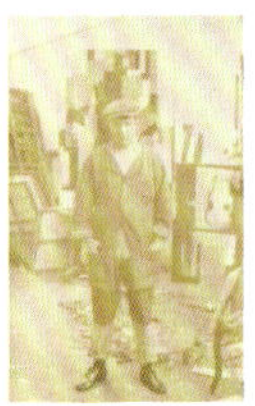

73 *Self-portrait with* **Man Leaning on a Table**, 5 bis Rue Schoelcher, Paris, 1915–16
Gelatin silver print, 188 x 116mm
Private Collection
(B, L)

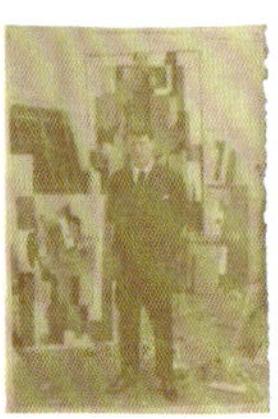

74 *Self-portrait with* **Man Leaning on a Table**, 5 bis Rue Schoelcher, Paris, 1915–16
Gelatin silver print, 188 x 118mm
Private Collection
(B, L)

75 *Sebastià Junyer i Vidal in front of* **Three Women**, Bateau-Lavoir, Paris, 1908
Gelatin silver print, 220 x 85mm
Archives Picasso. Musée national Picasso-Paris

76 ***Head of a Woman (Fernande Olivier)***, 1909
Oil on canvas, 650 x 545mm
Städel Museum, Frankfurt am Main

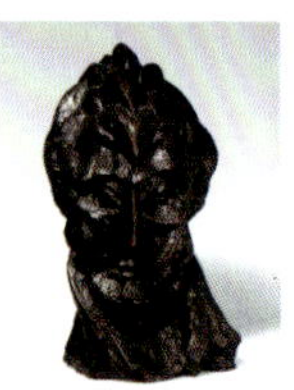

77 ***Head of a Woman (Fernande)***, 1909
Bronze, 413 x 248 x 267mm
Leonard A. Lauder Cubist Collection
(B, L)

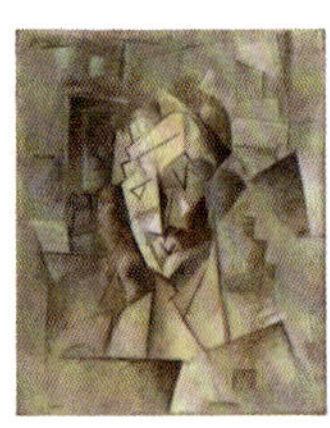

78 ***Cubist Head (Portrait of Fernande)***, 1909–10
Oil on canvas, 660 x 530mm
The Syndics of the Fitzwilliam Museum, Cambridge
(B, L)

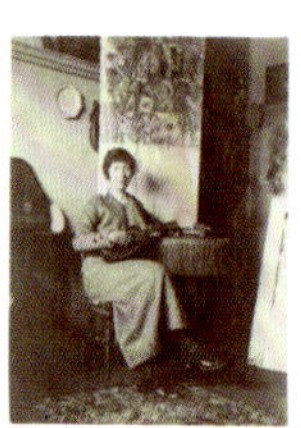

79 ***Marie Laurencin with* Man with a Mandolin**, 11 Boulevard de Clichy, Paris, 1911
Vintage photograph, 111 x 69mm
Private Collection. Courtesy Fundación Almine y Bernard Ruiz-Picasso para el Arte
(B, L)

80 ***Guillaume Apollinaire***, 11 Boulevard de Clichy, Paris, 1910
Gelatin silver print, 219 x 174mm
Archives Picasso. Musée national Picasso-Paris

81 ***Portrait of Ambroise Vollard***, 1910
Oil on canvas, 930 x 650mm
Pushkin State Museum of Fine Arts, Moscow

82 ***Daniel-Henry Kahnweiler***, 11 Boulevard de Clichy, Paris, 1910
Modern gelatin silver print from original glass negative no.45
Archives Picasso. Musée national Picasso-Paris

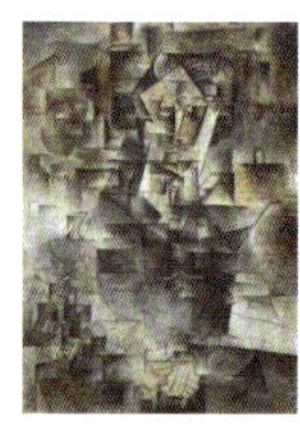

83 ***Daniel-Henry Kahnweiler***, autumn, 1910
Oil on canvas, 1004 x 724mm
The Art Institute of Chicago. Gift of Mrs. Gilbert W. Chapman in memory of Charles B. Goodspeed, 1948.561
(B, L)

4. Photography and the return to classic styles, 1915–1927

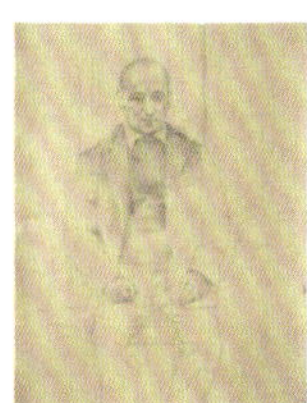

84 ***Portrait of Max Jacob***, 1915
Graphite on vellum paper, 325 x 248mm
Musée national Picasso-Paris
MP 1998-307
(B)

85 ***Portrait of an Unidentified Man***
Carte de visite by Charles-François Jalabert, 1860s
Albumen print
Archives Picasso. Musée national Picasso-Paris

86 *Portrait of an Unidentified Man*
Carte de visite by André-Adolphe-Eugène Disdéri, c.1860
Albumen print
Archives Picasso. Musée national Picasso-Paris

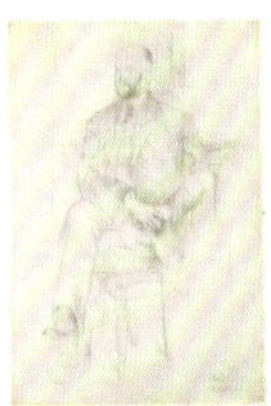

87 *Portrait of Ambroise Vollard*, 1915
Pencil on paper, 467 x 321mm
Metropolitan Museum of Art. The Elisha Whittelsey Collection, The Elisha Whittelsey Fund, 1947 (47.14)
(B)

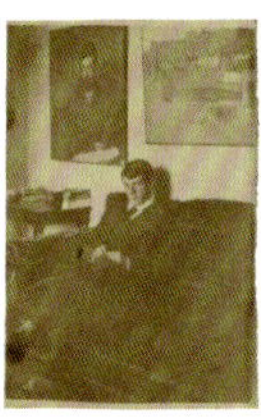

88 *Self-portrait with* Portrait of a Man, 5 bis Rue Schoelcher, Paris, 1915–16
Gelatin silver print, 172 x 119mm
Private Collection
(B, L)

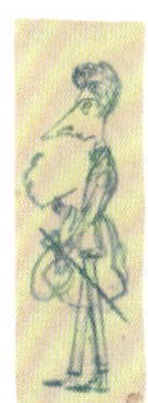

89 *Caricature of Jean Cocteau*, 1917
Gouache on textured vellum paper, 197 x 68mm
Musée national Picasso-Paris
MP 784
(B)

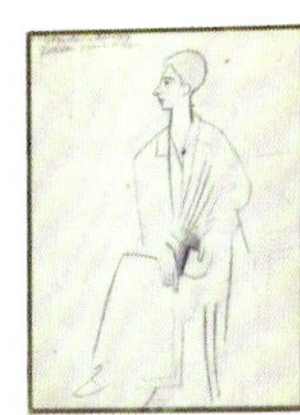

90 *Jean Cocteau*, 1917
Pencil on paper, 270 x 240mm
Collection Stéphane Dermit. Dépôt à la Maison Jean Cocteau, Milly-la-Forêt
(B, L)

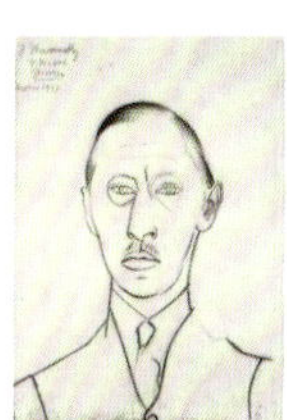

91 *Portrait of Igor Stravinsky*, Rome, 1917
Pencil on paper, 270 x 210mm
Private Collection
(L)

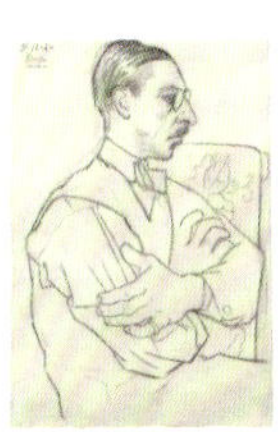

92 *Portrait of Igor Stravinsky in Profile*, 31 December 1920
Pencil on paper, 624 x 485mm
Private Collection
(B)

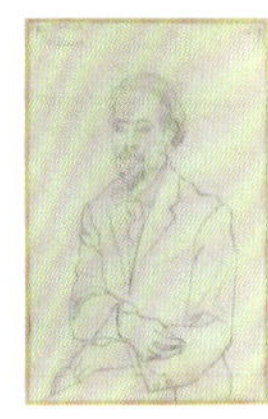

93 *Portrait of Vladimir Polunin*, 1919
Pencil on paper, 530 x 340mm
Private Collection
(L)

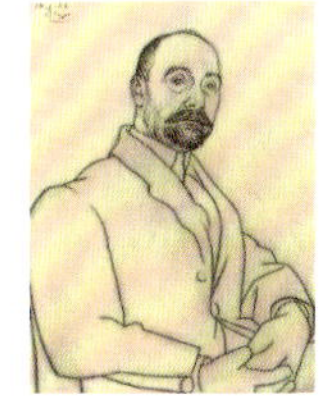

94 *Portrait of Élie Faure*, 14 June 1922
Graphite on paper, 320 x 260mm
Private Collection
(B, L)

95 *Portrait of Erik Satie*, 19 May 1920
Graphite and charcoal on laid paper, 620 x 480mm
Musée national Picasso-Paris
MP 910

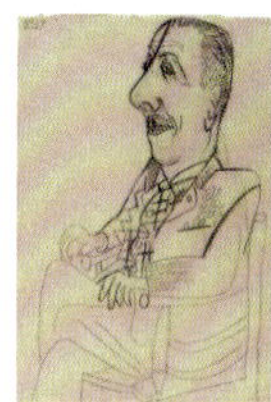

96 *Portrait of Francis Poulenc*, 13 March 1957
Graphite on thick vellum paper, page from a sketchbook, 540 x 370mm
Musée national Picasso-Paris
MP 1515
(L)

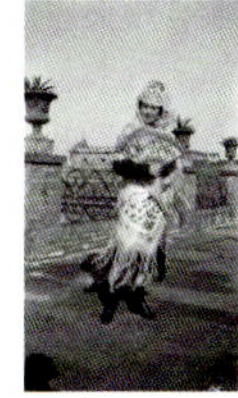

97 *Olga Khokhlova on the Roof of the Minerva Hotel*, Rome, 1917
Modern print from an original negative, 117 x 69mm
Private Collection. Courtesy Fundación Almine y Bernard Ruiz-Picasso para el Arte
(B, L)

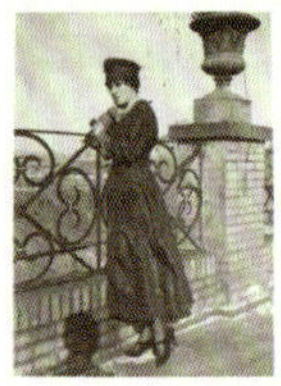

98 *Olga Khokhlova on the Roof of the Minerva Hotel*, Rome, 1917
Vintage photograph, 110 x 81mm
Private Collection. Courtesy Fundación Almine y Bernard Ruiz-Picasso para el Arte
(B, L)

99 *Olga with Her Hair Down*, Barcelona, 1917
Graphite on Ingres paper, page from a sketchbook, 230 x 153mm
Musée national Picasso-Paris
MP 1990-103.05r

100 *Olga on a Balcony Overlooking the Ramblas*, Barcelona, 1917
Graphite on Ingres paper, page from a sketchbook, 230 x 153mm
Musée national Picasso-Paris
MP 1990-103.13r

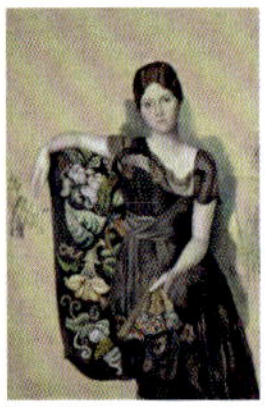

101 *Portrait of Olga in an Armchair*, spring 1918
Oil on canvas, 1300 x 888mm
Musée national Picasso-Paris
MP 55
(L)

102 *Madame Rivière* by Jean-Auguste-Dominique Ingres, 1806
Oil on canvas, 1165 x 817mm
Musée du Louvre

103 *Portrait of Olga, Seated*, 1918
Pencil on paper, 365 x 275mm
Private Collection. Courtesy Fundación Almine y Bernard Ruiz-Picasso para el Arte

104 *Olga Khokhlova in Picasso's Studio in Montrouge*
by an unknown photographer, 1918
Gelatin silver print, 225 x 165mm
Archives Picasso. Musée national Picasso-Paris

105 *Olga Khokhlova (reclining in the foreground) with Members of the Ballets Russes Corps de Ballet in* Les Sylphides, New York, 1916
Programme illustration
Jerome Robbins Dance Division, The New York Public Library for the Performing Arts, Astor, Lenox and Tilden Foundations

106 *Three Dancers*, 1919–20
Graphite on three joined sheets of laid paper, 375 x 320mm
Musée national Picasso-Paris
MP 840

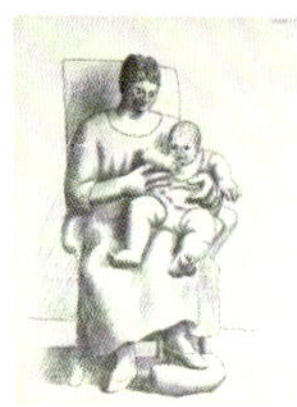

107 *Mother and Child (Olga and Paulo)*, 25 July 1921
Pencil on paper, 645 x 495mm
Private Collection. Courtesy Fundación Almine y Bernard Ruiz-Picasso para el Arte
(L)

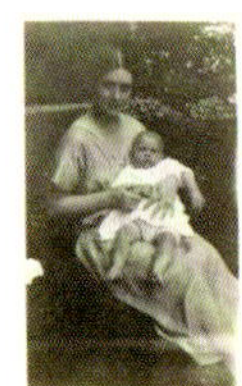

108 *Olga and Paulo, Fontainebleau*, 10 August 1921
Modern print from an original negative, 107 x 67mm
Private Collection. Courtesy Fundación Almine y Bernard Ruiz-Picasso para el Arte
(B, L)

109 [see 1, p.232]

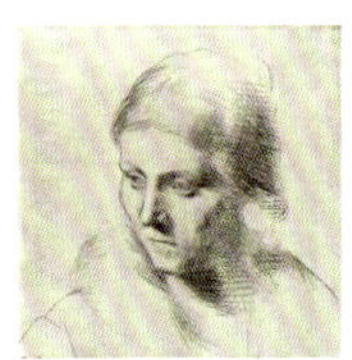

110 *Portrait of Olga with a Fur Collar*, 1923, printed 1955
Drypoint on zinc, 763 x 565mm (sheet)
The Museum of Modern Art, New York. Sue and Edgar Wachenheim III Fund; General Print Fund; Jerry I. Speyer in honor of Edgar Wachenheim III; Agnes Gund; Nelson Blitz, Jr. with Catherine Woodard and Perri and Allison Blitz, in honor of Riva Castleman's 80th birthday; Mary M. and Sash A. Spencer;The Orentreich Family Foundation in honor of Deborah Wye; Linda Barth Goldstein in honor of Deborah Wye; Sharon Percy Rockefeller; Maud and Jeffrey Welles in honor of Deborah Wye; and Roxanne H. Frank.
(B, L)

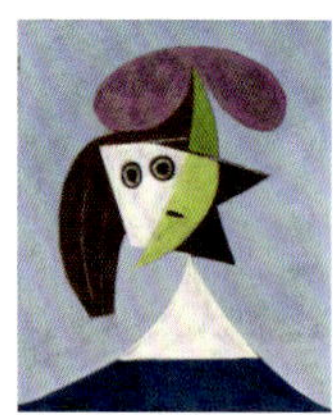

111 *Woman in a Hat (Olga)*, 1935
Oil on canvas, 600 x 500mm
Centre Pompidou, Paris. Musée national d'art moderne/Centre de création industrielle. Legs de M. Georges Salles en 1967
(inv. no. AM 4393 P)
(B, L)

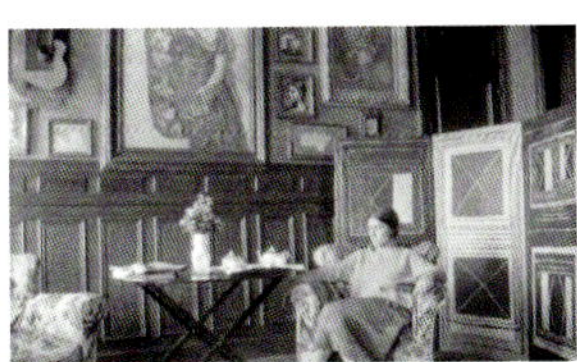

112 *Olga Picasso in the Living Room at 23 Rue La Boétie*, Paris, *c.*1923
Modern print from original negative, 69 x 121mm
Private Collection. Courtesy Fundación Almine y Bernard Ruiz-Picasso para el Arte
(B, L)

5. The many faces of Picasso's portraiture, 1927–1944

113 *Guitar Hanging on a Wall with Profile*, 1927
Oil on canvas, 268 x 346mm
Private Collection

114 *Marie-Thérèse Walter*, 1927
Pencil on paper, 394 x 257mm
Private Collection

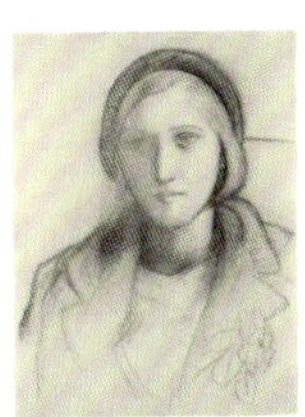

115 *Marie-Thérèse in a Beret*, c.1930
Charcoal on paper, 630 x 480mm
Private Collection
(B)

116 *La belle jardinière* by Raphael, 1507
Oil on panel, 1220 x 800mm
Musée du Louvre

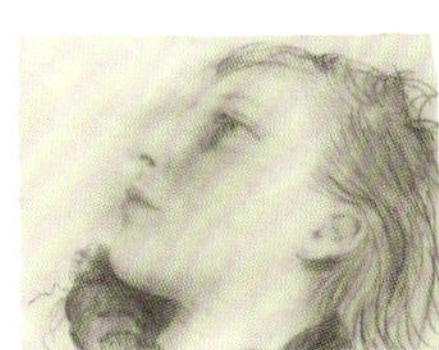

117 *Portrait of Marie-Thérèse*, 1935
Pencil on paper, 275 x 343mm
Private Collection
(L)

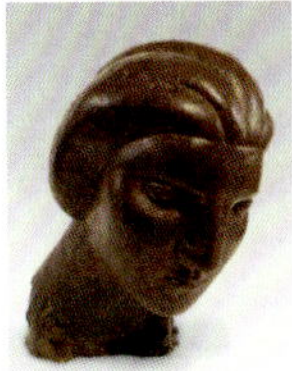

118 *Head of a Woman (Marie-Thérèse)*, 1931
Bronze, 500 x 310 x 270mm
Private Collection
(B, L)

119 *Marie-Thérèse, Full-face and Profile*, 1931
Oil and charcoal on canvas, 1110 x 810mm
Private Collection

120 *Woman with a Veil* by Henri Matisse, 1927
Oil on canvas, 615 x 502mm
The Museum of Modern Art, New York. The William S. Paley Collection
© Succession H. Matisse/ DACS 2016

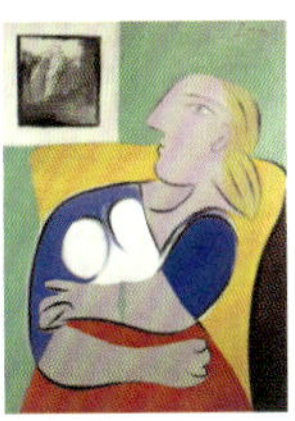

121 *Woman in a Yellow Armchair*, 1932
Oil on canvas, 1160 x 890mm
Private Collection
(L)

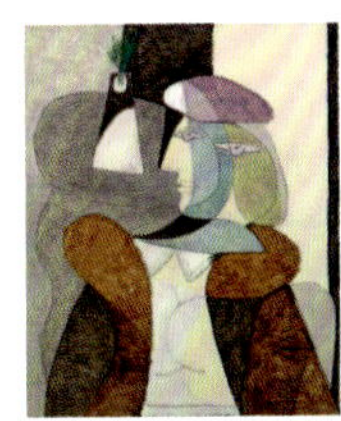

122 *Woman in a Beret and Fur Coat*, 3 February 1937
Oil and charcoal on canvas, 730 x 600mm
Private Collection
(B)

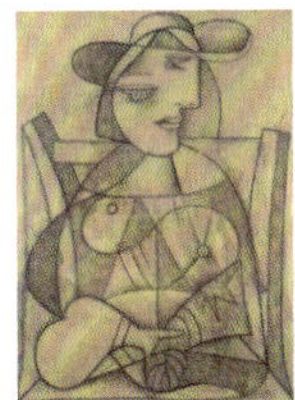

123 *Woman with Joined Hands (Marie-Thérèse Walter)*, 8 January 1938
Oil and wax crayon on canvas, 800 x 600mm
Collection Mr and Mrs J. Tomilson Hill
(B, L)

124 *Sleeping Nude*, 13 March 1932
Charcoal and oil on canvas, 1300 x 1620mm
Private Collection

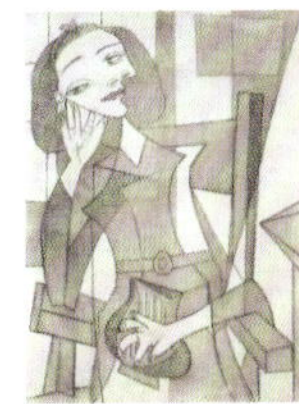

125 *Portrait of Nusch Éluard*, 9 February 1938
Pen and charcoal on canvas, 960 x 720mm
Private Collection
(B, L)

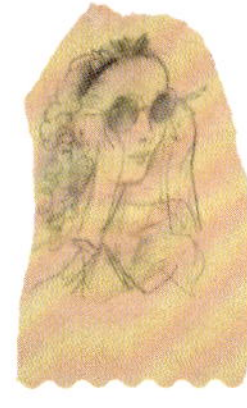

126 *Portrait of Nusch Éluard*, 1937
Crayon on paper table cloth, 240 x 145mm (irregular)
The Penrose Collection
(L)

127 *Woman with a Cat (Portrait of Paul Éluard)*, 30 August 1937
Oil on canvas, 810 x 655mm
Present whereabouts unknown

128 *Nusch Éluard*
Photograph by Lee Miller, 1937
Modern print from an original negative, 404 x 502mm
© Lee Miller Archives, England 2016. All rights reserved. www.leemiller.co.uk

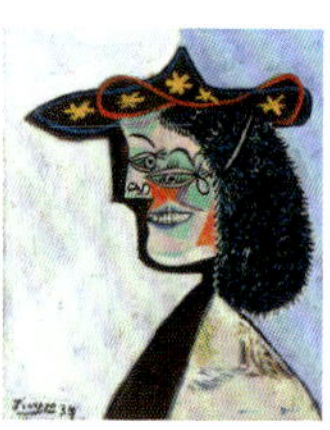

129 *Nusch Éluard*, 1937
Oil on canvas, 550x 460mm
Staatliche Museen zu Berlin, Nationalgalerie, Museum Berggruen
(B, L)

130 *Lee Miller*
Photograph by Man Ray, *c.*1930
Photogravure, 280 x 211mm
National Portrait Gallery, London (NPG x137153)
© Man Ray Trust/ADAGP, Paris and DACS, London 2016

131 *Mademoiselle Marcelle Lender, Half-Length* by Henri de Toulouse-Lautrec, 1895
Lithograph, 423 x 325mm
The British Museum, London

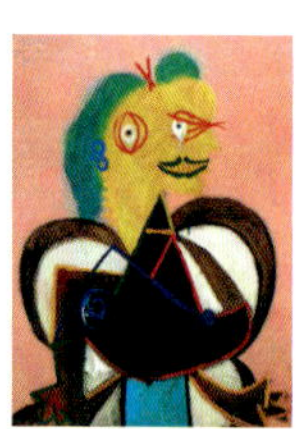

132 *Portrait of Lee Miller à l'Arlésienne*, 1937
Oil on canvas, 810 x 600mm
The Penrose Collection
(B, L)

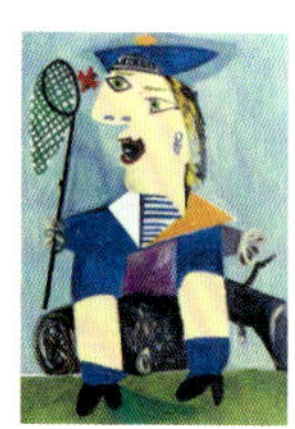

133 *Maya in a Sailor Suit*, 23 January 1938
Oil on canvas, 1216 x 863mm
The Museum of Modern Art, New York. Gift of Jacqueline Picasso in honor of the Museum's continuous commitment to Pablo Picasso's art, 1985
(B, L)

134 *The Artist's Daughter, Maya*, 29 August 1943
Charcoal and pastel on paper, 370 x 310mm
Private Collection

135 *Marguerite de France, Reine de Navarre* by François Clouet, *c.*1559
Chalk, gouache and watercolour on paper, 298 x 215mm
Musée Condé, Chantilly

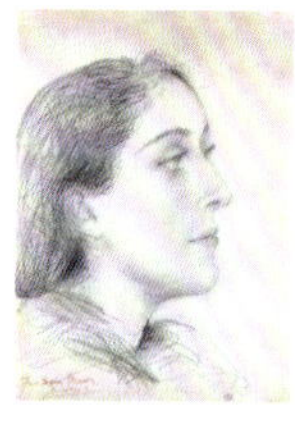

136 *Dora Maar*, *c.*1937
Pencil on paper, 410 x 305mm
Private Collection
(B, L)

137 *Dora Maar*, Paris
Photograph by Lee Miller, *c.*1956
Modern print from an original negative, 508 x 506mm
© Lee Miller Archives, England 2016. All rights reserved. www.leemiller.co.uk

138 *Thérèse Louise de Sureda* by Francisco de Goya, *c.*1803–4
Oil on canvas, 1197 x 794mm
National Gallery of Art, Washington
Gift of Mr. and Mrs. P.H.B. Frelinghuysen in memory of her father and mother, Mr. and Mrs. H.O. Havemeyer

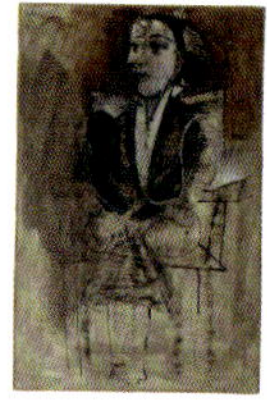

139 *Dora Maar Seated*, 13 May 1938
Ink, gouache and oil on paper on canvas, 689 x 625mm
Tate, Purchased 1960
(B, L)

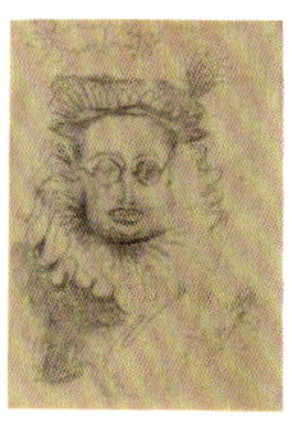

140 *Jaume Sabartés as a Gentleman of the Age of Philip II*, Paris, 25 December 1938
Graphite pencil on printed paper, 287 x 207mm (irregular)
Museu Picasso, Barcelona, Gift of Jaume Sabartés, 1962. MPB 70.231
(B)

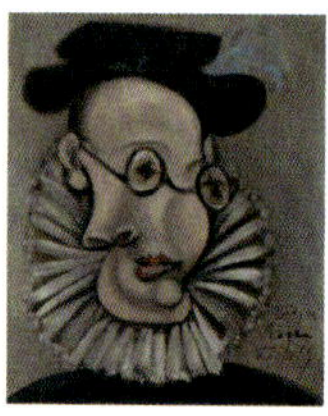

141 *Jaume Sabartés with Ruff and Cap*, Royan, 22 October 1939
Oil on canvas, 460 x 380mm
Museu Picasso, Barcelona, Gift of Jaume Sabartés, 1962. MPB 70.241
(B, L)

142 *The Intrigue* by James Ensor, 1890
Oil on canvas, 900 x 1500mm
Koninklijk Museum voor Schone Kunsten, Antwerp, Belgium
© DACS 2016

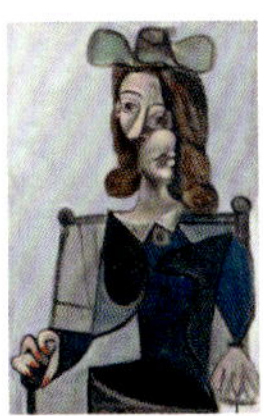

143 *Woman in a Hat*, 9 June 1941
Oil on canvas, 920 x 600mm
Musée national Picasso-Paris
MP 188
(B, L)

144 *Lee Miller, Roland Penrose, Louis Aragon; Pablo Picasso, Nusch Éluard, Paul Éluard and Elsa Triolet*
Photograph by Lee Miller, September 1944
Modern print from an original negative, 508 x 506mm

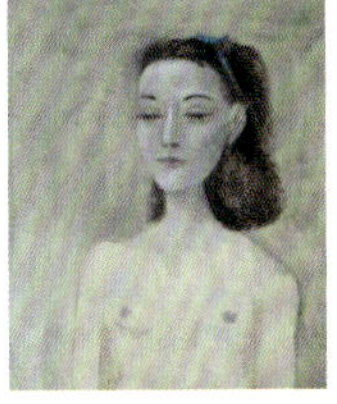

145 *Madame Paul Éluard*, 19 August 1941
Oil on canvas, 730 x 600mm
Centre Pompidou, Paris. Musée national d'art moderne/ Centre de création industrielle.
Don de M. Paul Éluard en 1947 (inv. no. AM 2745 P)
(B, L)

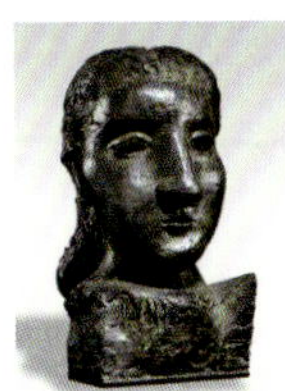

146 *Head of a Woman (Dora Maar)*, 1941
Bronze, 800 x 400 x 550mm
Private Collection
(B, L)

147 *Colossal Statue of Constantine: Head*, AD 313–24
Marble, height 2600mm
Musei Capitolini, Rome

148 *Picasso's Studio, 7 Rue des Grands-Augustins, Paris, with* Head of a Woman (Dora Maar) *and* Man with a Sheep
Photograph by Brassaï, 1943
Gelatin silver print

Paris, musée Picasso

6. Picasso's post-war portraiture

149 *La femme-fleur (Françoise Gilot)*, 5 May 1946
Oil on canvas, 1460 x 890mm
Private Collection, courtesy Thomas Ammann Fine Art AG Zürich

150 *'Pansy', Les fleurs animées* by J.J. Grandville, 1847
Hand-coloured engraving
Bibliothèque nationale de France

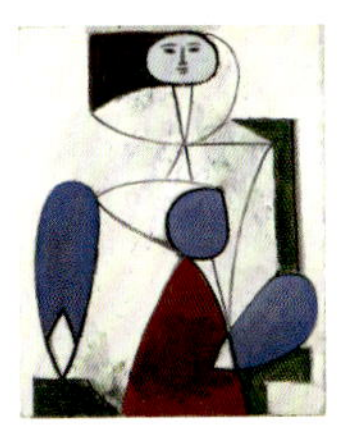

151 *Woman in an Armchair*, 2 April 1947
Oil on canvas, 920 x 725mm
Musée national Picasso-Paris
MP 1990-23
(B, L)

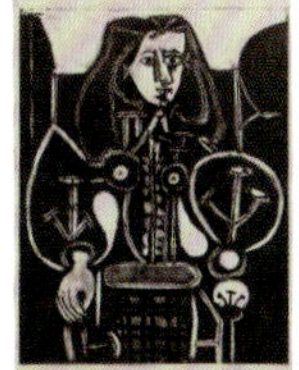

152 *Woman in an Armchair. No.4 (From the Violet)*, 3 January 1949
Lithograph. Sandpaper and brush on zinc, printed on Arches vellum paper (fifth and final state, unnumbered artist's proof), 760 x 565mm
Museu Picasso, Barcelona, Gift of Jaume Sabartés, 1962.
MPB 70.116
(B, L)

153 *Queen Mariana of Austria* by Diego Velázquez, 1652–3
Oil on canvas, 2342 x 1320mm
Museo Nacional del Prado, Madrid

154 *The Romanian Blouse* by Henri Matisse, 1939–40
Oil on canvas, 920 x 730mm
Centre Pompidou, Paris. Musée national d'art moderne/Centre de création industrielle

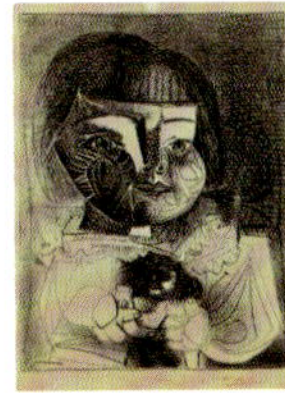

155 *Paloma and Her Doll on a Black Background*, Vallauris, 14 December 1952
Lithograph. Lithographic crayon and scraper on zinc, printed on Arches vellum paper (unnumbered artist's proof), 760 x 565mm
Museu Picasso, Barcelona, Gift of Jaume Sabartés, 1962.
MPB 70.099
(L)

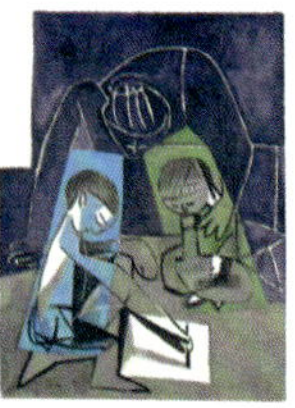

156 *Claude Drawing, Françoise and Paloma*, 17 May 1954
Oil on canvas, 1160 x 890mm
Musée national Picasso-Paris
MP 209
(B, L)

157 *Picasso Drawing with Claude and Paloma*
Photograph by Edward Quinn, La Galloise, Vallauris, 16 April 1953
Credit: Photo Edward Quinn, © edwardquinn.com/
© Succession Picasso

158 *Sylvette David*, 21 April 1954
Pencil on paper, 310 x 240mm
Musée national Picasso-Paris
MP 1428

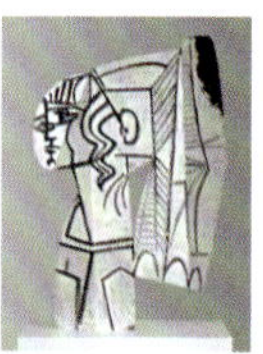
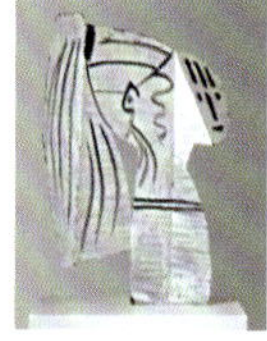

159 *Sylvette*, 1954
Sheet-metal, cut out, bent and painted on both sides, 699 x 470 x 76mm
Fondation Hubert Looser, Zürich
(B, L)

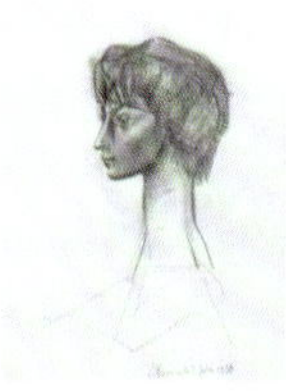

160 *Jacqueline*, 2 June 1954
Pencil on paper, 255 x 193mm
Private Collection
(B)

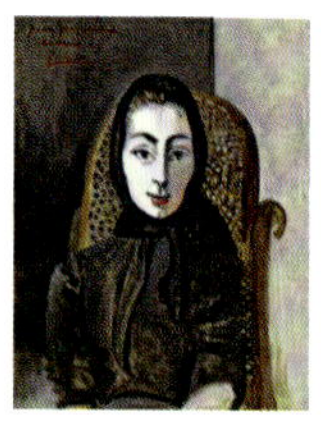

161 *Portrait of Jacqueline in a Black Scarf*, 11 October 1954
Oil on canvas, 920 x 730mm
Private Collection
(B, L)

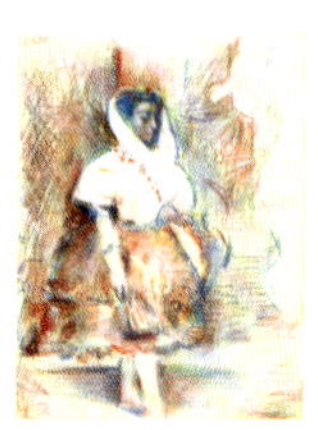

162 *Jacqueline (after* Lola de Valence *by Manet),* 6 October 1955
Coloured crayons on paper, 310 x 242 mm
Private Collection
(L)

163 *Lola de Valence*
by Édouard Manet, 1862
Oil on canvas, 1230 x 920mm
Musée d'Orsay, Paris. Bequest of Count Isaac de Camondo, 1911

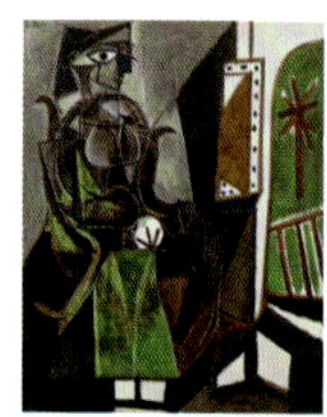

164 *Woman by a Window*, 11 June 1956
Oil on canvas, 1620 x 1300mm
The Museum of Modern Art, New York. Mrs Simon Guggenheim Fund, 1957
(B, L)

165 *Picasso with* Jacqueline with a Yellow Ribbon *in Notre-Dame-de-Vie, Mougins*
Photograph by Lee Miller, May 1963
Modern print from an original negative, 111 x 112mm
© Lee Miller Archives, England 2016.
All rights reserved. www.leemiller.co.uk

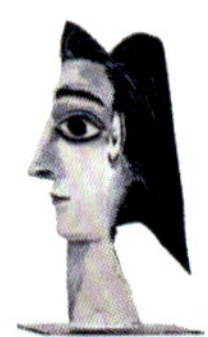
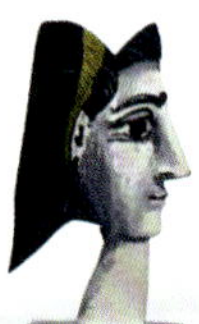

166 *Jacqueline with a Yellow Ribbon*, 1962
Sheet-metal, cut out, bent and painted on both sides, 510 x 290 x 220mm
National Gallery of Iceland
(L)

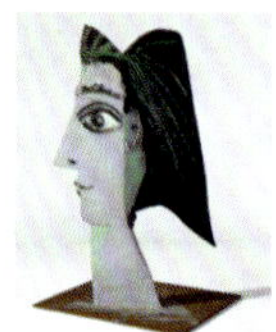
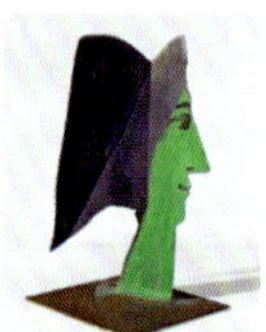

167 *Head of a Woman (Jacqueline)*, 1962
Sheet-metal, cut out, bent and painted on both sides, 510 x 300 x 255mm
Horst und Gabriele Siedle-Kunststiftung
(B)

168 *Portrait of Stalin*, 8 March 1953
Reproduced on the front cover of *Les Lettres françaises*, no.456, 12–19 March 1953
Archives Picasso. Musée national Picasso-Paris

169 *Dream and Lie of Franco I*, Paris, 8 January 1937
Etching and aquatint, 386 x 571mm (sheet)
Museu Picasso, Barcelona, Acquisition, 1982
MPB 112.423

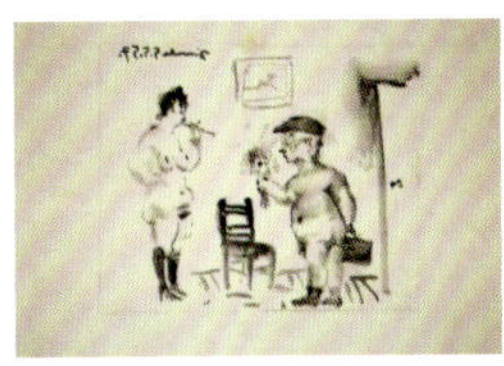

170 *Sabartés and His Neighbour*, 5 May 1957
Monotype on zinc, 222 x 273mm
Private Collection
(B, L)

171 *The Client* by Edgar Degas, c.1876–7
Monotype in black ink on white paper, 220 x 164mm
Musée national Picasso-Paris.
Picasso Gift
RF 35788

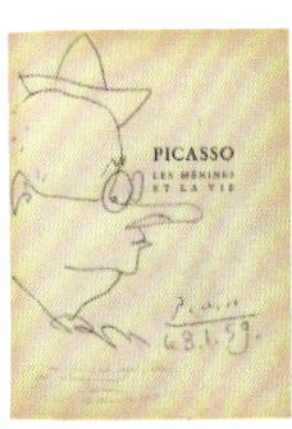

172 *Caricature of Jaume Sabartés*, 3 January 1959
Dedication on title-page of Jaime Sabartés, *Picasso. Les Ménines et la vie*, Paris, Éditions Cercle d'Art, 1958
Conté crayon on paper; book, 320 x 240mm
Museu Picasso, Barcelona,
Gift of Dr. Joseph Jaffé, 1970.
MPB 111.835
(B)

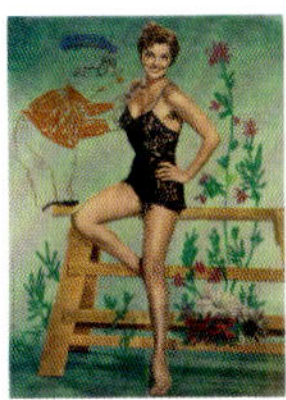

173 *Humorous Composition: Jaume Sabartés and Esther Williams*, Cannes, 23 May 1957
Coloured grease pencils on magazine printed paper, 356 x 265mm
Museu Picasso, Barcelona,
Gift of Jaume Sabartés, 1964.
MPB 70.675
(L)

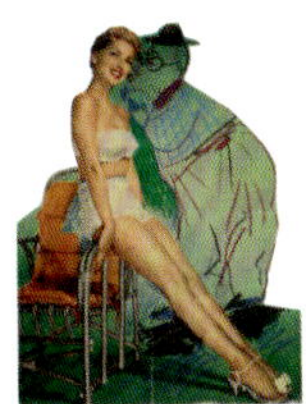

174 *Humorous Composition: Jaume Sabartés and Lana Turner*, Cannes, 22 May 1957
Coloured grease pencils on cut magazine printed paper, 345 x 261mm (irregular)
Museu Picasso, Barcelona,
Gift of Jaume Sabartés, 1964.
MPB 70.672
(B)

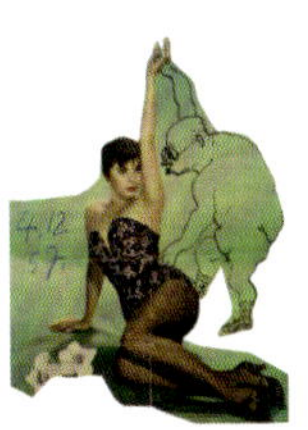

175 *Humorous Composition: Jaume Sabartés and Neile Adams*, Cannes, 4 December 1957
Brush and Indian ink on cut magazine printed paper, 356 x 260mm (irregular)
Museu Picasso, Barcelona,
Gift of Jaume Sabartés, 1964.
MPB 70.674
(B)

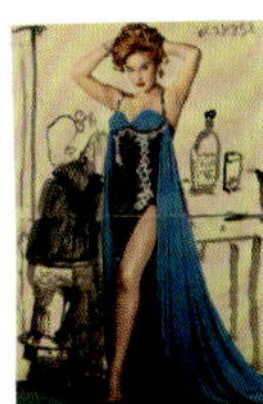

176 *Humorous Composition: Jaume Sabartés and Sylvia Lopez*, Cannes, 24 March 1958
Brush and Indian ink on magazine printed paper, 520 x 350mm
Museu Picasso, Barcelona,
Gift of Jaume Sabartés, 1964.
MPB 70.669
(L)

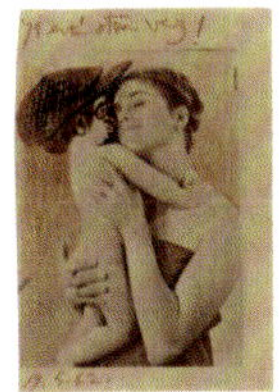

177 *Humorous Composition: Jaume Sabartés as a Baby and a Model*, 19 May 1962
Coloured pencils on magazine printed paper, 187 x 130mm (irregular)
Museu Picasso, Barcelona,
Gift of Jaume Sabartés, 1964.
MPB 70.677
(L)

7. Picasso with the old masters

178 *Las Meninas* by Diego Velázquez, 1656
Oil on canvas, 3180 x 2760mm
Museo Nacional del Prado, Madrid

179 *Las Meninas after Velázquez*, Cannes, 17 August 1957
Oil on canvas, 1940 x 2600mm
Museu Picasso, Barcelona,
Gift of Pablo Picasso, 1968.
MPB 70.433

180 *Photomontage with Velázquez's* Las Meninas*, dedicated to Joan Gaspar by Jaume Sabartés and Picasso*, 1 April 1959
Reproduction of the original, 180 x 240mm
Museu Picasso, Barcelona
Jaume Sabartés Fonds

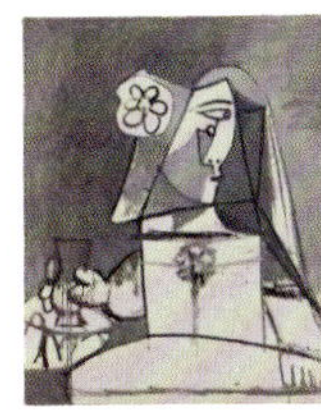

181 *Las Meninas (Infanta Margarita María)*, Cannes, 20 August 1957
Oil on canvas, 1000 x 810mm
Museu Picasso, Barcelona,
Gift of Pablo Picasso, 1968.
MPB 70.434
(B, L)

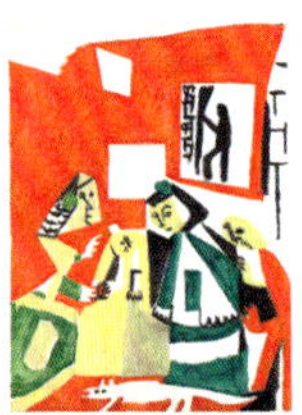

182 *Las Meninas*, Cannes, 15 November 1957
Oil on canvas, 1300 x 970mm
Museu Picasso, Barcelona, Gift of Pablo Picasso, 1968.
MPB 70.479
(B, L)

183 Detail from *The Burial of the Count of Orgaz* by El Greco, 1586–8
Oil on canvas, 4600 x 3600mm
Iglesia de Santo Tomé, Toledo

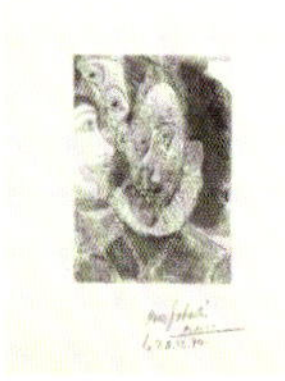

184 ***Caricature of One of the Characters in* The Burial of the Count of Orgaz*, Weeping. Suite 347*, plate 194**, 29 June 1968
Etching on copper, printed on Rives vellum paper (unnumbered artist's proof), 346 x 285mm (sheet)
Museu Picasso, Barcelona, Gift of Pablo Picasso, 1971.
MPB 111.967
(B)

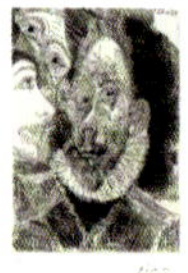

Suite 347*, plate 194 *(Caricature of One of the Characters in* The Burial of the Count of Orgaz*, Weeping), 29 June 1968
Etching on paper, 350 x 285mm (sheet)
On loan from the British Museum, London
(L)

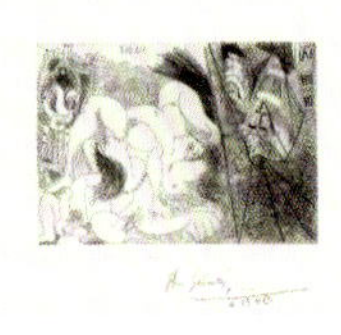

185 ***Raphael and the Fornarina IV: with the Pope Pulling Back the Curtain. Suite 347*, plate 299**, 31 August 1968
Etching on copper, printed on Rives vellum paper (unnumbered artist's proof), 375 x 469mm (sheet)
Museu Picasso, Barcelona, Gift of Pablo Picasso, 1970.
MPB 70.599
(B)

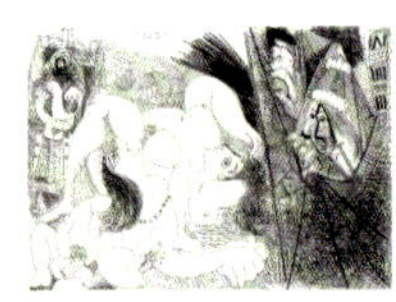

Suite 347*, plate 299. *(Raphael and the Fornarina IV with the Pope Pulling Back the Curtain), 31 August 1968
Etching on paper, 375 x 470mm (sheet)
On loan from the British Museum, London
(L)

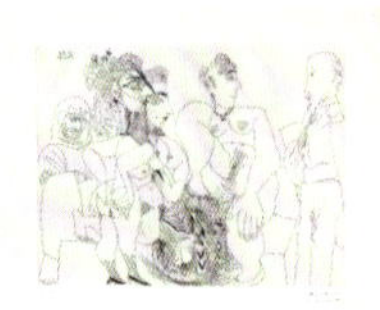

186 ***Brothel. Degas with His Sketchbook, Bawd, Three Prostitutes, and a Moroccan Pouffe. Suite 156*, plate 87**, 16 March 1971
Etching on copper, printed on Rives vellum paper (numbered artist's proof), 502 x 650mm (sheet)
Museu Picasso, Barcelona, Gift of the Estate of Pablo Picasso, 1980.
MPB 112.232
(B)

187 *The Madame's Name Day* by Edgar Degas, c.1876–7
Monotype in black ink with pastel on paper, 266 x 296mm
Musée national Picasso-Paris. Picasso Gift
RF 35791

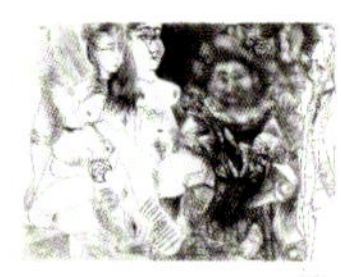

188 ***The Madame-Abortionist and Three Prostitutes. Degas with His Hands behind His Back. Suite 156*, plate 117**, 1–4 May 1971
Drypoint and scraping on copper, printed on Rives vellum paper (Second and final state, numbered artist's proof), 502 x 650mm
Museu Picasso, Barcelona, Gift of the Estate of Pablo Picasso, 1980.
MPB 112.234
(L)

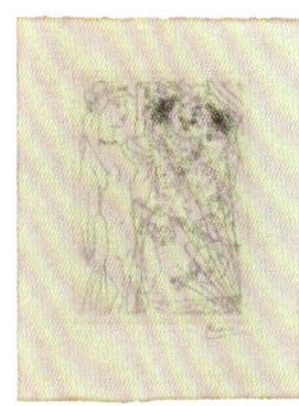

189 ***Rembrandt and Woman with Veil. Suite Vollard*, plate 36**, 31 January 1934
Etching on copper printed on Montval laid watermarked paper, 446 x 340mm (sheet)
Museu Picasso, Barcelona, Acquisition, 1989.
MPB 112.924
(B)

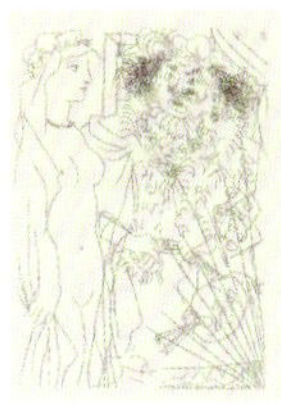

Suite Vollard, plate 36.
(Rembrandt Holding the Hand of a Young Woman with Veil),
31 January 1934
Etching on paper, 447 x 340mm (sheet)
On loan from the British Museum, London
(L)

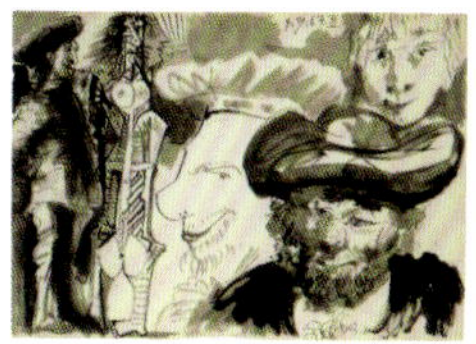

190 *Figure in the Style of Rembrandt*,
4 July 1967 (III)
Ink and watercolour, 355 x 525mm
Colección Telefónica
(B, L)

191 *Head of Rembrandt*, 17 May 1968
Pen, Indian ink and wash on paper,
328 x 250mm
Collection Angela Rosengart, Lucerne

192 *The Prodigal Son in a Tavern*
by Rembrandt, c.1635
Oil on canvas, 1610 x 1310mm
Staatliche Kunstsammlungen,
Gemäldegalerie Alte Meister, Dresden

193 *Couple*, 9 October 1970
Oil on canvas, 1950 x 1300mm
Private Collection

194 *Self-portrait*
by Vincent van Gogh, 1887
Oil on artist board mounted to wood panel, 349 x 267mm
Detroit Institute of Arts

195 *Self-portrait*
by Rembrandt, 1658
Oil on canvas, 1337 x 1038mm
The Frick Collection, New York

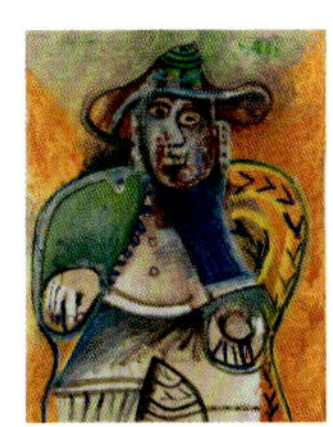

196 *Old Man Seated*, 26 September 1970–14 November 1971
Oil on canvas, 1455 x 1140mm
Musée national Picasso-Paris
MP 221
(B, L)

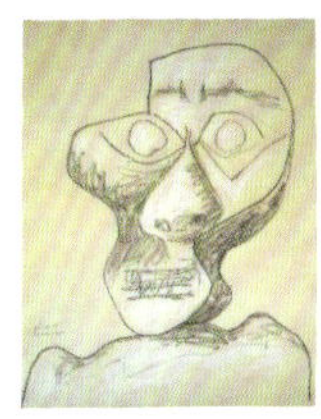

197 *Self-portrait*, 2 July 1972
Crayon on paper, 657 x 505mm
Private Collection
(L)

198 *Picasso in Notre-Dame-de-Vie*,
Mougins
Photograph by Lee Miller, late 1960s
Modern print from an original negative,
404 x 502mm

p.225 *Picasso with Jacqueline and Her Portrait*
Photograph by Edward Quinn, 1955
Credit: Photo Edward Quinn,
© edwardquinn.com/
© Succession Picasso

Additional works

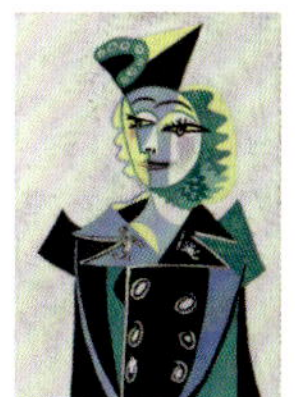

Portrait of Nusch Éluard, 1937
Oil on canvas, 920 x 652mm
Musée national Picasso-Paris
MP 1990-19
(B)

Guillaume Apollinaire, *Alcools, Poèmes 1898–1913*
Paris, Mercure de France, 1913
With frontispiece portrait of Apollinaire by Picasso
British Library
(L)

Photography credits

The photographs of all works that belong to the Museu Picasso, Barcelona (see pp.232–47), are credited to the Fundació Museu Picasso de Barcelona. Photographic reproductions by Gassull Fotografia.

p.10 *Picasso in Montmartre, place Ravignan*, *c.*1904
Photo © RMN-Grand Palais (Musée national Picasso-Paris)/Jacques Faujour

4 *Philip IV*, *c.*1653
© Museo Nacional del Prado

5 *Picasso with Henri Rousseau's Self-portrait and Portrait of the Artist's Second Wife* (both 1900–3)
Photo © RMN-Grand Palais (Musée national Picasso-Paris)/Droits réservés

6 *La Coruña*, 16 September 1894
Photo © RMN-Grand Palais (Musée national Picasso-Paris)/Béatrice Hatala

12 *Juan de Villanueva*, 1800–5
© Museo de la Real Academia de Bellas Artes de San Fernando, Madrid

14 *Self-portrait with Skeleton Arm*, 1895
© The Trustees of the British Museum

16 *Portrait of Pere Romeu*, 1897–9
© Museu Nacional d'Art de Catalunya, Barcelona 2016. Photo: Jordi Calveras

24 *Santiago Rusiñol*, 1900
Image copyright: The Metropolitan Museum of Art/Art Resource/Scala, Florence

25 *Joaquim Mir*, 1900
© 2015. Image copyright: The Metropolitan Museum of Art/Art Resource/Scala, Florence

26 *Portrait of Mir*, Reproduced *Pèl & Ploma*, no.81, 1 October 1901
© Museu Nacional d'Art de Catalunya, Barcelona 2016. Photo: Jordi Calveras

27 *Portrait of the Writer Frederic Pujulà i Vallès*, 1900
© Photo: Claude Germain

28 *Frederic Pujulà i Vallès*, 1900
Image copyright: The Metropolitan Museum of Art/Art Resource/Scala, Florence

30 *Ramon Pichot*, 1900
© 2015. Image copyright: The Metropolitan Museum of Art/Art Resource/Scala, Florence

32 *Pere Romeu in a Field of Irises*, *c.*1900
Image © Fundación Francisco Godia, Barcelona

35 *Carles Casagemas*, 1900
Image copyright: The Metropolitan Museum of Art/Art Resource/Scala, Florence

37 *Portrait of Dr Félix Rey*, 1889
Pushkin Museum, Moscow, Russia/ Bridgeman Images

38 *Self-portrait*, 1901
© Mike Bruce, courtesy Ordovas

41 *Self-portrait in His Studio*, 1901
Photo © RMN-Grand Palais (Musée national Picasso-Paris)/Michèle Bellot

42 *Gustave Coquiot*, 1901
© Centre Pompidou, MNAM-CCI, Dist. RMN-Grand Palais/Béatrice Hatala

44 *Portrait of the Poet Sabartés*, 1901
Pushkin Museum, Moscow, Russia/ Bridgeman Images

46 *In a Café (L'Absinthe)*, 1875–6
© RMN-Grand Palais (musée d'Orsay)/ Martine Beck-Coppola

47 *Portrait of Sebastià Junyer i Vidal*, 1903
© 2015. Digital Image Museum Associates/ LACMA/Art Resource NY/Scala, Florence

51 *Neither More Nor Less (Ni mas ni menos)*, 1799
© Museo Nacional del Prado

54 *Victor Hugo on His Death Bed*, 1885
Photo © RMN – Grand Palais (musée d'Orsay)/ Hervé Lewandowski

55 *Portrait of Jaume Sabartés*, 1904
Image © bpk/Nationalgalerie, SMB, Museum Berggruen/Jens Ziehe

57 *Caricatures of Paul Fort, Henri Delormel and André Salmon*, 1905
© RMN-Grand Palais (Musée national Picasso-Paris)/Droits réservés

58 *Portrait of André Salmon*, 1907
© Droits réservés Photo © RMN-Grand Palais (Musée national Picasso-Paris)/Thierry Le Mage

59 *Sketches Made During the Audience of 14 November (Court of Assizes)*, 1831
Bibliothèque nationale de France

60 *Guillaume Apollinaire, Bank Clerk*, 1905
Image © bpk/Jens Ziehe/Museum Berggruen, Private Collection | Jens Ziehe

63 *Portrait of Ricard Canals, 1904*
Photo © RMN-Grand Palais (Musée national Picasso-Paris)/Droits réservés

65 *Fernande Olivier,* Summer, 1905–6
© FABA Photo: Marc Domage

67 *Head of a Woman (Fernande)*, 1906
© Eric Emo/Musée d'Art Moderne/ Roger-Viollet

69 *Portrait of Gertrude Stein*, 1906
Image copyright: The Metropolitan Museum of Art/Art Resource/Scala, Florence

71 *Self-portrait with Palette*, 1906
Photograph and Digital Image
© Philadelphia Museum of Art
© Estate of Pablo Picasso/Artists Rights Society (ARS), New York

73 *Self-portrait with* Man Leaning on a Table, 5 bis Rue Schoelcher, 1915–16
M. Aeschimann

74 *Self-portrait with* Man Leaning on a Table, 5 bis Rue Schoelcher, Paris, 1915–16
M. Aeschimann

75 *Sebastià Junyer i Vidal in front of Three Women*, 1908
Photo © RMN-Grand Palais (Musée national Picasso-Paris)/Droits réservés

76 *Portrait of Fernande Olivier*, 1909
Photo © Städel Museum – ARTOTHEK

77 *Head of a Woman (Fernande)*, 1909
© Metropolitan Museum of Art

78 *Cubist Head (Portrait of Fernande),* 1909–10
The Fitzwilliam Museum Museum, University of Cambridge

80 *Guillaume Apollinaire*, 1910
Photo © RMN-Grand Palais (Musée national Picasso-Paris)/Droits réservés

81 *Portrait of Ambroise Vollard*, 1910
Pushkin Museum, Moscow, Russia/ Bridgeman Images

82 *Daniel-Henry Kahnweiler*, 1910
Photo © RMN-Grand Palais (Musée national Picasso-Paris)/Droits réservés

83 *Daniel-Henry Kahnweiler*, autumn 1910
© 2015 Estate of Pablo Picasso/Artists Rights Society (ARS), New York

84 *Portrait of Max Jacob*, 1915
© RMN-Grand Palais (Musée national Picasso-Paris)/Michèle Bellot

85 *Portrait of an Unidentified Man*, 1860s
Photo © RMN-Grand Palais (Musée national Picasso-Paris)/Michèle Bellot

86 *Portrait of an Unidentified Man*, *c.*1860
Photo © RMN-Grand Palais (Musée national Picasso-Paris)/Michèle Bellot

87 *Portrait of Ambroise Vollard*, 1915
© 2015. Image copyright Metropolitan Museum of Art/Art Resource/Scala, Florence

88 *Self-portrait with* Portrait of a Man, 5 bis Rue Schoelcher, Paris, 1915–16
M. Aeschimann

89 *Caricature of Jean Cocteau*, 1917
© RMN-Grand Palais (Musée national Picasso-Paris)/Thierry Le Mage

94 *Portrait of Élie Faure*, 14 June 1922
Image: © Private Collection (photographer: Tim Nighswander/IMAGING4ART)

95 *Portrait of Erik Satie, 19 May 1920*
Photo © RMN-Grand Palais (Musée national Picasso-Paris)/Béatrice Hatala

96 *Portrait of Francis Poulnec*, 13 March 1957
Photo © RMN-Grand Palais (Musée national Picasso-Paris)/Franck Raux

99 *Olga with Her Hair Down*, 1917
Photo © RMN-Grand Palais (Musée national Picasso-Paris)/Image RMN-GP

101 *Portrait of Olga in an Armchair*, 1918
Photo © RMN-Grand Palais (Musée national Picasso-Paris)/René-Gabriel Ojéda

102 *Madame Rivière*, 1806
© RMN-Grand Palais (musée du Louvre)/ Thierry Le Mage

103 *Portrait of Olga, Seated*, 1918
Courtesy Fundación Almine y Bernard Ruiz-Picasso para el Arte © FABA
Photo: Marc Domage

106 *Three Dancers*, 1919–20
© RMN-Grand Palais (Musée national Picasso-Paris)/Béatrice Hatala Agence Photographique de la Réunion des musées nationaux

107 *Mother and Child (Olga and Paulo)*, 25 July 1921
© FABA Photo: Marc Domage

110 *Portrait of Olga with a Fur Collar*, 1923
© 2015. Image copyright: The Museum of Modern Art, New York/Scala, Florence

111 *Woman in a Hat (Olga)*, 1935
© Centre Pompidou, MNAM-CCI, Dist. RMN-Grand Palais/Droits Réservés

116 *La belle jardinière*, 1507
© Musée du Louvre, Dist. RMN-Grand Palais/Angèle Dequier

120 *Woman with a Veil*, 1927
Copyright Digital image, The Museum of Modern Art, New York/Scala, Florence

122 *Woman in a Beret and Fur Coat*, 3 February 1937
© Photo: Claude Germain

124 *Sleeping Nude*, 13 March 1932
Photograph by Ellen Page Wilson, courtesy Pace Gallery

125 *Portrait of Nusch Éluard*, 9 February 1938
M. Aeschimann

126 *Portrait of Nusch Éluard*, 1937
Image: © Roland Penrose Estate, England 2014. All rights reserved

128 *Nusch Éluard*, 1937
© Lee Miller Archives, England 2016. All rights reserved. www.leemiller.co.uk

129 *Nusch Éluard*, 1937
Image © bpk/Nationalgalerie, SMB, Museum Berggruen/Jens Ziehe

130 *Lee Miller*, c.1930
© Man Ray Trust/ADAGP, Paris and DACS, London 2016

131 *Mademoiselle Marcelle Lender, Half-Length*, 1895
© The Trustees of the British Museum

132 *Portrait of Lee Miller à l'Arlesienne*, 1937
Image: © Roland Penrose Estate, England 2014. All rights reserved.

133 *Maya in a Sailor Suit*, 23 January 1938
© 2015. Image copyright: The Museum of Modern Art, New York/Scala, Florence

135 *Marguerite de France, Reine de Navarre*, c.1559
Photo © RMN-Grand Palais (domaine de Chantilly)/René-Gabriel Ojéda

137 *Dora Maar*, c.1956
© Lee Miller Archives, England 2016. All rights reserved. www.leemiller.co.uk

139 *Dora Maar Seated*, 13 May 1938
© Tate, London 2016

142 *The Intrigue*, 1890
© Lukas – Art in Flanders VZW/ Photo: Hugo Maertens

143 *Woman in a Hat*, 9 June 1941
© RMN-Grand Palais (Musée national Picasso-Paris)/Jean-Gilles Berizzi

144 *Lee Miller, Roland Penrose, Louis Aragon; Pablo Picasso, Nusch Éluard, Paul Éluard and Elsa Triolet*, September 1944
© Lee Miller Archives, England 2016. All rights reserved. www.leemiller.co.uk

145 *Madame Paul Éluard*, 19 August 1941
© Centre Pompidou, MNAM-CCI, Dist. RMN-Grand Palais/Droits Réservés

146 *Head of a Woman (Dora Maar)*, 1941
© Photo: Claude Germain

147 *Colossal Statue of Constantine: Head*, AD 313–24
Musei Capitolini, Rome, Italy/Bridgeman Images

148 *Picasso's Studio, 7 Rue des Grands-Augustins, Paris, with Head of a Woman (Dora Maar) and Man with a Sheep*, 1943
Photo © RMN-Grand Palais (Musée national Picasso-Paris)/Franck Raux

163 *Lola de Valence*, 1862
Photo © Musée d'Orsay, Dist. RMN-Grand Palais/Patrice Schmidt

150 *'Pansy', Les fleurs animées by J.J. Grandville*, 1847
Bibliothèque nationale de France

151 *Woman in an Armchair*, 2 April 1947
© RMN-Grand Palais/Gérard Blot

153 *Queen Mariana of Austria* by Diego Velázquez, 1652–3
© Museo Nacional del Prado

154 *The Romanian Blouse*, 1939–40
Photo © Centre Pompidou, MNAM-CCI, Dist. RMN-Grand Palais/Philippe Migeat

156 *Claude Drawing, Françoise and Paloma*, 17 May 1954
© RMN-Grand Palais (Musée national Picasso-Paris)/Jean-Gilles Berizzi

157 *Picasso Drawing with Claude and Paloma*
Credit: Photo Edward Quinn, © edwardquinn.com

158 *Sylvette David*, 21 April 1954
Photo © RMN-Grand Palais (Musée national Picasso-Paris)/Franck Raux

160 *Jacqueline*, 2 June 1954
© Photo: Claude Germain

161 *Portrait of Jacqueline in a Black Scarf*, 11 October 1954
© Photo: Claude Germain

162 *Jacqueline (after Lola de Valence by Manet)*, 6 October 1955
© Photo: Claude Germain

163 *Lola de Valence*, 1862
Photo © Musée d'Orsay, Dist. RMN-Grand Palais/Patrice Schmidt

164 *Woman by a Window*, 11 June 1956
© 2015. Digital image, The Museum of Modern Art, New York/Scala, Florence

165 *Picasso with Jacqueline with a Yellow Ribbon in Notre-Dame-de-Vie*, May 1963
© Lee Miller Archives, England 2016. All rights reserved. www.leemiller.co.uk

166 *Jacqueline with a Yellow Ribbon*, 1962
Photographer: Guðmundur Ingólfsson

168 *Portrait of Stalin*, 8 March 1953
Photo © RMN-Grand Palais (Musée national Picasso-Paris)/Adrien Didierjean Autorisations à demander aux Lettres Françaises

169 *Dream and Lie of Franco I*, 8 January 1937
Photograph Gasull Fotografia

170 *Sabartés and His Neighbour*, 5 May 1957
M. Aeschimann

171 *The Client*, c.1876–7
Photo © RMN-Grand Palais (Musée national Picasso-Paris)/Droits réservés

178 *Las Meninas*, 1656
© Museo Nacional del Prado

179 *Las Meninas after Velázquez*, 17 August 1957
Photograph: Gasull Fotografia

183 Detail from *The Burial of the Count of Orgaz*, 1586–8
Santo Tome, Toledo, Spain/Bridgeman Images

184 *Suite 347*, **plate 194**, 29 June 1968
© The Trustees of the British Museum

185 *Suite 347*, **plate 299**, 31 August 1968
© The Trustees of the British Museum

187 *The Madame's Name Day*, c.1876–7
Photo © RMN-Grand Palais (Musée national Picasso-Paris)/René-Gabriel Ojéda

189 *Suite Vollard*, **plate 36**, 31 January 1934
© The Trustees of the British Museum

190 *Figure in the Style of Rembrandt*, 4 July 1967 III
Image: © Fernando Maquieira

192 *The Prodigal Son in a Tavern*, c.1635
© bpk/Staatliche Kunstsammlungen Dresden/ Elke Estel/Hans-Peter Klut

193 *Couple*, 9 October 1970
Image: Eric Baudouin, courtesy Gagosian Gallery

194 *Self-portrait*, 1887
Detroit Institute of Arts, USA/City of Detroit Purchase/Bridgeman Images

195 *Self-portrait*, 1658
Copyright The Frick Collection

196 *Old Man Seated*, 26 September 1970–14 November 1971
© RMN-Grand Palais (Musée national Picasso-Paris)/Jean-Gilles Berizzi

198 *Picasso in Notre-Dame-de-Vie*, late 1960s
© Lee Miller Archives, England 2016. All rights reserved. www.leemiller.co.uk

p.225 *Picasso with Jacqueline and Her Portrait*, 1955
Credit: Photo Edward Quinn, © edwardquinn.com

Portrait of Nusch Éluard, 1937
Photo © RMN-Grand Palais (Musée national Picasso-Paris)/Gérard Blot

Indexes

Index of Picasso's works by title

Bold page numbers indicate illustrations.

General index

Bold page numbers indicate illustrations.

Published in Great Britain by
National Portrait Gallery Publications
St Martin's Place, London WC2H 0HE

Published to accompany the exhibition *Picasso Portraits* at the National Portrait Gallery, London, from 6 October 2016 to 5 February 2017 and the Museu Picasso, Barcelona, from 16 March to 25 June 2017.

This exhibition has been made possible by the provision of insurance through the Government Indemnity Scheme. The National Portrait Gallery, London, would like to thank HM Government for providing Government Indemnity and the Department for Culture, Media and Sport and Arts Council England for arranging the indemnity.

Every purchase supports the National Portrait Gallery, London. For a complete catalogue of current publications, please write to the National Portrait Gallery at the address above, or visit our website at www.npg.org/publications

ISBN 978 1 85514 542 9 (hardback)
ISBN 978 1 85514 760 7 (paperback)

A catalogue record for this book is available from the British Library.

10 9 8 7 6 5 4 3 2 1

Managing Editor: Christopher Tinker
Senior Editor: Sarah Ruddick
Editor: Andrew Roff
Copy-editor: Rebeka Cohen
Production Manager: Ruth Müller-Wirth
Designer: Jason Ellams

Printed in Italy

Page 2: *Nusch Éluard*, 1937
(detail of 129, page 149)

Page 4: *Self-portrait with Wig*, 1900
(detail of 11, page 25)

Page 10: *Picasso in Montmartre, place Ravignan*, by an unknown photographer *c.*1904

Page 18: *The Artist's Father, Joaquim Mir, Carles Casagemas and Various Caricatures*, 1899–1900
(detail of 20, page 37)

Page 48: *Gustave Coquiot*, 1901
(detail of 42, page 57)

Page 70: *Daniel-Henry Kahnweiler*, 1910
(detail of 83, page 97)

Page 100: *Portrait of Olga in an Armchair*, 1918
(detail of 101, page 118)

Page 130: *Woman in a Hat*, 9 June 1941
(detail of 143, page 163)

Page 170: *Woman by a Window*, 11 June 1956
(detail of 164, page 188)

Page 200: *Las Meninas*, 15 November 1957
(detail of 182, page 207)